REPORTING FOR THE PRINT MEDIA

Fourth Edition

FRED FEDLER
University of Central Florida

HARCOURT BRACE JOVANOVICH, PUBLISHERS

San Diego   New York   Chicago   Austin   Washington, D.C.
London Sydney Tokyo Toronto

Copyrights and Acknowledgments

The author gratefully acknowledges the following publishers and copyright holders for permission to use materials in this book:

JOAN DAVES   For "I Have a Dream" by Martin Luther King, Jr. Copyright © 1963 by Martin Luther King, Jr. Reprinted by permission of Joan Daves.

THE NEW YORK TIMES   For 16 excerpts from *The New York Times*. Copyright © by The New York Times Company. Reprinted by permission.

UNITED PRESS INTERNATIONAL   For leads and articles. Copyright © by United Press International. Reprinted by permission.

THE WALL STREET JOURNAL   For "Seaborne Smugglers Often Outfox Feds—But Not for Drugs" by Alfredo Corchado; "Most U.S. Firms Seek Extra Profits In Japan, At Expense of Sales" by Damon Darlin; "Cigarette Smoking Is Growing Hazardous to Careers in Business" by Alix M. Freedman; "Prices of Small Items, Services Rise Rapidly, Hint of New Inflation" by Constance Mitchell; "The Game Is at Stake as Wardens Combat Plague of Poachers" by Ken Slocum; and "Research on Impotence Upsets Idea That It Is Usually Psychological" by David Stipp. All copyright © 1987 by Dow Jones & Company, Inc. Reprinted by permission.

PHOTO CREDITS

Page 175 AP/Wide World; 182 Courtesy of The New-York Historical Society; 184 Photo by Chris O'Meara/THE LEDGER; 187 UPI/Bettmann Newsphotos; 210 © Alan Carey/The Image Works; 212 © Zimbel/Monkmeyer; 214 © Alan Carey/The Image Works; 215 © Ellis Herwig/Stock, Boston; 216 (left) © Olivier Rebbot 1980/Woodfin Camp & Assoc., (right) © Bob Daemmrich/The Image Works; 228 Courtesy Gannett Co.; 229 Courtesy THE WALL STREET JOURNAL/Dow Jones & Co., Inc.; 252 © Burk Uzzle/Woodfin Camp & Assoc.; 254 AP/Wide World; 268 Courtesy THE BAKERSFIELD CALIFORNIAN; 272 (top) Courtesy THE MIAMI HERALD, (middle left) AP/Wide World, (middle right) UPI/Bettmann Newsphotos, (bottom left) Courtesy NATIONAL ENQUIRER, (bottom right) © Bill Beebe; 273 Frank Micelotta/TIME Magazine; 275 AP/Wide World; 276 © Stanley Forman/BOSTON-HERALD AMERICAN/Pulitzer Prize 1976; 277 AP/Wide World; 278 (top) AP/Wide World, (bottom) UPI/Bettmann Newsphotos; 286 AP/Wide World; 287 NEW YORK DAILY NEWS; 384 AP/Wide World; 387 AP/Wide World; 424 © John Seakwood/Outline; 477 (top) George Skadding, LIFE MAGAZINE © 1955 TIME Inc., (bottom) UPI/Bettmann Newsphotos; 515 © Alan Carey/The Image Works; 540 © Kagan/Monkmeyer; 598 Courtesy USA TODAY.

To the Student

This book contains instructions, examples and exercises designed to help you learn how to write for the print media, particularly newspapers. However, the writing skills emphasized by this book—clarity, conciseness and accuracy—are also required in radio and television news and in the related fields of advertising and public relations.

Chapters 1 through 6 deal with the basic format and style used by newswriters. Chapters 7 through 10 discuss questions of good taste, ethics and responsibilities; the work of a typical reporter; and communication law. Because journalists are continually confronted by decisions concerning good taste, ethics and responsibilities, newswriting exercises throughout the book challenge your decision-making abilities. Chapters 11 through 21 discuss more advanced writing techniques and more specialized types of stories.

To make the exercises as realistic as possible, most resemble the assignments given to beginning reporters. Many present genuine documents: actual speeches, police reports and publicity releases, for example. In some of the exercises, you are given a few facts and asked to summarize them in acceptable newswriting style. In other exercises, the facts are more complex and require more sophisticated newswriting techniques. Still other exercises will send you out of your classroom to gather information firsthand.

To add to the realism, your instructor may impose deadlines that require you to finish your stories by a specified time. Your instructor may also require you to compose stories on a typewriter or computer terminal. Because composing a story in longhand takes too much time, reporters must learn to think and write at a typewriter or computer.

Mistakenly, students who spend hours working on their first take-home assignments often worry about their slowness. As you begin to write, accuracy and clarity are more important than speed. Good writing requires a great deal of time and effort, writing and rewriting. Few first drafts are so well written that they cannot be improved. To write well, you will have to develop the habit of rewriting your first draft, perhaps two, three or even four times. Through practice, you will develop speed naturally, over a period of time.

Unless it mentions another location, assume that every story in this book occurred on your campus or in your community. Also assume that every story will be published by a newspaper in your community.

Develop the habit of assessing every word and every sentence before using them in a story. Some exercises are intentionally disorganized and poorly worded so that they will require extensive revisions. Also remember that newswriting is based on fact, not fiction. Use only facts that you are given or are able to obtain or verify from other sources. Never make any assumptions, and never make up or create any facts.

Verify the spelling of names that appear in the exercises by consulting the city directory in Appendix A. So that you get in the habit of checking the spelling of every name, some names used in the exercises are intentionally misspelled. Only the spellings in the city directory are correct.

To achieve a consistent style of abbreviations, capitalization, punctuation and so forth, follow the guidelines suggested by The Associated Press Stylebook and Libel Manual. This style is used throughout "Reporting for the Print Media," and a summary of the stylebook's most commonly used rules appears in Appendix B. United Press International, the nation's second major news agency, uses an almost identical book, and most newspapers in the United States—both dailies and weeklies—follow the guidelines the news agencies recommend.

Some students may want to buy copies of The Associated Press Stylebook and Libel Manual. If it is not available at your campus bookstore, write to: Stylebook, AP Newsfeatures, 50 Rockefeller Plaza, New York, N.Y., 10020. Or, any local bookstore can order it for you.

Students using this textbook should also read a daily newspaper. Newspaper editors expect their reporters to be well informed about their communities and especially about their local governments. Reporters should know the names of local and national officials. They should also be able to ask intelligent questions, and to write accurately and knowledgeably about topics in the news.

Students who read newspapers, books and magazines are also likely to be better writers. Good readers become familiar with different styles of writing and can use the best styles as models for their own work. They are also more likely to recognize mistakes, including mistakes in their own writing.

Most students realize that athletes and musicians must practice several hours a day. However, many fail to realize that writers, too, must practice regularly and systematically. To improve their writing skills, they should submit their writing to an instructor or editor and then study the corrections made in their work. As author Sheila Hailey has observed:

> The one thing all professional writers have in common . . . is that they get down to it and write. They don't just talk about it, they don't wait for inspiration, they don't wish they had time to write. They make time and press on. Oh, there's often some pencil-sharpening and desk-tidying that goes on first. But sooner or later, they write, though never knowing with certainty if they are at work on a masterpiece or a disaster.*

This Fourth Edition of "Reporting for the Print Media" includes two new chapters: one on Alternative Leads and another on Ethics. The text has been edited, expanded and brought up to date, and many of the exercises are new.

The book's primary emphasis has not changed. Like previous editions, it provides both the instructions and the exercises needed to help students learn to write for the print media. The first chapters emphasize fundamentals: basic, introductory exercises for people with no prior experience in the field of journalism. Later chapters contain more complex exercises to challenge your developing skills.

Students who want some additional practice while studying Chapters 1 and 2 can complete the exercises labeled "Answer Key Provided" and correct their own work. The answers to those exercises appear in Appendix D.

Students should not expect to complete all the exercises. The book contains enough exercises for a full year, and some students may use it in both introductory and advanced reporting classes. Your instructor will select the chapters and exercises most appropriate for your class. If the class needs more practice in a particular area, the instructor can assign some of the extra exercises in that area. Or, you may complete the exercises on your own, and then ask your instructor to correct them. Some instructors will also supplement the exercises with assignments involving your campus and community.

A Personal Note

When I meet students using this book, many ask, "Who are you, and why did you write the book?"

Writing is hard work. It requires hours—even years—of lonely research, writing, editing and rewriting. But writing is also a challenging and enjoyable (and sometimes profitable) pursuit. The rewards arise when you have finished a piece and it appears in print: when you see your byline, receive your payment and hear from people who like your work.

I grew up in Wisconsin and, as an undergraduate, studied journalism at the University of Wisconsin at Madison. After graduating, I worked as a reporter and copy editor for newspapers in Dubuque and Davenport, Iowa, and Sacramento, Calif. I began to teach news reporting while working for my M.A. at the University of Kentucky in

---

*Sheila Hailey, *I Married a Best Seller* (Garden City, N.Y.: Doubleday, 1978), p. 95.

Lexington and for my Ph.D. at the University of Minnesota in Minneapolis. I now teach at the University of Central Florida in Orlando.

This was my first—and most successful—book. It seems to be the most popular reporting textbook in the country, used at 500 to 600 colleges and universities. I have also written an introductory textbook about the mass media and will soon publish a third book about media hoaxes. In a few years, I hope to start a fourth book about media humor.

Writing the first edition of this book took about nine months, but that edition contained only 256 pages. Each revision takes about a year. Many of the examples were written by students in the classes I teach. The exercises are based on actual news stories collected during the years between each new edition.

So that I can improve the next edition of this book, I would appreciate receiving your comments and suggestions. Please write to:

Fred Fedler
Department of Communication
University of Central Florida
Orlando, Fla. 32816

A Note of Thanks

Journalists are wonderful people. Most are young, enthusiastic and interesting. While writing this book, I asked dozens for help. Reporters, editors and photographers from Los Angeles to St. Louis, Miami and New York answered my letters and provided advice and samples of their work.

I would especially like to thank: Barry Bradley, executive editor and vice president of Maddux Publishing Inc. in St. Petersburg, Fla.; Roy Peter Clark, associate director of The Poynter Institute in St. Petersburg; John Harte, staff photographer for The Bakersfield Californian; Harry Levins, writing coach and chief copy editor for the St. Louis Post-Dispatch; Marty Murray, a friend and former student who shares her "out of body" experience in one of the exercises; M. Timothy O'Keefe, a freelance writer and professor at the University of Central Florida; Chris O'Meara, formerly a photographer for The Ledger in Lakeland, Fla., now with The Associated Press; Louis Michael Perez, executive editor of The Ledger; and Patrick S. Washburn, associate professor at Ohio University.

These newspapers and other news organizations also allowed me to quote their stories or republish their photographs: American Newspaper Publishers Association Foundation, The Arizona Daily Star, The Associated Press, Chicago Tribune, Dallas Times Herald, Deseret News, Salt Lake City, Doubleday & Company, Inc., KNT News Wire, McGraw-Hill Book Company, The Miami Herald, The Milwaukee Journal, The New York Times, Newsday, The Orlando Sentinel, Scripps Howard News Service, Society of Professional Journalists (Sigma Delta Chi), St. Petersburg Times, United Press International, Inc., USA Today, The Virginia-Pilot, Norfolk, The Wall Street Journal, Washington Journalism Review, and The Washington Post.

I would also like to thank the staff at Harcourt Brace Jovanovich—Marlane Miriello, acquisitions editor; David Watt, manuscript editor; Kim Svetich, production editor; Gina Sample, designer; Susan Holtz, art editor; and Lesley Lenox, production manager—for their part in the publication of this new edition of "Reporting for the Print Media."

Fred Fedler

Contents

1 Format and Style

Until the 1970s, newspaper reporters typed their stories on sheets of paper, then used a pencil to correct their errors. Since then, newspapers have experienced a period of rapid technological change. Most reporters now type their stories on computers or word processors with video display terminals. As they are typed, the stories appear on screens above the terminals' keyboards. Any errors can be corrected directly on the keyboards. The stories are stored in a computer until an editor is ready to summon them up on another video display terminal. Finally, the edited stories are transmitted to other machines, which set them in type. Everything is done electronically, and the system saves millions of dollars by eliminating the need for typesetters.

Although most newsrooms no longer contain typewriters, students must still learn the traditional news story format and copy-editing symbols, for a number of reasons. First, newspapers that have not installed the electronic equipment continue to use the traditional format and copy-editing symbols and to employ some typesetters. Second, reporters and editors may have to handle some typewritten copy from free-lance writers, public relations agencies and a variety of other sources. Finally, the traditional format and copy-editing symbols are still used by some magazines, book publishers and advertising agencies.

The journalism departments of many colleges have purchased video display terminals or other types of electronic equipment, but few use that equipment for every assignment in every reporting and editing class. Instead, journalism students continue to learn the basics—typing their stories on sheets of paper and using the traditional format and copy-editing symbols—because it is simpler and cheaper to do so, especially in introductory classes that attract large numbers of students whose work does not have to be set in type.

News Story Format

Reporters have developed a unique format for their stories, and each story you write should follow the guidelines suggested here. Although minor variations exist between one newspaper and another, most publications are remarkably consistent in their adherence to these rules.

Type each news story on separate 8½- by 11-inch sheets of paper. Avoid onionskin and other types of glossy or erasable bond paper because it is more difficult to write corrections on such paper.

Type your name, the date and a slugline in the upper left-hand corner of the first page. For example:

Fred Fedler
Jan. 12, 1992
Proxmire Speech

Editors use sluglines to help them identify and keep track of stories that are being prepared for publication. The sluglines also provide a quick summary of each story's topic. A story that reports a speech by your city's mayor might be slugged "Mayor's Speech"; a story about a fire at an elementary school might be slugged "School Fire." Sluglines should not exceed two or three words and should be as specific as possible. Vague sluglines, such as "Speech" or "Fire," might be used on more than one story, and the stories might then be confused with each other.

Also avoid jokes, sarcasm and statements of opinion that would cause embarrassment if the slugline were accidentally published, as sometimes happens. A reporter in California became irritated when asked to write about a party given by several prominent women. The reporter thought the story was unimportant and uninteresting. Angrily, he slugged it "Old Biddies." He was almost fired when, accidentally, the slugline appeared in print. Similarly, a writer at the Boston Globe wrote an editorial that criticized a speech given by President Carter. Another employee thought the writer's slugline was the headline—and an accurate one. It was set in type, so the lead editorial published the next morning bore the headline, "Mush from the Wimp."

Begin each story one-third to one-half of the way down the first page. When you write for a newspaper, the space at the top of the first page provides room for your byline, a headline and special instructions to your paper's typesetters. In class, the space provides room for your instructor to evaluate your work. Leave a one-inch margin on each side and at the bottom of every page.

Newspapers place a dateline at the beginning of the first line of each news story to indicate the story's geographical source. Datelines normally include the name of the city, printed entirely in capital letters and followed by a comma, the abbreviation for the state in upper/lower case and a dash (for example: LEXINGTON, Ky.— or PORTLAND, Ore.—). The names of major cities that most readers will immediately recognize (such as Boston, Chicago, Miami and Los Angeles) are used alone, without their state. Newspapers do not use datelines for any stories that originate within their own communities, and most newspapers use only the names of other cities within their own state, without adding the name of the state.

To save time, you will have to learn to type even the first draft of all news stories you write: you will not have enough time to write the stories in longhand first. Type and double-space each assignment so that it is neat, uniform and easy to read. Type on only one side of each page, and do not leave any extra space between paragraphs.

Do not divide a word at the end of a line. A typesetter might mistakenly assume that the hyphen was part of the word and incorrectly set it in type. Also avoid starting a sentence or paragraph at the bottom of one page and finishing it at the top of the next page. Each page should end with a complete paragraph so that typesetters can set the page in type immediately, without waiting for the rest of your story, and so that each page can be given to a different typesetter without loss of continuity.

If a story is continued on a second page, write the word "more" at the bottom of the first page and circle it to indicate that the word is not part of the story and should not be set in type. Begin the second page and all later pages about one inch from the top of the page. Type your last name, the page number and the slugline in the upper left-hand corner. For example:

Fedler
Proxmire Speech
Page 2

Instead of using the word "paragraph" while communicating with one another, the journalists at some newspapers shorten it to "graf." Similarly, instead of using the word "page," some journalists use "add" or "take." Also, some newspapers ask their reporters to triple-space rather than double-space their stories.

Copy-Editing Symbols

Reporters are expected to edit their stories and to correct all their errors before giving the stories to an editor (or instructor). Stories do not have to be typed perfectly, but they should be neat and easy to read. If you make a mistake while typing a story, or if you want to edit a story after typing it, use the copy-editing symbols shown here. Using the copy-editing symbols is faster and easier than using an eraser or retyping a story.

If several major errors appear in a paragraph or section of a story, you can retype that section and paste it over the original. If your corrections become too numerous and messy, retype the entire story.

Indent every paragraph in a news story, and mark the beginning of each paragraph with the proper copy-editing symbol:|_____ If you want to mark a paragraph to be divided into two shorter paragraphs, you can use either the same copy-editing symbol or this one: ⊄

If you indent a line and then decide that you do not want to start a new paragraph, link the lines together with a pencil, as shown here. ⌐
⌐The same symbol is used to link the remaining parts of a sentence or paragraph after a major deletion ~~involving the elimination of a great many words and more than one line of type, or even a complete sentence or two,~~ as shown here.

Always use a pencil, not a pen, to correct any errors that appear in your stories. If you make a mistake in correcting your story with a pen, the mistake will be difficult to correct.

Write "OK" or "cq" above facts or spellings that are so unusual that your editors are likely to question their accuracy, and circle the letters (for example: Neil Schneider became a millionaire at the age of 13). ⊙⃝ The notations "OK" and "cq" indicate that the information is correct, regardless of how unlikely or bizarre it may appear to be.

If you accidentally type an extra word or letter, cross out the word or ~~or~~ letter, then draw an arc above it to link the remaining portions of the sentence. An arc drawn above a deletion indicates that the remaining segments of the sentence or paragraph should be moved closer together, but a space should be left between them. To eliminate a space within a word, draw an arc both above and below it. To eliminate an unnecessary letter, draw an arc both above and below it, plus a *vertical* line through it.

When two words or letters are inverted, use|symbol|this|to indicate that they should be transposed. If you want to move an entire paragraph, retype that portion of the story. Particularly if the transposed paragraphs are on different pages, several errors are likely to occur if you fail to retype them.

draw three lines under a letter to indicate that it should be capitalized. If a letter is capitalized but should not be, draw a *slanted* line *T*hrough it. If two words are incorrectly run together, draw a *straight*, vertical line between them to indicate that a space|should be added.

If you make a correction and then decide that the correction is unnecessary or mistaken, write the word "stet" alongside the correction to indicate that you want to retain the original version. If you want to add or change a letter, word or phrase, write or type it above the line, then use a caret to indicate precisely where it fits into the sentence. Many punctuation marks, including colons, semicolons, exclamation points and question marks, are added in the same manner (for example: When will she arrive?).

To add a comma, draw a comma in the proper place and put a caret *over* it (for example: He is tall, intelligent and wealthy). If you add an apostrophe or quotation mark, place a caret *under* it (for example: He said, "Don't ignore these rules"). To add a period, draw either a dot or a small "x" and circle it. A hyphen is indicated by the symbol =, and a dash by the symbol ⊢⊣.

Never type over a letter. Also, place all corrections above (never below) the typed line and error.

Newspapers never underline because typesetters do not have a key to underline. However, you can use the symbol shown here to set type in italics, and you can use the symbol shown here to set type in boldface. You can use this symbol to center a line on the page: ⌐By Marcia Sirota.⌐

⌐ This symbol means flush left.   This symbol means flush right. ⌐

Spell out most numbers below 10 and use numerals for the number 10 and most larger numbers. Consult The Associated Press Stylebook and Libel Manual for more exact guidelines. If you type a numeral but want it spelled out, circle it (for example: He has 8 sisters). If you spell out a number but want to use the numeral, circle it (for example: He has thirteen sisters). Similarly, circle words that are spelled out but should be abbreviated (for example: He is from Madison, Wisconsin), and words that are abbreviated but should be spelled out (for example: He is from Minn.). Do not use a circle to indicate that a letter should or should not be capitalized.

Below the last line of each news story, in the center of the page, place one of these "end marks":

-30-

###

-0-

As a reporter, you will not normally be expected to write headlines for any of the stories you write, nor to put your own byline on the stories. Newspaper editors write the headlines after they determine the headlines' size and decide where to place the stories in their papers. Editors also control the use of bylines and generally add them only to stories they consider exceptionally good.

Accuracy of Facts and Spelling

Double check the accuracy of every fact reported in all the news stories you write. Errors will damage a newspaper's reputation and may seriously harm people mentioned in the stories. Because of the serious consequences, your instructor may lower your grade whenever you make a factual error. You will also be penalized for errors in diction, grammar and style. If your instructor accepts late assignments (many do not), your grades on them may also be lowered. Like all the other media, newspapers must meet rigid production schedules, and editors expect work to be turned in on time.

Be especially careful to check the spelling of people's names. Most misspellings are the result of carelessness, and they anger the victims. Most editors require their reporters to consult a second source, usually a telephone book or a city directory, to verify the way names are spelled.

Use the city directory that appears in Appendix A to verify the spelling of names used in this book, and place a box around the names to show that you have checked their spelling and that they are accurate (for example: Mayor Paula Novarro has resigned). To avoid inconsistent spellings, check and box names every time they appear in a news story, not just the first time they are used. Some names in later exercises have deliberately been altered, and you will misspell them if you fail to use the city directory.

Like other city directories, the directory in this book does not list people who live in other parts of the country. Thus, if a story mentions that someone lives in another city, you can assume that the person's name is spelled correctly; because the name will not be listed in the city directory, it will be impossible to check.

Finally, make and save a carbon or photocopy of each story you write. This copy will be invaluable if a story is lost, if questions arise about its content, or if you want to compare your original story with the edited version published by a newspaper or returned by your instructor.

Avoid Sexual and Other Stereotypes

In the past, news stories seemed to emphasize women's domestic and sexual role as wives, mothers, cooks, seamstresses, housekeepers and sex objects. During the 1960s and 1970s, women began to complain that such stereotypes are false and demeaning—that women are human beings, not primarily housewives and sex objects.

Partly in response to their criticisms, journalists are trying to avoid sexist titles and comments. Journalists no longer use occupational terms that exclude women: "fireman," "policeman" and "workman," for example. They substitute "firefighter," "police officer" and "worker." Similarly, they use "reporter" or "journalist" instead of "newsman."

Although some groups favor their use, The Associated Press Stylebook and Libel Manual recommends that journalists avoid coined words, such as "chairperson" and "spokesperson." Instead, journalists use "chairman" or "spokesman" when referring to a man or to the office in general. They use "chairwoman" or "spokeswoman" when referring to a woman. Or, if applicable, they use a neutral word such as "leader" or "representative."

As you begin to write, avoid using the words "female" and "woman" in places where you would not use the words "male" or "man" (for example: "woman doctor" or "female general"). Also avoid words such as "authoress," "aviatrix" and "coed." Use unisex substitutes, such as "author," "aviator" and "student." Women object to being called "girls" and being referred to by only their first names. News stories do not call men "boys," and use their last names—rarely their first.

As a newswriter, also avoid:

- Suggesting that homemaking is not work.
- Identifying a woman solely by her relationship with a man: for example, as a man's wife, daughter or secretary.
- Describing a woman's physical characteristics—her hair, dress, voice or figure—when her appearance is irrelevant to your story.
- Mentioning the fact that a woman has been divorced unless a similar story about a man would mention his marital status. When a woman's marital status is relevant, it seldom belongs in the lead. Avoid stories that begin: "A 35-year-old divorcee . . ."

Never assume that everyone involved in a story is male, that all people holding prestigious jobs are male, or that most women are housewives. Be especially careful to avoid using the pronouns "he," "his" and "him" while referring to a typical American or average person. Mistakenly, some readers will assume that you are referring exclusively to men—not to both men and women. However, you should not use the cumbersome and repetitive "he/she" or "he and she." The effort to rid the language of male bias should never become so strained that it distracts readers.

Although most journalists are becoming more sensitive to the problem, a recent headline announced, "Woman Exec Slain in Waldorf-Astoria." Critics said that the slain person's sex was irrelevant, and that few journalists would have written "Male Exec Slain." Similarly, a headline in The Washington Post read, "School Job May Go to Woman Educator." Critics asked editors at the Post why they used the term "woman educator," since they would never use "man educator." Moreover, the headline's wording suggested that it was unusual for a woman to achieve a position of importance.

A recent story published by The New York Times noted that a secretary "wore a full-length blue-tweed coat, leather boots and gold bangle bracelets." Yet the secretary's clothing was not unusual, nor relevant to her involvement in the news. Moreover, reporters would not have described the attire of a man in the same position.

Advertisements contain other stereotypes. Radio advertisements have urged women to ask their husbands for money so they could shop at the sponsor's stores. Other advertisements have urged mothers (but not fathers) to bring their children to an amusement park. A television advertisement urged women to buy the right brand of soap so their husbands would never be embarrassed by ring-around-the-collar. No one suggested that men should wash their own shirts—or their dirty necks.

Journalists are also trying to eliminate other stereotypes. They mention a person's race, religion, marital status or ethnic background only when that fact is clearly relevant. Employees at The New York Times are told: " . . . the writer—or the characters quoted in the story—must demonstrate the relevance of ethnic background or religion. It isn't enough to assume that readers will find the fact interesting or evocative; experience shows that many will find it offensive and suspect us of relying on stereotypes."

Veterans organizations have accused the media of creating another stereotype: of portraying the men and women who served in Vietnam as dangerous criminals—as violent and unstable. Why? Because the media often report that the person charged with a serious crime is "a Vietnam veteran," regardless of the fact's relevance. Also avoid such words as "wampum," "warpath," "powwow," "tepee," "brave" and "squaw" in stories about American Indians. The words are disparaging and offensive.

To avoid the stereotypes—especially sexist stereotypes—consider these guidelines:

1. Avoid sexist titles.

Most newsmen are college graduates.
REVISED: Most reporters are college graduates.

The Catholic church is delegating more work to laymen.
REVISED: The Catholic church is delegating more work to its congregations.

2. Substitute an article for the male pronoun.

To succeed, a gardener must fertilize his crop.
REVISED: To succeed, a gardener must fertilize a crop.

A college teacher is expected to serve his community.
REVISED: A college teacher is expected to serve the local community.

3. Substitute plural nouns and pronouns for male nouns and pronouns.

A reporter must cultivate his sources.
REVISED: Reporters must cultivate their sources.

A cautious investor will diversify his portfolio.
REVISED: Cautious investors will diversify their portfolios.

4. Alternate male and female pronouns or substitute descriptions or job titles for male nouns and pronouns.

He said that few men are satisfied with their salaries.
REVISED: Accountants say that few Americans are satisfied with their salaries.

A spokesman for the doctors said that most of their patients expect miracles: fast, painless cures.
REVISED: Doctors said that most of their patients expect miracles: fast, painless cures.

Copy Preparation Checklist

During this course, as you finish writing each of your news stories, consult the following checklist. If you answer "no" to any of these questions, your stories may have to be edited or retyped.

1. Have you started typing one-third to one-half of the way down the first page and one inch from the top of all following pages?
2. Do you have a slugline (no more than two or three words) that specifically describes your story's content?
3. Is the story typed and double-spaced, with only one story on a page?
4. Is each paragraph indented and marked?
5. Have you used a pencil and the proper copy-editing symbols to correct all your errors?
6. Have you made certain that no words are divided and hyphenated at the end of a line, and that no sentences or paragraphs are continued on another page?
7. If the story continues on a second page, have you: typed and circled "more" at the bottom of the first page; typed your name, page number and slugline at the top of the second page; and typed "-30-," "###" or "-0-" at the end of the story?
8. If the story originated outside your community, have you added the proper dateline?
9. Have you used the city directory to verify the spelling of all names used in the story and checked and drawn a box around those names every time they are used?
10. Have you been careful to avoid sexual and other stereotypes?

Reference Chart for Copy-Editing Symbols

1. Abbreviate   He was born on (August) 4 in Urbana, (Illinois.)

2. Boldface   This line should be set in boldface type.

3. Capitalize   An american won the nobel prize.

4. Center   ]Continued on Page 10[

5. Change letter   Their house is expensive.

6. Change word   She received three gifts. (four)

7. Close up space between words   Their car was totally destroyed.

8. Close up space within a word   Their children r an outsi de.

9. Continues on next page   (More)

10. Delete letter | They receiveed the monkey.

11. Delete phrase | They did not use ~~any unneeded or~~ unnecessary words.

12. Delete punctuation | They asked/ if he was safe/.

OR: They asked, if he was safe.

13. End of story | ###

OR: -30-

OR: -0-

14. Flush left | [The typesetter will begin this line at the left margin.

15. Flush right | The typesetter will end this line at the right margin.]

16. Ignore correction (Correct as written) | (Stet)

17. Insert apostrophe | It's good you're going home.

18. Insert colon | He set three goals: success, health and wealth.

19. Insert comma | The girl, 7, lives with her grandmother.

20. Insert dash | The score was 87 to 53—a disaster.

21. Insert exclamation point | "What! I don't believe it!" she exclaimed.

22. Insert hyphen | The 7-year-old girl lives with her mother.

23. Insert letter | Their car filed to start.

24. Insert period | John C. Kefalis received the scholarship.

OR: John C. Kefalis received the scholarship.

25. Insert quotation marks | "This is easy," he said.

26. Insert semicolon | Don't go; he needs your help.

27. Insert word | He often writes clever poetry.

28. Italic | Some publications set words in italics for emphasis.

29. Lowercase (Do not capitalize) | The Mayor failed To arrive.

30. No new paragraph | To generate more publicity, the candidate announced that he would work at 100 different jobs. He spent the remainder of his campaign

picking tomatoes, plucking chickens, hauling trash, digging ditches and driving trucks.

31. Separate words

Journalists are critical of political gimmickry.

32. Spell out numbers or words

He said ⑧ people will go to Ⓐⓛⓐ.

33. Start new paragraph

¶ Another man campaigned on roller skates. His wife explained: "We met at a roller skating rink, and we thought it would be a fun idea. He's going house to house, subdivision to subdivision on his skates, and people remember him."

34. Transpose letters

Typsits often transpoes letters.

35. Transpose words

Happily he accepted the award.

Suggested Readings

Copperud, Roy H. *American Usage and Style: The Consensus.* New York: Van Nostrand Reinhold Company, 1979.

Crump, Spencer. *The Stylebook for Newswriting.* Corona del Mar, Calif.: Trans-Anglo Publishing Co., 1979.

French, Christopher W., ed. *The Associated Press Stylebook and Libel Manual.* Reading, Mass.: Addison-Wesley Publishing Company, Inc., 1987.

Holley, Frederick S., ed. *Los Angeles Times Stylebook.* New York: New American Library, 1981.

Jordan, Lewis, ed. *The New York Times Manual of Style & Usage.* New York: Quadrangle/The New York Times Book Company, 1982.

Webb, Robert A., ed. *The Washington Post Deskbook on Style.* New York: McGraw-Hill, 1978.

EXERCISE 1
Sexism

SECTION I: TITLES Replace these titles with words that include both men and women.

1. Businessman	7. Man
2. Congressman	8. Mankind
3. Craftsman	9. Man-sized
4. Fatherland	10. Salesman
5. Founding Fathers	11. Statesman
6. Mailman	12. Workman

SECTION II: NOUNS AND PRONOUNS Rewrite the following sentences, avoiding the use of male nouns and pronouns.

1. A reporter is expected to protect his sources.

2. A good athlete often jogs to build his endurance.

3. Normally, every auto mechanic buys his own tools.

4. No one knows which of the nation's congressmen leaked the details to his wife and friends.

5. If a patient is clearly dying of cancer, doctors may give him enough drugs to ease the pain, and perhaps even enough to hasten his death.

SECTION III: STEREOTYPES Rewrite the following sentences, avoiding sexist language and comments.

1. A California man and his wife attended the reunion.

2. The bus driver, a woman, was blamed for the accident.

3. While the girls were playing tennis, their husbands were playing golf.

4. She is 56 years old and a petite grandmother but still plays tennis five days a week.

5. While her husband works, Valerie Dawkins raises their children and dabbles in politics.

6. Mrs. John Favata said she often discusses the stock market with other girls in her neighborhood.

7. Mike Deacosta, his wife and their two children—Mark and Amy—served as the hosts.

8. Councilman Alice Cycler, the attractive wife of a lawyer and mother of eight girls, is fighting to improve the city's parks.

9. In addition to raising their four children and caring for their home, Nikki Evans has also succeeded as a banker. Today, she was promoted to vice president.

10. An attractive young blonde, Elaine Gardepe, seems to be an unlikely person to write a book about auto mechanics, but it has become a best seller.

11. The 72-year-old spinster does not look the part but has become an expert on criminal law.

12. She is a quiet woman, but the 52-year-old divorcee has a reputation for being an aggressive competitor. Last year, she sold more homes than any other salesman in the city.

EXERCISE 2
Format and Style

INSTRUCTIONS: Using the proper copy-editing symbols, correct the mechanical, spelling and stylistic errors in the following stories. The stories also contain sexist titles and comments that should be corrected or eliminated. If necessary, turn to the reference chart for copy-editing symbols (included in this chapter) and to the stylebook in Appendix B.

Story 1: Minneapolis Family

minneapolis, minnesota—A women who police said taught her 4 children to shoplift has beeen convicted of Grand Theft ad child abuse. She will he sentenced next Monday and fa ces a maximum penalty nine years in Prison.

a jury convicted the woman, Jena Arvel, 29, after her four children testifiedthat she orde3red them to shoplift. The youngesT child is 6, and

the oldest 11.

Judge maggy Einhorn ordred mrs. Arvel held without bzond,.

Arvel and hre chiLdren were arrested at a dept. store with $410 dollars wortt of clothing that police said was stolin

Defene attorney james Vashem argue that the childrens Father taught them to steal. Vashemsaid Mrs. Arvel regainted custody of tee children a year ago and tried to brake them of te habit, but aparently . failed.

The children havve be en placed in Foster Homess.

###

Story 2: Arbor Law

Colorado Springs colorado—mayor Buck torcaso today announced that he favors an arbor ordinanca to protect the City's trees from removal by

developers.

"Its a shame to see trees one hundred or two hundred years old take down withot reason," Torcaso said. "It's happening all over the city."

he complained that osme builders "get theiir bulldozors into an area and rape the land."

Torcaso said he and other colorado springs ofic ials will stuDy the arber ordnances adoptedby neighborng communitites and draft an. ordinance in about six mo/nths.

Councilmen Mike Adk ins and Veronica levine said they will suppert his proposale. "Im a builder and a homesowner myself,and I prefer trees on a lot," Adkins said. "it beautifies an area and enrichs every?ones life. Some people complain about more government regulatixns, but you need some regulations tlo protect the public.

Torcaso sa id the ordinance might requirf build ers ot obtain a pearmit before they cut any trcees in the city. The ordinance might also require wbuilders plant 2 or three troees for every one they cutdown.

Story 3: Wasted Workday

FRESNO, CALIFORNIA—Rresearches at california S tate, Universityat Fresno have found that the averagae worker spends 32% percent of his day goofing off.

the researchors observed Men at work throughoout the state fond that thee employees at some busineses wa7sted as little as 10 percent of their time. However, the employes at other busineses wastde as much as 55 percenf.

Martha dutton, a business prof at the univer sity, said, "The averaga permanent employee we observed if paid to wirk 35.2 hours per week, but w astes 11 hours and 15 minutes . that adds up to c four months a year"

Dutton sai the statisticsreflect thea inefficiency of Americcan business and the absense of a strong work ethick among american workkers. "Its no wonder that we can't compete wtih the Japanese," she sad. "Or the KOREANS, or, almost anyone else in the wirld.

###

EXERCISE 3
Format and Style

INSTRUCTIONS: Using the proper copy-editing symbols, correct the mechanical, spelling and stylistic errors in the following sentences. The stories also contain sexist titles and comments that should be corrected or eliminated. If necessary, turn to the reference chart for copy-editing symbols (included in this chapter) and to the stylebook in Appendix B.

Story 1: Tobacco Addicts

Washington, d.c.—Newevidence sujjests that Tobacco is more addictive—and deadlier—than Alcohol or Heroin.

A Study inv olving 12,400 americans fount that smoknig is 8 tim es deadlier than the excessive use of alcohel. The STUDY also found that an addiction to tobaco is moredifficult to treat than an addiction to heroin

The directtor of the National Institute on drug ABuse discussed the study durnig apress conference at 8 AM todaay. The institte is urging DOCTORS to traet tobaccoaddicts with the some compassion and concrn givenn men addicted to otpher dangerous drugs.

The institute also , suggests that doctors recognize the use of tobacco as a fatal addiction—and tthat they begn treading it that way on death certificates, just as they would an overdos of street drugs?

sources in the institute added that the Tobacco Ind*ustry seems to be the only industry in the U.S. that manufacturse product likely to kill the man who use that product in it's intented manner.

###

Story 2: School Vandals

PORTLAND OREGON—The schol board will sues the parents of 5 teenagers accused of vandalizing Spring Lake Elementary Shl.

At a meeting lost night, the board voted9 to 0, to seeek $17,800 dollers in damages. The teenagers, aLL high school students, have been charfged climbing through a skylight, pouring paint and syrup on cla ssroom flors;

discharging fire extinguishrs; and destr)oying books furniture and ohter classroom furnishings

board atty Noel Holsombeck said state law allows scheel boards to sue parents for the malicious acts committed by their children.

HOlsombeck recommended that theboard file the lawsuit. "Inn this case, the parents se em able to afford
to paid," Holsombeck said. "also, the boird needs to show that it will nto tolerate this kind of behavior. Theres no reasons for it"

holsombeck added that: "Weve never sue anyone before, but usually the students andtheir parents' dont have the economic abilite to respond. Besides, this is the worst— the mostsenseless—case of vandlism we've ever had in tha the countyn."

Story 3: Rabbit Breeders

chicago—Members ofthe American Rabbit Breeders Assn. hope that Rabbit meat and fur will become the fooDd and fashion of the future

About 3200 memberss of the Assn. , are c onducting their 64th annuil convention in Chicago, and about One Hundred animal rights advocates are picketint their convention head quarters,.

some protetors wore T-shirts sayig "Love Animals, Don't Eat them." The protestors want dabbits freed, not caged nad killed for medicalexperments, fur and food.
Rowland Bukowski, Pres. of the assn., Responed that to many men thinkof rabbits as cute, cuddly cousins of the Easter Bunny, not as an inexpensive source of fooD.

Bukowski said that ravvit will be onmne of the most imporsant meats of the future because fo ri sing farm csts costs, dwindling agriculture lands and an

increasing world popultion. olther types of meet will becometoo costly, HE said, leaving rabbt as a majro source protein.

ABout forty million rabits are rised in captivity ea ch year. More than 6,000 of them—forty-two breed—are being shownat conventon.

###

EXERCISE 4
Format and Style

INSTRUCTIONS: Using the proper copy-editing symbols, correct the mechanical, spelling and stylistic errors in the following sentences.

1. Robert j. Curey junior, the Mayorof Eugene Oregon sa id thre media is to bias.d

2. Sandra Oliver, age six, is four feet Tall, weaghs 81 pds, and ivles on Elm boulevard.

3. Oliver Brooks, who ahs a Ph.d., wrote a book entitled Urban Terrorists.

4. After serving in the army he obtairned a B.A. and beCame a citizen of the U.S..

5. The girl, an 18 yearr old blond, sipped a coke, and read Time Magazine

6. The retired col. fought with the united states marines in vietnam durnig the 1960's.

7. The united states congrxess will meet at 10:00 A.M. tues. January 4th in the
   United States capital bludg.

8. Mr. Richard Harris, an Editor AT Newsweek Magagine, will fly north on Mon.
   Harris, was born in oct., 1942, and be gan wrok as areporter fr the Chicago Tribune.

9. Sen. Andrews, a democrat from New Hampsire, said hewill spend about fifty
   percent of his campaign funds—nearly $18,000,000—on radioand telivision
   advertiznig.

10. Prof. Myron Carey, of 614 North Highla?nd Dr. is Chairman of THE Dept. of
    Mathematics and hasanoffice in Rm. 407 of thehumanities bldg.

11. the temperature is zero. She is white; he is. Vietnamese.She earns $278.00 a week
    and spends 4fourty percent of her incgincome on food.

12. Prange Incoporated of Columbia, South carolina manufacsre widgets at a cost of
    fourty seven cents and sel,ls th hem for two dollars. Normaly, about two % are
    defective.

13. Ruth, who was borgborn duringg the 1960s will be
    a Sophmore this Fall and wants to join the republican parTY.

14. 8,000 persons weRe killed when a severe hurrican struck south florida during the
    eightheenth century.

15. At 10:00 A.M. This morning, the Vice-President said "The Federal Govt. is far too
    wastefal".

16. A presidential aide sa id its safe to assume that the criteria are so vague tha t neither
    therepublican nor the democratis parties will object to their content.

17. The source said Eleven College Students—five boys a nd six girls—are likely to
    attend the city council meetign.

18. 14 members of a Black Congression3l delega a tion visited the President in the Oval Office to day and demandedd that, as his Number One Priority, HE solve the unemployment problem.

19. Mr. Randolph R. Wilcox junior, of Columbus, Ohio a former presidential aide, will speak at the university of N. Carolina at 7:30 P.M. Friday November 6.

20. The senator, an alumnus of Harvard, complained that,he cannot afford to live in the nations capital,

21. He warned that, by the 1990s, the Federal Government will have to transfer $14,800,000,000 billion dollars from general tax revenues to save thw social security system.

22. the retired army sargeant, ag3 43, lives in Sacramento california with his wive and three children James, Randolph and Tricia.

23. Timothy Wagnor, age eight, of 418 Notrth Wilkes Road ATE some french fries and sipped a Coke.

24. A jury awa rded Mrs. Sarah Petersen $1,316,400 after a car was struck and totally destroyed by a van driven by a drunken driver, killing her husband.

EXERCISE 5
Format and Style

INSTRUCTIONS: Using the proper copy-editing symbols, correct the mechanical, spelling and stylistic errors in the following sentences.

1. The consultant was given $125,000 on Feb ruary 7th, 1980 in aust in texas

2. The temperature feyll to −14 aftre a blizzzard struck Denver colorado in december 1982.

3. Tom Becker, a black born in the south during the 1930s was elected Mayor of the Cit.y

4. a senior who will graduate next Spring said "history and english are my favoite subjects".

5. The girls elbow was injjured when ahe fell twelve feat at lincoln park at Noon yesterdy.

6. Susan Majorce, age seven, is five ft. tall and weighs eighty-seven lbs.

7. the caddccident Occurred on Interstate 80, about twleve miles West of Reno Nevada.

8. They moved from 438 North Sunset Drive to 318 Jamestown boulevard.last Thurs.

9. Mr. Carl r. zastrow junior, of Columbus Ohio, a former Presi(dential aide, will speak-at the university Thursday at 7:00 PM. on the 1st of next mnoth.

10. Atty. Martha Dilla, forgmerly liglived at 4062 South EastlanD DRIVE andworks fo r the Westinghouse coporation

11. the companys presidnet said his firm willProvide more than $100,000,000 dollars to develoxpe an electric car able to travel sixty miles per hour.

12. The yout,h a high School Sophomore, said the temperture in Idaho often falls below 0 during the WIntsr.

13. 50 women who met yesterday morning at 11 am said there children are entitled to use the new park on Vallrath Avenue.

14. The 5-member city council wantxxs ot canvass the towns voters to determene weather a large group favors the establishment ov a Civic Orchestra.

15. Dist. Atty. Paul Tartagila Junior, who was born in Mont. during the 1940s graduated from the Univarsit y ofNebraska.

16. Mrs. Marie Hyde, Asst. Supt. for Public Educatioon for the City, said the 16 year old girls were raised in athens georgia

17. The lady earned her beachelors degree from te university of Kentucky and her masters degr ee froum the Univertiy of Indiana during the 1960s.

18. The suspects were arested at 1602 North Highland Avenue, 64 East Wilshire Drive, and 3492 3rd Street.

19. Chris Repanski, of pocatello idaho will enrolled in the college as a Sophmore nxt fall and hopes to become an Attorney

20. The man, whose i n his mid 30s, joined the F.B.I. after Recieving a Ph.D. in Computer Science.

21. Afterwards, the Vice-President sayd hewill need $25 to $30 million dollars to win the Presidential Election next Fall.

22. Reverand Andrew Cisneros estimated that ⅓ of his parishioners contribute att leeast five per cent of their annuall income to the churchs general revenue fund.

23. The cops arrested four kids dirvng North on Michigan Ave. minutes atfer the restaurant was robed of $1640.83 last Friday.

24. The Catholic Priest that was elected to the city council by a vote of 8,437–8,197 said hehad expected to lose the elb electio.

25. the bill of rights was added to the unites states constitution durign the eightheenth century.

26. Since the 1940s, he has livedin five States Ws., Ken., Mass., N.Y., & Ca.

EXERCISE 6
Format and Style   **Answer Key Provided: See Appendix D**

INSTRUCTIONS: Using the proper copy-editing symbols, correct the mechanical, spelling and stylistic errors in the following sentences. You can correct your own work by comparing your answers with the answers printed at the back of this book.

1. The President of the U.S., a member of the republican party, announced yesterday that income taxes will be lowered eight per cent, effective at 12:01 a.m. on the morning of January 1st of next year. 1992

2. Atty James M. Murphy, of Detroit Michigan estimated that ⅓ of the members of the United states congress are lawers and members of the American Bar Assn.

3. time Magazine, which was established during the Twentieth Century, costs about two dollars $2 a copy, has a circulation of 5,500,000 5.5 million, and favors the Republican party.

4. Henry Kubisak, age eight, of 418 North Wilkes rd, sipped a coke at 11 AM yesterday morning Thursday while his father read a copy of the New York Times

5. The Jiffey Loan company, formerlylocated at 841 South Jefferson Boulevard, haS moved to the interssection of Colonial and Nye ro ads.

6. 12 police oficers hl helped captrue the 19 year old boy. One officer said the youth was carryingthree dollars, a bible, and a letter addressedd to the overnor governor of the State.

7. The girls, who were born in Austin Texas during the 1950s, sagreed to hold their first reunion in Fla. on December 21st at 7:30 p.m. in the evening.

8. After ser ving four years in the Army, became he a united states citzen and then earned a B.A. from Harvard universit.y

9. Asst. Prof. Saul Holmann, a meMber of the Political Science dept., said thee 1960s were a decade of turmoil, caused by a revolutin among blacks and youths opporsed to the Vietnam war.

10. Author Ralph toore, junior, who has an of fice in room 411 of the Lakeshore Heights Bldg., won a pulitzer prize for hsi first boook, whichis entitled Ecology and You.

11. Des?pite the tem perature, which Fell to twenty degrees below 0 in Minneapolis, Minnesota, 82% of the city's voters turnd out last tuesday and defeated Rev. Louis C. Salvaggio, an avowed homosexual candida te for mayor, by a vote of 142,619–81,710.

NAME _____ CLASS _____ DATE _____

EXERCISE 7
Format and Style   **Answer Key Provided: See Appendix D**

INSTRUCTIONS: Using the proper copy-editing symbols, correct the mechanical and stylistic errors in the following sentences. You can correct your own work by comparing your answers with the answers printed at the back of this book.

1. THe president, speaking in Wis., Minn., and Neb. lsat saturday, said he opposes any further increased in social security taxes during the 20th cenTtury.

2. Roger Ritzmann, cha ir man of the Better Schools Assn., scheduled the group's next meeting for Tuesday, March 21, at 7:00 P.M. The Association's ann#ual dues ar#e $25.00

3. Afterinheriting $2,300,600, the 20 year old girl established Fashions, Incorporated, a store at the intersection fo Conway and Anderson Sts.

4. Mr. Andrew c. Mears, a member of the republican party, said the Federal Government should give the army an additional $6 to $8 billion for the pur(hase of three thousand new Tanks

5. The city coun cil met at 12 noon last Tues. Afterwards, COuncilwoman Maggy delevaux said it will meet at 7:30 p.m. tomorrow night to c reconsdier theappointment of Mrs. Ralph Pinder as City Assessor.

6. Colonel Andrew Smith, who emnlisted inthe army as a private on December 7th, 1941, retired in Sept., 1976 at the age of fifty three and now lives on the west coast.

7. The Hospital, locat ed at 581 W. 89 Street, treatde one hundred person for food poisoning.

8. The woman is five feet, seven inches tall, weigghs 132 pounds AND has four sisters, Rosemary, Linda,Ruth, and Doris.

9. Mary Wilson, age eight, said "the baseball gme was rather dull".

10. John Jones, Junior, of Rock Island Illinois arrived September 1 and helped raised almost $1,400,000 for the church new.

11. Mr. John Adams, A wir writer from Mont. will re ceive his B.A. nextMonday and then fly to the midwest at 7:00 P.M. at night.

12. He is seven years old, four feet fall, weighs fifty-five pounds and has saved $74.00.

13. The pres ident of the u.s., his wive, and 2 daughtres have anounced plans to visit the citY on August 7

14. The gen., has retried from the army andis President of Globe Electronics company. The Compny has an officHe oN Central Avenue.

2 Newswriting Style

Newspapers serve a mass audience, and the members of that audience possess diverse capabilities and interests. To communicate effectively—to convey information to a mass audience—newswriters must learn to present that information in as interesting and simple a manner as possible so that almost everyone will want to read and be able to understand it.

Newspapers have consequently developed a distinctive style of writing, and every element of that style serves a specific purpose. Together, the elements enable newspapers to convey information to their readers clearly, concisely and impartially. At first the style may seem difficult and perhaps even awkward. It may also dismay some students because of its emphasis on facts; but newswriters are reporters, not creative writers.

As a first step, reporters must learn to avoid excessive formality. When they begin to write, people often become too formal, and their articles become awkward and pompous. A good writer should be able to present even the most complicated and important ideas simply—in clear, plain language that every reader is able to understand. If a reporter is unable to state an idea plainly, it is usually because the writer does not fully understand the idea or clearly know what needs to be said.

Test your stories by reading them aloud to yourself or to a friend. If your sentences sound awkward, or if you would not use them in a conversation with friends, they may have to be rewritten. Be particularly careful to avoid complex phrases and long, awkward sentences that you would not use in a normal conversation.

Simplify Words, Sentences and Paragraphs

To simplify stories, avoid long, unfamiliar words. Whenever possible, substitute shorter and simpler words that convey the same meaning. Use the word "about" rather than "approximately," "build" rather than "construct," "call" rather than "summon" and "home" rather than "residence." After an airplane crashed, an FAA official explained that its engines "were experiencing fuel starvation." His statement would have been clearer if he had said its engines "ran out of gas."

In addition to being clearer, simpler words also help save space:

> He gave assistance to the victims.
> REVISED: He helped the victims.

> His association with the bank began in 1976.
> REVISED: The bank hired him in 1976.

> Some women were engaged in conversation with their neighbors.
> REVISED: Some women were talking with their neighbors.

Newswriters use simple sentences as well as simple words, with the subject, verb and direct object usually appearing in that order. Notice how much clearer and more concise the following sentences become when they use this word order:

> Phillips was invited into the apartment by a woman.
> REVISED: A woman invited Phillips into the apartment.

> The amount that has been allocated by the city is $42,000.
> REVISED: The city allocated $42,000.

> Another of the terrorists' demands is that they be given permission to leave the country.
> REVISED: The terrorists are demanding permission to leave the country.

Too many clauses, particularly when they appear at the beginning of a sentence, make the sentence more difficult to understand. The clauses overload sentences, so their main points fail to receive enough emphasis; instead, they are buried amid the clutter:

> Left paralyzed on the left side of his body after brain surgery last summer, the 22-year-old is suing his doctor for $6 million.
> REVISED: The 22-year-old is suing his doctor for $6 million. He has been paralyzed on his left side since brain surgery last summer.

> Echoing parental complaints about the danger to children swimming in the pool, Mayor Marsha Palen-Saigol today closed it.
> REVISED: Mayor Marsha Palen-Saigol today closed the pool and explained that she agrees with parents who said it is unsafe.

Newswriters also use active verbs and strong nouns—not adjectives or adverbs, since they tend to be less forceful, vaguer and more opinionated. Writer Mark Twain warned, "When you catch an adjective, kill it." Similarly, Stanley Walker, editor of the old New York Herald Tribune, advised his staff to: "Select adjectives as you would a diamond or a mistress. Too many are dangerous."

A single verb can transform a drab sentence into an interesting one—or a horrifying one. Notice the impact of the word "plunged" in the first example and "danced" in the second, published by the Minneapolis Star and Tribune:

> He plunged the blade into his brother's stomach.

> While searchlights danced in the sky, thousands of fun-seekers converged on the Mississippi riverfront Wednesday night to mark the beginning of a new year.

Because it lacks a strong verb, the following sentence is vague and bland:

> The girl was on her way home.

A good writer would be more specific. How was the girl going home? The sentence becomes more interesting—and informative—when you substitute a more specific and descriptive verb:

The girl was *walking* home.
The girl was *jogging* home.
The girl was *staggering* home.
The girl was *carried* home.

Changing a single word—the verb—also changes the following sentence's impact and meaning:

He *got* a computer.
He *bought* a computer.
He *won* a computer.
He *stole* a computer.

Be particularly careful to avoid the repeated use of the passive verbs "is," "are," "was" and "were." These verbs are overused, weak and dull:

Filing the protest was a history teacher.
REVISED: A history teacher filed the protest.

A sharp criticism of the plan was voiced by the mayor.
REVISED: The mayor sharply criticized the plan.

Police officers were summoned to the scene by a neighbor.
REVISED: A neighbor called the police.

Also use short sentences and short paragraphs. Very long or awkward sentences should be rewritten and divided into shorter units that are easier to read and understand. Research has consistently found a strong correlation between readability and sentence length; the longer a sentence is, the more difficult it is to understand. One survey found that 75 percent of the people shown sentences that contained an average of 20 words were able to understand them, but the percentage dropped rapidly as the sentences became longer. Only 62 percent were able to understand stories with an average sentence length of 25 words, 47 percent understood stories with 30-word sentences, 33 percent understood stories with 35-word sentences, and 17 percent understood stories with 40-word sentences.*

Because of the strong correlation between readability and sentence length, publications quite obviously cater to their intended audiences. The sentences in comics contain an average of about eight words, whereas the sentences in publications for the general public contain an average of 15 to 20 words. Publications that contain 20 to 30 words per sentence are much more difficult to understand and appeal to more specialized and better-educated audiences. These publications include such magazines as Harper's and The Atlantic, and scholarly, scientific and professional journals.

Despite the importance of short sentences and short paragraphs, beginners often write 30-, 40- and even 50-word sentences. They place too many ideas—even unrelated ideas—in their sentences:

She was thrown on the ground, choked when she began to scream for help and robbed of her small black cloth purse containing $7 in coins, a $20 bill, two rings and a gold watch worth $200.
REVISED: The robber threw her on the ground and choked her when she screamed for help. He took a small black purse that contained $27, two rings and a gold watch worth $200.

*Carolyn Clark Reiley, "Can They Read What We Write?" *Seminar*, September, 1974, pp. 5-8.

A lawsuit the boy's parents filed against the two teachers, Bonnie Gumienny and Lynn Davis, charges that they took 11 children from the day care center to the private property of John Bledsoe, 330 S. Dean Road, to swim in a pond without a lifeguard or fencing, and that their son was submerged for almost 10 minutes before anyone noticed that he was missing.

REVISED: The boy's parents are suing two teachers at the day-care center: Bonnie Gumienny and Lynn Davis. Their lawsuit charges that the two teachers took 11 children to a pond without a lifeguard or fencing. The lawsuit also charges that the boy was submerged for almost 10 minutes before anyone noticed that he was missing.

Mistakenly, critics often accuse newspapers of oversimplifying news stories in the attempt to appeal to the least educated of their readers. However, scientific studies have found that newspaper stories are more likely to be too difficult, rather than too easy, for the public to read. One of these studies revealed that stories disseminated by The Associated Press are written at about a 10th-grade level, and that stories provided by United Press International are written at nearly the 11th-grade level.* Together, stories provided by the two news services compose about 40 percent of the news content in most daily newspapers.

Other critics have said that newspapers' emphasis on simplicity makes their stories dull, yet the exact opposite is true. When stories are well-written, simplicity makes them clearer and more interesting. Well-written stories contain no distracting clutter; instead, they emphasize the most important facts and report those facts in a clear, forceful manner.

Jerry Ballune, a California editor, has pointed out: "Our goal is to write . . . in short, understandable sentences. We talk in short sentences. Unless we're Einsteins, we think in short sentences. Readers understand our writing in short sentences. Even Einstein, who had less need for it than most of us, advised: 'Keep it simple.'" Harry Levins, a writing coach at the St. Louis Post-Dispatch, noted: "When we play games with the reader, he usually wins. He simply quits reading. Most readers want their information presented clearly and simply. They lack the time and patience to peel off the camouflage of indirection." (Both Ballune and Levins expressed their advice in bulletins written for their newspapers' staffs.)

There's another important reason for using short sentences and short paragraphs in news stories. Newspapers are printed in small type, with narrow columns, on cheap paper. Long paragraphs—large, gray blocks of type—discourage readers. So reporters divide stories into bite-sized chunks that are easy to read. Also, the white space left at the ends of paragraphs helps brighten each page.

Ernie Pyle, a correspondent during World War II, wrote simply, factually and without sentimentalism, and his work might serve as a model for students. Pyle wrote about individuals in the war, and his syndicated column became so popular that many newspapers published it on their front pages. The following column was reprinted in one of his books, "Here Is Your War":

Sergeant Fryer had an experience on one of the last few days of the campaign that will be worth telling to his grandchildren. He was in a foxhole on a steep hillside. An 88mm shell landed three feet away and blew him out of his hole. He rolled, out of control, 50 yards down the rocky hillside. He didn't seem to be wounded, but all his breath was gone. He couldn't move. He couldn't make a sound. His chest hurt. His legs wouldn't work.

A medic came past and poked him. Sergeant Fryer couldn't say anything, so the medic went on. Pretty soon two of Fryer's best friends walked past and he heard one of them say, "There's Sergeant Fryer. I guess he's dead." And they went right on too. It was more than an hour before Fryer could move, but within a few hours he was perfectly normal again. He said if his wife saw the story in print she would think for sure he was a hero.

(Scripps-Howard Newspapers)

*Ibid., p. 5.

The average sentence in this piece contains 10.6 words. Three sentences contain only three words, and two others contain only four words. Compare Pyle's work with the following single sentence from William L. Shirer's book "Gandhi: A Memoir":

> Clever lawyer that he was, Jinnah took the independence that Gandhi had wrestled for India from the British by rousing the masses to non-violent struggle and used it to set up his own independent but shaky Moslem nation of Pakistan, destined, I believed then, to break up, as shortly happened when the eastern Bengali part, separated from the western part by a thousand miles of India's territory, broke away to form Bangladesh; destined eventually, I believed, to simply disappear.

Because of its length and complexity, this sentence is much more difficult to understand. It contains 80 words. By comparison, the Bible starts simply, "In the beginning God created heaven and earth." The entire Lord's Prayer has only 71 words. The Ten Commandments have 297. The Gettysburg Address has 271. The legal marriage vow has 2 ("I do").

Eliminate Unnecessary Words

President Calvin Coolidge was known as a tight-lipped New Englander. Coolidge supposedly attended church in Washington one Sunday, without his wife. When he returned home, she asked what the minister had preached about.

> "Sin," Coolidge said.
> "What did he say about it?" she asked.
> "He was against it."

Like President Coolidge, newswriters must learn to be concise—to avoid using unnecessary words. However, newswriters must also be more specific, and detailed enough so their stories are informative—more informative than Coolidge's conversation with his wife.

Most newspapers can publish only a fraction of the information they receive each day; for example, an editor for The New York Times has estimated that the Times receives 1¼ to 1½ million words every day but has enough space to publish only one-tenth of that material. By writing concisely, reporters try to present as much information to readers as possible. Brevity also helps readers to grasp quickly the main ideas conveyed by each story, since it eliminates the need to spend time reading unnecessary words. Thus, writers who use two or more words when only one is necessary waste time and space. Moreover, they also exhibit a lack of alertness. Some words are almost always unnecessary: "that," "then," "currently," "now" and "presently," for example. Because the proper verb tells when an action occurred—in the past, present or future—it is redundant to add a second word that reiterates the time, such as "*past* history," "is *now*" and "*future* plans."

Notice how easily several unnecessary words can be deleted from the following sentences without rewriting them or changing their meaning:

> She was able to persuade him to leave.
> REVISED: She persuaded him to leave.

> He presently drives a distance of about 80 miles a day.
> REVISED: He drives about 80 miles a day.

> At the present time the restaurant opens for business at 6 a.m. every morning of the week.
> REVISED: The restaurant opens at 6 every morning.

Other sentences may have to be more extensively rewritten to eliminate unnecessary words and phrases:

A pilot said he thinks that the airplane is worth in the neighborhood of between approximately $34,000 and $36,500.
REVISED: A pilot said the airplane is worth $34,000 to $36,500.

Three drownings occurred in the waters of Crystal Lake this last summer.
REVISED: Three people drowned in Crystal Lake last summer.

Pointed out in the report is the fact that the problem of alcoholism is not fully understood by most Americans.
REVISED: The report says most Americans do not understand alcoholism.

Unnecessary repetition is another form of wordiness and waste. There is rarely any need to repeat the same fact two or three times in a single sentence or story. This problem often arises when writers introduce a topic, then present some specific information about it. In most cases, only the more specific information is needed:

Other injuries the man received include a broken arm.
REVISED: The man also suffered a broken arm.

In an attempt to put out the fire, two men tried to smother it with a blanket.
REVISED: Two men tried to smother the fire with a blanket.

A survey Monday concerning the fairness and accuracy of the news media revealed that four out of 10 students believe the media are unfair and inaccurate.
REVISED: Four out of 10 students surveyed Monday said the news media are unfair and inaccurate.

Repetition is even more common in longer passages that involve several sentences. Sentences that appear near the end of a paragraph should not repeat facts implied or mentioned earlier:

Workers digging a drainage ditch brought up more than dirt. They found the skeletons of three children.
REVISED: Workers digging a drainage ditch found the skeletons of three children.

This is not the first time he has been held up. He has been robbed three times in the past eight months.
REVISED: He has been robbed three times in the past eight months.

A burglary occurred Tuesday afternoon at the home of Clarence Dozier, 2347 Bentley Ave. A .38 caliber revolver and some food were stolen.
REVISED: Burglars took a .38 caliber revolver and some food from the home of Clarence Dozier, 2347 Bentley Ave., Tuesday afternoon.

Be Precise

To communicate effectively, reporters must also be precise, particularly in their selection and arrangement of words. Imprecision creates confusion and misunderstanding. Thomas Berry, author of "The Craft of Writing," has pointed out that the difference between mediocre writing and excellent writing is often the choice of words, and that the perfect choice can change the meaning of an entire sentence. The perfect choice also makes sentences more forceful and interesting.

Some words are simply inappropriate for use in news stories. Few editors permit the use of words such as "cop" or "kid" (unless you are referring to a goat), or derogatory terms about a person's race or religion. Editors allow profanity only when it is essential to a story's meaning and, even then, refuse to publish the most offensive terms. They prefer the word "woman" to the archaic "lady." Many ban the use of contractions, except in direct quotations. Editors also object to nouns used as verbs. They would not allow you to report that someone "authored" a book, "detailed" a plan, "hosted" a party, "headquartered" a company or "gunned" an enemy. Nor would they allow you to report that food prices were "upped," plans "finalized" nor cars "sirened" to a halt.

Other errors occur because reporters are unaware of words' exact meanings. Few newspapers would report that a car collided with a tree, that a funeral service was scheduled or held, that a gunman executed his victim or that a child was drowned in a lake. Why? Two objects can collide only if both are moving; thus, a car can strike a tree but can never "collide" with one. The term "funeral service" is redundant, and the word "execute" means that a person is being put to death in accordance with a legally imposed sentence; therefore, only a state—never a murderer—can execute anyone. A story which reported that a child "was drowned" would imply that someone held the child's head underwater until the victim died.

Such considerations may seem trivial, but journalists devote their lives to jobs that require a mastery of the English language, and most of them strive for perfection. Moreover, they realize that every word published by their newspapers may be read by thousands of people, and that many of those readers will notice any errors they make.

Double meanings are more difficult to detect. In writing a sentence, a reporter may intend to say one thing, yet—because of the reporter's inability to express the idea clearly and precisely—readers may interpret the sentence differently. Double meanings in the following headlines, all of which have actually been published by newspapers, illustrate the problem:

Albany Turns to Garbage
American Sentenced to Life in Scotland
Lawmen from Mexico Barbecue Guests
Drunk Gets Nine Months in Violin Case
Milk Drinkers Turn to Powder
Death Causes Loneliness, Feelings of Isolation
Juvenile Court to Try Shooting Defendant
Khrushchev Is Buried in Encyclopedia
Squad Helps Dog Bite Victim

Readers often consider the double meanings humorous, but few editors are amused when the errors appear in their newspapers. Nevertheless, similar errors often appear in news stories, again as a result of imprecise writing:

An Ohio man was found guilty of molesting his 9-year-old step-daughter in Circuit Court today.

The State Health Department is surveying hospitals around the state to ascertain whether women patients are being given pap tests to determine if they have uterine cancer as required by law.

(The New York Times)

Remain Objective

During the Revolutionary War, American newspapers were journals of opinion and frequently propagandized for or against the British. A colonial editor named Isaiah Thomas joined the militia that fired on British troops at Lexington, then reported the battle in his paper, the Massachusetts Spy. His story, published on May 3, 1775, began:

AMERICANS! forever bear in mind the BATTLE OF LEXINGTON!—where British troops, unmolested and unprovoked, wantonly and in a most inhuman manner, fired upon and killed a number of our countrymen, then robbed, ransacked, and burnt their houses! nor could the tears of defenseless women, some of whom were in the pains of childbirth, the cries of helpless babes, nor the prayers of old age, confined to beds of sickness, appease their thirst for blood!—or divert them from their DESIGN of MURDER and robbery!

Today, journalists strive to be as impartial or "objective" as possible. Editors and other newspaper employees can express their opinions in editorials and columns, but not in news stories. Newspaper reporters are expected to be neutral observers, not advocates or participants. Reporters cannot discriminate against any ideas or tell their readers what to think about these ideas.

While working as a reporter, assume that your readers are intelligent and capable of reaching their own conclusions about issues in the news. Your job as a reporter is to gather and report facts that your readers need to make wise decisions—not to make the decisions for them. Avoid adjectives and labels that reflect your opinions. Also avoid loaded words, such as "demagogue," "extremist," "radical," "racist," "segregationist" and "zealot." They are unnecessary, may be inaccurate and may unnecessarily infuriate readers who have opposite views.

Reporters can eliminate the opinion in some sentences by deleting a single word: "*alert* witness," "*famous* author," "*gala* reception," "*thoughtful* reply," "*tragic* accident":

> The tickets will cost only $14.
> REVISED: The tickets will cost $14.

> The tragic explosion injured seven students.
> REVISED: The explosion injured seven students.

Other sentences require more extensive revisions:

> Most people were apathetic; only 22 percent voted in the election.
> REVISED: Twenty-two percent of the eligible people voted in the election.

> About two dozen strikebreakers evaded the pickets by using a back door at the plant.
> REVISED: About two dozen workers avoided the pickets by using a back door at the plant.

Entire sentences sometimes convey opinions rather than facts. In most cases, the opinions are expressed as trite generalities, unsupported by facts. Such sentences must be avoided:

> House trailers are not cheap. The average price is $19,000.
> REVISED: The average house trailer costs $19,000.

> Most of us are not happy about going back to work on Monday. But Kris Wilcox was more than happy to return to work today. She just recovered from a kidney transplant.
> REVISED: Kris Wilcox returned to work today after recovering from a kidney transplant.

Still other sentences contain no facts, only the opinions of the reporters or of their sources. The entire sentences must be deleted:

> Their answers were thoughtful.
> The woman's poor judgment caused the $6,000 loss.
> This year's program will offer something to please everyone.

Review Questions

As you begin to write news stories, ask yourself the following questions. If you answer "no" to any of the questions, you may have to edit or rewrite your story.

1. Have I used short, familiar words?
2. Have I used short sentences and short paragraphs?
3. Have I used colorful, descriptive *active* verbs?
4. Have I eliminated unnecessary words, especially adverbs and adjectives?
5. Have I been precise? Is every word used correctly, and does every sentence say what I want it to say?
6. Have I avoided statements of opinion?
7. Have I avoided overloading my sentences? Does each sentence contain only a few *related* ideas?
8. Finally—and perhaps most importantly—have I used relatively simple sentences, with the normal word order: subject, verb, direct object?

Newsman Lou Bate and his colleagues on the city desk of the Deseret News in Salt Lake City compiled these examples of wordy phrases which appeared in their newspaper:

held a meeting	should be trimmed to	**met**
was a winner of	should be trimmed to	**won**
voted to appoint	should be trimmed to	**appointed**
was the recipient of	should be trimmed to	**received**
is presently studying	should be trimmed to	**is studying**
made a denouncement of	should be trimmed to	**denounced**
will give a lecture on	should be trimmed to	**will lecture on**
made a $10,000 donation	should be trimmed to	**donated $10,000**
conduct an evaluation of	should be trimmed to	**evaluate**
have come to a compromise	should be trimmed to	**have compromised**
come into compliance with	should be trimmed to	**comply with**
gave its tentative approval	should be trimmed to	**tentatively approved**
several members of the public	should be trimmed to	**several people**

Daily newspapers such as the St. Louis Post-Dispatch have begun to hire writing coaches to help reporters improve their writing. Many of the coaches also prepare bulletins, such as this one, that discuss common problems and provide examples of good and bad writing. More bulletins appear in following chapters.

Write & Wrong ST. LOUIS POST-DISPATCH

By Harry Levins
Post-Dispatch Writing Coach

Good writers try to shed adjectives and general nouns whenever they can. The writers rely instead on specific nouns. That's because specific nouns have a better chance of evoking specific images in the reader's mind.

Take, for example, a sentence that says, *He sped off in his car.* Well, a car is a car is a car. Refining the idea will reinforce the image:

He sped off in his sports car.

Better, but still vague. The car could be any one of a number of models. Is it a Porsche? A Fiat? So:

He sped off in his Corvette.

A Corvette is something concrete, something a reader can visualize. That vision comes even more easily with a bit more refinement:

He sped off in his red 1983 Corvette.

Now, the reader has the images he needs for an instant replay in his mind. Now, the hazy notion of "car" has taken on form and color. All of us know "red." Most of us have some idea of what a Corvette looks like. Some of us know precisely what a 1983 Corvette looks like. To some degree, we've all been served by specificity.

True, "red" and "1983" are adjectives. But they evoke *specific* images. A bad writer would have chosen adjectives like "sleek" and "costly." And that's where adjectives get writers into trouble.

What's "sleek"? Sleekness, like beauty, is in the eye of the beholder; some people (The Coach among them) regard the Corvette as squat and ungainly. Anyway, "sleek" is so hazy a notion that it can cover both Brooke Shields and the B-1 bomber.

And how costly is "costly"? A newspaperman thinks a Corvette is costly. But to a network anchorman, a Corvette qualifies as an impulse purchase. The writer who reaches for "costly" ought instead to reach for the telephone. The Coach did—and was told by a salesman at Don Reed Chevrolet that the average Corvette retails for about $24,000. Specific information like that can let each reader decide whether a Corvette is "costly."

The matter came to mind recently when The Coach read a story about an event at the Convention Center at which people strolled "from one end of the huge Exhibit Hall B to the other."

OK—how huge is "huge"?

One phone call by The Coach established that Hall B is 299 feet by 266 feet, 10 inches—79,782 square feet. That comes to 1.83 acres; the people at the Home Builders Association tell The Coach that the square footage is slightly more than the square footage of 51 average new homes in the suburbs.

Hey, 79,782 square feet is *big*. But is it *huge*?

Well, Gilley's, a country-and-western honkeytonk near Houston, Tex., has 174,240 square feet. Huge?

Well, the New Orleans Superdome has 566,280 square feet. Huge?

Well, the VBA flower growers' co-op in Aalsmeth, Netherlands, has 3,264,386. Huge?

Well, each tower of the World Trade Center in New York has 4,370,000. Huge?

Well, the Pentagon has 6,500,000. Huge?

Well, the Nizhnig tank plant in the Soviet Union has 8,899,326 square feet. It's the world's biggest building, so it's *huge*.

Maybe the reporter was thinking in terms of cubic feet. The Convention Center's Exhibit Hall B is 55 feet high. That gives it a cubic footage of 4,388,010. Not bad. But is it *huge*?

Well, the Goodyear airship hangar in Akron, Ohio, has 55,000,000 cubic feet. Is *that* huge?

Try the vehicle assembly building at Cape Canaveral, Fla. It has 129,482,000 cubic feet. Huge?

Not really. The main assembly plant at Boeing's complex in Everett, Wash., has 200,000,000 cubic feet. That's *huge*.

The point of this exercise? To show that adjectives like "huge" have two strikes against them:

1. They are relative, and thus subjective. What's "huge" from the viewpoint of a 2-year-old is tiny to an astronomer. What's "tiny" to a microchip assembler is infinitesimal to an autoworker. What seems "pretty" to a GI in Guam might be considered pretty grim along the bar at Friday's.

2. They are maddeningly vague. Telling the reader that Exhibit Hall B is "huge" tells him nothing. Telling the reader that Hall B has 79,782 square feet gives him something to chew on. Refining it further—noting that Hall B is almost as long as a football field, or that it covers 1.83 acres, or that it has more floor space than 51 new suburban homes—puts "huge" in terms that most readers can grasp.

And making the news understandable to the people who read it is a basic part of what we're supposed to be doing.

☆ ☆ ☆

Department of Dirty Words

Euphemisms are like weeds, or leftist insurrections: no sooner do you stamp one out than another one springs up. We've been doing well with some. "Senior citizen" seems to have waned in favor of "the elderly," "the aged" or "old people." Rare is the use of "indigent," "disadvantaged" or "economically deprived" for "poor." We hardly see "affirmative action" for "minority job program." But other euphemisms have arisen. Here are some that seem to be cropping up recently:

Certified personnel. In stories about schools—and such stories are almost always mother lodes of euphemisms—these are people who hold teaching certificates. We can call them "teachers." If we want to include administrators who hold teaching certificates, we can say "teachers and their supervisors." If we also want to include staff workers who hold teaching certificates, we can say, "Teachers, their supervisors and high-ranking staff workers"; that ought to differentiate the certified staff member from the little old lady who dishes out macaroni and cheese in the cafeteria. Moral: people in education know what "certified personnel" means, but lots of newspaper readers don't. Write for the people who read the news, not for the people who make it. Postscript: at all costs, avoid the word some educators use: "certificated."

Corrections officers. They stand guard in jails and prisons. Once, we knew them as "guards." Let's revive that term.

Executive session. This is what aldermen and school commissioners say when they decide to shut out the public. "Executive session" has a dignified ring, which is why the politicians like it. It also softens the truth, which is why the politicians use it. The truth: that the politicians went into *a closed session*. Use that phrase.

Sandinista. For some reason, we have made "Sandinista" a synonym for "Nicaraguan." The Coach suspects that in so doing, we are serving our readers poorly. A recent poll found a lot of confusion among the public about what's going on in Central America; a majority was unable to say whether we backed El Salvador and opposed Nicaragua, or whether it was the other way around. Sandinista is the name of a political party; it is to Nicaragua what the Communist Party is to the Soviet Union. But by no means is every institution "Sandinista" rather than "Nicaraguan." After The Coach read about the poll on Central America, he got the nagging suspicion that a dismaying number of Americans probably think "Sandinista" is a country sandwiched somewhere between Honduras and Costa Rica. So: where the word "Nicaraguan" will replace "Sandinista" with precision, use it.

Third World. This phrase is like an enduring marriage—so familiar that we overlook its shortcomings. If pressed to define it, a user might well hesitate, then say testily, "Well, you know what it means."

Do we? Trouble is, it's a catch phrase that means many things to many people.

Geopolitically, it means "nonaligned nations," those countries that choose not to choose sides in the East-West rivalry. But even that category is hardly hard and fast. Afghanistan once was solidly in the Third World; now, it's straddling the barbed wire between the Third World and the Soviet bloc. India's air force is a kissing cousin of the Soviet Union, yet India remains in the Third World. And what do we do about Yugoslavia? Or Albania?

(continued on next page)

Racially, it seems to mean most countries in which most of the people are not Caucasian. But again, we have exceptions. Many people in Central America and most in India are Caucasian, so here the difference is in language, or in shade of whiteness, or something.

Economically, "Third World" means several things. Wretchedly poor subsistence-farming countries like Honduras and Pakistan are considered a part of the Third World. But so are rapidly developing nations—Brazil, say, or Nigeria. Mexico seems to slide between both economic subcategories, depending on the writer's degree of optimism.

Excluded from the Third World are two countries now developing rapidly from a subsistence-farming past: South Korea, apparently because of its military alliance with the United States, and Ireland, apparently because of racial considerations. Sicily could be in the Third World but can't be, because it's part of Italy, which is part of the First World. Or is that the Second World?

Then, we have some judgment-call countries—Burma, for example, or Singapore, or Saudi Arabia, or Iran, or Malta. Are they Third World, or are they not? And if we don't know, what does that say about the term "Third World"?

Maybe that it's vague.

Those seeking precision might pin down a category—"nonaligned," "poor," "developing" or "nonwhite"—and use it in place of "Third World."

☆ ☆ ☆

A Note To The Reader

The Coach plans to spend much of October on vacation, picking nits in his reading and pulling crabgrass in his yard. He may or may not get to a November issue of *Write & Wrong*. But he'll be back for sure before you say "winter solstice."

Suggested Readings

Associated Press Staff, and Rene J. Cappon, eds. *The Associated Press Guide to Good Writing*. New York: The Associated Press, 1982.

Barzun, Jacques. *Simple & Direct: A Rhetoric for Writers*. New York: Harper & Row, Publishers, 1985.

Bernstein, Theodore M. *Do's, Don'ts, & Maybes of English Usage*. New York: Times Books, 1977.

———. *More Language That Needs Watching*. New York: Atheneum, 1964.

———. *Watch Your Language*. New York: Atheneum, 1981.

Burack, Sylvia K., ed. *The Writer's Handbook, 1986*. 50th ed. Boston, Mass.: The Writer, Inc., 1986.

Cheney, Theodore A. *Getting the Words Right: How to Revise, Edit & Rewrite*. Cincinnati, Ohio: Writer's Digest Books, 1983.

Grey, David L. *The Writing Process*. Belmont, Calif.: Wadsworth Publishing Company, 1972.

Hohenberg, John. *The Pulitzer Prize Story*. New York: Columbia University Press, 1959.

Newman, Edwin. *A Civil Tongue*. New York: Warner Books, 1977.

———. *Strictly Speaking*. New York: Warner Books, 1975.

Rivers, William L. *Writing: Craft and Art*. Englewood Cliffs, N.J.: Prentice-Hall, Inc., 1975.

Sale, Roger. *On Writing*. New York: Random House, 1969.

Shaw, Harry. *Twenty Steps to Better Writing*. Totowa, N.J.: Littlefield, Adams, 1978.

Yates, Edward D. *The Writing Craft*. 2nd ed. Raleigh, N.C.: Contemporary Publishing Company, 1985.

Zinsser, William. *On Writing Well; An Informal Guide to Writing Nonfiction*. rev. ed. New York: Harper & Row, 1985.

Advice from a Pro

"Some lucky stiffs, whom you will learn to envy if you're not one of them, have the facility for swift, painless writing. Others, the majority I believe—and you may count me in—find writing a labored agony of mental sweat. They figuratively have to flog themselves into starting, and they love it only for the satisfaction of having done it, never for any joy in doing it."

"Of course there is bad newspaper writing. There is terrible newspaper writing, just as there are terrible magazine stories and terrible books. But considering the speed and quantity with which they are produced, newspaper stories deserve a pretty high rating. . . . Some of the finest writing I have ever read has been in newspapers."

"Always, when time permits, read your story before submitting it. If you can't cut out at least a couple of words, you're not doing a sufficiently critical job of reading. One of the toughest things in the writing trade, and one of the best for a writer, is to cut your own copy."

"Don't try to increase your vocabulary, either. Decrease it. The only time a new word is worth using is when it will take the place of three or four others, and then don't try to use it fresh from the dictionary. Wait until you've become familiar with it by hearing or seeing it used. A thesaurus is a curse; don't have one in your desk. If it's handy, it will tempt you to use too many obscure words."

"The new reporter is always prone to use such words as 'contusions and abrasions,' which don't mean as much to the reader as 'cuts and bruises.'"

"One well-chosen verb packs more power than a string of adjectives and adverbs."

(From the book "Newspaperman" by Morton Sontheimer)

REVIEW: Writing Simply and Clearly

Before beginning the exercises on the following pages, review these examples and guidelines.

A key to good writing is simplicity. When people speak, they use simple words and simple sentences. Yet many people seem unable to write that way. Instead, their language becomes more formal and stilted. For example:

Can you afford me the opportunity to visit with you?
REVISED: Can I visit you?

He patterned it after programs successfully implemented in West Germany.
REVISED: He copied successful West German programs.

Most sentences use the normal word order: subject, verb and direct object—in that order. The following sentences are awkward because they fail to use that word order:

Cost of the breakfast will be $3.50.
REVISED: The breakfast will cost $3.50.

A declination to prosecute her husband was signed by the woman.
REVISED: The woman declined to prosecute her husband.

There are several advantages to using the normal word order. First, your sentences will be simpler and more readable. Second, they will be more concise. Third, because you can use an active verb, they will also be more interesting:

They are products that the public has come to know and trust.
REVISED: The public knows and trusts the products.

It is in violation of the law to use profanity, he said.
REVISED: Profanity violates the law, he said.

Mistakenly, students often begin their sentences with a long clause. The longer the clause, the more unreadable their sentences become. When sentences begin with a long clause, the most important information—the news—is usually buried near the end:

Scheduled to appear in court at 9 a.m. today for the death of an 8-year-old girl, a man hanged himself in the county jail last night.
REVISED: A man charged with the death of an 8-year-old girl hanged himself in the county jail last night. He was scheduled to appear in court at 9 a.m. today.

Calling NASA's practice of flying thousands of guests to Florida to watch its shuttle launches "one of the most expensive and wasteful public relations campaigns in the history of the federal government," Sen. William Proxmire demanded that it be stopped.
REVISED: Sen. William Proxmire demanded that NASA stop flying thousands of guests to Florida to watch its shuttle launches. He called it "one of the most expensive and wasteful public relations campaigns in the history of the federal government."

Also be certain that you are writing as concisely as possible. Delete words that are repetitious or that state the obvious:

The boys were in the water swimming together.
REVISED: The boys were swimming together.

The police do not have any suspects at this point in time.
REVISED: The police have no suspects.

You can often substitute a single word for a longer phrase:

She began to scream at the intruder.
REVISED: She screamed at the intruder.

The accident resulted in the death of one man.
REVISED: The accident killed one man.

Some experts advise writers to present only one idea in each sentence. However, that may be an extreme remedy. Instead, present only a few *related* ideas in each sentence. If a sentence contains too many ideas, eliminate some. Or, start a new sentence:

Eighty percent of the education majors who took the test last month passed all four parts, with women having an 82 percent passing rate compared to 76 percent for men.
REVISED: Eighty percent of the education majors who took the test last month passed all four parts. Eighty-two percent of the women passed the test, compared to 76 percent of the men.

Neighbors said that, at about 5:15 p.m., they heard Thomas Rawl and his girlfriend, Jean Marie Simkell, begin to argue in the front yard of a home they shared at 3168 Whisper Lake Lane, and they saw Rawl get a gun from his car, shoot Simkell, and then shoot himself, both fatally.
REVISED: Neighbors said they saw Thomas Rawl get a gun from his car and shoot and kill his girlfriend, Jean Marie Simkell, and then kill himself. Rawl and Simkell shared a home at 3168 Whisper Lake Lane. Neighbors said the couple had begun to argue in the front yard at about 5:15 p.m.

Finally, remember to remain objective. Report facts, not your opinion:

The school's athletic program is well-rounded, with 26 sports offered for men and 14 offered for women.
REVISED: The school offers 26 sports for men and 14 for women.

The lengthy 137-page report contains some interesting facts about cancer.
REVISED: The 137-page report contains facts about cancer.

EXERCISE 1
Selecting the Proper Word

SECTION I Substitute simpler and more common words for each of these words.

1. accelerate	11. community	21. originate
2. adjacent	12. conflagration	22. present
3. altercation	13. dilapidated	23. provide
4. anticipate	14. encounter	24. purchase *buy*
5. apprehend *caught*	15. finance	25. reimburse - *paid back*
6. ascertain	16. incarcerated	26. relocating
7. assist	17. instruct	27. request
8. attempt	18. intoxicated	28. residence
9. bequeath *gave/willed*	19. lacerations - *cuts*	29. roadways
10. commence	20. ordinance	30. terminate

SECTION II The following phrases are redundant. They do not have to be rewritten: simply cross off the unnecessary words.

1. abolish altogether	10. hanged down from	19. planning ahead
2. are in need of	11. hanged to death	20. proposed plans
3. are now	12. head up	21. return back home
4. are presently	13. honest truth	22. right here
5. bald headed	14. in an effort to	23. sat down
6. brilliant genius	15. is presently	24. seek to find
7. equally as good as	16. lifeless bodies	25. sent away for
8. first became	17. mental anguish	26. sum of $6,000
9. first discovered	18. now costs	27. terrible tragedy

SECTION III Use a single word to replace each of these phrases.

1. allows for	6. get underway	11. made their exit
2. are in agreement	7. in the course of	12. made a contribution
3. at present	8. is hopeful that	13. posed a question
4. gave chase to	9. made the ruling	14. proceeded to leave
5. gave their approval	10. made their escape	15. short distance away

SECTION IV Eliminate the nouns used as verbs in the following sentences.

1. She wants to author a book. _____

2. He was shotgunned to death. _____

3. She doctored her own illness. _____

4. The body will be autopsied Friday. _____

5. They trucked a load of furniture to their new home. _____

SECTION V List three stronger, more active and descriptive verbs to replace the verbs in the following sentences.

1. The book should have more information about Indians. _____

2. They got a computer for their home. _____

3. About 800 students are in the school. _____

4. Her scrapbook has many photographs. _____

5. The city council will ~~look into~~ study the library's annual budget. _____

SECTION VI Rewrite the following sentences, using stronger verbs. Also use the normal word order: subject, verb and direct object.

1. She said ~~it was~~ the defendant's ~~intent~~ tried to rob her client.

2. The girl had several teeth knocked out by her father.

3. He was fired because it is against company policy to have alcoholic beverages during work hours.

4. To obtain more money, she has three college students renting rooms in her house.

5. The teacher got a lemon meringue pie thrown in her face by an angry student.

EXERCISE 2
Writing Clearly and Concisely

SECTION I: REDUNDANCIES The following phrases are redundant. They do not have to be rewritten: simply cross off the unnecessary words.

1. are currently
2. brand new
3. first arrived
4. free of charge
5. future goals

6. giving away
7. jail facility
8. personal belief
9. personal habit
10. referred back to

11. set a new record
12. small in size
13. they both agree
14. unpaid debt
15. whether or not

SECTION II: WORDINESS Eliminate the unnecessary words from the following sentences. The sentences do not have to be rewritten; simply cross off the words that are not needed.

1. Firefighters reached the scene and extinguished the blaze.

2. Before the robbers left, they also took some liquor.

3. At the present time, about 100 students participate.

4. The center will have eight offices for different ministers to occupy.

5. The boy was submerged underwater for about 5 to 10 minutes.

6. The results showed that only 31 percent passed the test.

7. He was pinned in the car 40 minutes before he could be removed.

8. Since the inception of the program it has saved three lives.

9. Anyone may participate if they would like to.

10. The engineer said that, in his opinion, relatively few people actually use the road.

SECTION III: VERBS List three stronger, more active and descriptive verbs that can replace the verbs in the following sentences.

1. She had on a pink suit. _____

2. The newspaper will be made weekly. _____

3. The committee has had several meetings. _____

4. A study is being done by the school board. _____

5. Students made the lowest scores in mathematics. _____

6. The robber told her to give him her purse. _____

7. He is asking for $250,000 for the land. _____

8. The editor did a study of newsroom computerization. _____

9. The fire did $36,000 worth of damage. _____

10. Each journalism student is required to do an internship. _____

SECTION IV: CLARITY AND CONCISENESS The following sentences are passive, awkward and wordy. Rewrite the sentences, using the normal word order: subject, verb and direct object.

1. Her screams were heard by some men.

2. The governor's goal is to raise teachers' salaries.

3. The bike path is used by other people as an exercise track.

4. The purpose of the program will be to raise money for wildlife.

5. The program will feature pro and con speakers for and against a nuclear freeze.

6. He said the primary reason EDB is used is because it is the most effective pesticide.

7. Attempts to lift fingerprints off of the unlocked window had negative results.

8. One problem cited by the city planner is that the subdivision's developers failed to advise her of the drainage problems.

9. Arlene Einhorn was taken by ambulance to Memorial Hospital where she was treated for a broken right arm and shock.

10. Private citizens receiving the full expense-paid trips to Hawaii totaled 256 in number.

EXERCISE 3
Improving Your Newswriting Skills

SECTION I: REDUNDANCIES The following phrases are redundant. They do not have to be rewritten: simply cross off the unnecessary words.

1. burned in flames
2. combine together
3. continue on
4. crowd of people
5. foreign imports

6. join together
7. new discovery
8. new recruit
9. past experience
10. personal friend

11. right now
12. safe haven
13. totally destroyed
14. true facts
15. won a victory

SECTION II: VERBS AND SENTENCE STRUCTURE Rewrite the following sentences, using stronger, more descriptive verbs. Also use the normal word order: subject, verb and direct object.

1. Police suspect that the vandalism was done by children.
2. The woman had her purse snatched by a boy, about 16.
3. Included in the bag were one shirt, some shoes and two pairs of socks.
4. Their lawsuit complains that the bottle of soda had an insect in it.
5. Anxious to buy an engagement ring, the couple got a loan for it.

SECTION III: OBJECTIVITY Rewrite the following sentences, eliminating the expressions of opinion.

1. His speech was well received, as he was interrupted 17 times by applause.
2. Another important concept is the author's idea that it does not matter whether children begin to read before they are 10 years old.
3. When Mary Ellen Rodriguez left work Monday, she received a little surprise. Missing from her new Cadillac were both doors and all four hubcaps.
4. It should be kept in mind, however, that with the interstate highway only 10 miles away, the park is easily accessible to all the residents of the state.
5. They announced that residents of the city can look forward to the construction of a new $4.1 million library next year.

SECTION IV: SENTENCE STRUCTURE ERRORS Rewrite the following sentences, eliminating the errors made by other college students.

1. The car's driver suffered a concussion and scars on her legs.
2. A car stopped to help the accident victims and then called the police.
3. Paramedics came and took the victim to a hospital with minor cuts and bruises.

4. Both the speech and the breakfast are free to the public which begins at 7 a.m.

5. After robbing the convenience store, a waiting vehicle sped east on Northrup Road.

6. Sheriff's deputies said that skid marks on the road indicated that neither driver had time to step on their brakes.

7. Attorneys charged that he had an intoxicated driving record even before the accident Sunday.

8. The law will increase the fines given to every motorist convicted of speeding by 10 percent.

9. Foods sold in vending machines with a high sugar content will be replaced by foods considered more healthy.

10. The lawsuit states that she suffered massive scarring from the ant bites and loss of work.

SECTION V: CLARITY AND CONCISENESS Express the following ideas more clearly and concisely. As you rewrite the sentences, use the normal word order: subject, verb and direct object.

1. Durst was acquitted of the charges by a jury.

2. Kathy Tijoriwali is the owner of the hot dog stand.

3. The summer recreation program is set up so that the costs are paid by the city.

4. One problem cited in the report was that the mechanic failed to regularly inspect the airplane's engine.

5. He said that ladder trucks are needed by the fire department to reach taller buildings in the city.

6. The opinion of the students is that there should be more opportunities for them to complain about incompetent professors.

7. It is recommended by the article that the appointment should be temporary, lasting for only one year.

8. Miller testified that she was visited by Paddock on three occasions.

9. The turnout was fairly small. Only seven women attended the first meeting.

10. To make a story interesting, a good use of verbs can be extremely effective.

EXERCISE 4
Eliminating Unnecessary Words

SECTION I The following sentences do not have to be rewritten. Simply cross off the opinionated words and phrases.

1. Only 7 of the 94 people aboard the plane were killed.

2. The boy's grief-stricken father says he intends to sue the school.

3. Eighty-six women miraculously escaped injury when an alert pedestrian noticed the flames and quickly warned them to leave the dormitory.

4. In a powerful speech Monday, the governor insisted that the state must adopt needed laws to protect the endangered environment.

5. One of the most interesting facts he revealed was that the Chinese replace each barrel of oil with one barrel of water to ensure that all their oil is pumped out of the ground.

SECTION II The following sentences do not have to be rewritten. Simply cross off the unnecessary words.

1. Police responding to the call found that the assailants had kicked him in the face, neck and head.

2. The accident occurred when a pickup truck collided with an oncoming car.

3. The city council voted to go ahead and sue the builders.

4. There is a possibility that a TV monitor may be installed sometime later this month.

5. When the police arrived on the scene, they found only an empty shoe box—not a bomb.

SECTION III Substitute a single word for the longer phrases in the following sentences.

1. A gunman made off with about $700.

2. The gunman was described as wearing a blue jacket.

3. The operation left him in a state of paralysis.

4. Her medical bills are in excess of $10,000.

5. The other man then began to stab Hodgins.

6. Margaret Van Den Shruck addressed her speech to the Rotary Club.

7. Three of the 20 students said they are concerned about getting AIDS.

8. The new law will no longer allow tinted car windows.

9. The report goes on to say that he is asking for a new car.

10. He believes the program serves as a deterrent for drunken driving.

SECTION IV Rewrite these sentences, eliminating as many words as possible.

1. He said the cost of putting on the program will be about $500.

2. He criticized the president, calling him inconsistent and unrealistic.

3. The police officer opened fire, shooting six times at the suspect.

4. He responded by knocking the youth's hand away from his wallet.

5. The men demanded that Hodgins give them his wallet.

6. They said that another major problem with the program is that it has been poorly planned.

7. Of the 10 drivers interviewed, four felt that it is inevitable that you are going to have some injuries and deaths among the people participating in their stock car races.

8. The thieves were males about 16 years old and described to be of slim build.

9. Sanchez was taken to Memorial Hospital and is in fair condition there.

10. They told the midwife that there was not much time before the baby was due.

EXERCISE 5
Improving Your Newswriting Skills: Miscellaneous Exercises

SECTION I: SIMPLIFYING Rewrite the following sentences more simply and clearly.

1. He was the recipient of numerous awards and honors.
2. The police were summoned to the scene by a neighbor.
3. She said that their farm is in close proximity to the city.
4. Snow-removal vehicles are undertaking a cleanup of the city.
5. They said that a visit to their grandmother's was where they were going.

SECTION II: CONDENSING Edit or rewrite the following sentences more concisely.

1. The men were in the process of painting a house when they fell.
2. He said the water system is presently serving about 1,200 homes.
3. The chapel is interdenominational, serving worshippers of all religious faiths.
4. The police pursued a car traveling at a high rate of speed down the highway.
5. Sen. William Proxmire criticized the program and said it is a luxury which the country cannot afford.

SECTION III: IMPROVING THE WORD ORDER Rewrite the following sentences, using the normal word order: subject, verb and direct object.

1. It is estimated by police that the car was traveling 85 mph.
2. Raising the minister's salary to $42,600 a year was approved by the church's trustees.
3. The decision as to which student will be named editor will be made by the newspaper's own staff.
4. Another goal of Fidel Castro's was for Cuba to emerge as a leader of developing Third World countries.
5. A lack of interest in the tennis tournament resulted in a vote by the club members to cancel it in future years.

SECTION IV: SIMPLIFYING COMPLEX SENTENCES The following sentences are too long and complicated. Divide them into simpler, more concise sentences.

1. Two high school students, Joan Harnish and Sara Courhesne, were driving north on Carpenter Road at 10:30 p.m. when they came around a sharp curve in the road and noticed a wrecked motorcycle and, about 20 feet away, a man—apparently seriously injured—sprawled near a telephone pole.

2. In a 121-page report, the Department of Health and Human Services stated that drunken driving causes 28,000 traffic deaths a year, costing the nation $15 billion, and that nearly 9 million persons suffer from alcoholism or lesser drinking problems, a number that constitutes 10 percent of the U.S. work force.

3. Striking her head on the windshield when the truck sideswiped her car, Anna Schaufler passed out and, when she regained consciousness moments later, she found that a passenger in her small car was desperately reaching over her and trying to steer their car back onto the road.

4. Cynthia Allerson, who was driving the car, said she was taking four other students, including three exchange students from Germany, to a nearby shopping mall when another car smashed broadside into her vehicle at the intersection of Polle Street and Fuller Road, seriously injuring two of the exchange students.

5. Of the $126,000 estate, nearly $102,000 worth of stocks and cash was divided among Norbratten's son, daughter and wife, with the son, Ronald L. Norbratten, getting nearly $60,000, while Norbratten's daughter, Rosemary K. Norbratten, received half that amount, $32,000, and his wife, Maria N. Norbratten, received the remainder.

EXERCISE 6
Review   **Answer Key Provided: See Appendix D**

SECTION I: REDUNDANCIES The following phrases are redundant. They do not have to be rewritten: simply cross off the unnecessary words.

1. actual facts	6. free gifts	11. strangled to death
2. close down	7. in order to	12. tracked down
3. dead bodies	8. new innovation	13. very unique
4. dropped downward	9. past history	14. winter months
5. first began	10. revert back to	15. young child

SECTION II: WORDINESS Substitute a single word for each of the following phrases.

1. came to a stop	7. in the vicinity of
2. did not pay any attention to	8. is in possession of
3. due to the fact that	9. made an investigation of
4. hold the belief that	10. pursuing a study of
5. in advance of	11. took under consideration
6. in the near future	12. united in holy matrimony

SECTION III: SIMPLIFYING Rewrite the following sentences more simply and clearly.

1. The debt was then not nearly so large as it is today.

2. The mayor said that he is favorably disposed toward the passage of the new law.

3. The agency gave a favorable recommendation to a proposal to annex the 40 acres of land.

4. Students utilizing the library voiced their displeasure when two people engaged in a loud conversation.

5. The suspect maintained that he had been drinking and had no recollection at all of the events that transpired on the Saturday night in question.

SECTION IV: VERBS AND SENTENCE STRUCTURE Rewrite the following sentences, using stronger verbs and the normal word order: subject, verb and direct object.

1. The goal of the mental health clinic is to become self-supporting.

2. The cost of the chapel is estimated by church officials to be $320,000.

3. Her bachelor's degree is a goal she set for herself three years ago.

4. He said an investigation of the crime is being conducted by the police.

5. Another objective of the clinic is to offer individual and group counseling to abused women.

6. The car the woman escaped in was described by witnesses as a new Ford.

SECTION V: WORDINESS The following sentences are wordy and redundant. As you rewrite the sentences, eliminate unnecessary words. Also try to use stronger verbs.

1. The police said that burglars gained entry to the home by prying open the back door.

2. Mark Boggard, a freshman, does not feel the same way as Audrey Kuhlman does about abortion.

3. He said that the United States is inferior to the Soviet Union when it comes to their conventional military forces in Europe.

4. At a party given in her honor on the day of her retirement, co-workers celebrated the occasion by presenting the librarian with a trip to Paris.

5. It was brought out at the conference that the terms of the agreement are not in accordance with the desires of the people of Israel.

EXERCISE 7
Newswriting Style   **Answer Key Provided: See Appendix D**

REVIEW: WORDY AND PASSIVE SENTENCES

INSTRUCTIONS: The following sentences are wordy and passive. Most have weak verbs, using "is," "was," "are" and "were." Rewrite the sentences, using stronger, more active and more descriptive verbs. As you rewrite the sentences, eliminate unnecessary words.

1. The club is in need of more members.

2. The purpose of the new program is to provide medical services to the indigent.

3. A short circuit in electrical wiring at the church was the cause of the fire.

4. The plan of the youths was never to tell their parents about the near drowning.

5. The consensus of opinion among participants in the workshop is that formal classes in sex education are a necessity for high school students.

6. It was brought out by a teacher at the school that algebra is a course that is avoided by most students.

7. It was stated in the report that water skiing is a sport that can be enjoyed by anyone regardless of age.

8. Another practice the radio station engaged in was to bill customers twice for the same advertisements.

9. Speaking of the plan, the senator said what it would do would be to give the elderly more protection against the problem of inflation.

10. Police went on to say that entrance made into the locked car was probably done by using a hook-shaped wire jimmied through the vent window to pull up the door latch.

11. Financial problems were listed as one of the reasons why the city decided to abandon its plans to expand the school.

12. Pointed out in the report is the fact that there are 28,000 traffic deaths a year as a direct result of the consumption of alcoholic beverages in the United States.

13. The sheriff cited overcrowded conditions in the county jail as the main reason why he intends to resign.

14. There have been complaints from patrons that on numerous occasions city buses have failed to leave promptly on time.

15. The main reason why most people in the town do not get good television reception is that the nearest television station is located a total of 60 miles away.

EXERCISE 8
Newswriting Style   Answer Key Provided: See Appendix D

REVIEW: MISCELLANEOUS PROBLEMS

INSTRUCTIONS: Make any changes necessary to improve the following sentences. Some are too wordy. Others are awkward, passive or opinionated.

1. He suffered the loss of his right eye.

2. They reached a settlement of the debt.

3. Brown, a family man, has a wife and four children.

4. Berkeley, Calif., is the town harboring the school.

5. Not until late August did she finally receive the money.

6. A pay raise of 8 percent was received by the carpenters.

7. It is estimated by witnesses that the boys drowned at 4:10 p.m.

8. The purpose of this article will be to examine the problems of students.

9. The politician extended his appreciation to those who had supported him.

10. It will be up to the state Legislature to decide how to expend the funds.

11. Applications must be submitted on or before the deadline date of March 1.

12. The blaze initiated at about midnight in the area of the high school.

13. The loan was made to the couple for the purchase of a new home.

14. The woman testified that she suffered numerous beatings from her husband.

15. A spokesman said it is hoped that the medical program will be entirely self-supporting.

16. A total of eight persons, four men and four women, serve on the committee.

17. It should be kept in mind, however, that property taxes will be increased by 5 percent.

18. Auto sales are decreasing because of the fact that the vehicles are becoming more expensive.

19. It was not until 6 p.m. that evening that the police were able to find the child.

20. The building burned to the ground despite the valiant efforts of firemen to save the structure.

21. Legal action has been taken by the company, which obtained an injunction to halt the strike.

22. A group of eight men beat him about his face and body after he was elected to the position of sheriff.

3 Spelling and Vocabulary

People who devote their lives to journalism develop a respect for the English language. They learn to write with precision: clearly, concisely and accurately. They select the exact word needed to convey an idea, use the word properly, and place it in a sentence that is grammatically correct.

Journalists' emphasis on precision is essential to the media's success. Americans expect their newspapers to be accurate and to use the language properly—to serve as a model for the public. If a writer is careless, an editor must then spend time correcting the writer's stories. Inevitably, errors that the editor misses will be published, and they may be noticed by thousands of readers. If the errors are serious or become too numerous, they may damage a newspaper's reputation and perhaps even its credibility. The errors may also require the printing of costly and embarrassing corrections.

As a consequence, responsible editors do not tolerate sloppiness of any kind, and they are particularly critical of errors in such basic areas as grammar, spelling and word usage. To help guard against these errors, newspapers often give job applicants spelling, vocabulary and writing tests, and hire only those who produce the best work.

The following exercises are designed to help you avoid some of the most common vocabulary and spelling errors. Appendix C contains the rules for forming possessives, and you may want to consult it while completing the exercises.

Suggested Readings

Berner, R. Thomas. *Language Skills for Journalists*. 2nd ed. Boston, Mass.: Houghton Mifflin, 1983.

Bernstein, Theodore M. *Do's, Don'ts, and Maybes of English Usage*. New York: Times Books, 1977.

———. *Watch Your Language*. New York: Atheneum, 1981.

Berry, Thomas Elliott. *The Most Common Mistakes in English Usage*. New York: McGraw-Hill, 1971.

Callihan, E. L. *Grammar for Journalists*. 3rd ed. Radnor, Pa.: Chilton, 1979.

Hayakawa, S. I. *The Use and Misuse of Language*. Greenwich, Conn.: Fawcett Publications, 1962.

Hodges, John C., and Mary E. Whitten. *Harbrace College Handbook*. 10th ed. San Diego: Harcourt Brace Jovanovich, 1986.

Leggett, Glenn, David C. Mead, and William Charvat. *Handbook for Writers*. Englewood Cliffs, N.J.: Prentice-Hall, 1974.

Rivers, William L. *Writing: Craft and Art*. Englewood Cliffs, N.J.: Prentice-Hall, 1975.

Safire, William. *I Stand Corrected: More on Language*. New York: Times Books, 1984.

——. *On Language*. New York: Avon, 1981.

——. *What's the Good Word?* New York: Times Books, 1982.

Shaw, Harry. *Punctuate It Right!* New York: Harper & Row, 1986.

Strunk, William, Jr., and E. B. White. *The Elements of Style*. 3rd ed. New York: Macmillan, 1979.

EXERCISE 1
Spelling and Vocabulary

INSTRUCTIONS: These 10 words are the ones that journalism students misspell most frequently. Some of the words are spelled correctly; others are misspelled. Use the proper copy-editing symbols to correct all the misspelled words.

1. alot
2. ammendment
3. criticises
4. definately
5. develop

6. it's (possessive)
7. judgment
8. occured
9. receive
10. seperate

Here are 25 more words that journalism students frequently misspell. Use the proper copy-editing symbols to correct the words that are misspelled.

1. accidently
2. alledgedly
3. amoung
4. analysed
5. apparently
6. argument
7. broadcasted
8. calender (for dates)
9. catagorized
10. fourty
11. license
12. lightening
13. magizines

14. medias
15. occasionally
16. opportunity
17. payed
18. personel
19. priviledge
20. proffessional
21. reguardless
22. severly
23. sophmore
24. thier
25. truly

Five other words that students often misspell include: "criteria," "data," "graffiti," "media" and "phenomena." All five are plural forms. The singular forms are: "criterion," "datum," "graffito," "medium" and "phenomenon." Thus, it would be correct to say, "The four criteria are adequate" or "The datum is lost," but not, "The media is inaccurate" or "The phenomenon are unusual."

A final point: journalists tend to be formal in their spelling. For example, they normally use "until" rather than "till" and "although" rather than "though."

EXERCISE 2
Spelling and Vocabulary

INSTRUCTIONS: The following list contains 75 words that college students frequently misspell. Some of the words are spelled correctly, but many others are misspelled. Use the proper copy-editing symbols to correct all the misspelled words. If several letters need to be corrected in a single word, rewrite the entire word.

1. accommodate	26. diarrhea	51. picknicing
2. advertizing	27. eligable	52. pneumonia
3. alright	28. embarrass	53. practise
4. ammount	29. equipted	54. proceded
5. arithmatic	30. existence	55. pryed
6. athletics	31. explaination	56. pursuit
7. beliefs	32. fiery	57. realised
8. believeable	33. harrassment	58. re-elect
9. benifit	34. housewifes	59. restaurant
10. burglers	35. immitate	60. rhythm
11. canceled	36. indorsed	61. saleries
12. Caribbean	37. infered	62. sargeant
13. cemetary	38. irate	63. sattelites
14. changeable	39. labeled	64. sentance
15. cigarette	40. leisure	65. sherriff
16. conscious	41. lieutenant	66. sponser
17. controlled	42. likable	67. sueing
18. cryed	43. maintnance	68. surprizing
19. defendent	44. marijuana	69. survivors
20. descended	45. missles	70. tenative
21. description	46. mosquitos	71. trys
22. desparately	47. negligence	72. untill
23. dieing	48. ninety	73. vacuum
24. distroyed	49. noone	74. Wedesday
25. deterant	50. obscenity	75. worrys

EXERCISE 3
Spelling and Vocabulary

INSTRUCTIONS: The following list contains 75 words that college students frequently misspell. Some of the words are spelled correctly, but many others are misspelled. Use the proper copy-editing symbols to correct all the misspelled words. If several letters need to be corrected in a single word, rewrite the entire word.

1. abdomen	26. dormitories	51. nickles
2. activitys	27. elete	52. noticeable
3. alphabet	28. emphacize	53. occurrence
4. ambulence	29. encyclopedia	54. paniced
5. assault	30. favortism	55. parallel
6. basicly	31. foriegner	56. partys
7. becomming	32. forsee	57. persuasion
8. bureaucracy	33. fraternities	58. poisonous
9. catastrophe	34. fulfill	59. prepairing
10. champagne	35. govermental	60. quizes
11. changing	36. grammer	61. respondent
12. cheif	37. heros	62. schedule
13. coller	38. illegitimate	63. simplest
14. commited	39. inaugurate	64. sizable
15. compitition	40. irregardless	65. skiing
16. congratulations	41. janiter	66. souvenir
17. contraversial	42. kindergarden	67. subpoena
18. convenient	43. legitimate	68. summerize
19. credibility	44. likelyhood	69. taxy
20. curcuit	45. massacre	70. theives
21. delagates	46. mileage	71. usable
22. desirable	47. mispell	72. victum
23. detremental	48. municiple	73. villain
24. deviding	49. necessary	74. wintry
25. disasterous	50. neighbor	75. wreckless

EXERCISE 4
Spelling and Vocabulary

INSTRUCTIONS: The following pairs or groups of words often cause confusion because, although most look or sound alike, their meanings differ. In the space provided, define each of the words and explain how its usage differs from the other word or words. If necessary, use additional sheets of paper for your answers.

1. advice/advise ——————————————————————————————

———

2. affect/effect ——————————————————————————————

———

3. aid/aides ——————————————————————————————————

———

4. alumna/alumni/alumnus ——————————————————————————

———

5. average/mean/median/mode ————————————————————————

———

6. because/since ——————————————————————————————————

———

7. burglar/robber/swindler/thief ————————————————————————

———

8. capital/capitol ——————————————————————————————————

———

9. cite/sight/site ——————————————————————————————————

———

10. compose/comprise ————————————————————————————————

———

11. consul/council/counsel ————————————————————————————

———

12. decent/descent/dissent ————————————————————————————

———

13. farther/further ————————————————————————————————————

———

14. fewer/less ——————————————————————————————————————

———

15. hanged/hung _____

_____

16. its/it's _____

_____

17. lay/lie _____

_____

18. loose/lose _____

_____

19. ordinance/ordnance _____

_____

20. principal/principle _____

_____

21. statue/statute _____

_____

22. than/then _____

_____

23. that/which _____

_____

24. their/there/they're _____

_____

25. to/too _____

_____

26. who/whom _____

_____

EXERCISE 5
Spelling and Vocabulary

INSTRUCTIONS: The following pairs or groups of words often cause confusion because, although most look or sound alike, their meanings differ. In the space provided, define each of the words and explain how its usage differs from the other word or words. If necessary, use additional sheets of paper for your answers.

1. adapt/adept/adopt _____

_____

2. altar/alter _____

_____

3. bloc/block _____

_____

4. blond/blonde _____

_____

5. canvas/canvass _____

_____

6. censor/censure _____

_____

7. complement/compliment _____

_____

8. confidant/confident _____

_____

9. conscience/conscious _____

_____

10. elusive/illusive _____

_____

11. ensure/insure _____

_____

12. envelop/envelope _____

_____

13. finance/financee _____

_____

14. imply/infer _____

_____

15. incite/insight _____

_____

16. liable/libel _____

_____

17. marshal/marshall _____

_____

18. miner/minor _____

_____

19. naval/navel _____

_____

20. reign/rein _____

_____

21. role/roll _____

_____

22. titled/entitled _____

_____

23. trail/trial _____

_____

24. trustee/trusty _____

_____

25. who's/whose _____

_____

26. your/you're _____

_____

EXERCISE 6
Spelling and Vocabulary

INSTRUCTIONS: Some words in the following sentences have been placed in parentheses. The words often cause confusion because they look or sound like other words. You were asked to define many of the words in Exercises 4 and 5. Decide which of the words is correct here and circle it. Cross off all the other words.

The sentences also contain possessives that need correcting. If you need help, the rules for forming possessives appear in Appendix C.

1. The schools (principal/principle) criticized her two (aids/aides).

2. The story (implies/infers) that the girl (hanged/hung) herself.

3. He (adviced/advised) the city to find another (cite/sight/site).

4. She asked (who's/whose) jacket is (laying/lying) on the floor.

5. His (fiance/fiancee) said (its/it's) unlikely to succeed.

6. They asked (who's/whose) (role/roll) she will be given.

7. He said the (data/datum) eliminated by the (censor/censure) was mistaken.

8. They wondered why (your/you're) being so (elusive/illusive) about the issue.

9. He said the (statue/statute) is likely (to/too) be declared unconstitutional.

10. He is trying to raise more (capital/capitol) to (insure/ensure) the store's success.

11. They (complemented/complimented) the architect but want (fewer/less) windows.

12. He is (confidant/confident) that the movie, (titled/entitled) "Romance," will succeed.

13. They want to (altar/alter) the plans so the buildings are (farther/further) apart.

14. (Their/There/They're) inheritance will total (over/more than) $7 million.

15. The committee is (composed/comprised) of 14 nurses, and they addressed all 5,000 (envelops/envelopes).

16. They (canvased/canvassed) the neighborhood and learned that the problem is (miner/minor).

17. A (loose/lose) wheel (that/which) broke off the trailer caused the accident.

18. Representatives from one (media/medium) said the criteria (is/are) too strict.

19. The (blond/blonde) said that (burglars/robbers/swindlers/thieves) broke into his house.

20. Thousands of the schools (alumna/alumni/alumnus) voiced their (decent/descent/dissent).

21. The bank's (trustee/trusty) said she was unable to (affect/effect) the decision.

22. The (trail/trial) began three months after he was charged with (inciting/insighting) the riot.

23. They obtained more signatures (then/than) their rivals (because/since) they worked Sunday afternoon.

24. His statement (implies/infers) that the negotiations will not (affect/effect) us.

25. They wondered (who's/whose) (role/roll) will be (affected/effected) by the new law.

EXERCISE 7
Spelling and Vocabulary

INSTRUCTIONS: Correct all the errors in the following sentences, which contain a number of words that cause confusion because they look or sound like other words. You were asked to define many of the words in Exercises 4 and 5.

The sentences also contain possessives that need correcting. If you need help, the rules for forming possessives appear in Appendix C.

1. He adviced the city to adopt the ordinance.

2. The concept was to illusive to insure success.

3. Its rules were altered, but the affects were minor.

4. The blonds finance said there new home was robbed.

5. Who's statue was laying near you're construction cite?

6. Rather than dissenting, he agreed to study their advise.

7. The alumna, all men, said the dissent became to violent.

8. He censured the aides behavior and ignored their descent.

9. A prison trustee said its two miles further down the road.

10. The council was confidant that his advice would insure success.

11. The data was placed in envelops and sent to all the news medias.

12. The governors two aids were given offices in the capitol building.

13. The man was hung because he insited a riot which caused three deaths.

14. The portrait hung in his brother-in-laws office in the state capital building.

15. Six of the schools alumnus said there childrens curriculum should be altered.

16. The principle is liable to lose his students respect if he blocks their proposal.

17. The phenomenon were unusual and affected their son-in-laws roll in the family.

18. The board is composed of seven alumnus rather than seven students or teachers.

19. He sited three precedents and implied that the councils decision could be altered.

20. Thomas Alvarez, a tall blonde from California, said the governments data is false.

21. The councilor was confidant of victory but said his roll in the matter was minor.

22. The church alter lay on its side, less than a dozen feet from the broken statutes.

23. His insight, conscience and high principles ensured an excellent performance.

24. The schools principle threatened too censure the newspaper if it tries to publish an article advicing students on how to obtain an abortion.

25. Merchants, fearing that they would lose thousands of dollars, complained that the governments criteria is to difficult to implement.

4 Basic News Leads

The first paragraph in a news story is called the "lead." The lead (some people spell it "lede") is the most important part of a story—and the most difficult part to write. Traditionally, the lead summarizes an entire story so that readers can decide at a glance whether they want to read it. In this way, readers do not have to waste any time or effort. And—even if they read only the lead—they will receive a capsule account of the entire story.

Newspaper editors prefer the use of summary leads because their readers tend to be skimmers who glance from one story to another and read only what interests them. If a lead fails to interest readers—if it is confusing or dull—they will move on to another story rather than read any of the following paragraphs. Thus, a lead must do more than simply summarize the story; it must also arouse readers' interest and lure them into the story.

Before reporters can write an effective lead, they must first learn to recognize what is news. Leads that fail to emphasize the news—the most interesting and important details—cannot be used, regardless of how well they are written. After deciding which facts are most newsworthy, a reporter must then summarize those facts in sharp, clear sentences—a simple, straightforward account of what happened. On the night Abraham Lincoln was shot, a correspondent for The Associated Press wrote the following lead. Typically, it is concise and to-the-point:

WASHINGTON, FRIDAY, APRIL 14, 1865—The President was shot in a theater to-night, and perhaps mortally wounded.

Other leads have also provided clear, concise summaries of momentous events in the nation's history:

TOKYO, Dec. 8—Japan went to war against the United States and Great Britain today with air and sea attacks against Hawaii followed by a formal declaration of hostilities.

(The Associated Press)

DALLAS, Nov. 22—A sniper armed with a high-powered rifle assassinated President Kennedy today. Barely two hours after Mr. Kennedy's death, Vice President Johnson took the oath of office as the thirty-sixth President of the United States.

(The Associated Press)

WASHINGTON, D.C.—Richard Milhous Nixon announced his resignation last night as President of the United States, the first chief executive to resign in the Republic's 198-year history.

(San Francisco Chronicle)

The Questions a Lead Should Answer

In the past, every lead was expected to answer six questions: *Who? How? Where? Why? When?* and *What?* Newspapers have abandoned that rigid style because leads that answered all six questions became too long and complex. Also, answers to all the questions were not always important. Because few readers in large cities know the people involved in routine stories, the names of those people do not have to appear in leads. The exact time and place at which a story occurred may also be unimportant.

Today, leads emphasize answers only to the most important of the six questions, which vary from one story to another. The following examples, although slightly exaggerated, are traditional leads that attempt to answer all six questions. Their revisions, following the currently preferred style, answer only the most important questions:

Andrew A. Kernan, 18, a student at Central High School and the son of Mr. and Mrs. Harry Kernan of 1432 Hillmore Lane, died at about 3:30 p.m. Tuesday when his car overturned near a sharp curve on State Road 12.
REVISED: An 18-year-old student was killed Tuesday when his car overturned while he was driving home from high school.

Samuel Alston, assistant district attorney for Hennepin County, announced during a press conference in the Blackhawk Hotel at noon today that a prisoner, whom he did not identify, has confessed to the murder of a local liquor store owner seven years ago.
REVISED: A prisoner in the county jail has confessed to the murder of a local liquor store owner seven years ago.

To determine which questions are most important for a story you have been asked to write, consider the following points:

1. What is the most important information—what is the story's main point or topic?
2. What was said or done about the topic—what happened or what action was taken?
3. What are the most recent developments—what happened today or yesterday?
4. Which facts are most likely to affect or interest your readers?
5. Which facts are most unusual?

Each of the following leads emphasizes the answer to only one of the six basic questions—the question that seems to be most important for that particular story:

WHO: Three teen-agers, including a 14-year-old who is eight months pregnant, today were sentenced to 20 years in prison for robbing and murdering a cab driver.

HOW: A 15-year-old boy in the county jail ripped part of a sheet from his bedding and used it to hang himself from a coat hook in his cell.

WHERE: Turbulent air 35,000 feet above the state jolted an Eastern Airlines jet last night, injuring 23 passengers and 3 flight attendants.

WHY: Desperate over the breakup of his marriage and financial problems, Teddy Bruce Flichum killed his 2-year-old son, then committed suicide in a motel room Wednesday.

(The Orlando Sentinel)

WHEN: Moments after two young women left a jewelry store Monday afternoon, a salesman discovered that four gold bracelets valued at $1,840 were missing from a display case he had opened for them.

WHAT: PROVIDENCE, R.I.—Teen-age children in one out of 10 American families hit, beat, stab or shoot their parents, according to a survey released Monday by a University of Rhode Island sociologist.

(The Associated Press)

Sentence Structure in Leads

Most leads consist of a single sentence, and that sentence must follow all the normal rules for punctuation, grammar, word usage and verb tense. If an event occurred in the past, the lead must use the past, not the present, tense. Leads must be complete sentences and should include all the necessary articles (the words "a," "an" and "the"). Mistakenly, inexperienced reporters often use incomplete sentences and the present, rather than the past, tense. Some beginners also eliminate the articles, particularly when they appear at the beginning of a lead, a practice that is distracting and unnecessarily brusque:

> Man dies on railroad tracks.
> REVISED: A 19-year-old Detroit man was killed early Tuesday when he was hit by a train while lying on some railroad tracks just south of Nova Road.

> Party ends in tragedy as two die.
> REVISED: Two 7-year-old girls attending a friend's birthday party suffocated Monday after climbing into an unused freezer during a game of hide-and-seek.

Most leads contain only one sentence. Two- or three-sentence leads often become wordy, repetitious and choppy, particularly when all the sentences are very short. Like most multisentence leads, the following examples can be combined more concisely into a single sentence:

> The federal government issued a report about welfare recipients today. The report stated that the number of welfare recipients in the United States has risen to 14.4 million, a record high.
> REVISED: The federal government reported today that the number of welfare recipients in the United States has risen to 14.4 million, a record high.

> Two women robbed a shopper in a local supermarket Tuesday. One woman distracted the shopper and the second woman grabbed her purse, which contained about $50.
> REVISED: One woman distracted a shopper in a local supermarket Tuesday, and another woman grabbed her purse, which contained about $50.

The original leads were redundant. Before describing the report's content, the first lead said—unnecessarily—that the report was issued. The second lead reported that two women robbed a shopper, then described the robbery. Yet if a lead says that one woman distracted a shopper and another woman grabbed her purse, it is redundant to add that "two women robbed a shopper."

Reporters use two-sentence leads only when the need to do so is compelling. Often, the second sentence is used to emphasize an interesting or unusual fact of secondary importance. It may also be impossible to summarize all the necessary information about a complex topic in a single sentence. The following examples, both transmitted by The Associated Press, use a second sentence to summarize an unusual or secondary highlight:

> ST. MARY'S, W. Va. (AP)—Fifty-one construction workers plunged screaming to their deaths Thursday when a scaffold inside a power company cooling tower collapsed and crashed 168 feet to the ground. Nine of the victims were members of one family.

> OSSINING, N.Y. (AP)—Joseph and Edna Reyes were buried Wednesday beside their teen-age son, reunited in death with a beloved only child. They had chosen not to go on living without him.

Some problems with sentence structure arise because beginners confuse a story's lead with its headline. The lead is the first paragraph of a news story. The headline is a brief summary that appears in larger type above the story. Most headlines are written by editors, not reporters. To save space, the editors use only a few key words in each headline. However, that style of writing is not appropriate for leads.

While writing leads, reporters use a relatively simple sentence structure. Most leads begin with the subject, which is closely followed by an active verb and then by the object of the verb. Reporters deviate from that style only when they want to emphasize some other element of a story. Leads that begin with long qualifying clauses and phrases lack the clarity of simpler, more direct sentences. Long introductory clauses also clutter leads, burying the news amid a jumble of less significant details. Because they begin with clauses, the following leads fail to emphasize the most important facts and to report those facts clearly and immediately:

> While on a routine patrol, a police officer discovered that burglars had pried open the back door of a liquor store on Pennsylvania Avenue and stolen more than 100 cases of whiskey Thursday night.
> REVISED: Burglars pried open the back door of a liquor store on Pennsylvania Avenue and stole more than 100 cases of whiskey Thursday night.

> While a 42-year-old man was dropping off two women on West Jackson Street Tuesday night, he was robbed and punched in the face by three youths who opened a car door and took his wallet.
> REVISED: Three youths opened the door of a car stopped on West Jackson Street Tuesday night, robbed its driver and punched him in the face.

Before it was revised, the first lead emphasized the commonplace—the fact that a police officer discovered a burglary "while on a routine patrol." The second lead delayed the news—information about the robbery—until its eighteenth word.

How to Write an Effective Lead

Be Concise

Newspapers' concise style of writing makes it easier for the public to read and understand leads, but more difficult for reporters to write them. Typically, leads written by correspondents for the nation's two major news agencies, The Associated Press and United Press International, contain an average of only 18 to 20 words. Some journalists insist that no lead should exceed 30 words, but that limit is too rigid and forces reporters to stop and count the number of words in every lead. Slightly longer leads may be acceptable, if they are easy to read and understand. Also, it is easier to count the number of typed lines in leads instead of the number of words. Most leads contain about two typed lines, and some contain three. A lead that exceeds three typed lines is probably too long and should be critically examined to determine whether it is wordy or repetitious or contains facts that could be shifted to a later paragraph. A lead that exceeds four lines should always be rewritten and shortened.

Reporters shorten leads by eliminating unnecessary background information and the description of routine procedures; a lead should report a story's highlights, not all its minor details. Even more importantly, reporters must eliminate unnecessary words, always expressing their ideas as concisely as possible:

> A county education official Wednesday said she favors spanking elementary school children but admitted the practice should not be used on high school students.
> REVISED: A county educator Wednesday said she favors spanking elementary school children, but not high school students.

> A man who walked with a limp approached Laura Walker in the 1700 block of Michigan Avenue at about 5 p.m. Monday, drew a knife and forced her into a white van parked nearby, then took about $24 from her purse and beat her before letting her out and driving away.
> REVISED: A man who walked with a limp drew a knife, then robbed and beat a woman after forcing her into a van parked on Michigan Avenue Monday afternoon.

Reporters can also shorten leads by deleting unnecessary names, dates and locations. Leads should not contain too many names, particularly obscure names that readers are unlikely to recognize, or the names of people who played minor or routine roles in a story. If you include someone's name in a lead, you may also have to identify that person, and the identification will take up even more space. Reporters can often substitute descriptive phrases for names (for example: "a 16-year-old girl," "an Austin teacher," "a retired nurse"). Similarly, instead of reporting a story's precise time and location, a lead might mention only the day and city; the specific hour and street address could be reported in a later paragraph.

Thus, most leads should contain no more than two or three typed lines, and reporters can save space by eliminating minor details, unnecessary names and precise times and locations. However, there is no *minimum* length for leads; an effective lead may contain only four or five words (for example: "The president is dead," or "Man has landed on Mars"). Despite their brevity, editors at The New York Times have praised the following leads, written by members of their staff:

> Smallpox is about to be eradicated from the earth.

> Howard R. Hughes died today as mysteriously as he had lived.

Be Specific

Good leads contain interesting details and are so specific that readers can visualize the events they describe. As you read the following leads, you should be able to imagine the dramatic scenes they describe:

> MIAMI (UPI)—A "grandmother-type" 71-year-old woman who became annoyed when a teen-ager blew cigarette smoke in her face on a city bus, whipped out a can of Mace Friday and chased the youth down the aisle, her spray can going full blast.

> TAMPA (AP)—The parents, two lawyers, a doctor and a nurse looked on in tears as the respirator was unplugged. Forty minutes later, 14-month-old Andrew James Barry died in his mother's arms.

The following leads are less interesting because they are abstract and contain vague generalities. However, reporters can easily transform them into more interesting leads by adding more specific details:

> A Clark County woman is suing her former employer, charging sex discrimination.
> REVISED: A Clark County receptionist who says she was fired because she became pregnant is suing an optometrist for sexual discrimination.

Several agencies handle the large number of animals killed or injured on city and county roads.

REVISED: Each week, the Humane Society picks up about 50 animals killed or injured on city streets, and county employees bury hundreds of others at the spot where they are found.

A secretary whose child was born handicapped is suing a medical laboratory for what she says was negligence.

REVISED: A secretary whose child was born blind and deaf is suing a medical laboratory which failed to detect her exposure to measles. Because of the negative test results, she decided to continue her pregnancy.

A related (and lazy) way of summarizing a story is also too vague. Instead of presenting any specific details about a topic, some reporters write that "a step has been taken," or that someone has moved "one step closer" to a goal. These are vague, dull cliches:

The City Commission has taken a step to combine the city's police and fire departments under one boss.

REVISED: The City Commission voted to appoint a director of public safety to head both the police and fire departments.

The state is one step closer to the adoption of a tourism tax that will add $30 million to its promotional budget.

REVISED: A House subcommittee Monday passed a bill authorizing establishment of an 11-member tourism commission. The commission will impose a tax on tourism-related businesses and use the $30 million it raises each year to promote tourism.

Use Strong, Active Verbs

A single word—a descriptive verb—can transform a routine lead into a dramatic one. As you read the following lead, for example, you may be able to sense the drama (or agony) of a wounded deputy struggling to his feet:

PAHOKEE, Fla.—A deputy sheriff who was shot four times on a street in this town on Lake Okeechobee struggled to his feet and shot his assailant, who was trying to escape in the officer's patrol car.

(United Press International)

Avoid weaker, non-descriptive verbs, especially passive verbs such as "is," "are," "was" and "were." Strong, active verbs are more colorful, interesting and dramatic:

A 66-year-old woman *was* the victim of a purse snatching at a shopping center Saturday night.

REVISED: A man *leaning* out a car window *snatched* a 66-year-old woman's purse at a shopping center Saturday night.

One person *was killed* and four others *were injured* Sunday morning when their car, which *was traveling* west on Interstate 80, *hit* a cement bridge pillar and *was engulfed* in flames.

REVISED: A car *traveling* west on Interstate 80 *swerved* across two eastbound lanes, *slammed* into a cement bridge pillar and *burst* into flames, *killing* one person and *injuring* four others Sunday morning.

If you write a passive lead, you can easily convert it to the active voice. Simply rearrange the words, so that you begin by reporting: (1) who . . . (2) did what . . . (3) to whom. Instead of reporting that "Rocks and bottles were thrown at firefighters," report that "Rioters threw rocks and bottles at firefighters." Similarly, instead of reporting that "The contract was approved by teachers," report that "Teachers approved the contract."

Emphasize the Magnitude of the Story

If a story is important, reporters emphasize its size, or magnitude, in the lead, often by revealing the number of dollars, buildings or other objects it involves. When describing a major storm, reporters may emphasize the amount of rain or snow that fell. When describing a major fire, they may emphasize the amount of damage, the number of people left homeless or the number of injuries:

> PENSACOLA (AP)—A National Airlines Boeing 727 carrying 60 people plowed into Pensacola Bay on a landing approach late Monday night, killing at least one.

> A power failure plunged New York City and Westchester County into darkness last night, disrupting the lives of nearly nine million people.
>
> *(The New York Times)*

Most good leads emphasize the impact that stories have on their participants or readers. For example: the fact that a person was injured is considered more important than the fact that a car was destroyed or that a store was robbed. Thus, the following leads also emphasize the fate of people involved in the news:

> Two gunmen shot a customer in the chin while robbing a restaurant at 944 W. Colonial Drive Wednesday night.

> A policeman suffered a broken leg and a concussion when his motorcycle collided with a car Monday afternoon.

Stress the Unusual

Leads also emphasize the unusual. By definition, news involves deviations from the norm—the unusual rather than the routine. Newspapers are sometimes criticized for emphasizing the unusual, but the fact remains that the unusual is more interesting than the routine and is therefore more likely to attract and hold readers' attention. The unusual or unexpected also tends to be more important. The fact that someone was born, married, divorced, arrested, robbed, injured or honored is more interesting and more important than the fact that, on the same day, someone else did nothing out of the ordinary. Similarly, the fact that an airplane crashed is more important (and more interesting and unusual) than the fact that hundreds of other airplanes had routine flights.

Leads about a city council meeting should not report that the council met at 8 p.m. in the city council chambers in city hall and that the council began its meeting with a prayer and the Pledge of Allegiance. Those facts are routine and consequently not newsworthy. Most city councils meet at least once every week, usually at the same time and place, and many begin all their meetings with a prayer and the Pledge of Allegiance. Leads should emphasize the unique—the action that follows those routine formalities.

Normally, for example, newspapers do not report minor crimes, yet in one instance a $20 robbery became front-page news. A reporter learned that an attorney had gotten a client released from jail by convincing a judge that the man was a thief. The man had accepted $20 from an undercover officer and promised to give him some cocaine. Instead of delivering the cocaine, the man fled. He was arrested several days later and charged with the unlawful delivery of cocaine: a felony. Because the man did not have enough money for bail, he was locked in the county jail. During a preliminary hearing, his attorney argued that the man was a thief: that he never possessed any cocaine and never intended to deliver any. Instead, he had simply stolen the officer's $20. Because the theft of $20 is a less serious crime—a misdemeanor—the man was freed without bond.

Similarly, bank robberies are so common in big cities that newspapers normally devote only a few paragraphs to them. Yet a robbery at the Burlington National Bank in

Columbus, Ohio, became a front-page story, published by newspapers throughout the United States. A story transmitted by The Associated Press explained that:

> A 61-year-old man says he robbed an Ohio bank with a toy gun—he even told the FBI ahead of time when and where—because he wants to spend his golden years in federal prison.

After his arrest, the bank robber insisted that he did not want a lawyer. Instead, he wanted to immediately "plead guilty to anything." The man explained that he recently was divorced, had no family ties and was disabled with arthritis. He had spent time in at least three federal prisons and wanted to return to one of them. "I knew what I was doing," he insisted. "I wanted to get arrested, and I proceeded about it the best way I knew how."

To make the following leads more interesting, both have also been revised to emphasize the unusual:

> Four fire trucks responded to a blaze in a home at 871 N. Woodlawn Ave. at 7 a.m. today.
> REVISED: A widow and her five children smashed a window and jumped from the second floor as fire destroyed their new home at 871 N. Woodlawn Ave. at 7 a.m. today.

> A local restaurant was robbed of $62 early Tuesday morning.
> REVISED: An elderly woman who was armed with a knife and said she needed the money to buy Christmas toys for her grandchildren robbed a local restaurant of $62 Tuesday morning.

Stories may also involve other kinds of unusual details that reporters must learn to recognize and emphasize in their leads:

> A woman who claims several cans of peaches fell from a shelf and struck her head is suing a local supermarket for $25,000.

> MIAMI—Trials for motorists caught speeding by Florida Highway Patrol radar units in Dade County have been postponed because the devices were proven inaccurate—in one case clocking a tree at 86 mph.

> LANCASTER, Mass. (AP)—A volunteer firefighter who helped pull four charred bodies from a burning wreck was told hours later that one of the dead was his own son, relatives say.

Similarly, other leads emphasize the unexpected:

> MIAMI (AP)—Nineteen-year-old Jose Pico thought he was doing a good deed when he chased down a hit-and-run driver and held him at gunpoint until police arrived.
> He still can't understand why he was arrested and the driver was set free.

> GAINESVILLE, Fla. (AP)—When Eddie Lasco pulled a gun on Julie Black and robbed the hair styling parlor where she worked, she was impressed by his thoughtfulness and manners.
> A few months later, she married him.

Localize and Update Your Lead

Reporters are trained to localize and update their leads whenever possible. Reporters localize leads by emphasizing their communities' involvement in stories. Editors explain that readers are most interested in stories that affect their own lives and the lives of other people they know. To satisfy their readers' interests, newspaper editors emphasize stories that occur within their own communities and that mention people, places and events that their readers are familiar with. Consequently, when an editor in Kansas City was asked to define news, he replied, "The farther it is from Kansas City, the less it is news."

Reporters also try to localize stories that arise in other parts of the world. If Congress grants federal employees a raise, reporters may localize the story by reporting the number of federal employees in their communities who will benefit from the congressional action. Similarly, when the FBI reports on the number of violent crimes committed in the United States, reporters stress the statistics for their local communities:

The FBI reported today that the number of violent crimes in the United States rose 8.3 percent during the last year.
LOCALIZED: The number of violent crimes committed in the city last year rose 5.4 percent, compared to a national average of 8.3 percent, the FBI reported today.

Eighty-three people were killed today when their jet plunged into a field two miles south of an airport in Tokyo.
LOCALIZED: Eighty-three people, including three from this area, were killed today when their jet plunged into a field two miles south of an airport in Tokyo.

Reporters update a lead by stressing the latest developments in the story. Even a story that occurred only a few hours earlier can often be updated. Instead of reporting that a fire destroyed a local store the previous day, reporters may stress the fact that subsequently authorities have learned the fire's cause, identified the victims, arrested an arsonist or estimated the monetary loss. Stories are updated so they offer the public something new—facts not already reported by other newspapers or by local radio and television stations.

Major stories about such topics as economic trends, natural disasters, wars and political upheavals often remain in the news for several months and must also be updated. Reporters must always emphasize the latest developments—what happened today or yesterday, not several weeks or months ago—so that readers are given something new, facts they have not already heard from other sources:

Two men robbed the First National Bank, 1841 Main St., of about $20,000 yesterday and shot a police officer in the chest.
UPDATED: A police officer shot during a bank robbery is reported in critical condition today at Memorial Hospital.

Sheriff's deputies who received a complaint from an unidentified woman raided a poker game at a retirement home yesterday and charged eight men with gambling.
UPDATED: Eight men charged with gambling after sheriff's deputies raided a "nickel and dime" poker game at a retirement home said today that they will plead guilty to the charge.

Not every lead can be updated or localized. If a story has no new or local angles, report it in a simple, straightforward manner. Do not distort the story in any way or attempt to create any new or local angles that are fictional.

Be Objective and Attribute Opinions

Leads of news stories, like their bodies, must be objective. Reporters are expected to gather and to convey facts to their readers, not to comment, interpret or advocate. There is rarely any justification for labeling accidents "tragedies"; for calling the people involved in news stories "alert," "heroic" or "quick-thinking"; or for describing facts as "interesting" or "startling." These comments waste space and, when they are accurate, usually state the obvious. Leads composed entirely of opinion or interpretation must be rewritten to provide more factual, comprehensive accounts of the news:

An afternoon fishing trip turned into tragedy Wednesday when a 41-year-old mechanic drowned in Clear Lake.
REVISED: A 41-year-old mechanic drowned Wednesday after he apparently suffered a heart attack while fishing in Clear Lake and fell out of a small boat.

Speaking to the Downtown Rotary Club last night, Emil Plambeck, superintendent of the City Park Commission, discussed a topic of concern to all of us—the city's park system.

REVISED: Emil Plambeck, superintendent of the City Park Commission, wants developers to set aside 5 percent of the land in new subdivisions for parks.

It pays to be a friend. That is what Clarence and Edith Grafton of Birmingham, Ala., have learned.

REVISED: A retired minister has left his entire estate, valued at $280,000, to two friends: Clarence and Edith Grafton of Birmingham, Ala.

The first lead states the obvious by calling a 41-year-old man's sudden death a "tragedy." The second lead is weak because it refers to "a topic of concern to all of us." The reporter does not identify "us" and is wrong to assert that any topic concerns everyone. The third lead contains a cliché as well as opinion, and thus fails to give a clear report of what happened.

Although reporters cannot express their own opinions in stories, they often include the opinions of people involved in the news. A lead that contains a statement of opinion must be attributed so that readers clearly understand that the opinion is not the reporter's.

Often, beginners misplace the attribution in leads, use attribution when it is not necessary and fail to use attribution when it is needed. Attribution is usually necessary in leads that contain a quotation, charges or criticism of any kind, or other statements of opinion. The attribution should be expressed as concisely as possible and should be placed near the end, rather than at the beginning, of the lead. Leads should begin with the news—important details that reporters want to emphasize—as in the following examples:

NEW YORK (AP)—More American workers are dissatisfied with their jobs now than at any other time in the past 25 years, according to a survey released Tuesday.

NEW YORK (AP)—Up to 85 percent of all drowning victims are teen-aged males either showing off or testing their endurance, according to five leading doctors.

Reporters often use "blind leads" that do not specifically name their source. So they can devote more attention to the news, reporters use only a brief descriptive phrase (such as "leading doctors") in the lead, and present most of the attribution in the second or third paragraph. The attributions in the following leads are also brief, with the sources identified more fully in the subsequent paragraphs. Notice that only the biochemist's title is used in the first lead; his name appears in the second paragraph:

The mysterious process by which green plants turn sunlight into chemical energy can certainly be harnessed to help man solve the energy crisis and world hunger, a University of Kansas biochemist said Friday.

"When sunlight hits a leaf, it makes a small chemical battery," said Ralph Christoffersen. "If we knew the details of how that process occurs, there's no reason why we couldn't build a copy of the leaf."

(The Associated Press)

Childbirth is far more dangerous than generally believed and may be the 11th leading cause of death to women 15 through 44 years of age, a new federal study has disclosed.

The study, conducted in Georgia by the national Centers for Disease Control, supports earlier findings that deaths associated with pregnancy and childbirth may be 50 percent higher than currently reported.

(The Chicago Tribune)

Similarly, the following lead contains only seven words of attribution. More information about the source appears in the fourth paragraph:

WASHINGTON, D.C.—Teen-agers are more than twice as likely as adults to be victims of rape, robbery and assault, according to a government report issued Sunday.

The study shows that more than 60 of every 1,000 teen-agers are victims of violent crime each year, compared to just 27 of every 1,000 adults.

The study also found that teen-agers were nearly twice as likely as adults to be victimized by theft. The teen-age rate for theft was 123 per 1,000 compared to 65 per 1,000 for adults.

The report by the Justice Department's Bureau of Justice Statistics was compiled from twice-a-year surveys of 49,900 households. . . .

(The Associated Press)

A lead that contains an obvious fact or a fact that the reporter has witnessed, or can verify by some other means, generally does not require attribution. An editor at The New York Times, instructing reporters to "make the lead of a story as brief and clear as possible," has noted: "One thing that obstructs that aim is the inclusion of an unnecessary source of attribution . . . If the lead is controversial, an attribution is imperative. But if the lead is innocuous, forget it." Thus, if a lead states a fact that no one is likely to question, you can place the attribution in a later paragraph because none is necessary in the lead:

Seven children and both their parents were killed when their van slammed into the back of a truck parked along an Arizona highway late Friday night.

WASHINGTON (AP)—Children who murder their parents will no longer be able to collect Social Security survivors' benefits.

Avoiding Some Common Errors

The following pages discuss the errors that appear most often as students begin to write leads.

Emphasize the News

Mistakenly, some leads emphasize whatever occurred first. Yet the first events rarely are the most newsworthy. As you begin a story, decide which facts are most interesting and important—then begin your leads with those facts regardless of whether they occurred first, last or in the middle of the story:

A pollster who spoke to political scientists meeting today began by welcoming them to the city and by describing his accuracy in recent surveys.
REVISED: No woman is likely to be elected president of the United States during the next 50 years, pollster Lester Marshal predicted during a speech today.

The prosecution this morning opened its case against a 19-year-old man charged with murdering a cab driver last August.
REVISED: Two police officers who testified during a murder trial that opened today said they observed the defendant driving a stolen cab and found the driver's watch and wallet in his jacket pocket.

Other leads place too much emphasis upon the time and place a story occurred:

A retired engineer who hitchhiked a ride from three other men on Eastbrook Avenue after his car ran out of gas at 10 o'clock last night was robbed of everything, including all his clothes.
REVISED: Three men robbed a retired engineer of everything, including all his clothes, after he attempted to hitchhike on Eastbrook Avenue at 10 o'clock last night.

A country and western bar on Benson Avenue was the scene of a fight last night that left one man critically injured.
REVISED: A 41-year-old man is in critical condition after being stabbed by his brother-in-law outside a country and western bar on Benson Avenue.

Until it was revised, the first lead emphasized the fact that a man was hitchhiking because his car ran out of gas at 10 p.m. on Eastbrook Avenue. The lead failed to mention the news—the robbery—until the 27th word. The second lead emphasized the story's location rather than the victim's critical injuries (and the unusual fact that they were inflicted by his brother-in-law).

Organize Your Lead

After deciding which details are most newsworthy, place those details at the beginning—not the end—of your lead. An editor at The New York Times has explained that: "The lead is where you invite the reader into the story. So don't have a doormat that he trips on, and don't keep him waiting. Make the lead short, simple and direct, with the news right up front." Secondary matter can be reported briefly at the end of the lead or in a later paragraph.

Be particularly careful to avoid beginning with an attribution. Names and titles are dull and often unimportant. Moreover, if every lead begins with the attribution (or with the time and place a story occurred) all the leads will sound too much alike. Place the attribution at the beginning of a lead only when it is unusual or significant and deserves that emphasis:

> At a press conference in Washington, D.C., today, Neil A. Schuster, a spokesman for the U.S. Bureau of Labor Statistics, announced that last month the cost of living rose 2.83 percent, a record high.
> REVISED: The cost of living rose 2.83 percent last month, a record high, the U.S. Bureau of Labor Statistics reported today.

> In a speech before a statewide convention of the National Education Association in the state capital today, Gov. Ronald A. Harris revealed plans to raise the state sales tax by one penny and to use most of the money to improve the state's school system.
> REVISED: The governor plans to raise the state sales tax by one penny and to use most of the money to improve the state's school system.

Originally, the two leads devoted more space to the attribution than to the news. The first lead, as revised, emphasizes the news—the information revealed by the Bureau of Labor Statistics. The attribution has been condensed and can be reported more fully in a later paragraph. The second lead, as revised, stresses the governor's plans to raise the state sales tax, an idea that would affect virtually all of a newspaper's readers. The fact that the governor revealed the plans at a teachers' convention is less important and can be reported later.

If you are uncertain about what to emphasize, look for a story's action or consequences. The following lead, as revised, does more than report that four shotgun blasts were fired at a house; it also summarizes the consequences or damage caused by those shotgun blasts. Similarly, the second lead, as revised, stresses the consequences of the accident:

> Four shotgun blasts were fired into a home at 205 E. Mason Drive at 2 a.m. today.
> REVISED: Four shotgun blasts fired into a home at 205 E. Mason Drive at 2 a.m. today shattered several windows and damaged some furniture but did not injure the home's five occupants.

> A 15-year-old boy learning to drive his family's new car struck a gasoline pump in a service station on Hall Road late Tuesday afternoon.
> REVISED: A 15-year-old boy learning to drive his family's new car struck a gasoline pump in a service station on Hall Road late Tuesday afternoon, causing a fire that blocked traffic on the road for three hours.

Avoid "Label" Leads

Leads should report the substance of a story, not just its topic. A good lead will do more than report that a group met, held a press conference, issued a report or listened to someone speak. The lead will reveal what the group did at its meeting, or summarize what was said at the press conference, in the report or during the speech.

An introductory paragraph that fails to report the news—that mentions a topic but fails to reveal what was said or done about that topic—is called a "label" lead. Because they use similar words and phrases, label leads are easy to recognize and avoid. Many of the leads report that an issue "was the subject of" a speech or "the main topic of discussion." Other label leads report that people "spoke about," "delivered a speech about" or were "interviewed about" an issue. Typically, then, label leads emphasize the topic under consideration but fail to summarize the statements made about the topic or the action provoked by it:

LABEL LEAD: The Department of Health and Human Services issued a report on alcoholism today.
REVISED: Alcohol is the major drug problem in the United States, and one out of 10 working Americans suffers from alcoholism or a lesser drinking problem, the Department of Health and Human Services reported today.

LABEL LEAD: A police lieutenant spoke to the Methodist Women's Club last night about the danger of firearms.
REVISED: People who own guns are more likely to shoot themselves or members of their family than to shoot a prowler, a police lieutenant said last night.

Avoid Unfamiliar Terms

Make your leads as clear, simple and readable as possible. If your readers are unlikely to recognize a name or term, place it in a later paragraph, not the lead. Or, avoid it altogether. A lead that contains several unfamiliar names or terms is likely to be especially dull:

Police Officer Bruce Esterling told Prosecuting Attorney Leslie Hess on Monday that he spotted the defendant, Charles McLockland, 820 Randall St., attempting to flee from a store.
REVISED: A police officer testified Monday that he saw a young soldier running from a convenience store moments after a clerk was robbed and raped.

Health care for the poor is substandard in this county, according to medical health care experts who met at an AMA conference here. They hope that Vertical Integration Systems will help reverse that trend.
REVISED: To improve medical care in the county, experts want to establish eight clinics in poor neighborhoods and to refer only the most serious cases to specialists at County Hospital.

Avoid Lists

Avoid placing any lists in your leads. Most lists, like names, are dull. If you *must* use a list, place an explanation before it, never after it. If you begin with a list, your readers will not immediately understand its meaning or significance. The following example, published by a Denver newspaper, delays starting the explanation until the 20th word:

BOULDER, Colo.—Complaints about bicycle racing fans urinating on lawns, perching on the roofs of private homes and trampling flower beds may lead city officials to ask Coors Classic organizers to find a new setting next year for their Boulder criterium.

If you place the explanation before a list, your readers can immediately understand its meaning:

Their family home, a new Cadillac, $2,500 a month, and a 50 percent interest in their family business were awarded to Claire Marcial, who sued her husband for divorce.
REVISED: As part of the divorce settlement, a judge awarded Claire Marcial their family home, a new Cadillac, $2,500 a month and a 50 percent interest in their family business.

The company that made it, the store that sold it and the friend who lent it to him are being sued by a 24-year-old man whose spine was severed when a motorcycle overturned.

REVISED: A 24-year-old man whose spine was severed when a motorcycle overturned is suing the company that made the motorcycle, the store that sold it and the friend who lent it to him.

Avoid Stating the Obvious

Avoid stating the obvious, and avoid emphasizing routine procedures in your leads. If you write about a crime, you do not have to begin by reporting that police "were called to the scene" or that ambulances "rushed" the victims to a hospital "for treatment of their injuries." The following leads are ineffective for the same reason: they state the obvious or emphasize the routine. The first lead may be difficult to rewrite. If the Placement Center is not doing anything new, the story lacks a newsworthy angle. If, on the other hand, the Placement Center is offering a new service, the lead should describe that service:

The college's Placement Center has a wide variety of information and facts to help prepare students for their future careers.

REVISED: On Monday, the college's Placement Center will install computers in every building to inform students about new jobs and job interviews.

It can be a frightening experience to wake up and find an armed intruder in your bedroom. Just ask 20-year-old Stacy Hidde. It happened to her Tuesday.

REVISED: A 20-year-old college student was awakened at 2 a.m. Tuesday and saw a prowler, with a knife in one hand, searching her bedroom.

Avoid the Negative

When you write a lead, report what happened—not what failed to happen or what does not exist:

Americans over the age of 65 say that crime is not their greatest fear, two sociologists reported today.

REVISED: Americans over the age of 65 say their greatest fears are poor health and poverty, two sociologists reported today.

A 20-year-old woman was not seriously injured Tuesday night when a shotgun accidentally discharged in a pickup truck.

REVISED: A 20-year-old woman seated in a pickup truck bent down to light a cigarette Tuesday night just as a shotgun accidentally discharged two inches above her head, shattering a rear window and temporarily deafening her.

Avoid Exaggeration

Never exaggerate. If a story is weak, exaggeration is likely to make it weaker, not better. A simple summary of the facts can be more interesting (and shocking) than anything you might contrive:

A 78-year-old woman has left $3.2 million to the Salvation Army but only 2 cents to her son.

A jury today found a restaurant not guilty of serving a man and his wife a dead rat in a loaf of bread.

ST. PETERSBURG, Fla.—Saying it was "outrageous" that a man's body fell out of a casket before startled pallbearers, a jury awarded a widow and her family $240,000 in their suit against a funeral home and cemetery.

Avoid Misleading Readers

Every lead must be accurate and truthful. Never sensationalize, belittle or mislead. In addition to being factually accurate, a lead must also set a story's tone—accurately revealing, for example, whether the story that follows will be serious or whimsical. Most of the stories that you write as a beginning reporter will be routine, and many of their topics may not interest you. Yet, as a service to readers who *are* interested in them, report such stories as you would any others—as well as you possibly can.

Breaking the Rules

Occasionally, it pays to use your imagination, to try something a little different, perhaps reporting the facts more cleverly than any of your competitors. Two journalism students wrote the following leads. Both summarize the same story, yet the second lead is more effective. Why?

> FIRST STUDENT: A young woman was robbed of $2 Thursday on her way to work by a young man with a knife.
> SECOND STUDENT: After a man threatened her with a pocket knife, a young woman gave him all her money—all $2 of it.

The following are also factual summaries, but reported with more imagination than most:

> When a masked man walked into a convenience store and pounded a hammer on the counter, demanding money, clerk Brenda Kay Casey didn't argue with him. She handed it over.

> BOSTON (AP)—Here's a strategy for long life: Avoid the elevator and take the stairs. Each stair climbed could increase lifespan by about 4 seconds.

Rewriting

Finally, critically examine every lead you write, and rewrite it as often as necessary. First drafts are rarely so perfect that they cannot be improved. Even experienced professionals often rewrite their leads three or four times (or more).

Checklists for Writing Leads

Use the following checklists to evaluate all the leads you write. If you answer "No" to any of these questions, your leads may have to be rewritten.

Writing Style

1. Is your lead specific rather than vague and abstract?
2. Have you avoided stating the obvious or the negative?
3. Have you emphasized your story's most unusual or unexpected developments?
4. Have you emphasized your story's most interesting and important developments?
5. Have you emphasized your story's magnitude—and its impact upon its participants and readers?
6. Have you used a complete sentence, the proper tense and all the necessary articles ("a," "an" and "the")?
7. Is your lead concise? (If it exceeds three typed lines, examine the lead critically to determine whether it is wordy or repetitious or contains some unnecessary details. If your lead exceeds four typed lines, rewrite it.)
8. Have you avoided writing a label lead that reports your story's topic but not what was said or done about it?
9. Did you begin your lead with the news—the main point of the story? (If you began with attribution or the time and place your story occurred, rewrite it.)

10. Have you used a relatively simple sentence structure, exercising particular care to avoid beginning the lead with a long phrase or clause?

11. Have you used strong, active and descriptive verbs rather than passive verbs such as "is," "are," "was" and "were"?

12. Is every name that appears in the lead essential? (Avoid unfamiliar names—and names that require lengthy identification that could be reported in a later paragraph.)

13. If a lead contains a quotation or a statement of opinion, is it properly attributed?

14. Has the lead been localized, and does it emphasize the latest developments, preferably what happened today or yesterday?

15. Have you eliminated statements of opinion, including one-word labels such as "interesting" and "alert"?

16. If you have used two sentences, can you justify their use? Have you checked to be certain that they are concise and non-repetitive?

Finally, have you read the lead aloud to be certain that it is clear, concise and easy to understand?

Checklist for Format and Accuracy

1. If the story originated in a distant city, did you begin with a dateline?

2. Is the lead typed and double-spaced, and have you used the proper copy-editing symbols to correct all your errors?

3. Have you double-checked the facts to be certain that they are accurate, and have you used a telephone book or city directory to check the spelling of every name? (If the lead is mistaken, exaggerates, sensationalizes or misleads, rewrite it.)

A Comparison: The Communist Press

Compare the best leads in this chapter with the following leads which appeared in a single issue of a communist paper: the China Daily published in Beijing. The following leads are dull because they emphasize routine and abstract generalities:

> Retired Chinese Communist Party leaders have pledged to do everything in their power to help "newly-promoted officials and promote the current reforms."

> Soldiers should support the current reforms in various fields while carrying out the reform of the army itself, a senior Chinese army leader said yesterday.

> HARBIN—A Sino-Canadian agricultural program was described as "satisfactory" by Chinese and Canadian experts here recently.

> China is to build more apartments for sale to help solve the urban housing problem, an official of the Ministry of Urban and Rural Construction and Environmental Protection said in the capital on Thursday.

Write & Wrong ST. LOUIS POST-DISPATCH

By Harry Levins
Post-Dispatch Writing Coach

Who says wind is weightless? We load our readers with many burdens, but the heaviest may be windy sentences. Here's an all-too-typical example. It fell short of springing the scale but was needlessly weighty:

National Airport, opened in 1941 and operated by the Federal Aviation Administration, was the site of a crash by an Air Florida jet in January that killed 78 people.

Grammatical? Sure. Are the words spelled properly? You bet. Are the facts correct? More or less; the crash was a few miles from the airport proper, but the flight originated there.

So what's wrong?

Simple: the sentence meanders through two separate and distinct thoughts. One is the background on when the airport opened and who runs it. The other is the background on the crash. The ideal remains one idea per sentence. Two ideas should get one sentence apiece. Repairing the sentence above would have been a simple matter:

National Airport opened in 1941 and is operated by the Federal Aviation Administration. In January, an Air Florida jet crashed after taking off from the airport, killing 78 people.

Here's another windy sentence, one that gets tangled up in detail before it can make its point:

JEFFERSON CITY (UPI)—Gov. Christopher S. Bond's trip to New York City this week is part of a program to promote Missouri as a location for new business, to increase export sales, to bolster the state's stagnant economy and to provide jobs for unemployed workers.

Too many "to" verbs. The sentence has four, which suggests trouble. The writer tried to tell everything but merely produced an eye-glazer. We could have spared the reader by giving him one-idea sentences, leading with the general and then describing the specific:

JEFFERSON CITY (UPI)—Gov. Christopher S. Bond's trip to New York City this week is part of a three-point program aimed at boosting the state's economy. The governor hopes to:
—Promote Missouri as a site for new businesses.
—Increase exports of Missouri's goods.
—Provide more jobs.

At times, we go out of our way to complicate sentences. Here's an example from The New York Times News Service, a mother lode of complicated sentences:

WASHINGTON—John W. Hinckley Jr., complaining of restrictions placed by St. Elizabeth's Hospital on his contacts with reporters, has asked the American Civil Liberties for help.

The reader dips his toe in—and promptly loses it to the teeth of a nonrestrictive clause. Nonrestrictive clauses (phrases set off by commas) constitute one of the biggest roadblocks to readability. They interrupt the reader's train of thought, sidetracking him into a second idea that may or may not be crucial at that point.

At times, we're forced to use such clauses. But The Coach remains convinced that the nonrestrictive clause often represents a crutch for a writer who lacks the time, talent or inclination to recast his stuff. Sometimes, the sentence can be broken into two, each with its own idea. Sometimes, the information in the clause can be shifted deeper in the story, preferably in a sentence of its own.

And every so often, a two-idea sentence can be recast into something that more nearly meets the ideal of one idea per sentence. For example, that Hinckley lede could have read this way:

(continued on next page)

WASHINGTON—John W. Hinckley Jr. wants the American Civil Liberties to help him fight what he says are restrictions by St. Elizabeth's Hospital on his contacts with reporters.

Ah, well—at least The Times held itself to a two-idea sentence. Here's a locally produced sentence with *three* ideas:

Mayor Vincent C. Schoemehl Jr., who asked Hohman to come to St. Louis, said the study would not be directly related to Homer G. Phillips Center, which the mayor is trying to reopen as a full-service hospital.

Try diagramming *that*. The result looks like the genealogy of a family that practices incest. The writer overloaded the sentence with two nonrestrictive clauses—the ones beginning with "who" and "which." And all of those editors dumped it untouched onto the readers.

Somewhere, somebody could have broken off the first part as a single sentence:

Mayor Vincent C. Schoemehl Jr. invited Hohman to St. Louis.

One down, two to go:

The mayor said Hohman's study would not be directly related to Homer G. Phillips Center, an emergency room and clinic on the city's North Side.

Okay, that sentence has 1.6 ideas. Still, we're four-tenths of a point ahead. And now, Strike Three:

Schoemehl has been trying to re-establish Phillips as a full-service hospital.

But at times, the cure can be as vexing as the ailment. Here's a paragraph that The Coach suspects started life as one sentence:

The ILO's Committee on Freedom of Association will take up the case when it meets in Geneva, Switzerland, on Nov. 8 and 9, according to Stu Smith. He is executive director of the Capitol Employees Organizing Group.

Somebody deserves praise for making the effort. But somebody also deserves admonishment for doing it so clumsily. The last sentence reads like an afterthought. A bit more work would have made the transition smoother:

...meets in Geneva, Switzerland, on Nov. 8 and 9. The announcement was made by Stu Smith, executive director...

☆ ☆ ☆

The Coach's eye has been caught recently by some questionable wording. Here's a lede that probably grabbed many readers—and then dropped them in a hurry:

LONDON (AP)—Queen Elizabeth II is in a rage because her son, Prince Andrew, has flown to the Caribbean island of Mustique with American actress Koo Stark, the Sun newspaper reported today.

When the queen rages, that's news. But when a British tabloid makes up news, that's old stuff. Whose word have we on the queen's temper? Well, three paragraphs later, the story quotes an unidentified member of the queen's staff as saying, "The queen feels badly let down."

The next sentence: "The Sun added, 'The queen is in a rage.'"

So readers of the Post-Dispatch newspaper—why does that damned usage keep creeping into the paper?—got their lede from the editors of a British tabloid. These are the same editors who introduced topless photos on front pages and inflicted the current version of the *New York Post* newspaper—oops, there we go again—on that melancholy city.

Did we overstate our lede by using the word "rage"? Probably. All we know for sure is that the queen "feels badly let down." If we thought that royal rage deserved Page 2A notice, we could have least [sic] warned the reader by starting the story this way: *A British tabloid says Queen Elizabeth II is in a rage...* Moral: beware of loaded words. They hurt this sentence:

Schneider says his bill would modernize Missouri's badly outdated standards for motor fuel.

Presumably, Schneider called the standards badly outdated. But the way this sentence was worded, the Post-Dispatch newspaper—sorry, but it's catching—called the standards outdated. And that's an editorial judgment.

At least once a week, The Coach runs across a sentence like this:

Smith, 38, lives in rural Belleville.

What is "rural Belleville"? Or "rural Kirksville" or all the other "rurals" we write about? Presumably, we mean "outside Belleville" or "in a rural area near Kirksville." If so, we ought to say it that way. Otherwise, we are calling Belleville a bucolic village—a description to which 41,000 people might take exception.

☆ ☆ ☆

Some parting shots on words:

Ceremonies. This word almost always appears as a plural; it almost always should be singular. "The awards are to be presented in ceremonies in the rotunda of City Hall." Sorry, but *a ceremony* is all that's planned.

Jobless, joblessness. Here's more headlinese that has crept into copy. The word "jobless" is bad enough in a headline, but a copy editor can plead tight space. No such excuse extends to people who use "jobless" and "joblessness" in copy as substitutes for "unemployed" and "unemployment." We're better off repeating a good word than substituting something from the junkpile of journalese just for the sake of variety.

Plague. Early in the history of journalism, some clever writer seized upon the word as a synonym for "vex," "bother," "trouble," "annoy," "anger," "harass," etc. Very shortly thereafter in the history of journalism, everybody else starting using it. They turned the verb "plague" into a punchless piece of journalese. Let's retire it.

Suggested Readings

Brooks, Brian S., George Kennedy, Daryl R. Moen, and Don Ranly. *News Reporting and Writing.* 2nd ed. New York: St. Martin's Press, 1985.

Cappon, Rene J. *The Word: An Associated Press Guide to Good News Writing.* New York: The Associated Press, 1982.

Charnley, Mitchell V., and Blair Charnley. *Reporting.* 4th ed. New York: Holt, Rinehart and Winston, 1975.

Harriss, Julian, and B. Kelly Leiter. *The Complete Reporter.* 5th ed. New York: Macmillan, 1985.

Heyn, Howard C., and Warren J. Brier. *Writing for Newspapers and News Services.* New York: Funk & Wagnalls, 1969.

Hohenberg, John. *The Professional Journalist.* 5th ed. New York: Holt, Rinehart and Winston, 1983.

Hough, George A. *News Writing.* 3rd ed. Boston: Houghton Mifflin, 1984.

Metz, William. *Newswriting: From Lead to "30."* 2nd ed. Englewood Cliffs, N.J.: Prentice-Hall, 1985.

Metzler, Ken. *Newsgathering.* 2nd ed. Englewood Cliffs, N.J.: Prentice-Hall, 1986.

Stephens, Mitchell, and Gerald Lanson. *Writing & Reporting the News.* New York: Holt, Rinehart and Winston, 1986.

Ward, Hiley H. *Professional Newswriting.* San Diego: Harcourt Brace Jovanovich, 1985.

EXERCISE 1
Leads

EVALUATING GOOD AND BAD LEADS

INSTRUCTIONS: Critically evaluate the following leads. Select the best leads and explain why they are effective. In addition, point out the flaws in the remaining leads. As you evaluate each one, look for lessons that you can apply to your own work.

1. A re-organization bill signed by the president will affect college students' eligibility for financial aid. *→ how will it affect?*

2. "Faith in a Violent World" will be the theme for Religious Emphasis Week at the university next week, according to the director of the United Campus Ministry.

3. Even after 34 years on the police force, 63-year-old Chief William Casey has not lost sight of his goal to "protect and serve."

4. The city's public schools have come under fire since it was revealed that student test scores are declining. Now, the superintendent of schools has responded to the criticism.

5. Four shots from a high-powered rifle blasted through the front window of a liquor store last night.

6. The school board will offer a $30,000 settlement in exchange for the resignation of a teacher acquitted of sexually molesting two fifth-grade girls.

7. A new campus organization, the Student Tourism, Restaurant and Travel Association, held its initial meeting last night.

8. A new health insurance plan will pay city employees for staying well.

9. Elementary and high school students often know more about computers than their teachers, says Dr. James Orwigg.

10. A man who admitted slashing his neighbor with an 8-inch kitchen knife was acquitted Thursday of aggravated assault. A jury decided that the man had acted in self-defense.

11. Discussion on prohibiting advertising billboards received most of the attention during Monday night's City Council meeting.

12. Local schools have a lot of holiday activities planned for their youngsters.

13. A college student was left bound and gagged in her dormitory room last night after being robbed by a man who answered her advertisement in the campus newspaper.

14. A motorcyclist involved in an accident at about 5 p.m. Sunday suffered multiple injuries.

15. Carbon monoxide sucked into an air conditioning duct spread through a house at 105 Crown Point Drive early today, killing a couple and their five children.

16. The School Board has voted to give James Julastic a 12 percent raise and to extend his contract as school board superintendent for another three years.

17. Six automobiles were broken into Friday at the Midtown Motel, 929 W. Colonial Drive, and property valued at more than $1,600 was stolen.

18. Two people remain hospitalized after a collision on State Road 419 at 2:30 a.m. Thursday.

19. The City Council listened to preliminary plans Monday night for a $56 million high-rise condominium development on the shores of Lake Howell.

20. Three young men who paid $20,000 for a small weekly newspaper five years ago have transformed it into a $500,000 publishing company.

EXERCISE 2
Leads

EVALUATING GOOD AND BAD LEADS

INSTRUCTIONS: Critically evaluate the following leads. Select the best leads and explain why they are effective. In addition, point out the flaws in the remaining leads. As you evaluate each one, look for lessons that you can apply to your own work.

1. An unemployed construction worker was shot Saturday afternoon during a heated argument with another patron in the parking lot of the Melody Lounge, 844 Wilson Ave.

2. Circuit Court Judge Marilyn Picott today refused to allow James Roger Carrig to attend the funeral services for his parents, whom he is accused of murdering.

3. A school bus carrying 46 pupils to an elementary school in the city was involved in a collision on Jefferson Avenue at 8:10 a.m. today.

4. Offering what looked like a good deal on a new roof, two men persuaded an elderly couple to give them $3,000, then disappeared with their money.

5. Kennedy High School is the only school in the city that has a school-community liaison counselor.

6. Syndicated columnist Jack Anderson spoke Tuesday evening to a crowd of about 350 people in the Student Union.

7. A 42-year-old man was arrested and charged with cultivating marijuana Monday after his landlady discovered more than 300 plants in a house he rents from her.

8. One man fell 40 feet and another was left dangling from a drainpipe yesterday after a scaffold collapsed while they were painting a house at 48 Par Ave.

9. A small fire, started by a 13-year-old babysitter, caused more fear than damage Monday afternoon.

10. A 25-year prison sentence was handed down today by Judge Edward Kocembra after Marc Lubinskas pleaded guilty to a charge of armed robbery.

11. Children in this area will join more than 30 million other trick-or-treaters across the United States this Halloween in a night of make-believe and masquerade.

12. The prospects for the college's football team this coming season look good to coach Dennis Cramrad.

13. Six people were held at gunpoint when Denny's Restaurant at 4830 Oakhill Road was robbed of $2,400 Tuesday night.

14. New safety regulations concerning air bags in automobiles were announced during a press conference in Washington, D.C. this morning.

15. Telling an admitted member of a multicounty theft ring that he should have thought of his wife and two children before he burglarized a string of homes, a circuit court judge Monday sentenced the man to five years in prison.

16. The first-degree murder trial of Eldred L. Tontenot continued Thursday with testimony from the assistant county medical examiner, Dr. Guillermo Ruiz.

17. Most residents of the city are opposed to an increase in property taxes for several reasons, according to a survey released today.

18. In a startling report issued today by the city's Ministerial Alliance, it was charged that church members "spend more money on beer and cigarettes than on charity."

19. Barbara Denise Webb, author and columnist, will be the featured speaker at a meeting of the DAR scheduled for 8 p.m. Friday at Kennedy High School auditorium.

20. In a nationally televised speech to the American public last night, the president explained why he will not run for re-election.

EXERCISE 3
Leads

1-3 pt 1

IMPROVING WEAK LEADS

SECTION I: CONDENSING LENGTHY LEADS Condense each of these leads to no more than two typed lines: about 20 words.

1. ~~Maggie Baile, 28, of 810 N. Ontario Ave.,~~ an employee at the Halstini Manufacturing plant, ~~810 Hall Road,~~ suffered second and third degree burns at 2:15 p.m. yesterday when sparks from her welder's torch started a fire that quickly spread through the factory, causing nearly $1 million in damage.

2. During a regularly scheduled meeting in its chambers at 8 p.m. last night, the City Council voted 5 to 2, after nearly 3 hours of debate, in favor of a proposal which, for the convenience of pedestrians, will require developers to construct a sidewalk in front of every new home and subdivision.

3. At its annual awards banquet last night, the city's Chamber of Commerce named Marlene P. Gianangeli, the founder and owner of the city's largest pest control firm, the city's "Businessperson of the Year," and then elected Destiny Schifini, a vice president at the Sun Bank, to a two-year term as chamber president, to begin on the 1st of January.

SECTION II: USING PROPER SENTENCE STRUCTURE Rewrite the following leads, using the normal word order: subject, verb and direct object. Avoid starting the leads with a long clause or phrase. You may want to divide some leads into several sentences or paragraphs.

1. Saying that he had concluded that no benefit would come to anyone from the imprisonment of a 51-year-old woman who killed two teen-agers while driving while intoxicated last summer, Circuit Court Judge Thomas L. Levine today suspended the woman's driver's license for five years and sentenced her to one year in the county jail—but then suspended her jail sentence on the condition that she seek professional help for her chronic alcoholism.

2. Although the world has plenty of food due to great advances in agricultural techniques in recent years, the World Bank reports that about 700 million people in developing countries do not have enough to eat, primarily because they do not have sufficient funds to buy the food that is available.

3. Because the victim contributed to his own death by refusing medical attention that might have saved his life, James K. Arico, the 47-year-old man accused of stabbing him during an argument seven months ago, was allowed to plead guilty to assault today and was sentenced to six months in the county jail. He had been charged with murder.

SECTION III: USING STRONG VERBS Rewrite these leads, using stronger, more active and descriptive verbs.

1. A 75-year-old woman who was approached from behind while walking south on the 5200 block of Cypress Woods Drive was robbed by a teen-ager who threatened her with a stick Tuesday morning.

2. A German couple was upset because, after making their hotel reservations two months in advance, they were told by a clerk, upon their arrival at a hotel here shortly after 9 p.m. yesterday, that it had nothing available; all of its rooms were already occupied, and so the couple slept in their rented car.

3. A woman had a ring valued at $2,000 and some other belongings stolen from her home Tuesday after a thief entered her home through an unlocked bedroom window while she was at work. A videocassette recorder, a camera and two cats were also missing.

SECTION IV: USING ATTRIBUTION As you rewrite the following leads, emphasize the news, not the attribution. Limit the attributions to a few words and place them at the end, not the beginning, of the leads.

1. During a meeting in her office in Washington today, the secretary of Health and Human Services told a group of health care specialists that American men and women who practice "wellness," a program of health promotion and disease prevention, can expect to live 11 years longer than people who neglect their health.

2. According to Tracy R. Edwards and John W. Robitzsch, psychiatrists hired to testify for the defense at the murder trial of Tommy Ahrens in your community today, Ahrens was temporarily insane: too emotionally upset and distraught to think clearly when he shot his wife and her boyfriend last May.

3. Testifying before a congressional committee, Alan Greenspan, chairman of the Federal Reserve Board, today voiced a warning that the nation is likely to enter a severe and harmful recession unless Congress balances the federal budget.

EXERCISE 4
Leads

IMPROVING WEAK LEADS

SECTION I: REMAINING OBJECTIVE Rewrite the following leads, eliminating their conclusions and other statements of opinion.

1. If City Commissioner Cindy Kaehler has her way, the city will soon have speed bumps at intersections where stop signs have been poorly observed. Last night, she introduced a proposal to install the bumps at 12 intersections, all located in residential neighborhoods, to solve the problem.

2. More than 600 angry citizens, upset by the brutal murders of four helpless children during the past 12 months, last night attended a heated public meeting at which they criticized the police department's failure to solve the crimes.

3. A decision by the School Board last night not to replace teachers who resign or retire indicates the seriousness of the system's lack of funds. To balance its budget, the board will eliminate 5 percent of its current staff through a process of attrition.

SECTION II: EMPHASIZING THE POSITIVE Rewrite the following leads, stressing the positive—what happened—not what failed to happen.

1. Two months after fire damaged a furniture store, an insurance company is asking the U.S. District Court to declare that it is not liable for its insurance policy which covers the store on the grounds that the fire was deliberately set, and its policy states that the company does not have to pay for damage caused by an intentional fire.

2. A state trooper who was shot and seriously wounded while pursuing a car thief has filed a $3 million lawsuit for negligence. However, he is not suing the thief, whom he killed in the gunfight. Rather, he is suing the owner of the car on the grounds that the owner illegally left the keys in the ignition, thus contributing to the crime and his wounds.

3. No one was injured when a fire broke out in a cafeteria at Kennedy High School at 8:49 a.m. today, setting off fire alarms and resulting in the evacuation of more than 2,100 students who were then dismissed for the day.

SECTION III: COMBINING MULTISENTENCE LEADS Rewrite the following leads in a single sentence.

1. Acting on a tip, four detectives staked out a restaurant at 12:50 a.m. this morning and foiled an armed robbery. While posing as customers and employees, they observed two men with guns approach a cashier. The detectives captured both men.

2. Two city officials resigned today. Both had been criticized for abusing their positions. Mechanics at the city garage complained that both officials had them repair and wash and wax their cars. One of the city officials was the mayor. The other was her assistant.

3. The parade is scheduled for 9 a.m. tomorrow. The city's annual Memorial Day parade will proceed down Main Street to Wildwood Cemetery. Services there will honor the men and women killed in 20th century wars.

EXERCISE 5
Leads

INSTRUCTIONS: Write only a lead for each of the following stories. As you write the leads, consult the checklists on pages 87–88. This exercise—and others throughout this book—contain misspelled names and style errors that you will be expected to correct. To learn the proper spellings of the names, use the city directory in Appendix A. To check the proper style, consult The Associated Press Stylebook in Appendix B.

1. The man is Herman Weiskoph of 4817 Twin Lakes Boulevard in your city. The woman involved is Sharon Meyer of 810 Kalani Street. She is pregnant with his child. However, they are not married. At 9 a.m. next Monday morning, a judge in your county will hear his plea. The judge, JoAnne Kaeppler, today issued a temporary restraining order to prevent Meyer from having an abortion. The judge issued the order in response to a suit filed by Weiskoph. On Monday, the judge will decide whether to make the order permanent or to dissolve it. In his lawsuit, Weiskoph offers to marry Meyer, to pay all her medical expenses, and/or to take custody of the child after it is born. He bases his suit upon a claim "that a natural father has rights to the life of his child."

2. At its meeting last night, the Muncie city council in Indiana made another important but controversial decision. Not everyone agrees with it. After hearing from interested citizens during a 60-minute hearing, the council voted by a narrow margin, 4–3, to stop donating cats and dogs from the city pound to the University of Indiana. Proposed experiments there caused some controversy earlier this year. The controversy erupted when one researcher proposed suspending cats from their legs to test the effects of spaceflight on bones. Another controversy erupted when a researcher proposed drowning dogs to test methods of saving human drowning victims. Last year, the city donated about 1,400 cats and dogs picked up on the city's streets and held 10 days at the pound without being claimed. Now, instead, it will put the cats and dogs to sleep, as it does with other unclaimed animals. University officials said they are unhappy, and one researcher explained, "People don't understand, but our experiments with animals have resulted in great advances for mankind, providing life-saving medicines and other innovations that make all our lives healthier and safer."

3. There is a new study out, one conducted by your city's police department. The department questioned a random sample of 350 people living within your city and announced the results during a press conference held at 9 a.m. this morning. The chief of police made the announcement. He said the survey revealed that 65 percent of all the crimes occurring in your community are not reported to the police because the victims consider the incidents unimportant or believe that nothing can be done about them. About half the violent crimes of rape, robbery and assault seem to be reported, he said. The rates for reporting crimes ranged from 25 percent for household larceny to 69 percent for motor vehicle theft. Forty percent of those who reported crimes gave economic reasons, either to recover property or collect insurance money, for doing so. Thirty-five percent cited a sense of obligation.

4. Previously, if you parked in a parking spot reserved for the handicapped in your city you would be fined $10. However, your city council met last night and heard and discussed complaints that other motorists often use the spaces, so the handicapped are unable to shop or eat out or be entertained. As a result, the council voted 5–2 to raise the fine to $250—the highest in the state—to prevent able-bodied drivers from using the parking spots reserved for the handicapped. Those spaces normally are close to store entrances. Two members of the Paralyzed Veterans Association were

at the meeting to lobby for the stiff fine, saying it might be the only way to stop offenders. The new law will go into effect in 30 days. State law allows half of the money collected in such fines to go toward enforcing and administering the parking regulation. The rest may be used to build wheelchair ramps and other improvements to enhance access to public buildings.

5. It was a sad tragedy. Rescue workers got the call from neighbors shortly after 4:30 p.m. yesterday. Brenda Ward of 7214 Olin Way is divorced, with two children, Lindsay 3, and Michael, 5. Ward, 27, told police she was talking on the telephone. She received two calls, one from a friend and one from her mother. She thought her children were watching TV. Later, when she went into the living room, the TV set was on, but they weren't watching it. She called to them but got no answer. Then, growing more worried, she went to look for them. Neighbors called the police when they heard her screams of horror. The bodies of the two children were found by their mother inside the household clothes dryer, badly burned. They were declared dead on the scene.

6. Your city's fire chief today released copies of his proposed annual budget for next year. He will present the proposal to your City Council at its next regular meeting. Chief Sid Bellochi wants $4,943,612, a 19.8 percent increase, which he says is needed primarily to beef up protection on the east side. If fully funded, it would raise property owners' taxes for fire protection to 6.41 mills, or $6.41 for every $1,000 of taxable property value. Bellochi said he needs to hire eight new firefighters. The eight new firefighters would fill two round-the-clock positions. The department also wants to buy several pieces of equipment. "We are a manpower-intensive operation," he explained. "And some very expensive equipment is necessary to outfit these people." Bellochi added that, within the next five years, the city will have to build a new fire station and purchase at least three new trucks.

7. For 10 years, researchers at the University of Washington in Seattle have been studying a sample of 5,000 adult males. The researchers received a federal grant totalling $720,000 in amount to conduct the study, and they announced the results today. It was a study of heart attacks: who gets them, when and with what results. All the men were aged 50 to 60 at the time the study began 10 years ago. Now, many have retired. The researchers found that those who retired were more likely to suffer and die of a heart attack. "We found an 80 percent higher rate of death from coronary disease among those who had retired compared with those who had not," one of the medical researchers said. The researchers had set up the long-term study to determine men's physical and mental responses to retirement, and the results announced today were the first phase of their study. Other results will be announced next year. Another of the researchers added: "For some people, retirement is a reward for a lifetime's work, and they look forward to it. But for other people, it is a punishment for growing old. Those who feel that way perhaps might be the ones who are most likely to suffer bad health, but we don't have that breakdown yet."

8. J. T. Pinero is a developer in your community. He is planning to build 350 houses in a 120-acre subdivision which he has named "Deer Run." Yesterday he was cited by the city. The city also stopped all work on the development. The land had been wooded, and Pinero was charged with clearing the first 30 acres without obtaining city permits. Mayor Paula Novarro said it was the most flagrant violation of the city's tree protection code since her election five years ago. Pinero was cited for cutting down more than 500 pines, oaks, maple, birch and other trees. Under city codes, unauthorized destruction of each tree is punishable by a fine of up to $500. Novarro added that she and other city officials are negotiating with Pinero and his attorney for landscaping and replacement of all the trees. Pinero must also post a $100,000 bond or letter of credit to ensure restoration. If the work is done, Novarro said,

Pinero may not be fined for this, his first offense. Pinaro said he did not know of the land-clearing and tree-removal permits required by the city.

9. Liz Holten operates a doughnut shop at 2240 Broadway Avenue. Today, she was ordered to appear in court at 10 a.m. tomorrow. One of her employees is Mildred McCartney. McCartney was called for jury duty on Monday of last week and served the entire week. When she returned to work at 7 a.m. on Monday of this week she found that she had been replaced: fired because of her absence last week. State law prohibits an employer from firing or threatening to fire an employee called for jury duty, and Judge George C. LeClair has ordered Holten to appear in his courtroom to determine whether she should be held in contempt of court. Interviewed today, Holten said she did not know of the law. She said she works 12 to 16 hours a day in the doughnut shop, which she owns. McCartney is her only full-time employee, and she said she cannot afford to have her away for several days at a time—she is unable to run the business by herself with only her part-time help. If held in contempt, she could be fined up to $10,000 and sentenced to six months in jail.

10. Wesley Barlow is an inmate in a Nebraska state prison. He has been charged with swindling dozens of widows of thousands of dollars. Barlow, 32, is serving an 8-year sentence for burglary. Today he pleaded guilty to new charges against him and was sentenced to an additional 10 years. Barlow had mailed letters to men who recently died. The letters were then received by the men's widows. They sought payment— usually less than $100—"for maintenance and repairs." Some women paid because they assumed their dead husbands had some work done before their deaths, a detective said. Or, the women may have been too upset at the time to give the bills much thought. Barlow said he got their names from the obituaries in an Omaha newspaper. The scam was discovered when the mother of an Omaha detective received one of the letters.

11. Researchers at your college issued a report today. After three years of study, they found a link between drinking and birth defects. They warned that pregnant women who drink risk injury to their children. Because the scientists don't know how much alcohol may be safely consumed by pregnant women, they recommend absolute and total abstention from all alcoholic beverages during a woman's 9-month term of pregnancy. What the doctors found during their three years of study is that children born to pregnant women who drink have higher rates of mental and physical abnormalities. The most common problems among such infants are mental retardation and delays in their physical development. Pregnant women who drink also experience more miscarriages and premature births. The reason for the problems is that alcohol from a mother's system passes directly into the bloodstream of her developing child, and that the alcohol remains in the fetal system longer because it is not metabolized and excreted as fast as it is in the adult woman. Scientists call the problem the fetal alcohol syndrome.

12. Pollsters have asked a random cross-section of American adults their attitudes toward the nation's federal income taxes, and the results are contained in a 12-page report. The study was financed by the Internal Revenue Service, which released the results to reporters in the federal capital today. In general, the report concluded that the average American's respect for the federal income tax system is declining. A similar study conducted just 10 years ago found that, when Americans were asked to describe the tax they thought was most unfair, most mentioned their local property tax. But now, the new study released today found that a majority of the nation's adults consider their federal income tax most unfair. Guaranteed that their identities would not be revealed by the pollsters, 27% of the respondents said they themselves had cheated on their federal tax returns on at least one occasion during the past five years.

EXERCISE 6
Leads

INSTRUCTIONS: Write only a lead for each of the following stories. As you write the leads, consult the checklists on pages 87–88. This exercise—and others throughout this book—contain misspelled names and style errors that you will be expected to correct. To learn the proper spellings of the names, use the city directory in Appendix A. To check the proper style, consult The Associated Press Stylebook in Appendix B.

1. There was an accident occurring in your city at 7:10 this morning at the intersection of Post Road and Rollins Avenue. Charles R. Lydon was driving north on Post Road and proceeded to enter the intersection in his van at a speed estimated at 40 mph. His van struck a fire engine responding to an emergency call, with its lights and siren in operation. Two firemen aboard the vehicle were hospitalized; however, their condition is not known at this point in time. Lyden was killed instantly in the serious and tragic accident. Authorities have not yet determined who was at fault. The truck was traveling an estimated 25 mph and responding to a report of a store fire. However, it was a false alarm. Lyden's van was totally destroyed. Damage to the truck was estimated at $50,000.

2. A teen-ager is paralyzed. The teenager, Amy Claunch, 17, was struck by a bullet when a pistol fired accidentally. Yesterday, a jury awarded her $2 million in damages. Claunch, who is not married, sued both David Gianangeli, who fired the pistol, and the pistol's manufacturer. Gianangeli fired the gun accidentally while showing it to friends in the parking lot of Kennedy High School last spring. The jury found Gianangeli responsible for the shooting. It dismissed all the charges against the manufacturer. Claunch's attorney said she probably won't be able to collect even a penny of the award because Gianangeli does not have any money. He dropped out of the school, without graduating, and now works as a gardner, paid little more than the minimum wage. The jury deliberated almost 10 hours before reaching its decision. Claunch had attempted to prove that small handguns are so inherently dangerous that their makers and sellers should be held jointly responsible for harm caused by them, even when they are misused.

3. There was a report issued in Washington, D.C. today. It came from the Highway Loss Data Institute, an affiliate of the Insurance Institute for Highway Safety. It shows that there are advantages to driving big cars. A study by the institute found that small two-door models and many small or midsize sport or specialty cars have the worst injury and repair records. Many of these small cars show injury claim frequencies and repair losses at least 30 percent higher than average, while many large cars, station wagons and vans show 40 percent to 50 percent better-than-average claim records. According to the analysis, a motorist in a four-door Oldsmobile Delta 88, for example, is 41 percent less likely than average to be hurt in an accident.

4. An article appeared today in the Journal of the American Medical Association. The article concerns the dangers of hot dogs. "If you were trying to design something that would be perfect to block a child's airway, it would be a bite-size piece of hot dog," says a researcher. He concluded that children under 4 should "never be given a whole hot dog to eat," and that hot dogs should never be cut crosswise. The hot dogs are so dangerous that every five days, it is estimated, someone, somewhere in the United States, chokes to death on them. Other risky foods for young kids up to 9 years of age include: candy, nuts, grapes, apples, carrots and popcorn.

5. It's a smart idea, some people say, a way to solve a problem. Other people say it's a waste of taxpayers' money. The city council in Roseville, a small town near your community, adopted the idea last night. In the last municipal election there, only 23% of the city's registered voters cast a ballot in the race for mayor, a dismal record. It was the lowest percentage in your state. The Roseville city council wants to do something about it, so last night they decided to have a lottery. During the next municipal elections, scheduled for the fall of next year, the city will give away $5,000 in cash prizes. The winners' names will be drawn from a list of all the persons who cast a ballot in the election.

6. The family of Kristine Belcuore was grief-stricken. She was 51 years old and died of a heart attack last week. She left a husband and four children. Because her death was so sudden and unexpected, an autopsy had to be performed before the funeral last Saturday. It was a big funeral, costing more than $7,000. More than 100 friends and relatives were in attendance. Today, the family received an apologetic call from the county medical examiner. Mrs. Belcuor's body is still in the morgue. The body they buried was that of a woman whose corpse had been unclaimed for a month. The error was discovered after the medical examiner's office realized the month-old corpse had disappeared. Someone probably misread an identifying tag, they said. Also, the family never viewed the remains; they kept the casket closed throughout the proceedings. A relative said, "We went through all the pain and everything, all over the wrong body, and now we have to go through it again."

7. It's another statistical study, one that surprised researchers. For years, researchers thought that advanced education translated into greater marriage stability. Then they discovered that marital disruption is greater among more highly educated women than any other group (except those who haven't graduated from high school). Now a sociologist at Ohio State University has conducted a new study which explains some of the reasons why women with graduate degrees are more likely to be graduated from their marriages as well. The key fact seems to be timing. Women who married early, before they began graduate school, are more likely to have established traditional family roles which they find difficult to change. When the wife goes back to school and no longer wants to handle most of the housework, it causes resentment on the part of husbands. If the husband refuses to pitch in and do his share, it creates tension. Such unhappiness on both sides often leads to divorce. Indeed, a third of the women who began graduate school after they were married ended up separated or divorced. By comparison, only 15.6 percent of those who married after they had finished an advanced degree ended up divorced or separated. They seem more likely to find husbands supportive of their educational goals.

8. The Department of Justice, as it often does, conducted a crime-related survey. It questioned long-term prisoners. It found that new laws limiting the ownership of guns do not discourage handgun ownership by career criminals. The report concludes, however, that even though curbs on legitimate retail sales of guns have failed to attain the goal of keeping weapons out of the hands of criminals, the laws still may serve other useful functions. The report explains that criminals get their weapons most often by theft or under-the-counter deals. The department surveyed 1,874 men serving time for felonies in 11 state prisons and found that 75 percent said they would expect little or no trouble if they tried to get a handgun after their release from prison. Fifty-seven percent had owned a handgun at the time of their arrest. Thirty-two percent of their guns had been stolen, 26 percent acquired in black market deals, and others received as gifts from family and friends. Only 21 percent had been bought through legitimate retail outlets.

9. Thomas C. Ahl appeared in Circuit Court today. He pleaded guilty last week to robbing and murdering two restaurant employees. In return for pleading guilty,

prosecutors promised not to seek the death penalty. He was sentenced today. Ahl is 24 years old, and the judge sentenced him to two life terms, plus 300 years. It is the longest sentence ever given anyone in your state. Ahl will be 89 before he can be considered for parole. The judge explained that Ahl had a long history of violence and brutality, and that the public deserved to be protected from him. There had been no reason for him to shotgun the two employees to death. Ahl himself admitted that they had not resisted him in any way.

10. Sonya Barlow was born brain-dead. She lived about a month. Today, her mother, Mrs. Janet Barlow, 23, 2886 Moore Street, was charged with her death. Mrs. Bralow, who has two other daughters, is in jail. She is accused of being responsible for her infant daughter's death by taking drugs, consuming alcoholic beverages and recklessly disregarding medical instructions during pregnancy. Legal experts say this is the state's first criminal action for the crime, sometimes known as "fetal abuse." Prosecutors say the case will "foster a greater sense of parental responsibility for prenatal care."

11. Increasingly, people around the world are concerned about waste. One group, the Worldwatch Institute, issued a report about it today. It found little progress. Only about one-fourth of the world's paper, aluminum and steel is recycled, it found, a figure that has improved only slightly during the last 20 years. "This rate could be doubled or tripled for each material," the Institute said. "Steps must be taken to increase collections of recycled materials and to develop additional markets for the products made with them. In many cases, recycling costs only 20 percent the cost of manufacturing a totally new product—and the recycled product is just as good. There's no logical reason for the waste of our planet's meager resources. Eventually, we'll exhaust them."

12. The U.S. Justice Department issued a report in Washington, D.C. today about the number of prisoners in state and federal prisons. The department's Bureau of Justice Statistics reported that the number of prisoners in the prisons increased 9.9% last year, compared with an 8.6 percent increase during the previous year and an 8.1% increase the year before that. The four states with the largest prison populations were Texas with 35,345, California with 33,520, New York with 27,527 and Florida with 26,978. The total number of prisoners in all state and federal prisons as of the last day of last year reached an all-time record high of 405,371. The report says the number of prisoners is rising largely due to new state laws that impose mandatory sentences in serious crimes and that restrict parole, so that more people are being sentenced to prison and so that each prisoner tends to remain behind bars for a longer period of time.

EXERCISE 7
Leads

1-6 & 10-12

INSTRUCTIONS: Write only a lead for each of the following stories. As you write the leads, consult the checklists on pages 87–88. This exercise—and others throughout this book—contain misspelled names and style errors that you will be expected to correct. To learn the proper spellings of the names, use the city directory in Appendix A. To check the proper style, consult The Associated Press Stylebook in Appendix B.

1. Police received a call at 12:30 a.m. today from the manager of the Aloma Apartments, 4713 Bell Ave. The apartment manager told police someone had jumped into the apartment swimming pool and died a tragic death. Police investigating the case reported: "The pool had been closed since last Saturday night for repainting and was just being refilled with water. There were only 19 inches of water in the bottom of the pool at the time of the accident. The victim, Dr. Wesley Rue, apparently sustained a broken neck. He dove about 9 feet into the pool. The coroner pronounced him dead at the scene." Neighbors said that Dr. Rue often went swimming just before going to bed, and he apparently didn't look into the pool before diving into it last night.

2. The International Standardization Organization, which is composed of acoustics experts, today opened its annual convention. The convention is meeting in Geneva, Switzerland. Delegates from 51 countries are attending the convention, which will continue through Sunday. An annual report issued by the organization warned that noise levels in the world are rising by one decibel a year. If the increase continues, the report warned, "everyone living in cities could be stone deaf by the year 2000." The report also said that long-term exposure to a noise level of 100 decibels can cause deafness, yet a riveting gun reaches a level of 130 decibels and a jet aircraft 150.

3. The city's Human Rights Commission lost a battle last night. It wanted the City Council to ban a history book that it claims "deals erroneously and disparagingly" with American Indians. City Council members said they did not want to start banning books and refused to endorse the commission's efforts and refused to order school officials to remove the book from city schools.

4. Robert J. Horten was charged with evading income taxes some time ago. The Internal Revenue Service said that he has not filed a tax return since 1986 and that he owes $76,144 in back taxes. Horten is 37 years old. He appeared in U.S. District Court this morning and pleaded guilty to the charges against him. The judge delayed sentencing until next week. Horten has been district attorney in the city since 1978. He resigned five weeks ago.

5. A 19-year-old shoplifting suspect died last Saturday. Police identified him as Timothy Milan. He lived at 1112 Huron Avenue and was employed as a cook at a restaurant in the city. A guard at Panzer's Department Store told police he saw Milan stuff 2 sweaters down his pants legs, then walk past a checkout line and out of the department store. The guard then began to chase Milan, who ran, and 3 bystanders joined in the pursuit. They caught up with Milan, and, when he resisted, one of the bystanders applied a headlock to him. A police officer who arrived at the scene reported that Milan collapsed as he put handcuffs on him. An autopsy conducted to determine the cause of death revealed that Milan died due to a lack of oxygen to the brain. Police today said they do not plan to charge anyone involved in the case with a crime because it "was a case of excusable homicide." The police said the bystanders did not mean to injure Milan or to kill him, but that he was fighting

violently—punching and kicking at his captors and even trying to bite them—and that they were simply trying to restrain him and trying to help capture a suspected criminal, "which is just being a good citizen."

6. There was a fatal traffic accident on State Road 419 at about 7:00 o'clock this morning. Five persons were killed in the fiery crash. State highway patrolmen said a truck was attempting to pass a car about 2 miles west of your city. The truck clipped the back of the car, sending it into a complete spin. The spinning car came to rest in a ditch, and its driver was not injured. The truck then proceeded to skid out of control and crashed head-on into an oncoming car. The truck and the on-coming car that it hit burst into flames. All four persons in the car died. The truck driver, who was alone in his vehicle at the time, also died. A highway patrolman said the truck and second car "hit pretty hard, and their occupants probably died before the flames reached them." The patrolman added that all four persons in the car were tourists from Canada. The truck driver was a resident of your city. Police are withholding all their names pending notification of next of kin.

7. Alfred J. Piccioll, age 33, of 411 Robinson Road was pronounced dead at Memorial Hospital at 2 a.m. today after attempts to revive him were unsuccessful. He was rushed to the hospital from the county jail. A correction officer at the jail checks each cell in the jail each 15 minutes. At about 1:30 a.m. a correction officer saw Picciol lying on his bed. At 1:45 a.m., the same officer found that Picciol had tried to hang himself by ripping his pants into strips and making a noose that he tied to a bar in his cell. He was arrested last week and charged with speeding, drunken driving and manslaughter after his car struck and killed an 8-year-old girl riding her bicycle home from school. Picciol was to appear in court this afternoon.

8. Two researchers at your school, both psychologists, have studied births in your state for the past 10 years. They were particularly interested in children born to parents who live under airport landing patterns. Today, they finally issued their report. The report, which examines the frequency of birth defects, uncovered some interesting differences. The psychologists found that the rate of abnormal births is 42 percent higher among parents who live near airports. The researchers explained that the cause is stress suffered by pregnant women who are repeatedly exposed to the noise of loud jet aircraft overhead.

9. A child's life was saved yesterday. Max Rivera and Charles Fusner, employees of the local power company, are the heroes. Cheryl Nichols, 1287 Belgarde Avenue, told police she found her 3-year-old son, Richard, face down and motionless in the family's swimming pool at about 4:30 p.m. yesterday. She screamed and pulled him from the water. The boy had been riding his tricycle around the pool, and it apparently slipped over the edge, dumping him into the cold water. Rivera and Fusner, who were working on nearby electrical lines, heard her screams and rushed to help. Rivera breathed into the child's mouth and Fusner applied heart massage. A neighbor called the police and fire departments. Fusner said the child came to after 3 or 4 breaths. Paramedics responding to the calls for help said the boy was in good shape when their rescue unit arrived at the scene a few minutes later. They rushed the boy to St. Nicholas Hospital, where he was examined, then released in good condition. A spokesman for the power company said company employees are required to take training in cardiopulmonary resuscitation (CPR) because of the dangers they face while working around high-voltage lines.

10. Martin S. Sneiderman is the manager of the Beef and Ale Restaurant located at 3204 Forester Road. Other restaurant employees said a masked gunman entered the front door of the establishment at 11 p.m.—just a few minutes before it was scheduled to close—last night. The gunman ordered 7 employees and 3 customers

still in the restaurant to lie down on the floor, then scooped up about $2,300 from a cash register. As the gunman was scooping up the money, Sneiderman tried to get up and run out a back door for help. The gunman shot Sneiderman once in the back, but Sneiderman managed to stumble across the street to a convenience store and ask a clerk there to call for help. He collapsed while returning to the restaurant. After firing at Sneiderman, the gunman ran out the front door, jumped into a waiting getaway car driven by a woman and fled. Sneiderman is listed in fair condition at a local hospital. No one else was hurt.

11. Several English teachers at your city's junior and senior high schools require their students to read the controversial book, "The Adventures of Huckleberry Finn." The book was written by Mark Twain. Critics, including some parents, said last week that the book should be banned from all schools in the city because it is racist. After considering their complaints and discussing them with her staff, the superintendent of schools, Marcia Pagozalski, announced today that teachers will be allowed to require reading the book in high school English classes but not in any junior high school classes. Furthermore, the superintendent said that it will be the responsibility of the high school teachers who assign the book to assist students in understanding the historical setting of the book, the characters being depicted and the social context, including the prejudices which existed at the time depicted in the book. Although the book can no longer be used in any junior high school classes, the school superintendent said it will remain available in junior and senior high school libraries for students who want to read it voluntarily. The book describes the adventures of runaway Huck Finn and a fugitive slave named Jim as they float on a raft down the Mississippi River.

12. Jamie is a German shepherd dog. It has been accused of biting two people and of attacking at least four other pets in its neighborhood. Jamie is owned by Robert and Cathy M. Sobolewski of 1031 Hidden Lane. Since Jamie bit the second person two weeks ago, it has been held in an isolation cage at the county animal shelter. Today a county judge ordered the killing of the 4-year-old dog. The county's Animal Control Board will set an execution date after receiving the order signed by Judge Randall Pfaff. The dog will be destroyed by a lethal dose of sodium phenobarbital. The county's Animal Control Board recommended Jamie's execution to the judge after concluding that the dog was vicious and dangerous to the public. It was the first death recommendation made by the board since it was formed in 1972.

EXERCISE 8
Leads

EMPHASIZING THE UNUSUAL

INSTRUCTIONS: Write only the lead for each of the following stories. Each story contains an unusual or unexpected fact that should be emphasized in the lead.

1. A car was stolen at 7:45 a.m. this morning from a convenience store parking lot on Colonial Drive. It was a four-door Buick owned by Mr. and Mrs. David R. Guerria of 3418 North Oakland Boulevard. Mrs. Guerria went into the convenience store for a pack of cigarettes. Expecting to return in a few seconds, she said she left the engine running, with the keys in the ignition. Her 2-year-old daughter, Salley Anne, was sleeping in the back seat. When she returned, the car was gone—stolen. For 2 hours, she feared for her daughter's safety. Then, shortly before 10 a.m., the car was found abandoned with the baby safely in the back seat. Police said the thief almost certainly intended only to steal the car and probably did not, when he took the car, notice the girl in the back seat. When the car was found, she was still asleep.

2. Cremation is rising in popularity. Nearly 30 percent of the people who die in your state are now cremated. The Funeral Directors Assn. in your state met at noon yesterday and discussed a growing problem. The ashes of nearly 50 percent of those people they cremate are never claimed by family members, friends or anyone else, so they are stored in the funeral homes, and the directors want to dispose of them but are uncertain of their legal right to do so. They voted to ask the state legislature to pass a bill that spells out disposal procedures. The bill they propose would require funeral homes to make every possible effort to settle with the family of the deceased the desired disposal method. Families would have up to 90 days to pick up the remains or to specify what they want done with them. After 90 days, the funeral homes would be free to get rid of them either by burying them, even in a common container (in a properly designated cemetery) or by scattering them at sea or in a garden, forest or pond.

3. A home at 2481 Santana Avenue was burglarized between the hours of 1 p.m. and 4 p.m. yesterday afternoon. The owner of the home is Dorothy R. Elam, a sixth-grade teacher at Madison Elementary School. She said no one was home at the time. Neighbors said they saw a truck parked in the driveway but thought some repair-men were working at the home. The total loss is estimated at in excess of $5,000. The items stolen from the home include a color television set, a videocassette recorder, stereo, sewing machine, electric typewriter, 2 pistols and many small kitchen appliances. Also, a stamp collection valued at about $1,000, some clothes, silverware and lawn tools were taken. Roger A. Elam, Mrs. Elam's husband, died 2 days ago. The robbery occurred while she was attending his funeral at 2:30 p.m. yesterday at the Powell Funeral Chapel, 620 North Park Avenue. Elam died of cancer after a long illness.

4. A city health inspector today inspected several restaurants in the Colonial Mall, and his reports show that he found everything in those restaurants satisfactory. But while in the mall, the inspector, Randall Tillmann, said in a separate report that he noticed a popcorn stand which did not meet various city requirements for an establishment selling food to the public. As a consequence of his inspection and the deficiencies he noted in its operations and facilities, he ordered the popcorn stand closed. His report explains that it does not have a washroom or sink for its patrons. The stand is owned and operated by Mr. and Mrs. Herbert J. MacDonald, who pay

the sum of $100 a month for the right to operate the popcorn stand in one corner of the mall. The MacDonalds were not available for comment. They closed the stand immediately after Tillman's inspection early today.

5. Gladys Anne Riggs is 81 years old. Her husband, George, died 10 years ago. She is retired and normally receives about $600 a month in Social Security benefits. She complains she has not received her benefits for the past 4 months. When she inquired as to the reasons for the troubles, officials at a Social Security office in your city today explained that she is dead. Four months ago, her check was returned and marked "deceased," so all her benefits were canceled. Because of the error, Mrs. Riggs fears that her check for next month may also be late, and she says she needs the money to buy food and to pay her rent. She lives alone in a one-bedroom apartment and says she has already fallen behind in her rent and is afraid she will be evicted. Social Security officials said that they will correct the problem as soon as possible and that she will receive a check for all the benefits she has missed during the past 4 months, but that it may take several weeks to issue the check. They suggested that she apply for welfare until the check arrives.

6. Security personnel at a local discount store arrested another shoplifter yesterday. He was observed stealing a $9.98 pair of tennis shoes at about 3 p.m. A clerk said she saw him put the shoes in a lunch bucket, then leave the store without paying for them. She notified the store's manager, and he apprehended the shoplifter in the store's parking lot. The shoplifter did not offer any resistance. He did not even cry. Police were called to the scene and took the shoplifter to a home for delinquent children. Because of the youth's age, they were unable to release his name. He was 6 years old. The store filed a complaint against the boy. The police charged him with delinquency, then released him to his parents. Police say they believe he is the youngest person they ever arrested.

7. Sometime late yesterday afternoon or early evening, Glenn R. Beghor of 415 West Hazel Avenue was driving south on State Road 419, about a mile north of your city. He apparently suffered a heart attack, and his car swerved off the busy highway, jumped the curb and came to a dead stop in a field. Authorities said he had a history of heart trouble and was in his late 60s. Most passing motorists apparently did not notice his car. At about 8 p.m., the owner of a nearby store became curious and flagged down a patrol car and pointed the car out to them. Two officers in the car found that Beghor was dead but that at least one passer-by had noticed his car and stopped. Beghor's cash, jewelry and shoes were missing. His pockets were turned inside out, and all the money had been stolen from his wallet. Relatives said Behor's watch and credit cards also were missing. The police said they do not know whether Beghor was robbed while he was still alive, or whether he died instantly of a heart attack and was robbed after his death.

8. Melody Anne Pickaid is 7 years old and dying of cancer. She is expected to live only 5 to 10 more months. She and her mother, Margaret, live at 819 Superior Avenue in your city. There are 3 other children in the family, all under the age of 10. The children's father, Ralph R. Pickaid, was killed in a car accident a few years ago. Mrs. Pickaid is unemployed and receives about $920 a month in welfare payments. She says much of the money goes to help pay Melody Anne's various bills. News stories written about the family's plight last Christmas aroused widespread sympathy. The stories reported that the 4 children had not received any Christmas presents for 2 years and would not receive any again last Christmas due to the family's extreme poverty. Several persons gave the children toys valued at more than $1,000. The family also received other gifts: nearly $4,200 in cash, food, clothing and household furnishings. State welfare officials who learned of the gifts now say they are required to cut off the family's welfare payments and to ask Mrs. Pickaid to return

nearly $2,000 in past welfare payments. The officials today explained that new regulations intended to eliminate welfare fraud tightened the restrictions on outside income that can be received by welfare recipients. The regulations automatically cut the welfare payments of recipients who receive any income from outside sources, regardless of the purpose or circumstances.

9. There was a robbery which occurred at approximately 10:30 p.m. last night. A masked gunman entered a pizza parlor at 411 Michigan Avenue. There were three patrons and four employees in the establishment at the time. The gunman quickly emptied a cash register of about $350 in cash. A youth about to enter the pizza parlor noticed the robbery in progress. He immediately called the police. Just as the police arrived, the gunman ran from the pizza parlor and fled into a housing development behind it. The youth followed the gunman. The police released a police dog from their car and ordered it to attack the gunman. The dog caught and bit the youth four or five times in his right leg. The youth required 64 stitches in his leg. The gunman escaped.

10. Melanie Anne Hoffman is 23 years old. Her home address is 481 East Brittany Road. In the last five years, she has been arrested 47 times on prostitution charges. She has been found guilty 26 times. She has been found innocent 7 times. The other charges were dropped or are pending. Upon conviction in the past, she has usually been fined or sentenced to serve a few days in the county jail. She was just released from the jail two weeks ago after serving a 10-day sentence on one of the prostitution charges. She appeared in court again today on the 47th charge, and was convicted and given an unusual choice. The judge, Edward Kocembra, sentenced her to serve a total of 1,800 days in a state prison as a repeat offender. Or, the judge said he would suspend the sentence if she would leave the county and not come back for at least 5 years. The judge explained: "In view of the money it costs to continue to arrest you and hold you in jail, the county will save money if you leave. And it's obvious you're not being rehabilitated." The woman chose to leave. She will be held in the county jail until 8 a.m. tomorrow. Then a deputy sheriff will escort her to the airport and watch to be certain that she gets aboard a plane to the city of her choice: Los Angeles.

EXERCISE 9
Leads

SPECIAL PROBLEMS
(THE UNUSUAL, LOCALIZING AND UPDATING)

INSTRUCTIONS: Write only the lead for each of the following stories, following the guideline that precedes each group of stories. Some stories contain highly unusual facts that should be emphasized in their leads. Other stories will have to be localized or updated. Again, consult the checklists on pages 87–88.

Part I: Stress the Unusual

1. Daniel J. Silverbach is a policeman in your community. Last year, because of his heroic rescue of seven persons held at gunpoint during a robbery, Police Chief Martin Guidema named him the department's Police Officer of the Year. Guidema fired Silverbach when he reported for duty at 7 a.m. today. The department adopted certain grooming standards, and Guidema said Silverbach's mustache was a quarter inch too long and his sideburns a half inch too long, and he refused to trim them. Guidema added that he warned Silverbach a month ago to trim his hair, then ordered him to do so at the first of last week. He fired him for failing to obey the order of a superior officer.

2. Terri Snow of 3418 Hazel St. is a nurse at Mercy Hospital. She is married to Dale Snow, a former eighth-grade science teacher at Mays Junior High School. Snow was crippled after a diving accident three years ago, when his arms and legs were paralyzed. He met his wife at the hospital, where he was a patient, and they were married last month. Now state officials have suggested that they get a divorce. Before his marriage, Snow received $345 a month from the state's Department of Social Services and a monthly $792 federal Supplement Security Income payment. Because of his wife's income, he no longer is eligible for the payments, and the couple says without the payments they cannot afford to pay for Snow's continuing medical treatments and special diet. State officials have advised them that Snow will again become eligible for the aid if they get a divorce. The officials refused to talk to reporters, however.

3. Jeffrey DuFaull Junior lives in the house in which he was born. It was built in the year 1884 by a grandfather, and he plans to burn it down tomorrow. DuFaull explains that when his grandfather built the eight-room house, his property taxes were $18 a year. When DuFaull inherited the house from his father in 1952, the property taxes were $122 a year. This year the city raised his annual property taxes to $1,483, up from $816 last year. DuFaull said, "The town jumped my taxes $600 in a single year, and that's just too much." He said the remaining property—nearly four acres of land—will be sold and he will move into an apartment. The house is located at 1994 Hazel Lane.

Part II: Localize Your Lead

4. The state Department of Transportation today announced plans for next year. It will spend a total of $218 million to build new roads and to improve old ones. The amount represents a $14.5 million increase over last year's total. The money comes from a state gasoline tax amounting to 4 cents per gallon sold. The department allocates the

money on the basis of need, with the most congested and dangerous areas receiving the most help. Included in the allocations for next year are $7.8 million, allocated to widen from two to four lanes state highway 17–92, which runs through the south-eastern part of your city for a distance of approximately three miles. Construction work on the highway project is expected to begin in four months and to be completed within one and one-half years.

5. Three persons have been killed in the crash of a single-engine plane. Police have identified the victims as Mr. and Mrs. Joel Skurow of Atlanta, Georgia, and Melville Skurow of 4138 Hennessy Court in your community. Joel and Melville are brothers. The plane, flown by Joel, crashed on the outskirts of Atlanta at 7:30 a.m. today. Cause of the crash is unknown. No one on the ground was injured. Friends said Melville Skurow was visiting his brother, an attorney in Atlanta. Skurow is a carpenter and was thirty-seven years of age. The plane, valued at $14,800, was fully insured.

6. The annual Conference of U.S. Mayors is being held in New York City this week. Mayors from throughout the United States hold an annual convention to discuss problems of mutual interest. At the closing session today they elected their officers for the forthcoming year, and they elected your mayor, Paul Novarro, first vice president. Approximately 1,460 mayors were in attendance at the convention, which next year will be held in Las Vegas.

Part III: Update Your Lead

7. William MacDowell, 28, a housepainter who lives at 1429 Highland Drive, is being tried for the murder of a cocktail waitress, Ethel Shearer. His trial opened last Thursday, and witnesses last Friday said a ring found in MacDowell's home belonged to the murder victim. MacDowell took the stand today and said he knew the victim and had bought the ring from her for $60 for a girlfriend. If convicted, MacDowell could be sentenced to life in prison. He is currently on parole after spending 8 years in prison on an armed robbery charge.

8. There was a grinding head-on collision on Cheney Road yesterday. Two persons were killed: Rosemary Brennan, 27, and her infant daughter, Kelley, age 2, both of 1775 Nairn Dr. The driver of the second car involved in the accident, Anthony Murray, 17, of 1748 North 3 Street, was seriously injured, with multiple fractures. Police today announced that laboratory tests have confirmed the fact that Brennan was legally drunk at the time of the accident.

9. The state Legislature passed a law which prohibits doctors from performing abortions on girls under the age of 16 without the consent of their parents or guardians. The law specifies that doctors found guilty of violating the law can be fined up to $5,000 and can lose their licenses to practice medicine in the state. The law, which has been signed by the governor, will go into effect at midnight tonight. The Legislature adopted the law after news media in the state revealed that girls as young as the age of 11 had been given abortions without their parents' knowledge or consent. The law is intended to prevent that. The parents' consent must be in writing. The law stipulates that the girl who is pregnant must also agree to the abortion so that her parents cannot force her to have one unwillingly.

5 Alternative Leads

The previous chapter described basic summary leads. That type of lead is more common than any of the alternatives—and probably easier to write. While reading your local daily, you may find that 95 percent of its stories begin with a summary lead. Yet increasingly, experienced reporters are using newer and more controversial types of leads.

The alternatives are called "soft leads." There are at least a dozen variations, but most soft leads begin with a story's most interesting details—often a question, quotation, anecdote or description. A summary of the story's most important details may appear later, perhaps in the third or fourth paragraph. Or, the soft lead may move directly into a story without any attempt to summarize it.

When reporters finish a story, their editors expect it to be well written: clear, concise, accurate and interesting. If a story meets these criteria, editors are unlikely to object because its lead does not use the conventional summary form. However, beginners should use the alternative forms sparingly. Beginners who try to use the alternative forms before they have mastered the basic summary lead run the risk of making too many serious errors.

The Controversy

During the 1940s, The Wall Street Journal became one of the first daily newspapers to use soft leads. Since then, a few other dailies, such as the Los Angeles Times, The Miami Herald and the Boston Globe, have become known as "writers' newspapers." These dailies give their reporters more freedom to experiment with newer styles of writing. Many of their reporters use soft leads, and reporters at other dailies are following their example.

Proponents of soft leads argue that it does not matter whether a lead is hard or soft—only whether it works. They refer to the traditional summaries derogatorily as "suitcase leads." In the past, they explain, newspapers tried to jam too many details into the leads. They argue that summary leads and the inverted pyramid style are unnatural, making it more difficult for them to write a good story. They further explain that summary leads eliminate the possibility of surprise and make all their stories sound alike.

Reporters using soft leads see their stories as hourglass-shaped, with three parts: (1) an introduction; (2) a turn or transition; and (3) a narrative which tells the story, usually in chronological order. Roy Peter Clark, a proponent of more experimentation in writing, insists that the hourglass form is a more natural way to tell a story. Like good storytellers, the reporters start at the beginning of a tale and proceed to the end, thus presenting the facts in a normal, logical sequence. Clark adds that the key to a good story is the turn—the transition from the lead to the narrative.

The more literary style of soft leads may also help newspapers compete with television. The style's proponents explain that television can report the news more quickly than newspapers but that, by using soft leads, newspapers can make their stories more interesting.

Critics—primarily other reporters and editors—call the style "Jell-O Journalism." They complain that soft leads are inappropriate for most news stories: too artsy, literary, dangerous and unprofessional. Critics add that the soft leads are too long and fail to emphasize the news. If a story begins with several paragraphs of description or quotations, for example, the story's most important details may be lost: buried somewhere in a later paragraph. Critics also complain that some reporters seem to be straining to write fine literature, and that many lack the necessary ability. Their leads seem fashionable but dull. Some begin with minor but misleading details. Others "turn to mush."

Critics believe the traditional summary leads are clearer and more straightforward—and more appropriate for hard news stories. They do not expect reporters to begin every news story with a summary lead, but do not want the delays (the introductions) to be excruciatingly long.

Thus, some editors are trying to discourage soft leads: to limit the number of stories that start with color instead of the news. These editors are particularly critical of front-page stories that begin with soft leads that fail to deliver their main point until after the jump—the continuation on an inside page. Editors fear that, if readers have not learned the stories' main point by then, few will turn to the inside page.

Delayed or "Buried" Leads

"Delayed" leads seem to be the most common—and controversial—of the alternatives. Some reporters call them "buried" leads. Typically, these begin with an interesting example or anecdote that sets a story's theme. Then—perhaps in the third or fourth paragraph—a "nut graf" summarizes the story and provides a transition to the body. Thus, the nut graf moves the story from a single example or anecdote to the general issue or problem. Like a traditional lead, it summarizes the topic. In addition, it may explain why the topic is important. Here are two examples:

> Steve Good said he knew his father would rather be dead than spend the rest of his life behind bars.
> So when James Good needed one more bullet to use on himself after killing his girlfriend and firing at an Orange County deputy sheriff early Thursday, his 20-year-old son was there to lend a hand.
> "I helped him look for the bullet," Steve said later. "And I gave it to him. I knew what he wanted it for, and I didn't want him to do it. But he didn't want to do any time. He didn't want to get captured. He wanted the bullet."

Steve said he stood and watched his father shove the bullet into the revolver's chamber. They embraced, and his father went into his bedroom and shot himself in the head.

(The Orlando Sentinel)

BRENTWOOD, Pa.—Shana Racquel owns a mink coat, a dozen custom-made outfits (including a dress trimmed with ostrich feathers and a London Fog raincoat), gold bracelets; her own seamstress, chauffeur, nanny and beautician.

Unusual for a 13-year-old. Even stranger for a dog.

"This is the little girl I never had," Suzanne Brandau says of the brown-and-white English springer spaniel. "She always has the best—the best food, the best clothes, the best baby sitters."

Brandau is one of a growing number of pet lovers across the USA who are spoiling their animals to the hilt—and willing to pay for it.

(USA Today)

There are dozens of variations. Some delayed leads, such as the following example, contain even more of an "O. Henry touch," surprising their readers with an unusual twist. The following story begins in chronological order, hiding its twist until the fifth paragraph:

SAN JOSE, Calif.—The man who called the state Employment Development Department last week said he wanted to hire 70 or 80 people to tear down a vacant house in East San Jose in a hurry.

He got action.

About 75 men, jobless and hungry for the job, offered $5 an hour, set about the task with zeal. By Tuesday morning, only the foundation and the floor remained—and the floor was disappearing fast.

That's when the owner, Mark Campbell, showed up.

"He asked us, 'Who gave you permission to tear my house down?'" said Robert Robinson, one of the workers. "He told us to get the hell off his property. We didn't know we were tearing down somebody's house we weren't supposed to."

(Knight-Ridder Newspapers)

If a story is only three or four paragraphs long, journalists may save the twist for the last line. If a story is longer, they use the twist to lure readers to the nut graf, and it provides a transition to the following paragraphs.

Multiparagraph Leads

Other newswriters consider their leads a unit of thought. These writers continue to use summary leads, but their summaries include two or three paragraphs, as in the following examples:

LEOMINSTER, Mass. (UPI)—Two teen-age girls opened a bottle of champagne, shared it and left behind letters about how happy they were about to be.

Then they took out a 12-gauge shotgun and killed themselves.

Eugene W. Phillips stumbled and fell from his porch, punctured his back with a stick and slammed his head against the ground. It was about the nicest thing that ever happened to him.

Phillips had been blind most of the past 16 years. The accident a week ago helped him to partially regain his eyesight.

Rafael Morales promised he would show up for trial. His father promised. His mother promised. And his two sisters promised. His boss promised, too.

Morales, 33, a Hialeah salesman charged with cocaine trafficking, did not keep his promise. He jumped $75,000 bail and skedaddled. So Dade County Circuit Judge Margarita Esquiroz sent his father, mother, two sisters and his boss to jail Thursday for 30 days.

(KNT News Service)

Using Questions and Quotations

Reporters also use questions and quotations in leads—but sparingly. Reporters use a quotation only when a source has said something so effectively that the statement cannot possibly be improved. In addition, the quotation used in a lead should: (1) summarize the entire story, (2) be brief, and (3) be totally self-explanatory. As shown in the following examples, a quotation must satisfy not just one, but all three of these criteria:

> "Congress should immediately ban the sale of all tobacco products, especially cigarettes," the president of the American Cancer Society declared in a speech here last night.

> "Why does God hate me?" asked Alan McDonald after gunpowder exploded in his face and hands, burning him severely for the second time in his life.
>
> *(The Associated Press)*

> Having told a federal judge, "If I don't tell the truth, I will be punished by God," 9-year-old John Calzadilla walked calmly across a crowded courtroom here today and pointed a finger at two teen-agers charged with kidnapping him.
>
> *(The New York Times)*

Never use a quotation simply because it is sensational and likely to startle your readers. A quotation used in a lead should summarize the entire story, not just a small part of it. If the quotation fails to summarize the entire story—only a sensational detail—the main point of the story is likely to be unclear, and later paragraphs are likely to seem disorganized: unrelated to the sensational detail presented in the lead. If the quotation is not self-explanatory, it may confuse and discourage your readers. If the quotation is too long, your entire lead may become too long and complicated.

Be particularly careful to avoid quotations that begin with words that must be identified or explained in a later paragraph: words such as "he," "we," "it" and "this." If "he" or "we" is the first word in a story, readers have no way of knowing to whom the word refers. When the subject's identity is revealed later in a story, readers may have to stop, go back and reread the quotation to understand its meaning. Here is an example of that type of error:

> "If you don't cooperate, I'll blow your brains out," he told her as she walked to work this morning.
> REVISED: Lisa Vantorini was walking down Princeton Street when a young man approached her from behind and threatened to kill her unless she helped him rob a bank where she works as a cashier.

Leads that use a quotation can often be rewritten with a brief introduction placed *before* the quotation to enhance its clarity:

> "It was saucer-shaped and appeared to have a glass window section running around the center." That's how a woman described the flying object she saw hover above Crystal Lake on Monday and Tuesday nights.
> REVISED: A woman who saw a flying object hover above Crystal Lake on Monday and Tuesday nights said, "It was saucer-shaped and appeared to have a glass window section running around the center."

> "Forget it" is the advice a 20-year-old gave in an interview Monday to other youths who want to drive race cars.
> REVISED: A 20-year-old, who was crippled when his stock car collided with two other cars and struck a wall, Monday warned other youths who want to drive race cars to "forget it."

Instead of using a full quotation, reporters often quote only a key word or phrase in a lead:

LONDON—Cigarette smoking can lead to "smoker's face," a wrinkled, weary, haggard look that will give you away every time, a British doctor says.

(The Associated Press)

Dr. Margaret Mead, an authority on marriage and family life, Monday warned that student marriages are creating "a settled, security-loving, unadventurous people."

A police chief, speaking here today, accused sociologists of being "impractical, blind, maudlin sentimentalists," with unrealistic attitudes toward crime and criminals.

Questions also make effective leads but, again, are most appropriate for light, humorous stories—not serious news stories. In one case, members of a college psychology class disguised a student as an old man, placed him in a booth on campus and watched as he tried to give away dollar bills. Most passers-by refused to accept money from the "old man." A journalism student asked to write a story about the experiment typed this lead:

Students in a psychology class tried to give away dollar bills Friday but found that most of their classmates were unwilling to accept them.

Another student, given the same assignment, wrote this question lead:

Would you accept free dollar bills from an old man?

To be effective, question leads must be brief, simple, specific and provocative. The question should contain no more than a dozen words. Moreover, readers should feel absolutely compelled to answer it. Thus, the question should concern a controversial issue that readers are familiar with: an issue that interests and affects them. Avoid abstract or complicated questions that would require a great deal of explanation.

The following questions are ineffective because they are too abstract, long and complicated. Moreover, they fail to ask about issues that everyone is certain to care about:

Would you like to have a say in the physical and mental health care facilities offered in your city?

If you were on vacation miles from your house, and you thought the mechanic at a service station deliberately damaged your car, then demanded an exorbitant fee to repair it, would you be willing to file criminal charges against the mechanic and return to the area to testify at his trial?

The following questions also fail, but for different reasons. The first question asks about an issue unlikely to concern most readers. The second question is flippant, treating a serious topic as a trivial one. Moreover, no one can answer the question:

Have you thought about going to prison lately?
Someone was swindled today. Who'll be swindled tomorrow?

The following, more effective leads are short, specific and concern topics more likely to affect or interest large numbers of readers:

Why do people lie?

Why do some children become delinquents?

Are college professors giving too many As and Bs?

At what age should children start learning about sex?

Some editors prohibit the use of both quotation and question leads. The editors explain that most quotations lack clarity and, when used in leads, are too long and complicated. Some editors also believe that news stories should answer questions, not ask them.

Suspenseful Leads

Other leads are written to arouse readers' curiosity, create suspense or raise a question in their minds. By hinting at some mysterious development explained in a later paragraph, this type of lead compels readers to finish a story:

> Karen Martin no longer wonders who she is.

> Soon Joyce Simonton must die. Everyone has told her so.
>
> *(St. Petersburg Times)*

> Jean Driftmier was dead for a few moments Sunday morning.
>
> *(The Orlando Sentinel)*

> Three weeks ago Sue McCrady bought a stack of guidebooks to national parks, planning a cross-country trip she and her husband were to begin today. Two days later she bought a coffin.
>
> *(The New York Times)*

Descriptive Leads

A descriptive lead is one that begins with descriptive details and moves gradually into the action. The description should be colorful and interesting so that it arouses readers' interest in the topic. The description can also help summarize a story, as in the first example:

> An Ohio woman clutched a picture of her son and choked back tears as his killer was sentenced to 99 years in prison.

> There were row after row of gravestones—and they were knocked over, lying flat, more than 500 of them, under a chill sun yesterday at Mount Hebron Cemetery in Flushing, Queens.
> Ruth Kart, whose father-in-law's stone had been among those overturned and, in some cases, cracked by vandals during the night, remembered how she had been sickened when she saw a monument in Israel to the six million Jews who were murdered by the Nazis in World War II. The new sight, she said, "turned my stomach again."
> Jewish graves have not been the only target of cemetery vandals. . . .
>
> *(The New York Times)*

> It's Thursday morning, and the back room of the restaurant is filled with neatly dressed men holding earnest conversations over eggs and pancakes.
> Mimeographed pamphlets are handed out. A sex-education book is passed around, causing heads to shake negatively. A rousing prayer is delivered.
> The Decency in Education Committee of Lee County is holding its weekly meeting.
>
> *(The Associated Press)*

The following leads, which appeared on the front page of The New York Times on the same day, demonstrate the effectiveness of descriptive leads. The first lead *summarizes* a major story. The second lead *describes* the story. As you read the second lead, notice its effective use of descriptive verbs: "hit," "glided," "skidded" and "sank":

An Air Florida jetliner taking off from National Airport in a snowstorm crashed into a crowded bridge this afternoon and broke as it plunged into the Potomac River, leaving at least 10 people dead and more than 40 missing, according to unofficial police estimates.

It hit the bridge with a deafening roar and then, suddenly, there was silence. There was no sound at all, those who watched said later, as the Air Florida 737 jetliner glided into the river, skidded across the gray ice and sank slowly into the icy waters.

Shocking Leads—With a Twist

Reporters also like "shockers"—startling leads that immediately capture the attention of readers. The following examples, written by students, have an unusual twist that adds to their effectiveness.

A freight train carrying toxic chemicals smashed into a bus Thursday, killing two teenagers. "It was fun," said one 17-year-old. "I'd like to do it again next year."
Sharon Handler, a high school senior, could talk about her "death" because she and 59 other high school students volunteered to be the victims of a mock disaster.

An Edgewood patrolman today said that he would like to shoot people all day long if it would make the streets any safer.
"It's easy. Take the gun, aim and shoot—whammo, you've nailed 'em," said patrolman L. E. Dobbins.
He spends about two hours a day hidden in bushes or behind a building, waiting for the unsuspecting speedster to cross the sights of his radar gun.

Ironic Leads

Other leads, closely related to the shockers, present a startling or ironic contrast—again, details likely to arouse readers' curiosity, as in the following examples:

Civil Defense officials estimate there are 300 handicapped residents in the county who will need help during an emergency. So far, the officials have located only 50.

RALEIGH, N.C.—Velma Barfield, who crocheted dolls for her grandchildren and slipped fatal doses of arsenic to her mother and three other victims, was executed by lethal injection early today.
Wearing pink cotton pajamas and strapped to a stainless-steel gurney, Barfield became the first woman executed in the United States in 22 years shortly after 2 a.m. when a powerful muscle relaxer was pumped into her veins.

(The Orlando Sentinel)

Direct-Address Leads

Reporters occasionally use a form of direct address, speaking directly to their readers:

If you are convicted of drunken driving after Jan. 1, you will be fined $1,000 and sentenced to three days in prison.

If you live another 50 years, you are likely to be a millionaire. The Social Security Administration predicts that an average worker will earn $656,000 a year. However, a loaf of bread will cost $37.50, a car $281,000 and a home $3.4 million.

Unusual Words Used in Unusual Ways

If you are clever and have a good imagination (or a good grasp of literature), you might try to use a common word or phrase in an uncommon manner. However, the style is difficult because what seems funny or clever to one person may not be funny or clever to another:

Parole may be an idea whose time has gone.

(The New York Times)

A Beverly Hills bar poured the shot that may be heard round the nation.

(The Associated Press)

Two veteran motion picture industry executives were chosen today by the board of Walt Disney Productions to head the troubled company a mouse built.

(The New York Times)

The second story went on to explain that, after a serious auto accident, a Californian won a $2 million lawsuit filed against a Beverly Hills bar that served liquor to a drunken driver. A law in California makes bars liable for the actions of their patrons.

The following examples are less successful, perhaps because they seem contrived (or corny). Also, the subjects may be too serious for such a light touch:

A man who punched a highway patrolman in the face will pay through the nose for the blow.

A 15-year-old boy's errant throw at a baseball tryout landed him in court, but the jury found him safe and pitched the lawsuit.

Mark Mazur, once in a pickle over a cucumber, was a free man Wednesday after a judge suspended his six-month jail sentence and placed him on probation.

The first story went on to explain that a man had been ordered to pay $40,000 to a state trooper he punched in the face during a routine traffic stop. The trooper suffered a broken nose. The second story explained that a 15-year-old had been sued for $178,000 after a baseball he threw from first base struck an airline mechanic watching the game from near homeplate. The mechanic claimed that the baseball shattered his glasses, destroying 50 percent of the vision in his right eye. The third story described a man arrested and charged with theft after he ate a cucumber, some raw hamburger and bacon bits at a supermarket.

Chronological Order

As mentioned in Chapter 4, journalists like to tell some stories—even serious news stories—in chronological order. They consider chronological order a more natural way to tell a story. Here's an example from The Milwaukee Journal:

June Shore, 71, was getting ready to leave for church when the smoke alarm began to blare in her apartment building at 3414 W. Wisconsin Ave.

"All of a sudden, people were running around in robes yelling, 'There's a fire! There's a fire!'" Shore said in a telephone interview. "It was a horrendous thing, but everyone tried to help everyone else."

Although most of the building's 23 residents were at home when the three-alarm fire broke out about 8 a.m. Sunday, no one was injured. The fire caused about $170,000 in damage to the three-story brick building and its contents, Battalion Chief Dennis Michalowski said.

Other Unusual Leads

The following leads are difficult to categorize. All the leads are unusual, yet effective. Notice their simplicity, brevity and clarity. The average sentence contains fewer than 10 words. Also notice the leads' emphases upon the interesting and unusual:

Every week millions of drivers encounter trains at crossings nationwide. Hundreds of them never get across the tracks.

The winners who beat the trains get no prizes. The losers show up as statistics: 7,280 accidents, 649 deaths and about 2,900 injuries. . . .

(Journal of Commerce)

OCALA, Fla.—Nineteen years ago someone saved Selena Frank's life. Wednesday morning it was her turn.

(The Orlando Sentinel)

Save your sympathy, Glenn Stephens says. His blindness doesn't bother him. But ignorant clerks and waiters do.

(St. Petersburg Times)

NEW YORK—Police horses, police dogs and now—police seals?

Three harbor seals, taught to retrieve guns, tools and other objects and to enter a diving bell to take a breath, showed off their skills Wednesday before police and other public officials at a private research institute.

(Knight-Ridder Newspapers)

The man who stumbled out of the Miami Beach paddywagon into the county's alcoholic referral center at about 10 p.m. wore filthy, ragged dungarees.

He smelled of dirt and beer.

He was loud.

He was obnoxious.

He was a cop.

(The Miami Herald)

Write & Wrong ST. LOUIS POST-DISPATCH

By Harry Levins
Post-Dispatch Writing Coach

Most story-tellers swear by chronological order. Stories make more sense when they begin at the beginning and end at the end. The news usually dictates that reporters push chronological order aside, at least temporarily. But in the following lede, chronological order got pushed, shoved and stomped upon:

MILWAUKEE (AP)—A 39-year-old man who wanted to "scare" his wife was being held Tuesday on suspicion of setting fire to her shortly after he watched a television movie about a woman who had burned her abusive husband to death, police said.

The order of events was (1) the movie, (2) the burning and (3) the arrest. But we ran things backward, meaning that reading the story is like watching a movie in reverse. We could have said it this way:

MILWAUKEE (AP)—Shortly after the broadcast of a movie about a woman who fatally burns her abusive husband, a woman who had watched the movie on television with her husband was doused with gasoline and set afire.

The woman is in a hospital, and her husband was being held Tuesday in Milwaukee's city jail on suspicion of attempted murder. Police say the man insists he meant only to "scare" his wife.

Now, the order is 1-2-3, and the story makes more sense.

(continued on next page)

Granted, many stories won't lend themselves to this sort of treatment. But The Coach will again quote the writing expert who urges reporters to "get to chronological order as soon as your story, your editor and your conscience allow. Readers sigh in relief when they realize that the journalism is over and the story is about to begin."

☆ ☆ ☆

A Novel Approach

A recent story featured a woman who said something "with a brave smile" and admitted something else "a bit sheepishly."

This sort of wording fits in a novel, but not in a newspaper. A novelist is God; because he creates his characters, he can read their minds. But reporters gamble when they try to read minds. How can the reporter possibly know that a smile is "brave"? Similarly, how can he know that he's hearing sheepishness? That's a guess.

Postscript: the word "brave" turned up again in a curious sense when Walter Mondale campaigned in Columbia, Mo., on a cool, drizzly autumn day. One of the people on hand to greet him was a student who "braved the cool, wet weather."

Braved? People in Seattle "brave" this sort of weather almost every day. Please, let's ration the medals for bravery.

☆ ☆ ☆

Murky Modifiers

Clumsy placement of modifiers can make us look sloppy at best and absurd at worst. Some recent examples:

—A story about utility cutoffs said that *companies disconnected delinquent homes as soon as they legally could.* The homes are inanimate; the *customers* are delinquent.

—A People item described Arthur Hailey as the *best-selling author of "Hotel" and "Airport."* A book, not an author, is a best-seller. The only best-selling people in publishing are the high-pressure clerks at B. Dalton.

—*Fifteen percent of children tested for lead poisoning in St. Louis recently had toxic amounts of lead in the blood.* The writer meant that the testing had been done recently. But the reader could easily take the wording to mean that the children recently had lead in their blood. The solution: "Fifteen percent of the children tested recently in St. Louis for lead poisoning had . . ."

—A story on the Special School District said that *an investigation has turned up no evidence of fraudulent legal billings by two former lawyers.* How can something be both "fraudulent" and "legal"? Solution: drop the word "legal" and, in this case, let context carry the day.

—One story described the Veterans Day parade in St. Louis as *the largest patriotic observance of the national holiday in the nation.* Huh? Try, "the nation's largest observance of the holiday."

—A story on striking miners told of *two days of incidents at mine gates, including one in which four people were injured.* Literally, we're saying that four people were injured in one mine gate. That sort of tortured absurdity usually crops up when a writer tries to pack too many facts into one sentence. The solution: spread the facts over two sentences. ". . . two days of incidents at mine gates. In one of those incidents, four people were injured."

—We reported the theft *of a car given by the baseball Cardinals to their retiring equipment manager two years ago.* As a modifier, "retiring" means "quiet and withdrawn," which Butch Yatkeman was not. Try: ". . . a car that the baseball Cardinals gave to their equipment manager when he retired two years ago."

—From a wire story datelined Manila: *A report by the National Bar Association that was made public Tuesday says . . .* We meant to say that the report was made public Tuesday. But because of clumsy placement, we said that the National Bar Association was made public Tuesday. (To compound the folly, we singled out the association as the one "that was made public Tuesday," presumably to distinguish it from those that were made public on Wednesday and Thursday.) Solution: "A report made public Tuesday by the National Bar Association says . . ."

☆ ☆ ☆

Punctured Punctuation

Yes, essays on restrictive and non-restrictive clauses make for dull reading. But when we screw up the two—which we do, with dismaying regularity—the reader faces confusing reading.

A restrictive clause is one that's essential to the sentence. It starts with a "that" and is *not* set off by commas.

The noun **that starts this sentence** *is the subject.*

If you erase the "that" clause, you're left with a meaningless shell of a sentence:

"The noun is the subject." Well, *which* noun is the subject?

A non-restrictive clause contains useful but non-essential information. This clause starts with a "which" (or a "who") and is set off by a comma or commas. Example:

The noun, **which is a part of speech,** *is used to start many sentences.*

Even if you erase the "which" clause, the sentence makes sense.

Lately, we've been having trouble with sentences in which the "which" is omitted but nevertheless understood. Here's an example:

He was arrested early Sunday morning after the collision on U.S. Highway 40 at Hanley Road in Richmond Heights.

Everything after the word "collision" is part of a non-restrictive clause (a "comma-which" clause)—even with the "which" understood. In effect, we are saying:

. . . after the collision, **(which occurred)** *on U.S. Highway 40 . . .*

Yes, in a sentence like this, you may omit the "which." But no, you may not skip the comma. The reason: without a comma, the clause becomes a restrictive clause—a "that" clause. And if the clause is restrictive, the sentence becomes absurd.

Look at it this way: is the information in the clause crucial to the meaning of the sentence? No. Although the site of the crash is useful, the sentence makes sense without it.

But by omitting the comma, we made the information crucial to the meaning of the sentence. And the only possible sense in which this information would be crucial would be if the story described more than one accident—"the accident that occurred on U.S. Highway 40 *as opposed to* the accident that occurred on Interstate 70." But the story in question described only one accident. So a comma was vital.

No big deal? Well, the aim is to inform—not confuse—the reader. Missing commas cause confusion.

(Rule of thumb: in spoken English, most people pause in their conversation at points where commas would be used in written English. ". . . after the collision *(pause)*, on U.S. Highway 40 . . ." If you're in doubt about restrictive versus non-restrictive, read the sentence aloud, or at least mutter it under your breath. Wherever you pause, you're usually safe in inserting a comma.)

☆ ☆ ☆

First Things First

Sometimes, a writer reaching for a pronoun pokes the reader in the eye. An example:

Now that he's turned things around at Chrysler Corp., Lee Iacocca says he wouldn't mind taking a crack at the U.S. economy.

"Now that he . . ." Now that *who?* The reader has to wade through six more words before the identity of "he" becomes clear. The solution: hold off on the pronoun until you've used the name:

Now that Lee Iacocca has turned things around at Chrysler Corp., he says . . .

Here's an example in which the reader was kept in the dark even longer:

Although he has lost three times in his effort to have the U.S. Supreme Court consider the merits of the St. Louis area desegregation case, Attorney General John D. Ashcroft plans . . .

The solution: switch "he" and "Attorney General John D. Ashcroft."

At all costs, make sure that the pronoun refers back to the nearest noun. Here's a paragraph that strayed badly:

Ms. Goodwin said the appeal was the group's first fund drive. **It** *has been operating out of the pockets of its several most active members . . .*

What does "It" mean? The reader naturally looks back to the closest noun and assumes that "It" stands for "fund drive." Trouble is, the reader soon has to backtrack, because "fund drive" makes no sense. The reader might finally deduce through context that "It" means "the group."

Or he might set the paper aside and turn on the television news, which is painless.

☆ ☆ ☆

For The Record

Some sharp-eyed readers have noticed that The Coach skipped a September issue. He pleads innocent. Manpower problems in the composing room held up the September issue to the point where The Coach figured that the only graceful way out was to date it October.

Tips for the Top

Roy Peter Clark, a proponent of experimentation in writing, offers these tips for writing leads:

1. Keep leads short. Even a very long story can flow from one carefully crafted sentence.

2. Never forget the news. If it is not in the first paragraph, put it in a "nut graph" near the top of the story, and certainly before the jump.

3. If a lead is delayed you have a responsibility to give readers a reason to continue. Include elements that dramatize the news, foreshadow events, create a sense of foreboding or of anticipated surprise.

4. Even if you begin your story with hard news, look for an opportunity later to retell events in a chronological narrative.

5. Keep the lead honest. Don't begin with the most startling or sensational anecdote if it is not organically related to the news.

6. When you find a good lead that violates any or all of these rules, use it.

Suggested Readings

Clark, Roy Peter. "A New Shape for the News." *Washington Journalism Review*, March 1984, pp. 46–47. (Reprinted in *Best Newspaper Writing 1985*, ed. by Roy Peter Clark and Donald Fry. St. Petersburg, Fla.: Modern Media Institute, 1985, pp. 90–95.)

———. "Plotting the First Graph." *Washington Journalism Review*, October 1982, pp. 48–50.

Lanson, Gerald, and Mitchell Stephens. "Jell-O Journalism: Why Reporters Have Gone Soft in Their Leads." *Washington Journalism Review*, April 1982, pp. 21–23.

EXERCISE 1
Alternative Leads

EVALUATING ALTERNATIVE LEADS

INSTRUCTIONS: Critically evaluate the following leads, all of which use alternative forms. Select the best leads and explain why they succeed. Point out the flaws in the remaining leads. As you evaluate the leads, look for lessons—"do's and don't's"—that you can apply to your own work.

1. "I don't see any problems, and I never anticipated any," Judge Marlene Ostreicher said when asked about plans to televise a murder trial in her courtroom next week.

2. Could you swim 40 miles, jog 100 miles or bike 400 miles in one month?

3. Brenda DeVitini got up at dawn to jog. She planned to use a high school track two blocks from her house, a track she used every morning for the last 4 years.
   A paper carrier found her body there an hour later.

4. She is young, beautiful and a good athlete—but confined to a wheel chair.

5. "Indian education is a failure and a national disgrace," a California educator declared in a speech here today.

6. "I'll let you guys have it with both barrels," a member of the state Legislature told members of the Association of Secondary Teachers, who held their state convention in the city today.

7. A 16-year-old girl who says she "considers abortion murder" was placed in jail today because she refused to obey her mother and have an abortion.

8. Are you afraid of snakes?

9. "I'm not guilty, and that's all I can say," is how a 30-year-old man responded after being found guilty of burglary and six counts of grand theft.

10. "I felt mad and chased him with an ax," a 62-year-old woman said after noticing a prowler in her backyard Tuesday.

11. Should America's 1 million excess dairy cows be donated to impoverished nations, or destroyed as ordered by the federal government to maintain the prices of dairy products?

12. With tears forming in his eyes, Albert Chmielewski whispered goodbye to his mother.
    Moments later, Chmielewski was handcuffed and led from the courtroom on his way to prison. A jury of nine men and three women had just found him guilty of stealing a car.

13. On July 7, Rhonda Harmon attended a birthday party at a lounge on Princeton Street. She left at about midnight, and friends saw her get into a light-colored van.
    No one has seen or heard from her since.

14. Following his attorney's instructions, an accountant refused to appear at a grand jury hearing Monday. As a result, he was convicted of contempt of court and sentenced to 90 days in jail.

15.   Ten years ago, she lived in Vietnam and could not speak a word of English. Five years ago, she lived in Cambodia and still could not speak a word of English.

    Shortly after noon yesterday, she won the State Spelling Bee, surpassing more than 10,000 contestants in 400 schools throughout the state.

EXERCISE 2
Alternative Leads

WRITING LEADS WITH QUOTATIONS

INSTRUCTIONS: Use a full or partial quotation while writing a lead for each of these stories.

1. The senior United States senator from your state gave a speech in your community early today and, in the speech, he criticized the federal government's college student loan program. The progam is designed to help young people get a higher education. He complained that the program "teaches many student loan recipients to become deadbeats," since 21 percent of the students in your state, on the average, fail to repay their loans. Your senior senator added that the amount of student loans in default in your state alone "exceeds by 76% the total amount stolen in all bank robberies in the entire United States last year." The senator added, "It is truly disturbing that such a high percentage of the young, college-educated people in our state take a major financial obligation so lightly."

2. Ralph R. Palomino, 42, of 374 Douglass Road is a local businessman. He is also a candidate for mayor. He issued his campaign platform to the news media today. He promises, if elected, to hold taxes at their present level—or even to reduce them—by attacking the problem he considers most severe at the moment, the problem of mounting welfare costs. Palomino said, "Most people who receive welfare checks are bums and chiselers too damn lazy to work. Hard-working, decent Americans should not be forced to support these parasites."

3. Dr. Guy Alvarez gave a speech at a meeting of the county medical society last night. Alvarez works in Washington, D.C. for the Department of Health and Human Services. He said: "Thousands of Americans die every year because their diseases are not profitable. The country's major pharmaceutical firms refuse to conduct research and to produce drugs to combat serious diseases that strike only a small percentage of the American public because those drugs are not profitable. Instead, the drug companies are looking for types of medicines, such as tranquilizers, that 30 or 40 million people will take. Their approach is hard-hearted and mistaken. What's more, they admit to the practice but say it is necessary to recoup the cost of their research and development for new medicines."

4. Scientists at the Nielsen Institute in Oregon issued a report about marijuana today. It said: "There are 15 million regular marijuana smokers in the United States, and the use of marijuana has become part of America's cultural mainstream. Like alcohol, marijuana is an intoxicant, and the greatest danger in its use involves the operation of motor vehicles rather than the more widely publicized alarms about biological damage. There is little evidence to support charges that marijuana causes brain damage, chromosome breakage and adverse effects in the body's immune response and hormone levels. But as marijuana becomes more acceptable to society, more users are likely to drive cars under its influence, and that is the most serious problem. Our studies have shown that 39 percent of the drivers involved in fatal accidents in this state were intoxicated on alcohol, and 16 percent had recently used marijuana."

5. Marilyn Kubik is an English teacher at North High School and today she went to the police department and charged three students with vandalism: Herman Krueger, 16, Stephen Reeves, 15, and Fred Albertson, 15, all sophomores at the school. Kubik explained: "For years, students have been vandalizing the school and have gotten

away with it. They've caused thousands of dollars of damage, and no one's had the guts to do anything about it. We're not going to allow it anymore. We teachers have gotten together and have agreed that, whenever we see any vandalism, we're going to file criminal charges against the students responsible for it. It's not enough to just make them stay after school or pay for the damage. Money doesn't mean anything to some of these kids, and most of their parents don't give a damn, so they're no help."

6. The president of your state's medical association, Dr. Leonard Holmann, made a speech to your state Legislature in the state Capitol today. The speech concerned the topic of boxing and the medical risks incurred by the people who engage in that sport. He warned that, "New evidence shows that 15% of all boxers suffer brain damage. So nationwide, thousands of amateur and professional boxers wind up suffering from memory loss, slurred speech, tremors and abnormal gait. In the worst cases, boxers become punch-drunk. Their speech and walk become unsteady, their memories fade, and they lose their grasp of reality." The association's president added that: "Boxing is barbaric. The only purpose is to hurt someone—to knock him unconscious or to injure him so badly that he is physically incapable of continuing a fight." Dr. Hollman recommended that the state Legislature "immediately ban boxing to protect athletes from serious and permanent harm and possibly death."

7. A report released by researchers at the Annenberg School of Communications at the University of Pennsylvania today warned that "watching television can hurt your health." Their report explains that: "People who watch television many hours a day are likely to adopt the nonchalant, careless outlook of the characters who populate prime-time TV. The more people watch television, the more complacent they are about health and exercise, and the more confidence they have in the medical profession. There is an unrealistic belief in the magic powers of medicine. They say, 'If anything goes wrong, the doctor will take care of it.'" The characters shown on TV eat, drink or talk about food eight times an hour. They grab a fast snack almost as often as they eat breakfast, lunch and dinner combined. Despite these poor eating habits, less than 6 percent of the male TV characters and 2 percent of the female characters were overweight. The study also found that "the most common beverage on the tube is alcohol." Thirty-six percent of the characters drink, but only 1 percent are alcoholics.

8. It is a bright red sticker. It says, in large white letters: "Convicted DUI: Restricted License." The letters "DUI" stand for "Driving Under the Influence." Today a judge in your community announced that, effective immediately, he will require every person convicted of drunken driving in his courtroom to attach one of the stickers to the rear bumper of his car, and another to the front bumper. An attorney who opposes the idea responded that the notion is illegal, "like putting somebody in a pillory." A second judge, who also favors the idea, responded that, "The public deserves to be protected from these people—to know who they are and to be able to avoid them." Other proponents add that the stickers will serve as a deterrent "since most people would be embarrassed, so embarrassed that they'd be more careful about driving after drinking, and the ones convicted of drunken driving might stay off the roads to avoid being seen and identified as drunks." Even after their convictions nowadays, many drunk drivers are given "restricted licenses" that allow them to drive, but only to and from work. The proposal would apply mainly to them.

EXERCISE 3
Alternative Leads

INSTRUCTIONS: Write only the leads for the following stories—but not routine summary leads. Instead, write alternative leads: the types described in this chapter.

1. A branch of the U.S. government—the Census Bureau—issued some statistics today. In a report from Washington, it discussed the net worth of the richest Americans. It found that, by last year, 1 out of every 100 American families had a net worth of $1,000,000 dollars or more. That does not mean the families have an income of $1,000,000 dollars or more, but only that if they sold everything they owned and then paid their debts that they would have that amount left over. The report also drew a profile of the average American millionaire. The average millionaire, it found, is an entrepreneur: a white male in his early 60s, married to his first wife, with a business "catering to the ordinary needs of his neighbors." Most millionaires are from middle-class or working-class backgrounds and worked hard to get their money: 10 to 12 hours a day, six days a week, for 30 years or more. Washington, D.C. was tops, with 1.7 millionaires for every 100 households. The state of Connecticut was next, with 1.6.

2. It was one of those crazy contests that you sometimes read about. Everyone seems to enjoy them and lots of people buy tickets for them, hoping to win the grand prize. The grand prize was 3 minutes in a supermarket. The Optimist's Club in your city sponsored the contest. It wanted to raise money to buy playground equipment for a park. To raise the money, they had a charity raffle. They charged $1.00 a ticket. They said the winner would be allowed in a supermarket just before it normally opened for the day and would be allowed 3 minutes. In that time, the winner could grab everything he could get in grocery carts. The winner's name was drawn last Tuesday night: Allison Hesslin. She got her chance just before 9 this morning. In three minutes, she filled four carts with groceries. Club officials are shocked. Her bill was $1,024.91. "There goes the kids' money right out the door," said the club president. "We raised $980 and thought that was a lot. We figured the winner might get a few hundred dollars, but that'd still leave us a good profit. Now, we'll have to dig into our treasury to make up the difference, and there's nothing left for the playground." Mrs. Heslin filled the carts primarily with costly meats, cheese and wines that cost up to $29.99 a bottle. "I planned this out with my husband," she said. "We visited the store in advance, so I knew where everything was. You don't get a chance like this very often." The contest planners never specified that the winner could take only one of each thing; normally, that limits the bill to about $100 a minute.

3. The man's name is Howard Washington. At 12 noon yesterday, he was released from the county jail. At 12:45, he was arrested and charged with breaking and entering, burglary, and auto theft. The story started at about 12:15 when two deputies leaving for lunch observed him in the jail parking lot. Washington, 34, had originally been arrested on a trespassing charge. He was released without bond after 24 hours because the county jail was overcrowded. About 15 minutes later, the two deputies, Glenda London and Tiffany Wildez, observed him peering into several cars and jiggling door handles. Deciding that the suspect had not committed a crime, the detectives decided to help him along. They put London's uncover car in the parking lot with a wrong key in the ignition so it couldn't actually be started. After about five minutes, the suspect jumped in the car and tried to start it. At that time, the detectives arrested him. So less than an hour after his release, he was back behind bars. Jail officials put him in an isolation cell so he could be watched.

4. Mr. Theodore Deamud was in Circuit Court at 10 a.m. yesterday. He was there to witness the sentencing of his son, Frederick. Deamud is 72. His son is 24. The judge began to sentence Fredrick to 10 days in the county jail for shoplifting. Deamud didn't think that was enough. He asked permission to address the court. "This isn't going to do my son any good," he told the judge. "I don't know how to say this, but my son, he's on that crack, that crack cocaine stuff. He's been taking my stuff, my property, and selling it to get crack. He's promised me he wouldn't do that anymore, but he lies. He roams the street at night, and I'm scared if something isn't done now, he'll get into more trouble." Deamud then turned to his son and said: "You done it long enough. You deserve more than 10 days. I've talked and begged with you, and you lied to me. You need help." As a result of his father's comments, Fredrick was sentenced to 90 days in the county jail. In addition, the judge placed Fredrick on probation for three years. The judge added that Frederick would be tested in jail to determine if he needs treatment for drug abuse and will get that treatment if he needs it. As he left the courtroom, Frederick turned and said to his father, "Boy, you sure done me wrong."

5. There was a fire last Friday, very early that morning. It occurred in a mobile home owned by Linda Machtel in the Whispering Oaks Park. The mobile home burst into flames at about 1:30 Friday morning. Firefighters reached the scene "in just a few minutes." However, they were too late to save the structure—a common problem in mobile home fires, since fires often totally destroy them in 5 to 10 minutes. Mrs. Machtel, who is divorced, lived in the trailer with her two children, Todd, 3, and Jamie, 7. This morning, she got a $500 bill from the Township Fire Department. Fire Chief Henry Zotara explained that she had not paid her annual fire service bill of $15. "The bill is legal, and it's the standard rate," Zotara explained. "We're in the county— just outside the city limits—and you can't run a fire department without money. Every run costs us money, and it has to come from somewhere. If people pay in advance, and most do, we charge them $15 a year. That's a kind of insurance. It's only 30 cents a week. If people haven't paid, we charge them an amount equal to our expenses. Our gas bill for that fire is over $50, and we'll probably have $200 in medical bills for my man that was hurt there. He needed stitches in his hand, and he'll probably have a week of lost wages. That doesn't include the men's time and the cost of running the trucks out there. The problem is, people never think it can happen to them. No one expects a fire, so they spend their money on something else." Mrs. Machtel responded: "It's a disgrace. Here, I lost my home, our clothes, everything, and now the firemen expect me to have money left for them. It's crazy."

6. Ryan Bellini was 7 years old. His dad, Ed, was 30. Yesterday was planned as a big day for them. They were going on their first camping trip, and it was going to last two weeks. Just the two of them were going. Ed Bellini of 2047 Princeton Street is divorced from his former wife, Marie, of 1010 Bumby Avenue. He gets full-time custody of Ryan two weeks a year. During the rest of the year, they try to spend lots of time together: watching movies, swimming, golfing and playing soccer and base-ball. They started out at 9 a.m. yesterday. They were going to a campsite on Crystal Lake. As they neared the campsite they were stopped at a stop sign, and their car, a new Ford convertible they often washed together, was hit from behind by a truck. The truck driver was charged with drunken driving. Police identified him as Edgar Duncan of 533 Oak Park Way, Apt. 372. The police said his driver's license had been revoked for five years as the result of three previous convictions for drunken driving. Bellini had planned to teach his son how to scuba dive. "He just loved that kid and wanted to give him everything he could," a friend said. The truck driver has been arrested and charged with two counts of DUI manslaughter, since both Bellini and his son were killed. Duncan is being held in jail. Police estimated that his truck was going more than 60 mph when it struck the Bellini vehicle. The truck driver was not injured.

7. Two college students, David Kaeppler and Michael Hosokawa, dreamed of rafting down the Mississippi River, all the way from their homes in Minneapolis south to New Orleans. Using materials they said they "scrounged," they built the raft from old oil drums, lumber and inner tubes. They built a lean-to on its deck and added two stuffed chairs and a red sail. They estimated that the entire raft cost only $100 to construct. The two youths attended high school together in Minneapolis and plan to enroll in the University of Minnesota next fall. Both are 18 years old. Their sailing plans were reported in Minneapolis newspapers, and some Coast Guardsmen apparently read the news stories in the paper. They nabbed the two youths only a few miles into their journey this morning. The Coast Guardsmen said the 22-foot raft needs life preservers, electric lights, river charts and a radio so the two youths can communicate with other boats using the Mississippi River in order to avoid a serious collision. The Coast Guardsmen also complained that the raft does not have a motor, only two paddles. The youths were ordered to go ashore immediately and to remain ashore until they are equipped to obey all the Coast Guard orders. Because they have a small gas stove, they also need a fire extinguisher. Because they plan to live on the raft, they also need a toilet.

8. Nicklas H. Romain is a 47-year-old welder. He has been unemployed for a total of 8 months. He went to a state employment office in your city early yesterday and was in line when the office opened at 8 a.m. Because he has been out of work for so long, he says, he has had to put his boat and even his pickup truck up for sale in order to buy food for himself, his wife and his four children. After waiting in line for about 3 hours yesterday morning, he finally reached the clerk, whom police identified as Beth Snowden. Everyone agrees that she told Romaine that he was in the wrong line and would have to start over at the back of another line. Romaine complains that she was "real snotty-like" and that, "Something just snapped, and I just got so I couldn't take it anymore." Instead of getting in the second line, Romain tore up his computer card and went to a nearby supermarket and spent $4.79 for a lemon meringue pie. He hurried back and threw the pie in Snowdin's face. Snowdin said she is used to short tempers but that there are strict rules in the office, and that she is not supposed to deal with people in the wrong line. A good sport, she added that she understands his frustrations and would not charge him with assault, although for a moment she considered doing so.

6 The Body of a News Story

The portion of a news story that follows the lead is called the "body," and it normally presents facts in descending order of importance. After reporters summarize a story in the lead, they normally place the story's most important details in the second paragraph. They continue to add details in decreasing order of importance, until only the least important remain. Those details may be discarded or, if they are used, may be placed in the final paragraph.

The Inverted Pyramid Style

Reporters call this form of writing the "inverted pyramid" style. The lead in an inverted pyramid story summarizes the topic, and each of the following paragraphs presents some additional information about it: names, descriptions, quotations, conflicting viewpoints, explanations, background data and so forth. Most paragraphs are self-contained units that require no further explanation, and the only summary of the entire story appears in the lead. News stories end with their least important details—rarely with any type of conclusion.

The primary advantage of the inverted pyramid style is that if someone stops reading a story after only one or two paragraphs, that person will still learn the story's most important details. The inverted pyramid style also ensures that all the facts are immediately understandable. Moreover, if a story is too long, editors can easily shorten it by deleting one or more paragraphs from the end. However, the inverted pyramid style also has several disadvantages. First, because the lead summarizes facts that later paragraphs discuss in greater detail, some of those facts may be repeated. Second, a story that follows the inverted pyramid style rarely contains any surprises; the lead immediately reveals every major detail. Third, the style makes some stories more complex and more difficult to write. Despite these problems, reporters use the inverted pyramid style for most news stories.

If two cars collided, injuring several people, an inverted pyramid story about the accident might contain the following sequence of paragraphs:

Lead . . . . . . Summarizes the story
Paragraph 2 . . . . . . Identifies the injured
Paragraph 3 . . . . . . Explains how the accident occurred
Paragraph 4 . . . . . . Reports one driver was charged with speeding
Paragraph 5 . . . . . Quotes one driver, a police officer or witness
Paragraph 6 . . . . . Describes damage to the cars
Paragraph 7 . . . . . . Describes traffic problems caused by the accident
Paragraph 8 . . . . . . Background: reveals that several other accidents
                        have occurred at the same location

Normally, news media emphasize either the role that people play in a story or the story's impact on the lives of those people. As a consequence, paragraph 2 identifies the people who were injured. Damage to the cars—much less important—is reported later. Paragraph 3 describes the accident itself—the recent action and main point of the story. Quotations, such as the one used in paragraph 5, add detail and color as well as a pleasing change of pace. Paragraphs 6, 7 and 8 are less essential and might be deleted if little space is available for the story.

Not every reporter would present all the facts in exactly the same order; some variation is inevitable. However, most reporters would begin with a summary lead and then would present whichever of the remaining facts they considered most important— usually the victims' identity, particularly if they were seriously injured, and a description of the accident.

As another example of the inverted pyramid style, imagine that the police in your community arrested three high school students and charged them with auto theft. A newspaper reporter might write the following story:

1. Three students have been charged with the theft of a dozen cars from a faculty parking lot at Wilson High School.

2. Police arrested the youths last night after noticing a stolen car parked near a theater on Palmer Avenue.

3. The youths were apprehended when they returned to the car at 11:15 p.m. after watching a movie.

4. Police said the youths, all sophomores at the school, admitted stealing 12 cars from the faculty parking lot during the past year.

5. Each youth was charged with 12 counts of auto theft and was released to the custody of his parents. They are scheduled to appear in Juvenile Court at 11 a.m. Monday.

6. All the other cars were recovered within a week of being stolen. However, one had been involved in an accident and was badly damaged, and some parts had been stripped from the others.

7. Police did not identify the youths because they are juveniles.

Typically, the lead summarizes the story, and each of the following paragraphs presents some additional details about it, beginning with the most important—the youths' arrest and confessions (the action and the most recent developments). Later paragraphs report more routine details and background information. For example: paragraph 6 reports that all the cars stolen weeks or months earlier were recovered, and paragraph 7 reports that the youths' names were not revealed because they are juveniles, a common practice. If little space were available, both paragraphs 6 and 7 could be deleted.

The inverted pyramid style is most appropriate for short, simple stories that have only one source and one main topic. Notice how the leads in the following stories summarize their topics, and how the second and third paragraphs present their most important details. Neither story ends with a summary or conclusion; instead, the final paragraphs present the least important details. The stories are cohesive because their leads summarize their main topics and because each of the subsequent paragraphs presents additional information about those topics:

Burglars took an estimated $3,000 worth of appliances and jewelry from a home at 1424 Balchner Drive late Sunday morning.

The owners, Mr. and Mrs. Henry Ruiz, returned home at noon after taking their four children to church. They found a back door pried open and the house ransacked.

"I didn't know what to think," Mrs. Ruiz said. "The house was a mess, and we were afraid the burglars were still inside. It was really quite scary."

The burglars took a television set, a stereo, two cameras, jewelry and several kitchen appliances.

Neighbors said they saw an unfamiliar car parked in the driveway of the home at 11 a.m.

Two teen-agers were arrested Monday and charged with committing burglary and vandalism at Colonial High School.

Leon M. Davis, 18, and David Zukowski, 16, both students at the school, were charged with burglary, criminal mischief and grand theft.

Police say they recovered about $4,000 worth of audiovisual equipment taken during the burglary, which occurred last weekend.

Davis was taken to the County Jail, and his bail was set at $5,000. Zukowski was taken to the County Juvenile Detention Home.

The arrests followed a joint investigation by the police and the County Sheriff's Department.

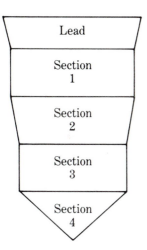

Because many of the facts reported in longer news stories are of approximately equal importance, those stories are more likely to resemble the diagram shown at the left rather than the perfect triangle shown on Page 136. Immediately after the diagram's summary lead, Section 1 presents several paragraphs that contain information of roughly equal importance. Those paragraphs may present some additional information about a single topic or information about several different, but related, subtopics. Section 2 presents other details in descending order of importance, and Section 3 presents more facts of approximately equal importance—but of less importance than the facts in Section 1. Section 4 contains the least important details, perhaps routine procedures, background information or a reminder of some related incidents that occurred in the past.

Writing the Second Paragraph

The second paragraph in a news story is almost as important as the lead—and as difficult to write. Like the lead, the second paragraph should emphasize the news. In addition, the second paragraph should provide a smooth, logical transition from the lead to the following paragraphs.

While writing their stories' second paragraphs, some reporters fail to emphasize the news. Other reporters fail to provide smooth transitions. As a result, their stories may seem dull or disorganized. The following pages discuss both problems—and their solutions.

Avoid Leapfrogging

Reporters often refer to an individual in their lead and begin their second paragraph with a name. However, many reporters fail to clearly link the two: to state that the individual referred to in their lead is the person named in their second paragraph. Readers are forced to guess, to make that assumption. They will usually—but not always—be right.

The problem is so common that it has been given a name: "leapfrogging." To avoid the problem, provide a one- or two-word transition from the lead to a name in the second paragraph:

> LEAPFROGGING: A 55-year-old man wept Wednesday after a Circuit Court jury found him not guilty of burglary and sexual battery.
> Gary Lee Phillips was arrested two months ago.
> REVISED: A 55-year-old man wept Wednesday after a Circuit Court jury found him not guilty of burglary and sexual battery.
> *The defendant*, Gary Lee Phillips, was arrested two months ago.

> LEAPFROGGING: The Norfolk City Council has denied a former mayor's request for the annexation and re-zoning of 19 acres located along Highway 50.
> E. E. "Sparky" Dawson threatened to sue the city.
> REVISED: The Norfolk City Council has denied a former mayor's request for the annexation and re-zoning of 19 acres located along Highway 50.
> *The former mayor*, E. E. "Sparky" Dawson, threatened to sue the city.

Continue With the News

After providing a smooth transition between the lead and second paragraph, continue with the news: more information about the topic summarized in your lead. Mistakenly, some reporters shift to a different topic—a decision certain to confuse their readers:

> CORVALLIS, Ore.—The police spend more of their time responding to domestic squabbles than to any other type of call.
> Merritt Tendall has been the police chief in Corvallis for 15 years. He has seen a lot of wrecks and a lot of crimes, but says he never wanted any other job.
> REVISED: CORVALLIS, Ore.—The police spend more of their time responding to domestic squabbles than to any other type of call.
> "We hate those calls," says Police Chief Merritt Tendall. "You never know what to expect. We settle most of the disputes in a few minutes. But people get angry and irrational, and some take their anger out on us. I've been the police chief here for 15 years, and it's my biggest problem."

> "No nation depends more upon its news media, and no media have more influence," Marty Cirocca said.
> Cirocca added that this small group of people decides which stories millions of Americans will receive each day.
> REVISED: "No nation depends more upon its news media, and no media have more influence," Marty Cirocca said.
> "Unfortunately," Cirocca continued, "a small group of people, located primarily in New York, controls the most influential media, and that small group decides which stories millions of Americans receive each day."

Before it was revised, the first story seemed to discuss two different topics. The lead summarizes a problem that confronts police officers everywhere: family disputes. The second paragraph shifts to the police chief: his career and goals. Until it was revised, the story's second paragraph failed to even mention the problem of family disputes. The second story seems disorganized because, originally, its second paragraph mentioned a "small group of people" but failed to identify them or to link them to anything mentioned in the lead.

Names, Names—Dull, Dull

Other reporters place too much emphasis upon their sources' identity. As a result, their second paragraphs fail to convey any information of interest to readers. The following examples have been revised to emphasize the news—what the sources said, saw or did—not who they are:

> A construction worker was killed Monday afternoon when a gust of wind toppled the frame for a new apartment building on Conway Road.
> Julian Prevatte, a carpenter for John McCormack & Sons, was an eyewitness to the accident.
> REVISED: A construction worker was killed Monday afternoon when a gust of wind toppled the frame for a new apartment building on Conway Road.
> Julian Prevatte, a carpenter at the site, said he tried to warn the victim when the frame began to collapse, but the noise made by a saw drowned out his shouts.

> Three gunmen who took $4,200 from a Safeway Supermarket at 1010 S. Broadway Ave. Friday were captured in a nearby motel room 20 minutes later.
> Kathy Laxalt, 21, of 1842 S. Gayle Road was one of two cashiers on duty when the men entered the store.
> REVISED: Three gunmen who took $4,200 from a Safeway Supermarket at 1010 S. Broadway Ave. Friday were captured in a nearby motel room 20 minutes later.
> Kathy Laxalt, a cashier at the supermarket, said the men stood near the entrance for five minutes before they came in, drew their pistols and forced an assistant manager to open the safe.

Background: Too Much Too Soon

Also avoid devoting your entire second paragraph to background information. That information is rarely interesting and rarely new. The second paragraphs in the following stories are dull because they emphasize that type of old, routine or insignificant detail:

> A state law designed to help police officers find hit-and-run drivers went into effect at 12:01 a.m. today.
> The law was passed by the state Legislature during its last session and was signed by the governor.

> "Rape is the most difficult crime to solve because of the insensitive treatment given to victims," District Attorney Russell Grant said during a seminar held last night at the YMCA.
> The seminar, the fourth presented in the county during the last year, was sponsored by the Rape Prevention Center, 1015 5th Ave., which offers counseling to rape victims and encourages them to prosecute their assailants.

The first example emphasizes the obvious: the fact that a state law was approved by the state Legislature and signed by the governor. The story's second paragraph fails to convey any news: the latest developments. It might have reported what occurred after the law went into effect "at 12:01 a.m. today." The second example fails to emphasize the district attorney's comments about rape. Instead, its second paragraph presents background information about the sponsor's identity and goals. Yet the same background information might have been reported in stories about the group's first, second and third seminars, held months earlier. Again, the background information should have been placed after an account of the news: a thorough summary of the district attorney's remarks.

Fortunately, the problem is easy to correct, as in this example:

> Six hundred children in the state needed foster homes last month, but only 220 new homes were licensed to care for them.
> Karen Hudgins of 2406 Eastbrook Road coordinates the program. She studied sociology in Tennessee and, after earning her master's degree there, moved here in 1984. She is married and has three children.
> REVISED: Six hundred children in the state needed foster homes last month, but only 220 new homes were licensed to care for them.
> Why? "With more women working, fewer are home and able to care for children, especially

problem children," an expert explained. "Also, it's a lot of work with no pay. The only reward is sharing a part of a child's life and knowing it's important—something that has to be done."

Before it was revised, the second paragraph shifted from a topic in the news (the shortage of foster homes) to background information about the person who administers the program. Again, that information should be moved to a later paragraph, preferably the story's final paragraph.

The following story, a better example, appeared in Newsday. Notice that the story's second paragraph continues to emphasize the news. Not unfamiliar names. Not unrelated ideas. Not the background:

> The American space program suffered its first airborne disaster yesterday when the shuttle Challenger exploded 74 seconds after liftoff from Cape Canaveral, Fla., killing all seven members of a crew that included high school teacher Christa McAuliffe.
> Authorities at the Kennedy Space Center said nothing seemed amiss until fire engulfed the $1.2 billion vehicle some 8 miles southeast of the launch pad. One official of the National Aeronautics and Space Administration said the explosion came "unexpectedly and with absolutely no warning."

Improving Your Later Paragraphs

Each paragraph, regardless of its placement in a story, should present only one idea or unit of thought. When reporters shift to a new topic or a new phase of the same topic, they should start a new paragraph. Because the quotation in the following example introduces a new idea—a fact unrelated to the topic of American norms—it should be placed in a new paragraph. At the same time, the topic of American norms might be expanded to explain or illustrate it more clearly:

> Living with his cousin has helped Faisal adjust to American norms. He added, "We often cook Middle Eastern dishes and invite our American friends over to our apartment."
> REVISED: Faisal said living with his cousin has helped him adjust to American norms. He explained: "Life is so much freer here than in the Middle East. My cousin explains your ways to me and shows me what to do."
> They often cook Middle Eastern dishes and invite American friends to their apartment.

Avoid generalities that have to be explained in a later paragraph. If you focus on a story's specific details, the generalities often become unnecessary. The following paragraphs illustrate that principle. Until they were revised, they emphasized general topics rather than any specific information that sources provided about those topics:

> She described the life she observed in New Zealand.
> REVISED: She said life in New Zealand is relaxed and carefree.
>
> He also talked about the economic hardships faced by unwed mothers.
> REVISED: He said 80 percent of unwed mothers under the age of 18 drop out of high school, and 84 percent become dependent on welfare.

If you are specific—if you report that someone said life in New Zealand "is relaxed and carefree"—you do not have to add that someone described the life in New Zealand. Similarly, if you report the specific problems of unwed mothers, you do not have to add that your source described the hardships they face. The following examples contain similar problems. Until they were revised, they presented only dull generalities:

> Two high school students managed to get a description of the gunmen's car.
> REVISED: Two high school students said the gunmen escaped in a white Chevrolet driven by an older woman.

The Rev. James Williams witnessed the mugging.

REVISED: The Rev. James Williams said a boy, about 16, knocked the woman down and tore the necklace from her body.

Also avoid reporting details within each paragraph in chronological order, especially if not reporting the overall story in chronological order. Instead, emphasize the news. Too many paragraphs report that a topic was discussed, then slowly proceed to the results. Consequently, the most important details are buried in the final line:

The second witness called by the prosecutor was Norman Chrzan, a private investigator. Chrzan testified that Mrs. Ehren hired him to follow her husband. "She thought her husband was seeing another woman," Chrzan said. "She wanted me to find out who she was." Chrzan said he never found another woman. But just two weeks before her husband's murder, Mrs. Ehren asked Chrzan for a gun.

REVISED: A private investigator, Norman Chrzan, testified that Mrs. Ehren asked him for a gun just two weeks before her husband's murder.

Chrzan said Mrs. Ehren hired him to follow her husband. "She thought her husband was seeing another woman," he testified. "She wanted me to find out who she was." But Chrzan never found another woman.

Next on its agenda, the City Council opened bids to determine who would receive a contract to construct the recreation center. The lowest bid was $1.5 million. The budget for the center was only $1,240,000. "It was very disappointing," the mayor said. "Now we'll have to go back over the plans with our architects and eliminate some of the options to lower its cost. It'll delay construction six to nine months."

REVISED: The construction of a recreation center will be delayed six to nine months because the bids were $260,000 more than budgeted for the work.

The city had allocated $1,240,000 for the work, but the lowest bid was $1.5 million. The mayor said that city officials will "have to go back over the plans with our architects and eliminate some of the options to lower its cost."

Improving Your Sentences (A Brief Review)

Write naturally, the way you talk. Be clear and direct. No one would use the following sentences in casual conversation with friends, yet beginners used them in news stories:

Killed in the accident was a 7-year-old girl.
The vehicle damage is estimated to be $4,000.
Angry words were exchanged between the two drivers, resulting in the fatal stabbing.

The sentences are awkward because they fail to use the normal word order: subject, verb and direct object. Moreover, all three used passive verbs: "was," "is" and "were."

Shorten Your Sentences

Beginners use sentences that are too long and complicated. Yet the longer a sentence, the more difficult it is to understand. Moreover, when too many ideas are crammed into a sentence, none receives the clarity and emphasis it deserves.

As you read the following sentences, you are likely to stop and to start again. Why? Both sentences contain more ideas than most readers can absorb at a glance. As you reread each, count the number of ideas it contains:

Thirty-year-old Melvin Holder, an employee at the McDonald's at 3710 Lake Ave., was cleaning the closed restaurant at 2:40 a.m. when the two men, one wearing a ski mask, knocked on a locked door, pointed a revolver at him and demanded to be let in.

Number of ideas in sentence:_____

Officer Kevin D. LaVigne, 25, of the Morgantown Police Department said he was walking in uniform through a parking lot near the 100 block of South Garland Avenue when a car, a late-model Chevrolet driven by John E. Ross, 27, 482 Mays Court, struck him from behind, knocking him to the pavement and breaking his left arm.

Number of ideas in sentence:_____

Readers may count as many as 12 ideas in the first sentence, and 14 in the second. To make your sentences more readable, shorten them:

A Catholic mother of three children—two daughters ages 27 and 22, and a son age 16—and a grandmother, Mrs. Johns explained that she opposes abortion because, since abortions have become legal, Americans next "might try to do away with the aged."

REVISED: Mrs. Johns, a Catholic, said she opposes abortion because, since abortions have become legal, Americans next "might try to do away with the aged." Mrs. Johns has two daughters, 27 and 22, and a son, 16. She also has three grandchildren.

A sentence does not have to be long to be overloaded. If the ideas it contains are unrelated, as in the following examples, even a very short sentence may have to be rewritten:

Born in New Hampshire, he has red hair.

Petrowski, who has a wife and six stepdaughters, was elected by only 27 votes: 382,917 to 382,890.

Avoid Choppy Sentences

A few writers go to the opposite extreme, using a series of very short, simple sentences. Although a typical sentence or paragraph should be short and simple, some variety is necessary to keep paragraphs from becoming too choppy and repetitive, as in the following example:

The youth was sentenced to prison at 9:45 a.m. today. The judge was C. R. Revere. The youth's attorney immediately appealed his conviction. The state Court of Appeals reversed the sentence. The youth was freed at 4:45 p.m.

REVISED: Judge C. R. Revere sentenced the youth to prison at 9:45 a.m. today, but his attorney immediately appealed the conviction. The state Court of Appeals reversed Judge Revere's decision, and the youth was freed at 4:45 p.m.

Vary your sentence length. Remember, however, that even the longer sentences should be uncomplicated, and it is better to err toward shortness than length.

Also vary your wording so that sentences and paragraphs do not begin with the same words, or with very similar words. When writing a story about a government report, for example, it may be tempting to begin several paragraphs with the words: "The report said . . ." "The report added . . ." "It said . . ." "The report also said . . ." "It continued . . . " and "The report concluded . . . " But if every sentence or paragraph begins with the same words, those words will become dull, distracting and repetitious.

Ignore the Routine and Unimportant

News stories should report what happened. Avoid reporting what has not happened. A list of everything that did not happen today would be endless; by tomorrow, the list would be dull and repetitive. Thus, as you write a story's final paragraphs, avoid the temptation to mention that:

No one was hurt.

No one was killed.

No one was arrested.

No one was able to describe the thief.

Similarly, an alert reporter or editor would eliminate the following statements because they state the obvious:

Police are looking for the thief.

Fire fighters called to the scene quickly extinguished the flames.

Of the 34 homicides in the city last year, five have not been solved.
The police hope to change that.

Other statements are ludicrous: so obvious and nonsensical that readers might laugh at the newspapers that published them. After reading the third example, readers might also complain that the newspapers are insensitive and sexist:

Joe Baker was sleeping in the front seat of his car when a man disturbed him early Friday. The man threatened Baker with a gun and took the car.

Margaret C. Scott, a retired teacher who died of a heart attack, left her estate to the relatives who survived her.

"I don't think I'd want to go through that again," a 23-year-old woman said after being tortured and raped.

Transitions

Transitions help stories move from one fact to the next in a smooth, logical order. Reporters introduce new ideas by relating them to ideas reported earlier in a story. Often, the natural progression of thought, or sequence of facts and action, is adequate. Or, reporters may repeat a key name or pronoun:

The company's president, Mark *Stoudnaurer*, opposed the plan.
Stoudnaurer said the company cannot afford to construct a new plant.

Lt. Lee Marey said the Navy is a small, elite force that offers an effective deterrent to nuclear war.
He added that submarines have become more important than battleships and aircraft carriers.

The first example repeats the name of the company president. In the second example, the pronoun "he" refers to the lieutenant mentioned in the preceding paragraph.
Reporters can also repeat other key words, ideas or phrases:

The company borrowed $52 million to pay for the *machinery*.
The *machinery* arrived in July and was operating by November.

Richard *Nolles*, editor of the Weekly Outlook, said the *newspaper* tries to report the truth even when its *readers* do not want to hear it.
"A *newspaper* that reports only what its *readers* want to hear is dodging its moral obligations," *Nolles* said.
In a speech Wednesday, *Nolles* added that many *readers* want to avoid unpleasant news and threaten to cancel their subscriptions when *he* reports it. "But if a problem exists, *they* need to know about it so they can correct it," *he* said. "Ignorant citizens can't make wise decisions."

Here is another example. Again, notice the repetition of several key words. Moreover, every sentence continues to discuss the topic summarized in the lead—downtown trees:

> *Sycamore trees* are sprouting along *Main Street* in the first phase of an effort to make the downtown shopping district more attractive and comfortable for pedestrians.
> The *trees* will line *Main Street* for five blocks between Jefferson and Jackson Avenues, according to Daisy *Lemkuehl* of the Downtown Development Board.
> "We chose *sycamore trees* because they're deciduous," *Lemkuehl* said. "In the summer they'll provide shade. In the winter they'll lose their leaves and let the sun warm the streets."
> *Lemkuehl* said the City Council provided the money, and all the *trees* will be planted within a week.
> *In addition to the trees*, *Lemkuehl* said the sidewalks in the five-block stretch of *Main Street* will be widened and paved with red *brick*.
> "We expect to start with the *brick* sidewalks in a month or so," *Lemkuehl* said.

Other Linkage Words

To provide smooth transitions from sentence to sentence and paragraph to paragraph, reporters also use linkage words such as "again," "also," "furthermore," "moreover" and "therefore." Other linkage words refer to:

- Comparisons, such as "likewise" and "similarly."
- Contrasts, such as "however," "conversely," "but" and "nevertheless."
- Geographical locations, such as "in the state Capitol," "at their home" or "on Main Street."
- The time, such as "earlier" and "later," "before" and "after" or "next winter."

Transitional Sentences

Transitional sentences link paragraphs that contain more diverse ideas, but the sentences should do more than report that another idea was "introduced" or "discussed." They should present some interesting details about the new topics so readers will be motivated to finish a story. Mistakenly, beginners often use vague generalities, such as:

> There were other developments as well.
> She also mentioned a drainage problem.
> Two people spoke in opposition to the resolution.

A good transitional sentence often summarizes the topic it introduces, revealing whatever was said or done about it. Then, the following paragraphs can discuss the topic in more detail:

> He also discussed the television coverage of the president's funeral.
> REVISED: He said the television coverage of the president's funeral was misleading.

> He also talked about the city's schools.
> REVISED: He said the city's schools are too old and overcrowded.

> Later, he discussed the other advantages of living in the South.
> REVISED: Later, he said that people living in the South enjoy a milder climate, lower taxes and newer, less crowded cities.

Questions As Transitions

Like leads, transitional sentences occasionally take the form of questions. The questions should be short and, as in the following examples, should be immediately followed by their answers—the new details or topics that reporters want to introduce:

> Where does she get the ideas for her books?
> "People," she said. "Most people can give you a good story. And I talk to everyone."

Forty-seven percent of the students enrolled in the university will earn a degree within the next six years, according to Dr. Robert McMahon, director of the Office of Institutional Research.

What about the other 53 percent? They will drop out or transfer to another institution.

Why? A study just completed by the Office of Institutional Research found that most students who drop out of school accept full-time jobs, get married, have children or say they lack the money needed to continue their education.

Did the rehabilitation program change their lives?

"Yes, it has," Kathy said. "I started to grow up. I feel so much older than other kids my age."

"Yes," Ellen agreed. "I realize now that I had better start controlling my life better."

"No," Jill said. "I can't say that it has changed my life, although my life has changed. I'm going to be married soon, and I'm very happy."

Chronological Order

Finally, reporters tell some stories in chronological order, and the natural sequence of events, from moment to moment, creates a smooth, logical flow of ideas. This example appeared in another of the stories that Newsday published about the shuttle disaster:

> . . . But then at 11:38 a.m., the gleaming ship rose from a new launch pad, a majestic 700-foot stream of snow-white vapor trailing behind. Onlookers cheered, as is the custom at space shots, and a NASA spokesman described the progress of the flight.
>
> Challenger reached a speed of 1,977 mph—three times that of sound—and was 10.4 miles over the Florida terrain. Mission Control in Houston sent the routine order: "Challenger, go throttle up."
>
> Commander Francis (Dick) Scobee increased power to the main engines as planned and then spoke what proved to be his final words: "Roger, go throttle up."
>
> At that point, officials said, Challenger, one of four U.S. space shuttles, was to enter a period when maximum force would be brought to bear on the vehicle by atmospheric condition and wind force.
>
> Television viewers then were able to see flames racing toward the space vehicle from an aft section, in the area of the craft's solid-fuel booster rockets. Almost immediately there was a titanic explosion, and Challenger, which had been carrying 526,000 gallons of highly volatile propellant, began rapid disintegration.
>
> A space center employee watching the flight said in horror: "It's too soon. It's too soon. It can't be separation (of the boosters)." Another said simply: "I can't believe it. . . ."

Conclusions

Reporters must resist the temptation to end news stories with a summary, conclusion or opinion of any kind. Experienced reporters present a story's least important details in the final paragraph and, if they have nothing more to add, stop. Reporters rarely place any important information in the final paragraph because too many readers will stop before they get that far. Reporters also know that, if their editor does not have enough space for an entire story, the editor is most likely to discard the story's final paragraphs. So the information placed at the end of a story is least likely to be published or read. Thus, the following conclusions are inappropriate:

> Is Miss Roth a good teacher? We certainly believe so.

> The remainder of the meeting was concerned primarily with the gripes and comments of those present about conditions at the hospital. Also discussed were some suggestions on ways those conditions could be resolved.

The first example contains an opinion rather than a fact. If the story was well written, and if it clearly described Miss Roth, her performance and her students' reaction to her, readers should not have to be told she is a good teacher. The facts reported earlier in the story should have made that obvious. The second example summarizes facts never discussed in the story. It fails to describe specifically the conditions that disturbed people and the suggestions made to resolve those conditions. Every topic mentioned in news stories must be fully explained, including topics mentioned in final paragraphs.

Other stories end too quickly. These stories are superficial because reporters sometimes fail to gather or to include enough information. When you write a news story, be thorough. Assume that your editor has enough space to report every important detail. If you are uncertain about a fact's importance and whether it should be included in a story, place that fact in the story's final paragraph. If your editor or instructor considers the fact unimportant, it can easily be deleted. But if you fail to include an important fact, it is difficult for your editor or instructor to find you, and for you to retrieve your notes, place the story back in your typewriter and then add the missing information.

Your Final Step

After finishing a story, edit it ruthlessly. Author Kurt Vonnegut recommends that, "If a sentence, no matter how excellent, does not illuminate your subject in some new and useful way, scratch it out." Vonnegut also urges writers to have mercy on their readers. Vonnegut explains: "Our audience requires us to be sympathetic and patient teachers, ever willing to simplify and clarify—whereas we would rather soar high above the crowd, singing like nightingales."

Alternatives to the Inverted Pyramid

Although most news stories follow the inverted pyramid style, several alternatives are available.

Chronological Order

Newspapers begin some stories with a summary lead, then shift to chronological order. That style provides a logical means of organizing short, simple stories, particularly stories about dramatic events. If necessary, some background information can be placed in the stories' final paragraphs:

> A gunman robbed a McDonald's restaurant at 2604 Forest Road Thursday night of $430 and 10 fish sandwiches.
> An employee said a man in a blue van appeared at a drive-through window and ordered the sandwiches, then paid for them with a $20 bill.
> When the employee opened a cash register to get some change, the gunman pointed a pistol at her and said: "I want all the money, and fast. Put it all in a bag, and don't forget my sandwiches. I want them, too."
> The employee put the money in a white paper bag and handed it to the gunman.
> The gunman then demanded the money in a second cash register at the drive-through window. When the employee showed him that it was empty, the gunman drove away.
> Witnesses said he was about 20 years old, 6 feet tall and weighed about 220 pounds. His van had a Nebraska license plate and a bumper sticker that said, "I read banned books."

> A telephone company repairman rescued two people from a burning truck on Conway Road early today.
> Police gave this account:
> Repairman Donald Matthews was climbing into a manhole when he saw a pickup truck driven by Mitchell Kanton, 24, collide with a garbage truck. Kanton's truck was knocked backward, and its engine burst into flames.
> Matthews ran to the burning truck, shut off its engine and helped Kanton and an unidentified passenger get out.

Matthews tried to put the fire out with an extinguisher but said, "It was no use." Moments later, the truck was engulfed in flames.

Firefighters said Kanton would have burned to death if he had remained in the truck another two or three minutes.

Kanton, 2335 N. 16th Ave., was admitted to Memorial Hospital and listed in fair condition.

The following stories are more unusual. Neither has a summary lead. Instead, both begin in chronological order:

MIDDLEBURG, Fla. (AP)—Samuel Warren Jr. was sitting in his kitchen about to eat breakfast when he heard a loud roar and then saw a Navy attack jet bearing down on the house.

"We looked out the window and saw the plane coming toward us," the 17-year-old recalled. "My dad tried to get my aunt to the ground. The blast (from the jet) knocked everyone down."

When it was all over Sunday, the charred wreckage of a single-engine A-7E Corsair 11 attack jet lay 30 feet from Warren's front door.

The pilot, Lt. j. g. Scott S. Scheurich, 25, of Excelsior, Minn., parachuted from the plane after it developed engine trouble six miles from its destination, Naval Air Station Cecil Field in Jacksonville, said Navy spokesman Nick Young.

The pilot's parachute was snared in a pine tree 300 yards from the crash site, and neighbors helped the pilot down, Young said. Scheurich was taken to Navy Regional Medical Center in Jacksonville for observation.

LAKE WORTH, Fla. (UPI)—Police patrolman Richard Marks was dispatched to a physician's clinic to make out a routine report on the death of a heart-attack victim.

"About 30 minutes after I got to the clinic, I went into the examination room with the guys from the funeral home," Marks said.

"As I walked in, the guy on the table started gasping, then quit, then gasped again."

Funeral home attendant Pat Leach, who had been sent to pick up the corpse, rushed forward at Marks' yell. The husky Leach had worked for three years as an aide in a hospital emergency ward. He shouted to a co-worker to call an ambulance.

Leach then began administering mouth-to-mouth resuscitation and massaging the elderly man's heart. A flicker of life returned to Ramon E. Lawrence, 68, and he was rushed to the intensive care ward of a nearby hospital.

Complex Stories

Stories that contain several major subtopics may be too complex to summarize in a brief lead. Each week it is in session, for example, the U.S. Supreme Court announces all its decisions on a single day, and several of those decisions may be highly important. To save space, most newspapers report all the decisions in a single story. However, reporters can mention only one or two of the most important decisions in their leads, so they often summarize the remaining decisions in the second, and sometimes the third, paragraphs of their stories:

WASHINGTON—The Supreme Court today upheld a controversial federal law that requires banks to report to the government large cash transactions made by their customers.

In other decisions, the Supreme Court said an Iowa newspaper reporter can be forced to disclose the notes she used while writing about a divorce, and it removed the last barrier to oil and natural gas exploration in the Atlantic Ocean off the East Coast.

The court refused to question the authority of states to ban homosexual acts between consenting adults.

After summarizing all the major decisions, reporters can then discuss each of them in more detail, starting with the most important. By mentioning all the decisions in their stories' opening paragraphs, reporters alert readers to the stories' entire content. So readers interested in the second or third decision immediately learn that it will be discussed later in the story. If, in contrast, the lead and following paragraphs mentioned only the most important decision, readers might mistakenly assume that the entire story concerned that one decision, and many might stop reading before reaching the discussion of other decisions that might be of greater interest to them.

The following Associated Press story begins by summarizing the Supreme Court's most important decision and then, in subsequent paragraphs, summarizes other decisions announced the same day.

High Court Keeps Ban on Teacher-Supervised Prayer at School

WASHINGTON (AP)—The Supreme Court shunted aside arguments by 24 U.S. senators on Monday and refused to let teacher-supervised student groups pray in public schools at Lubbock, Texas.

The justices, without comment, let stand a ruling that a prayer-accommodation policy devised for Lubbock schools crosses the constitutionally required separation of church and state.

At issue was whether Lubbock school officials could allow students to "gather at school with supervision either before or after regular school hours on the same basis as other groups . . . for any . . . religious . . . purposes so long as attendance at such meetings is voluntary."

A federal appeals court said no earlier this year, and the Supreme Court refused to disturb that ruling, despite the senators' urgings. They had submitted an extraordinary "friend-of-the-court" brief to the justices.

In other matters, the court:

• Refused by 7 to 2 to consider letting students at two Orthodox Jewish high schools in Chicago wear yarmulkes while playing basketball against other schools. The Illinois High School Association bars all headgear by basketball players, and the two Jewish schools say that rule violates their students' religious freedoms.

• Agreed to decide in a Minnesota case whether its Miranda rule protecting criminal suspects when questioned by police also applies when probation officers do the asking.

• Refused by 7 to 2 to speed up the review of a ruling against the government's continued collection of billions of dollars under the . . . windfall profits tax on oil.

• Refused to hear an appeal by the widow of the man executed for killing aviation hero Charles Lindbergh's infant son 47 years ago. Anna Hauptmann, 84, is seeking compensation for the "wrongful death" of her husband, Bruno.

• Agreed to hear the appeal of a Nebraska man who wants custody of his illegitimate child and is trying to prevent its mother from putting the baby up for adoption in Texas.

• Refused to free South Carolina officials from paying nearly $5 million to women illegally denied unemployment benefits because of pregnancy.

Reporters also use lists in news stories that involve a number of diverse ideas, subtopics or illustrative examples. If all the ideas or examples are of roughly equal importance, reporters may begin a news story by summarizing one or two main points, adding a brief transition, and then presenting the other ideas or examples in a simple, orderly list:

During a speech at the university last night, Dr. Joyce Brothers called alcohol "one of the most serious health problems in the United States."

Dr. Brothers, a psychologist, columnist and frequent talk-show guest, said, "There is no typical alcoholic." Recent studies, she explained, have shown that:

ONE—From one million to three million American women are alcoholics.

TWO—One out of every eight high school students is an alcoholic.

THREE—Two of every five men in the armed forces are actual or borderline alcoholics.

NEW YORK—"We seem to have turned the corner in the epidemic of heart disease," Dr. Robert T. Levy, director of the National Heart, Lung and Blood Institute, said at a recent American Heart Association meeting. He cited some impressive statistics:

• Since 1968, the death rate from heart and blood vessel disease has been declining in both men and women, blacks and whites.

• The 30 percent decline in the cardiovascular death rate since the early 1960s is nearly double the drop in deaths from other causes.

• Two years ago, despite an increasingly older and larger population, the total number of deaths from cardiovascular diseases dropped below 1 million for the first time since 1967.

(New York Times Dispatch)

Later in a story, reporters can discuss each of the points in greater detail. Of course, the initial summary may contain all the essential information about a topic; in that case, it may never again be mentioned.

Each item in a list must be in parallel form. If one item begins with a noun and uses an active verb and a complete sentence, then every item in that list must begin with a noun and use an active verb and a complete sentence. For example, each item in the first story below is an incomplete sentence that begins with a verb. Each item in the second story is a complete sentence that begins with "you" or "your":

The governor said he wants to raise the state's sales tax and to increase state spending on education.

He told the National Education Association he would use the money to:
• Raise teachers' salaries.
• Test new teachers to assess their competence.
• Place more emphasis on English, science and math.
• Reduce the number of students in each class.
• Give schools more money to educate gifted students.

Financial advisers say there are certain warning signals that you are about to experience a financial crisis and possibly bankruptcy:
• Your checkbook balance gets lower each month.
• You are behind on one or more installment payments.
• You don't know how much money you owe.
• You must obtain new loans to repay your debts.
• Your savings account is slowly disappearing or has already disappeared.

Reporters also use lists to summarize less important details placed at the end of news stories. Lists are particularly useful when the details are minor and concern a number of diverse topics that would be difficult to organize in any other manner. During the question-and-answer session after a speech, a celebrity may be asked to discuss a dozen unrelated topics:

Donald M. Schoen, Republican candidate for governor, last night promised to cut the state's budget and taxes by a "minimum of 10 percent."

Schoen, mayor of Madison for the past eight years, also promised to dismiss 10 percent of the state's employees.

"People complain that the government has become too big and that it imposes too many taxes and places too many restrictions on their lives," he said at a fund-raising dinner held last night at Pine Hills Country Club.

On other subjects, Schoen said:

EDUCATION—School budgets should be frozen until educators trim administrative costs and improve students' test scores.

CRIME—Only 19 percent of the serious crimes committed in the state are solved, and fewer than 2 percent of the criminals responsible for those crimes are convicted and sentenced to prison. Penalties should be harsher, and criminals should be kept in jail until they have served their full terms, without parole.

MEDIA COVERAGE—News media devote too much attention to staged campaign activities and "have failed to critically analyze candidates' qualifications and positions on major issues."

Similarly, after voting on one or two major proposals, a city council may act on several less important matters that must also be reported:

After a 5½-hour debate, the City Council last night voted 8 to 1 to fire Police Chief Walter M. Durrance and two of his aides.

All three men have been accused of misusing Police Department funds.

The aides are Capt. Anthony Escalon, who started as a patrolman 24 years ago, and Lt. Raymond Krellar, a 17-year veteran with the department.

Criminal charges have been filed against all three men, but their trials have not yet been scheduled.

The council appointed Capt. James R. Bolack acting police chief.

In other action last night, the council:

—Approved the establishment of a branch library in a rented building at 5801 Shoals Drive.

—Approved the hiring of seven additional firefighters, including one lieutenant, and the purchase of two rescue vehicles that will cost $38,400 apiece.

—Refused to reconsider a motion, defeated last week, to remove the parking meters along Jamestown Drive.

—Delayed until next week consideration of a proposal to require all elected officials to file copies of their income tax returns with the city clerk in an attempt to reveal possible conflicts of interest.

Some newspapers number each item in a list. Others mark each item with a dash, bullet, asterisk, check mark or some other typographical symbol.

Write & Wrong ST. LOUIS POST-DISPATCH

By Harry Levins
Post-Dispatch Writing Coach

—Get to chronological order as soon as your story, your editor and your conscience will allow.

—Every reader sighs with relief when he gets to that point in an article where the journalism ends and the story finally begins.

> —*Charlie McDowell,*
> *Chief Washington correspondent,*
> *Richmond (Va.) Times-Dispatch*

The Coach dug into his back files to revive those quotes after reading Jim Dustin's Page 1 piece on Sunday, Dec. 5, on the flooding in Old Monroe, Mo.

You'll recall that Jim got through the journalism in a hurry, and then set out—in strict chronological order—what was happening in Old Monroe as the water rose, inch by inch, hour by hour. The result was a fine story. The suspense went up along with the river, holding the reader's attention throughout.

Not all stories lend themselves to this approach. But whenever chronological order can be used, it ought to be. After all, that's the narrative tradition, the way most of us tell stories. Novelists begin at the beginning: "It was the best of times, it was the worst of times." Tale-spinners at a newspaper tavern do the same thing: "It all began when . . . And then . . . And finally . . ."

In all too many stories, we ignore chronological order. We weave back and forth in time, like a movie that depends on flashbacks. Characters are introduced out of sequence; events occur in a pattern of our making rather than in a natural flow. The result: a patchwork narrative that confuses when it should inform.

The nature of the Old Monroe story—a disaster in slow motion—let Jim use a simple technique. He led into each segment with the time and date set in boldface. This approach struck The Coach as ideal, although only the special circumstances of the story made it possible.

Still, writers working on complicated, highly detailed stories about events that stretch over a period of time can shift after the lede paragraphs to straight chronological order, even without typographical devices. The reader is helped greatly by a sequence of paragraphs that start with phrases like these:

"The problem began when . . ."
"The next sign of trouble was . . ."
"When officials heard that, they . . ."
"Things came to a head when . . ."

☆ ☆ ☆

But in speaking of chronological order, The Coach is reminded of a phrase someone once set forth as the unofficial British motto: "Moderation in all things, including moderation."

The phrase comes to mind most often when reading the Police/Courts report. There, chronological order tends to run amok. Here's an example:

Two young women were robbed of $3,000 in jewelry and cash at a downtown parking lot. Authorities said Tammie Smiley, 23, and Sandra Clem, 26, were leaving their pickup truck about 1 a.m. Sunday in a parking lot at 914 North Third Street when two men approached. One man grabbed Ms. Smiley and the other hit Ms. Clem on the head with a revolver, police reported. After the women gave the assailants jewels and money, the men fled north on foot. Both victims refused medical attention, authorities reported.

How much scene-setting do we need in a police item? Certainly not so much as this example offers. The writer and editors could have jumped over some of the events and written a tighter account:

Two women were robbed of $3,000 in jewelry and cash about 1 a.m. Sunday in a parking lot at 914 North Third Street, police said. One man grabbed Tammie Smiley, 23, while the other struck Sandra Clem, 26, on the head with a revolver. The men ran away; both women refused medical attention.

The Coach deleted the notice that robbers "approached." The approach is obvious in the context. After all, how many robbers stand 20 yards away and holler at the victims to hand over their money? (The same thinking obtains for sentences that begin "The robbers entered the bank . . ." Very few bank robbers operate from the sidewalk.)

In the example above, The Coach deleted "young" from "young women," figuring that the ages conveyed the sense. At any rate, some people would argue that a woman of 26 is past "young."

The writer followed his chronological nose to note deep in the item that the women handed over the cash and the jewelry. But the first sentence had already said precisely that. Why repeat it?

The Coach eliminated some details—the pickup truck, for example. In this item, what difference does the type of vehicle make? Parking lots are parking lots. And The Coach struck the direction in which the robbers fled. Does anybody think that by the time we printed the item, the trail still led north?

(Note that robbers seem always to "flee on foot." Can't they simply "run away" from time to time? In burglaries, the bad guys "gain entry" by breaking windows or door. Every so often, The Coach would like to see them simply "get in.")

Finally, The Coach struck the attribution from the final sentence. Victims who refuse medical treatment are neither rare nor controversial. When the sentence contains mundane facts, take the plunge and let the facts stand by themselves.

☆ ☆ ☆

Back To The Basics
(Part of a continuing series)

Some of us ignore basic grammar by tossing a comma into copy every time we see a sentence bisected with the words "and" and "but." The Coach sees at least one example of this every day. Here's an example:

Jett returned the money when questioned on the subject, but has refused to make a specific account of its use.

Whoever inserted the comma fashioned a compound sentence that isn't a compound sentence. A compound sentence is two sentences in one, joined by a conjunction—"and" or "but," for example. Each of the two parts must have its own subject and verb. Without a second subject, the sentence isn't compound—and the use of the comma is wrong. Here are some hypothetical examples:

Right: He took the money, and he ran away to Buffalo, N.Y. (Two subjects, "he" and "he," and two verbs, "took" and "ran.")

Even More Right: He took the money and ran away to Buffalo, N.Y. (It's even more right because it's smoother. Commas mean stop signs to readers. We must use them when necessary, but we ought to avoid erecting more stop signs than we need.)

Wrong: He took the money, and ran away to Buffalo, N.Y. (The sentence has only one subject—"he." That makes "took the money and ran" a single verb phrase, indivisible under God and the rules of English grammar.)

☆ ☆ ☆

Bad weather brings out the cliches in all of us. What do tornados and flooding rivers do? They *rampage*, of course. The Coach suspects that the word *rampage* lost its impact years ago. But even so, we seem to use it automatically, just as the wire services refer by reflex to the House Ways and Means Committee as *the powerful House Ways and Means Committee*. One of these days, the committee's secretary is going to answer the telephone by saying, "Good morning—powerful House Ways and Means Committee."

We are heading into winter, when The Mercury starts to Plummet. The Coach is thinking of starting a pool—everybody kicks in a buck and picks a date on which the words "white stuff" will first appear as a synonym for "snow."

The White Stuff is, of course, "dumped." By whom? By Old Man Winter. And when Old Man Winter Dumps White Stuff, what happens to us? If we're at home, we Dig Out. But if we're on the highway, we Get

(continued on next page)

Snarled, even though Weary Highway Crews Are Working Around The Clock.

Cliches like that have a life all their own. Ten minutes after they become cliches, they are incorporated into standard newspaper usage, as if our computers were programmed to insert them.

Take, for example, fires. What do they do? They invariably "sweep through" buildings, like some sort of semantic broom.

The wire services like cliches. They are fond of calling any military post "sprawling." All calm is "an uneasy calm," and it almost always "prevails." Labor reporters write of "grueling" or "marathon" negotiating sessions, aimed at "hammering out" a "new" contract. (Does anybody hammer out an *old* contract?)

Adjectives—"marathon" and "grueling"—are the tools of weak writers. Good writers rely on colorful nouns and, most important, on strong verbs. Once upon a time, "hammering out" was a strong verb. Now, it's a cliche. Here's a hypothetical labor-story sentence that sags with those cliches:

Both sides met in a marathon 12-hour negotiating session in an effort to hammer out a new contract.

And here's the same sentence stripped to its basics:

The session dragged on for 12 hours as negotiators tried to agree on a contract.

We must learn:

1. To recognize cliches, and
2. To replace cliches with standard English.

A writer who sits down to recount a fire may be unable to come up with a vivid replacement for "swept through." After all, fires are one of the things we write about most often. But the writer ought to recognize "swept through" for what it is— weary and stale formula writing. The readers will be better served with a story that starts flatly, "A fire destroyed . . ." or "A fire heavily damaged . . ."

Suggested Readings

Anderson, Douglas A. *Contemporary Sports Reporting*. Chicago: Nelson-Hall, 1985.

Best Newspaper Writing. St. Petersburg, Fla.: Poynter Institute. (This book, published every year since 1979, contains prize-winning articles, followed by the editor's comments and question-and-answer sessions with the writers.)

Cappon, Rene J. *The Word: An Associated Press Guide To Good News Writing*. New York: The Associated Press, 1982.

Dorfman, Ron, and Harry Fuller, Jr., eds. *Reporting/Writing/Editing*. Dubuque, Iowa: Kendall/Hunt Publishing Company, 1982.

Ghiglione, Loren, ed. *Improving Newswriting: The Best of The Bulletin of the American Society of Newspaper Editors*. Washington, D.C.: American Society of Newspaper Editors Foundation, 1982.

Hohenberg, John. *The Professional Journalist*. 5th ed. New York: Holt, Rinehart and Winston, 1983.

Kelsch, Mary Lynn, and Thomas Kelsch. *Writing Effectively: A Practical Guide*. Englewood Cliffs, N.J.: Prentice-Hall, 1982.

Murray, Donald. *Writing For Your Readers: Notes on the Writer's Craft from the Boston Globe*. Chester, Conn.: The Globe Pequot Press, 1983.

Rucker, Bryce W., ed. *Twentieth Century Reporting at Its Best*. Ames, Iowa: Iowa State University Press, 1964.

Scanlan, Christopher, ed. *How I Wrote the Story*. Rev. ed. Providence, R.I.: Providence Journal, 1986.

Sims, Norman, ed. *The Literary Journalists*. New York: Ballantine, 1984.

Sloan, William D., Valarie McCrary, and Johanna Cleary. *The Best of Pulitzer Prize News Writing*. Columbus, Ohio: Publishing Horizons, Inc., 1986.

Snyder, Louis L., and Richard B. Morris, eds. *A Treasury of Great Reporting*. 2nd ed. New York: Simon & Schuster, 1962.

Tarshis, Barry. *How to Write Like a Pro*. New York: New American Library, 1983.

Teel, Leonard R., and Ron Taylor. *Into the Newsroom: An Introduction to Journalism*. Englewood Cliffs, N.J.: Prentice-Hall, 1983.

EXERCISE 1
Body

EVALUATING SECOND PARAGRAPHS

INSTRUCTIONS: Critically evaluate the second paragraph in each of these stories. Which second paragraphs are most effective, and why? Which second paragraphs provide smooth transitions from the lead? Which second paragraphs are the most interesting? Which continue to develop the idea summarized in the lead?

1. Jewel C. Harris, 42, of 2245 E. Broadway Ave. was arrested and charged with aggravated battery after her car struck a bicyclist, police say.
    Jerry R. Harris, 24, also of 2245 E. Broadway Ave., was transported to Memorial Hospital with cuts, bruises and a broken leg.

2. Two men robbed a restaurant on Kirkman Road, holding a knife to one employee's throat and forcing another employee to open five cash registers.
    The amount of money stolen from the restaurant at 5400 Kirkman Road is unknown.

3. The School Board has expelled eight more students for using drugs, bringing the total this year to 81.
    Only one of the eight students appeared before the board last night to defend herself. She was accused of selling marijuana to a classmate.

4. The new Alcohol Information Center on campus acknowledges a slow start with its responsible drinking program. But program coordinators have plans to change that.
    Karen Dees is one of the program coordinators. She wants to make sure that students understand the philosophy of responsible drinking. "We're not affiliated with any religious sect," she said. "Our main goal is to keep heavy drinkers off the streets and keep them from harming themselves and others."

5. County Commissioner Janet Zlatkiss wants pornographic movies banned from cable TV.
    In an interview Friday, Zlatkiss said that watching pornography can be psychologically damaging to children. "I'm not talking about R-rated movies," she said. "I'm talking about hard-core stuff that shows animals, whips and chains used in sexual acts."

6. Mayor Myron Banks was sitting in his office when he heard a report on his police radio about a traffic problem at Washington Elementary School.
    The 55-year-old mayor got in his van and drove to the school. It was raining, and he found that hundreds of parents had driven to the school to pick up their children. The mayor got out and directed the traffic.

7. A man claiming to have a bomb tried to rob the First Federal Savings and Loan Co. at 9:05 a.m. today.
    A man carrying a brown paper bag told a teller that it contained a bomb and would kill everyone in the bank unless she gave him $10,000.

8. A 22-year-old auto mechanic and his wife delivered their firstborn child at home Monday because there was not time to drive to a birthing clinic.
    Barbara and Paul Wyman of 2020 Lorry Lane delivered their daughter, Jessica, at 5:30 a.m. The baby and her mother are reported in excellent condition.

9.   Three armed men forced customers to lie on the floor while they robbed a supermarket Wednesday.

   The incident occurred at 11 a.m. at the Kroeger supermarket on Conway Road.

10.   Complaining that college administrators are insensitive to their needs, 50 handicapped students, some in wheelchairs, picketed the Administration Building Friday.

   About 10 percent of the student population is handicapped, but there is no way of determining how many there really are. When the Rehabilitation Act of 1973 was passed, the disclosure of information about handicapped students was prohibited. The law is intended to ensure that a handicapped student is not discriminated against and denied entrance into a college.

11.   The police in Reno, Nev., feel safer and more confident since the PR-24 Baton replaced their night stick.

   Officer Jim Balliet said the concept of a baton was derived from a martial arts weapon called the tonfa. Lon Anderson, a New Hampshire police officer, developed the baton and brought the idea to a company to manufacture it, Balliet said.

12.   Two soldiers who were abducted, robbed and tied in a woods said their captors apologized, saying that they became robbers in order to feed their children.

   The young couple told the pair that they had also abducted other soldiers but did not enjoy doing it.

   The soldiers, Jerrod Whisenant and Julian Banks, gave the following account to police:

EXERCISE 2
Body

IMPROVING YOUR SENTENCES (REVIEW)

SECTION I: AVOIDING THE OBVIOUS Do not rewrite the following sentences. Simply cross off the words that are redundant or that state the obvious.

1. The victim died during surgery to save her life.

2. They could not describe what the suspect looked like.

3. They were taken to Memorial Hospital for treatment of their injuries.

4. The author said her book is profitable, and she hopes it will stay that way.

5. Police who arrived at the scene said the suspect had left the premises but was positively identified by three eye witnesses.

SECTION II: IMPROVING VERBS AND SENTENCE STRUCTURE Rewrite the following sentences, using stronger verbs and the normal word order (subject, verb and direct object).

1. A television set was stolen Saturday night when burglars broke into an appliance store on Wilson Avenue.

2. A 75-year-old woman who was walking south on Cypress Woods Drive was robbed by a teen-ager who threatened her with a knife and was given her purse.

3. A box carried by the bank robber was confiscated by the police and was found by them to contain several flares, not sticks of dynamite.

SECTION III: SIMPLIFYING OVERLOADED SENTENCES Shorten and simplify the following sentences, dividing them into two or three sentences, if necessary.

1. About 80 homeowners, all from the Country Creek subdivision, pleaded with the City Council at its meeting last night to help them get their developer to uphold his end of the subdivision's master plan by providing everything originally promised them, including landscaping, better drainage, and recreation areas that are supposed to include a swimming pool and four tennis courts.

2. Accepting arguments that he had been in no other trouble and needed a job to support his family, the seven members of the Bureau of Licenses voted unanimously Monday afternoon to make an exception to their rules by allowing 42-year-old Warren Schroeder, who was convicted and placed on probation only two years ago in Georgia for stealing a car—a felony—to obtain a chauffeur's license so he can drive a cab here.

3. A study, conducted by the National Institute of Education and released during a press conference in Washington, D.C. at 3 p.m. yesterday, revealed that incompetent teachers are a major problem in public education but are seldom fired after being granted tenure because school systems are wary of court fights that can cost as much as $100,000 and tie up a school board's members for years during the ensuing legal battles.

EXERCISE 3
Body

IMPROVING YOUR PARAGRAPHS

SECTION I: IMPROVING TRANSITIONS Improve the transitions between these leads and their second paragraphs:

1.   After three hours of detention and questioning Saturday afternoon, security officers at a downtown department store released a family they suspected of shoplifting.
      Joseph L. and Destiny Horvath filed a $50 million lawsuit in Circuit Court this morning on behalf of themselves and their two children, Paul and Sonya.

2.   "No one believed it. We thought it was a joke. Then they shot the cashier."
      These were the words today of Edward Duncan, describing the moment three gunmen entered and robbed Hedlinger's Restaurant shortly after 7 p.m. yesterday.

3.   Two young children were killed and their parents seriously injured when their car apparently lost a tire and tumbled out of control.
      Elias L. Yantorini was driving north on the Eisenhower Expressway shortly before 7 a.m.

SECTION II: EMPHASIZING THE NEWS Rewrite the following paragraphs, placing more emphasis upon the news: the action or results.

1.   The school board then turned to the second item on its agenda: a proposal to give school administrators a raise. Board member Jesse Alton moved that the administrators be given an 8.5 percent raise. The superintendent of schools, Marcia Pagozalski, supported the proposal. Without debate, the board accepted the motion by a vote of 6–1.

2.   The elderly man limped into the First Security Federal Bank, 810 Broadway Ave., at 2:50 yesterday afternoon. Witnesses estimate that the man was 65 years old. After waiting patiently in line almost 10 minutes, he reached a cashier, drew a pistol from under his shirt and threatened to shoot her. She gave him all her money: an estimated $10,000. While handing him the money, she sounded a silent alarm. The bank manager, seeing the old man, tried to stop him as he left. The gunman shot and killed the bank manager, then disappeared into a parking lot.

3.   Another section of the district attorney's report turned to the issue of the charity's financial management. The report recommended that the charity's books should be audited at the end of every year and that two people should be required to sign each of its checks to prevent any abuses. It also recommended the employment of a professional and bonded bookkeeper. In the past, the report revealed, these procedures were not followed, and about $20,000 in donations "disappeared" during the last year. No trace has been found of the money.

SECTION III: AVOIDING CHOPPY PARAGRAPHS Rewrite the following paragraphs, eliminating their choppiness.

1.   The man was at home. He entered a bedroom and locked the door. He then blocked the door with a chair. His wife tried to break into the bedroom. She failed and set the

door on fire. He opened a window and called for help. Neighbors called firefighters. They responded and doused the blaze. The fire caused $100 in damage to the door. The man declined to prosecute his wife. The police did not identify them. Police officers said both were drinking.

2. Buddy Kirby was home last night, watching television. Kirby heard someone breaking into his apartment. He went into a bedroom and saw someone entering through its window. Kirby fired his gun, a .38 caliber pistol, until it was empty. The intruder was hit by two bullets. He died. Police have not determined his identity. The police say Kirby did not violate the law. So he will not be charged. The law says you can use force to protect yourself. You must feel that your life is threatened. Or you may fear you are facing great bodily harm.

3. The meeting of the Dubuque City Council began at 8 p.m. last night. The council approved an increase in parking meter fees. The price downtown will go from 10 cents to 25 cents an hour. The fire department asked for a new truck. The fire chief said it would cost $96,400. The council voted against it. Council members told the chief to look for a used truck. They said a used truck would be cheaper.

EXERCISE 4
Body

IMPROVING POORLY WRITTEN STORIES

INSTRUCTIONS: The following stories contain many of the flaws discussed in this chapter. The stories' second paragraphs are weak. Their later paragraphs are poorly organized and poorly written, with inadequate transitions. Rewrite the stories, correcting all their errors.

1. A hammer-wielding masked man robbed a convenience store Wednesday night and made off with an unknown amount of money.

    Claire McAuliffe was the clerk on duty at the time of the robbery. She was working alone.

    The store is located at 100 N. Wilshire Avenue, and she told police that he entered the store at about 11 p.m. She described him as about 6 feet tall, 200 pounds, 30 years of age and balding.

    At first, he asked for a pack of cigarettes. Then he pulled out a knife from a pocket and threatened McAulife, saying he would cut her if she didn't give him all the money in the cash register. He reached into the register himself and began scooping out all the money, including all the change. He then ran out of the store, fleeing on foot.

    Police have no suspects. While cruising the neighborhood, they were unable to find anyone matching the description she provided.

2. An ex-teacher who taught at the elementary level and who claims she is the victim of sex discrimination today filed a lawsuit against the School Board.

    After graduating from college three years ago, Janet Hodgson was hired as a second grade teacher at Wilson Elementary School. Nineteen days after starting her 3rd year, she discovered that she was pregnant.

    According to her lawsuit, Mrs. Hodgson asked her principle for a leave of absence because she was suffering from pre-eclampsia toxemia of pregnancy.

    Her lawsuit adds that she was told by her principle that she could have a one-year leave of absence with the understanding that she would be eligible to return to her job at the start of the next school year, and that—if her performance was satisfactory—she would be granted tenure at the end of that year. Tenure is normally granted at the end of three full years of continuous service. Before that time, teachers are given only one-year contracts.

    About 9 months into her leave, Mrs. Hodgson wrote to her former principle, reminding him of her intent to return to her job.

    Mrs. Hodgson received a reply from the principle that said her job had been filled and the school had no intention of reappointing her. Mrs. Hodgson said the principle also refused to tell her of any other job openings.

    Mrs. Hodgson claims in her lawsuit that her discharge was carried out without notice, explanation or good cause. She claims that she has suffered mental anguish, loss of pride, emotional distress and financial hardship. She is seeking compensatory damages of $25,000 and punitive damages of $5 million.

3. A Memphis couple have filed suit against Cira Bazinet, M.D.; Memorial Hospital; and Zilow Needle Manufacturers, Inc., charging them with the negligent care of a patient.

    The couple's lawsuit charges that Stephen J. W. Dummerth was treated negligently which caused serious injury and damages to him. On May 2 of last year, Dummerth was admitted to Memorial Hospital for an operation. He charges that during the operation a Zilow needle was broken and that the tip, which broke off within his body, was not removed from his body during the operation.

The suit further charges that it was the duty of Dr. Bazinett to remove the needle from the patient which she did not do. The needle was left in Dummerth's body without his knowledge or consent as he was under anesthesia.

Dummerth and his wife, Ruth, charge that Bazinett breached the accepted standard of care for the kind and type of health care provided.

The couple is seeking $2.4 million in damages for the psychological as well as the physical pain and suffering caused by the doctor's negligence.

After the operation, the lawsuit adds, Mr. Dummerth suffered from continuing and severe pain that resulted in a very dangerous infection and the need for a second operation.

4.   Optimal nutrition and exercise are the two most important conditions to maintain top physical performance. This was the message in a speech Monday night in a program called "Fuel for Top Mental and Physical Power."

Dr. Brunson McFarland, executive director of the State Dairy and Food Nutrition Council, told students how to be a healthy person through diet and exercise.

This presentation was the first of the Health Improvement Series. They are designed to educate students on healthy living through proper nutrition and exercise.

Dr. McFarland emphasized the importance of eating well balanced meals. "A good diet consists of foods from the four basic food groups," Dr. McFarland said. The four food groups are the bread and cereal group, fruit and vegetables, meat, and milk and dairy products.

Dr. McFarland stated that people should have a balanced diet from the four major food groups. In doing so, they get all the vitamins and nutrients they need and eliminate the need for vitamin supplements. He warned people to be careful of vitamin supplements. "Most are unnecessary, a waste of money," he said. As an example, he said, vitamin E is not useful and can be harmful, especially for children. If a person went on a starvation diet, they'd die before they had a Vitamin E deficiency.

Calcium deficiency is just one of the many illnesses which can develop from not eating a well balanced diet, Dr. McFarland continued.

Osteoporosis is an illness which people get when they don't eat enough dairy products, cheese, milk, etc. Bones become brittle and break easily. Sixty percent of the women in the U.S. don't get enough dairy products in their diet. One out of every four of those women get osteoporosis.

Dr. McFarland gave many examples of foods from each of the four main groups. He also explained foods categorized as "others." These are foods which have no nutritional value. They just offer empty calories. Sodas are one example.

"If you're going to have a snack," Dr. McFarland said, "a cheese pizza has foods from all four food groups, so it's real good for you. The only problem is that it is high in calories."

Dr. McFarland emphasized throughout his speech the importance of exercise. "Please," said Dr. McFarland, "exercise, it's the only way to lose weight and keep it off.

"Stay away from fad diets," he said. "They're more harmful than good. Many of them stress staying away from whole food groups. In doing so, you become deficient of certain vitamins and nutrients. Sometimes you lose weight fast, but then you gain it all back as soon as you get off the diet. Sometimes you gain back even more weight than you lost. The best way to lose weight and to stay healthy is to reduce your caloric intake and start an exercise routine."

There will be two more programs to educate students on the ways to healthy living. The series is sponsored by the Speakers Committee of the Programming and Activities Council.

EXERCISE 5
Body

WRITING COMPLETE STORIES

INSTRUCTIONS: Write complete news stories based on the following information. Be thorough; include most of the information in your stories. Because much of the material is wordy, awkward and poorly organized, it will have to be extensively rewritten.

1. Historian Allen Whisenant of the University of Kansas gave a speech yesterday. This is what he said: "We can learn from history. Some old ideas are good ideas. There are reasons why we abandoned them, but there are even better reasons for returning to them. One of the ideas is banishment. Our society needs a banishment program, and we could have one in place within the next 2 to 3 years. It might start on a small scale, perhaps in one or two states, but would quickly spread across the United States. We might banish criminals who have received death sentences and, also, those criminals who have been determined to be dangerous and incorrigible. These criminals might be exiled to a remote island where they would live with no contact from the outside world. The exile of these criminals would have several advantages to society. First, the cost of maintaining death row prisoners would be eliminated. Also, litigation costs for these criminals would stop. Nationally, this could save $100 million a year. Second, by removing the incorrigible criminals from overcrowded prisons, rehabilitation of those who remain would be easier. Third, banishment would act as a deterrant. It would be swift, sure and permanent, and criminals would be aware of that. You also have to remember that the laws in a free society are very fragile, and their effectiveness depends on the faith that people have in them. Laws must not protect those who consistently abuse them. That would lead to a collapse of the law. Some people might express concern about what would happen to the criminals once they were on the island. But I'm talking about banishing someone who admitted raping over 100 women, another man who confessed to killing 10 or 20 people. I don't want these men on the street with my wife and daughters. I don't want to know anything about these men. I just want to get rid of them, and this is a better idea than trying to execute them, with appeals that drag on 10 or 15 years and cost us taxpayers millions of dollars. Banishment won't cost anything except the cost of transportation. You won't need any prisons or guards. These people can raise their own food and make their own clothes. That would be part of their punishment; they'll actually have to work to support themselves. We've got better things to do with our tax monies than spend them on people who want to rob, rape and murder us."

2. Under state law, it is a second-degree misdemeanor to publish or broadcast information that identifies rape victims or to cause such information to be published. The law is relevant to this case, which involves a daily newspaper: The Daily Courier in your city. The newspaper was sued by the victim of a rape. She is Paula Andrews, 52, of 4030 New Orleans Avenue. On the 20th of October, two years ago, the victim was raped, and she reported the crime to your city's police department. On the 22nd, The Daily Courier published the story, identifying her as the victim. She sued. A jury of 8 men and 4 women began to hear the case one week ago. At 4 p.m. yesterday, the presentation of evidence ended, and Circuit Court Judge Julian Strickland ordered the jury to find the newspaper negligent and to determine whether the victim deserved any financial damages. After a break for dinner, the jury immediately began its deliberations and, at 8:35 p.m., announced its verdict. The jury awarded the woman $75,000 compensation and an additional $250,000 in punitive damages. The publisher of the newspaper, Ricky Becker, testified during the trial that one of

his newspaper's reporters had violated the newspaper's policy and published the woman's name by mistake in a police briefs column, and that no one else noticed the error until after its publication. Becker said he "was amazed and dumbfounded" by the jury's verdict. "We'll appeal, of course," he said. "There's no justification for awarding anyone that kind of money. We were well within our First Amendment rights; the Constitution is supposed to protect us from this kind of harassment. Normally, we don't publish the name of a woman who's been raped, but the information's non-publication is a voluntary matter. The government can't mandate it." An attorney for the newspaper added that the state law is unconstitutional because it is equivalent to a prior restraint on the publication of truthful, legally obtained information that was part of a public record. The newspaper reporter obtained the information from a police report. Andrews, a widow, told reporters that she considers the award fair and hopes that it will discourage publication of rape victims' names by other newspapers.

3. It began with a routine inspection. Health inspectors in your city inspect every restaurant and bakery, normally twice a year. The inspections are a surprise. They are not announced in advance. Rather, the inspectors drop in by surprise. Last Friday, they dropped in at a bakery on Moore Street: the Kalani Bros. Bakery. It is one of the largest in the city, with 40 employees. It supplies more than 100 grocery stores and restaurants with bread, pies, cakes and other pastries. After the inspection Friday, the Health Department proceeded to suspend the bakery's license, effective immediately. The Kalani brothers, Charles and Andrew, say they will appeal to the city council, which meets at 8 p.m. tonight. During an inspection a year ago, health inspectors found cockroaches, mice droppings, flour beetles and other health problems. There have been two inspections since then, and they found that some problems were corrected, but new problems—such as inadequate refrigeration and garbage thrown on floors—had arisen. The inspectors returned again last Friday—a fourth time—to determine whether all the problems had been corrected. Under emergency provisions of city health laws, a business can be closed immediately—its license temporarily suspended—to protect the public health if a dangerous situation exists. After a hearing, the license can be permanently revoked. City inspectors said, despite their repeated warnings, the problems had not been corrected; some had gotten worse. So Friday, they temporarily suspended the license. Attorney Margie Allen, who represents the brothers, said she does not believe the sanitation problems are as bad as city officials allege and that most have been corrected and that the remainder are in the process of being corrected. She adds that the brothers are losing $13,000 a day in lost business and may permanently lose some customers, who are getting their bakery goods from rivals during the shutdown. "There has been no hearing here," Allen says. "Their business is being destroyed by an edict, without proper legal safeguards. We'll appeal tonight to the city council and, tomorrow, to the courts, if necessary."

4. There was another court hearing yesterday, one in Grand Forks, N.D. It involved a 13-year-old boy: Terry Aal. Terry is accused of helping Gregory and Robert Stanford, both of 824 Princeton Street, Apt. 4, kill his mother. Gregory is 15 and Robert 16. After the murder, Terry made an incriminating statement. Yesterday, a local judge ruled that the statement is inadmissible. It cannot be used at Terry's trial, nor at anyone else's, because the police did not meet their legal obligation to ensure that a parent, legal guardian or attorney for Terry was present when he was interrogated by detectives immediately following his arrest. Mrs. Aal was beaten and stabbed. Her first name is Vivian. Her husband, Ralph, a welder, has been dead 3 years, killed in a construction accident. The two older boys are being tried as adults. Their trial will begin on the first of next month. Authorities are still deciding how to handle Terry's case; however, he will probably be tried separately and treated as a juvenile.

During the hearing yesterday, an attorney representing Terry argued that he was not represented by an attorney during his questioning. There was a school teacher with him, a teacher he asked for. Terry's attorney said the teacher failed to meet the legal requirement for the type of guardian who should legally have been present. The teacher was a friend of Terry, not a guardian or custodian. The teacher advised Terry that, "Honesty is always the best policy; you should tell the truth." After receiving that advice, Terry admitted that he had helped plan the murder with the other two youths. They agreed to kill each others' mothers because they thought their mothers were too strict and unfair, always telling them what to do and not giving them enough money. Police say Terry apparently went to a movie while the other two waited for his mother, killing her in her house when she returned from work. In return, they expected Terry to kill their mother the next evening.

5. It's an idea being tried in many places. County commissioners want an impact fee. The county has been growing so rapidly, they point out, that it is impossible, without some additional sources of income, to provide the necessary services. The county needs more fire stations and more firefighters and sheriff's deputies. The county needs a bigger sewer system, a bigger jail, better roads, new schools and more teachers to accommodate all the new residents moving to the county. A task force of 12 county officials has been looking into the matter during the past three months, and they revealed their report at a press conference at 9 a.m. today. The county commissioners will consider the report at their next meeting: next Tuesday night at 8 p.m. The task force recommends that new people moving to the county should be required to pay for the expanded services they want and need. Taxes should not be raised. Rather, each time a new house is built, an "impact fee" should be assessed. The money would be used for needed capital improvements. New businesses would also be assessed: 5% of the cost of their construction. The plan is expected to raise about $18 million a year. The impact fee for hooking up to the county sewage system for a single-family home would cost $2,500. The impact fee for a water connection would be $1,000. The fees for apartment units would be $1,800 and $750, respectively. There would be other fees for roads, education and police protection. The county would then issue $260 million worth of bonds during the next five years to build three new sewer plants, a new water treatment plant, a jail, two fire stations, and several new schools, including a brand new high school. The impact fees would be used to repay the bonds. Developers object to the idea, saying that the proposed fees would raise the price of each new home more than $5,000 and that many people could not afford that kind of money. The county's goal is to get ahead of growth and to maintain a high quality of life for the county's residents. There will be a series of public hearings, the task force said, but no dates or locations have been set. The task force warns that, without new fees, growth will have to stop. The county will be forced to stop granting any new building permits because it will not have the water and sewage capacity to handle future growth. Roads and schools will become overcrowded, forcing double sessions at the schools. Police and fire protection will deteriorate.

EXERCISE 6
Body

WRITING COMPLETE NEWS STORIES

INSTRUCTIONS: Write complete news stories based on the following information. Be thorough: include most of the information in your stories. Because much of the material is wordy, awkward and poorly organized, it will have to be extensively rewritten.

1. There was a meeting of scientists at the University of Oklahoma today. They talked about dangers of nuclear war. The scientists represented many different fields, from biology to physics and meteorology. They concluded that the results of a nuclear war would be much worse than believed. Survivors may envy the dead. "We have very good reason to be scared," said one scientist about the long-term effects of nuclear war. More than 500 scientists from around the world—including Russia and China—attended the conference. Some concluded that a nuclear war between two major superpowers would result in the extinction of the human race. One said that even a relatively small nuclear war would trigger major changes in climate, which would destroy crops and endanger millions of people. A major nuclear war, they estimated, would kill more than 1 billion people and critically injure at least that number. A huge cloud of dust could be thrown into the atmosphere, cutting off sunlight and causing temperatures to drop well below freezing for weeks—possibly months or even years, so the world would be plunged into a new ice age. Much of the world's farmland would be covered with ice. People would freeze or starve in a dark, smoggy world. In a full-scale nuclear war, the Northern Hemisphere would be destroyed. Everyone there would suffer, not just the citizens of the warring nations. In fact, everyone there would be likely to die. The effects would spread across the equator to the Southern Hemisphere, so the entire globe would be affected. The predictions are based upon statistics concerning a nuclear war involving 5,000 megatons of explosives, or about one-third of the arsenal of the Soviet Union and the United States. The consequences would be more or less severe, depending upon the amount of weapons used and how they were used. A less severe war, a 3,000-megaton war, would lower the global average temperature by 8 degrees, which would be sufficient to wipe out all the world's grain production. The scientists said a Civil Defense program would save people's lives—but only for a few miserable weeks or months. Instead of being killed by the initial blasts, the survivors would die more slowly: of starvation, radiation, cold and disease. There would be no electricity or means of communication or transportation. Medicine and medical care would be unavailable. In parts of the United States, even water might be difficult or impossible to obtain.

2. It was an unusual case. It reached the Supreme Court in the State of New Hampshire, and the judges there reached their decision today. They ruled in favor of the doctor, not in favor of the couple filing the lawsuit. The couple are Wilbur and Martha Yantorini of Keene. Wilbur, the father of two other children, underwent a vasectomy two years ago to keep from fathering any more children, as he felt that was all that he could reasonably afford to raise. A year later, his wife, Martha, became pregnant. Three months ago, she gave birth to a third child, Fred. Wilbur then underwent a second vasectomy, as medical tests showed the first had been unsuccessful. The couple subsequently filed suit upon the doctor who performed the first operation, Dr. Richard Z. Abberger. They are demanding the costs of rearing the third child—a normal, healthy male. It is the first case of this kind to be filed in the state of New Hampshire, and perhaps the first in the nation. The couple demanded $500,000, calculated at the rate of $25,000 for 20 years to raise and educate Fred. They also

demanded all their legal expenses. The court reached its decision today. It ruled against the family and in favor of the doctor. The vote of the court was narrow: 4 to 3. The majority explained that, "Litigation cannot answer every question, and every question cannot be answered in terms of dollars and cents. We are convinced that the damage to the child will be significant: that to be an unwanted or 'emotional bastard' child who will someday learn that its parents did not want it and, in fact, went to court to force someone else to pay for its raising, will be harmful for that child. But we must also consider a ruling that could undermine society's need for a strong and healthy family relationship. Families have always been responsible for the care and upbringing of their children, and we are reluctant to alter that centuries-old tradition so basic to our society." If damages are to be awarded because an unwanted child was born, the court said, the state Legislature should take action, enacting a new law to settle the issue. The judges who dissented said forcing the issue on the legislature was a cop-out. They also said a policy of denying benefits in such cases would encourage abortion or adoption.

3. The case involves another unusual lawsuit. As a result of it, if you are blind, or going blind, you may have to wait longer to receive cornea transplants. Your state's supreme court ruled on the matter today. It issued a decision saying that medical examiners can no longer remove corneas from the eyes of a deceased without the permission of relatives. A state law, adopted in 1979, gave medical examiners the right to remove corneas—without permission of the family of the deceased. The law applied to bodies under the jurisdiction of medical examiners, such as victims of accidents, murders, suicides and other unexplained deaths. Since then, attorneys opposed to the law have argued that it violates a family's right to decide the disposition of a loved one's remains. There was a test case. It involved a woman who died two years ago, at the age of 31. She has not been identified, in part because she committed suicide. During the autopsy of her body, both corneas were removed from her eyes. Later, when her relatives learned of that action, they objected on the grounds of their religious beliefs. Your State Supreme Court, ruling on the case today, said the state law violates a family's right to decide the disposition of a loved one's remains. The ruling is expected to be appealed to the U.S. Supreme Court. People at an eye bank in your state say the decision could drastically affect cornea procurement. The director of the eye bank said the ruling could extend the waiting period for the sight-restoring surgery from a week or two to a year or longer. "I think this will have a disastrous effect on our ability to obtain an adequate number of corneas to serve our patients," said the medical director of the eye bank. On the other hand, presenting the other point of view, parents have complained that they did not even know about the law until after the corneas of their deceased children were removed. The law permitted the removal of the corneas, the transparent tissue forming the outer coating of the eye and covering the iris and pupil, as long as the family didn't object. The law did not require the medical examiner to notify the family of the procedure. So many families may not have objected because they did not know what was being done. About half of the 50 states have similar laws governing the procurement of corneas. In states where there is no law giving medical examiners the authority to remove corneas, the typical wait for a transplant is from three to six months. "In every state where there's a similar law, the waiting list is very small," a doctor said.

4. She is 27 years old and the mother of four young children: 1 girl and 3 boys. After dropping out of high school, she became a waitress. One of her boys, Greg, 6, owns a toy pistol. Today, the woman, Miriam Hotellin of 4112 American Street was convicted of the charge against her. She was charged with robbing the State Bank and Trust Company, 410 Broadway Avenue. On the morning of July 1 of last year, shortly after

9 a.m. that morning, when the bank opened, she walked in. She showed a teller her son's gun, pretending that it was real, and handed the teller a note saying that she was "despirate, with nothing too loose." She asked the teller for $5,000. The bank is only 6 blocks from her home, and she fled on foot and was chased from the bank by several bank employees and bank customers. The police quickly cordoned off the entire neighborhood around the bank, and she was arrested about two hours later after being found hiding in a parked car. Her purse was full of money, and witnesses who testified during her trial identified it as the money stolen from the bank. She has been held in prison since the robbery due to the fact that she was unable to post the $25,000 bail. She had no criminal record and entered the bank dressed in jeans, a T-shirt and sandals. Before being sentenced, she explained to the judge that she wanted the money for a down payment on a trailer in the country so she could get her family out of a government housing project in which they live. She said the bank she robbed had denied her a $5,000 loan she needed for the down payment. Her husband, who is disabled and confined to a wheelchair, knew nothing about the robbery and was shocked when he was visited at home by police investigating it after his wife's arrest. During her trial, her attorney entered a plea of "not guilty," and she did not take the stand. After her conviction today, the judge sentenced her to a term of five years in prison, with the time she has already served to count toward the five years. With time off for good behavior, she may be released in a year.

5. It was an unusual situation. Two police officers responding to an emergency call were involved in an automobile accident on the 14th of last month. Today they were fired. They were not fired for causing the accident, although they did. The chief of police announced their firing during a press conference in his office at 8 a.m. this morning. The chief complained that the two officers had lied in their official report about the accident and continued to lie to their superiors during subsequent questionings. That's why they were fired. The officers were Kevin Barlow and Wesley Zozuli. Barlow had been with the department for 3 years and Zozuli for 7. The chief said he reached his decision after receiving a report from his Internal Affairs Division, which had been in charge of the investigation. Since the accident—during the investigation—the officers have been assigned to the department's Traffic Patrol Division, directing traffic and checking parking violations. At the time of the accident, the two officers were responding to a report of a "burglary in progress, with officers in foot pursuit." They were situated about 2 miles from the scene and, upon notification that they were needed at the scene, informed the dispatcher that they were enroute. All agree that they activated their lights and siren while proceeding to the scene. At the intersection of Vine Street and Twin Lakes Boulevard, their squad car collided with a second vehicle. Fortunately, no one was injured in the collision, as everyone was wearing their safety belt. However, both vehicles were totally destroyed. A state trooper initially cited the driver of the other vehicle, a Toyota Celica, with failure to yield the right of way to an emergency vehicle but, upon further investigation and complaint from the driver of that vehicle, the charge was dropped. City police officers who conducted a routine investigation into the accident subsequently decided, from skid marks and other evidence at the scene, including the comments of four eyewitnesses to the collision, that the cruiser driven by Barlow had failed to stop as it was supposed to according to police department rules for cruisers entering an intersection against a red traffic signal. It is now estimated that the cruiser was traveling 30 to 35 mph when it entered the intersection. In their initial written account of the accident, the officers said they came to a complete stop. Chief Martin Guidemi, at his press conference this morning, revealed that both officers failed polygraph tests about the accident. When questioned about the accident and about the chief's decision after his press conference this morning, Barlow declined to

comment. Zozula commented: "I don't think it's right. We were trying to help another officer in need of assistance. There was no way we were going 30 mph, no way. We may not have come to a complete stop, but when another officer is chasing someone, and needs help, we try to get there as quick as possible. Everyone knows that. If we didn't, we wouldn't be good officers. We were doing our jobs, and the chief hasn't supported us like he's supposed to. That's his job. Sure, this collision was unfortunate, but that's a chance we take. Things like that happen. People would complain even more if we didn't get there fast when they needed help. It's the least we can do for another officer."

EXERCISE 7
Body

WRITING COMPLETE STORIES

INSTRUCTIONS: Write complete news stories based on the following information. Be thorough; include most of the information in your stories. Because much of the material is wordy, awkward and poorly organized, it will have to be extensively rewritten.

1. A new law that goes into effect next fall will affect elementary, junior high and high school students throughout the state. The state Legislature enacted the law, and the governor signed it today. Basically, the law prohibits the sale of so-called junk food at public schools. So, as a result of the law's passage, the content of all school vending machines will undergo a drastic change. The machines no longer will contain any candy bars, gum, soda or other foods with a high sugar content. Instead, they will be replaced by foods which are considered by many to be more healthy, foods such as canned soups and juices, jerky, toasted soy beans, sunflower seeds, yogurt, nuts, cheese, popcorn, pretzels, ice cream and milk. The law was supported by physicians, dentists and educators, who testified in legislative hearings that many students bought snacks and soft drinks from machines instead of eating the more nutritious meals served in school cafeterias. Other persons, primarily food manufacturers and vending-machine operators, opposed the law. Students, too, generally opposed it, claiming that their rights were being violated and that they were old enough to make their own decisions about what they want to eat. Some school principals also opposed the law, pointing out the fact that the law will be costly since they receive a percentage of the receipts of the vending machines located in their buildings. Some big high schools earn up to $20,000 a year from machines and use the money to buy materials that would not otherwise be available, such as supplemental textbooks, library materials, calculators for their mathematics laboratories, television cameras for their communications classes, and athletic equipment. School bands and athletic programs will be hurt most severely by the loss of revenue. The practice of showing free movies at some schools may also come to a quick end, since many were financed by vending machine revenues. Critics said it was inconsistent for schools to teach good nutrition in classes and then make food with a high sugar content easily available. The ban will be in effect only during school hours, so the junk food will still be able to be sold after school hours, such as during school dances and sports events, so schools can continue to earn a limited amount of money from their sale. One opponent added, "There's simply no sense in talking to kids about dental care and good nutrition and selling them junk food at the same time." Opponents responded that students will buy candy anyway, simply going off campus to buy it.

2. Thomas E. Richardson is 28 years old and a city policeman and alive today because while on duty he wears a bullet-proof vest supplied free of charge by the city. He lives at 5421 Jennings Road with his wife, Inez, and two children: Mary, 8, and Suanne, 5. He has been a policeman since leaving the Army 4 years ago. Without the vest, he might have died last night. Richardson went on duty at 4 p.m. and shortly after 10 p.m. the police received an anonymous phone call about a suspicious person loitering behind a restaurant at 640 Aloma Avenue. Responding to the call, Richardson spotted a man matching the description he was given and, when he pulled his patrol car to the curb and got out, he said without warning the man drew a .38-caliber revolver from a jacket pocket and without saying anything fired four shots at him. Two shots struck Richardson. Two struck his patrol car. The first two shots hit Richardson in the chest, and he was spun around and knocked against the car door by

the impact of those two shots. A third bullet shattered a left rear window of the patrol car and the fourth bullet entered the left rear door of the patrol car. After catching his breath, Richardson returned fire, blasting six shots at the suspect, who fell to the ground. Richardson was treated at Mercy Hospital for severe bruises on the chest, including one bruise that doctors say is directly above his heart, in a hospital emergency room. The suspect, who was killed in the exchange of gunfire, has not yet been identified. A police spokesman said they do not yet know why he opened fire at Richardson. The police department purchased bullet-proof vests for all its outside policemen last year, but wearing them is voluntary and many officers do not because they are heavy and uncomfortable, particularly during the hot summer months.

3. The police today celebrated the first anniversary of an innovative program. The program is for senior citizens—usually persons 65 and older, although any person who lives alone and is over the age of 55 can participate if that person wants to do so. The program is called "Project Reassurance." Each day, elderly persons who partici-pate in the program call Dorothy Morovchek, a clerk, and two aides at the police department between the hours of 7 and 9 a.m. If they do not call by 9:15 a.m., Miss Morovchek will dispatch a police officer to the person's home to determine whether the person is safe, and the officers have keys to each participant's home so they do not have to break their way in. Since the program started a year ago, Miss Morovchek says it has saved three lives, including the life of a woman who police officers found lying on the kitchen floor of her home after having suffered a heart attack before she was able to call the police that morning. Altogether, a total of 318 persons in the city participate in the program at the current time, and police say they will not impose any limitations on the number of participants in the future. Miss Morovchek adds that the elderly like the program for a second reason as well, since many feel alone, and it gives them someone to talk to every morning. One elderly person who uses the service says, "It's a thrill to hear a voice. My wife died four years ago, and I don't have anyone else to talk to. I also feel now like I have some security. I know someone's there to help if I need it."

4. Your city's fire department received a call for assistance at 8:17 p.m. yesterday. The dispatcher who took the call immediately sent three trucks and an assistant chief to Mario's Italian Restaurant, 1410 Dean Road. The call came from Mario Avossa, owner and chef, at the restaurant. Fire department records indicate that the first unit arrived at the scene at 8:21 p.m.—a response time of approximately 4 minutes. There was no fire, but the restaurant's roof collapsed. No one was injured. However, firemen found the ceiling had fallen onto and shattered the restaurant's tables and chairs, and food and dishes were littered over and about the floor. Because there was no fire and no injuries, two trucks and the assistant chief promptly returned to their stations. Three men assigned to one truck remained on the scene to assist in the draining of water from the restaurant and in the covering of its contents with waterproof tarpaulins to prevent further damage. Fire marshal N. B. Kazyk Junior reported that it had been raining throughout the day, and the rain water apparently collected on the flat roof of the restaurant during the storm, thus accumulating in weight during the daylight and the early evening hours. The weight of the water apparently caused a support beam in the roof to break. Kazyk said, "I've never seen anything like this in my 18 years in the fire service. There are several of these beams, and when one goes, the rest go. It's like a domino effect." Kazyk added that Avossa's quick thinking probably saved lives and averted injury. Avossa said he was in the restaurant at about 8:15 p.m. when he saw the interior roof begin to start sagging, and the ceiling began leaking, and he heard "popping and creaking" noises. Avossa said he immediately began to herd people out of the restaurant. Fourteen customers and five employees were on the premises at the time. "I heard a crack and thought it was lightning that had hit something nearby. Then I came out of the kitchen and saw

all the people looking up at the ceiling. I saw the roof sagging, and I yelled for everyone to run outside," Avossa explained.

5. A lone man robbed a bank in the city. He entered the Security Federal Bank, 814 North Main Street, at about 2:30 p.m. yesterday. Bank officials said he first went into the bank with the excuse of obtaining information about a loan, talked to a loan officer and then left. When he returned a few minutes later, he was brandishing a pistol and demanded money from the bank's tellers. Gladys Anne Higginbotham, the bank's manager, said he forced two tellers to lie on the floor. He then jumped behind a counter and scooped up the money from five cash drawers. As the gunman scooped up the money, he also scooped up a small exploding device disguised to look like a packet of money and stuffed it into his pockets along with the rest of the cash. The device contains red dye and tear gas and automatically explodes after a specified amount of time. The length of time before the explosion is determined by each individual bank using the device. The device is activated when someone walks out of a bank with it. As the gunman left the bank, he ordered four customers to lie down on the floor. Most of the customers were unaware of the robbery until told to get down on the floor. Witnesses believe the gunman sped away from the scene in a pickup truck parked behind the building. Police say they found a red stain in the rear parking lot and surmise that the device exploded just as the robber was getting into the truck. An eyewitness told police he saw a late-model black pickup truck a few blocks away with a red cloud coming out the window a few moments after the robbery but was unable to get the license number. Detective Myron A. Neeley said, "That guy should be covered with red. The money, too. Just look for a red man with red money. You can't wash that stuff off. It just has to wear off. It explodes all over the place—in your clothes, in your hair, on your hands, in your car. It's almost like getting in contact with a skunk." An FBI agent on the scene added that many banks now use the protective devices in an effort to foil bank robbers and that the stain will eventually wear off humans but stays on money forever. He estimated that the man will be covered with the red dye for at least the next two or three days. The man was described as a white man. He is between the ages of 25 and 30 years of age. He is about 6 feet tall. He weighs about 180 pounds. He has long blond hair. His attire includes wire-rimmed sunglasses, a gold wedding ring, a blue plaid shirt, blue jeans and brown sandals.

6. Your city's public library, with the assistance of local police, started a new policy yesterday. Dale Cranisky is director of the city's public libraries. During an interview yesterday he said that he is tired of people who fail to return library books. He said his office mails notices to people who fail to return books. If they still fail to return the books, his office mails them a second and then a third notice and, if they still fail to respond, then his office calls them. He said some people check out dozens of books and never return them, and other citizens are then unable to read those books as a consequence, yet the library has a tight budget and cannot afford to buy replacements for all the missing books. So Cranisky asked Police Chief Martin Guikema for help. Guikema sent out officers and they arrested 14 residents of your city yesterday. The officers are still seeking 7 other persons. All those arrested were charged with retention of library property after notice to return, a misdemeanor punishable by fines of up to $500 and/or 30 days in the county jail. All 14 were arrested at their homes or places of business and brought to jail. All 14 posted $100 bail and were released, pending hearings next week at which library officials will present their case. Guikema said several of the people were very angry about their arrests and said the punishment was too harsh for what they considered such a minor matter. Cranisky said the books belong to the taxpayers and not to individuals. He added: "I may be the first librarian in the state to do this, I'm not sure. But it's my job. I've got to be forceful." He added that all those persons arrested by the police and

still sought by the police had failed to respond to three mailed notices and all had books overdue a year or more.

7. Marie Terri Finkbeiner lives in a one-story home at 414 Ivanhoe Boulevard. She is 52 years old. Her former husband, Clayton Finkbeiner, is 47 and lives at 4718 Greenbrier Road. They were divorced 3 months ago. Finkbeiner is an architect with an office at 3316 Victory Drive. The couple had been married for a total of 27 years. They have 4 children. Capt. Al Guempil gave this account of what transpired yesterday. At about 2 p.m., Mrs. Finkbeiner went to her husband's office on Victory Drive and shot him 6 times. A partner and several office workers heard the shots and found Finkbeiner lying on his back on the floor behind his desk. He was still alive at the time. Fire department paramedics immediately rushed Finkbeiner by ambulance to Mercy Hospital for treatment of his injuries. Police officers found Mrs. Finkbeiner on a couch in a women's lounge in the building with a self-inflicted gunshot wound to the right side of her head. She, too, was still alive and was rushed by ambulance to Mercy Hospital for treatment of her injuries. Two letters written by Mrs. Finkbeiner were found by police on her husband's desk "indicating that she had given some thought to killing him and to taking her life; it was planned," Guempil said. Co-workers said they were shocked and taken by surprise because they were aware of the fact that the couple had divorced but thought the divorce was an amicable split and they had not detected any hostility between the two. Mrs. Finkbeiner died a few minutes after her arrival at the hospital. Her former husband died while being operated on for treatment of his injuries at 10:15 p.m. yesterday night.

8. Dr. Maurice Sasser spoke at 8:30 p.m. last night to a meeting of hearing specialists employed by the city's schools. Sasser began his speech by noting that noise can be harmful in a number of ways. It makes people more irritable and may result in an actual hearing loss. In fact, he said, hearing problems constitute the number one disability in the nation, affecting 16,500,000 persons. If people live long enough, practically everyone will suffer a hearing loss of some extent. High noise levels also cause hearing losses in addition to old age, he said. In the past, Sasser continued, concern has been expressed primarily about industrial noises, and standards set by the Occupational Safety and Health Administration stipulate that a worker may not be exposed to an average level of more than 90 decibels for more than eight hours a day. But now researchers are becoming more concerned about the noises encountered in a typical household, since continuous exposure to even 50 decibels of machine noise produce an annoyance factor that may increase a person's irritability. A vacuum cleaner used in a typical American home produces noise levels in the 75 to 85 decibel range. Power mowers, blenders and hair dryers, some of the loudest appliances in homes, give readings of 93, 92 and 90 decibels, respectively. Continuing, Sasser said a food mixer produces 83 decibels, a dishwasher 73, a sewing machine 64, a clothes dryer 63, a window fan 62, and a window air conditioner 60. Other noises are even louder. A stereo turned up so that the floor vibrates registers 95 decibels. Sasser said the problem of noise pollution is becoming so severe that some older persons who experience a hearing loss are reluctant to wear a hearing aid because, when given a proper hearing aid, they are surprised at how much noisier the world has become and are not certain they want to listen to it all. Finally, Sasser concluded by warning that hearing loss rarely is sudden. Rather, "The disability creeps up on you. It's painless and it's difficult to pin down where it comes from." Two things in homes are most dangerous to hearing, he concluded: stereos played at high levels over a long period and power mowers.

9. An unidentified gunman fired a pistol shot through a closed window and into a 1988 model Buick owned and driven by Francesca L. Giaimo, 42, of Bloomington, Indiana. She is visiting relatives in your city, and her car was parked at the Quality Inn, 7430

Woodside Drive in your city at the time, estimated to be about 11:30 p.m. last night. The bullet missed Giaimo. The gunman sustained undetermined injuries but was able to limp away on foot. Police searched the vicinity and checked area hospitals on the possibility they may have treated the man but were unable to find him. Giaimo had just parked her car outside the motel and had started to step outside the car and go to her rented room in the motel when the gunman approached her from behind and demanded her purse. But instead of giving him the purse, she promptly jumped back into the car, locked the car door and rolled up all the windows. When she refused to give him the purse despite his continued threats, the man fired a shot from his pistol into the passenger seat of her car. Afraid for her life, Giaimo then rolled down the window and handed him the purse, which contained an estimated $800, plus an assortment of 4 or 5 credit cards. All the while, her husband, Samuel, was in their nearby motel room, since he had felt ill and remained in the room all that evening while she was visiting the relatives. Mrs. Giaimo said she works hard for her money and became angry and, as the man began to run away, she started the car and followed him through the parking lot, then stepped on the gas and ran him down from behind. After hitting him at an estimated 10 to 15 miles an hour she said she got out of her car and proceeded to retrieve her purse which was lying on the ground near the man. But the man then got up. Later, she gave this statement to police: "I wasn't going fast when I hit him because I couldn't. There were too many cars in the parking lot, but I wasn't going to let him get away with my money. When I got out of my car and got my purse, he got up and hit me with his fists. I was scared, and I began yelling and crying. Someone must have heard me, because I heard some men shouting at him, and then he hobbled away. Now I've got my purse, and his gun, too. He must have dropped it when I hit him with the car, and I found it near my purse. I hope I hurt him bad, real bad. He could have killed me."

10. Marvin R. Fickett has been selected as the Libertarian Party candidate in the next presidential election. He spoke on your campus at 8 p.m. last night. His speech was open to the public free of charge. The audience was estimated to number about 600 persons, including several busloads of Libertarians who drove to the speech from a number of distant cities in your state. Fickett spoke about the federal government, saying that it has goals that are not good for the citizens of this nation. Fickett said that he favors a basic change in the political system. More specifically, he said: "We Libertarians favor more individual freedom and less government intervention. We intend to use every chance we can to get government out of our pocketbooks, out of our bedrooms and out of our lives."

Much of his talk centered about the issue of money. He said if he is elected president he will immediately implement a 50% reduction in all federal income taxes and will not tax any incomes below the amount of $25,000. Fickett said that the nation needs to abolish taxes for people in the middle- to lower-income levels so they are encouraged to get off or stay off welfare and get jobs, and that they will be more likely to work if they can keep all the money they earn. Raising the untaxed income level will put between 5,000,000 and 6,000,000 people to work at full-time jobs, he estimated. But to reduce taxes, you must also reduce government spending in order to avoid larger deficits. First on his list of reductions is the area of foreign military aid. He said: "In the American military budget next year, over $100 billion will go to subsidize the defense of Japan and Western Europe. After World War II, there may have been some need for that. Their economies were ruined, and they couldn't defend themselves. But unbeknowst to the Pentagon, both the Japanese and the Europeans have now recovered from World War II, and they can defend themselves. American taxpayers shouldn't have to pay for their defense."

Fickett warned that government monopolizing is almost as dangerous as too much government spending. He said that the government's monopoly on education has seriously injured Americans. To resolve the problem, he recommends a $1,000 tax credit for any parent sending a child to a private school. Continuing on that topic, Fickett said: "Choice and competition will improve education. Today's youths, for the first time in American history, are going to be less educated than their parents. That's because the public schools are no longer involved in really teaching. They've got lots of other social goals. Schools should be teaching reading, writing and arithmetic, not social goals or moral values." He said the problems won't be solved by the Republican or Democratic parties. Fickett said that the differences between those two parties are very small and that they both favor big government, a big military and big social programs that will lead the nation to bankruptcy or war. "We need new leaders—Libertarian leaders—but we also need a new system of government," Fickett said. "We've got to limit the power of the Supreme Court. It's making more changes in this nation's laws than Congress. But if you look at Congress, its record isn't very good either. Big government in the United States prohibits pornography, prostitution, gambling and marijuana. It also tells us we shouldn't smoke, but we should wear seat belts. Those are personal matters. They may not be good for us, but we should be able to decide that for ourselves. What I do in the privacy of my home is my business, not the government's. I'd abolish all those laws. The government has no business telling us how to run our personal lives. It's gotten to the point that the government isn't just trying to help people any longer; it's dictating to them. We don't need a federal Department of Education. Local people can run their own schools. We don't need an Energy Department. If energy conservation is a good idea, common sense and private enterprise will take care of it. We don't need a federal jobs program. We don't need federal subsidies and loans for farmers and college students and foreign governments. And I'd also get the government out of the welfare business. What right does the government have to take our money, and then give it to someone else? Let's end this big government. Support the Libertarian Party, and we'll help you accomplish that goal. Thank you."

7 Selecting and Reporting the News

On a typical day, more than two-thirds of all Americans aged 18 and over read at least part of a newspaper. One in eight reads two or more papers. By comparison, 52 percent watch a television newscast—but only 18 percent watch a network newscast. Fifty percent listen to radio news, and about 28 percent read a magazine. However, only 5 percent read a news magazine such as Time, Newsweek or U.S. News & World Report.

Researchers have also found that adults who use one source of news are likely to use a second source. One study revealed that 75 percent of the adults who watched a television news program on a particular day also read a newspaper. But only 59 percent of the adults who did not watch a television news program read a newspaper that day.

The majority of newspaper readers are whites who live in cities. Many have attended college, are middle-aged, hold white-collar jobs and earn more than the average American. The group least likely to read newspapers is adults aged 18 to 29. Young adults are also least likely to watch television news. Thus, they seem to be uninterested in the news, not just in newspapers.

Journalists do not expect every story they write to interest every reader. The average reader spends only 20 to 30 minutes a day looking at a paper. Many are in a hurry and read their papers on the run: while riding a bus, eating lunch, watching television or talking with friends. They skim each page, looking for stories of particular interest. They may pause to read a headline or lead. But if they encounter an obstacle— a dull or confusing paragraph—they quickly move on to another story.

Thus, one study found that only 56.7 percent of readers who start a story that contains just five paragraphs will finish it. The percentage declines as stories become longer. Only 39 percent will finish a story that contains 10 paragraphs, and only 28 percent will finish a story that contains 20 paragraphs.

Readership surveys have also identified the most popular types of stories. However, newspapers continue to publish many of the stories that attract only a few readers. Editors explain that, although unpopular, the stories are important or of great interest to those few readers.

A typical man looks at about 20 percent of all the items published by a newspaper. Younger men read fewer items, about 15 percent. Women read almost the same number of items as men and generally enjoy reading the same types of stories, except sports. A national survey involving 130 daily newspapers found that comics, the most popular item published by the newspapers, attracted 58.3 percent of their readers. The most popular news stories concerned wars, major crimes and disasters, the weather, human interest features, consumer information and scientific discoveries. The least popular news stories concerned business, agriculture, religion, minor crimes, state government, and art, music and literature.

Definitions of News

Newspapers do not have enough reporters, time or space to report everything that happens. Moreover, their subscribers could not afford to pay for all the news and would not have enough time or interest to read it. Instead, journalists serve as filters, or "gatekeepers." They evaluate potential news stories, then determine their fate. If journalists consider a story newsworthy, they may open the gates that allow the story to flow into the nation's news channels and, as a consequence, to reach the public. But if the journalists dislike a story, they may cut or kill it.

The gatekeeping process actually begins with a reporter's sources. The sources may see only a part of a story, understand and remember only a part of what they saw, and give the reporter only a part of what they remember. After receiving those fragments, the reporter may write a story that includes only the information that seems most newsworthy. Several editors may review the story, and each editor may trim or rewrite portions of it. If their newspaper does not have enough space to publish all the fragments that survived the editing process, the last editor to handle the story may throw out several more paragraphs.

The entire selection process is subjective: an art, not a science. Journalists do not have any scientific tests or measurements to help them judge a story's newsworthiness. Instead, they rely on their intuition: their instinct, experience and professional judgment. For most journalists, the process becomes automatic. They look at a story and instantly know whether or not it is news.

If you asked journalists to define the term "news," many would be unable to respond. Some might say definitions are unimportant. Others might say news is impossible to define because it is too diverse—because almost anything can become news. Faced with a similar dilemma, Supreme Court Justice Potter Stewart once confessed that he could not define the term "hard-core pornography." But, Stewart added, "I know it when I see it."

Journalists have tried to define news, but no single definition has won widespread acceptance. Also, no definition acknowledges all the factors that affect the selection process. Typical definitions include:

> News is a report of an event, containing timely (or at least hitherto unknown) information which has been accurately gathered and written by trained reporters for the purpose of serving the reader, listener or viewer.
>
> *(Phillip H. Ault and Edwin Emery*, Reporting the News*)*

> News is an account of an event which a newspaper prints in the belief that by so doing it will profit.
>
> *(Curtis MacDougall*, Newsroom Problems and Policies*)*

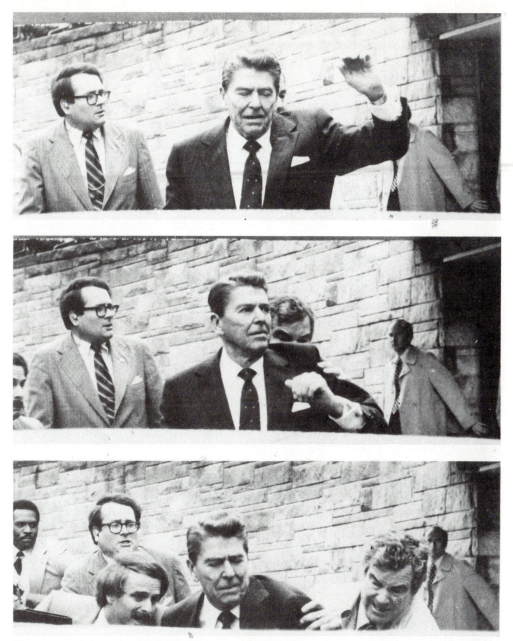

Photographs taken for The Associated Press show President Ronald Reagan as he was struck by a bullet while walking to his limousine just 3 months after taking office. The second photograph shows Reagan glancing toward his assailant, and the third shows him being shoved into the limousine. Doctors who saved his life at the George Washington University Hospital in Washington, D.C., found that the bullet struck Reagan under his left arm, then tore a 3-inch furrow through his left lung.

News is an account of a current idea, event or problem that interests people.
(*Laurence R. Campbell and Roland E. Wolseley,* How to Report and Write the News*)*

The news—what happens and what men think, do and feel about it—this is the first concern of the press.

(*James Wiggins in* Journalism Quarterly*)*

News . . . is current information made available to the public about what is going on—information often of vital importance to men and women trying to make up their minds about what to think and how to act. News is a timely, concise, accurate report of an event; it is not the event itself.

(Mitchell V. Charnley, "Reporting")

News has also been defined as "anything you didn't know yesterday," "what people talk about," "what readers want to know," "what a well-trained editor decides to put in his or her paper," "anything timely," "the report of an event" and "tomorrow's history."

Types of News

There are two major types of news: "hard" and "soft." The term "hard news" usually refers to serious, factual and timely stories about important topics. The stories may describe a major crime, fire, accident, speech, labor dispute or political campaign.

Hard news also may be called "spot news" or "straight news." A similar label, "breaking news," refers to events occurring, or "breaking," at the present moment.

The term "soft news" usually refers to feature or human-interest stories. Their topics may be old and unimportant—but never dull. Soft news is written to entertain rather than inform and appeals to its readers' emotions more than to their intellect. Such stories may make readers laugh or cry, love or hate, envy or pity. Such stories may also use a more colorful style of writing, with more anecdotes, quotations and descriptions.

An editor may instruct a reporter to find a "news peg" for a potential story whose topic seems too unimportant or uninteresting to be newsworthy at that moment. The reporter may look for a new or local angle. If none is available, the reporter may wait for a new development that thrusts the issue into the news. Readers may be uninterested in Civil Defense until a disaster demonstrates a need for it. They may be uninterested in a local artist until she succeeds. Or they may be uninterested in a local museum until it runs out of money and is forced to close.

Most Americans are more familiar with the terms "good" and "bad" news. Critics frequently charge that the media report too much bad news. One of those critics, Howard K. Smith of ABC News, has said the media do not "give the public a rounded, whole picture of the times they live in." Smith explains that journalists generally become interested in stories "only when things go wrong," and that a steady diet of negative news about the United States, whose history has been mainly successful, creates a false picture of life in the country.

Other journalists have defended the media's performance and insisted that they must report all the news, good or bad. During the war in Vietnam, Dr. Frank Stanton, president of CBS, acknowledged the fact that viewers said television brought the horrors of Vietnam too vividly into Americans' homes. However, Stanton also stated that: "The responsibility for the decisions made in Washington and culminating on a battlefield 10,000 miles away begin and end in that living room. Because that final responsibility rests with the people, they must have the facts—the bad news as well as the good, the unpleasant as well as the pleasant."

More systematic studies have found that readers exaggerate the amount of crime and violence reported by the media. Dozens of studies have examined the issue, and they revealed that individual newspapers devoted from 2 percent to 35 percent of their space to violence. On the average, one-tenth of newspaper content is concerned with violence.

Because of the public's complaints, journalists have tried to report more good news, but without much success. A retired journalist started a special service, called "Good News from Everywhere." He sent customers—about 200 newspapers, radio and television stations—10 "good news stories" a week. Many of the stories were about good Samaritans and animals. One story reported that a cat earned $7 a day by tasting cat food. Another described a law that would have required cats to wear bells so they could not quietly stalk and kill birds. The news service failed because its stories became too repetitious. Many of the stories were also unimportant, and editors wanted to devote their resources to stories they considered more newsworthy.

In Florida, the Miami News tried to eliminate all the violence from its editions for one day. It killed every violent feature, including three comics, and news stories about two armed robberies, a bloody campus riot and a boxing match. The newspaper's editors almost abandoned the experiment when a fugitive sought for murdering a policeman was captured in a shoot-out that morning, but instead, the paper's front page featured a strike by garbage workers and a waiter who had been awarded $3 million.

One of the newspaper's editors wrote a front-page explanation that concluded: "This de-emphasis of violence for this one day may demonstrate that we, as readers, would not receive from our paper an accurate and complete picture of the world around us if the paper practiced such deliberate selectivity every day and tried to shield us from reality."

Nevertheless, the criticisms continue. The Reagan administration accused the media of prolonging a recession by constantly reporting bad news about the nation's rising unemployment rate. Journalists responded that it was absurd to believe that a few news stories could affect anything so complex and massive as the nation's economy. But President Reagan urged the television networks to devote a week to good news, "then, if the ratings go down, they can go back to the bad news." CBS news anchorman Dan Rather responded that Reagan was blaming his administration's difficulties on "the people who call attention to the problems."

Good News—Bad News

In 1970, the late Will Winstead wrote this article for the Virginia-Pilot in Norfolk, Virginia. At the time, U.S. troops were fighting in Vietnam, and many Americans complained that the media were too critical of the war. Critics also objected to the media's coverage of anti-war demonstrations and other problems within the United States. Many of the critics insisted that the media should support the government during a war, that the publicity encouraged further demonstrations, and that the media emphasized the negative—what was wrong rather than what was right with America. Winstead's response to their criticisms helps explain the media's coverage of "bad news."

By Will Winstead

"Why," they ask, "do you print so much bad news?"

"Why don't you print the good news?"

"Why do you put big headlines and pictures concerning inflammatory incidents on the front page?"

"Is the press conspiring to wreck our society?"

So it always has been and always will be in every period of great national controversy—when a people are as divided as war, demonstrations, and riots have polarized America today—the tempo of letters and phone calls to newspapers increases proportionately to the magnitude of the unrest.

The readers ask, in brief, what is news?

It is a legitimate question. News is more than Webster's definition: "a report of a recent event; tidings" or "matters of interest to newspaper readers." News defies categorization as much as "right" or "wrong," "good" or "bad," for the interpretation often is in the eyes of the beholder.

News is many things.

It is natural phenomena and human endeavor. It is murder and rape and arson. It is births and marriages and deaths. It is war and pestilence and turmoil. It is progress and development and achievement.

News is magnified by drama, surprise, significance. That is why an underdog team that wins is worth a bigger headline and more space than a favorite that wins; why the assassination of a President is more newsworthy than the President's living another day, with routine comings and goings and meetings and statements. That is why the development of new math was news and millions of children learning multiplication tables was not, why the discovery of the Salk vaccine to control polio was worth the front page and another day of scientific experimentation without results was not.

Who would read a story about a bank that went through another day without being robbed, or about a taxi driver who got home from work without being mugged?

News is both the good and the evil that men do. And if it often seems that newspapers print more of the latter, remember that it was no less an observer of human nature than Shakespeare, who wrote:

The evil that men do lives after them.
The good is oft interred with their bones.

Evil, however, is too often an adjective for change, which today is wracking America. Change—at best orderly but, unfortunately, sometimes violent—is the keystone to the survival of a free society; otherwise there could be no adjustment to new demands and new needs. (The United States survived the Civil War, but it never could have survived with slavery.) A free, civilized society is founded on "good people," "the salt of the earth," a responsible citizenry; most Americans do not break the laws by which they are governed.

But the evil that men do, in the name of change or for whatever reason, can be wished away no more than could the calamitous developments in Europe that inexorably led the nation, even as it sought to ignore those events, into World War II. For a newspaper to ignore or gloss over today's debate or demonstrations about the war in Indochina, or the riots that have torn the nation's cities, would be for it to betray its function to inform. Those who would have a newspaper, ostrichlike, report only what they want to read are as foolish as they are potentially dangerous. Only those who are familiar with both sides of public issues, who are aware of the crimes and excesses of their fellows, can be intelligent citizens; only by learning of the "bad" can men make decisions for "good."

A free society and a controlled press can coexist no more than a dictatorship and a free press. It is that truth which was sanctioned by the First Amendment.

A newspaper occupies a unique position in American society, not only because of its constitutional protection but also because of its very nature: it is a private business that functions like a public institution. To exist, it must make money; but it could not long endure if making money were its only aim. It also must serve the public by reporting the news, what people would rather not know as well as what they want to read.

Thus, demonstrations and dissent are front-page news, not because of a "conspiracy," but because the cleavage of ideas in this country seldom has been greater—or the stakes higher. And riots get page-one display, not because newspapers seek to inflame opinion, but because the urgency for law and order is compelling.

The Characteristics of News

Although journalists cannot easily define news, most agree on its characteristics. Stories that actually get printed or broadcast are likely to possess the following characteristics:

Timeliness

Journalists stress current information—stories that occurred today or yesterday, not several days or weeks ago. Moreover, journalists try to report the stories ahead of their competitors. If a story occurred even one or two days earlier, journalists will look for a new angle or development to emphasize in their leads. If some background information is necessary, they usually keep it to a minimum and place it near the end of the story.

Importance

Reporters also stress important information: stories that affect, involve or interest thousands of readers. A plane crash that kills 180 people is more newsworthy than an automobile accident that kills two. Similarly, an increase in your city's property taxes is more newsworthy than an increase in the license fees for barbers and beauticians because the property tax increase would affect many more residents of your city.

As you evaluate potential news stories, you must consider their importance or magnitude. Ask yourself whether a story is about a *severe* storm, a *damaging* fire, a *deadly* accident, a *major* speech or an *interesting* organization. Also, you should usually consider stories with serious consequences more newsworthy than stories about more frivolous topics.

Prominence

Stories about prominent individuals, such as your mayor and governor, are more newsworthy than stories about people who play a less important role in civic affairs—and who have less power to make decisions that affect your readers' lives. Because he is the nation's leader, almost everything the president does is news. The president may veto a bill, fly to Europe, go swimming or seek a divorce. Because of his prominence, the media would report all four stories.

You may object to journalists' emphasis on celebrities, but the American public seems to have an insatiable appetite for more information about them. People magazine, to take just one example, has been phenomenally successful because it is filled with facts and photographs about the lives of famous people.

Proximity

Journalists consider local stories more newsworthy than stories that occur in distant places. Editors explain that readers are most interested in stories about their own communities because they are more likely to be affected by those stories and because they may know the people, places or issues mentioned in them. However, proximity may be psychological as well as physical. Two individuals who share the same characteristics or interests may want to know more about each other even though they are separated by thousands of miles. An American mother may sympathize with the problems of a mother in a distant country; American college students are likely to be interested in the concerns of college students elsewhere.

Oddities

Deviations from the normal—unexpected or unusual events, conflicts or controversies, drama or change—are more newsworthy than the commonplace. The fact that two people were killed in an automobile accident is more newsworthy than the fact that thousands of other commuters reached their destinations safely. Similarly, the fact that your mayor is squabbling with another city official is more newsworthy than the fact that two other officials are good friends.

Journalists must be alert for the unusual twists in otherwise mundane stories. Thus, most newspapers would not report a minor auto accident; but if journalists noticed that a car involved in the accident was driven by a 6-year-old girl, a new robot or a police chief, the story could become front-page news.

Critics charge that the media's emphasis on the unusual gives their audiences a distorted view of the world—that it does not accurately portray the life of normal people on a typical day in a typical community. Again, editors respond that, because they cannot report everything, they report problems that require the public's attention. Also, routine events are less important to, and therefore of less interest to, the public.

Other Characteristics

Dozens of other factors affect journalists' selection of news. However, most definitions of news acknowledge only a few of those factors. Journalists look for humorous stories—anything that will make their readers laugh. Journalists also tend to report simple events—fires, storms, earthquakes and assassinations—partly because such events are easier to recognize and report. Journalists are less adept at reporting more complicated phenomena: for example, the causes and consequences of crime, poverty, inflation, unemployment and discrimination. Journalists also have difficulty reporting stories that never culminate in obvious events. It would be difficult for anyone, journalists included, to assess the quality of education provided by your city's schools, the quality of life in the city, or the effectiveness of its judicial system.

Systematic studies have also found that journalists are most likely to report whatever stories they receive first. Why? Because they have more time and space to handle stories they receive at the beginning of the day. Other studies have found that many editors rely on the recommendations of the nation's news services as to which stories should be considered most newsworthy. Other editors follow the examples set by larger, more prestigious newspapers.

Definitions of news often vary from one medium to another. Daily newspapers report events that occurred in their communities during the last 24 hours. Weekly news magazines report events of national interest, often in more depth, and try to explain the events' significance. Television reports headline news: a few details about the day's major stories. Former CBS news anchorman Walter Cronkite has observed, "In an entire half hour news broadcast, we speak only as many words as there are on two-thirds of one page of a standard newspaper." Television journalists also look for visual stories that can be shown rather than read to viewers: colorful stories filled with action, drama and excitement.

A newspaper's selection of news is also affected by its size and by the size of the community it serves. A newspaper in a small town may report every local traffic accident; a newspaper in a medium-sized city may report only the accidents that cause an injury; and a newspaper in a large city may have enough space to report only the accidents that result in death. Similarly, newspapers in small cities often publish all wedding announcements and obituaries, whereas newspapers in larger cities are able to publish only those of prominent citizens.

If two stories are of approximately equal importance, newspapers are most likely to report the story that is easiest to obtain—a story that occurs nearby and that can be covered during normal working hours when reporters are easily available. The day of the week is important because newspapers publish more advertisements on Wednesdays, Thursdays and Sundays and consequently have more space for news stories on those three days. (Most newspapers attempt to maintain a specific ratio of advertisements and news, often about 65 percent advertisements to 35 percent news. So on the days they publish more advertisements, the newspapers also publish more news.)

Newspapers are also most likely to publish the types of stories that they have traditionally published. The Daily News in New York City has traditionally placed a greater emphasis on crime, sex, sports and photographs than The New York Times, which appeals to a more sophisticated audience and places a greater emphasis on political, business and foreign news. Similarly, some newspapers diligently investigate the problems in their communities, whereas others hesitate to publish any stories that might offend their readers or their advertisers.

Few publishers admit that they favor any individuals or organizations, yet most newspapers develop certain "dos" and "don'ts" that reporters call "policies" or "sacred cows." Sacred cows reflect the interests of a newspaper's publisher, editors and other executives; unfortunately, some use their power to distort the news. Publishers who are deeply involved in politics sometimes order their staffs to print only positive stories about their favorite candidates and political parties. Other publishers order reporters to suppress unfavorable stories about their friends and their advertisers.

It is difficult for people to detect all of a newspaper's sacred cows unless they actually work for it. Readers can see that a newspaper has published certain stories but seldom know why it did so, or whether in doing so it has deliberately left out any facts. Even in newspaper offices, sacred cows are never written down. Instead, reporters learn about them through more indirect means, often by talking to more experienced colleagues, by observing and listening to their editors and by noticing the changes made in the stories they have written.

Few journalists rebel against their newspapers' policies. Most like their jobs, respect their editors and are preoccupied with the task of gathering the news. Moreover, they want to advance in their profession. So they accept the sacred cows as a part of the job.

Clearly, however, newspaper policies—especially political biases—are becoming less common. A study conducted during the 1930s found that 47 percent of the correspondents in Washington agreed with the statement that it was impossible for them to be objective because of pressures to slant stories to fit their newspapers' policies. When the same study was replicated during the 1960s, only 9.5 percent of the correspondents in Washington agreed that their stories ever were cut, played down or killed for reasons of policy.

The Concept of Objectivity

A previous chapter noted that news stories must be objective, or free of bias. Journalists are expected to gather information and then to report that information as factually as possible. They cannot comment, interpret or evaluate. If an issue is controversial, journalists interview representatives for the opposing sides, then include all the conflicting opinions in a single story. Some of the representatives may be mistaken, and some may lie, but journalists cannot call their statements lies.

Journalists traditionally assumed, perhaps mistakenly, that if they reported all the conflicting opinions, their readers would think about those opinions and be able to determine which ones were most important and truthful. Because that has not always worked, newspapers now publish separate stories that analyze major issues in the news. The stories may be labeled "commentary" or "interpretation," and they critically evaluate the news in an effort to help readers better understand it.

No human can be totally objective. Like everyone else, reporters are influenced by their families, educations, personal interests and religious and political beliefs. Nevertheless, editors believe that objectivity is a worthwhile goal, and that journalists can be taught to be more objective.

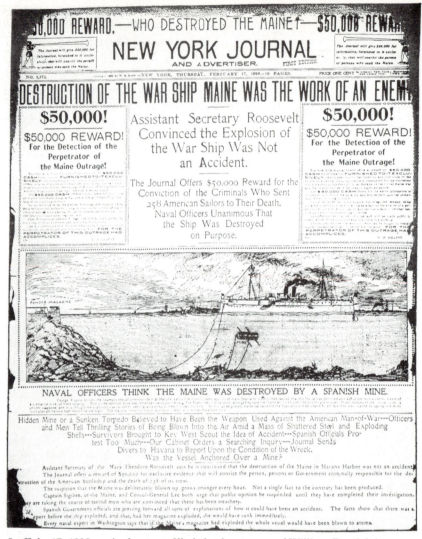

On Feb. 17, 1898, a single story filled the front page of William Randolph Hearst's New York Journal. The story reported that the USS Maine had been destroyed and 260 American seamen killed. Hearst wanted the United States to declare war against Spain and immediately suggested that Spaniards were responsible for the explosion. A Navy Court of Inquiry found that the explosion was caused by something outside the ship—but was unable to determine who was responsible for it.

Also, news stories rarely are the work of a single individual. Normally, an editor assigns a story and a reporter writes it. Several other editors may then evaluate and correct it. Each serves as a check on the others. If one slips and expresses an opinion in a story, another is likely to detect and eliminate that opinion.

The Changing Nature of News

Definitions of news are constantly changing. The newspapers published in Colonial America served rich and well-educated white males. Because the newspapers were expensive, only the rich could afford to buy them. Because the newspapers emphasized serious stories about business, politics and foreign affairs, they interested only the educated elite. Because women could not attend college, could not vote and had little or no money of their own, the newspapers ignored them.

On Sept. 3, 1833, Benjamin Day revolutionized American journalism by publishing the New York Sun for the city's workingmen. To appeal to workingmen, Day had to report the types of stories that would interest them. He began to discuss the problems of workingmen, to emphasize humor and local news, and to publish stories about crime, sex and sports. Day also published one of the most famous hoaxes in journalism history. A series of stories in the New York Sun reported that an astronomer using a powerful new telescope could see plants and amphibious creatures living on the moon. The most sensational story added that the astronomer also saw men and women living on the moon, and that those men and women had wings and were flying about the moon's surface.

Fifty years later, Joseph Pulitzer began to publish the New York World and again changed journalists' definitions of news. To attract more readers, Pulitzer emphasized lively news: sensational stories about crime, sex, disasters, gossip, scandals, oddities, monstrosities and sports. Pulitzer also published front-page illustrations of gruesome murders and more stories about children and animals, two topics that also attracted more readers.

If they were published today, many of the stories that appeared in the New York World would be considered sensational and irresponsible. The American public has become better educated and wants more serious and reliable information. Journalists also are better educated and, more than ever before, are dedicated to the task of informing citizens so they can govern themselves more wisely.

Journalists continued to modify their definitions of news during the 1970s and 1980s. To help their readers lead more comfortable and enjoyable lives, they began to publish more expert advice, consumer news, and what-to-do and how-to-do-it articles. Similarly, newspapers' society and women's pages have been replaced by new sections that appeal to a broader audience. Many of the sections have been renamed: "Outlook," "Emphasis," "People" or "Entertainment." Traditional stories on the women's pages discussed health and beauty hints, engagements, anniversaries, charities, clubs, recipes, fashions, homes and other society news. The new sections contain more stories about current issues and social problems. They discuss the problems of working mothers, the aged and the handicapped. Other stories concern modern families, personalities, medicine, the arts and entertainment.

Details Newspapers Are Reluctant to Publish

Reporters must learn to recognize the types of information that are not considered newsworthy and that newspapers rarely publish. Some of those types of information have been briefly described in Chapters 4, 5 and 6. Newspapers rarely mention routine procedures, such as the fact that a city council met in a city hall and began its meeting with a prayer and the Pledge of Allegiance. Newspapers rarely report what has not happened—the fact that no one was injured or arrested. They delete the obvious and the irrelevant: the fact that police officers were called to the scene of a traffic accident, and the fact that an ambulance was used to transport the injured to a hospital. Newspapers also hesitate to publish stories congratulating anyone. Journalists are in the business of reporting the news, not recognizing or praising people who deserve to be honored. If editors published all the stories submitted to them by publicity seekers, the stories might not only bore their readers but might completely fill their papers, leaving no space for the news.

Generally, newspaper editors omit all material that is obscene or in poor taste, usually on the grounds that their papers are family publications that are read by

A 13-year-old boy in Lakeland, Fla., was electrocuted while climbing a tree. The boy lost his footing, reached out and grabbed a high-voltage electric line. A Lakeland newspaper, *The Ledger*, published this photograph showing the victim's body being lowered from the tree, with his legs visible over the side of the bucket. Another photograph showed the boy's mother weeping and embracing a friend.

The Ledger's executive editor, Louis M. "Skip" Perez defended the photos—but wondered how the mother felt. "Nothing you did made me angry," she told Perez. Nor was she offended by the photos. "I appreciate having them now," she said. "They are the only photos I have of that day. You really couldn't see my son's face."

children as well as adults. Most newspapers also avoid sensationalism, but not sensational stories. Historically, the word "sensationalism" has been used to describe an emphasis on or exaggeration of stories dealing with crime, sex, oddities, disasters and sports. However, some stories are inherently sensational: stories about presidential assassinations, wars and other disasters. The media do not make those stories sensational and should not be accused of sensationalism when they report them. Because of their importance, such stories must be reported.

Newspapers also refuse to publish gruesome photographs, particularly when those photographs lack significance or show the body of someone killed in their own community (someone their readers might know). Newspapers report accidents, but not all their bloody details. Most refuse to identify juvenile delinquents or the victims of rape, even when they have a legal right to do so. Newspapers constantly search for humorous stories, but few make fun of another person's misfortune. When fire damaged the home of a minister in California, one journalist wrote this headline for the story, and an editor promptly ordered him to rewrite it:

Pastor's Study
Goes to Blazes

Journalists evaluating a potentially scandalous or sensational story must weigh several conflicting considerations and may ask themselves the following questions: "How seriously will this story harm the people it mentions?" "How will readers react to the information?" "Is the story newsworthy?" "Does the public need and have a right to this information?"

Newspapers are becoming less squeamish about the use of four-letter words, however. For years, newspapers referred to syphilis and gonorrhea as "social diseases" and used the terms "streetwalker" for "prostitute" and "operation" for "abortion." Editors also changed "damn" to "darn" or deleted it entirely. As society has become more candid, editors have begun to leave previously objectionable words in news stories, provided that they are needed to help readers understand an event or a person's character.

Newspapers rarely mention lotteries because the U.S. Postal Service can refuse to deliver any publication that advertises or promotes them. A lottery is any contest that involves a prize awarded by chance in exchange for a financial consideration, such as the price of a ticket. Because of the postal regulations, newspapers seldom report that a charitable organization will raffle off a television set or that a new car will be given to a ticketholder at a county fair. However, newspapers can mention a lottery after it has become newsworthy: for example, if a local teacher wins $50,000 in some sweepstakes or if a state legislature debates the establishment of a government lottery to raise money for education.

Newspapers also hesitate to mention trade names, usually on the grounds that the publication of trade names is unnecessary and provides free advertising for the products. When two cars collide, reporters rarely mention the fact that one of the cars is a Chevrolet and the other a Buick; their identity is irrelevant to the main point of the story—the accident and its consequences. When the types of products involved are important, reporters often substitute generic terms for trade names. They may report that someone bought a "soft drink" rather than a "Coke," "tissue paper" rather than "Kleenex," a "vacuum bottle" rather than a "Thermos bottle" or a "photocopy" rather than a "Xerox copy."

Manufacturers encourage journalists to use trade names properly. They place advertisements in magazines read by journalists to remind them to capitalize all trade names and to use trade names to describe only the products made by their companies—not similar products made by their competitors. If the public begins to use a trade name to describe every product within a certain category, the manufacturer will lose its exclusive right to use that trade name.

However, if carried to an extreme, the media's policy of avoiding trade names can have unfortunate results. When a small airplane crashed during a snowstorm in a mountainous area of Northern California, a family aboard the plane survived for three days by drinking melted snow and eating boxes of Cracker Jack carried by a child. In reporting the family's ordeal and rescue, some newspapers pointlessly substituted the term "candied popcorn" for Cracker Jack. A copy editor, disgusted because his paper refused to allow him to use the trade name "Jeep" in a story about several hundred people who had formed a caravan of Jeeps for a weekend camping trip (called a "Jeep Jamboree"), substituted the phrase "small truck-type four-wheel-drive vehicles of various manufacture." He did not expect his newspaper to print this circumlocution, but it did. The same newspaper substituted the term "small, beetle-shaped foreign car" for "Volkswagen."

Common sense should dictate whether or not a reporter uses a trade name. If you believe a trade name is pertinent, include it in your story.

These trade names have become generic terms. Their manufacturers lost the right to the words' exclusive use because the public began to use the words to describe every product of their type, not just the manufacturer's product:

aspirin	escalator	raisin bran
brassiere	kerosene	shredded wheat
cola	lanolin	tollhouse cookies
cornflakes	linoleum	trampoline
cube steak	nylon	yo-yo
dry ice		zipper

These words remain trade names. Thus, they should be capitalized and used only while referring to the specific product or brand:

Astroturf	Jacuzzi	Realtor
Baggies	Jeep	Saran Wrap
Band-Aid	Jell-O	Scotch tape
Caterpillar	Jockey (shorts)	Scotchgard
Coca-Cola	Kleenex	Styrofoam
Coke	Kool-Aid	Technicolor
Dacron	Life Savers	Teflon
Dictaphone	Liquid Paper	Vaseline
Ditto	Minute Rice	Velcro
Fiberglas	Muzak	Weight Watchers
Fig Newtons	Ping-Pong	Xerox
Formica	Plexiglas	Ziploc

The Importance of Accuracy

Accuracy in Facts

The information that appears in newspapers is more accurate than most Americans believe. Newspapers are managed by professionals who do their best to report the news as fairly and as accurately as possible, but journalists are not always able to convince the public of that fact. When reporters Bob Woodward and Carl Bernstein of The Washington Post investigated the Watergate scandals, they were required to confirm every important fact with at least two sources before reporting it. This policy is not uncommon among American newspapers. Editors insist on accuracy, and reporters will place a 100-mile telephone call to check a minor detail.

Errors occur, but less frequently than is generally imagined. Unfortunately, some have been stupendous. On Nov. 7, 1918, the president of the United Press Association, Roy Howard, reported that an armistice ending World War I had just been signed in

Journalists anxious to meet their deadlines—and to beat their rivals—sometimes guess at a story's outcome. In 1948, editors at the Chicago Tribune were certain that Thomas Dewey would defeat President Harry Truman. They rushed copies of this early—and mistaken—edition to the city's newsstands.

France. United Press relayed the story to newspapers throughout the United States; schools and factories closed and thousands of people paraded down their cities' main streets. Yet Howard was mistaken. The armistice was not signed until Nov. 11.

In a rush to be first with another story, columnist Jack Anderson announced that Sen. Thomas Eagleton of Missouri had been arrested several times and charged with drunken driving. It was 1972, and Eagleton was the Democratic Party's vice presidential candidate. Anderson had not seen the traffic citations but thought his source was reliable. However, Anderson never was able to verify the story and later apologized for it. At about the same time, other journalists revealed that Eagleton had been treated for a mental illness, and he was forced to resign during the middle of the campaign. All the stories, right and wrong, contributed to the Democrats' landslide defeat by Richard M. Nixon that fall.

The Saturday Evening Post lost $460,000 in a single libel suit because of its unprofessional handling of another story. The story charged that Wally Butts, athletic director at the University of Georgia, had conspired to fix a football game between Georgia and the University of Alabama. Despite the seriousness of the charge, journalists at the Post failed to look at the notes taken by its source (a man who had been placed on probation), to interview a second person who was supposed to have been with the source or to screen films of the game to determine whether the information it received was accurate.

Other factual errors are more embarrassing than costly. A daily newspaper in Iowa was forced to publish a correction after one of its reporters mistakenly quoted a dead sheriff. The reporter had called the sheriff's office to obtain some information about an accident and assumed that the man who answered the telephone was the sheriff. He was the sheriff, but a new one; his predecessor had died a few weeks earlier. In writing a story about the accident, the reporter—who failed to ask the sheriff his name—attributed all the information to his dead predecessor.

Most factual errors, like those just described, are caused by carelessness. After finishing a news story, reporters must learn to recheck their notes to be certain that the story is accurate. If reporters lack some information, they should consult their source again. If the source is unavailable, or is unable to provide the information, reporters may have to delete portions of their story or, in extreme cases, kill the entire story. Reporters should never guess or make any assumptions about the facts; they are too likely to make an error.

Reporters must also be certain that they understand a topic before they begin to write about it. Too often, when asked about a fuzzy sentence or paragraph, beginners respond, "I really didn't understand that myself." If you do not understand a topic, never try to write about it. Instead, go back to your source and ask for a better explanation. If that source is unable to help, find another.

To emphasize the need for accuracy, journalism teachers who find a factual error in a story usually lower its grade. At many schools, stories containing factual errors receive an automatic F.

Accuracy in Names

Newspapers are particularly careful in their handling of names. Spelling errors damage the papers' reputations and infuriate their readers, particularly when the misspelled names appear in wedding announcements and other stories that are likely to be clipped and saved. Consequently, many newspapers require their reporters to verify the spelling of every name that appears in local news stories by consulting a second source, usually a telephone book or city directory.

Most errors occur because reporters fail to consult a second source and to check their stories' internal consistency:

> Raymond Foote, editor of the newspaper, said minority groups often want publicity but do not know how to obtain it. Foot said he tries to be fair but does not have enough space to publicize the activities of every group in his community.

> Of the 10 men and women who were interviewed, five favored the proposal, three opposed it and three said they had not reached any decision.

Other errors arise because of reporters' carelessness. A source may say his name is "Karl" and, mistakenly, reporters may assume his name is spelled with a "C" rather than with a "K." Dozens of other common American names have two or more spellings, including, for example: Ann (Anne), Cathy (Cathie, Kathy), Fredric (Fredrick, Frederic or Frederick), Gail (Gayle), John (Jon), Linda (Lynda) and Susie (Suzy).

Obstacles to Accuracy

Some errors may be inevitable. Because of the need to meet strict deadlines, reporters must work quickly and often lack the time needed to perfect their stories. Reporters are also vulnerable to misinformation. They obtain much of their information from other people, yet some of those people may be mistaken, and reporters may unknowingly report their misstatements. If a prominent person discusses a matter of public importance, that discussion is news and must be reported, regardless of any doubts that journalists might have about the comments' validity. This definition of news required journalists to report President Lyndon Johnson's claims of victory in Vietnam and

President Richard Nixon's claims of innocence in Watergate. Other news stories written by journalists questioned the accuracy, and even the truthfulness, of both presidents, but those stories were not read by everyone and lacked the impact of the presidential speech or proclamation.

Historians can often be more accurate than journalists because they see more of a story before they begin work. Journalists deal with isolated fragments; they obtain stories piece by piece and cannot always predict their outcome or ultimate significance. For example, journalists failed to recognize immediately the significance of the break-in at the Democratic Party's headquarters in Washington in 1972. At the time, no one knew the break-in would lead to the resignation of President Nixon and the imprisonment of his top aides. Historians are aware of the consequences of that break-in from the outset of their work.

Other errors arise when stories are set in type. The word "house" may be typed "mouse"; "friend" may become "fiend"; and typesetters occasionally leave the "r" out of "shirt." One popular tale concerns a retired Army colonel who stormed into a newspaper office because a news story had accidentally called him "battle-scared" instead of "battle-scarred." The newspaper's editor apologized and published a correction—which called the colonel "bottle-scarred." Whole lines of type from different stories can become mixed together. One sentence about a wine festival in California appeared in a story about a new supermarket and suggested that the supermarket's theme would be "wine, women and song." Today, fortunately, computers that give journalists more control over the typesetting function in newspaper offices eliminate many errors.

Journalists might eliminate even more errors by giving the people named in news stories an opportunity to read and correct those stories before they are published. The idea has been discussed most seriously by science writers and by other journalists who deal with complex issues and have more time to write in-depth articles. However, most editors prohibit the practice; they fear that it would consume too much time and that people shown the stories would argue about matters of judgment and try to change all the statements they disagree with, not just factual errors.

Some newspapers give copies of their stories to sources *after* the stories have been published, then ask the sources to evaluate their accuracy. Researchers who have analyzed the sources' corrections have found that sources believe about half the stories contain an error. However, many of the perceived errors are judgmental rather than factual. Sources may interpret some facts differently from reporters or want to include, emphasize or de-emphasize different facts. Sources also may complain that they have been misquoted or that a headline distorts a story. Only about one-third of the errors marked by sources are typographical or factual errors. Most involve misspelled names and inaccurate times, dates, numbers, addresses, locations and titles.

The Need to Be Fair

News stories must be balanced and fair as well as accurate. Reporters who write about a controversial issue have an obligation to present every significant viewpoint fully and fairly, and they must exercise particular care when their stories might harm another person's reputation. A reckless or irresponsible charge might destroy an innocent person's reputation, marriage or career.

If a story contains information critical of an individual, that person should be given an opportunity to respond. It is not enough to call the victim after a story has been published and to report his or her response in a later story. Because not everyone who read the original criticism will see the second story, the victim's rebuttal should always be included in the original story. Typically, The New York Times has adopted a policy which requires that: ". . . a person mentioned derogatorily or critically in a story should immediately be given a chance to respond. If the person is unreachable, consideration should be given to holding the story over. If holding it over is deemed inadvisable, mention should be made in the story that efforts to reach the person were unavailing, and the efforts should be renewed the next day . . . this is a cardinal, unbreakable rule."

A typical story might report:

> The Better Business Bureau today warned consumers about "free inspections" offered to homeowners by Doss Furnace Repair, Inc.
>
> An employee at the bureau said it has received more than 200 complaints from homeowners during the past month. Some homeowners said they received bills for more than $300 after the company's representatives offered to inspect their furnaces for free.
>
> A vice president at the company said some customers apparently failed to read and understand its contracts. He said customers are always told that the inspections are free, but that they will be charged for necessary repairs, labor and replacement parts.

The following examples also present conflicting viewpoints. Notice how the second example integrates those viewpoints. Instead of presenting all the arguments voiced by one source, and then all the opposing arguments voiced by another source, the second example presents the sources' conflicting viewpoints about the first issue, then about the second issue and then about the third issue. As a consequence, readers immediately receive both points of view. Even the readers who fail to look at the entire story are likely to receive both viewpoints about a particular issue:

> Former officer Janet Wagner said she was fired because she is a woman and because the city's new police chief believes that men are stronger and more effective than women.
>
> However, Police Chief Myron Hanson said he fired Wagner because she "was arrogant, lazy and rude."

> After a special hearing that lasted 3½ hours Monday night, the City Council voted 6 to 1 to retain City Manager Ralph Kassarian.
>
> About 300 spectators who filled the council's meeting room applauded the decision and gave Kassarian a standing ovation.
>
> Councilman Albert O'Keefe, who had demanded the hearing, cast the only vote against Kassarian.
>
> During the hearing, O'Keefe criticized Kassarian's management techniques and "failure to control the work routine of city employees." O'Keefe said, "I've observed city employees sleeping in the back of a truck and quitting work during the middle of the afternoon and then just waiting around to punch out."
>
> Kassarian responded that the city employs fewer people than when he was hired three years ago, and that, "They get more work done now than back then, too.
>
> "My management philosophy is to trust my employees," Kassarian added. "Most are doing a good job and deserve that trust, especially when you consider the city's low pay and limited resources."
>
> O'Keefe also charged that Kassarian awarded a construction contract to a company that is not licensed to work in the state, and that a recreation building it erected in Midtown Park has a leaky roof and inadequate insulation.
>
> "That's just not right," Kassarian replied. "The contract was awarded at least 4 years ago, and I was working in another city then. I agree it's a terrible building, and we haven't been very successful in getting it repaired, but I didn't have anything to do with the original contract."
>
> O'Keefe later complained that Kassarian used cash instead of purchasing orders to pay for the city's supplies. Kassarian responded that it is faster and cheaper to pay cash, especially for purchases under $100.
>
> Former council member Margaret Smith supported Kassarian. "Many positive things have been done in this city because of Ralph Kassarian," she said. "I see no factual reasons for his dismissal. You've just got one councilman who doesn't like him."
>
> Several other citizens also praised Kassarian. "He's available, and he'll listen to you," said Thomas R. Luge of 2757 Edgewater Drive. Patti Mackown of 1047 Huron Ave. agreed, adding, "I was having trouble getting the street in front of my house repaired, and he had it taken care of the next day."

If the subject of a negative story is unavailable or refuses to respond, that fact should also be mentioned. A brief sentence might explain:

> Attempts to reach a company employee were unsuccessful.
> OR: A vice president at the company declined to comment about the charges.
> OR: Company officials failed to return eight phone calls made by reporters.

Newspapers are most likely to publish the criticisms voiced by normally reliable sources or that involve public figures or issues of public interest. Editors hesitate to report criticisms voiced by anonymous sources.

The Use of Reference Materials

No one expects reporters to be well-informed about every topic they might be asked to write about, but editors do expect them to know how to obtain more information about the topics. Journalists use hundreds of different reference books, and Exercise 2 in this chapter requires the use of several of the most important of those books. Reference books provide needed definitions, identify the people involved in news stories, explain unfamiliar concepts, supply additional background information and help verify the accuracy of facts that other people give journalists.

The most important reference books include dictionaries (general, medical and legal); telephone, city and government directories; postal guides, which list the correct spellings of U.S. cities; stylebooks; encyclopedias (general and biographical); atlases; almanacs; and maps.

By using just one of these books, a city directory, reporters can learn an adult's address, telephone number and occupation; spouse's name and occupation; and whether that adult is widowed or divorced, has lived at the present address for more than a year, and rents or owns the home. Using the same book, reporters can also learn the names of that person's neighbors and the same items of information about each of them. If someone is involved in a serious accident, reporters may consult a city directory to learn whether the person is prominent enough to merit a major news story. If a police radio reports a fire at the person's home, reporters can use a city directory to learn his or her neighbors' names and telephone numbers. Before any fire trucks reach the home, reporters can call one of the neighbors and ask for a description of the fire. If it is serious, they will rush to the scene with a photographer.

Most newspapers also maintain their own libraries, and the people working in them clip and file every story the papers publish. In the past, reporters called the libraries "morgues" because the libraries contain dead stories. Reporters can use these libraries to obtain background information, to verify facts and spellings and to learn whether or not their newspapers have already published stories about topics mentioned in the news. Many reporters also maintain their own files, clipping and saving all the stories they write. These personal files are useful when reporters are asked to write a second or third story about the same topic.

Suggested Readings

Articles

Breed, Warren. "Social Control in the News Room." *Social Forces*, vol. 33 (May 1955), 326–35. (Reprinted in *Mass Communications*, ed. by Wilbur Schramm. Urbana: University of Illinois Press, 1960.)
Gieber, Walter. "Across the Desk: A Study of 15 Telegraph Editors," *Journalism Quarterly*, 33 (1956), 423–32.

Lang, Kurt, and Gladys Engel Lang. "The Unique Perspective of Television and Its Effect: A Pilot Study." In *The Process and Effects of Mass Communication*. Rev. ed., ed. by Wilbur Schramm and Donald F. Roberts. Urbana: University of Illinois Press, 1971.

White, David. "The 'Gate Keeper': A Case Study in the Selection of News." *Journalism Quarterly*, 27 (1950), 383–90. (Reprinted in *People, Society, and Mass Communications*, ed. by Lewis A. Dexter and David M. White. New York: The Free Press, 1964.)

Books

Abel, Eli, ed. *What's News: The Media in American Society*. San Francisco: Institute for Contemporary Studies, 1981.

Dunn, Delmer D. *Public Officials and the Press*. Reading, Mass.: Addison-Wesley Publishing Company, 1969. (See Chapter 3, "What Is 'News'?")

Fishman, Mark. *Manufacturing the News*. Austin, Texas: University of Texas Press, 1980.

Gans, Herbert J. *Deciding What's News*. New York: Random House, 1980.

Modern Media Institute. *Making Sense of the News*. St. Petersburg, Fla.: Poynter Institute, 1983.

Monaco, James. *Celebrity*. New York: Delta, 1978.

Roshco, Bernard. *Newsmaking*. Chicago: The University of Chicago Press, 1975.

Schiller, Dan. *Objectivity and the News: The Public and the Rise of Commercial Journalism*. Philadelphia: University of Pennsylvania Press, 1981.

Schudson, Michael. *Discovering the News: A Social History of American Newspapers*. New York: Basic Books, Inc., 1981.

Tuchman, Gaye. *Making News: A Study in the Construction of Reality*. New York: The Free Press, 1980.

Winberg, Steve. *Trade Secrets of Washington Journalists*. Washington, D.C.: Acropolis Books, 1981.

EXERCISE 1
Selecting and Reporting the News

DISCUSSION QUESTIONS

1. Assume that a local politician today announced her candidacy for mayor. Which—if any—of these facts about her personal life would you include in a story about her candidacy:
   A. She is a millionaire.
   B. She is 57 years old.
   C. She is the mother of four children.
   D. She is 5 feet, 1 inch tall, has gray hair and weighs 180 pounds.
   E. Her first husband died, and she divorced her second.
   F. Her first husband committed suicide two years after their marriage.
   G. After her husband's death, she transformed a small restaurant they established into one of the largest and finest in the city.
   H. She now lives with a bank executive.
   I. The bank executive is 26 years old.
   J. One of her sons is a high-school teacher. Two help her in the restaurant. The fourth is in prison, convicted of rape.

2. Normally, your newspaper reports every birth in the city. As editor, would you include the births to unwed mothers?

3. As editor of your local daily, you normally avoid cheesecake: pictures of scantily-clad young women. But a student on a local campus won the Miss America preliminaries in your state and has flown to Atlantic City for the national finals. During the first day of competition there, your paper received only one photograph, and it shows her and two other contestants in bikinis at the beach. As editor, would you publish it? Why?

4. Assume that your mayor has often criticized the city's welfare system and the fact that some of the people it supports are able-bodied adults, without children. If you learned that the mayor's 27-year-old son (who does not live at home) was broke because of a business failure and applying for welfare, would you publish the story?

5. Assume that a member of your city council declared her candidacy for mayor. As part of her campaign, she spent one day "working" as a police officer: dressed in a uniform and walking a downtown beat. It is an obvious campaign stunt, designed to attract favorable publicity. But it is a local story, and unusual. As editor, would you cover it?

6. Imagine that a member of your city council, a Democrat, offered to give you information proving that store personnel had caught your mayor, a Republican, shoplifting. The store's owner declined to prosecute. Morever, the Democrat insists that you keep his identity a secret: that you never identify your source. The Democrat is a potential candidate for mayor—an obvious rival. Yet the information is genuine. How would you respond?

7. Assume that three local high-school students, each 15 years old, have been charged with arson; they started a fire that caused $50,000 in damage at their school, closing it for a day:
   A. If you obtained the students' names, and it was legal to do so, would you identify them in your story?

B. Before publishing the story, would you call and warn (or interview) the students or their parents?

8. Reporters are forced to make difficult decisions about what elements of a story are most newsworthy. Assume that, earlier today, two men robbed a local restaurant and shot a customer. During a high-speed chase through the city, a squad car skidded out of control and struck a pedestrian, a 17-year-old high-school student. Both the customer and the pedestrian have been hospitalized in serious condition.

    Which element would you emphasize in your lead: the customer shot by two robbers, or the pedestrian struck by police?

9. Should newspapers devote more space to worthwhile causes and organizations in their communities, recognizing and promoting their good work?

10. Do you agree with critics who say the media are too sensational? Why?

11. Assume that you edited your local daily and received the photographs reprinted in this chapter: the photographs showing an attempt to assassinate President Reagan and the 13-year-old boy's body being lowered from a tree.
    A. Would you publish the photographs on your newspaper's front page?
    B. How would you respond to the readers who accused you of sensationalism?

12. If a member of the American Nazi Party spoke in your community and criticized blacks, Jews or immigrants, would you report the story? How could you justify its publication or suppression?

13. Does the person who owns a daily newspaper possess the right to protect his or her friends and advertisers—or to give only favorable publicity to his or her favorite organizations? Why?

14. How would you respond if an editor told you to do something you consider unethical or irresponsible; for example, to interview a grieving mother about her child's death?

EXERCISE 2
Selecting and Reporting the News

REFERENCE MATERIALS

INSTRUCTIONS: Use the reference books listed below (books that reporters use most frequently) to find the answers to the questions that follow. If the books are not available in your classroom or department library, look for them in the main library on your campus.

1. *Almanac of American Politics*
2. *Ayer Directory of Publications*
3. *Bartlett's Familiar Quotations*
4. *Black's Law Dictionary*
5. *Broadcasting Yearbook*
6. *Congressional Staff Directory*
7. *Contemporary Authors*
8. *County and City Data Book*
9. *Editor and Publisher Yearbook*
10. *Encyclopedia of Associations*
11. *Encyclopedia of World History*
12. *Guinness Book of World Records*
13. *International Year Book and Statesmen's Who's Who?*
14. *The Municipal Year Book*
15. *National ZIP Code Directory*
16. *Official Congressional Directory*
17. *Oxford Dictionary of Quotations*
18. *Roget's International Thesaurus*
19. *Statistical Abstracts of the United States*
20. *The Statesman's Year-Book*
21. *Stedman's Medical Dictionary*
22. *United States Government Manual*
23. *Webster's Biographical Dictionary*
24. *Webster's Dictionary of Synonyms*
25. *Who's Who in America*
26. *Writer's Market*
27. Your state's most recent blue book, almanac and yearbook.
28. Also: an almanac, dictionary, atlas, encyclopedia, telephone book and city directory.

Section I: Community Data

1. What are the major sections in a city directory?

2. Who is the superintendent of your local school system?

3. Who are the superintendent's nearest neighbors? What are their names, addresses, telephone numbers and occupations?

4. Who in your community has a telephone number ending in the numerals 2641 or 7828?

5. What is the name of your city's police chief, and what is the name of the chief's spouse?

6. How many people are employed by your city's police and fire departments?

7. What is your city's annual budget? List the amounts received by the three departments which receive the largest shares of that budget.

8. What is the city's property tax rate, and how much would the owner of a house assessed at $120,000 pay each year?

9. What is the average temperature in your community? How many inches of rainfall does it receive each year? What is its largest industry?

10. What does the small "h" mean when it appears before an address in a city directory, and what does the asterisk (*) indicate when it appears after house numbers listed in the green pages?

Section II: State and Federal Data

1. Name the U.S. vice presidents who have become presidents.

2. What is the average income of people living in your state, and how does their income compare to the national average?

3. Who was the first governor of your state, and in what years did he or she serve?

4. Compare the number of votes cast for Richard Nixon in the 1972 presidential election with the number cast for Ronald Reagan in 1980—both in your state and nationally.

5. Check the spelling of these U.S. cities:
   A. Fellsberg, Kan.
   B. Massena, N.Y.
   C. Tibby, Ala.

6. Find the addresses and telephone numbers of the Federal Communications Commission and Selective Service System in Washington, D.C.

7. What are the three smallest states, by population, and who are their U.S. senators?

8. Name the press secretaries for your state's U.S. senators. Also find their telephone numbers.

9. What are the three largest cities in Maine?

10. List the governors of these states, their party affiliation and telephone numbers:
    A. Alaska
    B. Colorado
    C. Indiana

Section III: Miscellaneous Data

1. Assume that a news story from Europe reported that a ship is 214 meters long. What is its length in feet?

2. How many students are enrolled in Gallaudet College? Where is the college, and who operates it? Also, what is unusual about it?

3. How many students are enrolled in colleges and universities in the United States, and how does that figure compare to the figures in 1940, 1960 and 1980?

4. How severe must a storm become before it can be called a blizzard? What is the difference between a blizzard and a severe blizzard?

5. Explain the difference between a felony and a misdemeanor.

6. List all the media properties owned by the Hearst chain.

7. List all the radio and television stations that you might write to if you wanted to work for a station in the Albuquerque area. Also name the stations' owners and general managers.

8. What are the names of the daily newspapers in Fresno, Calif.; Evansville, Ind.; and Jackson, Miss.? Also list their owners, circulations and the names of their managing editors—the people you might write to if you wanted to apply for a job on their staff.

9. List the capitals and leaders in these countries. Also list their leaders' titles.
   A. Bulgaria
   B. Cyprus
   C. Ghana

10. Define these legal and medical terms:
    A. amicus curiae
    B. dysplasia
    C. naupathia
    D. nolo contendere
    E. teniacide

11. Compare the fuel economy of last year's models: which were the three best, and which were the three worst?

12. Find the addresses and telephone numbers of these companies and associations' national headquarters:
    A. General Electric Co.
    B. N.A.B.
    C. N.A.M.
    D. Xerox Corp.

13. Describe the types of free-lance articles sought by these magazines—and their payments for the articles:
    A. Good Housekeeping
    B. National Geographic
    C. Sports Illustrated

14. In what parts of the world are these places located?
    A. Great Slave Lake
    B. Orkney Island
    C. Sakkara

15. Identify the people who said:
    A. "As always, victory finds a hundred fathers but defeat is an orphan."
    B. "Those who make peaceful revolution impossible will make violent revolution inevitable."
    C. "The sole end for which mankind are warranted, individually or collectively, in interfering with the liberty of action of any of their number is self-protection."

EXERCISE 3
Selecting and Reporting the News

REPORTING CONTROVERSIAL STORIES
(QUOTING OPPOSING VIEWPOINTS)

INSTRUCTIONS: Write complete news stories about the following controversies. As you write the stories, present both sides of each controversy as fully and as fairly as possible. Also, try to integrate those conflicting viewpoints. Instead of reporting all the opinions voiced by the first source, and then all the conflicting opinions voiced by the second source, try—when appropriate—to report both opinions about the story's most important issue, and then both opinions about the second, third and fourth issues.

Story 1: Divorce Decree

FACTS: Marlene Ostreicher is a county judge. At 9 o'clock this morning she announced her decision in a divorce case involving Marilyn R. and Bruce C. Aparico. Bruce Aparico, a medical doctor, sued his wife, Marilyn, for divorce. In a countersuit, Mrs. Aparico sued her husband for a share of all his future earnings on the grounds that she had worked and sacrificed to help put him through medical school. In her decision today, Judge Ostreicher ruled: "Because the husband's degree was earned to a large extent by the contributions of the wife, the wife is entitled to an equitable distribution of an interest in the fruits of the husband's medical career. Therefore, I am awarding her 25 percent of her former husband's future income, to continue for the remainder of their lives, or until she remarries."

ONE SIDE: Roger Swidell was the attorney representing Mrs. Aparico. After the judge's decision was announced, Swidell said: "It's only fair. She contributed financially and domestically to the creation of an asset, and she deserves her fair share of that asset. I think it is an extremely enlightened decision." Mrs. Aparico herself added: "The ruling was fair, but I would have preferred staying married. You both struggle. You sacrifice, living with a student and counting every penny. You give the best years of yourself. Then you're not good enough any more. You're 30 years old, with two kids and no career. The only reason I did this was to secure my children's future; I have to think about them. I'm sorry that everything had to turn out this way. But I was attending college myself when we got married, studying to be a teacher. To help my husband get his medical degree, I dropped out and started working odd jobs and raised our children for six years while he was finishing his undergraduate work and then getting his medical degree. I always earned at least $10,000 a year, and sometimes more, so I contributed more than $60,000 or $70,000, plus all my time to support and nurture our family and help pay his school expenses."

THE OTHER SIDE: James Carlisle, an attorney representing Dr. Aparico, said: "It's the first time in the history of this state that a judge has awarded one spouse a portion of the other's future income in a divorce case such as this one. The ruling is unjust and oppressive. It puts my client in a position of involuntary servitude. Certainly we acknowledge that Mrs. Aparico is possibly entitled to something, but not this kind of money, and we intend to appeal." Dr. Aparico added: "The judge didn't understand, she just didn't understand the facts. She couldn't have considered the evidence. It's true we got married in college and my wife worked, but most of my expenses were paid by my parents and by student loans. On the day I graduated, I owed almost $25,000 in loans, and I still haven't started to pay them back. My parents gave me another $20,000 or $25,000. That's how I got through medical school, not by depending on my former wife."

Story 2: Fluoridation Debate

FACTS: Voters in your city will go to the polls next Tuesday to vote on the issue of fluoridating your city's water supply. It will be a straw ballot, not legally binding, but the City Council will consider the results and will officially vote on the issue at its next meeting, scheduled for the Monday after the election. Mayor Paula Novarro says that she and the council will vote according to the public's wishes as expressed by the outcome of the straw ballot. In an interview today, she said: "This issue has sparked more attention and debate than anything to come about in a long time. I have maintained neutrality on this issue and will vote according to what the people want, and the other council members have told me they intend to do the same." Fluoride is a chemical added to many toothpastes and to the water supply in many areas to help prevent tooth decay. Fluoridating the city's water has been an issue debated in three public hearings since the first of the year. The city has not fluoridated its water in the past. However, a new state program, called the State Fluoridation Project, is being sponsored by the Department of Dental Health. The terms of the program provide that the state will install in a city's water system the equipment needed to distribute fluoride. The state will also supply the city with all the fluoride it needs for two years. At the end of that period, the city would have to pick up the expense of continuing to fluoridate its water and pass those expenses on to city water users.

ONE SIDE: Randall Batchelder, a dentist, is the leading proponent of the project and heads an organization called Citizens for Fluoridation. In an interview earlier today, Batchelder said: "Thousands of studies have been conducted which show that fluoridating water makes teeth more resistant to tooth decay, especially in children. There is also evidence that it aids in the prevention of osteoporosis, which is a bone disease found in the elderly. We've been talking about the issue and debating the issue in this city for 20 years, but nothing's been done, and it's our children who suffer. They need this protection. Certainly the cost isn't the issue. Fluoridating the city's water would cost an average customer about 20 cents a year. Our opponents argue that high dosages of fluoride are toxic, but the doses to be put in the city's water supply are too low to cause any harm. The city's water supply has a natural fluoride content of three-tenths part per million. Under the proposed program, this content would be raised to eight-tenths part per million. The acute toxic dosage for fluoride is five grams, which means an individual would have to drink at one time 2,500 quarts of water to be poisoned."

THE OTHER SIDE: Margaret Rossi, the leading opponent of fluoridation, said in an interview today: "The type of fluoridation, sodium fluoride, proposed in the state program is not natural. It's a byproduct of aluminum and steel and is second only to arsenic in toxicity. It's an ingredient found in rat poisons, and it's dangerous to humans. But I want to be more organized about this. Let me say that I'm opposed to fluoridating our city's water for three reasons. One, it's accumulative, which means though it's taken in small dosages, those dosages accumulate in the body. Second, it's artificial and not naturally occurring. And third, there is no way to regulate how much someone is going to take into their body. If people want extra fluoride, they can take it by drops or tablets, or they can go have their dentist paint it on their teeth. But if they put it into the water, no one will have a choice whether they take it or not. We'll all be exposed to it. Some of my friends also worry about its being stored in the city. If the city starts putting fluoride into our water, it'll have to keep large tanks of fluoride somewhere in the city, and if there's an accident, or the tanks begin leaking, we'll have a serious situation on our hands."

Story 3: Police Response Time

FACTS: Two armed gunmen robbed the Jewelry Shoppe at 1118 Main Street at about noon yesterday. They escaped with about $1,200 in cash and with jewelry valued at about $35,000 to $40,000. The two gunmen, described as being in their mid-20s, wore business suits when they entered the store and said they wanted to look at a watch, then drew their handguns and forced the owner, Thomas Hoequist, to empty several cash registers and to open several display cases containing watches, rings, pearl earrings and necklaces, which they scooped up. "They knew what they wanted," Hoequist said. "They took only the best." Two clerks and five customers in the store at the time were made to lie face down on the floor.

ONE SIDE: Hoequist told reporters covering the robbery: "I'm very upset, very upset. The first police car didn't arrive until 10 minutes after I pushed a silent alarm button we have in the store, and it's connected directly to the police station. I pushed it as soon as I saw their guns, but the men escaped before the police arrived. We've had some false alarms in the past. I've pushed the button by mistake once or twice myself, and so have the employees. Then two or three police cars would come screeching into our parking lot in a minute or two. The officers would all jump out of their cars holding shotguns and revolvers. Yesterday, the only guns I saw were the ones pointed at me."

THE OTHER SIDE: Police Chief Martin Guidema, interviewed in his office late yesterday, said: "Our records show that 9 minutes elapsed before the first police car arrived on the scene, but all the units in that district were extremely busy on other calls. We aren't required to respond to calls within a specified length of time, and sometimes we can't. It's not uncommon for us to reach the scene of a complaint within 2 or 3 minutes, and that's what we try to do when it's a real emergency. That didn't happen yesterday because there was a four-minute delay before the first patrol car was dispatched to the store because all the cars in the district were extremely busy. It took another 5 minutes for the car to get there because it was miles away in another district at the time. We had a problem because, at the same time the call was received, several patrol cars were chasing a man driving a stolen car. Another car had just arrived at Midtown Park, where a young woman who had been severely beaten had just been found. It was a long dispatch time, but there are times when we are extremely busy. Every day, our heaviest volume of calls comes between 11 a.m. and midafternoon. It really comes down to a problem of money. Without more money, we can't put more cars on the road, but people say their taxes already are too high. It really wasn't a big factor here, but you've also got to consider that we've had 10 false alarms from this store in the last year. After a while, it's like crying wolf; you just don't believe them anymore. It makes you more reluctant to move an officer from where he's really needed."

Story 4: School Attendance Incentive Program

Marcia Pagozalski, superintendent of schools in your city, has adopted a unique but controversial pilot program. Last year, the city's school district lost $1,132,000 in state funds because it had an overall 6.4 percent absenteeism rate, compared to a statewide average of 5.3%. To try to solve the problem, Pagozalski persuaded the members of the school board to set up a $25,000 fund to pay students at Roosevelt High School the equivalent of 25 cents a day—a maximum of $5 a month. Last fall, students in the school began getting a coupon worth 25 cents for every day of attendance. Students can exchange their tokens in the school's student bookstore for school supplies such as notebooks and pencils. Since then, the absentee rate at the 1,410-student school has averaged about 13.7%, compared to 15.2% for the same period last year, when it had the worst attendance in the city.

ONE SIDE: In an interview in her office today, Supt. Pagozalski said: "We're trying this program out in one high school where our worst truancy problems exist. Then if it works, we may expand it to other schools. Under this program, a student can earn the equivalent of $5 a month just for being there—for attending school and compiling a perfect attendance record. They are credited with the equivalent of 25 cents for every day they make it to school and to all their classes on time. They don't actually get any cash. They get coupons they can use in the school store. We mark up the prices of goods sold in the store about 50%, so it really costs us a lot less than the students receive. So far as I know, the idea has been tried in only two or three other school districts, including one in San Diego, and I just thought we might try it here. We've really got nothing to lose. Some students just don't see any other reason to attend school. My responsibility is to give teachers an opportunity to teach the students, and getting them to attend class is a necessary first step. We already can see the results. Attendance is up, and inquiries have been pouring in from other school districts from all over the state and from news organizations as far away as England and Japan. There's a tremendous curiosity about it. It sort of shocks some parents to pay children to go to school, but nothing else has worked. If this works, it could save us thousands of dollars a year in lost state aid, and certainly the students are better off being in school."

THE OTHER SIDE: Stephen I. Wong is chairman of the city's School Advisory Committee, which is composed of one parent representative from each school in the city. Wong is opposed to the program. Today he said: "The program gambles with taxpayers' money. The 25 cents they give students comes out of our tax money. If attendance improves by 25 percent or more over a full year, we'll recover the money in increased state aid. But if the attendance figure remains low, we'll lose money. So we're gambling, and that just doesn't seem right. It's also materialistic and amounts to bribery. We shouldn't have to pay our children to do something as basic as going to school because then they expect to get paid for everything. Already, we've got some students in that high school complaining they aren't being paid enough, and students in other schools are demanding that they get paid, too. These kids are winding up with some very unrealistic ideas about how the world works and about what education is all about. Besides, the whole thing is cosmetic. It doesn't solve our real problems. The long-term remedies for truancy lie in more fundamental changes. I'll admit attendance is up so far this year, but not very much, and we don't know the real reason. It could be the money, or it could be something totally different. You also have to recognize that, once these students get to high school, they don't have to do well. They can flunk all their classes and still get paid. Some of these students also could be disruptive, so it may be better for other students if they don't come to school. It's a hell of a mess."

EXERCISE 4
Selecting and Reporting the News

REPORTING CONTROVERSIAL STORIES
(QUOTING OPPOSING VIEWPOINTS)

INSTRUCTIONS: Write complete news stories about the following controversies. As you write the stories, present both sides of each controversy as fully and as fairly as possible. Also, try to integrate those conflicting viewpoints. Instead of reporting all the opinions voiced by the first source, and then all the conflicting opinions voiced by the second source, try—when appropriate—to report both opinions about the story's most important issue, and then both opinions about the second, third and fourth issues.

Story 1: Banning Handguns

FACTS: In a close vote at a City Council meeting in your community last night, the council members voted 4 to 3 to ban the sale and possession of handguns, except by law enforcement officers and by those persons holding a permit issued by the chief of police. The law goes into effect on Jan. 1 of next year, and those persons now possessing handguns will, according to the law, have to dispose of them by that time. First-time offenders of the law will face a fine of $50 to $500. A second offense carries maximum penalties of up to six months in jail or a fine of up to $500, or both.

ONE SIDE: Councilman Luis Ramirez, who spoke and voted in favor of the law, said during last night's meeting: "There's no question, the law is valid and doesn't infringe on an individual's constitutional rights. We recognize the deep-seated convictions of a number of persons that they should be permitted to possess handguns for the purpose of protecting themselves and their families and property. But in this case the public interest outweighs the claim of personal interests. We're adopting this law for the overall good of the entire city, to help protect all its citizens from the careless and lawless use of handguns. I'm sure that hundreds of other cities are going to follow our example and consider similar measures. If they do, a lot of lives could be saved. There's no sense to the current slaughter. People can't use handguns to hunt with. Their only purpose is to shoot people. They're used mostly by criminals and, in this city alone, we have 8 or 10 people killed by guns every year and many more seriously injured. There also are hundreds and hundreds of robberies committed with handguns. This law will help put a stop to that. If people want to hunt, they can still buy a rifle or shotgun, and they can use a rifle or shotgun to protect themselves in their homes if they want. But it's harder for a criminal to conceal a weapon that large when he goes into a grocery store or restaurant with the intention of robbing it."

THE OTHER SIDE: Margaret Ungarient, an attorney representing the citizens opposed to the ban, said at the meeting: "We plan to appeal. The law infringes on citizens' constitutional right to keep and bear arms. It's also a matter of self-defense. Criminals do use some handguns in committing crimes. But that doesn't mean the solution is to take away everyone's gun. Law-abiding citizens would comply with this law, but criminals never would. So the criminals would be the only ones with guns, and everyone else would be at their mercy. The council has, in effect, ruled in favor of a minority element that has for a long time been trying to deny the rights of other individuals. We won't rest until this gets reversed in a court of law. If we have to, we'll take this all the way to the Supreme Court."

Story 2: Lie Detector Tests

FACTS: Memorial Hospital has begun to give its employees lie detector tests to prevent thefts. In the past, the hospital has been bothered by thefts of everything from food to bedsheets to drugs to expensive medical equipment. Estimates by hospital officials indicate that the thefts involve a total of $100,000 a year or more, and that most are committed by hospital employees. The hospital has 814 full-time employees and 187 part-time employees.

ONE SIDE: Hospital Administrator and Doctor Michael A. Ramirez discussed the new policy with reporters in his office this morning. He explained the adoption of the new policy this way: "It's not something we enjoy doing, but it's obviously necessary. It's a last resort. It's not just the hospital that's been hurt, but we're also trying to protect our employees and patients. We know that 99% of our employees are honest, and we've had a lot of them report that they've been the victims of crimes. Their purses have been taken, and some have been attacked and robbed in our parking lots. And every year we get dozens of complaints from our patients and from the families of patients. All sorts of things are stolen from their rooms, but mostly cash and jewelry and clothing. It may be taken when they're sleeping or sedated or out of their rooms for X-rays or something. The testing started two weeks ago. So far, we've tested about 100 employees, and it would be unfair to them to change the policy at this date. Besides, the testing's already proving effective. We're already experiencing a decline in theft reports. Every new employee is required to take the tests, and every existing employee will be retested once a year. That's hospital policy, and people who can't accept it can choose not to work here. That's their choice. We're convinced the tests are more than 90% accurate, and we wouldn't fire anyone on the basis of the tests alone. There are other things we're doing to corroborate the test results. In addition to reviewing the test results, we would counsel with someone whose test results showed deception in a serious fashion. We'll counsel with them, discuss the problem and listen to their version before any action is taken. We'll also determine if they had the opportunity to be involved in any thefts and look at their employment record and reputation and, if necessary, retest them. The last thing the hospital wants to do is fire an innocent person. We're just trying to weed out the undesirables. We've gotten rid of two so far. One quit, and we fired the other. The evidence in that case was just overwhelming, and there wasn't any question about it. We're also trying to use the tests in a nondiscriminatory fashion, testing everyone. We believe uniform testing of all employees is the fairest way to proceed, although selective testing could have been done. With uniform testing, no person should feel the stigma of being accused. Legally, we could select certain individuals or specific departments and require the tests. Also, remember that this is just one part of our security system. We have security guards, we provide lockers for our employees' belongings, and we restrict unauthorized people from wandering through our facilities. We want to design some new employee identification badges as additional security measures and, as soon as we can afford it, we want to add closed-circuit TV to cover some problem areas."

THE OTHER SIDE: Jo-Anne Fisher is chairwoman of a committee representing hospital employees in the matter. She says: "I don't know of any employee who favors this, not one. We're circulating a petition, and we've got more than 500 signatures opposed to this testing. We want to meet with the hospital's board of directors, and we want them to rescind this policy. We don't think it's fair, and we don't think it's legal to require people to take these tests, and then to fire them on the basis of the results, especially people who've worked here 10 or 20 years. The hospital's forcing us to take the tests to prove our innocence. That's not right. They should consider us innocent until we're proven guilty, not the reverse. Everyone knows these tests aren't very accurate, and that's why they can't be used in courts. It's also a terrible invasion of our privacy.

Once they get you hooked up to one of those machines, they could ask you almost anything about your private life. Then, if you refuse to answer, they'll fire you, just like that. There's one other point we think is important. It's discriminatory, terribly discriminatory. They're just testing staff members, not volunteer workers and not physicians, but those people have the same access to hospital property. Everyone knows we've got doctors who equip their private offices with what they steal from here. If they're going to test people, everyone with access to the facilities should be tested. We agree the hospital has some thefts and they should be stopped. But right away, the hospital administrators say, 'The employees did it.' We've got some volunteers and patients who are crooks, too, you know. Patients can wander just about anywhere in this hospital, and they've got a lot more time to rob someone than a technician or nurse who's kept busy on the job all day."

Story 3: Drinking Age Debate

FACTS: Your state Legislature is considering a bill that would raise the drinking age in your state from 18 to 21. There was a debate at a Rotary Club meeting in your city today about the issue. First, State Sen. Mildred Sobik spoke in favor of the proposal. Then local cocktail lounge owner Charles Welshans spoke in opposition to the proposal.

ONE SIDE: Sen. Sobik opened the debate with the following arguments: "Twenty years ago, the state's drinking age was lowered from 21 to 18, and that was a mistake. Alcohol abuse has become a serious problem since then, particularly among young people, even of high-school age. It's bad because if even one high schooler is old enough to buy alcohol, he'll buy it and pass it around to younger students, so now we've got 13- and 14-year-olds who're getting drunk and getting addicted to it. They just can't handle it at that age. They don't have the maturity, and they don't drink in moderation. But the biggest problem is that we're having more alcohol-related deaths in the state in the 18- to 20-age group than with any other. Last year in the United States 25,000 people died in alcohol-related highway accidents, and 4,484 of them were 16- to 24-year-olds. That's a scandal. We've got too many young people dying in these accidents, and raising the state's drinking age to 21 would reduce those statistics."

THE OTHER SIDE: Mr. Welshans said: "I have a real philosophical problem with saying someone 18 or 19 is old enough to get married but not old enough to drink champagne at his wedding. A lot of the people trying to force this law down our throats don't drink themselves, and they're trying to force their beliefs on everyone else. A higher drinking age would discriminate unfairly against responsible young people, foster contempt for the law and create very serious economic hardships. Even the statistics that are being quoted here today are misleading. If you look at the statistics again, you'll find there's no reason to discriminate against the young citizens of this state. Young drivers, those 18, 19 and 20 years old, are more responsible with drinking and driving than most older groups. A study done by the National Highway Traffic Safety Administration in 15 states of drivers killed in car accidents found that the death rate for drivers who had been drinking was slightly lower for 16- to 20-year-olds than for 22- to 44-year-olds. So young adults are getting a bum rap. Less than 48% of the young drivers killed in auto accidents had been drinking, and that's compared with a rate of 50.5% for the 22- to 44-year-olds. One reason why politicians are willing to consider raising the drinking age is because so few young people vote. There's no fear that the people it'll hurt will retaliate. There's also the argument that this will help solve a problem. That's just not true. It's going to create new problems and worse problems. There's no way to enforce a law like this. It just creates a disrespect for the law. It'll encourage teenagers to use more drugs as a substitute for alcohol. Drugs are as accessible as alcohol, easier to conceal and more difficult to trace in a person's system once they've been consumed. No one seems to realize it yet, but the law's also bad for business. Businesses that serve young adults in the state would lose $500 to $600 million a year if the drinking age were raised, and that would cost the state $25 to $30 million a year in lost sales taxes and even more in lost liquor taxes. A higher drinking age would also force hundreds of drinking establishments to close or to fire all their young employees. If young adults can't legally drink, they won't be allowed to work in places that sell liquor, so thousands of persons will lose their jobs. No one ever thinks about that."

Story 4: Housing Project

FACTS: Your City Council voted last night on a proposal to locate a low-income housing project in the 4200 block of Forest Boulevard, which is part of the Creekside Village subdivision. The project would consist of 14 two-story brick buildings. Each building would house 6 to 8 families. The project would cost $6 million and would be federally subsidized. It would serve the elderly, the handicapped and low-income families. After last night's meeting, at which many people loudly and vigorously objected to the plans, the City Council vetoed the proposal by a unanimous vote of 7 to 0. The plans were presented to the City Council by the Tri-County Housing Authority, which is a semi-autonomous public body but which needs the approval of local governing boards to locate its projects within the boundaries of their jurisdictions.

ONE SIDE: The director of the City Housing Authority, Tom Chinn Onn, told the City Council before the vote: "I'm really disappointed in the opposition here tonight. We have a backlog of over 900 applicants waiting to find public housing. This would go a long way toward meeting that need. Low-income people are the ones who'll be hurt, badly hurt, if this isn't approved. Everyone seems to be saying they want to help the poor, but no one wants them in their own neighborhoods. Everyone complains when we try to place them in a nice neighborhood. And a lot of what you're hearing tonight about this project is emotional rather than factual. It's all scare tactics. Studies done by Don Brame (the city's traffic operations engineer) show that the project would add only 600 to 800 additional vehicles on the area's roads on a daily basis, and that's a very liberal estimate considering that about a third of the units would be occupied by older people who probably wouldn't drive much. The elderly also wouldn't need other city facilities, like schools. Now, we've already spent more than $160,000 planning this project, and all the money will be wasted, just totally wasted, if you reject this proposal, and we've got nowhere else to go with it. Everyone says they want to help the poor, but they want to help them somewhere else. That's real hypocrisy. This is a chance for the members of this council to be real statesmen and do some real good for some needy people. This means a lot to them, so I ask you to approve these plans."

THE OTHER SIDE: Residents of the neighborhood voiced the following complaints during the council meeting. Frank D. Shadgett of 8472 Chestnut Drive said, "This thing would cause all sorts of problems: crowded roads, crowded schools, more kids in the streets. We don't have enough parks, and there's only one junior high school and one high school that serve our neighborhood, and both have been filled for years. Now, if you dump this project on us, you'll have to bus some of our children out of their neighborhood schools, or you'll have to bring in some portable classrooms. There are other places that could handle the project better. It just doesn't fit in our neighborhood. You should come out and look at the area before coming up with an idea like this. A lot of our homes cost $80,000 or $100,000 or more. You put this project in the middle of them, and it'll hurt our property values." Another person, James Lasater of 374 Walnut Drive, said: "The area is zoned for single-family homes, and that's why we invested here. We've got our life savings in our homes, and this will hurt us. We've got no lack of compassion for the cause, but it just doesn't belong here. We want to protect our neighborhood and

keep our neighborhood the way it is. We object to this bunch of bureaucrats coming in and changing its character. It's a good area to live in, and we don't want that to change."
An attorney representing the neighborhood, Michael Perakis, said: "The area is one of the most stable and beautiful single-family neighborhoods in the city, and these people are only interested in maintaining that status. Right now, you're in danger of violating your own laws if you put this project in Creekside Village. There's been no proper hearings to rezone the land, and this project doesn't fit its current zoning restrictions. The zoning laws are intended to prevent this very kind of thing, this invasion of a residential neighborhood with a nonconforming project of any type."

8 Careers in Journalism

Journalism continues to attract a record number of students. In years when enrollment in the nation's colleges and universities has grown only 1 percent, the enrollment in journalism (including mass communications) has grown 6 to 7 percent.

As recently as 1960, only 11,390 students in the United States were majoring in journalism. By 1970, the number had increased to 33,106, and by 1980 it had reached 75,000. Today, more than 90,000 students are studying journalism, and about 21,000 graduate every year.

Thousands of students have decided to major in journalism because the curriculum helps prepare them for specific jobs. Other students pick journalism because they like to write and believe that journalism is an enjoyable and important profession that provides an opportunity to serve the public. Some students hope to obtain glamorous, exciting, well-paid jobs, such as jobs in Washington or as foreign correspondents, and as free-lance writers.

There are enough journalism students to replace every reporter and editor currently employed by the nation's daily and weekly newspapers. But the term "journalism" includes more than just newspaper work. It also includes advertising, public relations, broadcasting, photography and magazine work, and many students seek jobs in one of these fields.

Of the 90,000 students now majoring in journalism, only 20 percent are preparing to work for newspapers. Each year, Paul V. Peterson of Ohio State University studies the nation's journalism students, and his most recent study revealed that 21.8 percent are majoring in advertising, 21.6 percent in broadcasting, 20.3 percent in news-editorial (newspaper) sequences and 14.8 percent in public relations. Other journalism students are majoring in photography, or magazine and general mass communication sequences, for example.

Enrollment in public relations has risen most rapidly, especially for women. Just 20

To save time, reporters often compose a story in their mind, then dictate it from rough notes. These reporters are calling in their stories about the release of 52 Americans held hostage for 444 days in Iran. The hostages were released on Jan. 20, 1981—minutes after Ronald Reagan's inauguration as president. In return, the United States agreed to return to Iran $8 billion in frozen assets.

years ago, most journalism students were male. Today, 61 percent of the students in news-editorial sequences are women. By comparison, 63 percent of the students in advertising and 71 percent of the students in public relations are women.

However, many graduates never try to find a job in their field. Peterson explains that: "Journalism continues to attract a number of young people who see such education as an excellent preparation for other endeavors, and it is simply not correct to assume that all persons majoring in journalism are going to seek media-related positions upon graduation." Some students go on to graduate or law school. Others enter the military, become teachers or seek jobs in sales or management.

Educational Philosophy

More than 300 American colleges and universities offer bachelor's degrees in journalism. About 90 of their programs are accredited by the Accrediting Council on Education for Journalism and Mass Communication (ACEJMC). Upon request, ACEJMC will send a team of educators and media professionals to examine an entire unit (a department, division, school or college). In the past, ACEJMC accredited individual sequences within a unit. Today, it accredits only the overall unit—not its sequences. Typically, the accreditation team will ask about the number of faculty members who teach in the unit, their qualifications and course requirements. The team will also examine the unit's physical facilities and its graduates' success in finding media jobs.

Other accreditation standards are more controversial. The ACEJMC recommends that only 25 percent of a student's courses should be in journalism or communications, with most of the remaining 75 percent in the liberal arts. So if a college student takes a total of 40 courses, only 10 will be in journalism. The ACEJMC also recommends that the journalism courses should be concentrated in the last two years of a four-year program and that the number of academic credits granted for media internships should be limited.

These accreditation requirements encourage students to obtain a broad liberal arts education so that they will learn how their communities function and will be able to understand and to write knowledgeably about a variety of topics. Traditionally, journalism majors have taken electives in anthropology, economics, English, history, philosophy, political science, psychology and sociology. Recently, newspaper editors have encouraged students to explore newer fields, such as computer science. Some editors also recommend courses in business administration, explaining that graduates who become news executives should be prepared to handle budgets and to supervise other employees.

The ACEJMC does not rate the schools it accredits, nor rank them in any order. Rather, "That a program is listed as accredited demonstrates that the administration and faculty of the school have passed a thorough examination by their peers." Committee member Maryann Yodelis-Smith of the University of Minnesota has added that: "Accreditation is a guarantee that a school has been reviewed by a body of peers and professionals and meets certain standards. It does not necessarily mean that non-accredited schools are not good. Some just don't seek accreditation. Perhaps they don't believe in it or can't afford it."

Some educators and newspaper editors argue that students should be required to take more journalism classes than the ACEJMC recommends, in order to sharpen their professional skills. Other critics charge that the accreditation requirements discourage diversity and experimentation; that, to be accredited, every program must conform to the same standards.

Most departments require journalism students to take several reporting and editing classes and to study the history of American journalism and communications law and ethics. In addition, they offer several journalism electives. The curriculum exposes students to the history and traditions of their profession. It also encourages students to learn something about the news media's problems; the news media's relationship to the government; and the news media's effects, responsibilities and functions within a democratic society.

Some good reporters and editors never took a journalism course, and some editors (apparently a declining number) argue that students interested in journalism should get a traditional liberal arts education, then learn newspaper work on the job. These editors say that they prefer graduates who majored in English, history, political science or economics rather than in journalism.

However, trying to become a journalist through on-the-job training involves some risks. Today few newspapers hire non-journalism majors, and most newspapers do not provide formal training programs for new employees because editors are too busy. If the editors notice a mistake in a reporter's story, it is easier to correct it themselves than to find the reporter, explain the mistake and then wait for the reporter to correct it. Even summer interns and regular staff writers complain that they do not receive enough constructive criticism or feedback from their editors.

Moreover, some topics—journalism history, law and ethics, for example—cannot easily be taught on the job. As a consequence, non-majors may be unprepared for the problems often encountered by reporters. Occasionally, an experienced reporter or sympathetic editor will teach a beginner some fundamentals, but many of the people trying to learn journalism through on-the-job training are likely to flounder.

What Editors Want in Job Applicants

Newspaper editors have often been asked to describe ideal applicants for positions on their staffs. Most editors say they want applicants who are intelligent and well-informed. Editors also want talented writers: good grammarians who can spell and who

Many reporters use portable word processors to write their stories, and telephone lines to transmit the stories to their offices, whether across town or across the country.

can write clearly and accurately. In addition, they look for applicants who are honest, curious, aggressive and able to act on their own initiative.

Newspaper editors also seek applicants who are dedicated: clearly committed to careers in journalism, willing to sacrifice and likely to stay in their jobs for several years. As evidence of that commitment, editors may look for applicants who have a long-term interest in journalism—who have worked for several student publications or who have sacrificed to obtain some additional experience, possibly in a summer internship.

Benjamin Bradlee, executive editor of The Washington Post, has said that he looks first for energy, for commitment to the news business and for people willing to take their work home with them. After that, he looks for knowledge, ability and judgment.

Asked to list applicants' major shortcomings, editors usually begin by complaining about the failure of many applicants to master the English language. Editors complain that too many applicants cannot write effectively and know too little about grammar, spelling and punctuation. Editors also complain that too many applicants are not familiar with city and county governments. They cannot type. They cannot cope with deadline pressures. They lack an adequate background in the fields of economics, history, literature, philosophy and science.

Editors frequently add that more than enough students are majoring in journalism and that schools should begin to place more emphasis on the quality, not the quantity, of their graduates. They want schools to weed out the least fit, and many schools are trying to do so. Dozens of schools now limit their enrollments, but for another reason as well. They simply cannot handle the thousands of students seeking admission to their programs. The nation's largest program, at Michigan State, has more than 3,800 students. The University of Texas at Austin is second, with 2,259. Syracuse is third with 2,155.

To be admitted as a journalism major, you may be required to pass an entrance examination—usually a grammar and spelling test. Some schools require prospective majors to have earned at least a C in several basic writing courses. Others require journalism majors to be juniors and to have a 2.5 or even a 3.0 (B) grade-point average and then to maintain that average in their journalism courses.

Who Actually Gets Newspaper Jobs?

Newspapers hire about 8,600 new reporters and editors every year. The largest percentage—48.5 percent—come from other newspapers. Newspapers like to hire reporters from other newspapers because those reporters have already been trained; they are experienced, productive professionals. Journalism schools provide about 28.5 percent of newspapers' new employees. Twelve percent come from other media jobs, 6 percent from other college majors and 4 percent from miscellaneous sources. These statistics reflect two major trends. First, newspapers no longer hire many people without a college degree. Second, journalism majors are getting more and more of the available jobs.

In 1970, only 10 percent of the new reporters and editors hired by the nation's daily newspapers did not have a college degree. Today, the percentage of new employees being hired without a degree has fallen so low that it is barely measurable.

A journalism degree gives graduates an obvious edge over non-majors trying to find their first job. Journalism majors also seem to obtain more rapid promotions. Three out of four news executives—76 percent—are journalism majors.

Why do newspapers hire so many journalism majors? Professor Warren W. Schwed suggests several reasons:*

> Journalism majors apply for the jobs at newspapers.
>
> Journalism majors obtain newspaper internships, then are hired for full-time jobs because of the experience they obtained as interns.
>
> Journalism majors do not require as much training, can show editors more writing samples and know how to operate the electronic equipment used in newsrooms.
>
> Journalism majors are motivated and understand what is expected of them.
>
> After moving into executive positions, journalism majors tend to hire other journalism majors.

Thus, the students who find jobs are the ones who prepared most intensively for them, and that trend seems to be true in every field of journalism. However, the media also tend to hire the graduates who earned the highest grades. In every field of journalism, graduates who maintained B+ or higher averages are more likely to find jobs than are students who earned lower grades.

Many daily newspapers are hiring more specialists, and editors seem to be impressed by new graduates who have developed an interest or some expertise in an area of specialization. Partly for that reason, many of the students who major in journalism minor in another field. Editors at smaller newspapers often hire applicants who can operate a 35mm camera and who can develop their own film, so all their reporters can also serve as photographers. Editors almost everywhere also look for good copy editors. Most newspapers pay their copy editors more than their reporters and are more likely to promote their copy editors; nevertheless, there seems to be a persistent and widespread shortage of copy editors, so it may be easier for journalism graduates to obtain jobs as copy editors than as reporters.

*Warren W. Schwed, "Hiring, Promotion, Salary, Longevity Trends Charted at Dailies," *Newspaper Research Journal*, vol. 3, no. 1 (October 1981), pp. 7–8.

A reporter and editor discuss a story.

The Recruitment of Minorities

Since the 1960s, newspapers have been trying to recruit more minorities. Minorities account for about 20 percent of the U.S. population. Yet newspapers employ 55,000 journalists, and only 3,600—about 6.5 percent—are minorities. The figure ranges from a low of 3 percent in the Midwest to a high of 9 percent in the Northeast. Radio and television stations are doing slightly better, but magazines are doing worse.

The American Society of Newspaper Editors has adopted a resolution urging the industry to employ more minorities so that, by the year 2000, newspaper staffs will have the same percentage of minorities as the U.S. population. However, newspapers seem unlikely to reach that goal—or even to come close. Recent surveys have found that 60 percent of the nation's daily newspapers still do not employ a single minority journalist.

Of all the minorities, blacks seem to be having the least success. During a recent 5-year period, the number of blacks employed in the nation's newsrooms increased 44 percent. By comparison, the increase for American Indians was 59 percent; for Hispanics, 74 percent; and for Asian Americans, 113 percent.

Journalism schools have joined the effort to recruit more minorities. About 7.5 percent of their students—a total of 6,600—are minorities. However, only 8.6 percent of those students are enrolled in news-editorial sequences. In 1986, 10.5 percent of the students graduating with a bachelor's degree in journalism were minorities. However, only 51.6 percent of the minority graduates accepted work at media-related companies.

Paul Peterson of Ohio State University concludes that: "It would appear there is no significant change in the number of minority students interested in journalism and

The features editor working at her desk at the Detroit Free Press.

mass communication, despite special attention paid by schools and the media. The area remains a concern, not only for journalism and mass communication, but for all areas in universities where, in general, minority enrollment has declined in the past several years.*

A second issue complicates the problem. Minorities employed by newspapers are more likely to become dissatisfied and quit. When minority journalists were interviewed, 40 percent said they expected to quit, compared to only 22 percent of the whites. When asked why they intended to quit, the minorities were most likely to mention their lack of opportunities for advancement. The whites were most likely to mention boredom or low pay.

All the media are run almost entirely by whites. Typically, fewer than 1 percent of the nation's newspaper executives are minorities. More than 1,600 daily newspapers are published in the United States, but only two have black publishers. Because of the media's apparent discrimination, some journalists have sued their employers, charging that they have been denied raises, assignments and promotions because they are black. Critics add that some newspapers have hired minorities to take the pressure off themselves, without any intention of ever promoting them.

Many newspapers have affirmative action plans, and some—especially the Gannett chain—have succeeded in hiring and promoting both women and minorities. But other newspapers have not. Some editors explain that they have been unable to find qualified applicants. Minority journalists respond that the applicants exist—if only the editors would look for them.

As the country's population changes, the employment of more minorities is becoming more than a matter of social justice. It is also good business. Minority consumers are

*Paul V. Peterson, "Enrollment up 7 percent in '86, outstripping university growth," *Journalism Educator*, vol. 42, no. 1 (Spring 1987), p. 6.

Until the 1960s, newspapers set their stories in lead type and arranged the type in narrow columns on their pages. Newspapers now save time and money by using computers to type their stories and by pasting the typed stories on dummy sheets. They make printing plates from a photographic image of the page.

a growing segment of the market, and the media will suffer if they fail to fulfill that market's needs: to satisfy its advertisers and readers.

In parts of the United States, a reporter unable to speak Spanish may be unable to obtain some stories. In California, for example, the San Bernardino Sun has begun to offer Spanish classes for its reporters and editors. The newspaper's executive editor, Robert W. Ritter, explains that about 30 percent of the 1.2 million people living in the Sun's circulation area are Hispanic, and that many speak little or no English. "Speaking and understanding Spanish is essential if we are to find, understand and write about these people," Ritter adds.

Because of the media's desire to recruit them, minority graduates are finding it easier to obtain jobs. In 1986, newspapers offered one job for every minority graduate with a news-editorial major. Because some graduates accepted jobs in other media (and non-media) fields, most who wanted a newspaper job should have been able to find one, and some were offered two or three.

Finding a Job

Each year, the Dow Jones Newspaper Fund surveys college graduates who majored in journalism. Within a few months after graduation, 51.4 percent of the 1986 graduates had found media jobs. About 28 percent had jobs with other employers, 7.5 percent had enrolled in graduate school and 12.5 percent were unemployed. The following statistics show more specifically where the graduates went:

Media		Non-Media	
Daily Newspaper	10.4	Sales/Clerical/Management	16.6
Advertising Agencies	9.7	Other Non-Media Jobs	12.0

Public Relations	8.7	Graduate/Law School	7.5
Other Media-Related Jobs	5.7	Unemployed, seeking work inside the media	9.6
Weekly Newspapers	4.9		
Television Stations	4.7	Unemployed, seeking work outside the media	2.0
Radio Stations	3.6		
Commercial Magazines	2.5	Unemployed, not seeking work	0.9
Free-lance Writer/Photographer	1.0		
News Service	0.2		

Newspapers and news services hired more journalism graduates than any other media-related employer—but there are still not enough jobs for every news-editorial graduate. The ratio of jobs to graduates in all the major fields included:

Newspapers jobs/News-editorial majors	1 to 1½
Broadcast jobs/Broadcast majors	1 to 2
Public relations jobs/Public relations majors	1 to 2½
Advertising jobs/Advertising majors	1 to 2½

Together, the news services and daily and weekly newspapers hired about 3,270 journalism majors. The number has not changed significantly during the last 10 years. Moreover, it accounts for only 42.7 percent of the news-editorial graduates. However, news-editorial graduates are unusually successful at obtaining jobs in other media fields, probably because of their writing skills. Eight percent of the news-editorial majors obtained jobs in public relations, 4.4 percent at commercial magazines, 3.5 percent at radio and television stations, and 2 percent at advertising agencies. About 5 percent became free-lancers or found other media jobs. Thus, 66.3 percent of the news-editorial majors found media-related work: a higher percentage than for any other major.

Thirty-five percent of the news-editorial graduates said they did not apply for a single newspaper or news service job. Of those who did find a newspaper job, almost 85 percent had two offers to choose from. More than 71 percent started work within one month of graduation.

About 17 percent of the news-editorial majors entered non-media fields, 8.8 percent enrolled in graduate school and 7.7 percent were unemployed.

Radio and television stations hired about 1,752 graduates, and 68 percent were broadcast majors. Yet only 31.8 percent of the broadcast majors found jobs in their chosen field. About 15 percent were unemployed.

Advertising agencies hired about 2,047 graduates, and employers in public relations hired 1,835. Women obtained nearly 79 percent of the jobs in advertising and 85 percent of the jobs in public relations. But only 33.5 percent of the advertising majors and 24.3 percent of the public relations majors found jobs in their fields. Twelve percent of the advertising majors and 16 percent of the public relations majors were unemployed.

Finally, nine out of 10 of the graduates who found media jobs said they would major in the same specialty again if they were beginning college next year.

Some new graduates encounter a situation called "the journalism merry-go-round." Newspaper editors refuse to hire the graduates because they do not have any experience. The graduates respond that they cannot get any experience because editors will not hire them.

Most journalism students can obtain some experience while still in school, and that experience provides a variety of benefits. It demonstrates their commitment to journalism. It improves their professional skills. It also provides the "clips" they need to obtain jobs. When journalism graduates apply for jobs, editors want to see samples of their work—clippings of stories that they wrote and published in newspapers or magazines.

Students usually begin by working for their campus publications. Later, they may free-lance or work part-time for a local paper. Summer internships may be even more valuable, enabling students to acquire more professional experience and to become better acquainted with the editors who hire newspapers' regular staff members.

About 18 percent of the reporters hired by daily newspapers have previously worked as interns at the same papers. Overall, the statistics are even more dramatic. Nearly three-fourths of journalism graduates who find media-related jobs have worked somewhere as interns. When asked what advice they would give future journalism students, graduates with media jobs are most likely to suggest that students obtain an internship or some other practical experience while still in school.

A newspaper editor explained: "It's just not enough to have a degree. We look for someone who has interned, worked for the school newspaper and who has a pile of clips so we don't have to play journalism school." Another news executive added that: "Somehow, some way, the real gutsy students will find a summer newspaper job. We are impressed with them. They show us that they are actively pursuing a journalism career. And they can offer us something other than a journalism degree—experience."

Summer Internships

The media employ thousands of interns every summer. Most internships are sponsored by individual newspapers, magazines, news services, and radio and television stations. However, too many students seek internships with a few prestigious media. Typically, The Washington Post receives more than 1,500 applications for the 20 internships it offers each summer. Other big dailies also receive hundreds of applications. Students are more likely to obtain internships with their hometown newspapers or with smaller newspapers in the area. To obtain the internships, students should get an early start and, in case they are rejected by one newspaper, should also apply at several others. Dailies often set a January or February deadline for applications, then select their summer interns during March or April.

Most schools encourage their journalism students to obtain internships, and some require them to. But it is difficult to ensure that every intern will benefit from the experience. Some interns are badly supervised, and some "internships" turn out to be routine clerical or secretarial jobs. Schools that grant students academic credit for their internships normally appoint a faculty adviser who may visit the students on the job, conduct weekly seminars and consult with their employers. The advisers try to eliminate internships that fail to develop students' professional skills.

Newspaper editors often expect interns to work for nothing. Some editors exploit interns, using them as free labor (often to replace vacationing employees). Other editors say that they could not afford to employ paid interns or that work performed by the interns does not merit a regular salary. Editors also insist that they are giving the interns valuable professional experience and that, when they were students, they too were expected to accept unpaid internships. Many schools encourage students to accept such internships because of the experience they provide. Others do not, and their administrators insist that interns should be treated (and paid) as professionals.

The best internships include formal training programs: orientation sessions, seminars with news executives, and regular reporting and editing duties. They also pay students the same salaries paid beginning reporters. Newspapers may provide internships because they feel an obligation to support journalism education and because they want to help students get ahead in the field. Editors also use internships to observe talented young journalists whom they might want to employ some day.

Seeking the First Job

New graduates looking for their first permanent jobs should set realistic goals for themselves. Most metropolitan newspapers and radio and television stations do not hire beginners, but look for people with several years of solid professional experience. Or if they do hire beginners, they assign them rather menial tasks. New graduates should contact weekly newspapers or small dailies, which receive fewer applications and are more likely to accept applicants with little experience. Moreover, jobs at smaller newspapers often provide better experience, since their reporters and editors are given a variety of assignments and greater responsibilities. Graduates who want to work in a metropolitan area are more likely to get jobs there after they have obtained some experience in the smaller markets.

Graduates seeking jobs in another state might consult Editor & Publisher, a weekly magazine that publishes several pages of help-wanted advertisements for newspaper reporters and editors, as well as some ads offering jobs in the field of public relations. Applicants should address their letters of application (individually typed, not duplicated) and résumés to the newspapers' managing editors, since they do the hiring and firing at most papers. Applicants can learn the managing editors' names by reading the newspapers or by consulting Editor & Publisher International Yearbook or the Ayer Directory of Publications.

Preparing a Résumé

A résumé should be neat, thorough and well-written. Even more important, every résumé should contain the types of information that employers consider most pertinent to the job applied for. Newspaper editors want to know whether applicants are qualified for specific jobs—for example, whether they possess the skills necessary to become good reporters. Editors also look for evidence of commitment, intelligence and initiative. They prefer applicants who are experienced and demonstrate a long-standing and active interest in journalism.

An expert estimates that: "The sad fact is that about one out of every 250 résumés that lands on someone's desk will result in an interview. That means your résumé has to dazzle editors or news directors—and it had better dazzle quickly because chances are that they see hundreds of résumés a year and give each one about 90 seconds."[1]

Normally, a résumé is short: only one or two pages long, either typed or typeset. In the past, many applicants began with personal data that included their age, height, weight and marital status. Today, many consider that information irrelevant.

Because of its importance, an applicant's journalism experience should be presented early in a résumé. A good résumé will begin with the applicant's current or most recent experience, including work on student publications, internships and part-time summer jobs. An applicant might also describe his or her duties and attach copies of his or her best stories (copies that do not have to be returned).

Employers are also interested in an applicant's education: in the applicant's major and minor, and the college he or she attended. In addition, an applicant might list his or her grade-point average: both overall and within the major.

Another portion of the résumé might list any honors or awards an applicant has received—anything that would help demonstrate the applicant's capabilities. An applicant might also list other skills and interests helpful in a career as a reporter or editor. For example: Can the applicant type? Use a camera and develop photographs? Operate the electronic equipment used in newsrooms? Speak a foreign language?

Other applicants provide:

- A statement of beliefs and professional goals. (Editors are skeptical of applicants who do not seem to know what they want, who claim that they can do everything, and who are obviously uninformed about a job and list unrealistic goals or salary demands.)
- Memberships and offices held, especially in media organizations.
- Years abroad, special programs, seminars and other unusual experiences.
- Descriptions of other (non-media) work experiences.

[1]Debra Bissinger, "Let your resume do the talking," *The Quill*, February 1986, p. 19.

- Military records, including ranks and duties.
- References, including the names of past editors and employers as well as the names of some journalism professors.
- Date of graduation and dates the applicant will be available for interviews—and available for work.
- A recent photograph.

There are a number of helpful guides to writing résumés, and some colleges and universities even offer résumé-writing seminars through their placement offices. Students preparing their first résumé would do well to use such services, though there is no single formula for a successful résumé.

Too many students list some of the information—their skills or experience, for example—but fail to present the information in parallel form. If the first item in a list begins with a verb, the following items should also begin with a verb. Similarly, if the first item uses the present tense, the following items should also use the present tense.

Other students leave gaps, failing to explain what they did for 1- or 2-year periods in their lives. Editors are skeptical of these as well as applicants who list too many former jobs, suggesting that they rarely stay anywhere more than a year or two.

Finally, an applicant should proofread a résumé several times, then ask several friends to proofread it. A single error in a résumé (a cliché, grammatical error or misspelled word) will destroy its effectiveness.

The two sample résumés reprinted on the following pages illustrate the format and content of an effective résumé.

Newspaper editors receive dozens of applications, including form letters addressed simply to "The Managing Editor." At many newspapers, all such applications are thrown away. Editors are also likely to throw away applications that contain spelling, typing or grammatical errors.

Several days after mailing an application, graduates might call the managing editor and request an interview. If the managing editor says the newspaper does not have any vacancies, graduates still might try to arrange an informational interview and offer to travel to the newspaper's offices at their own expense. That type of persistence may impress an editor. Also, because reporters are constantly moving to other jobs, a vacancy may develop a few days or weeks later. However, applicants should never walk in unannounced and expect an interview.

When applicants appear for interviews, they should bring evidence of their commitment and experience—especially clips or other samples of their work. An applicant's appearance is also important. Every applicant should be well-groomed: neat, clean and properly dressed. Applicants should be neither overdressed nor underdressed. For women, a coordinated jacket and skirt or a simple daytime dress with low-heeled shoes is most appropriate; makeup, if any, should be applied discreetly. Men should wear a dark suit or jacket and tie with slacks (no jeans) and well-polished shoes (no sneakers or running shoes). An editor recently complained that one college student appeared for an interview dressed in a T-shirt inscribed "Start a Movement—Eat a Prune." That student did not get the job.

Applicants who are turned down might continue to call the managing editor every two or three weeks to show that they are still interested in the newspaper and that they are aggressive and persistent. If, after three or four calls, the applicants have still not been offered a job, they should probably look elsewhere.

Applicants who are being seriously considered for employment may be given several tests and then asked to join the newspaper for a trial period. Recent surveys have found that two-thirds of the nation's dailies give job applicants one or more tests, most of which include sections on spelling, grammar and word usage. Applicants may also be

Thomas J. Wilke

PERSONAL DATA

Age: 22
Sex: Male
Height: 6' 2"
Weight: 175
Health: Excellent
Marital status: Single
Available to begin work:
    Immediately

Campus Address
1505 Yates Crescent, Apt. 42
Lexington, Kentucky 40505
Telephone: 606-257-2786

Home Address
1014 22nd Avenue
Morehead, Kentucky 40351
Telephone: 606-783-2649

JOURNALISM EXPERIENCE

Lexington Leader (daily).   Clerk responsible for delivering editorial material to and from newspaper editors; answering newsroom telephones; and writing obituaries, news briefs and weather forecasts. Extensive training on the newspaper's video display terminals. Worked 20 hours a week during junior and senior years of college.

The Wildcat (campus daily).   Managing editor during senior year, responsible for staff management, story assignments, editing and page layout. Earlier, worked as news editor, entertainment editor and general assignment reporter.

United Press International.   Campus stringer for three years.
Roseville Outlook (weekly).   Summer reporter/intern.
High school yearbook.   Editor-in-chief. Also worked as photo editor and staff writer.

OTHER WORK EXPERIENCE

Custom Painting & Decorating.   Job as house painter, three summers.
J.C. Penney Co., Inc.   Stockboy during high school.

EDUCATIONAL BACKGROUND

B.A. University of Kentucky.
Major: Journalism   Minor: Political Science
Grade point average in major: 3.54 on a 4.0 scale
Overall grade point average: 3.48 on a 4.0 scale
Graduated Cum Laude

AWARDS AND HONORS

Alumni Scholarship, two years.

Member, Phi Kappa Phi National Honor Society
Reader's Digest Grant for reporting project during junior year
Honorable mention in national Hearst newswriting contest, feature category

ACTIVITIES, HOBBIES

Member, Sigma Phi Epsilon social fraternity
Member, Society of Professional Journalists, SDX (Campus chapter)
Tennis, swimming, bowling, chess, reading

OTHER SKILLS

Typing: 55 words per minute
Photography: Own two 35mm Minolta cameras with wide angle and telephoto lenses and can develop black-and-white prints
Languages: Can speak and write Spanish (studied Spanish for three years in high school and for two years in college)

REFERENCES

Prof. Louis Murphy
School of Journalism
University of Kentucky
Lexington, Kentucky
Phone: 606-257-2786

Alice Stearman
City Editor
Lexington Leader
Lexington, Kentucky
Phone: 606-241-3765

Mike Tipton, Editor
Roseville Outlook
411 N. Lakeview Blvd.
Roseville, Kentucky
Phone: 606-365-6974

given some rough notes and asked to write them up into a story. Some newspapers give applicants current events and typing tests.

A growing number of major dailies ask applicants to work in their newsrooms for several days so that the editors can see how they handle everyday assignments. Most dailies pay the applicants, but editors may try out three or four before deciding which one will get the job.

Job Satisfaction—and Dissatisfaction

About 80 percent of the journalism graduates hired by newspapers say they are moderately to very satisfied with their jobs. Only 10 percent are very dissatisfied.

Why are journalists so satisfied with their work? One reason, they explain, is that their jobs are varied, creative, important and challenging. Perhaps more than anyone

Gail Anne Flemming

408 Langdon Street
Madison, Wis. 53706
608-262-1446

CAREER OBJECTIVES: To work as a newspaper reporter for several years and then to become a newspaper editor.

EDUCATION: Currently a senior majoring in journalism (news/editorial sequence) at the University of Wisconsin, Madison. Will graduate Dec. 12.
Minor: Sociology
GPA: 3.68 (Overall)
      3.81 (In major)
Graduated with honors from Plymouth High School, 12th in a class of 684. High school GPA: 3.86

MEDIA EXPERIENCE: Two summer internships covering county government for the Sheboygan Press.

Sold free-lance feature stories to seven daily newspapers in Wisconsin, including the Milwaukee Journal.

Worked four years as a reporter and editor for the university newspaper, the Daily Cardinal. Editor-in-chief during senior year.

Editor of high school newspaper and co-editor of the yearbook.

WORK EXPERIENCE: Office of Public Affairs, University of Wisconsin. Duties included writing articles for a faculty newsletter and an alumni magazine, writing press releases and arranging publicity for university events.

Wendy's Old Fashioned Hamburgers, Plymouth, Wis. Duties included serving as a cashier and all-purpose employee. Took customers' orders, operated a cash register, helped prepare each day's supply of food, made sandwiches and cleaned after closing time.

HONORS: Phi Kappa Phi National Honor Society
Regents' Scholar
High School Honor Society

else, journalists witness a kaleidoscope of the life within their communities: the good and the bad, the joyous and the tragic, the significant and the mundane. They are admitted everywhere and meet everyone. And, wherever they go, journalists share some of the power and prestige of the institutions they represent.

From a broader, more philosophical perspective, journalists represent the public when they cover a story. By providing citizens with the information they need to be well-informed, journalists perform a vital function within our democratic society.

In addition, newspaper jobs give journalists an opportunity to write. And writing a good story—being able to select the important facts, the correct words, the proper organization—is a highly creative process. It's also challenging. Within a few minutes, journalists may be expected to summarize a complex topic in a clear, accurate story that will interest the public. A few hours later, the entire story (and their byline) may appear on the front page of a newspaper read by thousands of people.

More systematic studies have found that journalists also like their jobs because they like their colleagues and have opportunities to learn something new every day, acquire new skills and play a role in improving their communities.

However, careers in journalism have several disadvantages. Reporters often complain about their low salaries, bad hours, deadline pressures and dull assignments. Much of their work is more routine than most people realize. For every reporter covering a major story, dozens of others are writing obituaries or covering the meetings of their local Rotary Clubs.

Studies have found that newspaper reporters are dissatisfied most with the way their stories are handled and with poor management practices, especially with a lack of direction from and communication with their editors. Reporters complain that too many of their stories are severely edited—that their stories are chopped and rewritten, and that they are rarely consulted beforehand or given an opportunity to correct their own errors. Reporters want more time to write their stories, more praise, more opportunities to talk with their editors, and more opportunities for advancement.

Some of these problems arise because few editors are trained in personnel management. Good reporters are offered jobs as copy editors, and the best copy editors become department editors. The editors are taught new professional skills, such as newspaper design, but few are taught how to supervise other people. Also, because of deadline pressures, editors may not have enough time to let reporters rewrite their own stories, nor to explain the changes they make in the reporters' stories.

Starting Salaries

The salaries paid beginning reporters are low, especially when compared to the salaries paid professionals in other fields, such as business, engineering and computer science. Even the teachers in many cities now earn more than reporters, and enjoy long summer vacations, too.

In 1986, the Dow Jones Newspaper Fund, Inc. reported that the median (midpoint) salary for beginners in public relations was $15,300 ($295 a week), and that advertising agencies paid beginners a median salary of $14,700 ($283/week). By comparison, daily newspapers paid $13,900 ($268/week), and radio and television stations paid $12,600 ($243/week). Other studies found that employers in all four fields will pay higher salaries to beginners who had internships and who earned high grades. Typically, those graduates earn $1,000 a year more than graduates who had B − or lower averages and no internships.

Why are beginning salaries so low? Some newspaper editors say they cannot afford to pay higher salaries. That seems implausible, however, since newspapers generally are more profitable than other types of businesses. Melvin Mencher, a professor at Columbia University's School of Journalism, speculates, "The supply of young people seems unlimited, and they will battle for even the lowest-paid jobs." In addition, the news business is not highly unionized. Many people go into the field knowing that its salaries are low but are willing to accept low salaries because they like the work, think it is important and are committed to serving the public.

Daily newspapers often hire new reporters on a probationary basis, then raise their salaries when they complete the probationary period satisfactorily. Good reporters may be able to double their salaries in five years, especially if they move to a larger paper. Also, many young journalists receive rapid promotions. It is not unusual for an ambitious and talented reporter to become a copy editor within two or three years, a department editor within four or five years and a city or managing editor by his or her late 20s or early 30s, receiving a raise with each promotion.

Few journalists make it that far, but the salaries paid by the nation's leading news media are phenomenally good. Journalists employed by the media in the nation's largest cities, by the newsmagazines, and by the radio and television networks may earn $50,000 to $100,000 or more a year. A very few journalists, such as Barbara Walters and Dan Rather, earn more than $1 million a year.

Newsroom Organization

Most news-editorial majors begin work as reporters. As new reporters, they often remain in their newspapers' offices, where they are given a variety of minor assignments—answering telephone calls, writing obituaries and rewriting publicity releases, for example. The work enables newcomers to become better acquainted with their newspapers' policies, and it enables editors—who are always nearby—to supervise their work more closely.

Because it requires less expertise than other areas, the police beat also may be assigned to a newspaper's newest and most inexperienced reporters. Police officers write reports about most of the calls they answer, and newspaper reporters are allowed to read most of those reports. Police departments in larger cities also provide special rooms for reporters and equip those rooms with typewriters, telephones and police radios. When reporters arrive at the police station each morning, they page through all the reports filed during the past 24 hours and take notes on the most newsworthy. In addition, reporters may ask whether any major crimes or accidents are being investigated at that moment. Because police reports contain all the information needed for routine stories, the reporters do not have to drive to the scene of every crime or accident, nor personally interview the victims.

Most newsrooms contain a police radio, and reporters listen to it while writing other stories. If a major story arises later in the morning, reporters will cover it themselves; they cannot wait for a police report, since it may not be completed until long after their newspapers' final deadlines. To save time, reporters try to cover the stories by telephone. If a store is robbed, they may call and ask a clerk to describe the robbery. If a student is injured, they may call the student's school and ask a teacher or principal to describe the injury. Reporters drive to the scene of major stories but, again to save time, may organize the facts in their minds, call their offices and dictate the stories to other reporters, thus saving the 20 or 30 minutes it might take to drive back to their offices.

This method of police coverage is not ideal, but it is efficient. Police officers complain that newspapers use the police beat as a training ground, forcing them to deal with a succession of novices who remain on the job only a few months before they are transferred to other beats. Some police officers are reluctant to trust inexperienced reporters and complain that the novices do not understand how police departments operate, are too inaccurate and sensational, and are not even good writers. However, other critics complain that newspapers obtain too much of their information from government offices and government officials and consequently emphasize the "official" version of most stories.

More experienced reporters also are assigned beats, often a specific building, such as the city hall, the county courthouse or the federal building. Other beats involve broader topics rather than a geographical location, and the most common of those beats are politics, business, education and religion. Larger newspapers establish dozens of more specialized beats, ranging from agriculture to art, from medicine to consumer affairs. The system promotes efficiency, since reporters become experts on the topics they cover and are able to cultivate important sources of information. Reporters often remain on the same beats for several years, become friends with those sources and obtain information from them more easily than they could if they were strangers. Each beat involves a topic that is especially newsworthy or a location where news is most likely to arise or be reported. When a serious problem arises, citizens usually report it to one of the government offices regularly visited by reporters.

On a typical day, the reporter assigned to cover, say, city hall for a medium-sized afternoon daily will begin work at about 8 a.m. and may spend the first hour in the paper's newsroom, writing minor stories left from the previous day, reading other newspapers published in the area, rewriting minor publicity releases or studying issues in the news. The reporter may confer with an editor about major stories expected to arise that day, then go to the city hall at about 9 a.m.; few important sources are likely to be in their offices before that time. During the next hour or two, the reporter will stop in all the major offices in the city hall, especially the offices of the mayor, council members, city clerk, city treasurer, city attorney and city planner. The mayor is the most newsworthy individual in most communities and may schedule a press conference in his or her office at the same time every morning to disseminate information about current developments (and to generate favorable publicity about himself or herself and the policies he or she favors).

The city hall reporter will return to the daily's newsroom at about 11 a.m. and, during the next hour or two, will quickly write stories that must be published that day. Other reporters, meanwhile, will have gathered information from the remaining beats; for example, the reporter covering the federal building may have seen the postmaster, local FBI agents, the federal marshal, federal court officials, the county agricultural agent, employees of the Internal Revenue Service and recruiters for the armed forces. News stories written by all the reporters may be due at noon, a common deadline for afternoon dailies. The deadline is rarely later than 1 p.m., since stories must be edited, set in type and printed, and the final product transported to subscribers' homes by 4 or 5 p.m. The deadline at some afternoon dailies is as early as 9 or 10 a.m., especially for early editions that must be transported to readers living in distant areas.

Some experienced writers are given jobs as general assignment reporters, and they cover stories that arise outside their papers' regular beats. The stories are more varied, often unexpected and often highly important. General assignment reporters might write about a circus arriving in town, a presidential candidate campaigning in the area, a train wreck or a speech given by a celebrity invited to the area.

Reporters compete for a number of other assignments, including jobs as feature and editorial writers and as columnists. Most of these jobs are given to a newspaper's most experienced writers, often people who have worked for the paper for 10 or 20 years. Some daily newspapers also hire correspondents to work in their state capitals, and larger dailies hire correspondents to work in Washington, D.C. However, the number of such jobs is limited, and they too are given only to experienced professionals.

Because they enjoy the work, some journalists remain reporters until they retire. Other journalists are promoted to the position of copy editor, and a few begin their careers as copy editors. Most copy editors check the stories written by reporters, write headlines for those stories and help with their newspaper's layout. Copy editors tend to be anonymous; they receive few bylines and spend most of their time indoors, working at a desk. Consequently, journalism students know less about their jobs and are less likely to seek such positions. Yet jobs as copy editors are often more plentiful than jobs as reporters, and the experience is essential for people seeking further promotions.

Newspapers appoint subeditors to supervise the various departments in their newsrooms, and many of those appointments are given to people who have learned the necessary editing skills by working as copy editors. The city or metropolitan editor— the most important of a newspaper's subeditors—is responsible for the coverage of local news and supervises a newspaper's staff of reporters. The city editor may assign the reporters' topics, edit their stories and then design the pages that contain local news.

Another major figure, the news or wire editor, handles stories transmitted by the news services, deciding which of the stories to use, editing them and arranging their placement in the paper. Small and medium-sized dailies also employ subeditors to supervise the following departments: sports, business, religion, entertainment, arts, regional or state news and Sunday editions. Larger dailies employ many more subeditors, and each of them may have several assistants.

The managing editor at most newspapers coordinates the subeditors' work and supervises the paper's day-to-day operations. Editors are responsible for budgets, policies, long-range planning and, at many smaller newspapers, writing all their papers' editorials (larger dailies employ specialists to write their editorials). Publishers, the chief executives in newspaper offices, supervise the work of all their major divisions, including their advertising, circulation and production departments. Publishers usually own their papers or are appointed by chains that own them.

The Electronic Revolution in the Newsroom

During the past 25 years, an electronic revolution has transformed the way news stories are written, edited and published. Just 25 years ago, reporters wrote their stories on typewriters, then used pencils to correct their errors. After proofreading a story, reporters pasted all its pages into one long strip, so none of the pages could be misplaced. Then reporters placed the story in a basket or impaled it on a sharp metal spike on their editor's desk. Editors used a pencil to correct the remaining errors. Then typesetters operating Linotype machines used molten lead to set the story in type, line by line, and proofreaders checked the type for errors. Other skilled craftsmen arranged the lead type in page forms and used those forms to make heavy metal plates that fit onto a newspaper's printing press.

Today, you may not be able to find any typewriters, typesetters, proofreaders or printers in a newspaper office. Instead, reporters type their stories on video display terminals (VDTs) that have keyboards like a typewriter's, plus a TV-like screen that displays stories as quickly as they are typed. VDTs resemble the computers that many Americans are buying for their homes.

If reporters make an error, they can correct it by pressing the proper combination of keys. Reporters can correct misspelled words, delete or insert other words, or re-

Newspapers use computers to write and edit their stories, but also to help with their layout. An editor using this combination of standard-size and large-screen monitors can edit and make up a full page before it is typeset and printed.

arrange entire sentences or paragraphs. When a reporter finishes writing a story, it is stored in a computer until the editor is ready to retrieve it. Working at another VDT, often a more sophisticated model, the editor can make additional corrections, trim the story, write a headline for it, then set the story's width, measure its precise length and feed it into a photocomposition machine that types it in narrow columns. Other employees paste the typed story onto a page form, photograph the entire page and make a lightweight printing plate from the negative.

Some VDTs have split screens, so editors can view two stories simultaneously. One story about an event may be written by a reporter, and another story about the same event may be provided by a news service. Editors can compare the two stories, then use the better one or combine the two stories, using the best of each. Other automated equipment enables editors to assemble entire pages on a screen: news stories, headlines, illustrations and advertisements. These new machines allow editors to see what an entire page will look like before it is set in type. They also eliminate the need for hand-drawn page dummies.

The new systems save millions of dollars in production costs, primarily because they eliminate the need for printers and other skilled craftsmen. News stories are typed only once, by reporters. Twenty-five years ago, The Washington Post had more than 500 printers, and The New York Times had about 800. Imagine how much money each of those newspapers could save by eliminating most of these positions, along with all the machinery, space, power and supplies needed to perform them.

The new systems are also faster and more accurate. A good Linotype operator could cast 6 to 8 lines of type a minute. Keypunch operators who replaced them could punch a tape that enabled Linotypes to set 14 lines a minute. Newer machines now set 500 lines a minute. Moreover, because the stories no longer have to be retyped by production workers after being typed and edited by journalists, they contain fewer errors, thus eliminating the need for most proofreaders.

Attaching printing plates to a press.

Editors hope that newspapers will use some of the money they save in production costs to improve their coverage of the news. Because the new systems are faster, they already enable editors to get more late-breaking stories into their newspapers. They also give journalists more control over their newspapers' production processes.

Some unionized papers have guaranteed their printers lifetime jobs in return for agreeing to install the latest labor-saving equipment; natural attrition then gradually reduces the number of printers. Some newspapers have also offered to retrain their printers for other jobs.

Free-Lance Writing

College students often dream of becoming free-lance writers. As free-lancers, the students imagine, they will be able to set their own hours, write about topics that interest them, pursue those topics in greater depth, sell their stories to prestigious national magazines and live comfortably on their earnings.

Some journalists supplement their incomes by writing for other publications, but free-lancing is more difficult than most people realize. It's been estimated that 25,000 Americans call themselves free-lance writers, but that only a few hundred earn a living at it. Most free-lancers hold another job or depend on the income of a husband or wife. To supplement their incomes, free-lancers may write speeches or books or work part-time in the field of public relations.

Why is free-lance work so difficult? One reason is that many of the big magazines that once bought articles from free-lancers have folded, and they have been replaced by smaller, special-interest magazines that pay much lower rates, most of which have not kept pace with inflation. Other magazines no longer accept any articles from free-lancers, instead using full-time staff writers exclusively. Editors can assign specific topics to staff writers and may consider them faster, more dependable and more talented than free-lancers.

Also, the competition among free-lancers is intense. Major publications receive hundreds of manuscripts for every one they accept. Even the best-written manuscripts may be rejected because they are inappropriate for a particular magazine or because the magazine has already accepted or published another article about the same topic or has received a similar article from a more famous writer whose byline will generate more publicity.

Free-lancers may spend days, weeks or even months working on an article, only to have it rejected by a dozen magazines. As a consequence, the free-lancers may collect enough rejection slips (usually impersonal, pre-printed forms) to paper every wall in their offices. Even if an article is accepted, it may be severely edited, or the free-lancer may be asked to rewrite it.

Free-lancers also complain that magazines pay too little and too late. After submitting an article, a free-lancer may have to wait several months until it is accepted. Then he or she may be told that the magazine pays "on publication," which means that the free-lancer will not receive any income from the article until it is published months later. Hundreds of magazines pay by the word: often 5 to 10 cents for each word they publish. Other magazines pay a specified flat fee, often less than $100 per article. Relatively few magazines pay more than $400 or $500 an article. There are exceptions: Harper's Magazine pays 50 cents to $1 a word for articles up to 6,000 words. Esquire pays up to $3,000, and Playboy pays a minimum of $3,000 for 3,000- to 5,000-word articles about topics "of interest to the urban male." Some major publications pay a "kill fee," usually about 25 percent of their normal rate, for articles they have commissioned free-lancers to write but then have decided not to publish.

In addition to all the other problems, free-lancers must provide and equip their own offices. A few large magazines pay some of their expenses, but most magazines do not. Travel is expensive. Even telephone, postage and supply bills can consume thousands of dollars a year. Many magazines prefer articles that are accompanied by several illustrations, so successful free-lancers may also have to be skilled photographers—which involves spending hundreds of dollars for cameras, film and developing costs. Moreover, free-lancers receive no fringe benefits: no medical or life insurance, no paid vacations, no pensions. On the other hand, they can deduct many of their expenses, including part of their rent and utility bills, while calculating their income taxes.

Few literary agents are willing to take on beginning free-lancers as clients. Typically, the Scott Meredith Literary Agency in New York advises potential clients, "If you are selling fiction or articles regularly to major national magazines, or have sold a book or screenplay or teleplay to a major publisher or producer within the last year, we'll be happy to discuss handling your output on standard commission basis of 10% on all American sales and 20% on British and all foreign sales." But if you are a beginner, you may have to pay an agent to handle your articles. The Scott Meredith Agency explains: "As recompense for working with beginners or newer writers until you begin to earn your keep through sales, our fee, which should accompany material, is $100 minimum charge per magazine story or article under 5,000 words. . . ."

Most literary agents prefer to handle books. After spending two or three days selling a book, the agents may collect 10 percent of a $50,000 fee. But with articles, they may work two or three days, then collect 10 percent of a $3,000 sale.

Despite all these problems, free-lance writing can be an enjoyable hobby or part-time pursuit. It provides another outlet for people who like to write and enables them to supplement their incomes from other jobs. However, beginners are most likely to sell their articles to smaller, less prestigious publications. Those publications may not pay as much as Harper's or Playboy, but they receive fewer manuscripts and are much less demanding. Aside from a typewriter, a successful free-lancer's indispensable tool is Writer's Market, published annually, which lists more than 4,000 markets for free-lancers. Writer's Market also describes the types of articles that each publication wants to buy and the amounts that it pays for those articles.

Suggested Readings

Historical Works

Abbot, Willis J. *Watching the World Go By.* Woodstock, N.Y.: Beekman Pub., 1974.
Hohenberg, John. *Foreign Correspondence: The Great Reporters and Their Times.* New York: Columbia University Press, 1967.
McPhaul, John J. *Deadlines and Monkeyshines.* Englewood Cliffs, N.J.: Prentice-Hall, 1962.
Mencken, H. L. *Newspaper Days.* New York: Knopf, 1941.
Murray, George. *The Madhouse on Madison Street.* Chicago, Ill.: Follett, 1965.
O'Connor, Richard. *The Scandalous Mr. Bennett.* Garden City, N.Y.: Doubleday, 1962.
Ross, Isabel. *Ladies of the Press: The Story of Women in Journalism by an Insider.* New York: Harper, 1936.
Salisbury, William. *The Career of a Journalist.* New York: Dodge, 1908.
Smith, H. Allen. *The Life and Legend of Gene Fowler.* New York: Morris, 1977.
St. John, Robert. *This Was My World.* New York: Doubleday, 1953.
Swanberg, W. A. *Citizen Hearst.* New York: Charles Scribner's, 1961.
———. *Luce and His Empire: A Biography.* New York: Charles Scribner's, 1975.
———. *Pulitzer.* New York: Charles Scribner's, 1967.
Walsh, Justin E. *To Print the News and Raise Hell!* Chapel Hill, N.C.: University of North Carolina Press, 1968.

Current Works

Anderson, Jack, with James Boyd. *Confessions of a Muckraker.* New York: Ballantine Books, 1979.
Bernstein, Carl, and Bob Woodward. *All The President's Men.* New York: Warner Books, 1976.
Brendon, Piers. *The Life and Death of the Press Barons.* New York: Atheneum, 1983.
Broder, David S. *Behind the Front Page: A Candid Look at How the News Is Made.* New York: Simon and Schuster, 1987.
Cannon, Lou. *Reporting: An Inside View.* Sacramento, Calif.: California Journal Press, 1977.
Chancellor, John, and Walter R. Mears. *The News Business.* New York: New American Library, 1984.
Crouse, Timothy. *The Boys on the Bus: Riding with the Campaign Press Corps.* New York: Ballantine, 1976.
Halberstam, David. *The Powers That Be.* New York: Alfred A. Knopf, 1979.
Hynds, Ernest C. *American Newspapers in the 1980's.* New York: Hastings House, 1980.
Kendrick, Alexander. *Prime Time: The Life of Edward R. Murrow.* New York: Avon, 1967.
Phelan, James. *Scandals, Scamps, and Scoundrels: The Casebook of an Investigative Reporter.* New York: Random House, 1982.
Salisbury, Harrison E. *A Journey for Our Times: A Memoir.* New York: Harper & Row, 1983.
Sevareid, Eric. *Not So Wild a Dream.* New York: Atheneum, 1978.
Talese, Gay. *The Kingdom and the Power.* New York: Dell, 1981.
Weaver, David H., and G. Cleveland Wilhoit. *The American Journalist: A Portrait of U.S. News People and Their Work.* Bloomington: Indiana University Press, 1986.
Weinberg, Steve. *Trade Secrets of Washington Journalists.* Washington, D.C.: Acropolis Books, 1981.
White, Theodore H. *In Search of History: A Personal Adventure.* New York: Harper & Row, 1978.

Careers and Scholarship Information

For more information about careers in journalism, write to the Dow Jones Newspaper Fund, P.O. Box 300, Princeton, N.J. 08540. The Dow Jones Newspaper Fund is a foundation that encourages young people to consider careers in journalism. Its programs include scholarships, internships, workshops, career information and an editor-in-residence program that it co-sponsors with the American Society of Newspaper Editors.

Each year, the Newspaper Fund lists more than $3 million in scholarships available to journalism and communications majors. The latest edition of its Career and Scholarship Guide includes a College Search Questionnaire for students interested in finding the colleges and universities that would best suit their needs and interests.

The Newspaper Fund also distributes a Minority Journalism Career Guide.

Careers in Journalism: Miscellaneous Assignments

1. Study the sample résumés in this chapter, then prepare your own résumé.

2. Write a three- to four-page paper that compares the appearance, content and style of four major journalism magazines: Editor & Publisher, Columbia Journalism Review, Journalism Quarterly and Quill.

3. Obtain a copy of Writer's Market, then describe the types of articles published by 10 magazines which interest you and list the amount each magazine pays for articles.

4. Critically analyze the content of the help-wanted ads that Editor & Publisher magazine publishes for newspaper reporters and editors. What types of jobs seem to be most plentiful? What are the requirements for those jobs? In what parts of the country are the jobs available? Write a two- to three-page paper that summarizes all your findings.

5. Conduct a survey of all the daily newspapers in your state to determine which newspapers hire summer interns and how many interns they hire. Ask each paper for additional information, such as the name and title of the person to whom applicants should write, what the newspaper's deadline is, and how much it pays interns. After gathering and writing up the information, you might distribute copies of your report to journalism students in other classes and schools.

6. Conduct a survey of all the daily newspapers in your state to determine how many of them give tests to applicants for their reporting and editing jobs, what types of tests they give, and whether they ask applicants to try out for several days before offering them jobs.

7. Survey minority students on your campus to determine their impressions of the news media and why they are or are not interested in careers as journalists.

8. Conduct a survey of all the media in your area to learn their starting salaries for college graduates. Also, ask how many new graduates they hire every year.

9. Conduct a survey of last year's graduates from your school. Where are they now, and what do they like and dislike about their new jobs? Also, what were their starting salaries?

9 Communication Law

Congress shall make no law respecting an establishment of religion, or prohibiting the free exercise thereof; or abridging the freedom of speech, or of the press; or the right of the people peaceably to assemble, and to petition the Government for redress of grievances.

(The First Amendment)

Although the First Amendment to the U.S. Constitution declares that "Congress shall make no law . . . abridging the freedom of speech, or of the press," these freedoms are not absolute. Some restrictions are necessary because they sometimes conflict with other rights that are also protected by the Constitution. For example: the Constitution protects Americans' reputations and privacy, yet some news stories may damage their reputations and invade their privacy.

Each time a conflict between two constitutional rights arises, it is up to the courts to try to balance them. The courts determine which right should be the preferred or dominating right in a particular case, and their decisions provide guidelines that can be applied in other cases.

The Constitution has been amended only 26 times. Nevertheless, the law is constantly evolving. As our society changes, its needs also change, and courts reinterpret the Constitution and apply it in new ways. Interpretations of the Constitution are also affected by new appointments to the U.S. Supreme Court. The Court's decisions may change significantly from one decade to another because of the appointment of new justices whose philosophies are more liberal or more conservative than those of their predecessors.

This chapter will examine recent decisions involving the First Amendment and the effect of those decisions on journalists. The decisions involve six legal issues of particular interest to journalists: libel, privacy, the free press/fair trial dilemma, the government's use of subpoenas to obtain information, the adoption of shield laws to protect journalists, and censorship.

Libel

Every reporter and editor is expected to understand the problem of libel and to help their newspapers avoid it. However, generalizations about libel are difficult. Libel laws are adopted by the 50 states, not by the federal government, and consequently vary from one area to another. Moreover, as new cases reach the Supreme Court, its decisions change, often dramatically. A series of favorable decisions that began in 1964 encouraged journalists to believe that the laws of libel were being repealed—that it had become almost impossible for responsible journalists to lose a libel suit. In an effort to encourage a free and vigorous discussion of public issues, the Supreme Court protected even news stories that contained obvious factual errors, so long as the errors were not malicious. However, a series of more recent decisions has created new guidelines that now make it easier for individuals, especially private citizens, to sue the media for libel.

Filing a Libel Suit

"Libel" has been defined as a written statement that exposes a person to hatred, ridicule or contempt, that causes other people to avoid the victim, or that impairs the victim's ability to earn a living. Stated more simply, a libel is a written statement that damages a person's reputation. The libel may appear anywhere in a newspaper: in a news story, headline, photograph, advertisement, editorial or letter to the editor. Depending upon the circumstances, citizens can also sue the broadcast media for slander, which is oral rather than written. Because it is less permanent, slander is usually considered less serious than libel.

An individual who believes that a printed statement has damaged his or her reputation can file a civil lawsuit against the publication. The courts hearing the suit will balance two conflicting rights: the media's right to gather and report the news and the individual's right to protect his or her reputation. If the courts find that the individual's reputation was indeed damaged unfairly, they usually award that person a sum of money to be paid by the publication to compensate for the damage.

The person who claims to have been libeled (the plaintiff) usually files a suit against a newspaper's publisher and against the company that owns the paper, since they can afford to pay the largest possible settlements. However, each person who handles a story can be held personally liable for its content, and suits may also name the reporter who wrote the story and the editor who checked it.

To win a libel suit, the plaintiff has traditionally been required to prove three points: (1) that he or she has been identified; (2) that he or she has been defamed; and (3) that the libel has been published.

Identification.

In order to win a libel suit, the plaintiff does not have to be identified by name if other facts in a story enable even a few readers to guess the victim's identity. However, only the person who is identified can file a libel suit; the victim's relatives cannot, even though they may be embarrassed by a story's publication. If the victim is dead, usually no one can file a suit for libel—so both journalists and historians are free to criticize the dead.

Reporters can avoid some libel suits by not identifying people who might be embarrassed by a story's publication. Thus, a reporter who wants to write about a humorous event or minor incident likely to interest readers may report that "a local woman" lost her swimsuit while diving into a pool, or that "a young father" suffered a broken nose while teaching his 4-year-old son how to box. Such stories do not libel anyone because they do not reveal the participants' exact identities.

However, journalists cannot always protect themselves so easily. The identity of people involved in the news is usually more important, and their names must be included in stories. For example, newspapers normally identify people who have been arrested and charged with serious crimes; their identities are news and a matter of public interest.

Defamation.

The plaintiff cannot win a libel suit simply because a story is false. To be actionable, the falsehood must damage the plaintiff's reputation. For example, courts have ruled that it is usually not libelous to report mistakenly that a married woman is pregnant, nor to report mistakenly that a person is dead. Judges have explained that it is not a disgrace for a married woman to become pregnant, nor for anyone to die. However, it would be libelous to report falsely that an unmarried woman was pregnant.

Publication.

The third proof requirement in libel suits, publication, occurs when a potentially libelous story appears in a newspaper and that newspaper is distributed to readers. If they discover a possible libel quickly enough, newspapers may be able to protect themselves by recalling and destroying all the copies that contain it.

The Defenses in Libel Suits

The presumption of innocence is reversed in libel suits, so that a newspaper is presumed guilty until it proves its innocence. The plaintiff is not required to prove that he or she is innocent (that the newspaper's charges are untrue). As the accuser of the plaintiff, the newspaper must prove that the charges it published are true. Publications may also rely on two other defenses, known as "fair comment" and "privilege."

Truth.

In many ways, truth is the best defense in a libel suit, but it may be difficult to prove to a judge or jury that the facts reported in a news story are true. In many states, truth alone is an adequate defense. If a newspaper in those states can prove that the statements it published are true, it will win a libel suit. Newspapers in the remaining states must prove not only that the statements they published are true but also that they published those statements for good reason—on a proper occasion and for some justifiable purpose. Truth in those states is not an adequate defense if a newspaper published a story needlessly or maliciously. For example, a newspaper in those states could not report that a prominent individual committed a crime 10 or 20 years earlier unless something that person did recently made the past record a matter of public interest.

Newspapers cannot defend themselves in a libel suit by proving that they attributed a statement to someone else, nor by proving that they accurately quoted someone else. Newspapers that rely on the defense of truth must prove that a statement is true in and of itself, not just that the statement is an accurate account of what someone else said. Thus, if a police officer accused someone of committing a crime, a newspaper that reported the accusation would have to prove that the person actually did commit the crime, not just that the police officer said the person did.

Newspapers that accuse the plaintiff of a crime must also prove that the plaintiff is guilty of the specific crime they mentioned, not of any other crimes. Moreover, newspapers usually cannot protect themselves by saying that a story is "reportedly" or "allegedly" true. To win a libel suit, they must prove that it *is* true.

Thus, newspapers are legally responsible for everything they publish. It does not matter whether a libelous statement was provided by a reporter, advertiser, news service, press release or police officer, nor that it was published in a direct quotation or letter to an editor. The fact that a newspaper published a libelous statement accidentally or unknowingly (or that its reporter obtained the libelous material from another person) will not absolve it of guilt.

Privilege.

Government officials (presidents, legislators and judges, for example) enjoy an absolute privilege while acting in their official capacities. Regardless of whether their statements are true or false, defamatory or not, the officials cannot be sued for libel. Everyone participating in a judicial proceeding, such as a trial, also enjoys an absolute privilege. Courts grant that privilege because they believe it is important that certain people be allowed to speak freely and fearlessly.

Reporters enjoy a "qualified privilege" to report the statements made during those official government proceedings. To be protected by that privilege, their stories must be full, fair and accurate. Courts grant reporters immunity from libel suits in instances when the need to inform citizens about public affairs is more important than the need to protect an individual's reputation.

However, reporters can invoke the defense only while reporting official government proceedings. The proceedings include almost everything the president says and does, congressional and legislative sessions, and trials. However, the qualified privilege does not protect statements that government officials make outside those proceedings—the statements a police officer makes at the scene of a crime, for example. It also excludes statements made at the meetings of private organizations.

Fair Comment.

"Fair comment" is a legal doctrine that enables newspapers to express their *opinions* about matters of public interest. Because of that doctrine, newspapers are free to criticize public figures and public officials, including politicians, actors and actresses, inventors, writers, astronauts and athletes. Newspapers are also free to criticize the work of public figures, including radio and television programs, speeches, plays, movies, books, paintings and athletic events. Even the meals served by restaurants and the cars manufactured in Detroit are subject to public criticism. Courts have explained that people who deliberately go before the public, who seek the public's approval, and whose own actions invite public interest in their lives, must be willing to accept unfavorable as well as favorable publicity.

Some people are thrust into the news unwillingly, and newspapers are free to comment on the actions and lives of these people. They may be involved in an accident or other newsworthy event that makes them public figures, however fleetingly.

Journalists who invoke the defense of fair comment do not have to prove that their criticisms are true. Because the criticisms involve matters of opinion rather than fact, it may be impossible for anyone to prove that the criticisms are either true or false. Furthermore, the criticisms may be unpopular and harsh. A recent review of the book "Always on Sunday" by Peggy Whedon began: "This is a remarkably dreadful book . . . Actually, it is a mish-mash of unrelated trivia and girlish revelations." Similarly, a movie review in Newsweek magazine began:

> They say that if a million monkeys sat down at typewriters, one of them would eventually produce "War and Peace." Well, one of them—bearing the name of Jeremy Joe Kronsberg—seems to have written *Every Which Way But Loose*, a Clint Eastwood "comedy" that could not possibly have been created by human hands.

Two Additional Defenses.

As two additional but less common defenses, newspapers may try to prove that the plaintiff consented to a story's publication or that the statute of limitations has expired. The statute of limitations varies from state to state. In most states, libel suits must be filed within one, two or three years of a defamatory story's publication.

Secondary Defenses in Libel Suits

Some secondary defenses are available to newspapers sued for libel. However, those defenses are used less frequently and normally offer less protection than truth, privilege and fair comment. The secondary defenses do not absolve newspapers of guilt but may lessen the amount they are required to pay in damages.

Newspapers will do everything possible to show that they did not injure a victim intentionally—that they made an honest error, that they sincerely regret the error, and that they have retracted or corrected it. Newspapers may try to show that they obtained their information from a normally reliable source, had no way of knowing that it was false, were at least partially correct, innocently republished a statement that had already been printed elsewhere, or accidentally identified the wrong person.

As another defense, newspapers may attempt to prove that a plaintiff's reputation was already so bad that it could not be damaged any further by the story they published.

Types of Damages

Normally, juries award successful plaintiffs "compensatory" or "general" damages to compensate for their emotional suffering, the damage to their reputations and their financial losses. Plaintiffs do not have to prove that they actually suffered any harm. If newspapers obviously libeled someone—if they called someone a Communist, criminal, drug addict, prostitute or quack—courts assume that the victim suffered some harm and award compensatory damages.

Juries can award "special" damages to plaintiffs able to prove that they suffered some additional or specific losses to their reputations or businesses.

Juries award "punitive" damages to punish publications found guilty of irresponsible conduct and to discourage the conduct's recurrence. To win punitive damages, plaintiffs must prove that the publication acted with malice. Both special and punitive damages can be awarded in addition to compensatory damages.

New York Times vs. *Sullivan*

In 1964 the U.S. Supreme Court made it virtually impossible for public officials to sue the media for libel. The Supreme Court ruled that public officials cannot be awarded any damages, not even for stories that contain obvious factual errors, so long as the media do not act maliciously.

The New York Times had published an advertisement for a civil rights group, and the advertisement charged that police officers armed with shotguns and tear gas had ringed an Alabama campus. The advertisement did not name L. B. Sullivan, the commissioner for public affairs in Montgomery, but Sullivan was responsible for the city's police department. He complained that the advertisement contained several errors, sued The New York Times for libel and was awarded $500,000. The Alabama State Supreme Court upheld the decision, but the U.S. Supreme Court ruled against Sullivan.

The U.S. Supreme Court said it considered the case "against the background of a profound national commitment to the principle that debate on public issues should be uninhibited, robust, and wide-open, and that it may well include vehement, caustic and sometimes unpleasantly sharp attacks on government officials." Justice William Brennan Jr., in writing the majority opinion, added:

We are required for the first time in this case to determine the extent to which the constitutional protections for speech and press limit a state's power to award damages in a libel action brought by a public official against the critics of his official conduct. . . .

The constitutional guarantees require, we think, a federal rule that prohibits a public official from recovering damages for a defamatory falsehood relating to his official conduct unless he proves that the statement was made with "actual malice," that is, with the knowledge that it was false or with a reckless disregard of whether it was false or not.

This ruling remains in effect today: To win a libel suit, a public official must prove that the publication acted with "actual malice," which the Supreme Court defined as the publication of a defamatory statement that the media knew was false or that the media published "with a reckless disregard of whether it was false or not." This doctrine has become known as the "New York Times rule." The Supreme Court adopted the rule to encourage debate on public issues. The Court feared that if the media could be punished for honest mistakes, they would become more hesitant to discuss important issues and to publish even truthful criticisms of public officials.

Expanding the Media's Freedom

In 1967 the U.S. Supreme Court declared that the New York Times rule applied to public figures as well as to public officials. In 1971, the court added that the rule also applied to private citizens who become involved in matters of public interest. Thus, the media no longer had to determine whether an individual was a public official, a public figure or a private citizen. If anyone became involved in an issue of public interest, the media were free to report on that issue with an almost total immunity from libel suits.

Combining two cases, on June 12, 1967, the Supreme Court ruled on both *Butts* vs. *Curtis Publishing Co.* and *Associated Press* vs. *Walker*. The Curtis Publishing Co. owned the Saturday Evening Post, which reported that Wallace Butts, the athletic director at the University of Georgia, had conspired to fix a football game. The Post charged that Butts had given his team's plays and defensive patterns to the University of Alabama. Butts sued the Curtis Publishing Co. for libel, and a jury awarded him $60,000 in general and $3 million in punitive damages.

The Supreme Court ruled that Butts was a public figure but upheld the award because the Saturday Evening Post had acted with a "reckless disregard for the truth"—a violation of the New York Times rule. The Court explained that the story was not "hot news," and the magazine's editors could have taken time to conduct a more thorough investigation but failed to do so. The editors knew that their source was on probation for bad-check charges but failed to examine his notes, failed to interview a second witness and failed to screen films of the game to determine whether the source's information was accurate. The editors also failed to determine whether Alabama changed its game plans after allegedly receiving the information. Moreover, "The Post writer assigned to the story was not a football expert, and no attempt was made to check the story with someone knowledgeable in the sport." The Court concluded, "In short, the evidence is ample to support a finding of highly unreasonable conduct constituting an extreme departure from the standards of investigation and reporting ordinarily adhered to by responsible publishers." Butts eventually settled for $460,000.

In the other suit, however, the Supreme Court ruled against Walker, a former Army general. The Associated Press reported that Walker had assumed command of some students and led a charge against federal marshals trying to help James Meredith, a black student, enter the University of Mississippi. The story also reported that Walker encouraged the rioters to use violence and instructed them on ways to avoid the effects of tear gas. The Court found that the story contained some factual errors, but it concluded that, "Under any reasoning, Gen. Walker was a public man in whose conduct society and the press had a legitimate and substantial interest." Moreover, an AP reporter was at the scene, seemed to be trustworthy and competent, and wrote a story that required immediate dissemination. The Court found that: "Nothing in this series of events gives the slightest hint of a severe departure from accepted publishing standards. We therefore conclude that Gen. Walker should not be entitled to damages from The Associated Press."

In *Rosenbloom* vs. *Metromedia, Inc.* (1971), the Supreme Court applied the New York Times rule to a private citizen involved in matters of public interest. The police in Philadelphia had arrested George A. Rosenbloom and charged him with distributing nudist magazines. Radio station WIP reported his arrest, said the magazines were obscene and added that the city was cracking down on "smut merchants." After being acquitted, Rosenbloom sued Metromedia, Inc., the company that owned WIP. A jury awarded Rosenbloom both general and punitive damages, but the Supreme Court overturned the award.

Rosenbloom was not a public official nor a public figure. Nevertheless, Justice William Brennan said:

> If a matter is a subject of public or general interest, it cannot suddenly become less so merely because a private individual is involved, or because in some sense the individual did not "voluntarily" choose to become involved. . . .
>
> We honor the commitment to robust debate on public issues, which is embodied in the First Amendment, by extending constitutional protection to all discussion and communication involving matters of public or general concern, without regard to whether the persons are famous or anonymous. . . .
>
> We thus hold that a libel action, as here by a private individual against a licensed radio station for a defamatory falsehood in a newscast relating to his involvement in an event of public or general concern, may be sustained only upon clear and convincing proof that the defamatory falsehood was published with knowledge that it was false or with reckless disregard of whether it was false or not.

Gertz vs. *Welch*

In 1974 the Supreme Court seemed to change its mind in *Gertz* vs. *Welch*. Its decision in that case now makes it easier for private citizens to sue the media for libel.

A Chicago policeman shot and killed a youth in 1968, and the victim's family hired attorney Elmer Gertz to file a civil suit against the policeman. American Opinion, a monthly magazine published by the John Birch Society, called Gertz a "Communist-fronter," implied that he had a criminal record and said that he had designed a national campaign to discredit the police. Gertz sued for libel, and a jury awarded him $50,000. The Supreme Court upheld that award by a vote of 5–4.

In the Gertz case, the Supreme Court said that private citizens deserve more protection than public officials and public figures. Public officials and public figures must prove actual malice because they have given up some of their privacy voluntarily. The Court ruled that Gertz was a private citizen, not a public official or public figure, because he did not have "general fame or notoriety in the community" and did not "thrust himself into the vortex of this public issue, nor did he engage the public's attention in an attempt to influence its outcome."

The Court added that private citizens are entitled to damages if they can prove that a statement was false and defamatory and published as the result of negligence or carelessness. It defined the criterion for negligence as whether a "reasonable person" would have done the same thing as the publisher under the same circumstances.

Time, Inc. vs. *Firestone* and *Hutchinson* vs. *Proxmire*

In 1976 the Supreme Court further narrowed its definition of public figures in *Time, Inc.* vs. *Firestone*. Time magazine had reported that tire-company heir Russell Firestone was granted a divorce from his wife, Mary Alice Firestone, on grounds of "extreme cruelty and adultery." Because the court had made no finding of adultery, Mrs.

Firestone sued Time and was awarded $100,000. Time appealed, arguing that Mrs. Firestone was a public figure—a prominent socialite involved in a highly publicized divorce—and that she had even held press conferences during the divorce proceedings. As a public figure, Time argued, she should be required to prove actual malice.

The Supreme Court ruled that Mrs. Firestone was not a public figure because "she did not assume any role of special prominence in the affairs of society, other than perhaps Palm Beach society, and she did not thrust herself to the forefront of any particular public controversy in order to influence resolution of the issues involved in it."

Similarly, in *Hutchinson* vs. *Proxmire* (1979), the Supreme Court ruled that a scientist conducting research funded by the federal government is not a public figure. Sen. William Proxmire, D-Wis., had given his monthly Golden Fleece Award for wasteful government spending to Ronald R. Hutchinson. Hutchinson sued, and the Court ruled that he was not a public figure or public official because, under the Gertz rule, he "did not thrust himself or his views into public controversy to influence others." Proxmire's statements would have been privileged if he had spoken on the Senate floor; however, statements published in his 100,000-circulation newsletter were not privileged.

Thus, the plaintiff's burden in a libel suit depends on his or her identity. Every plaintiff must prove publication, identification and defamation. Public officials and public figures must prove, in addition, that the publisher knew a statement was false or acted with a reckless disregard for whether it was false or not. Private citizens need only prove, in addition, that the publisher acted negligently.

The 1980s: Applying Gertz and Sullivan

The outcome of three major cases heard during the 1980s depended upon rules formulated during the 1960s and 1970s. The media seemed to win two of the cases. However, both victories were expensive—and controversial.

Dun & Bradstreet, Inc. vs. *Greenmoss Builders*

During the 1980s, a closely divided court ruled that non-public figures do not have to prove that the media acted with malice—if the libelous material concerns *private* matters. The vote was 5–4, but the justices wrote four separate opinions. Only three signed the prevailing opinion.

Dun & Bradstreet issued a credit report stating that Greenmoss, a building contractor in Vermont, had filed for bankruptcy. Dun & Bradstreet obtained the information from a part-time employee: a 17-year-old high-school student. The student misinterpreted a bankruptcy petition filed by a former Greenmoss employee. The student thought that Greenmoss itself had filed for bankruptcy. After receiving the information, Dun & Bradstreet failed to follow its own rules about verifying the data.

Dun & Bradstreet sent its credit report to five subscribers, and Greenmoss learned about it while talking to a banker. Greenmoss asked Dun & Bradstreet for a correction and for the names of everyone who received the report. After checking and determining that it was mistaken, Dun & Bradstreet sent a corrective notice to the subscribers. Greenmoss was dissatisfied with its correction and again asked for the five names. Because Dun & Bradstreet again refused, Greenmoss sued for libel.

A Vermont jury awarded Greenmoss $50,000 in compensatory damages for the harm it suffered and $300,000 in punitive damages to punish Dun & Bradstreet for its handling of the matter. Dun & Bradstreet appealed, insisting that—under the Gertz rule—it should not have to pay anything because it had not acted with malice. In Gertz, the Supreme Court had ruled that a non-public plaintiff could recover some damages by proving that he or she had been harmed by a defamatory statement made negligently. To collect punitive damages, a non-public plaintiff had to prove that a statement had been made with actual malice.

The Supreme Court based its decision on what was said. The court ruled that a jury can award punitive damages, without proof of malice, if the libelous material does not involve a "matter of public concern." Justice Lewis F. Powell, who wrote the court's decision, explained: "We have long recognized that not all speech is of equal First Amendment importance. It is speech on 'matters of public concern' that is 'at the heart of the First Amendment's protection.' . . . Speech on matters of purely private concern is of less First Amendment concern."

Thus, the court upheld the punitive damages against Dun & Bradstreet because its credit report was not in the public interest. Rather, it was "solely in the individual interest of the speaker and its specific business audience." The court failed to define "public concern," and its decision alarmed journalists. They fear that other judges will begin to second-guess their news judgment: to rule on whether other stories they publish truly involve matters of public concern.

Ariel Sharon vs. *Time, Inc.*

Israel's former defense minister, Ariel Sharon, filed a $50 million libel suit against Time, Inc. Time reported that Christian Phalangist militiamen killed 700 Arabs two days after the assassination of Lebanese President-elect Bashir Gemayel. The Phalangists drove into Palestinian refugee camps in West Beirut, supposedly searching for terrorists, but instead, they massacred hundreds of unarmed men, women and children.

The Israeli government appointed a commission to investigate the massacre, and it found that Sharon bore an "indirect responsibility" for the deaths. The commission explained that Sharon allowed Phalangists into the Arab camps, despite warnings that they might seek revenge.

Time also reported that, after Gemayel's assassination, Sharon visited the Gemayel family to express his condolences. Time added that a classified appendix to the commission's report indicated that during Sharon's visit, he discussed the Phalangists' need for revenge.

Sharon admitted meeting with the Gemayel family but insisted that he never discussed revenge. Sharon also insisted that the secret appendix did not, as Time claimed, say that he had talked about revenge. He sued Time, charging that its story implied that he had deliberately encouraged the massacre—an accusation well beyond the commission's public findings.

As a public figure, Sharon had to prove actual malice. Sharon's lawyers charged that David Halevy, Time's correspondent in Jerusalem, was unreliable and prejudiced against Sharon. The lawyers accused Halevy of inventing portions of his story, and they accused Time's staff in New York of failing to verify the details. Halevy responded that he relied on four sources, including an Israeli intelligence officer who took notes during Sharon's condolence call.

At first, the Israeli government refused to let Time's lawyers examine the secret appendix. Israel later relented, and attorneys for both sides looked at it. The appendix never mentioned a conversation about revenge, so Time was forced to admit—in court—that it had been mistaken. However, Time continued to insist that its error had been a minor one.

The trial lasted six weeks. Sharon called only 13 witnesses, and Time did not call any defense witnesses.

The judge instructed the jury to reach its verdict in three steps. First, the jury had to decide whether Sharon was defamed. Did Time say that Sharon encouraged the massacre, or only that he knew it might occur? The jury concluded that Time defamed Sharon.

Second, the jury had to decide the question of truth or falsity. Was Time accurate when it described Sharon's condolence call? The jury concluded that Time was mistaken. Thus, the jury found Time guilty of both defamation and falsehood. However, Time continued to hope that the jury would rule in its favor on the third question: whether it acted with malice. For Sharon to win, the jury had to answer all three questions in his favor.

The jury criticized Time for acting "negligently and carelessly" while reporting and verifying its information, but nevertheless ruled in its favor. Sharon had failed to prove that Time acted with a reckless disregard for the truth. Thus, the jury concluded that Time's story was defamatory and false, but that Time was careless rather than reckless.

Both sides claimed victory. Sharon did not receive any money but said that he filed the libel suit to clear his reputation and to prove that Time had lied. Time won the legal battle, but its reputation suffered. Many Americans could not understand—or agree with—the jury's verdict. Sharon proved that he was defamed, and that Time reported false information, yet he still lost.

Gen. William Westmoreland vs. CBS News

In 1982, the CBS television network broadcast a 90-minute documentary titled "The Uncounted Enemy: A Vietnam Deception." It charged that Gen. William Westmoreland, who commanded the U.S. forces in South Vietnam from 1964 to 1968, engaged in a deliberate conspiracy to mislead his superiors, including President Lyndon Johnson, about the number of enemy soldiers in Vietnam (and about his success in defeating them). The documentary accused Westmoreland of telling President Johnson and the Joint Chiefs of Staff that there were about 300,000 Viet Cong, yet many intelligence officers believed there were 500,000, or perhaps even 600,000. The documentary also charged that Westmoreland and his staff failed to report that nearly 25,000 North Vietnamese troops were infiltrating the South each month.

The war in Vietnam was America's longest and costliest war—and a war of attrition. There seemed to be only one measure of success: the "body count," or number of Viet Cong killed each month. Westmoreland was trying to kill the Viet Cong faster than they could be replaced.

The documentary charged that Westmoreland minimized the enemy's strength to make it appear that he was winning the war. CBS added that Americans learned the truth—the enemy's real strength—during the Tet offensive in January, 1968. The offensive showed that the Communists were able to strike anywhere in South Vietnam, including Saigon.

Westmoreland sued CBS for $120 million, though he was counseled that it would be difficult for him to win. Like Sharon, he would have to prove malice. Westmoreland charged that CBS news producer George Crile and CBS correspondent Mike Wallace were wrong, and that they knew they were wrong. Westmoreland also claimed that he had been "ambushed." He charged that CBS tricked him into the interview by promising a fair and educational study of the Tet offensive. Westmoreland's lawyers also tried to show that CBS failed to present a balanced account.

CBS seemed to be in trouble even before the trial started. Critics—including other journalists—accused CBS of treating Westmoreland unfairly: of taking some quotes out of context, of ignoring facts that conflicted with its own conclusions, and of retaping an interview with a source critical of the general. Because of the criticisms, CBS conducted an internal investigation, and it revealed that people working on the documentary had violated the network's own rules.

In court, Westmoreland testified that there was no deceit or conspiracy. He insisted that CIA and military analysts genuinely disagreed about whether they should count the Viet Cong's irregular, self-defense forces. Westmoreland's count did not include those forces, and he explained that they were part-time and often untrained civilians: mainly old men, women and youths. He considered them a home guard with no offensive capability: poorly armed and badly organized, not dangerous fighters to be killed.

The trial ended abruptly, just a few days before it was scheduled to go to the jury.

Westmoreland withdrew, and the two sides issued a joint statement saying, in part, "CBS respects Gen. Westmoreland's long and faithful service to his country and never intended to assert, and does not believe, that Gen. Westmoreland was unpatriotic or disloyal in performing his duties as he saw fit."

Westmoreland claimed that he had won, yet he received no money and no retraction: only the statement saying that CBS did not think he was disloyal. Westmoreland called it an apology that affirmed his honor, yet CBS never admitted that its documentary was mistaken. Moreover, CBS had reportedly offered to make a similar statement a year earlier.

Why did Westmoreland withdraw? It appeared that CBS was proving, in court, that its documentary was basically true. Several of Westmoreland's subordinates from his duty in Vietnam and CIA officials testified that estimates of the enemy's troop strength were tainted by politics. Even Westmoreland's former intelligence chief, a retired major general, testified that Westmoreland withheld information because it would cause a "political bombshell" in Washington. Some testimony was even more harmful for Westmoreland than the statements aired during the CBS documentary.

As the testimony turned against Westmoreland, his supporters seemed to become confused and demoralized. Some feared the jury would rule that CBS had not acted with malice, and even worse, might rule that the documentary was accurate—that Westmoreland had lied to his superiors. The Capital Legal Foundation, a conservative public-interest firm based in Washington, D.C., had offered to represent Westmoreland and to pay most of his legal expenses. But it began to run out of money, and may have been reluctant to invest any more in a case that it seemed to be losing. (During interviews conducted after the settlement the jurors indicated that they would have voted in favor of CBS.)

Westmoreland had filed the libel suit to vindicate himself; instead, it vindicated CBS. Thus, he turned a publicity victory into a courtroom defeat. He was worse off after the trial than before it. Stories published before the trial favored him, charging that CBS acted unfairly. If Westmoreland never filed his lawsuit, millions of Americans might continue to believe that CBS was both unfair and mistaken.

It seemed to be a major victory for CBS—but an expensive one. CBS spent about $250,000 to produce the documentary and millions to defend it. The network never revealed its legal expenses, but experts estimated that the two sides spent $7 million to $9 million in legal fees. Of that, Westmoreland's costs were estimated at $3.5 million. Moreover, some of the testimony harmed CBS, suggesting that, although accurate, the documentary may not have been fair.

Experts disagree about whether the results of *Sharon* vs. *Time, Inc.* and *Westmoreland* vs. *CBS News* will discourage other libel suits. Victories for Sharon and Westmoreland might have encouraged other public figures to file more libel suits against the media, but because they lost, others may conclude that libel suits are too expensive and difficult to win. Both cases also showed that the media can put up a strong defense. In addition, Westmoreland's case showed that plaintiffs may actually harm their reputations. The media may prove their cases in court even more effectively than they did in print.

Yet the two cases also show that plaintiffs can impose an expensive burden upon the media. The media may have to spend millions of dollars to defend themselves, and their executives may be embroiled in litigation for years.

Libel's Chilling Effect

The high cost of libel suits has a chilling effect on the media. Even the threat of a libel suit may make the media more timid. While larger media, such as the CBS television network, are able to protect themselves, smaller newspapers and broadcasting stations are more vulnerable. A single libel suit could force the smaller media into bankruptcy. To avoid this, some editors now censor themselves. They avoid investigative stories or remove the stories' most controversial details. Even book publishers seem frightened by the threat of libel. Many now edit their manuscripts to avoid anything even potentially dangerous.

Twenty years ago, the jury in a successful libel case awarded the plaintiff an average of $20,000. The first million-dollar verdict was awarded in 1976. By the early 1980s, the *average* award was close to $2.2 million.

However, plaintiffs rarely collect that much. Recent studies show that 74 percent of all the libel suits filed against the media never reach a jury. During the mid-1980s, newspapers lost 64 percent of the libel suits that did reach a jury. But that was an improvement: newspapers had lost 83 percent of the cases that went to jury during the previous four years. Moreover, at least 75 percent of the jury awards are overturned on appeal. Another 10 percent are substantially reduced, to an average of about $60,000.

The media can protect themselves by purchasing libel insurance, but it is expensive. A small weekly, published in a rural area, can buy libel insurance for $500 a year. Small dailies can buy a $10 million policy for $1,300, but larger dailies may have to pay $50,000. Newspapers already sued for libel are considered poor risks and pay up to $200,000.

Many of the libel policies have deductibles that require newspapers to pay the first $20,000 or $30,000. Due to rising legal costs, some insurance companies also require newspapers to pay 20 percent of *all* their legal costs, even beyond the $20,000 or $30,000 deductibles.

The Alton (Ill.) Telegraph, a daily with a circulation of 37,831, was forced into bankruptcy in 1981 by a libel suit resulting from a memo that it never published. Two of the newspaper's reporters sent a Justice Department lawyer a memo which said that their sources linked a local building contractor to the underworld. The charge was never substantiated, and the newspaper never published a story about it. However, when the contractor learned about the memo, he sued the Telegraph, and a jury awarded him $9.2 million, the largest amount a daily newspaper has ever been ordered to pay in a libel suit. The case was settled out of court for $1.4 million. Bankruptcy laws allowed the Telegraph to continue publication throughout the litigation, and the settlement enabled it to remain in business.

Similarly, in 1981, a California jury ordered the National Enquirer to pay actress Carol Burnett $1.6 million. The newspaper reported that:

> At a Washington restaurant, a boisterous Carol Burnett had a loud argument with another diner, Henry Kissinger. She traipsed around the place offering everyone a bite of her dessert. But Carol really raised eyebrows when she accidentally knocked a glass of wine over one diner and started giggling instead of apologizing. The guy wasn't amused and "accidentally" spilled a glass of water over Carol's dress.

Miss Burnett complained that the story was false, and the National Enquirer published a correction. Nevertheless, she sued the newspaper for libel, and a jury awarded her $300,000 in actual damages and $1.3 million in punitive damages. Witnesses testified that Miss Burnett had not been boisterous, had not argued, had not traipsed around and had not offered "everyone" a bite of her dessert. Moreover, she is a teetotaler, and the story implied that she was tipsy.

Many Americans consider the National Enquirer a sensational, even a disreputable, newspaper, and its story obviously contained several errors. But should any newspaper, regardless of its popularity, be ordered to pay $1.6 million because of the publication of a single story? Columnist James J. Kilpatrick said he was not concerned about the National Enquirer, "a penny-dreadful magazine that has grown fat on journalistic garbage." But he feared that "an award of $1.6 million is simply grotesque. The Enquirer's earnings reportedly are slightly under $2 million a year. Two or three such verdicts, and it's goodbye Enquirer." (A judge later reduced the award.)

Even newspapers that win libel suits may find their victories prohibitively expensive. Consider The Milkweed, a monthly newsletter that reports on the milk marketing industry for dairy farmers. In 1981, the Eastern Milk Producers Cooperative filed a $20 million libel suit against the newsletter, which had only 1,200 subscribers. Eastern, one of the largest dairy cooperatives in the Northeast, charged that the newsletter contained defamatory and inaccurate statements, including a prediction that the cooperative would lose more than $10 million. A federal judge dismissed the suit, but the newsletter's editor and publisher, Peter Hardin, feared that he was "in danger of winning the war but losing the peace." His legal expenses and other defense costs were nearly $20,000, or more than half of the newsletter's annual income.

Why Are the Media Being Sued?

Americans seem to believe that the media are too large, powerful, arrogant, sensational, inaccurate and irresponsible. Consequently, people are more willing to sue the media for libel. But libel suits are also part of a growing trend. More Americans are also suing doctors for malpractice and manufacturers for the injuries caused by defective products. Even lawyers are experiencing rising malpractice insurance as their own clients sue them.

People are outraged when the media publish stories critical of them. They file most libel suits to restore their reputations and to obtain some compensation for the harm they have suffered. In court, the plaintiffs usually claim that their reputations were ruined or their careers destroyed. Jurors seem to sympathize with the plaintiffs, especially when a story is obviously mistaken or unfair. The plaintiffs may hope to win millions of dollars and feel they have nothing to lose. They can engage attorneys to represent them on a contingency basis. If their cases fail, the plaintiffs pay their attorneys nothing. If they win, the attorneys receive a share of their award or settlement.

Other libel suits—a growing number—are being filed by public officials. The officials may realize that public opinion is shifting in their favor (and against the media). Also, some officials may want to punish or intimidate the media.

Paul Laxalt, a former U.S. senator from Nevada and former chairman of the Republican Party, sued The Sacramento (Calif.) Bee for $250 million. The McClatchy Newspaper Group publishes several newspapers, including The Bee, and in 1984 reported that some illegal "skimming" had occurred at a casino that Laxalt owned. The story also mentioned some alleged ties to organized crime.

Within a week, McClatchy filed a $6 million countersuit. Frank McCulloch, the group's executive editor, explained that: "Basically, it was our conviction that Sen. Laxalt sued us for the purpose of keeping CBS and ABC from doing programs on the same topic. . . . We felt he was trying to intimidate the rest of the press, and we filed suit for that purpose. Also, as far as we know, there were no errors whatsoever in our story, so we were persuaded that his suit was abuse of process."

Laxalt and the McClatchy Newspapers settled out of court 3 1/2 years later. Both sides claimed victory.

Laxalt agreed to dismiss his $250 million libel suit, and McClatchy agreed to drop its $6 million countersuit. The two sides issued a joint statement saying that discovery proceedings in the libel action failed to uncover any evidence of skimming at the Laxalt casino. The two sides also agreed to let a panel of three retired judges decide whether the newspapers should reimburse Laxalt for his attorneys' fees.

Laxalt announced, "We've received everything we wanted." He explained that the McClatchy Newspapers had spent millions of dollars investigating the case, but "came up with zip." With the legal fight ended, Laxalt announced plans to seek the Republican Party's nomination for president.

C. K. McClatchy, president of the McClatchy Newspapers, issued a separate statement insisting that the newspapers had not retracted their story. "We are the winners as far as I'm concerned," McClatchy said. "We have not retracted, we have not apologized, and we have not paid any damages." Despite his apparent victory, McClatchy said he feared that the case would encourage other politicians to use the same tactic: to intimidate newspapers by threatening to sue them for libel.

Elsewhere around the country, city council members, legislators, judges, mayors, governors and other public officials are increasingly bringing suits against the media, sometimes for amounts excessively greater than the net worth of those media, in litigations that can drag on for 8 to 10 years, even before the appeal process starts.

However, the media are not the only victims. More libel suits—perhaps 1,000 a year—are being filed against private citizens and other institutions, often by public officials. Anyone can be sued: a citizen who accuses the police of brutality, an environmental group that accuses a developer of pollution or a politician who accuses a rival of corruption.

When they fight the suits, the media usually win. In 1979, The Washington Post reported that William Tavoulareas, president of Mobil Corp., used his influence to set up his son, Peter, in business. Both Tavoulareas and his son sued the Post for libel. In 1982, a federal jury in Washington found that the Post had defamed the elder Tavoulareas, but not his son. The jury awarded Tavoulareas $2,050,000. A federal judge threw out the verdict, but a panel of three judges later reinstated it. In 1987—eight years after the story's publication—the full appeals court reversed their decision. By a vote of 7–1, the appeals court ruled that Tavoulareas had failed to prove that the Post acted with malice. The appeals court also found that the Post's story was essentially correct. By then, the Post's legal fees exceeded $1 million.

Avoiding and Discouraging Legal Action

Journalists can avoid libel suits by striving to be fairer and more accurate. When they do make a mistake, they should admit their error and publish a correction as quickly as possible. Researchers at the University of Iowa interviewed plaintiffs involved in libel suits during a 10-year period and found that more than half of the suits could have been avoided. The plaintiffs said that when they first went to the media to complain, they were insulted or ignored. The Iowa study also found that many plaintiffs did not care about the money they might win. They filed the suits to protect or restore their reputations—or to punish the media.

Some newspapers assign a single individual, called an "ombudsman," to handle all the complaints they receive. The ombudsman is usually an experienced and impartial editor who investigates the complaints and has the power to publish a correction or retraction whenever a newspaper has erred.

To discourage libel suits, newspapers are also filing more countersuits. As a matter of policy, the Charleston (W. Va.) Gazette files a countersuit whenever it considers a libel suit frivolous or an attempt to intimidate it. After countersuing for malicious prosecution, the Gazette received a $12,500 settlement from a lawyer. In another countersuit, also filed against a lawyer, the Hollywood (Fla.) Sun-Tattler won $25,097 in legal fees and court costs.

A third countersuit, filed in California, was even more successful for the media. In 1979, the Port Reyes Light, a weekly with a circulation of 3,100, won a Pulitzer Prize for a series of articles about Synanon, a drug rehabilitation center. Synanon responded by suing the Light's publisher, David Mitchell, and his former wife, Cathy. Four libel suits filed against the Light demanded a total of more than $1 billion. The Mitchells countersued, charging that Synanon's libel suits were attempts at harassment and intimidation. Synanon settled out of court, reportedly paying the Mitchells $100,000 for "defamation, abuse of process and malicious prosecution." As part of the settlement, both sides dropped their lawsuits.

To avoid libel suits and to protect the reputation of innocent persons, reporters rarely suggest that anyone mentioned in a news story was negligent or guilty of a crime. Reporters can say that a person has been arrested and charged with a crime (a fact that is easily proved), but not that the person actually committed the crime. If an automobile accident injured several people, journalists would report only that two cars collided; few would attempt to determine which driver was responsible for the collision. That is the job of the police and the courts. Even if several witnesses said one driver was drunk and sped through a stop sign, journalists normally would not report their allegations. The driver must be presumed innocent until convicted in a court of law, not by the people standing on a streetcorner:

> LIBELOUS: Thomas was drunk when his car sped through the stop sign and struck the van.
> REVISED: Police charged Thomas with failure to stop for a red light, speeding and drunken driving.

If the police did not file any charges against Thomas, the allegations could not be reported. Similarly, newspapers could not safely report:

> Sheriff Gus DiCesare said he caught two thieves, William Johnson and Marvin Wilke, both of 2107 N. Ninth St., red-handed as they broke into a service station at 802 Jefferson Ave. last night.

The sentence calls the men thieves, yet the only proof of that is the sheriff's statement. The men are not public figures, there has been no official governmental proceeding, and they have not been convicted by a judge or jury. If the men sued a newspaper after it reported the sheriff's allegations, the newspaper would be required to prove that the men were thieves, not just that the sheriff said they were. Yet the sheriff might be mistaken, charges against the men might be reduced or dropped, or a jury might find the men innocent. Reporters could avoid a libel suit by reporting only that the suspects had been arrested and charged with the crime:

> Sheriff Gus DiCesare charged William Johnson and Marvin Wilke, both of 2107 N. Ninth St., with breaking into a service station last night.
> DiCesare said a service station at 802 Jefferson Ave. was broken into and $80 was taken from a cash drawer.

As rewritten, the story no longer reports that Johnson and Wilke are guilty, only that a service station was broken into and that they have been charged with the crime—again, facts that are easily proved.

Newspapers will not usually report the charges that one private citizen makes about another. The charges are likely to be libelous and, in most cases, of little interest to the public. Charges voiced during family disputes, including divorces, are among the most common examples. Women beaten by their boyfriends or husbands often call the police and, if newspapers reported their allegations and were later sued for libel, they would be forced to rely on the women's testimony. Yet the men would be likely to deny their charges, making the situation one person's word against another's; moreover, some women might be afraid to testify against the men.

Thus, reporters who write stories that damage another person's reputation must exercise extreme caution. They might ask themselves: "Is this story true, and can I prove its truth in a courtroom?" "Is the person involved a public figure or a public official?" "Was the person involved in an official governmental proceeding, such as a trial or a legislative session?" If reporters are unable to answer "yes" to at least one of those questions (that is, if they are unable to rely on the defenses of truth, privilege or fair comment), they should eliminate the libelous comments from their stories or kill the stories.

Alternatives

Many journalists would like the courts to order the losers in every libel suit to pay the winners' legal fees. Journalists believe that fewer people would file frivolous suits if, after losing, they were ordered to pay the media's legal fees.

Other journalists would like the courts to make it impossible for any public official to sue the media for libel. A few justices on the U.S. Supreme Court—but never a majority—have advocated this sweeping of a doctrine.

Journalists have also proposed less costly alternatives to libel suits. The legal system might be changed so that plaintiffs sue, not to recover damages, but only to determine a story's truth or falsity. The plaintiffs who won their cases would be entitled to a retraction and their legal costs, but not huge damage awards. However, none of the plaintiffs—not even public officials—would have to prove that the media acted with malice.

Other journalists and legal scholars want judges to negotiate more pretrial settlements, or to have more libel cases taken out of courtrooms and arbitrated by some other means. Again, the emphasis might be on retractions and the correction of errors rather than on the award of damages. By avoiding the legal system, cases might be decided in a few weeks rather than years. Moreover, neither side would have to pay thousands of dollars in legal fees.

Other journalists are turning to their state legislatures for help. For example: the South Carolina Press Association supported a bill that would have limited punitive damages in the state to $250,000. However, that type of remedy seems unlikely to succeed. People libeled by the media believe they have a right to some compensation for the harm to their reputations, and other Americans sympathize with them. Americans are unlikely to support legislation that seems to favor the media rather than the citizens they libel.

A few trials have already ended with verdicts that cleared the plaintiffs' reputations—but awarded them only a token sum.

In 1956, William Shockley shared the Nobel Prize for physics. Shockley's interests later shifted to genetics, and he concluded that overbreeding among the "genetically disadvantaged" was responsible for a general decline in intelligence. Shockley also concluded that blacks are genetically inferior in intelligence to whites. To improve the population, he proposed a voluntary sterilization plan. Shockley suggested that people with low IQs might be paid as an incentive to be sterilized. Shockley also proposed sterilizing people with genetically transmitted disorders, such as hemophilia and sickle-cell anemia.

In 1980, a health and science writer for the Atlanta Constitution wrote that "the Shockley program was tried in Germany during World War II." Shockley called the comparison a "damnable, evil lie," and he filed a $1.25 million libel suit against the Constitution and its writer, Roger Witherspoon. Shockley charged the Constitution with malice, arguing that it knew, at the time it published Witherspoon's story, that it was false.

After deliberating 3 1/2 hours, the jury concluded that Shockley had been libeled—but awarded him only $1 for the harm to his reputation.

Privacy

Americans' right to privacy has been defined as "the right to be let alone." Writer Bruce W. Sanford explains, "Whereas the law of libel protects primarily a person's character and reputation, the right of privacy protects primarily a person's peace of mind, spirit, sensibilities and feelings."

The right of privacy is relatively new and, like the nation's libel laws, requires courts to balance two conflicting values: newspapers' right to gather and report the news, and citizens' right to prevent the unwarranted and unauthorized publication of facts about their private lives.

For years, there was no legal right to privacy in the United States. When sensational news stories about his private social affairs angered Samuel D. Warren, a Boston attorney, he and his law partner, Louis D. Brandeis (who later became a Supreme Court justice), submitted an article to the Harvard Law Review in 1890. The article denounced sensational "yellow journalism," charging that, "The press is overstepping in every direction the obvious bounds of propriety and decency." The article argued that individuals have a right to privacy and that invasions of their privacy subject them "to mental pain and distress, far greater than could be inflicted by mere bodily injury." After publication of this article, courts slowly began to recognize a right to privacy, and some states adopted new laws to protect that right.

In 1902, however, a young woman in Albany, N.Y., learned that her picture was being used without her consent on posters for Franklin Mills flour. She sued for an invasion of her privacy but lost. A court of appeals explained that she could not collect any money from the company because there was no law or precedent which established a right of privacy. In 1903, New York adopted the nation's first privacy law, but the law simply prohibited the use of a person's name or likeness for advertising.

The right of privacy is not mentioned in the U.S. Constitution, but the Supreme Court has recognized a constitutional right to privacy. Writers Harold L. Nelson and Dwight L. Teeter explain:

> Although privacy was not mentioned by the Constitution by name, its first eight amendments, plus the Fourteenth Amendment, include the right to be secure against unreasonable search and seizure and the principle of due process of law. Taken together with the Declaration of Independence's demands for the right to "life, liberty and the pursuit of happiness," it can be seen that the men who founded the nation had a lively concern for something like the "right to be let alone."

Types of Violations of Privacy

The media can invade Americans' privacy in four ways: (1) by intruding into their private lives, (2) by publishing private facts about their lives, (3) by placing them in a false light and (4) by using their identities for commercial purposes.

Intrusion.

Reporters cannot intrude on an individual's private affairs or property. Intrusion often involves some type of physical surveillance: the use of tape recorders, wiretaps, telephoto lenses and other electronic eavesdropping devices to spy on individuals in private places, such as their homes or offices. The offense occurs at the moment of intrusion, so it may not involve the actual publication of any information. Actually, most intrusion cases do not involve the media because they are unlikely to use wiretaps and other surveillance devices.

Publishing Private Facts.

The media cannot publish embarrassing facts about the life of a private citizen, regardless of whether those facts are true. For example, they cannot publish facts about an individual's health, idiosyncrasies or sexual habits. The media are freer to discuss the private lives of public figures and public officials.

Falsity.

Courts have ruled that the media cannot publish anything that would mislead the public about an individual or place an individual in a "false light." Falsity may occur when reporters fictionalize a true story in an effort to make it more interesting or dramatic. The story does not have to harm an individual's reputation. If it suggests that an individual said or did something the person never actually said or did, it casts that person in a false light.

Misappropriation.

Finally, the media cannot use an individual's name or image in advertisements, nor for any other commercial purposes, without that individual's permission.

Defenses against Privacy Suits

Truth is not an adequate defense in privacy cases; however, newspapers sued for an invasion of privacy can defend themselves by proving that a story was newsworthy or that the plaintiff consented to its publication.

The primary defense in privacy cases is "newsworthiness." Courts are reluctant to punish newspapers for reporting the truth and have been quite liberal in defining the term. So newspapers normally enjoy a broad freedom to publish whatever they want about people, so long as they can show that the topic interests the public.

Newspapers are also free to publish the names and photographs of public officials and public figures and even to discuss their private lives. Private citizens who become involved in newsworthy events or in other matters of public interest, whether willingly or unwillingly, also forfeit their right to privacy. In addition, newspapers normally have the right to take photographs in any public place and to publish those photographs, regardless of whom or what they show.

Finally, people who consent to an invasion of their privacy cannot later sue the media for an invasion of privacy. However, it may be difficult for the media to obtain an individual's consent or to prove that an individual gave that consent. People may consent to publication of a story or photograph but later revoke that consent, or they may attach certain restrictions to publication of a story or a photograph.

Court Decisions

Few privacy cases have reached the U.S. Supreme Court, but state courts have ruled on several cases. In 1972, for example, Jacqueline Kennedy Onassis, widow of President John F. Kennedy, sued photographer Ron Galella for intrusion, and a New York court found that his constant surveillance and interference in her daily life violated her privacy. For years, Galella had followed Mrs. Onassis everywhere. Her lawsuit charged that he had once jumped from behind a wall, frightening her son and causing the boy to lose control of his bike; had pursued Mrs. Onassis into the lobby of a friend's apartment building; had chased her at dangerous speeds in a car; had fired flashbulbs suddenly on lonely black nights; and had cruised so close as she was swimming that she feared being cut by his boat's propeller. The court found that:

> He was like a shadow: everywhere she went he followed her and engaged in offensive conduct; nothing was sacred to him, whether plaintiff went to church, funeral services, theatre, school, restaurant or aboard a yacht in a foreign land. While defendant denied so deporting himself, his admissions clearly spell out his harassment of her and her children.

As a result of the lawsuit, the court ordered Galella to keep at least 25 feet away from Mrs. Onassis and 30 feet from her children and to keep from blocking their movements or from doing anything else that might harm or endanger them.

Another privacy case involved a former child prodigy. William James Sidis had attracted national attention when he graduated from Harvard in 1910 at the age of 16. In 1937, The New Yorker magazine published a brief biographical sketch describing Sidis' life since then, revealing that he had held several menial jobs. The article was accurate, but Sidis sued The New Yorker for invading his privacy. The court ruled against Sidis, explaining that:

> He had cloaked himself in obscurity but his subsequent history containing as it did the answer to the question of whether or not he had fulfilled his early promise, was still a matter of public concern. The article . . . sketched the life of an unusual personality, and it possessed considerable popular news interest.

However, in another invasion of privacy suit, a woman sued a newspaper after it published a picture showing her leaving the fun house at a county fair. A photographer took the picture the moment a jet of air blew her dress up over her head. She charged that publication of the picture caused her immense embarrassment and that it was only minimally newsworthy. The court found in her favor (*Daily Times Democrat* vs. *Graham*, 1962).

Another woman won a $3,000 privacy suit against Time magazine. The woman had been admitted to a Kansas City hospital because of an unusual disease: she ate constantly but still lost weight. A photographer took her picture against her will in the hospital. Time published the picture and called her a "starving glutton" (*Barber* vs. *Time, Inc.*, 1948).

Other privacy cases have involved fictionalization. A newspaper legally published a photograph showing a 10-year-old girl who had been struck by a careless motorist. Twenty months later, the Saturday Evening Post used the same photograph to illustrate a story about children injured because of their own carelessness. The Saturday Evening Post was found liable for damages because it placed the child in a false light as a careless pedestrian (*Leverton* vs. *Curtis Publishing Co.*, 1951).

The U.S. Supreme Court ruled on its first privacy case involving the news media in 1967 but was closely split. James J. Hill, his wife and children were held hostage in their home by three escaped convicts but were released, unharmed, after 19 hours. Less than a year later, a novel titled "The Desperate Hours" described a family of four held hostage in its home by three escaped convicts. However, the convicts in the fictional story treated the hostages more violently. The book was made into a play and then into a movie.

Life magazine reported that the play described the Hill family's ordeal. Moreover, Life published several photographs staged in the Hills' former home. Hill sued for invasion of privacy, charging that the article "was intended to, and did, give the impression that the play mirrored the Hill family's experience, which to the knowledge of the defendant . . . was false and untrue." Attorneys representing Life responded that the topic was of legitimate news interest; however, a jury disagreed and awarded the Hills $75,000.

On appeal, the Supreme Court weighed the family's right to privacy against the media's First Amendment right to publish. Justice Brennan, who wrote the Court's majority opinion, said that truth is a complete defense for reports about newsworthy people or events, and that Hill was a newsworthy person "substantially without a right to privacy" regarding his hostage experience. However, Brennan added that Hill was entitled to sue for an invasion of privacy if he could prove that Life fictionalized and exploited the story for commercial benefit. The Court then applied the malice rule from *New York Times* vs. *Sullivan*, and Hill lost the case because the Court found no evidence of malice. Justice Brennan explained:

> We hold that the constitutional protections for speech and press preclude the application of the New York statute to redress false reports of matters of public interest in the absence of

This photograph demonstrates the dangers of fictionalization. The original caption accurately described its content, explaining that, "When parents reach old age, they and their children (like this 98-year-old man and his daughter) sometimes experience a sharp role reversal as children take care of their parents." However, the woman shown in the picture sued a national magazine that later used the photograph to illustrate an article about Alzheimer's disease.

proof that the defendant published the report with knowledge of its falsity or in reckless disregard of the truth.

Justices Hugo Black and William Douglas concurred with the majority and were even more outspoken in their defense of the press's freedom:

> Life's conduct here was at most a mere understandable and incidental error of fact in reporting a newsworthy event. One does not have to be a prophet to foresee that judgments like the one we here reverse can frighten and punish the press so much that publishers will cease trying to report news in a lively and readable fashion as long as there is—and there always will be—doubt as to the complete accuracy of the newsworthy facts. Such a consummation hardly seems consistent with the clearly expressed purpose of the Founders to guarantee the press a favored spot in our free society.

The Free Press/Fair Trial Dilemma

Another constitutional dilemma arises when journalists report local crimes. Journalists believe that the public has "a right to know," and that the news media have an obligation to keep citizens fully informed about important events that occur in their communities. The media report local crimes because they are important and because they interest readers. In addition, citizens are entitled to know whether their local judicial systems are working properly—whether honest citizens are being protected and whether criminals are being apprehended, convicted and given appropriate punishments.

However, attorneys and other court officials are concerned about the effect of news stories on the reputations of defendants in criminal cases and on the minds of potential jurors. The Sixth Amendment to the U.S. Constitution guarantees that "in all criminal prosecutions, the accused shall enjoy the right to a speedy and public trial by an impartial jury." Jurors should not be influenced by the content of news stories, nor by anything else said or done outside a courtroom. But news stories about a sensational crime may convince some potential jurors that a suspect is guilty. Moreover, the stories may contain information that would not be admissible as evidence during a trial— for example, a description of a suspect's prior criminal record or the results of a lie detector test.

Journalists call this conflict between the public's right to know and a defendant's right to a fair trial the "free press/fair trial" controversy.

Supreme Court Decisions

In 1961, for the first time in U.S. history, the Supreme Court overturned the conviction of a criminal in a state court solely because prejudicial publicity had made it impossible for him to obtain a fair trial. Justice Thomas Clark, who wrote the majority decision, declared that jurors do not have to be totally ignorant of the facts and issues in a case: "It is sufficient if the juror can lay aside his impression or opinion and render a verdict based on the evidence presented in court." But in *Irvin* vs. *Dowd*, the buildup of prejudice was clear and convincing.

Parolee Leslie Irvin had been arrested and charged with six murders. A government prosecutor issued press releases calling him "Mad Dog Irvin" and reporting that he had confessed to all six murders. The court called 430 people as potential jurors, but 375 said they already believed Irvin was guilty. Of the 12 jurors selected to hear Irvin's case, eight said they believed he was guilty even before the trial began. Not unexpectedly, the jury convicted Irvin, and he was sentenced to death.

Irvin was granted a new trial after the Supreme Court overturned his conviction. He was convicted for a second time but was sentenced to life imprisonment rather than to death.

A second case involving prejudicial publicity became even more notorious. Dr. Samuel Sheppard, a Cleveland osteopath, was accused of murdering his pregnant wife, Marilyn, on July 4, 1954. Sheppard told police he was sleeping on a couch in their lakeside home, heard his wife scream and went upstairs to help. According to Sheppard, he struggled with his wife's assailant but was knocked unconscious. When Sheppard regained consciousness, he found his wife on a bedroom floor, bludgeoned to death.

News stories reported that Sheppard refused to take a lie detector test, and editorials charged that someone was "getting away with murder." Other editorials asked why Sheppard was not in jail. Authorities held the inquest in a school gymnasium, and local television stations broadcast it live. At the start of Sheppard's trial, newspapers published the names and addresses of all his jurors, thus exposing them to the public.

Much of the space inside the courtroom during Sheppard's trial was set aside for journalists, including a large area inside the bar. Normally, that area is reserved for the defendant, attorneys and other court officials. The presence of journalists inside the bar made it difficult for Sheppard to talk confidentially with his attorney. Noise created by the journalists moving in and out of the courtroom also made it difficult for everyone to hear. Moreover, almost everyone involved in the case talked to journalists outside the courtroom. Some of the information journalists received and published incriminated Sheppard but never was introduced as evidence during his trial. The judge, who was running for re-election, did nothing to correct these problems.

Sheppard was convicted of murder and sentenced to life in prison. An appellate court called his trial a Roman holiday and an orgy of press sensationalism. The case reached the U.S. Supreme Court in 1966, and it threw out Sheppard's conviction, declaring that massive and highly inflammatory pretrial publicity had violated his right to a fair trial. Justice Thomas Clark noted: "Newsmen took over practically the entire courtroom, hounding most of the participants in the trial, especially Sheppard." The Supreme Court blamed the judge for allowing such a "carnival atmosphere" to prevail during Sheppard's trial.

Reporters and photographers smoked, played cards and swapped yarns as they lounged in the courtroom, waiting for the jury to finish its deliberations in the trial of Dr. Samuel Sheppard.

In 1963 the Supreme Court also reversed the conviction of a Louisiana defendant whose interrogation was filmed, then broadcast by a local television station. The defendant, Wilbert Rideau, was charged with robbing a bank, kidnapping three bank employees and killing one of the employees. The morning after Rideau's arrest, he was interrogated by the sheriff, and television station photographers filmed the 20-minute session. Rideau admitted the robbery, kidnapping and murder, and a television station broadcast his confession three times during the next three days. Three of Rideau's jurors saw and heard the confession; two other jurors were deputy sheriffs. Rideau was convicted and sentenced to death, but the Supreme Court overturned his conviction, saying, "Any subsequent court proceeding in a community so pervasively exposed to such a spectacle could be but a hollow formality."

Attempts to Resolve the Dilemma

Since the Sheppard case, judges in dozens of cities have met with journalists and attorneys to formulate and adopt voluntary guidelines to prevent the publication of prejudicial information. Judges, prosecutors and defense attorneys can question potential jurors to determine whether they are impartial or whether they have been influenced by the content of news stories. After jury selection, judges can instruct the jurors to avoid news stories and conversations about the cases they are scheduled to hear.

Judges can take several additional precautions to minimize the impact of prejudicial publicity, but each precaution creates new problems. Judges can postpone sensational trials until the emotions inflamed by prejudicial publicity have subsided. But if a trial is postponed, the defendant will not receive a speedy trial and may have to spend several months in jail. Judges can grant a change of venue, moving sensational trials to distant locations that did not receive as much prejudicial publicity. But a change of venue is expensive, since the government must pay for some participants' transportation, room and board. As another alternative, judges can sequester a jury. That is, if a trial is likely to attract extreme publicity, judges can lock up the jury so that during the entire trial, the jurors eat and live together, usually at a hotel near the courthouse. Their telephone calls, even visits from their families, may be monitored by court officials. Court officials also screen all the news media they receive, eliminating any stories about the trial. This procedure, too, is expensive. In addition, it may anger jurors to be kept away from their families and jobs for weeks or months.

During the 1970s, journalists began to complain that some judges were going too far in their efforts to avoid prejudicial publicity. Because of the Supreme Court's apparent mandate in the Sheppard case—because the Court clearly stated that judges have a responsibility to protect defendants—judges began to issue "gag orders" forbidding journalists to report some facts.

In 1976, for example, police charged a suspect with murdering six members of a Nebraska family, and Judge Hugh Stuart instructed journalists covering the case not to publish any information about: (1) a confession, (2) statements the suspect had made to other people, (3) a note the suspect had written, (4) some medical testimony at a preliminary hearing and (5) the nature of a sexual assault and the identity of its victim.

In a unanimous decision, the U.S. Supreme Court ruled that the judge had exceeded his authority and that the gag order was unconstitutional. Chief Justice Warren Burger explained, "Any prior restraint on expression comes to this Court with a 'heavy presumption against its constitutional validity.'" In writing the majority opinion, Burger added:

> We reaffirm that the guarantees of freedom of expression are not an absolute prohibition under all circumstances, but the barriers to prior restraint remain high and the presumption against its use continues intact. We hold that, with respect to the order entered in this case prohibiting reporting or commentary on judicial proceedings held in public, the barriers have not been overcome; to the extent that this order restrained publication of such material, it is clearly invalid. To the extent that it prohibited publication based on information gained from other sources, we conclude that the heavy burden imposed as a condition to securing a prior restraint was not met and the judgment of the Nebraska Supreme Court is therefore reversed.

Despite that decision, journalists continue to complain that courts are closing more and more judicial proceedings to the public and are gagging other people (not journalists) involved in those proceedings. Some proceedings, such as juvenile and divorce hearings, have long been closed to the public. But recently, judges have also closed preliminary hearings in some criminal cases because they feared that publication of information revealed at those hearings would make it more difficult for the defendants to obtain fair trials. Judges have ordered police officers, prosecutors, defense attorneys and other court officials not to speak to journalists outside a courtroom about some cases. Anyone who violates the orders can be cited for contempt of court.

Other Areas of Conflict

Until the 1960s, government officials rarely subpoenaed journalists. But the 1960s and 1970s were decades of social unrest caused by the civil rights movement, the movement opposing the Vietnam war, women's struggle for equality, changes in the lifestyles of young adults, the growing use of drugs and a variety of other tumultuous transformations in our society. Journalists witnessed those changes and interviewed their participants, including some people suspected of violating state and federal laws.

Government officials began to subpoena reporters to ask for the identity of their sources, and to ask for copies of information they gathered in the form of notes, tape recordings and photographs. Some prosecutors also asked reporters to testify at trials and to describe crimes they had witnessed. The prosecutors were often unable to obtain information in any other way, and they insisted that reporters who possessed information necessary to find, identify or prosecute criminals had an obligation, as citizens, to give that information to the appropriate law enforcement officials.

Journalists disagreed, insisting that their right to gather and report the news is protected by the First Amendment and that such subpoenas interfere with their responsibility to inform the public. Journalists explain that they must protect their sources to obtain confidential information. If they are forced to reveal sources' identities, fewer people will talk to them, thus curtailing the flow of information to the American public. So a new conflict has arisen between reporters' desire to protect their sources and the judicial system's desire to obtain information.

The journalists' demands are not unique. Spouses cannot be required to testify against each other. The relationship between attorneys and their clients is privileged. Relationships between doctors and their patients, and between ministers and penitents, are also privileged in many states. Yet journalists who disobeyed subpoenas and other court orders have been found guilty of contempt of court and sentenced to prison terms—usually indeterminate, with judges saying that the journalists would have to remain in prison until they were ready to identify their sources or to provide other information demanded by prosecutors. In reality, however, few journalists have been kept in jail more than 30 days.

In 1972, a case involving reporter Earl Caldwell reached the U.S. Supreme Court. Caldwell was assigned to The New York Times' bureau in San Francisco and often wrote about the Black Panthers, a militant black organization. Because of his knowledge of the Panthers, Caldwell was ordered to appear before a grand jury investigating the organization and to bring his notes and tape recordings of some interviews. Caldwell refused to appear, saying that even if he did not answer any questions, simply entering the grand jury room would destroy his credibility with the Black Panthers because they would never know what he said or did in the privacy of that room.

In a 5–4 decision, the Supreme Court ruled that journalists can be forced to provide information about criminal activities. It explained that, "The great weight of authority is that newsmen are not exempt from the normal duty of appearing before a grand jury and answering questions relevant to a criminal investigation." Justice Byron R. White, in writing the majority opinion, added:

> The sole issue before us is the obligation of reporters to respond to grand jury subpoenas as other citizens do and answer questions relevant to an investigation into the commission of crime. Citizens generally are not constitutionally immune from grand jury subpoenas; and neither the First Amendment nor other constitutional provisions protects the average citizen from disclosing to a grand jury information that he has received in confidence.

Shield Laws

Journalists do not enjoy many special legal privileges, but "shield laws" are an important exception. Most shield laws are new, adopted because of the recent conflicts between journalists and the nation's judicial system. Courts ruling on those conflicts have said that either state legislatures or the U.S. Congress could adopt new laws to protect a journalist's privilege to withhold information from government officials. At least 26 states have adopted shield laws, and those laws usually protect only journalists, not any other citizens.

The shield laws vary from state to state. Most shield laws are limited; they declare that reporters cannot be forced to reveal the identities of confidential sources. Some shield laws offer more protection, declaring that reporters cannot be forced to reveal the identities of confidential sources, nor to give government officials any other information or materials, such as notes or photographs.

Congress has failed to adopt a federal shield law, perhaps because too many questions remain unanswered. For example: Who is a "journalist"? Should a federal shield law protect only people employed by newspapers and by radio and television stations? Or should it also protect free-lance writers, authors of books and other writers? Also, what should a federal shield law protect—only the identities of sources, or all information journalists gather, including information about serious crimes? Similarly, if Congress adopts a federal shield law, should it apply to every court, or should it be limited to federal courts?

Journalists themselves are divided, and their disagreement may have made Congress more hesitant to act. Some journalists favor a qualified shield law. Others favor an absolute shield law. Still others do not want Congress to adopt any laws involving the news media. They fear that if Congress adopts one law to protect journalists, it later may adopt other laws that limit journalists' freedom. Some journalists insist that a federal shield law is unnecessary because the First Amendment already protects the media. They argue that, despite the Supreme Court's decision in the Caldwell case, the First Amendment protects reporters, and its protection is absolute. Proponents of that argument add that it would be foolish to endorse a qualified shield law if the First Amendment already grants journalists absolute protection.

Censorship

Hazelwood School District vs. *Kuhlmeier*

Another recent decision gave administrators a broad power to censor high-school newspapers. In 1988, the U.S. Supreme Court decided, by a vote of 5–3, that administrators can censor high-school publications so long as the censorship has a "valid educational purpose."

As part of a journalism class, students at Hazelwood East High School in Missouri wrote about student pregnancies and about the children of divorced parents. Their principal, Robert Reynolds, complained that the first story failed to adequately disguise the identity of several pregnant students, and that the story's references to sexual experiences and birth control were inappropriate for the school's younger students. Reynolds complained that the second story failed to adequately disguise the identity of a parent who was getting divorced. He deleted two pages from the student paper and explained that, because of a printer's deadline, he did not have enough time to ask the students to rewrite their stories.

The Supreme Court's decision, written by Justice Byron White, declared that, "Educators do not offend the First Amendment by exercising editorial control over the style and content of student speech in school-sponsored expressive activities so long as their actions are reasonably related to legitimate pedagogical concerns." Thus, the court will allow school officials to impose "reasonable restrictions on the speech of students, teachers and other members of the school community."

White distinguished between a school's obligation to *tolerate* student speech and its obligation to *promote* such speech. In this case, the school funded and published the paper. Under those circumstances, White said, school officials had a right to set and maintain standards—especially since the paper was produced by a class that was subject to the supervision of teachers and administrators.

A dissenter, Justice William Brennan, called Reynolds' conduct an act of "brutal censorship." Brennan complained that Reynolds "violated the First Amendment's prohibitions against censorship of any student expression that neither disrupts classwork nor invades the rights of others." Furthermore, Brennan warned that the majority decision could convert public schools into "enclaves of totalitarianism. . . ."

Journalists who agreed with Brennan's dissent complained that the majority decision turned students into second-class citizens. Journalists said the decision seemed to say that students can study the First Amendment in high school—but cannot practice it there. Journalists also complained that the decision gave school administrators too much power, and that it would encourage the administrators of other schools to censor controversial stories.

But many daily newspapers, including The New York Times, agreed with the court's decision. Daily newspapers explained that the decision provided a realistic lesson for students. The First Amendment has never given reporters and editors the right to print stories that their publishers do not want to print. The men and women who own the press—not their employees—decide which stories should be published. Newspapers supporting the court's decision added that school boards are no different from other publishers, and that high-school students are not entitled to more freedom than working journalists. Thus, students have no right to demand that their stories be printed without editing.

Moreover, newspaper publishers—not their employees—are held responsible for their papers' content. School boards serve as the publishers of student newspapers and can be held responsible for their content. If, for example, a school paper libels someone, the victim is likely to sue the school board—not a poor student.

The case seems unlikely to affect college papers, however. College students are adults, and courts have usually granted them the full protection of the First Amendment.

Suggested Readings

Denniston, Lyle W. *The Reporter and the Law: Techniques of Covering the Courts.* New York: Hastings House, 1980.

Devol, Kenneth S., ed. *Mass Media and the Supreme Court.* 3rd ed. New York: Hastings House, 1982.

Diamond, Sidney A. *Trademark Problems and How to Avoid Them.* 2nd ed. Chicago: Crain Communications, 1981.

Dill, Barbara. *The Journalist's Handbook On Libel and Privacy.* New York: The Free Press, 1986.

Francois, William E. *Mass Media Law and Regulation.* 4th ed. New York: John Wiley & Sons, 1986.

Franklin, Marc A. *Cases and Materials on Mass Media Law.* Mineola, N.Y.: Foundation Press, 1977.

Franklin, Marc A., with Ruth Korzenik Franklin. *The First Amendment and the Fourth Estate.* 2nd ed. Mineola, N.Y.: Foundation Press, 1981.

Galvin, Katherine M. *Media Law: A Legal Handbook for the Working Journalist.* Berkeley, Calif.: Nolo, 1984.

Gerald, Edward J. *News of Crime: Courts and Press in Conflict.* Westport, Conn.: Greenwood Press, 1983.

Gillmor, Donald M., and Jerome A. Barron. *Mass Communication Law: Cases and Comment.* 4th ed. St. Paul: West, 1979.

Ingelhart, Louis E. *Freedom for the College Student Press: Court Cases and Related Decisions Defining the Campus Fourth Estate Boundaries.* Westport, Conn.: Greenwood Press, 1985.

Nelson, Harold L., and Dwight L. Teeter. *Law of Mass Communications.* 4th ed. Mineola, N.Y.: Foundation Press, 1982.

Pember, Don R. *Mass Media Law.* 3rd ed. Dubuque, Iowa: Wm. C. Brown, 1984.

———. *Privacy and the Press.* Seattle: University of Washington Press, 1972.

Phelps, Robert H., and E. Douglas Hamilton. *Libel.* New York: Collier Books, 1966.

Sanford, Bruce W. *Libel and Privacy Litigation: Prevention and Defenses.* New York: Law & Business, Inc./Harcourt Brace Jovanovich, 1983.

———. *Synopsis of the Law of Libel and the Right of Privacy.* N.Y.: Newspaper Enterprises, 1986.

Schmidt, Benno C., Jr. *Freedom of the Press vs. Public Access.* New York: Praeger, 1976.

Spencer, Dale R. *Law for the Newsman.* 5th ed. Columbia, Mo.: Lucas Brothers, 1980.

Zuckman, Harvey L., and Martin J. Gaynes. *Mass Communications Law in a Nutshell.* 2nd ed. St. Paul: West, 1983.

EXERCISE 1
Libel

INSTRUCTIONS: Decide which of the following sentences and paragraphs are libelous. Place an "L" in the space preceding each statement that is libelous, and an "N" in the space preceding each statement that is not libelous.

1. _____ The police officers said they shot and killed Ira Andrews, a 41-year-old auto mechanic, because he was rushing toward them with a knife.

2. _____ Testifying during the second day of his trial, Mrs. Andrea Cross said her husband, Lee, never intended to embezzle the $70,000, but that a secretary, Allison O'Hara, persuaded him that their actions were legal. Her husband thought they were borrowing the money, she said, and that they would double it by investing in real estate.

3. _____ Store employees told the police that they detained Martha Jacbos, 23, 1889 32nd St., after she attempted to leave the supermarket with $8 worth of groceries that she allegedly failed to pay for.

4. _____ A 72-year-old woman, Kelli Kasandra of 9847 Eastbrook Lane, has been charged with attempting to pass a counterfeit $20 bill. A convenience store clerk called the police shortly after 8 a.m. today and said that she had received "a suspicious-looking bill." The clerk added that she had written down the license number of a car leaving the store. The police confirmed the fact that the $20 bill was counterfeit and arrested Mrs. Kasandra at her home about an hour later.

5. _____ Margaret Dwyer said a thief, a boy about 14, grabbed her purse as she was walking to her car in a parking lot behind Memorial Hospital. The boy punched her in the face, apparently because she began to scream and refused to let go of her purse. She said he was blond, wore glasses, weighed about 120 pounds and was about 5 feet 6 inches tall.

6. _____ Sheriff's deputies said that Terry Smythe "appeared to have been exceeding the 45 mph speed limit." They also suspect that he may have been drinking. The results of his breath and urinalysis tests are expected in a week.

7. _____ Four police officers teamed up late yesterday to arrest a man who sold them crack cocaine. The police arrested Michael Allen, 32, and charged him with the possession, sale and delivery of cocaine.

8. _____ The manager of the Plaza Book Shoppe announced today that it is bankrupt and will close—permanently—at 5 p.m. Saturday. The store's manager explained: "We still don't know exactly how she managed to do it, but one of our clerks embezzled more than $100,000. In three months since we hired her, she drained all our accounts, so we can't buy any new merchandise; we can't pay for it. We've turned the matter over to the district attorney and are asking other merchants in the area to consider hiring our six other employees. They're good, hard-working people and shouldn't have to suffer like this. It's awful."

9. _____ Police said the victim, Catherine White of 4218 Bell Ave., was too intoxicated to be able to describe her assailant.

10. _____ A 41-year-old high-school teacher is free on $2,300 bail. Police officers stopped the teacher, Leon Basis, after he sped through a red light. Basis struck one of the officers and was charged with driving while intoxicated, resisting arrest, and assault and battery upon a police officer.

11. _____ Alderman Martha Hernandez complained that the mayor acted irresponsibly, and that his decision to hire a second administrative aide "is another example of his squandering of the city's tax revenues."

12. _____ A judge in the beauty contest explained that no one favored Emily Goree, the 17-year-old representing North High School, because she was too plump and poorly groomed.

EXERCISE 2
Libel

INSTRUCTIONS: Decide which of the following sentences and paragraphs are libelous. Place an "L" in the space preceding each statement that is libelous, and an "N" in the space preceding each statement that is not libelous.

1. _____ "I've never lived in a city where the officials are so corrupt," Joyce Andrews, a Cleveland developer, complained. "If you don't contribute to their campaigns, they won't do anything for you. They won't even talk to you. You have to buy their support."

2. _____ The political scientist said that Americans seem unable to elect a competent president. "Look at who they've elected," she said. "I'm convinced that Lyndon Johnson was a liar. Nixon was a crook. Carter was incompetent, and Reagan was the worst of all: too lazy and senile to be even a mediocre president."

3. _____ The newspaper's restaurant reviewer complained: "I've had poor service before, but nothing this incompetent. The service at The Heritage Inn wasn't just slow; it was awful. When she finally did get to us, the waitress didn't seem to know what was on the menu. Then she brought us the wrong drinks. When we finally got our food, it was cold and tasteless. I wouldn't feed it to my dog. In fact, my dog wouldn't eat it. The stuff didn't even smell good."

4. _____ Police Chief Marvin Rudnick said: "We've been after Guiterman for years. He's the biggest drug dealer in the city, but it took months to gather the evidence and infiltrate his operations. His arrest last night was the result of good police work, and we've got the evidence to send him away for 20 or 30 years."

5. _____ Dennis A. Shatuck, 20, of 532 Third St. was arrested at 1 a.m. and charged with trespassing and possession of a controlled substance. A deputy said he spotted Shatuck parked behind a shopping center, and found him with a small amount of marijuana in his possession.

6. _____ George Adcock reported that he was robbed while withdrawing $50 from an automatic teller outside the First National Bank late Monday. A man, about 20, had been waiting in line behind him. When Adcock withdrew the money, the robber opened his jacket, revealed a shotgun strapped to his shoulder and asked Adcock whether he wanted to die. After taking the $50, the robber ordered Adcock to begin walking south along Grand Avenue.

7. _____ A police officer in your city, George Ruiz, today filed a $100,000 personal injury suit against Albert Tifton, charging that Tifton punched him in the nose last month while the police were responding to a call about a domestic dispute at Tifton's home. "It's the third time I've been hit this year," Ruiz said. "I'm tired of being used as a punching bag by these criminals, and I'm doing what I can to stop it."

8. _____ There was an emergency meeting at the Wisconsin Avenue branch of the YMCA at 8 p.m. yesterday, with its director, Marty Willging, presiding. About 100 angry parents were in attendance. Willging said he called the meeting to calm the parents' fears and to respond to rumors spreading among them. A parent asked whether it was true that the YMCA's janitor had been dismissed for molesting several boys. Willging responded that there had been some unfortunate incidents, and that the janitor had been discharged—but that some of the allegations were grossly exaggerated. When asked whether the police had been called in, Willging answered that they had, and that their investigation is continuing. Parents should have faith in the YMCA, he said. He assured them that it will see that the matter is resolved in an appropriate manner.

EXERCISE 3
Libel

INSTRUCTIONS: The following stories contain information that is potentially libelous. Write a news story for each set of facts, carefully avoiding the danger of libel. Remember that you can report that an individual has been *charged* with a crime. Normally, you cannot report that an individual is guilty until after that person has been convicted by a judge or jury.

Thus, you should describe each crime—but avoid saying that the person charged with the crime is the person who committed it.

1. Andrew J. Herman, an unemployed accountant, is in jail. The police have charged him with robbing a convenience store of $83. A store clerk, Vivian Hoffman, said Herman entered the store while she was alone shortly after 7 a.m. today and asked for a pack of cigarettes. He then drew a revolver. When he began firing the revolver, she ran into a back room and locked herself in it. The gunman then proceeded to scoop all the money from a cash register and fled on foot. Police arrested Herman driving north on Parkway Drive about 3 miles from the store and charged him with armed robbery.

2. Mildred R. Thistel is a counselor at Roosevelt High School. On Sunday afternoon, she was charged with shoplifting at a local department store. Two clerks told the police that they personally saw Thistel, 41, place a bottle of perfume valued at $32 in her purse and then leave without paying for it. A security officer apprehended Thistel outside the store and held her until police arrived. She was charged with shoplifting and released on $100 bond. School officials declined to immediately comment on her case, saying they need more time to gather information about the matter but that she might be suspended, with pay, until her case is cleared up.

3. Moments after reaching your office today, you received a call from an irate mother: Lisa Kopez of 1067 Eastland Avenue. Mrs. Kopez complained that, yesterday afternoon, her 8-year-old son, Brandon, was beaten by Florence Hendricks, a teacher at Risser Elementary School. "He was spanked and slapped," Mrs. Kopez said of her son. "And he was slapped hard. He was crying when he came home, and you could still see the ruler marks on his buttocks. What his teacher did was against the law; no one has a right to beat children, not even their teachers." Mrs. Kopez further added that she complained to the principal, and if nothing is done about the matter she fully intends to go to the police. When you called the principal, Collette Mejia, she responded: "Mrs. Kopez did call me, and I'm looking into the matter. At this point, it wouldn't be appropriate for me to make any other comments about the matter. I'll be meeting with the teacher involved later today—when she's got a free period. That's all I can say about it at this point in time."

4. Thieves entered a clothing store at the Colonial Shopping Center early today. A report filed by patrolman Wayne Warniky says: "I noticed the suspect, James Wilke, now incarcerated on charges of burglary, at the shopping center, sitting in a parked car in a suspicious manner at 3 a.m. As I drove up, Wilke started to drive away, with his car's headlights still turned off. I proceeded to force Wilke to stop his vehicle and asked him to step out. Several articles visible in the back seat of Wilke's car were identified as items stolen from a clothing store in the mall, and other perpetrators are also thought to have been involved, since more merchandise is missing from the store. Wilke's accomplices may have escaped while I was questioning him. We think there was also a second vehicle involved and are following several leads in the case."

5. Jack R. Denboar, 40, of 1415 Idaho Avenue, was arrested at 9 p.m. yesterday. The police have charged him with spouse abuse, aggravated assault on a police officer, and resisting arrest with violence. Police reports show that Denboar's wife, Anne, called for help. She told a dispatcher that her husband had beaten her and was threatening to set their house on fire. Officers responding to her call said her husband came to the door, ordered them to leave, and slammed the door shut. He then poked his fist through the window portion of the door, cutting his right fist. While the officers were attempting to subdue Mr. Denboare, Mrs. DenBoare ran out a back door. The officers said that, after entering the premises, they had to wrestle a butcher knife from her husband and subdued him with a chemical spray. They then allowed Mrs. Denboare to return to the house to pick up some clothing, as she was dressed only in a nightgown.

6. The police arrested Russell Kernan, 59, of 168 Lake Street at 3:20 p.m. and charged him with aggravated assault. The police were responding to a call from a 17-year-old boy. The youth said he had been struck by a BB pellet on his left cheek, causing it to bleed. When Officer Allison Biaggi turned onto Lake Street, a group of about 10 juveniles waved at her and informed her that a man in a nearby garage had confronted them with a gun. Biagi then questioned Kernan, and the victims identified him as their assailant. Kernan admitted that he had argued with the juveniles about their behavior and the loud music on their radios, but denied pointing or firing a BB gun at them. Kernan, who is on parole, is being held in the county jail. He was unable to post a $1,000 bond.

7. Police say that a trio of three men broke a 2- by 4-foot hole in the back of a convenience store. An official police report said that two of the men, Marvin Kehoe, 26, 182 West Broadway Road, and Thomas Murhara, 23, 40 West Hiller Avenue, were crawling out of the hole as the police officers responded to an anonymous call reporting a burglary in progress. The two men admitted to the officers that they had been robbing the store and also admitted that there was another person involved who was waiting in a van a short distance away. The third man, Grady Smith, 23, 8213 Perch Street, drove away before the police were able to apprehend him. He was arrested at his home a short time later. The men had 18 six-packs of beer piled outside the hole. Next to the beer were a tire iron, screwdriver, sledge hammer and other burglar tools used to assist in the crime. All three men were charged with burglary.

EXERCISE 4
Libel

INSTRUCTIONS: The following stories contain information that is potentially libelous. Write a news story for each set of facts, carefully avoiding the danger of libel. Remember that you can report that an individual has been *charged* with a crime. Normally, you cannot report that an individual is guilty until after that person has been convicted by a judge or jury.

Thus, you should describe each crime—but avoid saying that the person charged with the crime is the person who committed it.

1. Police have charged the estranged husband of an elementary school teacher with trying to forcibly kidnap her at gunpoint. The teacher, Tina Marie Alvarez, 28, told the police that her car was parked in a school parking lot, and she was approaching her car—leaving work for the day—at about 3:40 p.m. yesterday afternoon. Her husband, Harold Alvarez, 47, confronted her, she told investigating officers, and ordered her to get into his car, which was parked in the same parking lot. Mrs. Alvarez said she refused, and her husband then proceeded to produce a gun and said, "Get in or I'll blow your head off." Mrs. Alvarez tried to flee, but her husband grabbed her and knocked her down, police said. Mrs. Alvarez told police that her husband held the gun to her ribs and told her that he was going to take her away and that she would learn to love him again. Another teacher, Nancy Webber, 62, 44 East Princeton Street, witnessed the struggle and alerted a school secretary, who immediately called the police. A patrol car happened to be in the neighborhood and reached the school in less than a minute. Apparently hearing their siren as they approached, Alvarez threw his wife to the ground and fled, alone, in his car. His wife's purse, containing $70, was in the car when he fled. He is still at large.

2. There was a public hearing last night in the fellowship hall at Redeemer Lutheran Church, 6400 Hall Road. About 300 people were in attendance, primarily residents of the Deer Run Estates subdivision on Hall Road. They met with developer Richard Haselfe, who last week revealed plans for a shopping center, business park, and apartment complex directly adjacent to the subdivision's northern boundary. Haselfe told the residents that his development would not affect them adversely: that he would leave a 25-foot buffer between the subdivision and his development. "This should be an asset to the neighborhood," he said. "It's going to be a high-class, high-rent development, with a park-like atmosphere and establishments—stores and fine restaurants—that you people will be anxious to patronize." Residents accused him of lowering their property values and destroying the neighborhood. "You developers are all alike," one homeowner said. She identified herself as Bev Halso. "You come in, bulldoze everything in sight, and slap together a shopping center no one wants, with a huge, ugly asphalt parking lot. That's not a park. That's crap." Another resident, Anne Abare, said: "We're tired of your lies. We work hard for our money, and then you developers come in and cheat us. When we moved in, our developer said all the land around us was zoned for single-family homes, and we believed and trusted him. He lied to us then, and you're lying to us now. This won't help our neighborhood. It'll destroy it. You're all a bunch of crooks."

3. Two police officers in your city arrested a 53-year-old woman at a supermarket at 4340 North Howell Drive at 4:20 p.m. yesterday. This is exactly what the officers' reports say: "We were called to the store by an assistant manager, Richard E.

Propes. Mr. Propes explained to us that he saw the woman leave the store without paying for two pizzas, which cost $4.99 each. He followed her to the parking lot and asked her to pay for them. She refused, according to Propes, and shoved him to the ground while attempting to flee. Mr. Propes and two other store employees then stopped and detained the woman until we arrived. Identification she produced for us revealed her identity: Gumersinda Sanchez, 19, of 173 Burgass Road. We brought her in on charges of shoplifting. She was released on $500 bond."

4. Another couple seemed to work as a team. A security officer at a department store in your community reported that a man tried to steal five dresses last evening. The security officer, Margaret Hammar, said she observed a man and a woman, each about 30, select five dresses from a rack of clothing and put them in a shopping bag. The man and woman then split up, and he allegedly left the store carrying the bag. A second security officer stopped the man outside the store after he left without paying for the merchandise. The two security officers then held the man, whom the police arrested and charged with grand theft. He is 33-year-old Jonnie Lewis, 1840 Maldrin Avenue. The police do not know the identity of his accomplice, who escaped.

5. Patrolman Roger Temple was on a routine patrol shortly after 1 a.m. today when he noticed a shattered rear window at a restaurant, The Heritage Inn, 310 North Park Avenue. Temple summoned help, and other officers arrived with a K-9 unit. A dog was sent into the building and, when it began to bark, the police officers proceeded to enter the premises and found a man attempting to hide in a washroom. After being handcuffed and read his rights, the man was arrested on charges of burglary. Police said they found burglar tools in his possession and about $1,000 worth of liquor in his car, which was parked in the restaurant parking lot. The suspect was unarmed. Other restaurant supplies, including more liquor, were piled up inside the restaurant, very near the broken window. This morning, his bail was set at $8,600. The suspect is Ralph Beasley, 23, 810 Howard Street.

6. James D. Allen of 28 Rio Grande Road has been charged with the possession, delivery and sale of cocaine. Allen's problems began last night when he flagged down a car containing two undercover police officers. One of the officers told Allen that he needed a $20 "piece." According to a report filed by the officers, Allen took their money, which was marked, and returned with the cocaine. The officers took the cocaine and met with Sgt. Bill Jacobs and Officer Jeffrey Haille. Jacobs and Haille returned to the scene of the sale and arrested Allen. They reported finding in his possession the marked $20 bill given him by the other two officers. In addition, they reported finding and confiscating cocaine valued at more than $5,000 in his car, which was parked nearby. The police told reporters they did not know why Allen had such an unusually large amount of the drug in his possession.

7. Ronald Raintree, 18, and Thomas R. Haber, 19, both of 366 Clemson Drive, were arrested at 9:10 p.m. yesterday at the Springs Plaza by sheriff's deputies. Both were charged with possession of an alcoholic beverage by a person under 21. In addition, Raintree was charged with fleeing to elude a law enforcement officer, driving without headlights, and assault with a deadly weapon. Haber was additionally charged with dumping trash on a highway. A report filed by the sheriff's deputies provided this account of the incident: "As we were approaching the shopping center, we saw the two perpetrators running from a convenience store. The suspects jumped into a pickup truck which proceeded in a reckless manner to exit the parking lot. Activating our siren and flashing lights, we pursued said vehicle, forcing it to stop. At this time, Deputy Mauine Becker saw Haber throw a beer can onto the highway. As Deputy

Myron Hanzle stepped out to question the occupants, the truck sped forward, brushing against Hanzle and throwing him violently to the ground. As the truck tried to speed away, it struck an oncoming vehicle. None of the persons involved in the collision were injured. Store employees subsequently informed us that the two men had attempted to steal several six-packs of beer from a display without paying for it, and that they dropped said merchandise on the floor and fled when they were discovered. Deputy Hanzle suffered lacerations and contusions which did not require medical treatment or hospitalization."

10 Ethics

Ethical problems arise at every step in a journalist's work. Editors must decide which stories their newspapers should cover, how to cover those stories, and how the stories should be presented to the public. In questionable instances, reporters may ask the editors for permission to discuss a rumor or to quote an anonymous source, and a photographer may have to ponder the ethics of showing a mother grieving over a dead child.

No matter what the editors decide, some readers are likely to criticize their choices. People complain that the press is too critical, and filled with too much bad news. Americans also complain that the press is too big, powerful, arrogant and insensitive. At times, it seems to act sensationally, and to be more interested in its own profits than in serving the public.

The public also questions the techniques that reporters use to obtain the news. Rude, aggressive reporters seem willing to do anything to get a good story. They seem to invade the privacy of other individuals, to invent some details, to slant other details, and to interview the victims of crimes and accidents while they are still in shock.

Some may remember Janet Cooke, The Washington Post reporter who won a Pulitzer Prize for a story she fabricated about a young heroin addict. Or the photographers who chased jurors as they left a Los Angeles courtroom during the drug trial of John De Lorean. While the jurors were still deliberating, a television producer called six of them at their homes. The caller, a producer for ABC's "Good Morning America," wanted to schedule interviews to be conducted after the jurors reached their verdict. De Lorean's attorney was outraged by the producer's actions. "This is an idiotic, irresponsible person," he complained. To control the journalists, a judge issued an order warning that: "All persons are prohibited from contacting or attempting to contact jurors during the deliberations in this case, including attempts to establish interviews following the verdict."

A 5-year-old boy drowned while swimming in Bakersfield, Calif., and this controversial photograph shows a rescue worker trying to console the victim's mother and siblings. The victim's father is on his knees. Robert Bentley, managing editor of *The Bakersfield Californian*, said, "I ran the picture because it was a powerful photograph, and it was news, and I'm a newsman." The picture also appeared in other newspapers, from Salt Lake City to Boston and Tampa.

The Californian received more than 400 telephone calls and 500 letters. A bomb threat forced employees to evacuate their office, and 80 readers canceled their subscriptions. People complained that the photograph showed a callous disrespect for the victim, and that it invaded the family's privacy at a moment of grief and shock. Bentley apologized, admitting that he had made a mistake. Photographer John Harte disagreed. "The picture should have run," Harte said. "It was a very good picture. This was an area where there have been a lot of drownings, and the photograph will have long-term benefits in making people aware of water safety and swimming safety."

Other Americans may remember R. Foster Winans, a writer for the Wall Street Journal. Winans was assigned to "Heard on the Street," an influential stock column published by the Journal. He leaked information about the column to a stockbroker, and the broker then bought or sold stocks before the information was published. As a result, Winans and two other men were charged with insider trading. Prosecutors said one of the brokers grossed $675,000 in profits, and that Winans and a roommate received $31,000. In court, Winans admitted that he leaked information to the stockbrokers. He also admitted that his actions may have been unethical. Although he insisted that he did nothing illegal, Winans was convicted, fined $5,000 and sentenced to 18 months in prison.

Journalists have defended the profession by responding that these were isolated incidents, the unfortunate acts of a few individuals, and that they should not be used to condemn the entire profession.

But other problems compound the public's misunderstanding and criticisms of the press. Journalists want to report stories they feel the public needs to know, not just stories the public wants to read. Journalists feel an obligation to inform the public about every important event occurring in their communities. The public, on the other hand, worries more about the stories' effects. Some Americans want journalists to suppress stories that seem unpleasant, harmful or controversial.

Journalists reject the notion that they have a responsibility to suppress any stories. John Chancellor of NBC News explained that, "Too much of the public doesn't understand that just because we report a story does not mean we are in sympathy with what we are reporting." Katharine Graham of The Washington Post has added that: "To say the press ought to suppress some news, if we deem it too bad or too unsettling, is to make the press into the censor or the nursemaid of a weak and immature society. We cannot serve ourselves and our heritage by running away from our troubles. . . . National security does not rest on national ignorance. This is hardly the faith of a free people."

Even columnist Andy Rooney has commented on the problem. Rooney declared that: "Whether a journalist is reporting a war or a grocery store holdup, it is not his business to consider whether the story will do good or harm. He has to have faith that, in the long run, the truth will do good."

Despite the public's criticisms, journalists are acting more ethically and professionally than ever before. They are better educated and better paid. They are also devoting more attention to their ethical standards—and doing more to improve them.

In the past, reporters slanted some stories and invented others. Some stole pictures from the homes of people involved in the news. Others have been known to impersonate police officers, or accept expensive gifts from the people they wrote about. Today, these reporters would be fired, just as The Washington Post fired Janet Cooke. But the public rarely remembers that part of the story: journalists themselves exposed and denounced Janet Cooke.

Today's journalists generally agree that it is unethical to fabricate a story or to accept anything of value from a source. Other issues are more complex because of conflicting values. A journalist may want to report an important story but he or she may fear that it would intrude upon an individual's privacy. Or, a journalist may want to publish an important document, but he or she may hesitate because a source stole the document, or because the government considers it a "state secret."

Each problem is unique, and journalists must consider each individually, trying to balance the conflicting values or to decide which value is most important. While covering one story, journalists may decide to protect an individual's privacy. While covering another story, journalists may decide that a community's need to be informed about an issue is more important than any individual considerations.

Deceit: When Is It Justified?

Journalists want everyone to believe in and trust them. But to obtain some stories, journalists feel compelled to lie. Often, there seems to be no alternative.

Many journalists insist that anonymity is essential to their job. Though they may not lie about their identities, they may not reveal them. Restaurant reviewers, for instance, would be ineffective if everyone knew their identities. Restaurant owners, anxious to obtain more favorable publicity, would cater to the reviewers, offering them special meals and special service. As a result, the reviewers would be unable to describe the meals served to the restaurants' other customers.

Other reporters may want to shop anonymously at a store whose employees have been accused of misleading customers. Or, the reporters may want to visit a fortune-teller or attend a protest rally. If protesters realized that several reporters were present, they might act more cautiously. Or, they might perform for the reporters, acting more loudly, angrily or violently to ensure that they got into the news. Other protesters might harass or attack the reporters.

A few reporters sometimes lie about their identities, depending on their needs in gathering information for a particular story. They may pose as patients while gathering information about a mental hospital. Or, they may pose as laborers while writing about migrant workers and their exposure to the chemicals sprayed on farm crops.

A reporter for The Milwaukee Journal recently posed as a high-school student. The Journal had covered more routine stories about the area's schools, but its metropolitan editor, Patrick Graham, wanted to get closer to the students: to learn "what they're thinking, what they're saying, what their likes and dislikes are, what their cherished aspirations might be." Graham also hoped to learn: "What do they really think about drugs and alcohol? About sex? About going to college? About what they'll be doing or want to do after school?"

Reporter Vivian S. Toy agreed to enroll in a suburban high school. Toy, who was 25 but looked much younger, explained: "There's a natural wariness of any adult. I couldn't have broken through that." A suburban school board gave the Journal permission to go under cover. However, the Journal had to notify the school's principal and teachers. Later, while writing her story, Toy felt ethically obliged not to identify the students she talked to.

A Chicago paper lost a Pulitzer Prize because other journalists objected to its use of a more elaborate disguise. To expose corruption in the city, the Sun-Times bought a tavern and, appropriately, renamed it the Mirage bar. With the help of the Better Government Association, the Sun-Times used the bar to photograph and tape record city inspectors who, in return for payoffs, ignored its violations of city health and safety standards.

A panel nominated the Sun-Times for a Pulitzer Prize. Benjamin C. Bradlee, executive editor of The Washington Post, served on a board that actually selected that year's prize winners, and Bradlee opposed the Sun-Times' nomination. Bradlee and other critics objected that the Sun-Times had created the story, and that its reporters had become active participants in it. Critics agreed there was a need to expose the city's corruption, but insisted that the Sun-Times did not have to buy a bar to obtain the story.

Other disguises are more obviously unethical. Two reporters for the National Enquirer dressed as priests during Bing Crosby's funeral. While pretending to comfort Crosby's widow, the "priests" were actually trying to get an exclusive story from her.

Typically, editors allow their reporters to use a disguise only when a story is very important and there is no other way to safely obtain it. While writing their stories, the reporters are expected to admit their use of deception and to explain why it was necessary. The reporters are also expected to call everyone involved in the stories and give them an opportunity to respond.

Journalists are more reluctant to secretly record their conversations, which may seem devious and unfair. Journalists also fear that, if their sources learn that they record conversations, they may become more reluctant to speak candidly, if at all.

Journalists in most states can legally record their conversations. Or, they can ask someone else to record a conversation and to give them a copy. Imagine, for example, that several women complained of sexual harassment while applying for city jobs. An editor might want to send out an attractive female reporter with a hidden recorder to document their allegations.

Other reporters might want to use tape recorders to protect themselves in case they were accused of lying. The reporters might fear that, after giving them information, their sources may claim that they were misquoted, or that the reporters fabricated entire interviews. Some sources honestly forget what they said. Others are shocked by how awful their statements appear in print. If their statements become too controversial, the sources may claim that the reporters are mistaken. If reporters recorded their interviews, they would be able to prove that their stories are accurate. Reporters who tape their interviews are also able to protect themselves more easily in libel suits.

Invasions of Privacy

Journalists may intrude upon the privacy of other individuals. But although they usually have a legal right to intrude, do they have the moral or ethical right?

Newspapers report the important events occurring in their communities, including every birth, engagement, marriage, divorce and bankruptcy. When people die, newspapers also publish their obituaries, and some newspapers include everyone's age and cause of death. Many Americans consider the publicity embarrassing. They do not want anyone to know their age, or that they are divorced or bankrupt. Many people are embarrassed when the media publish the cause of a relative's death, especially suicides or illnesses that have social stigmas attached to them, like AIDS.

Other stories are more obviously newsworthy: major lawsuits, crimes and accidents, for example. If you become involved in one of the stories, even unintentionally, the media are free to report it.

Other decisions are more difficult. Newspapers usually do not identify juvenile delinquents. But if several teen-agers are arrested and charged with committing a series of rapes and burglaries that terrorized an entire neighborhood, editors may be tempted to identify the teen-agers, and perhaps to also identify their parents. Editors may decide that their obligation to inform the neighborhood about the arrests outweighs their normal obligation to protect the teen-agers and their families.

In the past, journalists were more reluctant to discuss personal lives, even of public officials. The officials' personal lives may have seemed irrelevant to their fitness for public office. Thus, journalists ignored the fact that some officials were profane, liked to gamble, and told dirty jokes. Even after he was elected president, for instance, journalists never reported on President John F. Kennedy's womanizing. They also ignored Wilbur Mills' drinking problems. Mills was chairman of the House Ways and Means Committee, yet no one reported Mills' problem until he became publicly involved with the police and a striptease dancer named Fanne Foxe.

Journalists are still hesitant to intrude upon the lives of private citizens. However, they are becoming more aggressive about reporting on the lives of public figures and public officials. They are most likely to publish details that can be verified and that might affect the officials' work. Although Liberace denied it, journalists reported that he was dying of AIDS. They also reported that a hero in San Francisco was gay. A bystander may have saved President Gerald Ford's life by grabbing a woman's arm as she tried to shoot him. News stories described the man's heroism, and some also reported that he was gay. Editors explained that the man had been active in the area's gay community, and that the details were a relevant part of his life story.

Similarly, when Geraldine Ferraro became the Democratic candidate for vice president, journalists reported that her husband, John A. Zaccaro, had been appointed the legal conservator of an estate and had improperly borrowed $175,000 from it. Other stories claimed that Zaccaro had done some business with people involved in the Mafia. Editors said the stories were a relevant part of their coverage of Ferraro's campaign, especially since she might someday become president. Other editors avoided using the words "mob" and "Mafia." Some also deleted the details that were never clearly substantiated. Critics considered their publication irrelevant, irresponsible, unproven and unfair. Months after Ferraro's defeat, journalists also reported that her son had been charged with selling drugs.

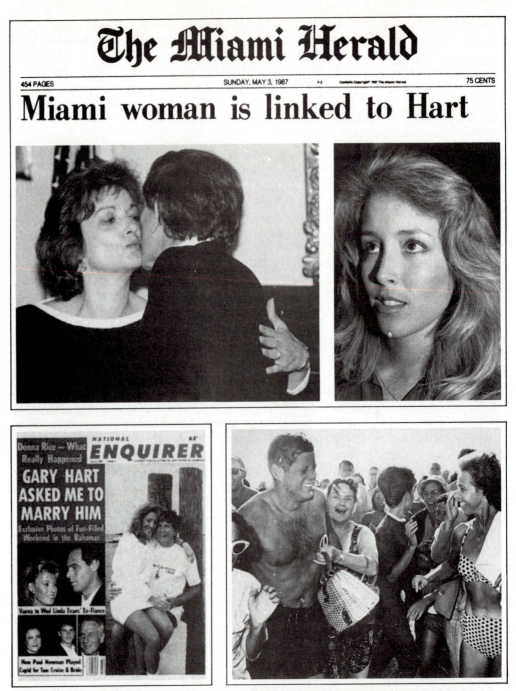

The Miami Herald

Miami woman is linked to Hart

Gary Hart withdrew—but only temporarily—from the 1988 presidential election after newspapers revealed his relationship with Donna Rice, a Miami actress. The National Enquirer published two photos that showed Hart and Rice vacationing together in Bimini.

After his death, Americans learned that John F. Kennedy also enjoyed the company of attractive young women, even after his election as president. Some journalists knew about Kennedy's relationships but, at the time, considered them a private matter.

Four years later, reporters were criticized for "staking out" Gary Hart and ending his presidential campaign.

Hart's wife was standing at his side when he announced his candidacy, promising "the very highest standards of integrity and ethics, and soundness of judgment." Polls

With his wife standing nearby (at the right), Gary Hart announces that he is withdrawing from the 1988 presidential campaign.

showed that Hart was the leading Democratic candidate, and likely to receive 65 percent of the votes cast in the Iowa primary. But there were questions about Hart's character, especially about discrepancies concerning his age and a change in the spelling of his name, for example.

For years, there had also been rumors about Hart's womanizing. A telephone tip from a woman who claimed to have information about Hart in an extramarital affair sent Miami Herald reporters on a stakeout to Hart's home in Washington. They discovered Hart leaving his house with a young woman, later identified as Donna Rice, and returning with her to the house late in the evening. The Herald published this information, and within a week Hart withdrew from the presidential campaign.

After Hart's withdrawal, the National Enquirer published two photographs showing him with Rice in Bimini. In one, the pair is cuddling on a dock, with Rice sitting on Hart's lap, one arm around him. The second photo showed Hart, Rice and another couple partying at a Bimini nightspot. The National Enquirer obtained the photos from one of Rice's friends, paying a reported $25,000 for them.

Although the scandal forced Hart temporarily from the presidential race, after a period of time he returned. But his unpopular image endured, and he again withdrew from the race.

Was it good journalism—or an invasion of Hart's privacy?

Some Americans were outraged by the stories' publication. They complained that journalists went too far in following a presidential candidate and in invading his personal life. Critics (including some journalists) were especially scathing in their remarks about the Herald's stakeout techniques.

Yet the Herald admitted that its stakeout was imperfect, and many Americans supported the paper. They thought that Hart himself was responsible for the Herald's surveillance because of his comments, behavior and "flagrant flaunting of fundamental rules of our society."

Hart knew that he was being observed and that his personal life was an issue in the campaign. Under the circumstances, journalists considered his behavior reckless and arrogant. Why would any presidential candidate (especially a married man) openly continue his relationship with an attractive young woman? And why would he pose for the photographs in Bimini? Thus, Americans disappointed by Hart's behavior complained that he betrayed his family, staff and supporters. For them, the issue was not just Hart's morality, but his attitude toward women, his self-discipline and his sense of responsibility toward other people. They were also disappointed by Hart's response to the news media: by Hart's belligerence and failure to accept any responsibility for his own actions and their consequences.*

Journalists have become involved in similar controversies after overhearing—and reporting—remarks not meant for publication. Their victims were outraged and accused the journalists of invading their privacy, and of acting unfairly and unethically. Journalists responded that the remarks were newsworthy—that they revealed more about speakers' true feelings, character and behavior. Some journalists have added that public officials should be more cautious about what they say—that the officials should not say anything in public that they would be ashamed to see in print.

When President Ronald Reagan joked about bombing the Soviet Union, journalists reported the story. Reagan told the joke just before a radio broadcast, and it was accidentally transmitted to a pressroom. During Jesse Jackson's campaign for the presidency, journalists also overheard—and reported—his derogatory remarks about Jews.

The media's probing may have an unfortunate result. Some Americans are reluctant to run for public office because they do not want to be exposed to media scrutiny. In Seattle, John Jamison was asked to run for mayor and declined because he did not want to surrender his privacy, nor that of his family. "I was not willing to make myself a target for the hostility of the press," Jamison said. He complained that political leaders are perpetually under attack and that he did not want to spend his time "defending this or that two-bit issue" dredged up by the press.

Jamison added that he found other people—men and women across the country—making similar decisions. He concluded that the country may be losing some of its best leaders because of their fear of the press.

Photographs: What's Newsworthy—What's Sensational?

Newspaper editors usually decide to publish a photograph because it tells an important story. Readers upset by the editors' decisions accuse them of acting unethically, of being sensationalists more interested in selling newspapers than in helping people in distress. Readers are concerned about the photographs' effects: whether some photographs may be too unpleasant, tasteless or upsetting. Criticism is greatest of photographs showing human grief, such as a picture of a mother grieving over her child's body.

Yet some photographs are so compelling—so filled with fresh, hard news—that editors publish them regardless of the criticism they may arouse. The problem often arose during the war in Vietnam. Editors used pictures that portrayed the horrors of war. One of the pictures showed a Buddhist monk burning himself to death on a Saigon street. Another showed a South Vietnamese police chief shooting a prisoner.

Stanley Forman of Boston's Herald-American snapped a series of horrifying photos that showed a young woman and a little girl about to be rescued from a fire escape. The fire escape collapsed, and the photos also showed the two in midair, falling to the ground. The woman died, yet newspapers throughout the world published Forman's photographs, and he received a Pulitzer Prize for them. Predictably, some readers accused the newspapers of sensationalism: of poor taste, insensitivity, an invasion of the victims' privacy, and a tasteless display of human tragedy to sell newspapers.

*For a firsthand account of the Herald's stakeout and coverage, see: "The Gary Hart story: How it happened," *The Miami Herald*, May 10, 1987, p. 1.

Eddie Adams, a photographer for The Associated Press, won a Pulitzer Prize for this photograph, which shows the chief of the South Vietnamese National Police executing a captured Viet Cong officer on a Saigon street. Adams took the photograph during the 1968 Tet offensive, and it has become one of the most widely circulated photographs in history. Some newspaper editors were reluctant to publish this and other controversial photographs taken during the Vietnam War. Other editors decided to publish photographs of violence and human suffering, but not on their newspapers' front pages.

Journalists in Pennsylvania faced a similar dilemma. The state treasurer, R. Budd Dwyer, shot and killed himself during a press conference. Dwyer, 47, was convicted in a bribery scandal and faced up to 55 years in prison. He began the press conference by insisting that he was innocent and by accusing other government officials of conspiring against him. Near the end of a rambling 30-minute account, Dwyer also began to attack the press. Then he opened a manila envelope, pulled out a gun and fired one shot into his mouth.

The entire episode—from the moment Dwyer pulled out the gun until he shot himself—took only 21 seconds. There were about 35 witnesses, primarily reporters and photographers.

WHTM-TV in Harrisburg broadcast the entire videotape, and so did two stations in Pittsburgh. Viewers outraged by the broadcast complained that some children saw the suicide before their parents were able to change channels. Newscasters responded that the media should not sugarcoat reality. Another journalist explained: "The feeling was, this was a major news event and it was at a public press conference. It captures the horror of the story in terms everyone can understand and see. Pictures are part of the story."

Stations elsewhere generally edited or discarded the videotape. Their edited versions showed Dwyer holding the gun, but not putting it into his mouth and pulling the trigger.

This series of prize-winning photos shows a Boston firefighter trying to rescue a young woman and a little girl. The fire escape collapsed just as he reached them, and the young woman died in the fall. Some readers objected to the photograph's publication.

Citizen vs. Journalist

After accepting a job with the news media, you may find that your duties occasionally conflict with your normal responsibilities as a citizen. Journalists believe that their primary responsibility is to report the news. To do so, they may have to set aside some responsibilities that conflict with their work. When journalists in Vietnam photographed the Buddhist monk burning himself, readers wondered why the journalists failed to lay down their cameras and extinguish the flames. Readers also wondered why the journalists failed to notify the authorities so they could prevent the suicide.

Journalists are reluctant to become involved in the stories they cover. They want to remain neutral bystanders—not to prevent, encourage or change a story. Yet this puzzles and sometimes outrages other citizens, who believe that journalists should help people in distress, cooperate with the police and support the president. They also want journalists to suppress harmful stories.

Journalists occasionally suppress some stories, but only in extreme cases; for example, when a life is in danger. The police in El Paso, Texas, recently asked journalists there to suppress news of a kidnapping until the victim was rescued. The journalists agreed, and an editor explained, "No story is worth the lives of children." Other journalists knew that some Americans were hiding in a Canadian embassy in Iran while the Iranians were holding 52 other Americans as hostages. No one reported the story.

However, "NBC Nightly News" decided to broadcast a film taken by a free-lancer who lived with Communist guerrillas in the Philippine countryside. The free-lancer, Jon

Would you publish these photographs in a daily newspaper? Does it matter that the man was a state official and killed himself during a press conference attended by about 35 reporters and photographers? Some newspapers used these photographs, but not a fourth taken after the official fired a single shot into his mouth.

This photo, perhaps the most famous taken during the war in Vietnam, shows a 73-year-old Buddhist monk protesting government policies he considered oppressive. The monk's self-immolation on a Saigon street succeeded in turning the world's attention to the issue.

Alpert, showed the guerrillas pointing to a map and explaining how they planned to ambush a convoy of Philippine soldiers. Alpert's film also showed the actual ambush, where 15 soldiers were killed. Some viewers called NBC to ask whether the film was real. Others wanted to know why Alpert referred to the government soldiers as "the enemy." Still others wondered why Alpert failed to prevent the killings, to warn the soldiers of the danger. Yet when other journalists slipped into Afghanistan, no one objected when they showed rebels there attacking Soviet troops.

NBC was criticized even more vehemently after it broadcast an interview with a suspected terrorist: Abul Abbas. Three countries were looking for Abbas after the hijacking of a ship and the murder of an American tourist. NBC agreed to conceal his location; it seemed to be the only way to persuade him to talk. During the interview, Abbas said the Palestinians now consider the United States, not Israel, their chief enemy. Abbas then threatened to conduct his next terrorist operations in the United States.

An official at the State Department called NBC's decision "reprehensible," and charged that the network had become an accomplice to terror. Another government official complained that the publicity NBC gave Abbas "encourages the terrorist activities we're all seeking to deter."

The Chicago Tribune called NBC's story "an abysmal disgrace to journalism." An editorial written by Tribune editor James D. Squires argued that Abbas' location was the only new and important element of the story, yet NBC agreed to keep it a secret. Squires added that, "If The Chicago Tribune could find Abbas we would turn him in." The Tribune would accept Abbas' offer for an interview and then tell the government his location.

Other journalists also criticized NBC's decision to interview Abbas—but were more critical of The Chicago Tribune's plan to betray him. They feared that, if a newspaper broke its word with Abbas, other sources would become more suspicious of every

Associated Press photographer Nick Ut took this picture of Vietnamese children fleeing a napalm bomb attack.

journalist and more reluctant to talk with them. Sources in other countries might also feel freer to harm the journalists, especially if they seemed to be cooperating with their governments.

Conflicts of Interest

After years of confusion and opposing standards, there seems to be a growing consensus about what constitutes a conflict of interest. Most journalists agree that financial corruption is unethical and that they should not accept money or other valuables from the people they write about. An editor at The Washington Post has explained that: "It is rather generally accepted among newspaper people that financial corruption is probably sinful, that editors and reporters ought not take money or other things of value from people and organizations that are in the news. On some newspapers (this one included), the acceptance of a bribe—for that is what it is—is a firing offense."

In the past, reporters often accepted gifts, called "freebies." Some reporters considered the gifts as fringe benefits. They received free tickets to every attraction in their communities. Each Christmas, a political reporter might receive a carload of gifts from the officials in city hall. After writing about a jewelry store, another reporter might receive a free watch from its owner.

Free trips, called "junkets," were also common. Fashion writers were invited with all expenses paid to New York, and television critics to Hollywood. Sports writers accompanied their local teams to games in distant cities at the teams' expense.

Journalists accepting the gifts insisted that they could not be corrupted because they were trained to remain objective. They also explained that most of the gifts were insignificant: small tokens of appreciation for their work. Some journalists added that they would be less willing to accept the gifts if they were better paid and could afford to buy the items for themselves. Similarly, journalists accepting the junkets insisted that the main issue should be the public's right to know. Journalists added that smaller newspapers and broadcasting stations could not afford to send their reporters to distant cities, and that the junkets helped them obtain stories that, otherwise, would be unavailable.

Most newspapers now prohibit their reporters and editors from accepting anything of value. Other newspapers allow their newspeople to accept small items worth only a few dollars: a cup of coffee or souvenir T-shirt, for example. Some newspapers also allow their newspeople to accept free tickets to sports events, theaters and movies. However, newspapers generally prohibit their newspeople from calling a press agent to ask for the tickets.

Increasingly, newspapers also prohibit outside work and activities that might conflict with their reporters' objectivity. Editors explain that reporters' first obligation should be to their primary employer, and that the reporters continue to represent their employers even after they have left work for the day.

Editors generally agree that reporters should not hold any public office, either elected or appointed. Most editors also agree that reporters should not serve as party officials, or help with anyone's campaign. They want to avoid even the appearance of a conflict. For example: there might not be a direct conflict if a business writer ran for city council; a business writer might never cover the city council. But the newspaper's readers might suspect that its other writers slanted the news in favor of their colleague's campaign.

The reporters at most newspapers are free to accept other types of second jobs, provided that they do not create any conflicts. Typically, reporters and photographers can work as free-lancers, but cannot sell their work to their employers' competitors, such as other media in the same market. Similarly, newspapers may allow their sports writers to teach at a community college, but not to serve as scorekeepers at the games they cover. As scorekeepers, the writers would become part of the stories they were covering. Their decisions might be controversial and might determine the outcome of some games. Thus, the writers would have to report on their own actions. Similarly, newspapers might tell their sports editor to stop serving as the host of a local radio program and to avoid appearing on local television programs, especially for pay.

Increasingly, journalists also face a newer conflict: their spouse's employment or position. To avoid the conflict, editors usually do not allow reporters to cover any story in which their spouse is involved.

Other conflicts arise when journalists become involved in the organizations they report on. Some editors, particularly those on small newspapers, encourage their employees to become involved in community affairs: to join the Kiwanis, Lions or Rotary Club, and to help the Cancer Society or Salvation Army. Other editors insist that their reporters do not have to belong to anything to do a good job. The editors fear that if their reporters become too involved, they may lose their objectivity.

Another problem, called "hobnobbery journalism," arises when journalists become good friends with their sources. Walter Lippmann, one of the nation's most respected columnists, insisted that: "Newspapermen can't be the cronies of great men. There always has to be a certain distance between high public officials and newspapermen." The problem often arises in Washington and was especially common during the Kennedy administration, when some journalists became the president's friends and, because of their friendship, may have been reluctant to criticize him. Some may have even feared losing his friendship.

A recent survey, conducted by the Ethics Committee of the American Society of Newspaper Editors, revealed that 30 journalists were suspended and 48 fired during the last three years because of their unethical behavior. The two most common problems involved: (1) journalists' social contacts with newsmakers and, (2) journalists who rewrote their competitors' stories without first verifying the details. Other ethical violations involved plagiarism, the fabrication of entire stories, the use of unpublished material for financial gain, and the acceptance of discounts from companies the journalists wrote about.

Other conflicts can affect an entire state or industry. In 1972, The Newspaper Guild endorsed George McGovern, the Democratic candidate for president. The Guild is a union representing thousands of the nation's journalists. After its endorsement, critics asked whether the Guild's members would be able to remain impartial while covering that year's presidential election, or whether its members had lost their objectivity. Because of the controversy, the Guild did not endorse a candidate in 1976 or 1980. However, in 1984 it endorsed Walter F. Mondale.

In 1978, Florida's largest daily newspapers opposed a proposal to legalize casino gambling in the state. The newspapers used their editorial pages to denounce the proposal. In addition, they contributed almost $150,000 to the campaign to defeat it. Large dailies contributed up to $25,000 apiece. The proposal was defeated but reappeared on Florida's 1986 ballot. In 1986, the dailies declined to donate any money to help defeat the proposal, partly because of the controversy caused by their earlier donations.

A Disney Bribe?

Walt Disney World invited thousands of journalists to fly to Orlando to celebrate its 15th anniversary and, supposedly, to also celebrate the 200th anniversary of the U.S. Constitution. Each journalist was allowed to bring one guest.

More than 5,000 people accepted Disney's invitation. Some were disc jockeys or worked in management, advertising or promotion. They flew to Orlando from all 50 states, and were joined by several hundred Canadians, about 200 Europeans and 20 Japanese.

The junket cost about $7.5 million, but Disney contributed only $1.5 million. Seventeen airlines offered their services for free or at reduced rates. Hotels donated 5,000 rooms and free breakfasts. The state of Florida and several local groups, all established to promote tourism in Central Florida, contributed an additional $350,000 apiece. They spent $600,000 for a single party in downtown Orlando. The journalists were also treated to a concert and a fireworks display, and they spent an entire evening in Disney's Magic Kingdom.

Disney insisted that there were no strings attached, that the journalists were not under any obligation to give it any favorable publicity. Moreover, Disney offered the journalists three options:

They could accept the free trip.
They could pay $150 a day to cover a portion of their expenses.
They could accept Disney's offer but pay the entire cost of their travel, food and lodging.

Disney refused to provide a list of the journalists who accepted its invitation. However, about one-third seemed to be employed by newspapers and magazines, and about two-thirds seemed to be employed by the broadcast media. Their acceptance renewed a controversy that many journalists thought ended years earlier. Hundreds of newspapers and broadcasting stations had adopted codes of ethics that prohibited the acceptance of anything of value. Almost every major organization in the field of journalism had adopted a similar code. Yet, when offered a junket that violated their codes, thousands of journalists accepted it.

Why? Journalists employed by smaller newspapers and broadcast stations explained that they would have been unable to cover the story without Disney's subsidy. Larger newspapers may have accepted Disney's subsidy because it would cost $100,000 or more if they paid all of a travel writer's expenses for one year. Other journalists said they accepted because they were not required to do anything in return. Still others insisted that, as trained professionals, they would remain objective: they would not be corrupted by Disney's subsidy.

A writer for The Orlando Sentinel responded that, "This generosity is no better than a bribe to get puffy coverage, and the so-called journalists who accept it are a disgrace." A second critic complained that Disney "exposed dramatically the seamy side of the journalism profession." Disney's offer seemed to prove "that a great deal of favorable publicity is, without question, for sale by a significant percentage of this country's media."

Even the critics overlooked a more fundamental issue. Was the party newsworthy? Was Disney's 15th anniversary important enough to justify coverage by 5,000 media employees? Or, did the recipients use Disney's anniversary as an excuse to accept a free vacation?

Disney obviously wanted publicity. Why else would it invite so many journalists to Orlando? Moreover, it succeeded. A Disney representative called it "the biggest marketing project we have ever undertaken." Within three months, Disney estimated that it had received $9 million worth of free publicity. Television stations broadcast 186 live reports during the extravaganza, and radio stations provided 1,000 hours of live coverage. Even major networks covered the story. Both ABC's "Good Morning America" and NBC's "Today" were on-the-air live from Disney.

Publicists at Disney also collected a two-foot stack of press clippings. The extravaganza was supposed to observe the 200th anniversary of the signing of the U.S. Constitution, but most of the stories described Disney World. Moreover, the Constitution was only 199—not 200—years old.

Thus, Disney exploited journalists' greed, but the journalists decided to accept its offer. The real issue may have been the journalists' credibility. Other journalists warned that the public might not trust any of the stories written by newspeople who accept gifts and trips from their sources.

Contests—Another Evil?

Journalists also worry about a newer conflict: a proliferation of contests. Editors do not want their employees to accept gifts from the people they write about. But each year, journalists are encouraged to enter hundreds of contests, including some that offer thousands of dollars in prizes. Together, these contests offer nearly $500,000 in prizes.

Initially, the contests encouraged excellence in journalism. But newer contests, established by non-journalists, seem intended to attract favorable publicity for their sponsors.

Editor & Publisher magazine publishes an annual directory that lists more than 500 awards, scholarships and prizes available to journalists. Typically, the Thoroughbred Racing Association gives "Eclipse Awards" for the best coverage of thoroughbred horse racing, while the Korea National Tourism Corp. gives "Heavenly Horse Awards" for travel writing about the Republic of Korea.

Other sponsors specify that, to be eligible for a prize, the publicity must be favorable. The International Association of Fire Fighters "honors news media for reporting and photography that best portray the professional and hazardous work of the firefighters in the United States and Canada." Similarly, the Mexican Government Tourist Office gives $2,750 in cash, silver trophies and trips for articles "that promote travel to Mexico."

Before allowing their employees to compete for any of the prizes, many editors now screen the contests and ask:

Who sponsors them?
Must the publicity be favorable?
How do journalists benefit from them?
Who are the judges?
Who selects the judges and screens the initial entries?

Rumors: Gossip or News?

Journalists are supposed to publish facts, but are tempted to publish some rumors. If everyone in their community seems to be talking about a rumor, the journalists may want to comment on it. Yet some rumors are impossible to verify. Journalists fear that, by publishing the rumors, they may encourage their repetition, and even though they explain that the rumors are "unconfirmed," some readers will fail to notice or remember their disclaimers.

Some rumors are little more than gossip. They may insist that a celebrity is gay, getting divorced or dying of AIDS. Other rumors have insisted that some celebrities were already dead. Similarly, people in a community may claim that a restaurant is adding horse or kangaroo meat (or even worms) to its hamburgers. Or, that someone shopping for Oriental rugs at a local department store was bitten and killed by a poisonous snake hiding in the rugs.

Other rumors concern topics of greater importance: topics that might affect an entire community. They may claim that a new building is unsafe, or that a major business plans to move.

Journalists report on some rumors because they are obviously false, and harm innocent people. For example, dozens of stories have attempted to refute the rumor that Proctor & Gamble Company's trademark is a symbol of Satanism. Yet some Americans still believe the rumor and are boycotting the company's products. People repeating the rumor usually claim that a Proctor & Gamble official appeared on a nationally televised talk show and admitted that he had made a deal with the devil. The official supposedly confessed that he agreed to work for the devil in return for the devil's help in making him a millionaire. Proctor & Gamble has no idea who started the rumor. To stop it, the company is filing libel suits against those who have reprinted it. The company is also eliminating the symbol, showing several stars and the moon, from its packages.

Another rumor confronted Stanley Dearman, editor of The Neshoba Democrat in Philadelphia, Miss. Dearman said he heard persistent rumors that three local men—a businessman, a law enforcement official and a pilot—had been arrested with a planeload of cocaine. Dearman checked the story and found that it was false, yet readers continued to call and ask why he failed to report it. Some readers suspected that Dearman was paid off. The callers were certain that the story had been broadcast by a television station; however, none had actually seen it. Finally, Dearman published an editorial offering a $500 reward to anyone able to prove that the story was true. He also promised to publish all the details. No one claimed the money, and the rumor died.

Censoring Media Ads

For almost 200 years, newspapers published every advertisement submitted to them. Editors rarely felt responsible for their content. Rather, the editors' philosophy was *caveat emptor*: "Let the buyer beware."

During the last century, newspapers in both the North and the South published advertisements for slaves. Perhaps unknowingly, some also published advertisements for prostitutes. Advertisements for quack medicines were even more common. Some medicines contained enough alcohol to inebriate the people using them. Others contained enough cocaine, heroin or morphine to make the people using them addicts. Even the "soothing syrups" sold for babies were spiked with heroin, morphine, opium and cocaine, so that some babies may have died from drug overdoses.

A single medicine might be advertised as the cure for dozens of ailments, including headaches, tuberculosis, malaria, poison ivy, ulcers, varicose veins, cancer, syphillis, hay fever and diarrhea. People felt better after taking the medicines, but only because some were nearly pure cocaine. Instead of wanting to cure their patients, manufacturers may have wanted to make them addicts, so they would buy more of their products.

During the 1880s, a few periodicals began to protect their readers from fraudulent advertising. When Cyrus H. K. Curtis took over the Saturday Evening Post in 1897, he began to reject advertisements for liquor and patent medicines. During the 20th century, newspapers began to reject advertisements for the medicines and for get-rich-quick financial schemes, especially schemes that required a large down payment. The St. Louis Post-Dispatch was a leader in the campaign to clean up newspapers' advertising columns. It lost thousands of dollars in revenue, but its publisher never objected.

Editors now reject advertisements that seem distasteful or that promote products that seem illegal, immoral or harmful. They want to act ethically, to do what is right. Some explain that they have always felt responsible for the content of their news columns, routinely deleting anything that seemed tasteless, inaccurate, unfair, libelous or obscene. Now, the editors say, they are accepting a similar responsibility for the content of their advertising columns. Many readers agree with the editors' decisions. Others accuse them of censorship.

More than 100 daily newspapers reject advertisements for alcoholic beverages, especially hard liquor. Other dailies reject advertisements for X-rated movies, mail order goods and fortunetellers. A few dailies reject advertisements for abortions and handguns. Some also reject advertisements for massage parlors and escort services which, in some cities, have been fronts for prostitution.

But of the nation's 1,674 daily newspapers, only a dozen or two reject advertisements for cigarettes. Scientists have proven that tobacco causes cancer, and the U.S. Surgeon General has called smoking "the chief single avoidable cause of death in our society and the most important public-health issue of our time." The American Lung Association estimates that smoking causes 350,000 deaths in the United States every year, an average of almost 1,000 a day. If its estimate is correct, smoking causes more deaths than all of the following causes combined: alcohol, illegal drugs, traffic accidents, suicide and murder. Moreover, the advertisements for tobacco products often seem to be aimed at teen-agers. Many show healthy, athletic young people, engaged in happy, glamorous activities.

In 1965, manufacturers were forced to place health warnings on cigarette packs. In 1971, Congress banned cigarette advertisements on radio and television. Since then, the tobacco industry has turned to other media, especially newspapers and magazines.

Why do newspapers and magazines continue to accept the advertisements? Some journalists do not believe that smoking causes cancer. Still others seem reluctant to offend smokers (or the tobacco industry). Each year, the industry spends more than $2 billion on advertising in the United States.

Many editors add that it would be unethical or irresponsible for them to reject the advertisements. The editors say they are hesitant to withhold information from the public simply because they happen to disagree with it. As long as the tobacco industry's advertisements are truthful and legal, the editors add, they want to protect Americans' freedom to make their own decisions, however good or bad. However, critics respond that the editors' arguments are nonsense—that the editors are selfishly protecting a major source of advertising revenue.

Moreover, new issues are constantly arising. Some newspapers, concerned about their readers' health and safety, no longer accept advertisements for "happy hours" (for cheap or free drinks). Bars usually advertise the "happy hours" during the late afternoon and early evening, when people begin to drive home after work. Editors fear that the advertisements will contribute to heavy drinking and drunken driving.

Newspapers in the Northeast have also been troubled by advertisements for babies. Typically, the advertisements promise to pay $10,000 or more for "a white newborn." Because of the use of contraceptives and the growing number of abortions, few healthy babies are available for adoption. Couples unwilling to wait several years at a conventional adoption agency may turn to a newspaper's classified advertising columns. To persuade mothers to put their babies up for adoption, the couples promise to give their babies loving and secure homes. In addition, they also promise to pay each mother thousands of dollars.

Do Journalists Encourage Terrorism?

Striking at random, terrorists kidnap tourists, assassinate diplomats and hijack airplanes. Their causes may seem obscure, yet the terrorists seem willing to die for them. They also seem willing to kill hundreds of other people. Because of their fanaticism, entire nations seem helpless against them.

The terrorists usually want publicity and have learned to create news so compelling that television is unable to ignore it. The terrorists provide genuine drama: hijackings, demands, deadlines and the threat of mass murder. They can add to the drama by moving from one place to another and by releasing (or murdering) a few of their hostages.

To attract even more publicity, the terrorists have learned to conduct formal press conferences. Some allow journalists to photograph and interview their helpless captives. Others make videotapes of their captives, typically showing the captives pleading for their lives, reading the terrorists' demands, and warning that, if the demands are not met, they will be killed.

Critics insist that television does more than cover the terrorists: it also encourages them. They believe that if the media ignored terrorists they would be discouraged and abandon their acts of violence. British Prime Minister Margaret Thatcher has urged journalists to stop covering terrorists, to starve them of the "oxygen of publicity." The critics want journalists to adopt a voluntary code that would limit their coverage. But that may be impossible. No one seems able to develop a code acceptable to thousands of journalists in dozens of countries. It also seems impossible to develop guidelines that would cover every possible situation.

Moreover, most journalists oppose the idea. They are reluctant to accept any guidelines that would limit their coverage of an important story—or their freedom. Journalists add that Americans have a right to know what is happening in the world, and that a blackout might be worse, because rumors about the terrorists' activities might become more frightening than the truth. Journalists also fear that, if the terrorists were ignored, some would escalate their violence. Instead of hijacking one plane, they might hijack two or three. Instead of using a small bomb to kill a single individual, the terrorists might use a larger bomb to kill hundreds. Eventually, the media would be forced to cover them.

Thus, journalists seem unable (and unwilling) to censor themselves. Some governments might censor the media. But in the United States, government censorship would be illegal. Journalists add that it would also be unwise. Any government that censored the media would be limiting the freedom—that is, the free access to knowledge—of the people it was trying to protect.

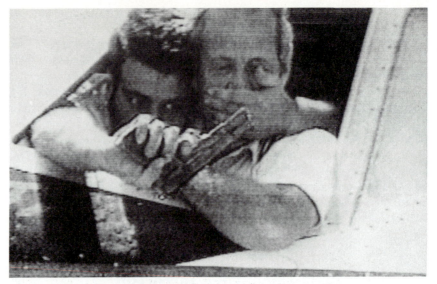

Most terrorists want publicity—and succeed in obtaining it. Here, a terrorist holds a gun on TWA pilot John Testrake as he was interviewed after the plane was hijacked to Beirut. One passenger was killed, but Testrake, his crew and the remaining passengers were released after days of negotiations (and intensive television coverage).

Codes of Ethics

Every major organization in the field of journalism has adopted a code of ethics, but there is little evidence that any of their codes are effective. None are enforced. Also, some organizations adopted their codes merely for self-protection: to convince the public that they are doing a good job of regulating themselves, and that government regulation is unnecessary.

The American Society of Newspaper Editors (ASNE) adopted one of the industry's first codes, the Canons of Journalism, in 1923. The Canons did not prohibit anything; rather, they told newspaper editors what they should do. Among other things they declared that newspapers should act responsibly: that they should be truthful, sincere, impartial, decent and fair. However, the Canons were so vague that even the most sincere journalists might disagree about their meaning.

In fact, the ASNE rejected attempts to enforce the Canons. In one case, during President Harding's administration, Frederick Bonfils, co-publisher of The Denver Post, ignored the Teapot Dome scandal in return for a bribe. When the ASNE learned about the bribe, it considered expelling Bonfils, but abandoned the idea. Instead, the ASNE decided to encourage editors to voluntarily comply with the Canons of Journalism. Its members were divided over the issue and feared that if they tried to expel Bonfils, the organization might be destroyed.

The Society of Professional Journalists, Sigma Delta Chi, adopted a revised code at its national convention in 1973. The code declares that journalists must seek the truth and have a responsibility to "perform with intelligence, objectivity, accuracy and fairness." The code adds that journalists should accept "nothing of value" because gifts and special favors might compromise their integrity. The code also recommends that journalists avoid second jobs and political involvement that might cause a conflict of interest.

The code's most controversial section directed that journalists who violated the code should be censured. The section explained that, "Journalists should actively censure and try to prevent violations of these standards, and they should encourage their obser-

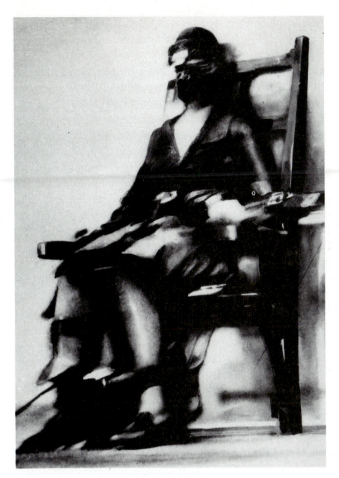

A photographer practiced for a month before secretly taking this picture of Ruth Snyder as she was electrocuted for murdering her husband. The photo appeared in a sensational tabloid, the New York Daily News. A mask was placed over Snyder's head after she was strapped into Sing Sing's electric chair on the night of Jan. 12, 1928. To avoid detection, the photographer—who posed as a reporter—tied a miniature camera to one ankle. He lifted a pants cuff and used a remote control to snap one photo as the first jolt of electricity surged through Snyder's body, and to snap another photo at the second jolt.

vance by all news people." Yet few violators were censured, and the society never adopted any formal procedures to censure them. In 1987, delegates at the society's national convention voted to eliminate that section of the code. (A copy of the society's code, including the controversial section, appears at the end of this chapter.)

During the 1980s, journalists began to call for an end to the hypocrisy. They wanted to eliminate the censure clause or to adopt the procedures necessary to enforce it. Other journalists opposed the idea. They wanted to encourage—not enforce—ethical conduct. Journalists seemed reluctant to infringe upon their colleagues' freedom, to tell them how to act or to publicly condemn their decisions.

Recent surveys have found that at least half of the nation's daily newspapers and broadcasting stations have adopted codes to govern their own employees. Most of the media codes are designed to prevent conflicts of interest, and many are strictly enforced. Typically, they prohibit the acceptance of anything of value, including gifts, favors, tickets and trips. Most also prohibit any outside work, political involvement or other activities that would conflict with their employees' coverage of the news.

A recent poll of 34 newspapers in the Northeast revealed that 51 percent had adopted a written code, and that:

- 90 percent did not allow their newsroom employees to accept gifts.
- 90 percent did not allow their newsroom employees to become involved in politics.
- 79 percent did not allow their newsroom employees to accept tickets to dinners.
- 63 percent did not allow their newsroom employees to accept tickets to artistic events.

- 57 percent did not allow their newsroom employees to accept tickets to athletic events.
- 27 percent did not allow their newsroom employees to accept books for review.

Reporters have responded that the codes infringe upon their freedom and that, as citizens, they have a responsibility to become involved in their communities. Reporters have also complained of a double standard in journalism. The codes limit their freedom, yet many editors and publishers seem to do as they please. Some continue to head charities, and some serve on the boards of local schools and businesses. Similarly, a publisher can write editorials that endorse a politician's candidacy, but reporters cannot sign petitions, march in rallies or provide any other help for a politician's campaign.

To prevent any conflicts, The Chicago Tribune requires its employees to fill out an annual disclosure statement that lists all their outside sources of income and that describes their involvement in civic and political groups. Yet the Tribune itself owns the Chicago Cubs, and that may be the greatest conflict of all. Readers who know that a newspaper owns a baseball team may distrust its coverage of that team.

Thus, the standards in journalism are improving. Journalists are becoming better educated, more responsible and more ethical. But it is difficult to convince the public of that fact. Journalists are forced to make too many controversial decisions, and the decisions are more complex than most people imagine.

Also, journalists and their readers often disagree about which stories the media should report and about how those stories should be presented to the public. Journalists are reluctant to suppress any stories, while readers worry more about the stories' effects on the people reported about, as well as on other readers.

Journalists are adopting codes of ethics to eliminate the most obvious abuses, especially conflicts of interest. But the codes cannot solve every problem. There are too many problems, and the problems are too diverse. Thus, decisions will always vary from one newspaper to another—but that may be one of our system's greatest strengths. Every journalist is free to decide what is right or wrong, ethical or unethical. Inevitably, some journalists will be mistaken. But any effort to change the system—to force every journalist to conform to a predetermined standard—would limit the media's diversity and freedom. It would also limit Americans' access to some information.

Suggested Readings

Christians, Clifford G., Kim B. Rotzoll and Mark Fackler. *Media Ethics: Cases and Moral Reasoning.* 2nd ed. New York: Longman, Inc., 1983.

Goldstein, Tom. *The News at Any Cost: How Journalists Compromise Their Ethics to Shape the News.* New York: Simon and Schuster, 1986.

Goodwin, H. Eugene. *Groping for Ethics in Journalism.* 2nd ed. Ames: Iowa State University Press, 1987.

Hulteng, John L. *The Messenger's Motives: Ethical Problems of the News Media.* 2nd ed. Englewood Cliffs, N.J.: Prentice-Hall, 1985.

———. *Playing It Straight: A Practical Discussion of the Ethical Principles of the American Society of Newspaper Editors.* Chester, Conn.: The Globe Pequot Press, 1981.

Lambeth, Edmund B. *Committed Journalism: An Ethic for the Profession.* Bloomington, Ind.: Indiana University Press, 1986.

Merrill, John C., and Ralph D. Barney, eds. *Ethics and the Press: Readings in Mass Morality.* New York: Hastings House, 1975.

Pfaff, Daniel W. *Joseph Pulitzer II and Advertising Censorship, 1929–1939.* Journalism Monographs, No. 77. Columbia, S.C.: Association for Education in Journalism, 1982.

Rivers, William L., and Wilbur Schramm. *Responsibility in Mass Communication.* 3rd ed. New York: Harper & Row, 1980.

Schmuhl, Robert, ed. *The Responsibilities of Journalism.* Notre Dame, Ind.: University of Notre Dame Press, 1985.

Shaw, David. *Press Watch: A Provocative Look at How Newspapers Report the News.* New York: MacMillan Publishing Company, 1984.

Swain, Bruce M. *Reporters' Ethics*. Ames, Iowa: Iowa State University Press, 1978.
Thayer, Lee. *Ethics, Morality and the Media*. New York: Hastings House, 1980.

These publications also frequently address ethical issues in journalism:

Columbia Journalism Review
The Quill
Washington Journalism Review

The Society of Professional Journalists, Sigma Delta Chi

Code of Ethics

THE SOCIETY of Professional Journalists, Sigma Delta Chi believes the duty of journalists is to serve the truth.

WE BELIEVE the agencies of mass communication are carriers of public discussion and information, acting on their Constitutional mandate and freedom to learn and report the facts.

WE BELIEVE in public enlightenment as the forerunner of justice and in our Constitutional role to seek the truth as part of the public's right to know the truth.

WE BELIEVE those responsibilities carry obligations that require journalists to perform with intelligence, objectivity, accuracy and fairness.

To these ends, we declare acceptance of the standards of practice here set forth:

RESPONSIBILITY:

The public's right to know of events of importance and interest is the overriding mission of the mass media. The purpose of distributing news and enlightened opinion is to serve the general welfare. Journalists who use their professional status as representatives of the public for selfish or other unworthy motives violate a high trust.

FREEDOM OF THE PRESS:

Freedom of the press is to be guarded as an inalienable right of people in a free society. It carries with it the freedom and the responsibility to discuss, question and challenge actions and utterances of our government and of our public and private institutions. Journalists uphold the right to speak unpopular opinions and the privilege to agree with the majority.

ETHICS:

Journalists must be free of obligation to any interest other than the public's right to know the truth.

1. Gifts, favors, free travel, special treatment or privileges can compromise the integrity of journalists and their employers. Nothing of value should be accepted.

2. Secondary employment, political involvement, holding public office and service in community organizations should be avoided if it compromises the integrity of journalists and their employers. Journalists and their employers should conduct their personal lives in a manner that protects them from conflict of interest, real or apparent. Their responsibilities to the public are paramount. This is the nature of their profession.

3. So-called news communications from private sources should not be published or broadcast without substantiation of their claims to news value.

4. Journalists will seek news that serves the public interest, despite the obstacles. They will make constant efforts to ensure that the public's business is conducted in public and that public records are open to public inspection.

5. Journalists acknowledge the newsman's ethic of protecting confidential sources of information.

6. Plagiarism is dishonest and unacceptable.

ACCURACY AND OBJECTIVITY:

Good faith with the public is the foundation of all worthy journalism.

1. Truth is our ultimate goal.

2. Objectivity in reporting the news is another goal that serves as the mark of an experienced professional. It is a standard of performance toward which we strive. We honor those who achieve it.

3. There is no excuse for inaccuracies or lack of thoroughness.

4. Newspaper headlines should be fully warranted by the contents of the articles they accompany. Photographs and telecasts should give an accurate picture of an event and not highlight a minor incident out of context.

5. Sound practice makes clear distinction between news reports and expressions of opinion. News reports should be free of opinion or bias and represent all sides of an issue.

6. Partisanship in editorial comment that knowingly departs from the truth violates the spirit of American journalism.

7. Journalists recognize their responsibility for offering informed analysis, comment and editorial opinion on public events and issues. They accept the obligation to present such material by individuals whose competence, experience and judgment qualify them for it.

8. Special articles or presentations devoted to advocacy or the writer's own conclusions and interpretations should be labeled as such.

FAIR PLAY:

Journalists at all times will show respect for the dignity, privacy, rights and well-being of people encountered in the course of gathering and presenting the news.

1. The news media should not communicate unofficial charges affecting reputation or moral character without giving the accused a chance to reply.

2. The news media must guard against invading a person's right to privacy.

3. The media should not pander to morbid curiosity about details of vice and crime.

4. It is the duty of news media to make prompt and complete correction of their errors.

5. Journalists should be accountable to the public for their reports and the public should be encouraged to voice its grievances against the media. Open dialogue with our readers, viewers and listeners should be fostered.

PLEDGE:

Journalists should actively censure and try to prevent violations of these standards, and they should encourage their observance by all newspeople. Adherence to this code of ethics is intended to preserve the bond of mutual trust and respect between American journalists and the American people.

Adopted 1926. Revised 1973, 1984.

Code of Ethics
The Washington Post

Benjamin Bradlee, executive editor of The Washington Post, drafted the Post's guidelines—"Standards and Ethics"—for newsroom employees. They state, in part:

THE REPORTER'S ROLE

Although it has become increasingly difficult for this newspaper and for the press generally to do so since Watergate, reporters should make every effort to remain in the audience, to stay off the stage, to report history, not to make history.

ERRORS

This newspaper is pledged to minimize errors, and to correct them when they occur. Accuracy is our goal; candor is our defense.

ATTRIBUTION OF SOURCES

This newspaper is pledged to discuss the source of all information unless disclosure would endanger the source's security. When we agree to protect a source's identity, that identity will not be made known to anyone outside the Post.

Before any information is accepted without full attribution, reporters must make every reasonable effort to get it on the record. If that is not possible, reporters should consider seeking the information elsewhere. If that in turn is not possible, reporters should request an on-the-record reason for restricting the source's identity, and should include the reason in the story.

In any case, some kind of identification is almost always possible—by department or by position, for example—and should be reported.

FAIRNESS

Reporters and editors of the Post are committed to fairness. While arguments about objectivity are endless, the concept of fairness is something that editors and reporters can easily understand and pursue. Fairness results from a few simple practices:

- No story is fair if it omits facts of major importance or significance. So fairness includes completeness.
- No story is fair if it includes essentially irrelevant information at the expense of significant facts. So fairness includes relevance.
- No story is fair if it consciously or unconsciously misleads or even deceives the reader. So fairness includes honesty—leveling with the reader.
- No story is fair if reporters hide their biases or emotions behind such subtly pejorative words as "refused," "despite," "admit," and "massive." So fairness requires straightforwardness ahead of flashiness.

Reporters and editors should routinely ask themselves at the end of every story: "Have I been as fair as I can be?"

OPINION

On this newspaper, the separation of news columns from the editorial and opposite-editorial pages is solemn and complete. This separation is intended to serve the reader, who is entitled to the facts in the news columns and to opinions on the editorial and "op-ed" pages. But nothing in this separation of function and powers is intended to eliminate from the news columns honest, in-depth reporting, or analysis, or commentary, when such departures from strictly factual reporting are plainly labeled.

TASTE

The Washington Post as a newspaper respects taste and decency, understanding that society's concepts of taste and decency are constantly changing. A word offensive to the last generation can be part of the next generation's common vocabulary. But we shall avoid prurience. We shall avoid profanities and obscenities unless their use is so essential to a story of significance that its meaning is lost without them. In no case shall obscenities be used without the approval of the executive editor or the managing editor or his deputy.

EXERCISE 1
Ethics

Discussion Questions

1. If you were a journalist, and Disney World invited you and a companion to fly to Orlando for its 15th anniversary, would you accept? Why?

2. If you served on the board that awards Pulitzer Prizes, would you have given a prize to the Sun-Times for its exposure of corruption in Chicago? Or, would you have objected to the Sun-Times' purchase of its own tavern to obtain the story?

3. How would you respond to the Seattle man who declined to run for mayor because he disliked being subject to the media's scrutiny and criticisms? Are his fears justified? Why?

4. Imagine that you worked as the news director at a Pennsylvania television station on the day the state treasurer, R. Budd Dwyer, shot and killed himself during a press conference. If one of your photographers returned with a 21-second videotape of his suicide, what would you do with it?

5. The Newspaper Guild, a union that represents thousands of newspeople, endorsed a candidate in several presidential elections. Do you agree with its policy? Why?

   If newspaper owners can endorse candidates on their editorial pages, why shouldn't reporters be able to endorse candidates through their unions?

6. Imagine that, as the editor of your local daily, you learned that one of your copy editors, working at home during her spare time, had written an article about a local celebrity. Would you allow her to sell the story to a magazine published in your city?

7. If you were the editor of your campus newspaper, would you accept and publish the advertisements submitted by companies that sell term papers? From discussions with friends, you know that some students submit the papers as their own work.

8. As the editor of a daily newspaper, would you report every birth, death, marriage, divorce, lawsuit and bankruptcy in your community?

   Would you also report every suicide, and every arrest and conviction for drunken driving?

9. Normally, the newspaper you edit avoids pictures of human grief. But imagine that a driver was killed during a stock car race at your county fair. More than 10,000 people saw the crash, and your photographer snapped a picture showing the driver's wife, holding his hand and crying as his body was cut from the wreckage. It is not a bloody scene, but you can see much of the driver's body and face. Would you publish the picture? Why?

10. Each year, you send a photographer to the graduation ceremonies at a local high school. Your photographer noticed several students misbehaving, and you published a picture of them because it seemed interesting and unusual. School administrators complained that the picture was not representative of the entire graduating class and that it may encourage other students to misbehave during next year's ceremonies. As a newspaper editor, you want to be fair but wonder whether it is your responsibility to encourage high-school students to behave at their graduation ceremonies. What instructions, if any, would you give the photographer who covers next year's ceremonies?

11.   You have just become the news director at a local television station and give each of your leading newspeople an allowance of $5,000 a year to purchase their wardrobes. The manager of a clothing store calls and offers to provide all their clothing for free. In return, the manager wants a brief "credit" broadcast at the end of each program. By accepting, you would be able to save $50,000 a year and could use the money to hire another newscaster and raise the salaries of your other employees. Would you accept the store's offer? Why?

12.   Your police reporter has learned that a prominent minister has been charged with shoplifting, a crime that you normally report. The police reveal that it is the minister's third arrest during the last year, but charges in the first two cases were dropped by the stores. The minister has learned that your reporter is working on the story. He calls and warns you that, if you publish the story, he will be forced to kill himself. How would you handle the situation?

EXERCISE 2
Ethics

Setting Your Newspaper's Policies
(What Would You Permit?)

1. If you published your city's daily newspaper, would you accept advertisements for all these products? If not, which ones would you ban, and how would you explain that ban to your readers? Similarly, how would you explain your decision to publish the other advertisements?
    A. X-rated movies.
    B. Massage parlors.
    C. Abortion clinics.
    D. Some or all alcoholic beverages.
    E. Cigarettes and other tobacco products.

2. As the editor of a daily newspaper, you have been asked to write a code of ethics for your reporters. You want to be fair, but you also want to prevent any conflicts that might affect your staff's coverage of the news, or that might harm your paper's credibility. Would you allow:
    A. Your science writer to date the mayor?
    B. Your science writer to run for the city council?
    C. Any of your reporters to sign a petition urging the mayor to resign?
    D. Your publisher to write an editorial endorsing the mayor's campaign for re-election?
    E. Your publisher to donate $1,000 to the mayor's re-election campaign?
    F. Your political reporter to volunteer his time each Saturday, helping supervise a fund drive for the Salvation Army?
    G. Your political reporter to volunteer his time each Saturday, writing publicity releases for the Salvation Army?
    H. Your political reporter to accept $100 for occasional appearances as a panelist on a Sunday morning television program?

3. Normally, your newspaper reports every birth, death, divorce and bankruptcy in your community. You also identify everyone charged with drunken driving, and your obituaries include everyone's age and the cause of their death. You rarely approve any exceptions to the policies. You want to protect your paper's reputation and avoid charges of favoritism. As editor, would you agree to help any of these people?
    A. A 74-year-old woman mails you a letter explaining that she is dying of cancer and does not want you to report her age in her obituary. Her friends think she is 65. She is embarrassed by the matter and does not want them to know that she lied.
    B. A man's family calls and asks you to not report the cause of his death: cirrhosis of the liver. They admit that he was an alcoholic but see no reason to inform the entire community of that fact.
    C. A local couple with four children asks you to not report their marriage. Their children have always thought that they were married, and the news that they are finally getting married would upset and embarrass everyone in the family.
    D. A minister charged with drunken driving pleads that he is innocent, that he was taking some drugs prescribed by a doctor, and that drugs made him dizzy. He insists that, in three or four days, breath and urinalysis tests conducted by the police will prove his innocence. Normally, you report everyone's arrest at the time of their apprehension, and later report the outcome of each case.

4. Robbers entered a local jewelry store just before 9 a.m. today, shot one clerk and seized seven hostages. Police have surrounded the store and cordoned off the entire block. It is your biggest story in years. As the news director at a local television station, would you instruct your staff to:
   A. Call and interview the hostages' relatives?
   B. Call the store and try to interview the robbers?
   C. Televise the confrontation live from across the street?
   D. If the robbers requested it, agree to let your leading newscaster serve as an intermediary between them and the police?
   E. In return for the robbers' promise to surrender and to release all seven hostages, agree to let them appear on the air—live and unedited—for three minutes after their surrender?

5. The police have shot a 15-year-old boy who broke into a liquor store. Police officers responding to a silent alarm surrounded the store and ordered the intruder to come out. At the time, they did not know his age. The intruder fired a .22 caliber pistol at the officers. They returned the fire, killing him. As a reporter, which of these details would you include in your story:
   A. The boy was an Eagle Scout: the highest rank in scouting.
   B. Other teen-agers—the boy's friends—say he was often drunk and may have been an alcoholic; however, the boy's parents deny it.
   C. The boy had committed dozens of other crimes, starting when he was 8, and spent three years in a home for delinquents.
   D. The boy's parents are separated but not divorced. He lived with his mother and her boyfriend.
   E. The boy's father is unemployed and an admitted alcoholic, fired from at least a dozen jobs. Relatives say he rarely saw his son.

6. Each year, book publishers hoping for favorable reviews send your newspaper thousands of free books. You could not afford to buy the books and could not afford to hire a full-time reviewer. Instead, you place all the books on shelves in your newsroom and encourage your regular staffers to read and review the ones they like. By the end of the year, your shelves are filled with the books. How would you get rid of them?
   A. Throw them in the trash.
   B. Return them to the publishers.
   C. Allow any reporter or editor who reviews a book to keep it.
   D. Donate all the leftover books to a local charity.
   E. Sell the leftover books to a bookstore and donate the money to a local charity, or divide it among your staffers as a payment for their reviews.

EXERCISE 3
Ethics

What's Your Decision?
(Solving the Media's Ethical Dilemmas)

1. As the editor of a daily newspaper, you know that the city has awarded several million-dollar contracts to a company run by the mayor's brother. The company submitted the low bids. The mayor insists that she has no connection with the company and never profited from her brother's success. Now, a secretary in the mayor's office secretly (and perhaps illegally) copied the mayor's tax returns and sent the copies to your paper. They reveal that the mayor receives $50,000 a year for her work as a "consultant" for the company. Would you publish the documents?
    At what point, if any, would you change your mind?
    A. When you confront the mayor, she admits that the documents are genuine but threatens to prosecute you for accepting stolen property.
    B. You learn that the secretary also sent copies of the mayor's tax returns to another newspaper, a magazine and at least three television stations in your community.
    C. The mayor is nearing the end of her first term in office and announces, a week later, that she will seek a second term.
    D. During her campaign for re-election, the mayor again publicly states that she has never benefited from her brother's success.
    E. Other stolen documents sent along with the mayor's tax returns clearly prove that she illegally gave her brother copies of the bids submitted by other companies so that he would be able to submit lower bids.

2. Late Saturday morning, an aide for the Democratic candidate for mayor gives your political reporter evidence clearly proving that the Republican candidate has been treated twice for an addiction to cocaine. In return for the evidence, your political reporter promised never to reveal its source. The election is next Tuesday, and it is only a half hour before your Saturday deadline: too late to find and question the Republican. Moreover, you do not publish a Sunday edition. As editor, what would you do?
    A. Ignore the story as unfair and a political smear.
    B. Because of its importance, publish the story immediately. Then, on Monday, publish a second story reporting the Republican's response.
    C. Publish the story immediately, but overrule your political reporter and identify its source, so your readers understand that it is a political smear.
    D. Wait until Monday—the day before the election—and then report both the charges and the Republican's response, all in the same story.
    E. Publish the story immediately. But in a column on your editorial page, identify and denounce its source, pointing out that he seemed to have deliberately waited until the last minute so the Republican would be unable to respond.

3. The crime rate in your city's downtown shopping district has been rising, along with an increase in prostitution. Customers are hesitant to visit the area, especially at night, and merchants are demanding better police protection. A major developer is considering a proposal to invest millions of dollars to revitalize the area, but is worried about its sordid reputation. The police and other city officials ask your newspaper for help. In the past, your paper has reported the names of women arrested for prostitution. Now, to discourage their customers, the police want you to

also publish the names of the prostitutes' customers, their "Johns." Which of these policies would you adopt?

    A. Respond that you sympathize with the officials' problems, but that your newspaper is not an arm of the police, with an obligation to help enforce the city's laws. Thus, you will not publish the men's names.

    B. Decline to publish any names, but publish news stories and editorials about the problem, encouraging the legal system (the police and courts) to solve the problem.

    C. Publish a warning, an editorial announcing your new policy: that in one week, you will begin to comply with the officials' request to publish the name of every "John" arrested in the area.

    D. Announce that you plan to begin publishing everyone's name, but not because the police asked you to. Explain, truthfully, that you discussed the problem with your staff, and that several reporters pointed out that it was discriminatory to publish the women's names, but not the men's. (Or, as an alternative, announce that you will no longer publish any names.)

    E. Respond that the campaign is senseless, and that the prostitutes and their "Johns" will simply move to another part of the city. Thus, the proposal will not solve the problem of prostitution in your community.

4.   Normally, your newspaper never reports suicides. As editor, you consider suicides a personal and private matter. Moreover, you are reluctant to add to a family's grief and embarrassment. But during the past year, three teen-agers—all high school students in your community—have killed themselves. Last night, a fourth teen-ager (a well-known athlete) shot himself. There were no witnesses. What would you do?

    A. Ignore the fourth suicide, just as you ignored the first three.

    B. Assign a reporter to write a story about the problem of teen-age suicides and to mention the four local deaths, but without using any of the teen-agers' names.

    C. Report the story as fully as possible, but identify only the latest victim, the prominent athlete.

    D. Call the teen-agers' parents and ask for their permission to report the story as a warning to other parents and teen-agers. Then write a story about the problem and identify only the teen-agers whose parents are willing to cooperate with you.

    E. Report the story as fully as possible, identifying all four victims.

5.   You are the editor of your local daily and accepted an invitation to a party at the mayor's home. During the evening, you overheard the mayor tell several jokes critical of the racial and religious minorities in your community. The mayor is a WASP (a white, Anglo-Saxon Protestant) and has often been accused of insensitivity to the problems of other groups in the city. In the past, the mayor always denied the charges. You were a guest in his home and were listening in—unnoticed—to his conversation with friends. Yet the mayor invited you to his home and never said the party was "off the record." What would you do?

    A. Not publish the jokes.

    B. Not publish the jokes but warn the mayor that, in the future, you will feel obligated to report that type of story. Then, to prevent additional conflicts, immediately sever all your social contacts with the mayor and other sources.

    C. Publish a story about the jokes but attribute them to "a city official," without identifying the mayor.

    D. Instruct a reporter to call other participants in the conversation and to get the story from them.

    E. Inform the mayor that you overheard the jokes and feel obligated to report them. Then ask the mayor to respond and include his response in your story, even if he insists that you are mistaken or lying.

6.   A photographer on your staff has covered a series of major fires during the past month. The police and fire fighters want to see all the photographer's pictures, including dozens never published by your newspaper. They explain that the fires were set by an arsonist, and that the arsonist probably returned to watch them. Thus, he may appear in the pictures. As editor, would you cooperate with the authorities?

    At what point, if any, would you change your mind?

A. The police say they have no other leads.

B. The police insist that you have a civic duty to help them and that, if you refuse, they will publicly denounce you and your newspaper.

C. Many of your readers fear that their homes and businesses may be the next to be burned.

D. The arsonist has sent letters to the local media, threatening to destroy the entire city.

E. A fire set last night caused two deaths. Both victims were children.

EXERCISE 4
Ethics

What's Your Solution?
(Solving the Media's Ethical Dilemmas)

1. Normally, your newspaper never identifies the victim of a rape. At what point, if any, would you change your mind?
   A. The victim appeared in court, identifying and testifying against a suspect.
   B. The suspect insists that he is innocent and, in court, testifies that the woman is lying—that she consented to their sexual relationship and is trying to destroy his reputation.
   C. The victim was staying in a hotel and later sues the hotel for $1 million, charging that its negligence enabled the rapist to enter her room.
   D. The victim's husband breaks out of a locked room, then shoots and kills the intruder in their home.
   E. After being raped, the victim was also robbed and strangled. Her assailant is convicted and sentenced to 120 years in prison, an unusually harsh punishment for murder.

2. As the editor of a major daily, you suspect that a politician is an alcoholic. You have heard rumors about the problem, and several of your reporters have seen the politician drinking, apparently heavily. After returning from a two-week vacation, the politician announces plans to run for a higher office. The next day, you receive an envelope in the mail. It contains medical recordings showing that the politician spent the two-week "vacation" at a hospital, being treated for alcoholism. The medical records were supposed to be confidential, and you have no idea who mailed them to you. When asked about the documents, the politician admits that they are genuine but insists that the treatment was successful. Would you publish the story?
   At what point, if any, would you change your mind?
   A. The politician is a candidate for mayor.
   B. The politician is a candidate for sheriff.
   C. The politician is a candidate for governor.
   D. The politician is a candidate for vice president.
   E. The politician is a candidate for president.

3. Normally, your newspaper is reluctant to discuss a public official's personal life and family problems. But last night, the police were called to the home of a local high-school principal to break up a family fight. There is no evidence that the marital discord has affected his work. Would you report the story?
   At what point, if any, would you change your mind?
   A. The principal and his wife admit that he struck her, but add that it is their problem—a personal matter—and that they are seeing a marriage counselor to solve it.
   B. The principal's wife charges her husband with assault. But early the next morning, she returns to the police station and drops the charges.
   C. The police say this is the third time they have been called to the couple's home. Neighbors placed all three calls after hearing the wife's screams for help.
   D. The principal's wife files for a divorce, charging that she was often beaten and that she suffered a broken nose and mild concussion.
   E. Three months later, the principal announces that he is a candidate for superintendent of schools.

4. As a reporter/photographer, you are invited inside a welfare office seized by its clients. The protesters want you to report their grievances and encourage you to interview and photograph everyone there. As you leave, police who surrounded the

building ask you how many people are inside, whether they are armed, and whether they seem likely to use their weapons. What would you do?

    A. Decline to answer any of their questions.

    B. Tell the police that you cannot answer their questions, but that your story and photographs will appear in the next morning's paper.

    C. Give the police only the information that you plan to publish in the next morning's paper.

    D. Answer all the officers' questions.

    E. Answer all the officers' questions and give them copies of all your pictures.

5.   You produce the evening news for a local television station, and one of your photographers has filmed the fire that destroyed a famous old apartment building. The film shows a woman, her clothing in flames, run out the front door, screaming in pain. Before anyone can reach her, the woman collapses and dies. No one knows who she is, and her identity may never be known. The building was supposed to be vacant; the city condemned it because of numerous fire, health and safety violations. However, transients and other homeless people lived in it and continue to live in many of your city's other condemned and abandoned buildings. Some of their occupants even build small fires to cook with and keep warm. The city has been criticized for failing to help the homeless, and this story seems to illustrate their plight. What would you do?

    A. Have a newscaster describe the story and then show the fire, but never the woman.

    B. Use only the first few seconds of the film, showing the woman alive and running out of the building, but not collapsing and dying.

    C. Warn your viewers that you are about to show something unpleasant but important. Then broadcast the entire film, hoping that it will warn other viewers of the danger and encourage the city to help them.

    D. Broadcast only a portion of the film on your 6 p.m. newscast, but broadcast the entire film at 11 p.m., when fewer children are watching.

6.   As a reporter, you regularly cover an environmentalist group in your city. Frustrated by their past failures, the environmentalists are becoming more militant. You discover that they plan to kidnap a 7-year-old girl, the daughter of a local developer. They intend to hold the girl hostage until her father agrees to stop polluting a river. You have covered the environmentalists for years, and they confided in you because you never betrayed their trust. What would you do?

    A. Say nothing.

    B. Warn the environmentalists that, because an innocent girl's life is in danger, you cannot remain silent. You will have to notify the police if they do not change their plans.

    C. Call the developer and warn him that his family is in danger, but without identifying the kidnappers.

    D. Call the police and inform them that someone plans to kidnap the girl, but without identifying the kidnappers.

    E. Call the police and tell them everything you know.

7.   As a foreign correspondent employed by a major television network, you learn that terrorists at a nearby airport have seized an airplane carrying 184 passengers and 12 crew members. The captives include 23 Americans. What would you do?

    A. Ignore the hijacking.

    B. Attend a press conference held by the hijackers.

    C. Arrange to have your network broadcast it live.

    D. Interview three hostages whom the hijackers provide for you.

    E. Interview the hostages' families when they fly to a nearby airport.

    F. Report that the U.S. Army's anti-terrorist squad has landed at a nearby airport.

You Be the Editor

The Miami Herald published these hypothetical cases. After reading the cases, decide what your decision would be if you were the editor. Check the most appropriate box in each example. You may make additional comments in the space provided or on a separate sheet of paper.

1. A woman on the county commission is raped. The afternoon paper reports she was hospitalized following an assault but does not indicate it was a sexual attack. A conservative and anti-feminist, she has blocked the expenditure of public monies for a rape crisis center at the county hospital. This has been a much publicized local controversy for the past six months. But now she tells you that she plans to rethink her position on the crisis center. She also makes clear the deep personal trauma she is suffering as a result of the assault and asks that you not say she was raped.

☐ Do you go ahead with the story, including her change of mind, recognizing that the shift is a significant public policy development?

☐ Do you say no more than the afternoon paper did?

☐ Do you refer to the attack simply as an assault but report that the convalescing commissioner is rethinking her position on the crisis center, thus suggesting the nature of the attack?

☐ Do you report the assault and say nothing about the rape now, but decide that when she actually votes for the rape crisis center you will report the reasons for her change of mind, whether or not she wants to talk about it?

2. The mayor is a hardliner on crime. He has made local drug enforcement a major issue. You learn that his 19-year-old son, who lives at home and attends a local junior college, has been arrested for possession of a small quantity of marijuana, a misdemeanor if convicted.

(a.) Would you run a story on the arrest?
☐ Yes.
☐ No.

(b.) Would you run a story if the arrest were for selling a pound of marijuana?
☐ Yes.
☐ No.

(c.) Would you run a story if the arrest were for using cocaine?
☐ Yes.
☐ No.

(d.) Would you run a story if the arrest were for selling cocaine?
☐ Yes.
☐ No.

3. A prominent businessman identified with United Way and many other charitable causes is discovered to have embezzled $25,000 from one of the charities he heads. There is no question about his guilt, although charges have not yet been filed. The story is yours alone. When your reporter contacts him for comment, the man says there are extenuating circumstances he cannot go into and that he will make full restitution if given a chance. He pleads that no story be written, saying his wife suffered a serious heart attack, is in critical condition at a local hospital and he fears that public disclosure of what he has done could kill her.

☐ Would you run the story, now?

☐ Would you wait until you have had an opportunity to talk with the hospital's doctors and are confident the woman is out of immediate danger, then run the story?

☐ Would you give him an opportunity to make restitution and, if this is done, write nothing?

4. A businessman donates $5 million to the University of Miami to build a new football stadium. Checking his background, you learn that the man was arrested at age 18 for armed robbery and avoided prison only by volunteering for military duty in World War II. His record, as far as you can discover, has been spotless since. He refuses to talk about the incident, says he has never even told his closest friends and threatens to withdraw his contribution to the university if you print the story. University officials are shocked and urge that you write nothing.

☐ Do you print the information on the arrest as one element in an over-all profile of the man and who he is?

☐ Do you hold off on the arrest information until the UM has the money?

☐ Do you take the position that the information is not relevant and discard it?

11 Quotations and Attribution

Reporters obtain much of their information by listening to other people, and they can convey that information to readers in the form of (1) direct, (2) indirect or (3) partial quotations. Direct quotations present a source's exact words and consequently are placed entirely in quotation marks. Indirect quotations do not use a source's exact words and consequently are not placed inside quotation marks; instead, reporters use their own words to summarize, or paraphrase, the source's remarks. Partial quotations use key phrases from a source's statement and quote them directly.

> INDIRECT QUOTATION: Mrs. Ambrose said journalism students should deal with ideas, not mechanical techniques.

> PARTIAL QUOTATION: Mrs. Ambrose criticized the "trade school atmosphere" in journalism schools and said students should study ideas, not mechanical techniques.

> DIRECT QUOTATION: Mrs. Ambrose said: "Journalism students should be dealing with ideas of a social, economic and political nature. There's too much of a trade school atmosphere in journalism schools today. One spends too much time on minor technical and mechanical things, like learning how to write headlines."

When do reporters use the different types of quotations? Reporters use direct quotations when their sources say something important or controversial and state their ideas in an interesting, unusual or colorful manner. To be quoted directly, sources must also state their ideas so effectively that their wording cannot be improved. For example:

> In his second inaugural address, President Franklin D. Roosevelt said, "The test of our progress is not whether we add more to the abundance of those who have much; it is whether we provide enough for those who have too little."

A famous singer said: "Perhaps I've found the secret for an unhappy private life. Every three years I go and marry a girl who doesn't love me, and then she proceeds to take all my money."

No matter where you live or work, the sources in your community will provide other interesting quotations:

"One of my roommates had to have an abortion," Katie said. "She went through hell—all bummed out and depressed. As her best friend, I really felt badly, too."

Kim, a junior majoring in nursing, said: "It's my job to care for the sick. I may have to take care of an AIDS patient someday, and it scares the hell out of me. I'm not satisfied with what's known about AIDS, about how AIDS is transmitted. I'm afraid of bringing it home to my family—my children."

A witness said four men clutching rifles advanced toward the shoppers, shouting, "Everyone get on the floor." A fifth man opened the supermarket's cash registers and scooped out the money.
Shoppers and employees cooperated with the gunmen. "No one wanted to be a hero," the witness said.

Direct quotations bring sources to life, clearly reporting their opinions in their exact words, with all their original flavor, emotions, color and drama. Quotations also help reveal the sources' character and give readers a sense of rapport with them—a sense that they have talked directly with the sources. The following quotations also help reveal the sources' humor:

Mark Twain said: "Always do right. This will gratify some people and astonish the rest."

Will Rogers said, "What the country needs is dirtier fingernails and a cleaner mind."

Direct quotations do not have to be long. Four words spoken by President Richard M. Nixon during the Watergate scandals fascinated the American public not only because of what the president said but also because of the very fact that he felt a need to say it: "I'm not a crook."
Reporters use indirect quotations when their sources have not stated their ideas effectively. By using indirect quotations, reporters can rephrase their sources' remarks, stating them more clearly and concisely. Reporters can also emphasize the sources' most significant remarks and reword or eliminate remarks that are unclear, irrelevant, libelous, pretentious or otherwise unprintable:

ORIGINAL STATEMENT: He said, "I fully intend to resign from my position as mayor of this city."
PARAPHRASED: The mayor said he plans to resign.

ORIGINAL STATEMENT: Mrs. Czarski said, "Women do not get the same tax and insurance benefits that men receive, and they do not receive maternity benefits that even start to cover what they should."
PARAPHRASED: Mrs. Czarski said women do not receive the same tax and insurance benefits as men, nor adequate maternity benefits.

Reporters generally avoid partial, or fragmentary, quotations. Most partial quotations are awkward, wordy or unnecessary. Sentences that contain several partial quotations are particularly distracting. The phrases should be paraphrased or used in indirect constructions, with the quotation marks simply eliminated:

FRAGMENT: Andrews said he expects to finish the job "sometime within the next month."
REVISED: Andrews said he expects to finish the job next month.

FRAGMENT: He said the press barons "such as William Randolph Hearst" created "an amazingly rich variety" of newspapers.
REVISED: He said the press barons such as William Randolph Hearst created an amazingly rich variety of newspapers.

Reporters also avoid "orphan" quotes—the practice of placing quotation marks around an isolated word or two used in an ordinary way. The addition of quotation marks to emphasize individual words is inappropriate. Similarly, there is no reason to place quotation marks around profanities, slang, clichés or grammatical errors:

He complained that no one "understands" his problem.
REVISED: He complained that no one understands his problem.

She said that having to watch her child die was worse than "hell" could possibly be.
REVISED: She said that having to watch her child die was worse than hell could possibly be.

Reporters use partial quotations only for statements that are particularly controversial, important or interesting. The use of partial quotations also helps attribute the statements more clearly to their sources:

He called the welfare recipients "lazy, no-good bums."

Hendricks said he killed the girls "because they laughed at me."

Using Direct Quotations Effectively

Direct quotations should be used to illustrate a point, not to tell an entire story. Stories composed entirely of quotations become too tiresome and often seem poorly organized because they lack natural transitions. The following stories contain a pleasing combination of quotations and paraphrases:

Zukowski said he did not see the car because he had opened his van's glove compartment and was looking for a cigarette.
"It was a dumb move, yeah," he said. "But just because I drove into a parked car doesn't mean I was drunk."
Zukowski challenged the accuracy of a breathalyzer test administered by the police. "Those things aren't reliable," he said. "I've heard of people taking mouthwash and then being recorded as drunk."
Witnesses said he had consumed six to eight beers, but Zukowski said he had "only a few, maybe three at the most."

She started dancing six months ago after a friend told her about the job. Debbie (who does not want her last name used) said: "I knew my friend was dancing topless, but I didn't think I could ever do it. At the time, though, I was desperate to find a job, so I agreed to try it."
Debbie said she felt guilty the first time she appeared topless in front of other people but "after the first time, it seemed there was nothing to hide anymore."
Now, after dancing topless for half a year, Debbie says: "I really enjoy it because there is no actual work involved. I love to dance anyway and I can pick my own hours around my class schedule and, with tips, earn $600 a week."
Few of Debbie's classmates know about the job. She explains: "It's not that I'm ashamed of what I do. It just makes it easier for me to know that no one in the audience will be sitting beside me in a class the next morning. I know the general public thinks that what I do is pretty low, and I don't want other students to say, 'There goes that topless dancer.'"

Quotations should be used only when they provide some additional information about a topic, not when they repeat facts reported earlier in a story. Reporters often summarize a major point, then use a direct quotation to explain the idea or to provide more specific details about it:

Medically, he was dead for three or four minutes. "His pupils were fixed and dilated. There was no pulse, no respiration and he had turned blue," Dr. Holman said.

Karcher's girlfriend was instructing a class of lifeguards and asked him to help administer their final test. Karcher said: "My job was to go out in the lake and act like I was drowning. I was to bite, scratch, tear—anything to keep them from rescuing me."

Quotations also help describe a story's most dramatic moments. Because of their importance, those moments should be described in detail, and that description should be placed near the beginning of a story. The following quotations are so interesting and dramatic that they would compel most readers to finish the entire stories:

As the grease and flames spread, she panicked and poured water on them. "That just made the flames go higher," she cried. "I knew the whole house was going to burn down, so I picked up my baby and ran outside."

"After the accident I must have passed out for a minute," she said. "Then I woke up and realized the car was on fire. I thought I was going to die. I wasn't badly hurt, but I couldn't get out. I couldn't move."

"I was confused," the girl said. "I woke up at about 2 a.m. and saw this strange man standing near my bed. I didn't know why he was there, and at first I thought my parents had visitors or something. Then I realized he was a prowler, and I screamed."

Quotations also help to reveal the personalities of people mentioned in news stories, showing them to be unique, interesting individuals. A story about a middle-aged woman who returned to college included this revealing quotation:

"Very practically, I came back to college to get my degree in education because I wanted to be busy and couldn't quite see myself as a 40-year-old checkout clerk in some supermarket. Fifteen years of my life consisted of runny noses and coffee klatches with the neighbors. Now my kids wipe their own noses and the neighbors are still having their coffee klatches, and I'm going to be a senior next term."

Quotations, combined with descriptions, create even more revealing pictures for readers:

A graduate student said he is "not particularly enthused" about the women's movement. "I kind of enjoy the situation the way it is now," he said, smiling at his girlfriend. She smiled back, raised a clenched fist and walked away.

She smiled, got out her photo album and thumbed through it. Then she said: "Fortunately for me, my mind is still there. One of the saddest things about old age is realizing that some day your mind might deteriorate before your body finally dies.
"I can still look at these pictures and remember who all the people are and exactly when and where the pictures were taken. The day I forget one is the day I'll give up."

Using Exact Words and Ellipses

Some reporters (the "pragmatists") insist that their only responsibility is to convey a source's thought and meaning—not the source's exact words. The pragmatists explain that people rarely speak with precision in clean, complete sentences. Rather, they pause, stutter and repeat themselves. To eliminate the errors (and anything else they dislike) the pragmatists will "improve" a statement's wording. The pragmatists will also correct obvious factual errors. They call it "doctoring," "massaging" or "cleaning up" a quote. The pragmatists explain that reporters should use their common sense and correct obvious slips of the tongue: quotations that would make a source look foolish, or that would make their readers' job more difficult.

Other reporters (the "purists") insist that quotation marks are sacrosanct—that every word placed inside quotation marks should be a source's exact words. They fear that if they alter a quotation, they may be accused of fictionalizing or lying to their readers. Purists add that the practice of doctoring quotations destroys their unique flavor: their richness and originality. Moreover, the reporters who doctor quotations make their sources sound better than they really are. Finally, the purists fear that readers do not understand the practice, and that the changes made in quotations make it easier for sources to claim that they were misquoted.

To avoid the problems, use your source's exact words. Most editors will insist that you do. If you are uncertain about the source's exact words (or think a statement needs rewriting), use an indirect rather than direct quotation. If you try to doctor a quotation and make a mistake—however unintentionally—you may seriously injure your source's reputation as well as your own.

There are only a few exceptions to the principle of using a person's exact words in direct quotations. Those exceptions usually involve the deletion of unnecessary words, grammatical errors or profanities. Even the purists delete unnecessary words, provided that their deletion does not change the meaning of what has been said:

> ORIGINAL STATEMENT: He said, "Look, you know I think nuclear power is safe, absolutely safe."
> QUOTATION: He said, "Nuclear power is safe, absolutely safe."
>
> ORIGINAL STATEMENT: Dr. Tausche said, "Uh, all the problems will be solved, you know, and, uh, solved effectively, when the new hospital is completed."
> QUOTATION: Dr. Tausche said, "All the problems will be solved, and solved effectively, when the new hospital is completed."

If they delete a significant number of words (entire phrases or sentences), reporters may add an ellipsis (three periods). An ellipsis that appears at the end rather than in the middle of a sentence uses four periods when the phrase preceding the ellipsis constitutes a complete sentence, in the original or in the condensation. However, policies vary from newspaper to newspaper, and some journalists—as in the previous examples—do not use ellipses in reporting ordinary interviews. However, they may use them in quoting selectively from longer and more formal statements:

> ORIGINAL STATEMENT: Sen. William Proxmire, D-Wis., said: "I have long advocated that the Law Enforcement Assistance Administration be abolished. Last year I was one of only two U.S. senators to vote against its reauthorization. Why? Because LEAA has failed miserably to meet its responsibilities for reducing crime and improving the criminal justice system. As I said in my letter to the president, LEAA has spent nearly $6 billion since its inception in 1969. But over the same time span, according to FBI statistics, the crime rate has increased an alarming 43 percent. Clearly, LEAA has been totally ineffective in trying to solve the problem of crime and violence in America."
> ELLIPSES: Sen. William Proxmire, D-Wis., said: "I have long advocated that the Law Enforcement Assistance Administration be abolished. . . . Why? Because LEAA has failed miserably to meet its responsibilities for reducing crime and improving the criminal justice system. As I said in my letter to the president, LEAA has spent nearly $6 billion since its inception in 1969. But over the same time span . . . the crime rate has increased an alarming 43 percent. Clearly, LEAA has been totally ineffective. . . ."

Correcting Grammatical Errors

Reporters correct most of the grammatical errors in direct quotations. The Associated Press Stylebook explains, "Quotations should be corrected to avoid the errors in grammar and word usage that often occur unnoticed in speech, but are embarrassing in print":

> GRAMMATICAL ERROR: The woman said, "The fire kept spreading, and my husband and me couldn't put it out."
> REVISED: The woman said, "The fire kept spreading, and my husband and I couldn't put it out."
>
> GRAMMATICAL ERROR: An usher said, "The people started pouring in, and there wasn't no way to stop them."
> REVISED: An usher said, "The people started pouring in, and there wasn't any way to stop them."

Reporters are most likely to correct the infrequent grammatical errors made by sources they interview for serious news stories. However, reporters may publish the errors made by sources they interview for human-interest stories, especially if the sources make several errors and if publication of those errors helps reveal the sources' character and habitual manner of speaking.

Deleting Profanities

Reporters also delete most profanities. Editors explain that newspapers are family publications that go into their readers' homes and are seen by a variety of people. Some children read daily newspapers, but even some adults are likely to be offended by the publication of four-letter words. Newspapers are becoming more candid, and many now publish mild profanities that are essential to a story. However, most forbid the publication of casual profanities—those used habitually and unnecessarily by many people:

> PROFANITY: The youth told police, "Hell, that man tried to cheat me."
> REVISED: The youth told police, "That man tried to cheat me."
>
> PROFANITY: "Shit, I wasn't going to try to stop that damned idiot," the witness testified. "He had a knife."
> REVISED: "I wasn't going to try to stop that idiot," the witness testified. "He had a knife."

Using Dialogue

With practice, writers can begin to use dialogue to let the characters in their stories reveal more information about themselves and about their most newsworthy experiences. For example: after a major airline crash, federal investigators usually release a transcript of the crew's final conversation. Reporters may publish the transcript as a separate story, or they may quote the crew members in a conventional news story. Because a storm dumped a heavy coating of snow onto the plane's fuselage and wings, Air Florida's Flight 90 crashed into the Potomac River during takeoff. As the plane began speeding down a runway at Washington's National Airport, co-pilot Roger Pettit noticed that they did not seem to have enough power. A story about that moment quoted the conversation between Pettit and Capt. Larry Wheaton:

> "God, look at that thing," Pettit said, apparently referring to a needle gauge that displayed the power being developed by the engines. "That don't seem right, does it?"
> "Yes it is," Wheaton said.
> "Naw, I don't think that's right," Pettit said. "Maybe it is, I don't know."
> The plane rose into the air 1,900 feet farther down the runway and 15 seconds later than normal. Moments later, it began to shudder, lose speed and fall.
> "Larry, we're going down, Larry," Pettit said.
> "I know it," Wheaton replied.

This story, transmitted by The Associated Press, also relies heavily—and effectively—upon dialogue:

> CAMDEN, N.J.—A 26-year-old woman pleaded guilty Tuesday to murdering her four children, describing how she placed them into a rain-swollen, polluted river.
>
> . . . Though Wright did not explain her motive, she described for the first time how the drownings occurred as she sat Nov. 10 with her children along a railroad track beside the Cooper River.
>
> "It was about 11:30 or 12 o'clock at night. I was sitting on a wooden plank. I sat there for quite a few hours trying to think. I did away with them," she said.
>
> "How?" Superior Court Judge Rudolph J. Rossetti asked.
>
> "By them drowning," she said.
>
> "Did you throw them into the river?" the judge asked.
>
> "I laid them," she answered. "I was sitting at the edge of the river, and put them in one at a time."
>
> Wright said her children—aged 11 months to 7 years—had fallen asleep near the river and were still asleep when she put them in the water. . . .

Stressing Answers, Not Questions

When reporters quote someone, they normally stress their source's answers, not the questions the source was asked. The use of both the questions and the answers is usually unnecessary, repetitive and dull. Reporters can either omit the questions or incorporate them into the answers:

> He then asked her, "What's your name?" She said, "Mary Delaveux."
> REVISED: She said her name is Mary Delaveux.

> The president was asked whether he plans to seek a second term, and he responded that he will not announce his plans until next winter.
> REVISED: The president said he will not announce his plans for a second term until next winter.
> OR: In response to a question, the president said he will not announce his plans for a second term until next winter.
> OR: During a question-and-answer session after his speech, the president said he will not announce his plans for a second term until next winter.

Explaining Quotations

If a quotation requires some explanation, that explanation should be placed before the quotation—not after it—so that readers can immediately understand what is being said:

> "Without them, we might have been hit by another vehicle," she said. "Everyone should carry a half dozen in their car." She was referring to flares.
> REVISED: She said everyone should carry a half dozen flares in their car. "Without them, we might have been hit by another vehicle," she said.

> "Many of our neighbors have had accidents because of it, and my son almost was killed when a truck hit his bike," said one homeowner complaining that State Route 15A is too narrow.
> REVISED: A homeowner complaining that State Route 15A is too narrow said, "Many of our neighbors have had accidents because of it, and my son almost was killed when a truck hit his bike."

If the information needed to clarify a quotation is brief, it can be inserted in parentheses:

> An attorney said, "He (Mayor Wilson) is almost certain to be indicted by the grand jury."

Dr. Harold Termid, who performed the operation, said, "The technique dates back before the 20th century, when it was first used by the French to study ruminants (cud-chewing animals)."

"He's working on (recuperating from) his third heart attack," the doctor said. "Usually people on their third heart attack have a better chance of survival than they had on their first, so his chances are good."

Reporters use such parenthetical matter sparingly, however. If reporters peppered their stories with parenthetical explanations, the stories would become more difficult to read. Each bit of parenthetical matter is an obstacle that forces readers to pause and absorb some additional information. Most stories will become more readable if reporters rewrite the sentences:

"They (members of the school board) have strong objections to the plan," he said.
REVISED: He said school board members "have strong objections to the plan."

She said, "They (police) are the last line between us and chaos."
REVISED: She said the police "are the last line between us and chaos."

Avoiding Weak Quotations

In an effort to brighten their stories, some reporters use whatever quotations happen to be available. Yet a weak quotation is worse than none. If a quotation bores or confuses people, many will stop reading a story at that point. Reporters can never justify a weak quotation by responding, "But that's what my source said." The quotations used in a story reflect the reporters' judgment and the reporters' interviewing techniques.

If a quotation is long, dull and self-serving, discard it. Similarly, if a quotation states the obvious or contains a cliché, discard it:

"They're going to have a lot of headaches," Gomez said. "At least we've paved the way."

Lyons called her program a success. "We had a terrific crowd," she said, "and a particularly good turnout."

The director of the school's library said she is "very excited and confident about the library's direction."

The first quotation contains two meaningless clichés. The second quotation is self-serving. It allows a source to praise her own program without any evidence of its success. Her quotation is also vague (What is "terrific" and "good"?). Similarly, the third quote is self-serving and vague. It also states the obvious: the fact that a head librarian thinks she is doing a good job.

The Need for Attribution

Statements That Require Attention

As mentioned in an earlier chapter, reporters do not have to attribute statements that report undisputed facts, such as that World War II ended in 1945, that Boston is in Massachusetts or that three people died in an accident. Attribution is also unnecessary in stories that reporters personally witness. However, reporters must attribute most information given to them by other people. They also attribute: (1) statements about controversial issues, (2) statements of opinion and (3) all direct and indirect quotations. If reporters fail to attribute such statements, news stories will seem to present their personal opinions rather than the opinions of their sources. One or two words of attribution are usually adequate:

> Insurance companies cannot lower their rates because they are not making enough money.
> ATTRIBUTED: The state insurance commissioner said insurance companies cannot lower their rates because they are not making enough money.

> The workers were fooling around while they were loading the hay. Suddenly Frey's jacket sleeve became tangled in the machinery, and his hand was crushed.
> ATTRIBUTED: Sheriff's deputies said Frey's jacket sleeve became tangled in the machinery while the workers were loading hay, and his hand was crushed.

Attribution is particularly important in the second example because it implies that the workers were careless. Consequently, most editors would delete the phrase "fooling around."

Statements that criticize a person or an organization should also be attributed. Again, reporters must clearly indicate that they are reporting what someone else has said and not expressing their own opinions or those of the newspaper they work for:

> Congress has failed to deal effectively with the problem of unemployment.
> ATTRIBUTED: The Republicans said Congress has failed to deal effectively with the problem of unemployment.

> He is cocky, aggressive and hot-tempered; but most of all, he is unpredictable.
> ATTRIBUTED: The coach said he is cocky, aggressive, hot-tempered and, most of all, unpredictable.

Attribution also helps readers determine the credibility of statements reported by news media. Readers may accept the statements made by some sources but distrust others. For example, although each of the following statements reports the same basic allegation, American readers would be least likely to believe the second statement and most likely to believe the third:

> The U.S. government is ignoring millions of hungry and jobless citizens.

> The Soviet newspaper Pravda charged Tuesday that the U.S. government is ignoring millions of hungry and jobless citizens.

> During a congressional hearing, Sen. Edward Kennedy testified Tuesday that the U.S. government is ignoring millions of hungry and jobless citizens.

The Placement and Frequency of Attribution

An attribution can be placed at the beginning or at the end of a sentence, or at a natural break within it. However, it should never interrupt a thought:

> "I shall," Gen. MacArthur said, "return."
> REVISED: Gen. MacArthur said, "I shall return."

> "Hard work," he said, "builds character."
> REVISED: "Hard work builds character," he said.

Readers should be told who is speaking as soon as is conveniently possible; they should never have to guess. If a quotation is long, the attribution should be placed at the beginning or end of the first sentence or after the first meaningful clause in that sentence. The attribution should not be delayed until the end of the second or third sentence. Similarly, if a quotation contains only one sentence, but that sentence is long, the attribution should be placed at or near the beginning of that sentence—not at the end:

"Of each dollar spent on personal auto liability insurance, only about 45 cents end up in the hands of accident victims, while 30 cents are used to pay insurance companies' selling and administrative costs, and more than 20 cents of the premium dollar are burned up in legal battles," he said.

REVISED: "Of each dollar spent on personal auto liability insurance," he said, "only about 45 cents end up in the hands of accident victims, while 30 cents are used to pay insurance companies' selling and administrative costs, and more than 20 cents of the premium dollar are burned up in legal battles."

"However close we sometimes seem to that dark and final abyss, let no man of peace and freedom despair. For he does not stand alone. If we all can persevere, if we can in every land and office look beyond our shores and ambitions, then surely the age will dawn in which the strong are just and the weak secure and the peace preserved," the president said.

REVISED: "However close we sometimes seem to that dark and final abyss," the president said, "let no man of peace and freedom despair. For he does not stand alone. If we all can persevere, if we can in every land and office look beyond our shores and ambitions, then surely the age will dawn in which the strong are just and the weak secure and the peace preserved."

A direct quotation should be attributed only once, regardless of the number of sentences it contains:

"I planned to shoot them and then shoot myself," Horwitz told the judge. "They kept telling me lies," he explained. "They were plotting to get rid of me, to take away my job, and I made up my mind I wouldn't let them," he continued.

REVISED: "I planned to shoot them and then myself," Horwitz told the judge. "They kept telling me lies. They were plotting to get rid of me, to take away my job, and I made up my mind I wouldn't let them."

"I'm opposed to any laws that prohibit the sale of pornography," the attorney said. "The restriction of pornography infringes on Americans' First Amendment rights," he explained. "I like to picture myself as a good guy defending a sleazy thing," he concluded.

REVISED: "I'm opposed to any laws that prohibit the sale of pornography," the attorney said. "The restriction of pornography infringes on Americans' First Amendment rights. I like to picture myself as a good guy defending a sleazy thing."

Even quotations that continue for several paragraphs need to be attributed only once:

Capt. Bonventre eliminated the police department's motorcycle squad. "The main reason is that there are more injuries to motorcycle policemen," he said. "I want to protect my officers. They think there's no danger on a cycle. Well, that's just optimistic thinking; there's a real danger.

"Officers have much more protection in a car. I think that's pretty obvious. If an officer gets in a hot pursuit and crashes, he stands a better chance of escaping injury when he's in a car.

"Also, almost any situation, even traffic, can be handled better in a patrol car than on a motorcycle. There are some places a motorcycle can go more easily, but a car certainly commands more respect."

A single phrase may unnecessarily attribute a quotation twice. For example: the first of the following sentences reports that a fire chief made an announcement, then adds that he "said":

In making the announcement, the fire chief said arsonists caused 20 percent of the blazes reported in the city last year.

REVISED: The fire chief said arsonists caused 20 percent of the blazes reported in the city last year.

"We need to raise the speed limit," R. L. Wirtz said, speaking at a meeting Thursday night.

REVISED: "We need to raise the speed limit," R. L. Wirtz said at a meeting Thursday night.

Reporters also must learn to avoid "floating" quotations: a summary followed by a direct quotation which appears in a separate sentence and is not attributed. Every direct quotation must be attributed, even when the speaker is identified in a previous sentence. If a quotation is not clearly attributed, readers may be momentarily uncertain about its source. The source may be the person mentioned in the last sentence, but some readers may assume that the source is some other person who will be identified in the following paragraph. The attribution also provides a smooth transition from one sentence to the next. In short, quotations should be attributed even when readers already know or can guess who is speaking:

Columnist Jack Anderson said investigative reporters dig up what government officials are trying to hide. "I've never known a government official who'd admit mistakes."

ATTRIBUTED: Columnist Jack Anderson said investigative reporters dig up what government officials are trying to hide. He added, "I've never known a government official who'd admit mistakes."

Margaret Mead said there is a trend toward vocationalism on college campuses.

"Many students now demand from college not a chance to think, but a chance to become qualified for some job."

ATTRIBUTED: Margaret Mead said there is a trend toward vocationalism on college campuses.

"Many students now demand from college not a chance to think, but a chance to become qualified for some job," Mead said.

Another practice causes even more confusion. Some reporters use a quotation, then attribute it in the following paragraph:

"I was scared to death. I knew I was hurt, and I wanted someone to help."

These were the words today of an 18-year-old student trapped in her wrecked car.

REVISED: An 18-year-old student trapped in her wrecked car said: "I was scared to death. I knew I was hurt, and I wanted someone to help."

"All a lottery would do is take money from the poor. Poor people would spend every dollar on lottery tickets instead of buying a loaf of bread. They would risk everything for that one-in-a-million chance."

The Rev. Arthur K. DeZego voiced that opinion today during a speech to the Rotary Club.

REVISED: Speaking to the Rotary Club today, the Rev. Arthur K. DeZego said: "All a lottery would do is take money from the poor. Poor people would spend every dollar on lottery tickets instead of buying a loaf of bread. They would risk everything for that one-in-a-million chance."

Reporters must also provide transitions between statements made by different people, particularly when the statements are contradictory or appear in succeeding paragraphs. If reporters fail to attribute and separate the statements clearly, readers may not understand which of the two people is speaking:

The newspaper's editor said he no longer will accept advertisements for X-rated movies. He explained: "These movies are worthless. They contribute nothing to society and offend our readers. They're depressing and pornographic."

"Newspapers have no right to pass judgment on matters of taste. If they do, they should also ban the advertisements for other products considered harmful: cigarettes, liquor and pollutants like automobiles," a theater owner responded.

These two paragraphs are confusing. People beginning the second paragraph might mistakenly assume, at least momentarily, that the editor has suddenly begun to contradict himself—to criticize newspapers and the position he just endorsed. The confusion can be easily avoided by placing a brief transition at the beginning of the second paragraph. The paragraph might begin: "However, a local theater owner responded that: 'Newspapers have no right to pass judgment on matters of taste. . . .'"

Even more attribution is necessary for indirect quotations than for direct quotations. Every idea or opinion in an indirect quotation—sometimes every sentence—must be attributed. Moreover, the attribution must be varied because paragraphs would become too clumsy and repetitive if reporters simply added the words "he said" at the end of all the sentences they contain:

> The police chief insisted that the death penalty must be retained. The death penalty, harsh as it may seem, is a form of justice designed to protect the lives and rights of law-abiding citizens. Without it, criminals' rights are overly protected. Because of the almost endless mechanisms of the appeal system, it is unlikely that an innocent person would be put to death.
> REVISED: The police chief insisted that the death penalty must be retained. He said the death penalty may seem harsh, but it is a form of justice designed to protect the lives and rights of law-abiding citizens. Without it, he added, the criminals' rights are overly protected. Because of the endless mechanisms of the appeal system, he said, it is unlikely that an innocent person would be put to death.

Journalists cannot attribute the police chief's remarks by placing the entire paragraph within quotation marks because they have no way of knowing for certain that the remarks they have been given are his exact words—they may be someone else's summary of what the police chief said. Similarly, editors cannot convert an indirect quotation (a paraphrase) written by a newspaper reporter into a direct quotation. However, editors can take a statement out of quotation marks and then reword it, provided they do not change the statement's meaning.

Guidelines for Capitalizing and Punctuating Quotations

Quotations must be capitalized and punctuated properly. The first word in a quotation that is a complete sentence is capitalized, but the first word in a partial quotation is not capitalized:

> He said, "life is just one damned thing after another."
> REVISED: He said, "Life is just one damned thing after another."
>
> He called journalism "Literature in a hurry."
> REVISED: He called journalism "literature in a hurry."

If the attribution is placed before a quotation that contains one full sentence, the attribution should be followed by a comma. If the attribution is placed before a quotation that contains two or more sentences, the attribution should be followed by a colon. The attribution is not followed by a period in either case:

> James Thurber said: "It is better to know some of the questions than all of the answers."
> REVISED: James Thurber said, "It is better to know some of the questions than all of the answers."
>
> Mark Twain said, "I apologize for writing a long letter. If I'd had more time, I'd have written a shorter one."
> REVISED: Mark Twain said: "I apologize for writing a long letter. If I'd had more time, I'd have written a shorter one."

When reporters place the attribution after a quotation, they use a comma (not a period) after the last word in the quotation:

"I'm feeling better." she said.
REVISED: "I'm feeling better," she said.

"He was always trying to help somebody." his wife said.
REVISED: "He was always trying to help somebody," his wife said.

The comma or period at the end of a quotation should always be placed *inside* the quotation marks. There are no exceptions to this rule:

Benjamin Franklin said, "A penny saved is a penny earned".
REVISED: Benjamin Franklin said, "A penny saved is a penny earned."

"Nothing can now be believed that is seen in a newspaper", he said.
REVISED: "Nothing can now be believed that is seen in a newspaper," he said.

Place the words of attribution in their normal order, with the subject appearing before the verb:

Said Ronald Reagan, "I've noticed that everybody who's for abortion has already been born."

REVISED: Ronald Reagan said, "I've noticed that everybody who's for abortion has already been born."

"Hard work is good for you. Nobody ever drowned in sweat," insisted the executive.
REVISED: "Hard work is good for you. Nobody ever drowned in sweat," the executive insisted.

Only the quotation—never the attribution—should be placed inside the quotation marks:

"Mrs. Johnson said, A politician should be born an orphan and remain a bachelor."
REVISED: Mrs. Johnson said, "A politician should be born an orphan and remain a bachelor."

"The motorcycle slid sideways and skidded about 100 feet, she said. The driver was killed."
REVISED: "The motorcycle slid sideways and skidded about 100 feet," she said. "The driver was killed."

If a quotation continues for several sentences, all the sentences should be enclosed within a single set of quotation marks; quotation marks do not have to be placed at the beginning and at the end of every sentence in the quotation:

The report said: "The land is too expensive." "Its price doubled in five years."
REVISED: The report said: "The land is too expensive. Its price doubled in five years."

"I did not see the car when I stepped out onto the street." "But when I saw the headlights coming at me, I knew it was going to hit me," she said.
REVISED: "I did not see the car when I stepped out onto the street. But when I saw the headlights coming at me, I knew it was going to hit me," she said.

Like any other part of a news story, a long quotation should be divided into short paragraphs to make it easier to read. Reporters divide long quotations at natural breaks, usually changes in topic, however slight. The paragraphs' lengths should vary, with few exceeding five or six typed lines. Reporters place a quotation mark at the beginning of a long quotation and before every new paragraph. However, they place a closing quotation mark only at the end of the entire quotation—not at the end of every paragraph:

> The senator added: "Perhaps the most shocking example of the insensitivity of the Bureau of Indian Affairs' educational system is the manner in which boarding school dormitories have been administered.
> "Psychiatrists familiar with the problems of Indian children have told us that a properly run dormitory system is the most crucial aspect of boarding school life, particularly in the elementary schools.
> "Yet, when a 6-year-old Navajo child enters one of the boarding schools and becomes lonely or homesick, he must seek comfort from an instructional aide who has no training in child guidance and who is responsible for as many as 100 other unhappy children.
> "This aide spends most of his time performing custodial chores. At night, the situation worsens as the ratio of dorm aides to children decreases."

When a quotation appears within another quotation, the first is enclosed in double quotation marks, and the second is enclosed in single quotation marks (use an apostrophe for a single quotation mark):

> Mrs. Veen said: "My breathing was shallow, my heartbeat weak and my pulse faint. That's when the doctor told my husband, 'I think she may die.'"

> During his 1960 presidential campaign, John F. Kennedy joked, "I got a wire from my father that said: 'Dear Jack, Don't buy one vote more than necessary. I'll be damned if I'll pay for a landslide.'"

Identifying Sources

After attributing information to a source, reporters should identify that source as fully as possible. Normally, reporters provide the source's name, occupation or position and other identification relevant to the story.

Some reporters, especially those in Washington, attribute their stories to anonymous sources—to "government employees," "congressional aides," "reliable sources in the State Department" and "high government officials." Asked to justify that practice, reporters might respond: "If we identified all our sources, some would be embarrassed by the publication of their statements, and some would lose their jobs. But if we protect their anonymity, the sources will speak more freely and give us more information. So by protecting our sources, we obtain more information and can do a better job of informing the public."

Because the practice is often abused, editors are becoming more critical of the use of anonymous sources. Some government officials use anonymous quotations to launch "trial balloons." They may release a plan or other information anonymously, then watch the public's response. If the response is favorable, the officials will publicly endorse the plan and take the credit for its success. If, on the other hand, the response is unfavorable, the officials will abandon or even publicly denounce the plan. No one (except reporters) will know that the officials are denouncing their own plan. Reporters are helpless because they cannot identify their source. Thus, reporters cannot hold the officials accountable for their statements: not if the officials are wrong, and not even if they deliberately lie.

Other sources "leak" information to the press. Leaks occur when someone who wants to remain anonymous reveals some confidential information. Some leaks are unsolicited and provide important stories. Reporters dig for other leaks, but officials misuse them. The officials leak information that will help their own careers and policies—or harm their rivals'.

Because the practice is so easy to exploit, reporters are becoming more reluctant to quote anonymous sources unless the information they provide is obviously factual and important. Critics believe that, if reporters placed more pressure on their sources—if reporters threatened to ignore all the information provided by anonymous sources—more sources would agree to the publication of their names. If some still refused, reporters might seek the same information from other sources who *were* willing to be identified.

Editors also warn that the use of anonymous sources threatens the media's credibility. If reporters fail to identify their sources, readers may wonder whether the sources really exist. Readers may also wonder whether the "informed sources" mentioned by reporters are truly informed, and whether the information they provide is accurate, important and objective.

Thus, a bulletin published for employees of The Miami Herald commented:

> Why do we so often use the phrase "who refused to be identified?" Because of lazy and sloppy reporting, that's why.
>
> There are exceptions, sure. But it is a bad habit. Every time we print the phrase, we suggest to others that they, too, can use it. It is for weasels. We hurt our own credibility, not someone else's.
>
> When a reporter grants a source anonymity in type, he is asking for trouble. To the source, anonymity can be an invitation to embroider, embellish, take the cheap shot.
>
> Most of the time it is not necessary. An astute reporter should be able to persuade the source to say what he thinks up-front. If not, go elsewhere.

If reporters use a fictitious name to hide a source's identity, they should inform readers of that fact clearly and immediately and explain why the fictitious name is being used. Even more important, no source should be allowed to engage in anonymous attacks on individuals or groups. A bulletin published for reporters and editors at The New York Times explained:

> People who have nice things to say about someone will usually not mind being named in a story, but those who attack someone often request anonymity. It is the anonymous detractors that we—as editors as well as reporters—must, as a matter of fairness, keep out of stories whenever possible. It may not be possible when the attack is crucial to the story. But in all other instances, we should strive to identify the attacker at least by his position or his relationship to the attacked person. If we cannot do that, the attack should not be reported.

On rare occasions, there may be some justification for the use of anonymous sources. The information they offer may be extremely important, and reporters may have no other way to obtain that information. But even then, the editors at several major dailies have instructed their staffs to use the following guidelines:

- Consult an editor and give your source's name to the editor. The editor will determine whether the information provided by your source is important to your newspaper's readers, and whether you could obtain the same information from a source willing to be identified.
- Identify sources as specifically as possible without revealing their identities so that readers can judge their importance and reliability. For example, instead of attributing information to "an informed source" or "a key official," you might attribute it to "an elected city official."
- Explain in your story why the source does not want to be identified.
- Try to corroborate the information with at least one other source.

Reservations about the use of anonymous sources are not new. During the 1940s, Americans concerned about the media's performance established the Commission on Freedom of the Press. After three years of study, the commission attempted to list the media's responsibilities. As part of its effort, the commission recommended that the press "ought to identify the sources of its facts, opinions and arguments so that the reader or listener can judge them." The commission explained: "Persons who are presented with facts, opinions and arguments are properly influenced by the general reliability of those who offer them. If the veracity of statements is to be appraised, those who offer them must be known."

More recently, Benjamin Bradlee called the continued abuse of unattributed information "a professional disgrace." Bradlee, executive editor of The Washington Post, added: "Why, then, do we go along so complacently with withholding the identity of public officials? I'm damned if I know. I do know that by doing so, we shamelessly do other people's bidding; we knowingly let ourselves be used. . . . In short, we demean our profession."

Word Choice in Attributing Statements

The words used to attribute statements must be accurate and impartial. The verb "said" is used most often; however, reporters also use verbs such as "commented," "replied," "declared," "added," "explained," "stated," "continued," "pointed out," "noted," "urged," "suggested" and "warned." Each of these words has a more specific meaning than "said" and can be used only when it accurately reflects the source's actual behavior. Reporters cannot say that a source "explained" anything unless the person's remarks actually explain some point mentioned in the story. They cannot use the word "added" unless the source has made some additional comments about a point already discussed in the story. Similarly, words such as "declare" and "state" are more emphatic and formal than "said." Few people "declare," "state," "announce" or "reveal" anything; most simply answer the questions asked by reporters.

Many editors also object to the use of verbs such as "hopes," "feels," "believes," "wants" and "thinks." Editors explain that reporters know only what sources tell them, not what sources hope, feel, believe, want or think. Other words are even more inappropriate. People speak words—they do not "grin," "smile," "chuckle," "laugh," "sigh" or "cough" them. Such words are particularly undesirable because they are easily misused:

> "We were bleeding all over the floor," she giggled.

> "It was my father," she smiled. "He had a heart attack."

Reporters should rephrase such sentences:

> "It's a wonderful movie," she smiled.
> REVISED: "It's a wonderful movie," she said.
> OR: "It's a wonderful movie," she said with a smile.
> OR: Smiling, she said, "It's a wonderful movie."

The words "claimed" and "admitted" are even more troublesome. The word "claimed" casts doubt on a source's remarks. It suggests that the remarks are controversial and possibly wrong. Similarly, the word "admitted" implies that a source conceded some point or reluctantly confessed to an error, charge or crime. By comparison, the word "said" is almost always appropriate. It may sound awkward at first, but "said" is a neutral term, and reporters can use it any number of times in a single story.

Attribution should also be concise. Each of the following phrases (which have actually appeared in news stories) can be replaced by a single word: either "said" or "added":

made it clear that	said that he feels that
further stated that	brought out the idea that

went on to say that	went on to say that in his opinion
let it be known that	in making the announcement said that
also pointed out that	continued the speech by urging that
emphasized the fact that	responded to the question by saying that
stated in the report that	concluded the speech with the comment that
offered the opinion that	

The following examples illustrate a similar problem—wordy attribution:

He concluded by saying that, in his opinion, most teachers are underpaid.
REVISED: He said most teachers are underpaid.

Colbourne said that he feels that it is a serious mistake to hire more city employees.
REVISED: Colbourne said it is a serious mistake to hire more city employees.

Some Final Guidelines for Attributions and Quotations

Reporters can attribute information to people, but not to places or institutions. For example, reporters can quote a hospital official, but not a hospital:

The hospital said the epidemic has ended.
REVISED: A hospital spokesperson said the epidemic has ended.

Atlanta announced that all city offices will be closed next Monday.
REVISED: The mayor of Atlanta announced that all city offices will be closed next Monday.

To avoid awkward combinations, separate partial quotations from complete sentences that are also being quoted. You can solve the problem most easily by (1) placing some attribution between the partial quotation and the full-sentence quotation or (2) by paraphrasing the partial quotation:

His mother said life is "a simple matter. I told all my children that if they really believe in God, they have nothing to fear."
REVISED: His mother said life is "a simple matter." She explained, "I told all my children that if they really believe in God, they have nothing to fear."
OR: His mother said life is a simple matter. "I told all my children that if they really believe in God, they have nothing to fear," she explained.

Ross said he expects to find a job "within a few weeks. And when I do get a job, the first thing I'm going to buy is a new car."
REVISED: Ross said he expects to find a job "within a few weeks." He added, "And when I do get a job, the first thing I'm going to buy is a new car."
OR: Ross said he expects to find a new job within a few weeks. "And when I do get a job, the first thing I'm going to buy is a new car," he added.

Reporters rarely add that a source "told reporters" or "informed this newspaper." Most news is transmitted through reporters, and it is unnecessary to say so. If reporters included the phrases in all their stories, they would become too repetitive and consume too much space:

He told reporters that the city is bankrupt.
REVISED: He said the city is bankrupt.

During an interview today, she informed this newspaper that the city must release some prisoners because its jails are overcrowded.
REVISED: During an interview today, she said the city must release some prisoners because its jails are overcrowded.

Also avoid unintentional editorials. If worded carelessly, partial quotes, and even attribution, can express an opinion:

> The mayor made it clear that the city cannot afford to give its employees a raise.
> REVISED: The mayor said the city cannot afford to give its employees a raise.

> Each month, Sen. William Proxmire presents the Golden Fleece Award "for the biggest, most ironic or most ridiculous example of wasteful government spending."
> REVISED: Each month, Sen. William Proxmire presents the Golden Fleece Award for what he considers "the biggest, most ironic or most ridiculous example of wasteful government spending."

The first sentence concluded that the mayor "made it clear"—that she expressed her opinion in a clear, convincing manner. The second sentence reported as fact Proxmire's claim that all the recipients of his "award" have wasted the government's money, yet many of the recipients have disagreed, and some have provided convincing evidence that Proxmire was wrong.

Finally, do not attribute a direct quotation to more than one person. Instead, eliminate the quotation marks. Two or more people rarely use exactly the same words.

Checklists for Quotations and Attribution

Consult the following checklists when using quotations and attribution. If you can answer "No" to any of these questions, the quotations or attribution in your stories may have to be revised.

Quotations

1. Have you used quotations sparingly—for emphasis and for a change of pace rather than to tell an entire story?
2. Are all the words that you have placed in quotation marks your source's exact words?
3. Does each quotation serve a purpose? Does it help reveal the source's character; explain, describe or emphasize an important point; or present additional details about that point?
4. Are all the direct quotations clear, concise, relevant and effective? If not, they should probably be paraphrased or discarded.
5. Have you reported only the source's answers, not the questions the source was asked?
6. If a quotation includes several sentences, have you placed quotation marks only at the beginning and the end of the entire quotation—not at the beginning and the end of every sentence?
7. Have you divided long quotations into shorter paragraphs, with quotation marks appearing at the beginning of every paragraph and at the end of only the final paragraph?
8. Do quotations that appear within other quotations use single quotation marks?
9. Have you avoided the use of orphan quotes?
10. Are you certain that none of the quotations repeat facts reported elsewhere in your story?

Attribution

1. Have you attributed second-hand information, criticisms, statements about controversial issues, other statements of opinion and all direct and indirect quotations—but not undisputed facts?
2. Have you punctuated the attribution properly? Have you used a comma before one-sentence quotations and a colon before quotations that contain two or more sentences? Also, have all the commas and periods been placed inside the quotation marks?
3. Have you capitalized the first letter in all full sentences—but not sentence fragments—that are quoted?

4. Has the attribution been placed at or near the beginning of all long quotations?

5. If the attribution appears in the middle of a sentence, does it appear at a natural break in the sentence rather than interrupt a thought?

6. Have you varied your sentences and paragraphs so most do not begin with the attribution?

7. Have you placed the attribution outside the quotation marks?

8. Have you attributed continuing quotations only once?

9. Have you attributed each separate statement of opinion expressed in indirect quotations?

10. Have you quoted only people, not places or institutions?

11. Have you avoided awkward combinations of partial and complete quotations?

12. Have you provided transitions to separate the statements made by different people, particularly if one of those statements is quoted immediately after the other?

13. Have you selected the proper words of attribution—words that accurately convey the speaker's actual meaning and behavior?

14. Have you avoided words of attribution such as "hopes," "feels," "believes," "laughs," "coughs" and "cries"?

15. Is the attribution as concise as possible?

If you would like more practice using these rules, complete Exercise 4, then compare your answers with the answers provided in Appendix D.

EXERCISE 1
Quotations and Attribution

MISCELLANEOUS EXERCISES:
IMPROVING YOUR QUOTATIONS AND ATTRIBUTION

SECTION I: AVOIDING WORDY ATTRIBUTION Condense each of these phrases to two or three words.

1. She went on to say that
2. She told the audience that
3. She concluded by saying that
4. She said that, in her opinion
5. She expressed her belief that

6. He also made mention of
7. He also pointed out that
8. He revealed the fact that
9. They were quick to point out that
10. The author made the remark that

SECTION II: AVOIDING DOUBLE ATTRIBUTION Mistakenly, each of these statements is attributed twice. Rewrite the statements, attributing them only once.

1. In her speech, she also said the city has dozens of beautiful old homes.
2. In a report issued today, the researchers revealed that the disease is spreading.
3. In a speech to the community, the senator announced that he will seek federal funds to repair the bridge.
4. According to the mayor in a speech she gave Wednesday, it would cost too much to widen the highway.
5. Slater said that, in his opinion, he is convinced that no one could have prevented the girl's death.

SECTION III: PLACEMENT Correct the placement and punctuation of the attribution in the following sentences.

1. "Nice guys" Leo Durocher said "finish last."
2. Said Gen. William Tecumseh Sherman: "War is hell".
3. "Another important step" she said "is to proofread everything you write".
4. "People under 18," she insisted "should never be allowed to drive".
5. "The federal government is like an alcoholic who has to hit rock bottom before he decides to seek help." Anders said in reference to the federal deficit.

SECTION IV: ADDING ATTRIBUTION Provide the proper attribution for the first statement, which is paraphrased, and for the second, which is a direct quotation. Also divide each statement into several shorter paragraphs.

1. Republican Eugene McIntry said tuition rates at the state's colleges and universities are too low, and he went on to make all of the following points as well. The tuition rates that students are charged cover only one-fifth the cost of their college educations, and taxpayers are forced to make up the difference. No taxpayer struggling to

support a family should have to help subsidize healthy young college students; students should pay their own bills. What we have, in effect, is a form of welfare, since other citizens are forced to help college students pay their bills. It's unjust. Students can work full-time summers and part-time during the school year and take out loans that they can repay when they graduate and find high-paying jobs.

2. The teen-ager said: "We were at the beach, and suddenly it began to rain. The lightning was falling, hitting all around us. There was no place to go, nowhere to hide, and I was absolutely terrified. All of a sudden I felt something hit me. I turned around because I thought my boyfriend had thrown something at me. I thought he had thrown a rock because it hurt so bad. From the small of my back down to the bottom of my feet I felt pain, like somebody had slapped me. The pain moved downward and concentrated in my feet. It was lightning, and it hit me. I think the only reason it didn't kill me was because I was wearing rubber track shoes."

SECTION V: MISCELLANEOUS ERRORS Correct the errors in the following sentences.

1. Ball, 20, said the Jeep was crushed to about half its normal size. "It was just a box of metal". he said. "Everything in the Jeep was totally crushed," he added, "except for the two front seats".

2. He said, "We're hoping it (the water level) will increase back (to normal)."

3. Margaret Hamill, a senior, claimed that she often went home and cried after the algebra class. "I wanted to quit." she said. "There wasn't enough time to ask questions," she explained. "Each day I got more and more confused."

4. He described himself as, "A church-going person who neither smokes nor drinks."

5. "I think it's kind of ridiculous." he explained about the high cost of a new home.

6. A specialist said: "in one third of all heart attack fatalities, the first symptom is death."

7. "Patriotism is the last refuge of a scoundrel," argued Samuel Johnson.

8. "I'm doing better." "Not hitting as many spectators." Former president Gerald Ford announced today while describing his golf game.

9. More women are becoming alcoholics, according to two sociologists who spoke at your school Friday.

10. He urged his listeners to remember one critical point: that high schools do not exist for the purpose of preparing every student to enter college.

EXERCISE 2
Quotations and Attribution

WORDING, PLACEMENT AND PUNCTUATION

INSTRUCTIONS: Make any changes necessary to improve the attribution in the following sentences and paragraphs, and correct matters of style.

1. "Our goal is peace". claimed the president.

2. Benjamin Franklin said: "death takes no bribes".

3. She said her son refers to her literary endeavors as, "mom's writing thing".

4. He is a scuba diver and pilot. He also enjoys skydiving. "I like challenge, something exciting."

5. "The dangers promise to be of indefinite duration." the president said referring to Communism.

6. "Freedom of the press is not merely freedom to publish news." "It is also freedom to gather the news. We cannot publish what we cannot gather." said columnist Jack Anderson during a speech last night.

7. Jesse Owens expressed the opinion that "I think that America has become too athletic." "From Little League to the pro leagues, sports are no longer recreation." "They are big business, and they're drudgery." he continued.

8. The man smiled, "It's a great deal for me." "I expect to double my money," he explained.

9. When asked what she likes most about her job as a newspaper reporter, the woman responded by saying—"I'm not paid much, but the work is important. And it's varied and exciting." She grinned: "Also, I like seeing my byline in the paper."

10. The librarian announced to reporters that the new building "will cost somewhere in the neighborhood of about $4.6 million."

11. "Thousands of the poor in the United States," said the professor, "die every year of diseases we can easily cure." "It's a crime," he said, "but no one ever is punished for their deaths."

12. Thomas said students should never be spanked. "A young boy or girl who gets spanked in front of peers becomes embarrassed and the object of ridicule."

13. The lawyer said, "He ripped the life-sustaining respirator tubes from his throat three times in an effort to die. He is simply a man" the lawyer continued "who rejects medical treatment regardless of the consequences. He wants to die and has a constitutional right to do so."

14. Bobby Knight, the basketball coach at Indiana University, said. "Everyone has the will to win." "Few have the will to prepare." Knight added that. "It is the preparation that counts."

15. She said she firmly believes that the federal government "must do more" to help cities "support and retrain" the chronically unemployed.

EXERCISE 3
Quotations and Attribution

WORDING, PLACEMENT AND PUNCTUATION

INSTRUCTIONS: Make any changes necessary to improve the attribution in the following sentences and paragraphs.

1. "Let's go to the game." she announced.

2. "My youngest daughter was married today". he smiled.

3. It was the funniest thing I've ever seen, laughed the woman.

4. The teacher was unhappy. "I wasn't given a raise this year."

5. He accused the newspaper of "sensationalism" and "poor taste."

6. "Three may keep a secret, if two of them are dead." added Benjamin Franklin.

7. "Those who sit," he said, "and wait for things accomplish nothing."

8. "My husband is a no-good bum." she sobbed. "He beats me." she explained.

9. The store announced that it will be closed for "at least a week" because of the fire.

10. "It was a tough course." he claimed. "Students are lucky to get a C." he explained.

11. He continued talking about the issue and pointed out the fact that elementary and high schools are unable to recruit enough math and science teachers.

12. The shortstop said the umpire was mistaken. "He couldn't possibly have seen the play." "He was too damned far away".

13. "I was standing behind the counter when the gunman came in and demanded all the money, the clerk added. "I gave it to him, and then he run out the back door."

14. When asked whether there are plans to construct any more public swimming pools in the city, the mayor responded, "Not right now."

15. According to forecasts, there is "a 20 percent chance of rain today. Tomorrow, the probability of rain rises to nearly 80 percent."

16. The senior smiled, "I'd really like to become a flight attendant." She added: "My sister has a job with Delta, and she really likes it."

17. The nurse said, "A cancer patient asked me, "Why won't you let me die?" I didn't know how to answer her," the nurse declared.

18. Adlai Stevenson said. "In America, any boy may become president." Stevenson continued by saying, "I suppose that is just one of the risks he takes."

19. "People who don't like a TV program should turn it off." "I have yet to hear of a TV set made that doesn't have an on-off switch." "People who blame the TV networks and the industry because they think TV harms their children are lazy and ignorant". claimed the producer.

EXERCISE 4
Quotations and Attribution   Answer Key Provided: See Appendix D

PLACEMENT AND PUNCTUATION

INSTRUCTIONS: Make any changes necessary to improve the attribution in the following sentences and paragraphs. Not every sentence necessarily contains an error. You can correct your own work by comparing your answers with the answers printed in Appendix D.

1. "We can't wait any longer." he said.

2. He said: "no one was seriously injured".

3. Smith said he is "not very happy. My wife is divorcing me," he explained.

4. He found the plane in a woods a half mile away and saw two people inside, both "dead".

5. "At least two he said and perhaps three people will be charged with fraud."

6. The girl smiled, "Yes, I'll marry you." She explained, "I've always loved you."

7. "I know I shouldn't smoke," the girl coughed. "But I can't help myself."

8. She said she hates college. "The teachers make us memorize." "They don't teach us how to think".

9. Thompsen, asked about her feelings as she received the award as the school's outstanding journalism student, said, "it's the biggest surprise of my life."

10. When asked whether he would teach next year, the art professor responded, "I think so. I like having a steady income, and I haven't been able to earn enough from the sale of my paintings," he explained.

11. The student grinned. "I really don't enjoy college, but I don't know what else to do." "Perhaps I should just quit school and look for a job."

12. The woman claimed that "only a few" of her friends are happy as housewives and that "most want to find a job. They want to make some money and become less dependent on their husbands."

13. The city council voted 7 to 2 against a proposal to give police officers a 12 percent raise. "It's just too much," Mayor Paula Novarro said. "Policemen are already overpaid." She added that "police officers just aren't worth $25,000 a year."

14. "My daddy will give me a dime." the girl declared as she ran home.

15. When asked whether he planned to run for another term, the governor responded, "I'm not going to speculate about that now." It's too early," he said.

16. Tests showed that "low" or "moderate" speed, rear-end collisions involving the car resulted in "massive" fuel leaks and fires, the magazine reported.

EXERCISE 5
Quotations and Attribution

USING QUOTES IN NEWS STORIES

INSTRUCTIONS: Write complete news stories based on the following information. Use some quotations in each story to emphasize its highlights, but do not use quotations to tell the entire story. Use the most interesting, important and revealing quotations, not just those that happen to appear first.

1. Carlos Vacante is a police officer who has worked 3 years for your city's police department. Last night he had an unusual experience. This is his story, as he told it to you in an interview today: "I remember his eyes. They were cold, the eyes of a killer. He was pointing a gun at me, and it fired. I smelled the gunpowder and waited for the pain. I thought I was dead. The whole thing had started at about 11 p.m. This man was suspected of stealing from parked cars, and I'd gotten his description by radio. Then I spotted him in a parking lot. This morning we learned he's wanted in the robbery and murder of a service station attendant in Tennessee. There's no doubt in my mind he wanted to kill me last night just because I stopped him. I was an object in his way. I'd gotten out of my car and called to him. He started turning around and I spotted a handgun in his waistband. As he drew the gun and fired, I leaned to the right and dropped to one knee. It was just a reflex that saved my life. When I heard the shot, I thought he hit me. I couldn't believe it was actually happening to me. I thought I was going to cash everything in. Then I was running—zig-zagging—behind some cars. He fired another shot, but my backup arrived, and he fled. Maybe 60 seconds had passed from the time I spotted him. Five minutes later, we found him at the back door to a house, trying to break in and hide. I ordered him to stop, and he put his hands up and said, 'You got me.' I still smell the gunpowder this morning. I thought I was dead."

2. County Judge Edward Johnson provided this story during an interview this morning. This is what he said: "I sentenced 42 men and one woman to jail yesterday, all for not making their child support payments. They've all been found in contempt of court. The jail's just bulging now. We're expecting more, so the sheriff is bringing in extra mattresses and wood cots. I'm scheduled to hear 40 more cases tomorrow. Normally, I hear about a dozen of these cases a month, and three to four are sentenced to jail. But the problem's been getting worse, and we decided the only way to deal with it was to crack down on these people. We've got hundreds of people in this county behind on their child support. Nothing's usually done about it, so people figure they can get away with it. Then their families starve or go on welfare. This is the last resort to get these people to place first priority on their children's support and care. We find that most of the offenders could have made their payments. They have the money. The maximum penalty is 179 days, but most are sentenced to pay what they owe or serve 90 days in jail. I'm told that yesterday seventeen of the defendants, including the woman, made all their back payments and were released. Others are in the process of raising the money they owe and will be released today. We decided to start with the worst offenders, the people farthest behind in their payments, so the majority of the offenders being brought in are $1,000 or more behind. There was one yesterday who was in arrears by $40,000. I think in general I've tried to be very firm and fair to get across to these people that this has to be their first priority, ahead of car payments or anything else. They have to take care of their children. I'm not really trying to punish them. I'm just trying to get their attention, and I believe the system works. I can't see how anyone can neglect their children."

3. There was a trial yesterday. It was a rape trial that lasted 6 hours and that ended in the conviction by an 8-man, 4-woman jury of Lonnie T. Ward, 20, who was then sentenced to a term of 28 years in prison. The main witness against him was the victim, Ashley Deyo. This is what she told the court: "I was alone in my apartment that night and had been asleep when I woke and found this man standing by the bed. He was nude, and I think I tried to scream because I opened my mouth, but nothing came out. He slapped me. Then he put his hand over my mouth and told me not to talk. He said if I cooperated, he wouldn't hurt me, but he had a knife. Then he touched me and raped me, using all kinds of nasty, filthy, four-letter words. He said he had done it lots of times before. I was scared to death, so that I literally could not move. He threatened to stab me if I resisted. I was petrified. I thought he was going to kill me. I just didn't think he'd do what he did and let me live to tell about it. It's ruined my life. My marriage has fallen apart, and I've had to move to another city, but I never forget. Never, not for a day, not for an hour. Never."

4. At their meeting last night, your city commissioners shut down a pet store: Kim's Pets located in the Colonial Mall. The commission revoked the owner's occupational license. They had received numerous complaints from customers, police and Humane Society officials that the store sold sick animals and did not take proper care of its animals. During a hearing before the commission, representatives of the County Humane Society, police officers and several unhappy customers complained about the store and its owner, Kim Rybinski. Rybinski claimed she has never knowingly sold sick animals or improperly cared for them. She said the Humane Society has been harassing her, and that its harassment "has been unbelievable." Serving as a spokesman for dissatisfied customers and other complainants, Michael Jeffries, director of the Humane Society, said: "She's not running her business in the fashion that other pet stores are being run. We have about 40 documented cases of improper business practices, including the sale of sick animals and improper care. We're also investigating complaints that she sold animals which she claimed were registered with the American Kennel Club. After selling the animals, she's been unable to deliver registration papers to the pets' owners. She's allowed sick pets to remain in cages with healthy pets, and she keeps large animals in small cages. We had to sue her over a sick cat that was for sale. It's in our custody now, and we're trying to find a home for her. At first, we were trying to help her, but she's never cooperated with us and orders me out of her store. We get more complaints about her than any other pet store in the area. We get complaints about other pet stores, but they're generally unfounded or involve passing conditions that can be corrected. We got a complaint the first month Rybinski opened, and we're still getting complaints about her. The problem is, she's looking at the almighty dollar and not at the welfare of her animals."

5. The city's Ministerial Alliance spoke out today against the death penalty. A copy of a resolution it adopted will be sent to the governor and to every member of the state legislature. As its spokesman, the Rev. Stuart Adler declared: "None of us is soft on crime. There must be just punishment for those who commit violent crimes, but what we are saying is we stop short of taking another person's life. We object because several independent studies have concluded that the death penalty is no deterrent to crime, rather the violence of the death penalty only breeds more violence. Also, the method of sentencing people is inconsistent. There is a great disparity between the victim being black or white. Defendants accused of killing black victims often are not sentenced to death, but when the victim is white, the death penalty is often imposed. People are frightened by the amount of violence in our society, and they've been sold a bill of goods. They've been told that the death penalty is a deterrent, and yet every major study disproves that reality. We're not getting at the deeper causes. We're a violent society, and getting more violent. Half the households in this city have guns, and it's inevitable some are going to use them. If we're really serious about stopping

crime and violence, we have to recognize and correct its root causes: poverty, racial and sexual discrimination, broken homes and unloved children. Also drugs and alcohol. That's what's responsible for most crimes. And television. Studies show the average child in America witnesses, on television, 200,000 acts of violence by age 16. So we're against the death penalty. It's not going to solve our problems, and it's not fair, not fairly applied. It'll take time, but we intend to abolish it, and we'll persist. We're already beginning to stimulate discussion, and we expect that discussion to spread."

6. Tommy Crosby, 16, and Richard Picardo, 15, are sophomores at Grant High School in your community. Yesterday they were water-skiing on Elkhart Lake. Crosby, whose family owns the boat, was pulling Picardo, who was water-skiing. This is what Crosby said in an interview describing Picardo's death: "We were taking turns water-skiing, and lightning hit him. He's my best friend, and I saw him die. It was about 4 o'clock, and we could see a storm east of us. We heard thunder, but it was in the distance, like maybe it would miss us. It never did rain, so we thought the storm would miss us. Dick was on one ski—he's pretty good at that. Then, uh, at first, I didn't know what happened. I was looking ahead, uh, watching for other boats. There was a flash, a bright flash, but at first it was like I still didn't know what was happening. I didn't hear any thunder then. Nothing. When I turned around, Dick was in the water. At first, I thought he had fallen, but he was face down."

BACKGROUND: The force of the bolt shredded the youth's bathing suit and caused first- and second-degree burns from his chin to his navel. When firefighters arrived, the victim had been pulled into a boat and taken to shore. An off-duty firefighter tried to revive him there. County firefighters applied advanced life-support procedures, but he was pronounced dead a short time later at Park Regional Hospital. Deaths caused by water-related lightning strikes run second only to those in open fields. Usually, however, the victims are in boats at the time the lightning strikes. Authorities in the county said they can't remember lightning ever hitting anyone else on water skis.

EXERCISE 6
Quotations and Attribution

USING QUOTES IN NEWS STORIES

INSTRUCTIONS: Write complete news stories based on the following information. Use some quotations in each of your stories to emphasize its highlights, but do not use quotations to tell the entire story. Use the most interesting, important and revealing quotations, not just those that happen to appear first.

1. Gus DiCesare is the county sheriff. During an interview in his office this morning he discussed the problem of motorists who leave self-service gasoline stations without paying their bills. DiCesare made the following remarks: "It's a growing problem and getting worse every year. We're getting at least 30 complaints a week from gas stations about the problem. How often a station is robbed depends a great deal on its location and popularity. The larger stations, especially those located near major highways and those with transient customers, are hit most frequently since drivers can quickly lose themselves on the highways. The small, neighborhood service station gets hit least often because its attendants know their regular customers. Station owners are trying to solve the problem, but there's only a limited number of things they can do. Most require employees who let a customer get away without paying to pay the bill out of their own pockets, and the employees at some large stations lose as much as $60 a week from their salaries because of customers leaving without paying. It gets busy at these big stations, and the employees just can't watch everyone. Some drivers speed away even when the employees are watching. A lot of the self-service stations are beginning to make you pay first, before you get your gas, and that cuts down on the thefts. We also recommend a number of other safeguards. We suggest that they service only one vehicle at a time, and that employees keep a pencil and paper handy to write down license numbers and a description of the drivers for later identification purposes. Attendants should pay closer attention to cars, and owners should do a better job of lighting their stations at night. But as the price of gas increases, we expect that the number of thefts will also continue increasing."

2. Norma J. Holtzclaw is a local realtor, and she spoke to the Rotary Club last evening. During the speech, she focused on the growing trend for single people to buy property. She told the club members: "The singles market in some areas now exceeds 25% of all home sales, but the trend isn't that pronounced in this area. Locally, about 10% of all the homes being sold are sold to singles, and that percentage seems to be increasing. It includes the sale of co-ops and condominiums as well as detached single-family dwellings. A lot of my clients say they're buying property for the tax benefits and as an investment. Usually, by the time they buy a house, singles are in their 30s or 40s, although I've had a few in their middle and late 20s. Other factors are contributing to the upswing in these sales. Because of the baby boom after World War II, there are a lot more people in the home-buying age range. More people seem to be living alone; many are divorced. More people also are getting married later in life, and more people 65 and older are living alone. Overall, townhouses are the most popular type of housing for singles, since their owners don't have to worry as much about the upkeep and maintenance; it's all done for them. Condominiums rank second with single buyers. Single-family homes are third, and mobile homes a poor fourth."

3. The American Medical Association issued a report in Philadelphia today. It concerns the results of a three-year study of medical treatment in United States jails. The

American Medical Association surveyed one thousand inmates at thirty jails across the country. Its report states: "Although these are only preliminary findings, they are indicative of a high percentage of undetected illnesses among the jail population of the country. Only 37% of the jails surveyed had medical clinics, and only 13 percent of the jails gave all their inmates routine physicals on admission. Treatment facilities for mentally ill offenders were available in 43% of the jails. As examples of our findings, 15% of the inmates examined in an Indiana jail had positive tuberculosis skin tests, and in a small jail in Washington state, 15% of the prisoners examined had positive X-ray readings for TB. 66% of the inmates in a Georgia jail had abnormal urinalysis tests. The initial findings show a shocking lack of medical manpower and services throughout the country. The ultimate objective of the program is the collection of information to be used for the development of a national certification system for jail medical programs, using approaches similar to those applied to the certification of hospitals and medical schools." Each of the thousand prisoners was given a physical examination as part of the American Medical Association study, and the prisoner's medical history was taken. The study is financed by a federal grant and will run for an additional two years. The grant provides an annual budget of $497,652. It started one year ago.

4. A rise in insurance rates is being blamed for a rise in hit-and-run motor vehicle accidents within the state. Richard Byrum, state insurance commissioner, discussed the problem during a press conference in his office today. He said, "The problem is serious. At first, we thought it was a police problem, but police in the state have asked my office to look into it. There has been a dramatic increase in hit-and-run accidents in the state, particularly in big cities where you find the higher insurance rates. I'm told that last year we had nearly 28,000 motor vehicle accidents in the state, and 4,500 were hit-and-run. People are taking chances driving without proper insurance coverage, or they're afraid of a premium increase if they have insurance and stop and report an accident. They seem to think, 'What the heck, no one saw it, and I won't get caught,' and they just bug out of there. If you look at the insurance rates in the state, it's practically impossible for some people to pay them, and as insurance rates go up, the rate of leaving the scene of an accident increases. Drivers with the worst records—those with several accidents and traffic citations—pay as much as $3,000 a year in insurance premiums, and they may pay even more than that if they are young or have a high-powered car. Even good drivers found at fault in an accident may find their rates going up several hundred dollars for the next three to five years. So leaving the scene of an accident is definitely tied to the economic situation, yet the insurance company people I've talked to say they can't do anything about it. It's just not realistic to expect them to lower their rates; they aren't making that much money. Right now, I'm not sure what we'll do about the situation. In the meantime, we can expect more hit-and-run accidents and more drivers going without any insurance coverage because of its high cost."

EXERCISE 7
Quotations and Attribution

USING QUOTES IN NEWS STORIES

INSTRUCTIONS: Write complete news stories based on the following information. Use some quotations in each story to emphasize its highlights, but do not use quotations to tell the entire story. Use the most interesting, important and revealing quotations, not just those that happen to appear first.

1. Michael Ernest Layoux, 22, is a clerk at a ~~convenience store at 1284 East Forest Boulevard~~. He was robbed late yesterday. Here is his account of the incident: "First, you have to understand where the store is. It's located in a remote area in the northeast corner of town. There's nothing around that's open at night, so I'm all alone in the store. I started carrying a gun to work last year after I read where two clerks at another convenience store in the city were robbed and killed. Carrying a gun is against company policy, but I figured I had to protect myself. We're open 24 hours, and the store has a history of holdups, particularly at night when there aren't any customers in the store. But it never happened to me personally before. Just after 11, when the store was empty except for me last night, this guy walks in and asks for a pack of Winston cigarettes. I handed him a pack, and then he pulled a gun and says, "You see what I got?" He had a pistol, and he held it low, level with his hip, so no one outside the store could look in and see it. Then he asked me for the money, and I gave it to him. We never have more than $30 in cash in the register. It's company policy. We put all the big bills we get into a floor safe we can't open. So he didn't get much, maybe $20. Then he motioned for me to move toward the cooler. We have a big cooler in the back for beer and soda and other stuff we have to keep cold. When he started shoving me toward the cooler I really got scared. There's no lock on the cooler, so he couldn't lock me in while he was getting away. There's no reason for him to put me in the cooler; I could walk right out. The only thing I could figure was that he wanted to shoot me, and he wanted to do it in some place where no one could see what was happening. That's where the two other clerks were shot last year, in a cooler in their store. Since they were killed, I've kept a .25-caliber pistol under the counter, and when he motioned for me to get into the cooler I shot him. He'd started turning toward the cooler, and then he must have heard me cocking the pistol because he started jerking his head back around toward me. I shot him 3 times in the chest and side, but I didn't know right away that I hit him. He just ran out through the front door. He didn't even open it. He ran right through the glass. I called the police, and they found his body in a field about 200 yards away. He was dead, and now I've lost my job. But I wouldn't do it any different. The police talked to me for almost two hours, and they said it was OK, that I acted in self-defense. Then this morning, just after 8, I got a call at home from my district manager, and he said I'm fired because it's against company policy to have a gun in the store. It's a real shame, because I'm still a college student, and I need the job. I can attend classes during the day and then work at night at the store. I've been doing it for 4 years now, and I want to graduate in a couple more months. But I can understand the company's rules. Most people don't know how to handle guns. I do. I've been around them and using them all my life."

   Company officials refused to comment about the robbery or the firing.

2. Lillian Shisenaunt is a pharmacist. She was elected president of your County Pharmacists Association at a meeting held last night. During an interview with you today, she talked about an issue of concern to pharmacists, one that the pharmacists talked

about at their meeting last night, along with possible solutions. She said: "We find that we've got an awful lot of older people taking three or four or five different drugs all at once. If they think that's going to do them any good, they're fooling themselves. We find that, in many cases, the medicine—the dosage and the way it's taken—are all wrong. Patients, especially the elderly, sometimes get all their different drugs confused, and then they take two of one and none of the others. Even when the elderly take all the right pills, sometimes the different drugs nullify each other. Different doctors these people see give them prescriptions without knowing what else a patient is taking for some other problem. So some of these oldsters become real junkies, and they don't even know it. As they get older and have more problems, they take more and more medication. After a few years, their children think their minds are going because they're so heavily sedated all the time. But if they get a good doctor, or a good druggist, they probably can stop taking some of the medicines, and then they don't actually have all the problems people think they have. A lot of these older people aren't senile; they just take too many different drugs, and it hits them like senility. Drug companies don't help. If you look at most drug companies, they test their products on healthy young adults, a 25-year-old, 180-pound male. Then the companies set a normal adult dosage based on the clinical tests with these young adults. But the things that determine how drugs affect you change with age, so what the drug companies set as a normal daily dosage doesn't always fit an older person with a number of conditions. If you look at studies of hospital emergency rooms, you'll find that people over 60 are admitted twice as often for adverse drug reactions as the young. Most people don't know that. They think about all the problems of the young, not the old. But most of the problems can be solved, and without too much effort. People should talk to a good pharmacist or physician. Unfortunately, we find that most people are scared of their doctors and don't ask them enough questions and don't understand what their pharmacists have to offer. Patients also should make a list of all their different medicines and dosages each time they go to a doctor and tell him what they're taking. Then when they get a new prescription, they should write down the doctor's instructions, and they should get all their prescriptions from just one pharmacist so the pharmacist knows everything they're taking and can watch for any problems. If they ask, the pharmacist can color code their pill bottles so they can't be confused. But patients also have a responsibility for their own health care. Each morning, they should sort out all that day's pills ahead of time, and then they'd be less likely to make a mistake."

3. Assume that you obtained the following information by interviewing Sheriff's Captain Mark Durrance in his office early today. Durrence said: "Most people don't know it, but rustling's becoming a big problem in this county. As beef prices rise, the problem gets worse and worse. Thefts of cattle are up 25% over last year, mainly because of the economy and because of the increase in the county's population. The thefts are sporadic but usually pick up in the summer after the cattle have been fattened. The thefts also go up when more people are unemployed and when the price of beef goes up. We figure there are 50,000 head of cattle in the county, and the largest concentration is in the southeastern area. Most thefts aren't large. The largest one we had last year was 50 head from a pasture in the Moss Park area. Someone probably drove them away in a truck. Usually the rustlers take only one or two, and they slaughter them on the spot and take only the best meat. They take the hindquarters, front shoulder and parts of the back, then leave the rest. The average rustler can kill and skin one out in 15 to 20 minutes. If they use a .22-caliber rifle to kill a cow, and a chain saw to cut it up, it takes only 4 or 5 minutes, so they can get away pretty fast. If you look at how it's done, you can usually tell what they'll use the meat for. If it's a sloppy job, it's for personal use. If it's a clean, professional job, it's for resale to other people. It's a felony, and we usually get a couple convictions every

year. A hundred years ago, it used to be a hanging offense. But today, most rustlers we catch just get put on probation, and maybe the judge orders them to pay for the cows they got caught stealing, if they got any money. It's not easy catching them. There's usually a big lapse of time between the time the crime occurs and the time when it's reported. It may be days, or even weeks, before the ranchers find a carcass and report the rustling to us. By then, the evidence is gone. What's left of the cow is mostly rotten or eaten away, and there's not much we can see or do, especially if it's rained. After a week or two, you can't find a good tire track or anything. The ranchers are screaming for us to do more, but there's only so much we can do. Manpower is our number one problem. We're trying to cover 260,000 acres with an 8-man detail assigned to rustling. We'd like to expand our patrols this year, but there's not enough money in our budget. We usually have some officers staked out in various parts of the county at night, and we have some patrolling the county in helicopters, in four-wheel drive vehicles and on horseback. And then some ranchers patrol their own land at night. Just seeing a set of headlights can be a deterrent. We're trying to get the ranchers to do more. Every year, we have programs that tell them their responsibilities under the law and their rights to protect their property. We've shown ranchers what they can do for crime scene preservation, and we're also going into some aspects of marking and branding. Ranchers are starting to take more interest in the branding laws, and they're meeting more with law enforcement officials. It's really a national problem. You go to a convention anywhere, and you'll find law enforcement people talking about it. So it's not just this county. Everyone is getting hit by rustlers, and it seems to be getting worse every year. Rustlers know there isn't much chance they'll get caught in the act, and then, in a couple of days, someone usually eats the evidence."

4. Marcia Baugh, a consumer advocate employed by the state, spoke at Kennedy High School this morning and discussed the problem of fat. She told an assembly of students at the school that: "Americans spend $10 billion a year to fight fat. It's estimated that 70 million Americans are overweight, and they seem willing to try almost anything to shed some pounds. But they want it to be easy. Every year, they spend millions of dollars on appetite suppressants, anti-obesity prescriptions, reducing pills, diet books, mechanical devices, health spas and all sorts of related items, much of it outright quackery. Women constitute 90 percent of the weight-reducing market, and much of their money is wasted. Dieters need more will power, not more pills. The best way to lose weight is simply cut down on the amount you eat and to eat more nutritious types of food. Fewer sweets and smaller portions. And exercise, lots of exercise. Doctors estimate that obesity is a secondary cause in the deaths of 50,000 people every year. But people who are overweight usually don't go to see their family doctors because they're embarrassed about the problem. Instead, they buy over-the-counter products. 90% of these diet products are sold in supermarkets and drugstores, which makes them super easy to get."

12 Improving Newsgathering and Writing Skills

When a major event occurs, dozens and sometimes hundreds of journalists rush to the scene, gather information and then transmit that information to the public. All the journalists write about the same event, but some of their stories are much better than others. Why?

Some reporters are particularly adept at gathering the information needed to write exceptional stories. They go beyond the superficial, critically examine all the information they are given and ask probing questions. They also search for alternative sources of information and are good observers. These reporters notice and record minor details that help reveal the truth and make their stories more colorful, descriptive and interesting.

Other reporters produce exceptional stories because of their mastery of the English language. Their language is vivid and forceful, and their stories are written so clearly and simply that everyone can understand them. These reporters describe the people, places and events involved in news stories and use quotations that enable those people to speak directly to the public. Their stories are so descriptive and specific—their images so vivid—that readers are able to picture in their own minds the scenes they describe.

Skilled reporters can transform even routine events into front-page stories. A reporter who is unimaginative about or indifferent to a topic may write a three-paragraph story that, because of its mediocrity, will not be used. Another reporter, excited by the same topic, may go beyond the superficial—may ask more questions, uncover some unusual developments and inject more color into the story. The second reporter may write a three-page story about the topic and, because of its excellence, the story may be published at the top of Page 1.

A young reporter named Barry Bradley uncovered and wrote that type of exceptional front-page story. Asked to describe his coverage of it, Bradley said:

Sometimes the best news stories are those you might have missed had you not done a little extra snooping or asked that one extra question. The old saying 'leave no stone unturned' applies to no business as much as it applies to the news business.

I picked up a press release at the local police station. These releases contain the barest essentials regarding police activities that might be of interest to reporters. Many times a set of facts on a press release may seem dull. But a little effort can turn these facts into an interesting story.

The facts said an elderly man was robbed at knife-point. I did some nosing around and found out the man lived in a nursing home. How did the robber get into a nursing home? And why did the robber choose such an unlikely spot? I also discovered the man was 71 years old and in a wheelchair. The story looked much better now than it did when I first looked at the bare facts.

Then I found out the man lost $4 and a pocketknife in the robbery. To make matters worse, that was about all he had. That little tidbit was enough to warrant front-page space.

I went to the nursing home, interviewed him and took some pictures. I found out he beat the mugger soundly with his cane before the mugger got away with his cash and belongings. He was a feisty gent who had been in three wars and wounded in two. This made the story good enough for my editors to submit it to an annual writers' contest sponsored by the local press club. I didn't win any awards, but it was still a good story. And I would have missed it if I hadn't been nosey enough that day.

Bradley's lead reported that:

Seventy-one-year-old Joseph L. Hill has been through a lot during his last 32 years confined to a wheelchair, but he never expected to be robbed at knife-point while watching television at a nursing home.

The same principles might be applied to any type of story—to stories about the awarding of a scholarship, the celebration of an anniversary or retirement, the construction of a new school, the election of a mayor or the damage caused by a storm. A good reporter will always begin by obtaining as much information about a topic as possible. The reporter may interview witnesses, consult experts, visit the scene or examine some documents, always observing and recording details of even minor significance—details that will help readers understand the topic and make it more interesting.

To help you improve your newsgathering and writing techniques, the remainder of this chapter will discuss those techniques in more detail.

Writing More Clearly

When they hire new reporters, editors are most interested in finding people who have mastered the English language—people who understand the language's usage and treat it with respect. They want reporters who possess a knowledge of spelling and grammar, who have developed an extensive vocabulary and who have learned to write in a clear, interesting manner. Editors also want reporters who will respect their newspapers' deadlines, are able to conduct effective interviews and can type clean copy with reasonable speed.

As a first step, students entering the field of journalism must expand their vocabularies and learn to be more selective in their choice of words—to use words that are strong, descriptive, specific and interesting:

Firefighters had to make a hole in the roof to get at the flames.
REVISED: Firefighters used power saws to cut through the roof and reach the flames.

The children were done with the dessert.
REVISED: After using spoons to scoop out most of the ice cream, the two boys picked up their bowls and licked them clean.

Reporters must also be certain that they use each word properly; if they do not, they may confuse or irritate their readers:

> Police gave the youth to juvenile authorities.
> REVISED: Police transferred the youth to juvenile authorities.

> She received a limp.
> REVISED: She suffered a broken leg and now walks with a limp.

Related words and ideas should be placed as close together as possible. For example: modifiers should be kept close to the words they are intended to modify. If the words are separated, the sentences containing them will become more difficult to understand; the sentences' meaning may also be changed:

> The gunmen tied the victim and left him with his hands and feet taped and lying on the back seat.
> REVISED: The gunmen tied the victim and left him lying on the back seat, with his hands and feet taped.

> He is now trying to make a list of all the empty lots in the neighborhood to track down the owners and ask if he can plant them next summer.
> REVISED: Because he wants to plant all the empty lots in the neighborhood next summer, he is making a list of them and trying to track down their owners.

Placement errors of this type are particularly common in leads and often involve modifiers of time and place, as in the following examples:

> The police said today that Mr. Bush told them that he had strangled Miss Watson after stabbing her in a marshy, undeveloped area off Meade Avenue.

> A 62-year-old woman was convicted Monday of embezzling $143,000 in Circuit Court.

In the first example, the murderer obviously did not stab his victim "in a marshy, undeveloped area" of her body, as the sentence suggests, and the 62-year-old woman mentioned in the second example was convicted in Circuit Court—she did not embezzle the money there.

Other sentences and paragraphs are awkward and even nonsensical because reporters sometimes fail to express their ideas with clarity and precision:

> The campus police are open 24 hours a day.
> REVISED: The campus police station is open 24 hours a day.

> The kitchen of a local restaurant caught fire Tuesday but caused little damage.
> REVISED: A fire that started in the kitchen of a local restaurant Tuesday caused little damage.

Before it was rewritten, the sentence about the restaurant suggested that the kitchen, not the fire, caused the damage.

Like some of the examples above, sentences that are poorly worded or ambiguous often have double meanings. Readers consequently misinterpret the sentences, and reporters are embarrassed by their publication. The problem is not limited to newspapers; the following examples appeared in church bulletins:

> This being Easter Sunday, we will ask Mrs. Johnson to come forward and lay an egg on the altar.

> This afternoon there will be a meeting in the North and South ends of the church. Children will be baptized at both ends.

Because their meanings are often unclear, words such as "it," "this," "these," "those" and "that" should be used with caution. Reporters must be particularly careful to avoid starting a sentence or paragraph with one of these words unless its antecedent is obvious. To avoid unnecessary confusion, reporters can briefly repeat a key word or phrase or rewrite a foggy sentence to clarify its meaning:

> He said: "Only childless couples will be admitted, so there won't be any noise and the trailer park won't affect schools in the area. We expect the average trailer in the park to cost $30,000, and some will cost twice that much."
> Some members of the audience disagreed with this.
> REVISED: He said: "Only childless couples will be admitted, so there won't be any noise and the trailer park won't affect schools in the area. We expect the average trailer in the park to cost $30,000, and some will cost twice that much."
> Some members of the audience disagreed, saying the trailer park would be too noisy and would lower the value of property in the area.

> Commissioner Ben Benham, who represents Scott County on the Transit Authority, said the bus system is no longer losing money. He attributed this to the elimination of routes that had consistently shown losses.
> REVISED: Commissioner Ben Benham, who represents Scott County on the Transit Authority, said the bus system is no longer losing money because routes that had consistently shown losses have been eliminated.

For clarity, new stories should also be emphatic. Facts that are important should never be slipped into stories as minor clauses or phrases that receive little emphasis:

> James Loach admitted that he robbed Anders of $170 and said he tied the Vanguard Theater employee's hands with a rope, but he denied that he killed the son of Central High School Principal Robert Anders.
> REVISED: James Loach admitted that he robbed Anders of $170 and said he tied Anders' hands with a rope, but he denied that he killed the youth.
> Anders, the son of Central High School Principal Robert Anders, worked at the Vanguard Theater.

The first sentence began by mentioning Anders but later referred to "the Vanguard Theater employee" and to "the son of Central High School Principal Robert Anders." The sentence failed to clearly explain that Anders himself was the theater employee and the son of the high-school principal. At best, the inclusion of these facts was confusing. At worst, it was misleading, since readers might assume that the story was describing three different people.

Be Specific, Detailed and Thorough

Good writing is specific, and good writers fill their stories with illustrative details. Generalities are less interesting and a sign of hasty writing. To be specific, reporters must take more time and be more perceptive in gathering information and in presenting that information in their stories.

Reporters must avoid vague qualifiers, words such as "young" and "old," "big" and "little," "early" and "late," "high" and "low," "fast" and "slow." Other vague qualifiers include: "rather," "very," "much," "quickly," "awhile" and "a lot." Entire phrases may be too vague, as in the following examples:

at an early age	only recently
in a lot of pain	too time-consuming
for several years	within a short time
in her later years	traveled extensively
he rested for a while	never finished his formal education

What is "an early age," for example? Readers are forced to guess, and one reader might guess two months and another eight years. Similarly, one reader might assume that "a short time" means five minutes whereas another might assume that it means 10 days. And someone who "never finished his formal education" might have left school after the sixth grade or after his junior year of high school.

The following sentences also need to be rewritten because they are too vague and consequently fail to convey any meaningful information to their readers:

One of the men was short.	They traveled extensively.
Police were on the scene quickly.	He led a controversial life.
Many of the students were involved.	The loss was kept to a minimum.
The customers were very cooperative.	She attended school erratically.
The response to the exhibit was great.	The mayor instituted numerous reforms.

When more specific details are added to sentences, the sentences become more interesting, as well as clearer:

They said the land used to be cheap but now is at a premium.
REVISED: They said speculators bought the land for $320 an acre 10 years ago and are now selling it for an average of $6,800 an acre. A bank paid $42,000 an acre for a corner lot, and developers paid $48,000 an acre for the land needed to build a shopping center.

He had not traveled very far when his troubles began.
REVISED: The youth paid $3,795 for his first car, a 4-year-old convertible, and began to drive it home. A tire went flat 2 miles from the used car lot. The youth quickly changed the tire, but the brakes failed when he tried to stop at the next intersection. Two days later, the car's transmission failed.

The following generalities were written by students. The revisions contain more specific details that the students had included later in their stories:

He said local legislators responded very positively to the city's needs.
REVISED: He said local legislators agreed to help the city obtain state funds for the construction of a community college.

Several improvements have been made in order to make the weekly newspaper more interesting for its readers.
REVISED: To attract more readers, its three owners began to emphasize local issues, to publish more feature stories about interesting residents of the city and to write editorials about controversial topics.

Reporters who understand a topic sometimes forget that their readers know less about it than they do. Consequently, they sometimes fail to provide a clear explanation:

A reporter covering Indiana's U.S. senators devoted all the coverage to the senior senator because the senator had done a favor for the reporter concerning a drunken driving incident.
REVISED: Goligoski said the reporter for an Indiana newspaper was charged with drunken driving and put in a Washington, D.C. jail.
The senior senator from Indiana quietly arranged for the reporter's release, and the reporter began to publish a great many favorable stories about the senator.
"It was obvious that the reporter was paying back the favor," Goligoski said.

Before the paragraph was revised, it failed to explain the incident adequately. The paragraph mentioned "a favor" but did not specifically describe it. It also mentioned "a drunken driving incident" but failed to provide any meaningful information about that incident.

News stories should be so detailed and so thorough that all the questions readers might logically ask about their topic are answered. As pointed out in Chapter 4, reporters no longer attempt to answer six major questions in leads: "who," "how," "where," "why," "what" and "when." Nevertheless, the answers to all six questions should be presented somewhere in every story. Reporters must also answer all the questions raised by their stories' subtopics. Yet stories that contained the following statements failed to answer questions they obviously raise:

> She said the institution of marriage should be abolished. (Why?)

> She said women should not be given the same opportunities as men. (Why?)

> He was reluctant to reveal his name because the FBI had taken his photograph. (When? Where? Why?)

Sentences and paragraphs should be so thorough and phrased so clearly and specifically that they do not require any later explanation. Notice how easily the following sentences can be rewritten to clarify their meaning:

> Tipton remarked that he has never had a problem like this before.
> REVISED: Tipton said it is the first time he has been accused of shoplifting.

> The girl and her boyfriend tried to obtain a marriage license but were turned down because of the age requirements.
> REVISED: The girl and her boyfriend tried to obtain a marriage license but were turned down because neither is 17, the minimum age for marriages in the state.

Before they were revised, the first sentence vaguely referred to a "problem like this," and the second sentence mentioned "the age requirements." Neither sentence explained the terms' meaning.

The same problem arises when stories report that a topic was "mentioned" or "discussed." If a topic is important enough to be included in a news story, that topic should be fully explained. Stories should reveal what was said—the substance of the discussion—not just the fact that a discussion took place. The error appears often in leads but may arise anywhere in a news story:

> He said blood donors must be 17 to 65 years old. Also, he mentioned a checklist of diseases that a potential donor may not have had.
> REVISED: He said blood donors must be 17 to 65 years old. He added that the blood bank rejects donors who have had malaria, hepatitis, diabetes or venereal diseases.

> He also discussed the federal tax structure.
> REVISED: He said the federal tax structure places too heavy a burden on middle-income families.

As an alternative, you may be able to delete the portions of a sentence or quotation that are too vague:

> He said the county fair will feature 25 rides and various other activities.
> REVISED: He said the county fair will feature 25 rides.

> The YWCA counselor said, "We have 800 girls participating in the program, and it's meeting with a large measure of success."
> REVISED: The YWCA counselor said, "We have 800 girls participating in the program."

Mistakenly, beginners often end their stories with other generalities that mention rather than summarize the stories' least important details. Again, reporters and editors should delete those generalities:

In other action, the council discussed the cost of health insurance.

Before adjourning, the mayor expressed his gratitude for the community's support during his personal ordeal.

How can you tell whether a statement is too vague? Ask yourself: "Can readers understand it?" "Does it contain specific, concrete details that readers can visualize?" "Does the statement answer every question that readers are likely to ask about the topic?" If the answer to even one of those questions is no, the statement may have to be rewritten or eliminated.

Identify, Define and Explain

Reporters should never assume that their readers are already familiar with a topic. Newspapers may have published earlier stories about the topic, but not every reader will have seen those stories. Consequently, reporters must always identify, define and explain unfamiliar topics. The information should be expressed as simply and briefly as possible; often, it can be stated in a short phrase or sentence.

Reporters identify virtually all the people mentioned in news stories, and they usually present the identification the first or second time a person is mentioned. Readers should not be forced to guess a person's identity nor wait until the end of a story to learn who the person is. Newspapers identify most people by reporting their ages, occupations and addresses. However, they report specific street addresses only for the people who live in their communities. If someone lives outside the area in which a newspaper circulates, the paper will report only the person's hometown.

Reporters also use a variety of other descriptive phrases to identify the people mentioned in news stories. Military papers use soldiers' ranks, and college papers list students' years in school, majors and hometowns. Stories that mention a child usually identify the child's parents, since readers are more likely to know them. Other stories describe people's achievements, goals and physical characteristics.

If a title is short, reporters place it before a name. For example: "Sheriff Keith Kirby" or "Sen. Claire Valle." If reporters refer to the same person later in a story, they use only the person's last name; they do not repeat the title. If a title is longer, reporters place it after a name or in the following sentence:

Associate Superintendent for Planning and Government Relations Gordon Marinelli said Friday the school is unsafe.

REVISED: Gordon Marinelli, the associate superintendent for planning and government relations, said the school is unsafe.

Assistant Deputy Commander for District II Ralph Phillips said the American Legion's membership is declining.

REVISED: An American Legion official, Ralph Phillips, said the organization's membership is declining. Phillips is the assistant deputy commander for District II, which includes California, Arizona and New Mexico.

If a person has several titles, place no more than one before a name, regardless of how short the titles may be:

Dr. and Human Resources Committee chair Ruth Heebner said she opposes the fee.

REVISED: Dr. Ruth Heebner said she opposes the fee. Heebner chairs the Human Resources Committee.

Junior medical technology major and former Peace Corps volunteer Susan Glenn said she expects to graduate next June.

REVISED: Susan Glenn, a junior majoring in medical technology, said she expects to graduate next June. She served with the Peace Corps in Africa.

Reporters have several reasons for identifying so specifically the people mentioned in news stories. Because some sources are more believable than others, a source's identity may affect a news story's credibility. Some people are more interesting than others, and reporters may attract more readers if they identify a prominent or popular person involved in a story. Reporters also identify the people involved in news stories to protect the innocent from adverse publicity. Because it failed to adequately identify the man mentioned in several stories, a newspaper in Orlando, Fla., was forced to publish a separate story to exonerate an innocent bystander. The first stories reported that a man named Kenneth Bray was remodeling a famous hotel in the city and that the hotel would appeal to a homosexual clientele. Angry citizens began to call Kenneth Lee Bray, a U.S. probation officer living in Orlando, yet the hotel was owned by another man, Kenneth Edward Bray. The newspaper had failed to fully identify Kenneth Edward Bray—to report his middle name, age or address—in all its earlier stories.

In extreme cases, proper identification protects newspapers from libel suits. If newspapers report that a man named Ralph Ussery has been charged with rape, but fail to provide any further identification, the papers may libel every local resident named Ralph Ussery, and the Ralph Usserys who have not been charged with rape might sue the papers for libel. But if the newspapers report that Ralph Ussery, 47, of 481 Georgia Ave. has been charged with rape, they identify a single individual, the Ralph Ussery who is 47 years old and who lives at that address.

Reporters must also identify or define unfamiliar places and locations. They should try to avoid words that are not used in everyday conversation. When an unfamiliar word is necessary, reporters must immediately define it. Eileen Shanahan, who writes about business and financial matters for The New York Times, has been praised for her ability to explain unfamiliar concepts in elementary terms. When she used the term "reserve requirements" in a news story, she promptly explained that it means "the amount of money that banks must keep on hand to back up deposits." Similarly, when she used the phrase "poor liquidity position," she explained that it means "lack of ready cash."

Stories that fail to define unfamiliar terms may annoy as well as puzzle readers. A story about a 19-year-old football player who collapsed and died before a practice session at the University of South Carolina reported that he died of clinical terminal cardiac arrythmia. The story placed the term in quotation marks but failed to define it. Yet many readers would be interested in the death of a college football player and would wonder why an apparently healthy young athlete had died. Because the story failed to define the term, it failed to satisfy their curiosity about the cause of the young man's death.

Reporters can use any of several techniques to provide definitions or explanations. Reporters may quote the formal definition provided by a dictionary. Or they may define the term in a phrase or clause immediately following the term, setting it off with commas, dashes or parentheses:

Ralph and Suzanne Hargis, 1574 Carlton Drive, filed for bankruptcy under Chapter 13, which allows them to repay their creditors in monthly installments over a 3-year period.

About 800 foreign students at the university are on F-1 student visas—which means that they are allowed to stay in the United States only until their educations are complete.

Reporters can place a definition or explanation in a separate sentence following the sentence in which the term is used:

About half the addicts are on a methadone-maintenance program. Methadone is a synthetic narcotic used to break heroin addiction.

The major banks lowered their prime rate to 12.5 percent. The prime rate is the interest rate that banks charge their best customers.

Instead of using an unfamiliar term and then defining it, it's often better to eliminate the term and to use only the definition or explanation:

He wants to improve the student-teacher ratio to 1:18.
REVISED: He wants to provide one teacher for every 18 students.

She said the school will have K–6 facilities.
REVISED: She said the school will accept children from kindergarten through the sixth grade.

Another story reported that a new hospital had "138 private rooms, 72 semi-private rooms and 16 ICU/CCU units distributed over two patient floors." Most readers might know the difference between a private and a semi-private room. Some would not, however, and others would stumble over the terms "ICU/CCU" and "two patient floors." All four terms can easily be avoided:

The hospital has 138 rooms that contain one bed, 72 rooms that contain two beds, and 16 intensive-care and critical-care units. All rooms for patients are located on two floors.

Reporters using these techniques can make even the most complicated stories understandable for their readers. For example, after President Ronald Reagan was shot, Newsweek magazine provided this clear description of his treatment:

The first order of business was peritoneal lavage, a procedure to double-check for injuries in the abdominal cavity. Giordano [the surgeon] made a small incision under the navel and pumped a clear liquid into the abdomen. The liquid that drained back out seemed free of blood, showing that no organs had been damaged.

Similarly, an environmental reporter for the Arizona Daily Star in Tucson wrote about several wells contaminated by trichloroethylene. The topic was complex, yet reporter Jane Kay's stories were clear and dramatic. Kay explained that the chemical, also called "TCE," is an industrial degreaser that may cause cancer in humans. The wells contaminated by TCE were closed, and government officials assured people that their drinking water was safe. But after hundreds of interviews, Kay discovered that, "For 10 to 30 years, many southside Tucson residents unknowingly got minute quantities of TCE almost every time they turned on the water tap." As many as 20,000 people "drank TCE at home, inhaled it in the shower and absorbed it through their skin when they washed the dishes."
Kay explained that:

TCE is a tasteless, odorless, colorless—and very toxic—chemical. It is volatile, meaning that it evaporates quickly, much like common household cleaning fluids.
Only a teaspoon of it poured into 250,000 gallons of water—about the amount used by five people in an entire year—would create a taint slightly beyond the 5 parts per billion suggested as a guideline for safety by the state Department of Health Services.

Apparently as a result of the TCE contamination, residents of Tucson's southside suffered from an unusual number of serious illnesses, including cancer.

The Importance of Examples

Specific examples make stories more interesting, personalize them and help readers understand them more easily. If a city's property taxes rise 4.2 percent, reporters might explain that this increase means that the tax on an average home will rise $34.02 to a total of $884.02 a year. When the national debt passed $1 trillion, a story distributed by The Associated Press noted that:

> It's about $4,700 for every American man, woman and child. And it's such a big number that if someone were to count it out, one dollar every second, he would be 31,668 years old by the time he finished.

When pills contaminated by one-half part per million of mercury were recalled, The Associated Press explained that the fraction "is comparable, proportionately, to a jigger of vermouth in a tank car of gin." Similarly, if you wrote about a teen-ager who became an alcoholic and flunked out of college, you might describe specific examples of the problems she experienced:

> She said school became unimportant, adding that: "I can remember staying up all night before my public health final. When I took the test I was smashed. And if that wasn't bad enough, then I ran the entire 10 blocks back to my apartment so I could drink some more. Of course, I flunked public health."

Specific examples are especially important in stories about abstract issues. If you wrote about the lives of people who drop out of college, you would have to report the percentage of students who drop out of college nationally, their reasons for dropping out and what they do afterward: join the military, get married, find a job or enroll in another school. In addition to reporting the general trends, a good writer would illustrate the story by describing the lives of two or three dropouts—specific examples of the trend. Similarly, The New York Times began a story about the chemical contamination of fish by describing the story's impact on a single person:

> Sitting in his Fulton Fish Market office one morning, Abe Haymes swallowed his shot of scotch from a small paper cup, slapped his chest and declared:
> "I've been eating fish every day of the week for the past 40 years. Do I look sick?"
> Like the rest of the city's fish dealers, Abe Haymes is angry about recent publicity concerning mercury and DDT contamination of fish. . . .

Following the same style, Fortune magazine began a story about the interstate highway system by describing the system's impact on a single truck driver. Notice the story's use of specific details:

> Five days a week, Cecil Irvin swings up into the cab of his truck, carefully fits his sunglasses and leather gloves, and then starts the heavily loaded twin trailers behind him down the narrow streets of St. Louis.
> Six blocks later, he turns up a ramp leading to Interstate 70 and then, shifting up through 10 gears, he gradually picks up speed toward Kansas City.
> In Irvin's 250-mile trip westward, one sees in capsule form much of the impact, good and bad, of the $70 billion interstate highway system.

The following story, published by The Miami Herald, uses three examples to illustrate the impact of a paralyzing disease. Ironically, the disease was caused by a vaccination program intended to protect Americans from a dreaded strain of influenza:

> WASHINGTON—At first none of them believed anything significant was happening. Their fingers tingled because the weather was bad. They were "coming down with something." That's what caused the tender areas on their heads.
> Then the symptoms came with savage swiftness.
> • Judi Roberts of Lakeland, Fla., tried to wiggle her toes in a tight-fitting pair of sandals and found she couldn't feel them. She took off her shoes—and found she couldn't feel her feet.
> • Maryalice Beauton of Chula Vista, Calif., was eating a hamburger. Astonished, she realized she hadn't tasted anything.

• Herman Bauer of Pittsburgh was shopping with his wife when his legs began to buckle. Confused and embarrassed, he grabbed onto a wall and called for help.

They didn't know it yet, but for these people and hundreds of other Americans, the preliminary stages of a paralyzing disease known as Guillain-Barré syndrome had just begun. . . .

The Use of Description

Descriptions, like quotations, make stories more interesting and help readers visualize scenes more easily. But many reporters are reluctant to use descriptive phrases; they summarize whatever they hear but are less likely to describe what they see, feel, taste and smell. Typically, a student who attended a speech by a controversial priest handed her instructor a note that said:

> The question-and-answer period was very brief. Father Groppi answered only three questions because he had to catch a train because the State of Wisconsin would only let him leave Wisconsin for a brief time until the legal charges against him are settled.

Despite the unusual circumstances, the student failed to describe Father Groppi's legal problems and early departure in her story.

When students begin to use descriptive phrases, most rely too heavily on adverbs and adjectives. Verbs and nouns are more effective. Their impact is demonstrated in "The Death of Captain Waskow" by Ernie Pyle, a correspondent during World War II. The story describes the death of Henry T. Waskow, a popular company commander who was killed in Italy. Pyle won a Pulitzer Prize in 1944, with this among his entries:

> One soldier came and looked down, and he said out loud, "God damn it!" That's all he said, and then he walked away.
>
> Another one came, and he said, "God damn it, to hell, anyway." He looked down for a few last moments and then turned and left.
>
> Another man came. I think he was an officer. It was hard to tell officers from men in the dim light, for everybody was bearded and grimy. The man looked down into the dead captain's face and then spoke directly to him, as though he were alive, "I'm sorry, old man."
>
> Then a soldier came and stood beside the officer and bent over, and he too spoke to his dead captain, not a whisper but awfully tenderly, and he said, "I sure am sorry, sir."
>
> Then the first man squatted down, and he reached down and took the captain's hand and he sat there for a full five minutes holding the dead hand in his own and looking intently into the dead face. And he never uttered a sound all the time he sat there.
>
> Finally he put the hand down. He reached over and gently straightened the points of the captain's shirt collar, and then he sort of rearranged the tattered edges of the uniform around the wound, and then he got up and walked away down the road in the moonlight, all alone.
>
> *(Scripps-Howard Newspapers)*

Adverbs and adjectives are more opinionated than verbs and nouns, and are often redundant. After Pyle's description, there is no need to add that war is unfortunate, tragic, deadly or wasteful. Nor is there any reason to state that the men were upset or that they loved and respected the captain.

Another journalist, William L. Laurence, won two Pulitzer Prizes for his work at The New York Times. Laurence was aboard the plane that dropped an atomic bomb on Nagasaki during World War II, and he wrote a story that contained this description of that event:

> Captain Bock swung around to get out of range; but even though we were turning away in the opposite direction, and despite the fact that it was broad daylight in our cabin, all of us became aware of a giant flash that broke through the dark barrier of our arc welder's lenses and flooded our cabin with intense light.

We removed our glasses after the first flash, but the light still lingered on, a bluish-green light that illuminated the entire sky all around. A tremendous blast wave struck our ship and made it tremble from nose to tail. This was followed by four more blasts in rapid succession, each resounding like the boom of cannon fire hitting our plane from all directions.

Observers in the tail of our ship saw a giant ball of fire rise as though from the bowels of the earth, belching forth enormous white smoke rings. Next they saw a giant pillar of purple fire, ten thousand feet high, shooting skyward with enormous speed.

Reporters who want to describe an object must learn to use concrete, factual details as opposed to trite generalities. When a black man and his white wife applied for an apartment, a journalism student reported that the rental agent "seemed nervous," yet in her story the student failed to provide any facts to support her conclusion. Later, she explained in class that the rental agent lit a cigarette, tapped a pencil against her desk, began to speak more rapidly and frequently repeated herself after the couple entered her office. The rental agent also insisted that she had no vacancies.

The following sentences, written by students who were asked to describe their campus, are also too vague:

The library casts a knowledgeable shadow.

The art complex appears to be a temporary structure.

Here man has altered nature, but he has not destroyed it.

The campus is a lesson in harmony between man and his natural surroundings.

The students seemed relaxed as they studied under the trees on the large lawn.

Most of the buildings have few windows. Those few windows are small and cleverly designed.

The first sentence presents an opinion rather than a verifiable fact; it's also absurd. How can a shadow be "knowledgeable"? The second sentence calls the art complex "a temporary structure" but fails to explain why the reporter reached that conclusion. Another sentence concludes that students studying beneath some trees "seemed relaxed" but fails to provide any specific details to support that observation. The same sentence refers to a "large lawn" but never estimates its exact size.

To be effective, description must be so factual and detailed that readers can visualize the scene in their minds:

VAGUE: A 6-foot fence surrounds the construction site.
BETTER: The construction site is surrounded by a 6-foot chain-link fence topped by three strands of barbed wire.

VAGUE: There were about 50 men working in the area.
BETTER: About 50 men were working in the area, and most wore hard hats, some yellow, some white and others red. Four of the men had tied nail pouches around their waists. Others smoked cigarettes and looked weary in their dirty white T-shirts, jeans and sunglasses.

The same problems arise when reporters attempt to describe other people. Instead of presenting factual details, some reporters mistakenly present generalities or their personal impressions of those people's appearance and character, as in the following (often contradictory) examples, written about a man and a woman:

He spoke with authority.	Her eyes lit up.
He gave a cool, casual speech.	Her face has a healthy glow.
He was frank about his duties.	She is a very animated speaker.
He appeared comfortable and relaxed.	Kay gestured freely with both hands.
He appeared unprepared for the occasion.	There was an awkwardness to her appearance.
He immediately took control of the situation.	She seemed to enjoy talking about her work.

None of these sentences is an actual description. The first sentence concludes that the man spoke "with authority" but fails to explain why the writer reached that conclusion. The second sentence reports that he gave a "cool and casual" speech but does not specifically describe either the speaker or his speech.

Generalities are often inconsistent. One student reported that a woman "seemed relaxed and very sure of herself." Everything about her "conveyed calmness." Yet another student concluded that, "She seemed nervous, perhaps embarrassed." The students could have avoided the problem by reporting specific details as opposed to their impressions, opinions and conclusions.

Reporters must learn to observe and describe specific details, including a person's height, weight, age, clothing, voice, mannerisms, facial expressions, hair, glasses, jewelry, posture, gestures, family and surroundings. Each factor can be described in detail; for example, a reporter describing a person's hair might mention its color, length, thickness, neatness and style. Thus, when you are asked to describe another person, look at the person carefully, then report specific facts about that person. Avoid generalities and conclusions:

> VAGUE: He is a large man.
> BETTER: He is 6 feet tall and weighs 210 pounds.

> VAGUE: Butler was dressed casually.
> BETTER: Butler was dressed in a maroon shirt that was left unbuttoned near the collar, striped pants and black shoes. He wore no jewelry, not even a watch or ring.

Reporters can include a descriptive word or phrase almost anywhere in a news story, or they can devote an entire sentence or paragraph to description:

> The audience applauded Galbraith, a tall, gray-haired man.

> Mrs. Ambrose, a former newspaper editor, arrived breathless and five minutes late for her speech.

> He leaned back in his chair, laced his fingers together across his round belly and clenched the cigar in the corner of his mouth.

> They sat across the table from each other. The girl, who had long, blonde hair, picked at her hamburger, tearing it into bite-sized bits. Her boyfriend, who was wearing a gold shirt and brown shorts, was nibbling french fries from a bag.

> She is 70 years old, but her thick brown hair is only slightly graying. As she spoke, she leaned back on a pillow and nervously smoked a cigarette. She has only a small table and a cot in her living room, and both are covered with knickknacks. She takes her guests into her bedroom to sit and talk.

Study the following examples. Both help reveal the character of the people they describe. The first example, reprinted from The Miami Herald, describes a 79-year-old city commissioner. The second example, reprinted from the Louisville Times, describes the mayor of Louisville. An editor who praised the second example explained that: "Those details paint a picture. They show the reader Harvey Sloane. They add life and meaning."

> She has white hair, red lips, clip-on earrings, good manners and a dog named Muffy. She sews, has arthritis, says "dear," and points her finger when she talks.

> He wore Nike running shoes, mud-splattered pants and the Santa-red parka that's been his insignia since his walk to win election as mayor of Louisville. . . .
> Sloane is physically slight. His dark hair is lightly streaked with gray. He is about 45 but looks younger. He is a millionaire by inheritance. He jogs. He has three little children, a chic wife and a classy renovated home in Old Louisville staffed with servants.

The Use of Humor

Editors constantly look for humorous stories and often place those stories on Page 1. But for most writers, humorous stories are particularly difficult to write. Reporters should not try to inject humor into stories that are not obviously humorous. If a story is funny, the humor should be apparent from the facts themselves. Reporters should not have to exaggerate or point out the humor by labeling it "funny" or "comical." Author and economist John Kenneth Galbraith has explained: "Humor is an intensely personal, largely internal thing. What pleases some, including the source, does not please others." Thus, although some people may laugh at a story, others are likely to see nothing funny in it.

When columnist James J. Kilpatrick wrote an article about conservative William Buckley, he did more than report that Buckley "had a good sense of humor." He gave a specific example of Buckley's wit. Kilpatrick reported that Buckley had once run for mayor of New York City and, when asked what he would do if he won, replied, "Ask for a recount."

Similarly, a story about the peculiar laws still in effect in some cities never called the laws "peculiar" or "funny." Instead, it simply listed them so that readers could judge the humor of the laws for themselves. The laws made it illegal to:

Hire a neighbor's cook
Take a cow on a school bus
Allow a fly into a motel room
Roll a barrel down a city street
Take a bath without a bathing suit
Break more than three dishes in a single day
Ride a horse that had not been equipped with a horn and taillight

Try to include some humor in your stories when appropriate, but remember that understatement is more effective than exaggeration. Simply report the facts that you think are humorous, then hope that your readers will laugh.

Newswriting Habits to Avoid

Avoid Stating the Obvious

Dull, trite remarks are called "platitudes," and reporters must learn to avoid them. News stories should not state obvious facts that readers already know. Reporters who write about a serious automobile accident do not have to say "police were called to the scene," since the police routinely respond to serious accidents, and that fact is common knowledge. Other platitudes that have appeared in news stories include:

As it has in most areas of modern life, science has entered the profession of firefighting in recent years.

Superhighways, high-speed automobiles and jet planes are common objects of the modern era.

The second example appeared in a story about technological changes that occurred during the life of a 100-year-old woman. The sentence would have been more interesting if it had described the changes in more specific detail and clearly related them to the woman's life, such as:

Mrs. Hansen, who once spent six days on a train to visit relatives in California, now flies to California in five hours every Christmas.

A student writing about attempts to control the birth rate of pigeons began the story this way:

Pigeons are common in large cities and even in small towns across the country. They are social birds and establish stable communities.

It seems acceptable that they are social and stable. However, citizens are annoyed by the messiness of pigeons and would rather not have so many around.

A more interesting lead would have avoided the obvious—the fact that pigeons are common and messy—and immediately emphasized the latest developments and main point of the story:

Cities are experimenting with the use of drugs to prevent pigeons from breeding.

Other students have included these platitudes in their stories:

Counselors help students with their problems.

The mayor said he was pleased by the warm reception.

The sponsors hope the art show will attract a large crowd.

She said she is looking forward to the challenge of her new job.

The principal said he has a staff of hard-working, dedicated teachers.

The university is constantly changing to meet the needs of its students.

The car's driver said he was relieved that the two girls he struck were not seriously injured.

The sources in these stories stated the obvious and said what they were expected to say. Their statements sound familiar because these platitudes have been used before, perhaps millions of times.

Other platitudes appear in direct quotations. However, that does not justify their use. Such dull quotes should be deleted:

The newly-elected mayor said, "I hope to do a good job."

A secretary said, "My boss is very kind and hard-working."

The athlete said, "I owe a lot of my success to my father and my coach."

The committee chairman said, "Homecoming is going to be big and exciting."

The teacher said, "My students are a great bunch of kids and have a lot of enthusiasm."

When people stop reading a story, they rarely think about the reasons why it bored them. If people re-examined the story, they might find not just one, but a series of the platitudes. The following platitudes (and a half-dozen others) appeared in an interview with a football coach:

"College is a great experience—an education," Coach Smith said. "Everybody should have the opportunity to experience college life."

Smith added that it is important for a person to go to college and learn how to interact with other people, even if he does not pass all his courses.

Even if some athletes do not get a degree, Smith said, they will still learn a lot on a college campus.

To avoid platitudes, reporters must be more alert, particularly when conducting interviews. Sources often give obvious, commonplace answers to the questions they are asked. If a bartender is robbed at gunpoint, there is no reason to quote him as saying that he "was scared." Most people confronted by gunmen are scared, and they often say so. If reporters wanted to quote the bartender—or any other source—they would have to ask more penetrating questions and to continue their interview until they received more specific, interesting or unusual details.

Avoid Slang and Clichés

Because they eliminate the need for thought, clichés have been called the greatest labor-saving devices ever invented. Clichés are words or phrases that we have heard before and copied. Many are 200 or 300 years old—so old and so overused that they have lost their original impact and meaning. They no longer startle, amuse or interest the public.

People use clichés automatically, without thinking. Journalists use them as short-cuts or crutches when they do not have enough time (or talent) to be more specific, descriptive or original. A writer for the Chicago Tribune has explained that, "Intelligent men and women working under intense time pressures often have to grab for any metaphor that comes to mind, stale or not."

Journalists may write that a fire "swept through" a building, that an explosion "rocked" a city, that rescue workers "sifted through the rubble" or that a judge "handed down" a decision. Or they may write that a major storm "left a trail of death and destruction"—a cliché so general and so vague that it could be used to describe hundreds of blizzards, hurricanes, thunderstorms and tornadoes every year. More capable writers might observe and describe specific or unique details about the storm's passage and consequences.

Other clichés exaggerate. Despite the clichés, few people are "blind as a bat," "cool as a cucumber," "light as a feather," "neat as a pin," "straight as an arrow," "thin as a rail" or "white as a sheet."

Political journalists often report that candidates are nominated in "smoke-filled rooms," then "test the waters" before they "toss their hats into the ring." The candidates launch "whirlwind campaigns" and "hammer away" at their opponents, usually in an attempt to "win the public's support" and to "take over the reins of government." Some candidates "straddle the fence" on "burning issues of the day," but few are willing to "give up without a fight."

Editors may accept an occasional cliché. But stories that contain several clichés sound old and stale. The clichés should be replaced by more specific details:

> He said the store's financial losses are a thing of the past.
> REVISED: He said the store is no longer losing money.

> A picnic ended in tragedy Sunday for two university students.
> REVISED: Two university students drowned Sunday afternoon while swimming to a boat anchored 150 feet from shore.

Other clichés that journalists should recognize and avoid appear in the box on the following page.

Journalists also avoid slang, which tends to be more faddish than clichés. Slang may be used occasionally in feature stories and personality profiles, but it is inappropriate and annoying in straight news stories. Moreover, a slang word may baffle readers, since not everyone understands its meaning. And slang rapidly becomes dated, so that a slang term used in a story may already be obsolete.

Clichés

There are thousands of clichés and slang phrases that reporters must learn to recognize and avoid. Some of the most common are listed here.

a keen mind
ambulance rushed
around the clock
arrived at the scene
at long last
at this point in time
baptism of fire
bare minimum
beginning a new life
behind the wheel
benefit of the doubt
bigger and better
blanket of snow
blessing in disguise
called to the scene
calm before the storm
came to their rescue
came to rest
came under attack
came under fire
cast aside
caught red-handed
clear-cut issue
colorful scene
complete stranger
complete success
coveted title
crystal clear
dead and buried
decide the fate
devoured by flames
dime a dozen
doomed to failure
dread disease
dream come true
drop in the bucket
dying breed
erupted in violence
escaped death
exchanged gunfire
faced an uphill battle
fell on deaf ears

few and far between
foreseeable future
gained ground
gave it their blessing
get a good look
go to the polls
got off to a good start
grief-stricken
ground to a halt
hail of bullets
heated argument
heed the warning
high-speed chase
hits the spot
in his new position
in the wake of
landed the job
last but not least
last-ditch stand
left their mark
leveled an attack
limped into port
line of fire
lingering illness
lodge a complaint
lucky to be alive
made off with
made their escape
made their way home
miraculous escape
Mother Nature
necessary evil
never a dull moment
no relief in sight
notified next of kin
once in a lifetime
one step closer
only time will tell
opened fire
paved the way
pillar of strength
pinpointed the cause

pitched battle
police dragnet
pose a challenge
proud parents
proves conclusively
pushed for legislation
quick thinking
real challenge
reign of terror
see-saw battle
set to work
smell a rat
sped to the scene
spread like wildfire
start their mission
still at large
stranger than fiction
strike a nerve
sudden death
sweep under the rug
take it easy
talk is cheap
tempers flared
time will tell
tip of the iceberg
tipped the scales
took its toll
too late to turn back
tower of strength
tracked down
traveled the globe
tried their luck
under siege
under their noses
undertaking a study
up in the air
view with alarm
went to great lengths
won a reputation
word of caution
words of wisdom
word to the wise

Since the war in Vietnam, politicians—and reporters—have worried that if one country falls "under the communist yoke," its neighbors will do likewise, toppling "like dominoes." Broadcasters, borrowing from comedians, often announce that they have "some good news and some bad news." Broadcasters criticized for reporting too much bad news often respond that Americans "blame the messengers" for the bad news they deliver.

In recent years young people have abused such terms as "cool," "freaked out," "heavy," "like" and "you know" until they became clichés. Likewise, young people complain that they are unable to "get it together" and do not know "where they are at," yet they want to "tell it like it is." They also want "a piece of the action" and admire people who are "mellow," "laid back" and able to "go with the flow."

In short, journalists must guard against slang as well as clichés:

The youths trashed a school.
REVISED: The youths vandalized a school.

The women said they had been ripped off.
REVISED: The women said two girls had stolen their purses.

Inflation will be the hardest nut to crack.
REVISED: Inflation will be the most difficult problem to solve.

Avoid Euphemisms

Reporters avoid "euphemisms," vague expressions used in place of harsher, more offensive terms. Euphemisms enable people to avoid words that seem rude, tasteless, embarrassing or ugly. Prudishly, Americans often say that a woman is "expecting" rather than "pregnant," and that they have to "go to the bathroom" rather than "go to the toilet" or, even more candidly, to urinate or defecate.

Americans also use euphemisms in talking about death. Many say that a friend or relative has "passed on" or is "no longer with us," not that their friend or relative has died and been buried. Funeral directors object to being called morticians—which itself was originally a euphemism for "undertakers." While talking to a dead person's family, the funeral directors refer to the dead body as "the deceased" or "the loved one" and offer to incinerate (never to "burn") the remains (never the "corpse") in a crematorium (never a "furnace").

Similarly, Americans rarely have their unwanted or dying pets killed. Instead, they have the animals "put to sleep." Even hunters now "harvest" rather than kill deer and other game animals.

Airlines use another set of euphemisms before every takeoff. Flight attendants demonstrate the use of oxygen masks that will pop from a plane's ceiling "in case of need." Attendants also demonstrate the use of life jackets hidden under each seat and point out the location of emergency exits. They explain that all the gadgets are there "for passenger comfort," never because the plane might crash.

Americans seem reluctant to speak candidly or to use unpleasant labels for individuals or groups within our society:

Americans are not old. Instead, they are senior citizens, the aged, the elderly, retirees or golden-agers.

Americans are not poor. Instead, they are indigent, underprivileged, financially disadvantaged or culturally deprived.

Americans are not fat. Instead, they are heavy, stocky, plump or (in extreme cases) obese. Other Americans may be lean or slender, but rarely skinny or scrawny.

Americans are not dumb. Instead, they are exceptional, slow learners or academic underachievers.

Americans are not fired from their jobs. Instead, they are dehired, de-employed, terminated, furloughed or phased out.

Americans do not live in slums or ghettos. Instead, they live in substandard housing, inner cities, central cities or depressed areas.

Teachers in the public schools of Cheyenne, Wyo., have been told to be more tactful while criticizing their students. Instead of saying a student is a bully, the teachers have been urged to write that the student has "qualities of leadership but needs help in learning how to use them democratically." A student who lies has "difficulty in distinguishing between imaginary and factual circumstances," and a noisy student needs "to develop quieter habits of communication."

Other examples of euphemisms include Americans' use of "donkey" for "ass," "intestinal fortitude" for "guts" and "affirmative action" for "minority hiring."

Some of the prestigious titles that Americans are giving themselves also seem to be euphemisms. Garbagemen call themselves "sanitation workers," prison guards have become "corrections officers" and dogcatchers have become "animal welfare officers." Barbers have become "hair stylists" and salespeople have become "account executives."

Still other euphemisms help businesses enhance their images and the images of products and services they offer the public. They sell "pre-owned" rather than used cars and report their "retained income" rather than their profits. The U.S. Department of Agriculture recently began to permit the sale of hot dogs, bologna and other processed meats containing small bits of bone. However, meat processors did not want to report that their products contain "ground bone." Instead, their labels now report the amount of calcium in an average serving.

The armed forces use many euphemisms. Nuclear weapons aimed at the Soviet Union are called "Peacekeeper missiles." Armies no longer retreat. Instead, they move to the rear, engage in a strategic withdrawal or occupy new territory in accordance with plan. The government of Argentina never admitted that its armed forces in the Falkland Islands were defeated by the British. To avoid words like "surrender," the Argentine government reported a "cease-fire" and "withdrawal."

Journalists call euphemisms "weasel words." Nevertheless, some journalists still use them in news stories. Moreover, journalists have created some euphemisms of their own. Apparently because it would be too unpopular, journalists rarely called presidents Lyndon Johnson and Richard Nixon liars, although both did lie. Instead, journalists reported a White House "credibility gap." The large chains that own several newspapers call themselves "groups." And editors who give free papers to the public call their publications "controlled-circulation newspapers," not shoppers or throwaways.

Avoid Technical Language and Jargon

Reporters must learn to avoid technical language and jargon. Critics call such language gobbledygook, bafflegab, doublespeak, legalese and bureaucratese. Most jargon is abstract, wordy, repetitious and confusing. It is often used to impress or to confuse rather than to inform the public.

The Occupational Safety and Health Administration defined a stairwell as "that portion of a means of egress which is separated from all other spaces of the building or structure by construction or equipment as required in the sub-part to provide a protected way of travel to the exit discharge." Similarly, a recent government report warned that, "There exists at the intersection a traffic condition which constitutes an intolerable, dangerous hazard to the health and safety of property and persons utilizing such intersection for pedestrian and vehicular movement." A good journalist could summarize this statement in four words: "The intersection is dangerous."

Americans expect teachers to set a good example and to show their students how to write more clearly and accurately. But even teachers use jargon. Some teachers call themselves "educators" or "instructional units." Desks have become "pupil stations," and libraries have become "instructional resource centers." A principal in Houston reportedly sent this note home to parents: "Our school's cross-graded, multi-ethnic, individualized learning program is designed to enhance the concept of an open-ended learning program with emphasis on a continuum of multi-ethnic, academically enriched learning using the identified intellectually gifted child as the agent or director of his own learning."

People using such jargon seem pompous. They use long, weighty words that make everything (especially themselves) seem more important. Other examples include:

"subsequently" instead of "later"
"in the near future" instead of "soon"
"in view of the fact that" instead of "because"
"eliminate the possibility of" instead of "prevent"
"ingress" and "egress" instead of "entrance" and "exit"

Readers can usually decipher the writers' meaning—but not easily:

Classic democratic theory holds that voting is the most common behavioral manifestation of a citizen's interest in politics.

All interviews were prefaced with the interviewer inquiring as to whether or not the respondent was at least 18 years of age. In the event that the respondent was not 18 years of age, he or she was thanked and the interviewer then proceeded to initiate another randomly placed telephone call.

Other bits of jargon are almost impossible to understand:

A workshop on Situational Leadership is being offered to administrators on Oct. 9 and 10. Participants will learn to diagnose the demands of a situation and determine the amount of task behavior and relationship behavior required to address the needs of the worksite.

You may also recognize the following, currently fashionable words and phrases—but be unable to explain what they mean:

ballpark figure	infrastructure	role model
bottom line	input	role playing
cognitive	interface	scenario
conceptualize	maximize	state of the art
effectuate	ongoing	surrogate
dialogue	optimize	thrust
feedback	parameter	viability
finalize	prioritize	zero growth

Play with these 24 words, using any five or six of them in a single sentence. They may sound meaningful at first, but they are gibberish:

The thrust of role playing will help conceptualize the feedback.

Their scenario calls for optimizing and prioritizing the variables to interface the parameters.

Technical language is appropriate in some specialized publications written for experts in a particular field. But it is not appropriate in newspapers written for a mass audience. Reporters' jobs are difficult because they obtain information from many different sources: doctors, lawyers, business people, press releases, technical reports, and police and court records. Many of those sources use jargon, and reporters must learn to recognize and avoid it. Good reporters reword their stories in everyday terms that readers can easily understand. Unfortunately, some reporters fail. The following sentence recently appeared in the Deseret (Salt Lake City) News. The second example was written by a student:

> The superintendent said the district has made a number of changes to accommodate constructive input and will remain in a dynamic state to respond to its constituency, for that is the posture of the administration and board of education.

> The City Council Tuesday endorsed the proposed planned-development zoning category with almost no minimum requirements and no specific examples.

The second story also mentioned "the city's growth management plan," "the first conceptual meeting," "an optional conceptual approval meeting" and "a site plan model." Few readers would understand any of that jargon.

Most jargon can easily be eliminated or rewritten:

> JARGON: The official said Montana may be in non-compliance with the federal guidelines.
> REVISED: The official said Montana may be violating the federal guidelines.

> JARGON: Police said two male subjects gained entrance to the house by breaking a window.
> REVISED: Police said two men entered the house by breaking a window.

> JARGON: Dr. Stewart McKay said, "Ethnic groups that subsist on a vegetarian diet and practically no meat products seem to have a much lower level of serum cholesterol and a very low incidence of ischemic diseases arising from atherosclerotic disease."
> REVISED: Dr. Stewart McKay said races that eat few meats have low rates of coronary heart attacks and related illnesses.

If the jargon appears in a lead, look for clearer and more specific details that would be more likely to interest your readers. Often, they appear in a later paragraph:

> Bit by bit, elementary schools are incorporating computers into their classroom curricula as auxiliary learning tols.
> REVISED: Elementary schools are using computers to help their students overcome weaknesses in grammar, punctuation, spelling and arithmetic.

> A proposal to rezone 722 acres for use as a planned unit development has been placed on the agenda of the County Commission's work session.
> REVISED: County commissioners will review plans for a 722-acre development that will house 2,000 families and provide land for an elementary school, an 18-hole golf course and four parks, each with its own tennis courts and swimming pool.

Journalists are not the only Americans concerned about the problem of jargon. Secretary of Commerce Malcolm Baldrige, a one-time cowboy, argued for plain talk in the federal government. Baldrige said he wanted lean sentences with active verbs, and fewer unnecessary adjectives. To enforce that edict, he had word processors fixed to discourage the use of more than 40 objectionable words and phrases. If someone tried to use them, the processors stopped and flashed, "Don't Use This Word" on their television-like screens. The forbidden words and phrases included:

I share your concern	as you are aware	however
contingent upon	as you know	image
effectuated	at the present time	input
inappropriate	best wishes	institutionalize
management regime	bottom line	interface
mutually beneficial	delighted	it is my intention
responsive	different than	maximize
specificity	enclosed herewith	meanwhile

thrust	finalize	more importantly
utilize	glad	needless to say
I would hope	great majority	new initiatives
I would like to express	happy	ongoing
my appreciation	hereinafter	orient
as I am sure you know	hopefully	parameter
personally	share	to optimize
reviewed	subject matter	untimely death
prior to	therein	very much
prioritized	to impact	viable
serious crisis		

Avoid Gush

Reporters also avoid "gush"—writing with exaggerated enthusiasm. They write news stories to inform their readers, not to please their sources. Thus, news stories should report useful information. They should not praise nor advocate.

Because it is fast and easy, too many reporters obtain all their information from a single source, often an official responsible for the issue being discussed. Officials try to use reporters. They would be foolish not to. Few officials are foolish enough to criticize their own programs. Instead, most try to impress or manipulate reporters in an attempt to obtain more favorable publicity, and often they succeed. They reveal only the information that makes them, their policies and their institutions look good.

To avoid this problem, reporters must talk to several sources to obtain a variety of viewpoints and to verify statements made by officials. Reporters must also prepare for each interview so that they can ask more knowledgeable questions and recognize evasive responses. Perhaps even more important, reporters must learn to ask for more specific details that support the officials' claims. The following statements lack those details and consequently enable the officials to engage in self-praise:

"Our program is very respected and well-run," the director said.

"We feel we are providing quality recreational programs for both adults and children," Holden said.

Police Chief Martin Guidema said the city's mounted horse patrol, which began one year ago, has become a great success.

When a reporter finishes an article, it should sound like a news story, not a press release. One travel story gushed that Mexico is "a land of lush valleys and marvelous people." Another story reported that some films "are in great demand, and the school is fortunate in being able to offer them to the community." Other examples of gush include:

The fair will offer bigger and better attractions than ever before.

The event will provide fun and surprises for everyone who attends.

Free beer will be provided, along with contests and games that will add to the excitement.

This gush cannot be rewritten because there is nothing of substance to rewrite. It should simply be deleted.

Avoid Journalese

Critics accuse reporters who abuse the language of writing "journalese." The critics charge that reporters have developed their own vocabulary, and that the vocabulary distorts, dramatizes and exaggerates. News stories describe fires that "rage," temperatures that "soar," earthquakes that "rumble" and people who "vow." Any new activity is "kicked off." Rivers "go on a rampage." Opponents are "hit" and proposals "killed."

Other reporters write that:

The program is geared toward college students.

The auditorium is tagged for demolition next fall.

Officials gave the go-ahead to the city's upcoming plans.

Journalese is especially common on sports pages. Because it would be too repetitive, writers are reluctant to report that a team "won" its game. Instead (especially in headlines) they report that one team "ambushed" another. Or, sportswriters may use words like "blanked," "blitzed," "bombed," "clobbered," "crushed," "doomed," "flattened," "humbled," "marched," "mauled," "nabbed," "nipped," "outlasted," "outscored," "overpowered," "ripped," "romped," "routed," "scorched," "shocked," "slammed," "slugged," "smothered," "spoiled," "stung," "stunned," "swamped," "thrashed," "topped," "toppled," "trampled," "tripped," "walloped" or "whipped."

Critics of journalese also mention the other problems discussed in this chapter: journalists' grammatical and vocabulary errors, misplaced modifiers, double meanings, clichés and jargon. In short, they consider journalese a fast, sloppy, careless use of the language.

Avoid Vague Time References and the Present Tense

Unless your instructor suggests otherwise, do not use the words "yesterday," "today" and "tomorrow" in news stories; you are too likely to mislead your readers. Instead, use the specific days of the week: "Sunday," "Monday," "Tuesday" and so forth. Many of the stories that appear in newspapers are written the day before their publication or even earlier. For example, the reporters employed by morning papers often work from about 2 until 11 p.m. and, if a fire destroyed a home at 5 p.m. Tuesday, the reporters would write a story about the fire later Tuesday night. The reporters could not say the fire occurred "today" because readers who received the papers Wednesday morning would assume that "today" meant that day—Wednesday. Thus, even though the fire occurred on Tuesday and reporters wrote the story on Tuesday, they would have to tell readers the fire occurred "yesterday." To avoid the confusion and errors that invariably arise, always use the name of the day of the week instead of "today," "yesterday" and "tomorrow." Because it is too vague, reporters avoid the word "recently."

Because many of the events that newspapers report end before readers receive the papers, newswriters also avoid the present tense and terms such as "at the present time." Even though it is true, a reporter working at deadline should not say, "A fire at the Grand Hotel threatens to destroy the entire block." Firefighters would almost certainly extinguish the blaze before readers received the paper hours later. For the same reason, a reporter covering a fatal accident should not say, "The victim's identity is not known." Police might learn the victim's identity in a few hours, and local radio and television stations might broadcast the person's name before subscribers received their papers. Consequently, reporters must use the past tense, clearly indicating that the situations they are describing existed at some time in the past:

A fire at the Grand Hotel threatens to destroy the entire block.
REVISED: At 11:30 p.m. Tuesday, a fire at the Grand Hotel was still threatening to destroy the entire block.

The victim's identity is not known.
REVISED: Police were unable to learn the victim's identity immediately.

Other Problems to Avoid

Reporters also avoid exaggeration, excessive punctuation and contrived labels. Exaggeration in news stories is artificial, wordy and ineffective. It also tends to be trite and to state the obvious. There is no need to report that an explosion was "violent," that a murder was "brutal" or that an ambulance "rushed" someone to a hospital. The adjectives waste newspapers' space and readers' time.

Sweeping generalizations, another form of exaggeration, are impossible to verify and often wrong. Consequently, few good reporters will claim that everyone in a community considers an issue important, that everyone mourns the death of a prominent person or that everyone is celebrating a holiday.

Reporters avoid excessive punctuation, particularly exclamation points and parentheses. Exclamation points are rarely necessary and should never be used after every sentence in a story, regardless of that story's importance. Reporters avoid parenthetical matter because it creates an obstacle that makes reading more difficult. Parentheses interrupt the flow of ideas and force readers to pause and assimilate some additional, often jarring bits of information.

Some students attach their own labels to subjects, yet most of those labels are unnecessary, opinionated and awkward. Many are also ridiculous. One writer referred to a young girl with an unusual illness as "the diseased student." Other students have referred to "a preliminary plant plan," "a two-motorcycle, three-person accident" and "the county's school bond-financed building program." If a label is so artificial that you have never heard or used it before, and would not use it in a conversation with friends, do not use it in a news story.

Thus, the following labels also are unnecessary and inappropriate:

apathetic students	the well-patrolled parking lot
mysterious break-in	a tentatively approved program
ambitious sneak thief	an estimated $3.6-million building
daring daylight robbery	the newly named university annual fund
unpleasant experience	drive committee

The labels—also called "false titles"—often appear as a jumble of modifiers piled before a name:

Twenty-year-old Seminole Junior College business major Nina Thomas won the $5,000 prize.
REVISED: Nina Thomas, a 20-year-old business major at Seminole Junior College, won the $5,000 prize.

The German measles vaccination program aimed at adolescent girls will begin Monday.
REVISED: A vaccination program intended to protect adolescent girls from German measles will begin Monday.

The labels are even more difficult to understand when reporters try to use their possessive forms:

The fleeing 22-year-old robbery suspect's red sports car was found abandoned near his home.
REVISED: The 22-year-old robbery suspect fled, and police found his red sports car abandoned near his home.

The American Association of Political Scientists' annual summer convention will be held in San Diego.
REVISED: The American Association of Political Scientists will hold its annual summer convention in San Diego.

Some Final Guidelines

1. Before you begin to write a news story, prepare an outline. Decide which facts are most important and decide how you want to organize those facts. Also plan the transitions between those facts and the point at which you want to end the story.

2. Place the information you want to emphasize at the beginning or end of a sentence. Avoid burying it in the middle of a sentence, since it receives less emphasis there. Because readers are most likely to remember whatever they saw last, many experts believe that information placed at the end of a sentence is likely to have the greatest impact on readers.

3. Use the articles "a," "an" and "the" correctly. The words "a" and "an" are indefinite articles, used to refer to one member of a broad category or class of objects (for example, "They want to buy a table"). The word "the" is a definite article, used to refer to a specific person or object (for example, "That is the table they want to buy"). As a general rule, you should use an indefinite article in referring to a person or object that has not been mentioned earlier in a story. Use the definite article in referring to a person or object that has been mentioned earlier in a story—when you are referring to a specific object, one that your readers are already familiar with (the person or the object mentioned earlier).

If it is misused, the definite article may mislead readers, since it often suggests that the object being referred to is the only such object in existence. If a story reports that three people were taken to "the hospital," yet the story has not mentioned the hospital previously, the sentence implies that the area has only one hospital, the hospital at which those people are being treated.

4. If your subject is singular, use a singular verb, and if your subject is plural, use a plural verb:

> The groups failed in its attempt to obtain more money.
> REVISED: The groups failed in their attempt to obtain more money.

> A team of researchers have been gathering the information.
> REVISED: A team of researchers has been gathering the information.

5. Again, use strong, active and descriptive verbs:

> After the game, they had three beers.
> REVISED: After the game, they drank (gulped, sipped) three beers.

> The radio station did a survey of 500 homes.
> REVISED: The radio station conducted (organized, supervised) a survey of 500 homes.

6. For clarity, sentences should be constructed in positive, rather than negative, form, as in the following examples:

> The student did not often come to class.
> REVISED: The student rarely came to class.

> It was not the first time the plane's engine failed.
> REVISED: It was the third time the plane's engine failed.

Sentences that contain two or three negatives are even more difficult to decipher. As you read the following examples, you may have to pause and struggle to determine what they mean:

The senator said he will not accept any campaign contributions from people who do not live in his district.
REVISED: The senator said he will accept campaign contributions only from people who live in his district.

The women said they are not disinclined to use butter.
REVISED: The women said they will use butter.

7. Every item listed in a series must be in parallel form. If one verb in a series uses the past tense, every verb must use the past tense. If one ends in "ing," all must end in "ing."

The woman was running away from the dog, crying and bled.
PARALLEL FORM: The woman was running away from the dog, crying and bleeding.

The woman suffered a severe concussion, internal injuries and both of her legs were broken.
PARALLEL FORM: The woman suffered a severe concussion, internal injuries and two broken legs.

Police said plastic handcuffs are less bulky, less expensive and no key is necessary to remove them from a suspect's wrists.
PARALLEL FORM: Police said plastic handcuffs are less bulky, less expensive and less difficult to remove from a suspect's wrists.

8. When you list several items in a sentence, place an explanation before the list, not after it. If the explanation does not appear before the list, readers may not immediately understand the relationship between the items or the significance of the list:

Attempting to elude a police officer, no driver's license, fleeing the scene of an accident and driving while intoxicated were the charges filed against him.
REVISED: He was charged with attempting to elude a police officer, driving without a license, fleeing the scene of an accident and driving while intoxicated.

Overcrowded, unsafe and inhumane conditions in the county jail were cited by the sheriff as his reasons for resigning.
REVISED: The sheriff said he is resigning because of overcrowded, unsafe and inhumane conditions in the county jail.

9. Be consistent in your description of, or reference to, topics. If you write about a hospital, use the hospital's full name the first time you mention it. Later in the story, refer to it as "the hospital" (you do not have to repeat its full name). Do not call the building a "hospital" the first time you mention it and later refer to it as a "structure," "building," "medical facility" or "health center." The different labels might confuse your readers.

10. Avoid loaded words that might prejudice your readers for or against a subject. When they attribute statements, reporters avoid the word "claim" because it implies doubt, suggesting that the statements may be false. The word "only" is even more troublesome. If a reporter comments that, "Only three of the 94 people aboard the plane were killed," the use of "only" suggests that those deaths were unimportant.

11. Use the words "who" and "whom" only when referring to a person or to an animal that has a proper name. Use the words "that" and "which" when referring to inanimate objects and to animals that do not have a name.

12. Avoid overusing the words "that" and "then"; both words can usually be deleted. "Then" is especially troublesome, since some writers habitually add it to most of their sentences.

13. Except in extraordinary circumstances, reporters should remain neutral bystanders. They should not mention themselves in news stories. Reporters should not have to use the words "I," "me," "we" or "us," except in direct quotations (when they are quoting some other person). When they appear outside quotation marks, the words are likely to confuse readers. Reporters who use the word "we" rarely explain who they are referring to, yet their subject is not always clear, and it is a mistake for reporters to assume that all their readers will fit into the category they are describing:

> He said we must work harder to improve the schools.
> REVISED: He said residents of the city must work harder to improve the schools.
>
> The president said we are being hurt by inflation.
> REVISED: The president said Americans are being hurt by inflation.

14. Avoid contractions—"doesn't," "hadn't" and so on. Many newspapers prohibit their use except in direct quotations.

15. If you use a specific figure, such as 41 or 8,471, do not use approximations such as "about." Use approximations only when you round off a figure, such as: "About 700 people attended the concert."

16. Avoid using too many pronouns in a sentence. They become confusing and repetitive, as in these examples:

> He said he had a bomb in the bag he was carrying, and he threatened to blow up the bank if he did not get their money.
>
> She said she would be happy to help him if they could finish their work after their test.

17. Also avoid bloody details. Report that someone suffered severe cuts, a concussion or broken leg. You do not have to add that, "A witness said he was bleeding from the mouth, nose and ears."

18. When you mention several objects or numbers in a story, always check their arithmetical consistency. If, for example, you report that seven people received awards, then list their names, count to be certain that you have listed seven, not six or eight, recipients.

19. Tell your readers how or where you obtained the information presented in each story: from a press conference, speech, interview or telephone conversation. The source does not have to be emphasized or placed in a story's lead, but it should be included somewhere, perhaps in a brief phrase or sentence (for example, "During a press conference in his office, the governor said he opposes legalized gambling in the state").

20. If you are unable to obtain an important fact or some information that your readers might expect or need, explain why you did not include that information in your story:

> University officials said it will take several days to calculate the average faculty member's salary.

Company officials said it would be impossible to determine how the food became contaminated.

Rescue workers said they will not know how many people were killed until all the water is pumped out and they can search the entire mine.

21. Never create or manufacture any information; report only the facts you obtain from reliable sources. If you need some additional information, research your topic more thoroughly; never make up any of that information. News stories are based on fact, not fiction.

22. Be original. Go out and personally gather the information you need for a story. Do not rewrite information that has already been reported by other media. By the time you copy it, the information is likely to be old, and many of your readers may have seen or heard it before. Moreover, some readers may accuse you of plagiarism.

Checklist for Improving Newsgathering and Writing Skills

1. Are the words used in your story strong, descriptive, specific and interesting? Are they used properly, and are related words and ideas placed as close together as possible?
2. Have you expressed your ideas with clarity and precision, eliminating sentences that have double meanings?
3. Have you started any sentences with the words "it," "this," "these" or "that"? If so, are the antecedents of these words clear?
4. Have you eliminated vague generalities and vague qualifiers: words such as "young," "big," "late," "fast," "very" and "a lot"?
5. Is your story so detailed and thorough that it answers all the questions that readers might logically ask about the topic?
6. Are sentences and paragraphs so thorough and phrased so clearly and specifically that they do not require any further explanation?
7. Have you identified everyone mentioned in the story, defined unfamiliar words and explained unfamiliar concepts? Also, have you identified people only once—normally, the first time you mention them in the story?
8. Have you used examples to personalize the topic and to explain abstract concepts?
9. If you have described the objects or people mentioned in your story, have you provided specific, factual details as opposed to generalities and personal impressions?
10. If you included some humor, did you present that humor in a clear, straightforward manner, without labels or exaggeration?
11. Have you used verbs and nouns rather than adverbs and adjectives?
12. Have you avoided platitudes, slang, clichés, euphemisms, technical jargon, gush and journalese?
13. Have you avoided misleading statements about the time the story occurred? Did you use the specific day of the week (not "yesterday," "today" or "tomorrow") and avoided suggesting that the story will continue indefinitely?
14. Have you avoided exaggeration, excessive punctuation and artificial labels?
15. Did you prepare an outline?
16. Have you buried important facts in the middle of a sentence or paragraph?
17. Have you used the articles "a," "an" and "the" correctly?
18. Have you used singular verbs with singular subjects, and plural verbs with plural subjects?
19. Are your sentences worded in positive rather than negative forms?
20. Do the items listed in series appear in parallel form?
21. Have you placed the explanation before rather than after items in lists?
22. Is your reference to topics consistent, and have you avoided loaded words and opinionated or artificial labels?

23. Do you use the words "who" and "whom" only in referring to people and to animals that have been given a proper name?

24. Have you avoided contractions and avoided overusing the words "that" and "then"?

25. Have you avoided mentioning yourself in the story and avoided the use of "I," "me," "we," "us" and "our" except in direct quotations?

26. Have you revealed how or where you obtained your information? Also, if you were unable to include some important information, have you explained the reason for its omission?

27. Is your story original and based entirely on facts that you are able to verify—not "facts" you made up?

Journalists have witnessed and reported hundreds of executions. Yet few stories are as powerful as this one, published by the Dallas Times Herald. As you read it, the story is likely to arouse feelings of anger, curiosity, fascination, repulsion or horror. What techniques has the reporter used to create such compelling and vivid images?

As killer lay dying, 'Oh! It's hurting'

DALLAS TIMES HERALD

HUNTSVILLE, Texas — Convicted murderer James David Autry, declaring in his last moments that he loved a Dallas woman who came to witness his death, was killed with a lethal injection early Wednesday for the slaying of a convenience store clerk four years ago.

Autry, convicted in the 1980 slaying of Shirley Drouet, told prison officials as he lay strapped to a gurney in the death chamber that he had no last words.

But then he turned to Shirley Tadlock, the Dallas woman who befriended him in letters after his Oct. 5 execution was stayed, and declared, "I love you," witnesses said.

"I love you, too. I love you so much, so awful much," the 32-year-old blond office manager responded.

But his last thoughts also were of pain.

"Oh! It's hurting," he cried out after the dose of lethal drugs began entering his bloodstream, according to Michael Graczyk, an Associated Press reporter and one of the witnesses.

As the drugs began to take effect, witnesses said, Autry began twitching. He began to breathe deeply and his knees jerked upward, they said.

"He grunted a bit and sighed. His stomach began to expand. He winced a bit. His eyes looked cloudy," Graczyk said.

Tadlock, a mother of three children whose husband accompanied her to Huntsville, was weeping and began to repeat, "Oh God. God. God."

After Dr. L. A. Masters pronounced him dead, witnesses said, Tadlock asked that his eyes be closed. Masters tried but the lids reopened, witnesses said.

Prison chaplain Carroll Pickett turned to the woman and said, "He's with God." She asked to hug Autry, but received no response from prison officials.

The death was announced to members of the press by Department of Corrections spokesman Rick Hartley at 12:50 a.m.

The death was not announced to a crowd of about 200 spectators who had gathered outside the Huntsville Prison Unit just before midnight. Word circulated among the spectators, however, and after a short time they dispersed.

Autry was pronounced dead at 12:40 a.m., 38 minutes after prison officials began the final procedures for his death.

According to a TDC official at the scene who maintained an open telephone line to the attorney general's office in Austin, the process began at 12:02 a.m. when Assistant Attorney General Leslie Benitez notified prison officials in Huntsville that no stays had been granted.

At 12:03, Autry was strapped on the gurney in the 12-by-18-foot death chamber. At 12:05, a needle was inserted in his left arm, and at 12:10 a needle was inserted in his right arm.

A saline solution was released into intravenous tubes connected to the needles at 12:15. A minute later, the witnesses were admitted to the death chamber.

(continued on next page)

The lethal chemicals, injected into the tubes from behind a wall that shielded the identity of those administering the drugs, were administered at 12:25. Under Texas procedures, several persons injected different solutions into the tubes so none knew who had administered the fatal dosage.

Autry had spent his last hours listening to the radio, prison officials said. They said he was irritated at reports that he was upset.

"He asked me to tell you (reporters) that he is taking this very calmly, very strong-willed," the TDC's Hartley said at 10 p.m.

But earlier Tuesday, Tadlock had emerged from a two-hour meeting with him and said, "He's very frightened. We got on our knees and prayed."

Five reporters selected by the state, five guests of Autry and at least 13 state officials—including Attorney General Jim Mattox and two TDC board members—witnessed Autry's last moments. A federal appeals court had refused his request to have his execution televised.

Autry's last chance to escape death passed at 11:30 p.m. Tuesday, when Gov. Mark White turned down his request for a 30-day reprieve. The U.S. Supreme Court refused Tuesday afternoon to review Autry's case, despite his claims he had endured cruel and unusual punishment with his last-minute stay of execution. His stay that time came from U.S. Supreme Court Justice Byron White, because the high court was considering a California case that might have affected his.

It was the 5th U.S. Circuit Court of Appeals in New Orleans that turned down his request to have his execution televised. He said in an affidavit filed with the suit that he wanted the broadcast "because it may help stop someone else from being put to death on death row, and maybe someone will see my execution and decide the death penalty isn't right."

Write & Wrong ST. LOUIS POST-DISPATCH

By Harry Levins
Post-Dispatch Writing Coach

Good writing draws a clear picture in the writer's mind. When a reader can see a sharp image in his mind, the writing comes alive.

But vague writing blurs the image, throwing it out of focus. Writers who rely on adjectives often blur their images. True, an adjective can evoke a specific image in the *writer's* mind. After all, the writer was on the scene; when he writes of a "giant ice-cream cone," as one reporter recently did, the word "giant" recalls to the writer the three-scoop diet-buster (or whatever it was) that somebody was eating.

But the reader was elsewhere; the reader never *saw* the ice-cream cone in question. As a result, the reader must grapple with a vague word: "giant." How giant is giant? One reader's "giant" ice-cream cone is another's appetizer.

Here's a lede in which the writer made an effort to fix a sharp image in the reader's mind:

Laurie Ann Oilar of Kahoka, Mo., was a large, red-haired woman who liked to fix autos, tend farm animals and play with her baby daughter.

It worked, except for one word—"large." What does "large" mean?
Does it mean that Ms. Oilar was fat?
Does it mean that Ms. Oilar was tall?
Does it mean that Ms. Oilar was buxom?
Does it mean that Ms. Oilar was Junoesque?

"Large" could fit any number of attributes. In this case, nobody knows which one—except for the writer (and, of course, Ms. Oilar's acquaintances, who needed no word pictures). We would have served the reader better with precision:

Laurie Ann Oilar of Kohoka, Mo., was a 325-pound, red-haired woman who . . .
Or:
Laurie Ann Oilar of Kahoka, Mo., was a 6-foot, 2-inch woman who . . .

Or whatever fits in the context. Even such relatively vague adjectives as "heavy-set" or "plump" or "tall" would have been more precise than "large." Moral: make sure that the picture in *your* mind can be developed in the reader's mind as well.

Sometimes, we're vague because we assume that the reader knows as much as we do—always a dangerous assumption. Here's an example, from a political story in which mayoral contenders were talking about appointing blacks to high-level city jobs:

Bosley said the number of blacks in such positions should be proportionate to the city's black population.
Jackson would not put a specific number on the percentage of blacks he would place in such posts . . .

And neither would the writer, which was unfortunate. Blacks make up about 47 percent of the city's population. Had we used that figure and the number of jobs in question, the reader would have had some idea of how many blacks Bosley was talking about.

Similarly, a story on the recovery by the police of some stolen goods ended with this paragraph:

Sgt. Stewart said many of the stolen goods had been sold at tremendous discounts. "For example, we learned that they were selling cigarettes at $30 a case," he said.

But unless we know the retail value of a case of cigarettes, this information is worthless. How much of a discount does $30 represent? Fifty percent? Ninety percent? Who knows? The Coach has few equals as a consumer of cigarettes, but even he has no idea how many packages or cartons of cigarettes make up a case.

At times we're vague through a poor choice of words. A recent lede provides an example:

A number of major road construction projects in the St. Louis area have been affected by the strike of Teamsters union truck drivers against the Material Dealers Association.

What is "a number of"? Answer: anything from one to infinity. What does "have been affected" mean? Some effects are good, some are neutral, some are bad. Some effects are slight, some are moderate, some are severe. What information did this lede convey? That from one to countless road projects is or are being affected in some way or other to some sort of degree. Conclusion: mush.

On the other hand, the sort of information that readers need was contained in (or perhaps was edited into) a recent AP story on asbestos exposure. The story said current government regulations limited asbestos at places of work "to two fibers for each cubic centimeter of air." Then it added:

That volume is about the size of a small sugar cube.

Most Americans know little about the metric system. So the sentence about the sugar cube took a hard fact and put it into terms that readers can understand.

Martha Shirk took the same extra step in a story about the sales tax increase proposed in the city. After noting that the increase would add three-eighths of a cent to the tax, she wrote:

The sales tax increase would add $18.75 to the price of a $5,000 automobile and 37½ cents to the cost of a $100 suit.

She needed only a moment to calculate the figures and a few words to convey them. But the beneficial impact can be way out of proportion to the effort. Numbers are abstractions; cars and suits are real.

☆ ☆ ☆

Adding It Up

Any newsroom has more than its share of people uncomfortable with mathematics. On election night, their cries ring out: "How do you figure percentages? Is it the big number into the little? Or the other way around?" Still, simple multiplication and division should be within our grasp.

Recently, when Florissant's water supply went bad, Anheuser-Busch gave that community 25,000 cases of canned water—and gave the Post-Dispatch a press release. It spoke of "56,000 gallons in 600,000 cans." The reporter took the brewery at its word, which was unfortunate. The brewery makes good beer but bad numbers.

Six hundred thousand 12-ounce cans equals 7,200,000 fluid ounces. At 128 ounces to the gallon, that comes to 56,250 gallons. The brewery's figure was 250 gallons short. The shortage was caught before the story saw print, but it was a near-run thing.

(continued on next page)

No big deal, you might say. Two hundred and fifty gallons of beer is one thing, but what's 250 gallons of water?

Well, remember that the vast and anonymous crowd we call "readers" includes people who read every story, notice every detail and catch every mistake. Even if only five or six of them notice that we're 250 gallons short, that's five or six people who wonder whether we know what we're doing.

You may recall the story of the clerk a few years back who was fretting late one Saturday morning because the weather machine had jammed just before the world temperatures moved. The deadline for the early Sunday edition was at hand, and the clerk had nothing to offer but a blank weather form.

Still, he had imagination—not judgment, but imagination. He went to the bound volumes and copied down the temperatures from the preceding week's early Sunday edition. And nobody noticed—nobody except the one reader who follows the world temperatures closely.

That reader found it odd that from Aberdeen to Winnipeg, the temperatures on one Saturday were precisely the same as the temperatures the Saturday before. He found it so odd that he brought it to the attention of the Reader's Advocate.

Moral No. 1: Somebody out there reads *everything*.

Moral No. 2: Recheck the math.

☆ ☆ ☆

To Be Or Not To Be

Here's an all-too common sort of sentence:

Mrs. Clark's problem is that a city ordinance forced her to run as an independent in a special election last month.

A purist might note that Mrs. Clark ran by choice, not because a city ordinance forced her to. But The Coach had more problems with the writer's use of the verb "is."

Verbs represent the strongest words in English. Verbs propel a sentence. But among English verbs, "to be" in any of its forms is the weakest. With "to be," nothing *happens*; things merely *are*. Nothing *moves*; things merely *exist*.

Naturally, some sentences require "to be." But in many instances, we can replace "to be" with a more active verb:

Mrs. Clark's problem stems from a city ordinance that barred her from running as a Democrat in a special election last month.

Another example:

. . . for Tammy Beckham, 16, of St. Louis, who is in need of a liver transplant operation.

The solution:

. . . For Tammy Beckham, 16, of St. Louis, who needs . . .

☆ ☆ ☆

Department of Niceties

• In a negative construction, watch out for "as . . . as." The following sentence had it wrong: *Jackson said he had not performed as well as he had expected.* In the negative sense, it should be "so . . . as." *Jackson said he had not performed **so** well **as** expected.*

• Lazlo Domjan points out that in our election stories, we are using the word "margin" when we mean "ratio." When Smith gets 60,000 votes and Jones gets 40,000, Smith's *margin* of victory is 20,000 votes. His *ratio* of victory is 3–2.

• Be on guard for partial quotes that backfire. We've had a run on bloopers of this sort: *Peach said he "appreciates the offer, but I'm a big boy, and I can do it myself."* George Peach may speak rashly but never ungrammatically. Literally, we have him saying here, "I appreciates the offer." And we appreciates good grammar. Solution: *Peach said that although he appreciated the offer, "I'm a big boy . . ."*

• Now that we are in the waning years of the 20th century, references to the 21st century will appear with increasing frequency. Please remember that the new century starts on January 1, 2001. The year 2000 will be the last year of the 20th century, not the first year of the 21st. (The reason: We had no Year 0. The First Century began on Jan. 1 in the year 1; it ran a full 100 years, ending on Dec. 31, 100. The Second Century began on Jan. 1, 101, and so on.)

• A recent lede told how a line of vicious thunderstorms had raked the metropolitan area, blowing down trees and taking off roofs—and then ended, "according to authorities." Why attribute an event that 2.3 million people witnessed? We can say on our own that it rained.

Suggested Readings

Armour, Richard, ed. *How to Write Better*. Boston: Christian Science Publishing Society, 1980.

Babb, Laura Longley, ed. *Writing in Style*. Boston, Mass.: Houghton Mifflin, 1975.

Bernstein, Theodore M. *The Careful Writer*. Boston: Atheneum, 1965.

Berry, Thomas Elliott. *The Craft of Writing*. New York: McGraw-Hill, 1974.

Fensch, Thomas. *The Hardest Parts: Techniques for Effective Non-Fiction*. Austin, Texas: Lander Moore Books, 1984.

Galbraith, John Kenneth. "Writing, Typing and Economic$," *The Atlantic*, March 1978, pp. 102–05.

Ghiglione, Loren, ed. *Improving Newswriting*. Washington, D.C.: American Society of Newspaper Editors Foundation, 1982.

Grey, David L. *The Writing Process*. Belmont, Calif.: Wadsworth, 1972.

Hall, Donald. *Writing Well*. 5th ed. Boston: Little, Brown, 1985.

Hohenberg, John, ed. *The Pulitzer Prize Story II*. New York: Columbia University Press, 1980.

Keir, Gerry, Maxwell McCombs and Donald L. Shaw. *Advanced Reporting: Beyond News Events*. New York: Longman, 1986.

Kilpatrick, James J. *The Writer's Art*. Kansas City, Mo.: Andrews, McMeel & Parker, 1984.

Murray, Donald M. *Writing for Your Readers: Notes on the Writer's Craft from The Boston Globe*. Chester, Conn.: Globe Pequot, 1983.

Rucker, Bryce W. *Twentieth Century Reporting at Its Best*. Ames, Iowa: Iowa State University Press, 1964.

Shaw, David. "The Use and the Abuse of Language," *The Los Angeles Times*, April 19, 1981. (Reprinted in pamphlet form.)

Shaw, Harry. *20 Steps to Better Writing*. Totowa, N.J.: Littlefield, Adams, 1978.

Sloan, William David, Valarie McCrary and Johanna Cleary. *The Best of Pulitzer Prize News Writing*. Columbus, Ohio: Publishing Horizons, Inc., 1986.

Snyder, Louis L., and Richard B. Morris, eds. *A Treasury of Great Reporting*. 2nd ed. New York: Simon & Schuster, 1962.

Tarshis, Barry. *How to Write Like a Pro*. New York: New American Library, 1985.

Zinsser, William K. *On Writing Well*. 3rd ed., rev. New York: Harper & Row, 1988.

EXERCISE 1
Improving Newsgathering and Writing Skills

RECOGNIZING AND CORRECTING ERRORS

SECTION I: RECOGNIZING EUPHEMISMS List five euphemisms for each of these words.

1. Drunk _____

2. Lie _____

3. Mistake _____

4. Steal _____

5. Toilet _____

SECTION II: AVOIDING FALSE TITLES Rewrite these sentences, eliminating their false and contrived titles.

1. President of the Michigan Avenue boat shop Robert Ellerbee reported the fire.

2. The door of the new home of the two Dallas men was pried open Sunday.

3. Assistant solid waste disposal director Carlos Alicea said he opposes the fee.

4. A burglarized carpet manufacturing company on Seventh Avenue lost $800 in merchandise.

5. Americans spend 37 percent of their weekly food-budgeted dollars in restaurants.

SECTION III: AVOIDING THE NEGATIVE Rewrite the following sentences in positive form.

1. He was not unaware of the restaurant's unpopularity.

2. There will be no lack of opportunities for more difficulties to arise.

3. The students do not have any limitations on which songs they can choose.

4. The mayor said he does not feel the decision will have a negative impact on the town.

5. Homeowners said the developers are reneging on their promise not to negatively impact the creek.

SECTION IV: USING PARALLEL FORM Rewrite these sentences in parallel form.

1. He said the gunman is white, about 50, had a moustache and almost bald.

2. She suffered a concussion, broken nose and required 45 stitches in her mouth.

3. The man was described as being 35 to 40 years old, black hair, brown eyes, 6 feet tall and 160 pounds.

4. They say the bracket was improperly installed, not thoroughly inspected or tested, and lacked sufficient warnings of possible danger.

5. She said the other advantages of owning her own business include being independent, not having a boss, flexible hours and less stress.

SECTION V: AVOIDING JOURNALESE Rewrite these sentences, eliminating the slang and journalese.

1. She racked up $30,000 in medical expenses.

2. He gave an OK to spending the $5,000 figure.

3. The program is geared toward high-school students.

4. The proposal met with opposition from three council members.

5. The new building will carry a price tag of about $6 million.

SECTION VI: KEEPING RELATED WORDS AND IDEAS TOGETHER Rewrite these sentences, improving their wording.

1. The girl was taken to a hospital for observation by her parents and a police officer.

2. Two suspects were arrested after a high-speed chase Thursday for the murder of a 58-year-old man.

3. The school board voted to ban seven books from schools which may contain racist statements.

4. The man, described by witnesses to be in his late 40s, balding and carrying a golf club, was arrested.

5. Robert Allen Wiese was placed on probation after pleading guilty to violating probation and burglary by Circuit Court Judge Samuel McGregor.

SECTION VII: AVOIDING GRAMMATICAL ERRORS Correct the subject/verb disagreement in the following sentences.

1. The basketball team won their game by a score of 88–42.

2. The school board used their attorney to prepare the documents.

3. He said the small concentrations found in drinking water is not harmful.

4. There is not much a student can do to prevent cheating except cover their exam paper.

5. Speaking for the highway patrol, Lucas said they would like new and larger cars.

EXERCISE 2
Improving Newsgathering and Writing Skills

RECOGNIZING AND CORRECTING ERRORS

INSTRUCTIONS: Rewrite the following sentences, correcting all the errors and problems they contain. Some sentences contain more than one error or problem.

SECTION I: SIMPLIFYING

1. The license is renewed on an annual basis.

2. He warned, "There is a minimum of human interface opportunities in the job."

3. Leonard Weiner said students are not disadvantaged by the absence of a campus newspaper.

4. The governor said he is gratified by citizens' willingness to assist in his endeavor to provide enhanced medical care for the indigent.

5. He said it is the responsibility of public television stations to make their programs of benefit to the viewing public.

SECTION II: AVOIDING SLANG AND CLICHÉS

1. The club president said he plans to call it quits.

2. The bank cashier admitted coming up $11,000 short in his account.

3. She said the student has a long way to go before he can graduate.

4. The mayor painted a rosy picture of the city's financial situation.

5. The exercise trail is geared toward the average adult citizen who is serious about getting in shape.

SECTION III: AVOIDING FAULTY WORDING

1. The $24.4 million hospital will consist of 226 beds.

2. Smaller grocery stores usually know their customers.

3. Minutes after the man left the bar, he collided with another car.

4. After paying a $25 fine, the dog was free to go home with its owner.

5. The attorney noted that William L. Williamson had an intoxicated driving record.

SECTION IV: KEEPING RELATED WORDS TOGETHER

1. A police officer saw a man fitting the description of the suspect he had been given.

2. The youth said he suffered from an allergy during his hospital stay which prevented him from taking pain medication.

3. He is constructing a housing project close to the school which will include 200 homes.

4. Religious Emphasis Week is scheduled to feature a guest speaker from Princeton University who recently visited Vietnam.

5. The coach said he felt pretty good about the season his team had in an interview Tuesday.

SECTION V: AVOIDING THE NEGATIVE

1. The restaurant was not far away.

2. He does not like candy as much as he likes fruit.

3. High-school students are not as likely to watch TV newscasts as entertainment programs.

4. She said that she is no longer in favor of not raising the state sales tax.

5. The more physically fit one is the less likely he is to injure himself while engaging in a sporting activity.

SECTION VI: USING PARALLEL FORM

1. He was charged with drunken driving and an expired driver's license.

2. She charges that her injuries include a broken left arm, permanent blindness in her left eye, an 84-day hospital stay and bills exceeding $40,000.

3. The purpose of the paper is to summarize the basic writing skills for all good writers, whether they be journalists, writers of prose or the simple task of writing a letter.

4. To join the club, one must be a sophomore, junior or senior, study journalism, be in good academic standing and have shown professional journalistic ability.

5. The youth must obey his parents, seek further education, not possess drugs or associate with people who do, and he is restricted from drinking alcohol under the conditions of his probation.

SECTION VII: AVOIDING JARGON

1. He wants to show teachers how to use computers as an instructional tool in their classrooms.

2. The university president said he is looking to the private sector for funds to construct several dormitories.

3. Teresa Phillips, a/k/a Marie Frank, testified that she helped the defendant steal an unknown quantity of jewelry on or about the 9th of last month.

4. Brown's lawsuit charges that, as a result of the auto accident, he is suffering from bodily injury, disability, disfigurement and mental anguish. Brown's lawsuit also charges that he has lost his ability to earn a living and that the accident aggravated a previous condition.

EXERCISE 3
Improving Newsgathering and Writing Skills

RECOGNIZING AND CORRECTING ERRORS

INSTRUCTIONS: Rewrite the following sentences, correcting all the errors and problems they contain. Some sentences contain more than one error or problem.

1. He said the book is a good read.

2. The council chairman cast a strong no vote for the $52,000 expenditure.

3. Two guitar players, a lute player, strolling minstrels and jugglers will provide the entertainment.

4. The article went on to add that none of today's most popular comedians are women.

5. The latest fire occurred Sunday night in a basement room used by the school band, causing an estimated $15,000 damage and destroyed 80 band uniforms.

6. The views of all the students were similar in that they felt that unless the cost of tuition is not subject to further increases, fewer youths will be able to afford to attend college.

7. He wants to establish a program where convicted juveniles would be required to perform some sort of community service and not go to jail.

8. Assistant director for instruction and research in the Division of Computer Services Abraham Cohen said every elementary school should teach their students how to use a computer.

9. The auditorium costs $600 a day to rent. This is the reason for the program's $6 admission fee.

10. John Adles said the possible deformity of the child is the only circumstance in which he feels that abortion should be legal.

11. Academic reputation and school location were the two major reasons listed by college students as their reasons for attending a particular college.

12. Community Action Center's executive director Dan Friendly announced that there are 1,492 dues paying members currently affiliated with the center.

13. Eight people agreed that the only crimes serious enough to receive capital punishment as a penalty are those involving murder.

14. He said that before marijuana is legalized, there has to be more extensive research pointing in the direction of its being a harmless drug.

EXERCISE 4
Improving Newsgathering and Writing Skills

WRITING NEWS STORIES

INSTRUCTIONS: Write complete news stories based on the following information. Critically examine the information's language and organization, improving it whenever possible. To provide a pleasing change of pace, use some quotations in the stories. Go beyond the superficial; unless your instructor tells you otherwise, assume that you have enough space to report every important and interesting detail in the stories.

1. Seven people died in high-speed police chases in the state last year. Three of the dead people were innocent bystanders whose cars were struck by vehicles being pursued by the police. Three victims were the drivers of or passengers in the vehicles being pursued by the police. One victim was a state highway patrolman. Other people were injured, including several additional police officers. Because of the mishaps, a committee composed of law enforcement officials from throughout the entire state studied the matter, and they issued a report today. Their report says the accidents are "unfortunate," but it does not recommend any major policy changes. The report goes on to explain that: "The decision to chase a motorist must be left to the officer on the scene. The officer must decide if the situation warrants a chase, how fast and how far the chase should continue." The report acknowledges the fact that the officer involved must also consider factors such as traffic and weather conditions.

   None of last year's fatalities occurred in this city, and when he was interviewed after the report was issued today, the local police chief, Martin Guidema, said he takes a more conservative approach to high-speed chases. Guidema said: "Is the offense worth the degree of risk? In most cases, the danger outweighs the need for pursuit. An officer does not need to match the speed of the fleeing motorist in most cases. The officer need only keep the suspect's car in sight because he will receive assistance from fellow officers. Also, in general, there is no justification for giving chase to traffic violators who fail to stop. The officer can jot down the tag number, take out a warrant and arrest the driver later. You don't have to pursue traffic violators at the same breakneck speed as bank robbers; you can push a person into taking actions he wouldn't normally take. In the case of a robbery or some other serious crime, it is more important that the suspect be stopped as soon as possible. In that case, the officer involved has to take a look at the immediate situation and decide whether it's practical to chase the guy and whether he can do so safely. It's a judgment call."

   In Roseville, a neighboring town, Police Chief Alton Gunter was also interviewed by reporters, and he said: "Officers are held strictly accountable for their decision to pursue a traffic violator or felon. We've never had anyone killed in a high-speed chase here, and we don't intend for it to happen. It's just not worth it. Most crimes aren't serious enough to risk endangering the lives of innocent motorists. When no serious threat is posed to the public, I've ordered my officers to discontinue a pursuit and attempt to arrest the driver later with a warrant."

2. Janet C. Herholtz is a professor of sociology at the University of Wyoming. She was in town today to give a speech at the annual convention of the American Association of Sociologists. During her speech, she discussed the topic of murder, about which she wrote her Ph.D. dissertation. She is also in the process of writing a book about murder and, at the University of Wyoming, teaches an unusual course titled "The Epidemic of Murder." She explains that each year one out of every 10,000 Americans is murdered, and that in five years more Americans are murdered than were killed

during the entire war in Vietnam. Yet, she said, many popular stereotypes about murder are false, totally without foundation. "The most likely murderer is a victim's relative," she explained. "Almost a third of all victims are related to their killers. The murderers are husbands, wives, lovers, neighbors, friends and acquaintances—people who can no longer endure chronic frustrations. Most murders are committed by men in their 20s—often because they blame other people rather than themselves for their problems. In two-thirds of the murders, they use guns. I should mention the fact that the probability of being murdered varies from one area of the country to another and from one race to another. People in the South are three times more likely to be murdered than people living in New England, and people who live in a large city are twice as likely to be murdered as people living in a suburb or rural area. Also, black men are 10 times more likely to be murdered than white men, and black women five times more than white women. In 90 percent of the cases, blacks are murdered by blacks, and whites by whites. When racial lines are crossed, it is usually a white who kills a black." Dr. Herholtz blames the use of alcohol for many murders, along with rising frustrations, permissive parents, joblessness and marital instability.

3. The school board met at 7:30 p.m. last night for its regular bimonthly meeting and, during the course of the meeting, approved a new "Vandal Watch Program." The program is similar to programs started in more than 100 other cities throughout the United States and is expected to cut down on vandalism in city schools. Supt. of Schools Marcia Pagozalski reported at last night's meeting that vandals caused more than $920,000 damage last year, and the figure for the previous year was $825,000. For a start, the new vandal watchers will be installed at half of the city's elementary schools next year. The following year, they will be located at the remaining elementary schools. The program will be reviewed at the end of the first two years to determine its cost effectiveness and, if the program is effective, it will be expanded to junior high schools in the third year and to senior high schools in the fourth year, so that every school in the city will eventually have a vandal watcher. Pagozalski explained the program this way: "We will invite responsible adults, who we'll carefully screen, to move trailers onto the school grounds, and they will act as 24-hour-a-day watchmen to discourage intruders. Entire families can live in these trailers, and the school system will provide a free lot, chain link fence, patio area and utilities for the families. The vandal watchers must provide their own trailers; the county does not pay for them, nor does it pay the vandal watchers any salaries. When schools close at night, burglar alarms will be turned on, as they have in the past, and the vandal watchers will be instructed to call the police if any trouble arises. School intercoms will be left on, and they will be hooked up to the trailers, so that the vandal watchers can hear anyone who gets into the schools and enters a classroom." Pagozalski said the program will more than pay for itself, since she expects the damage caused by vandals to drop by more than 80 percent. "Schools have gotten good results elsewhere," she said. "There's no reason why we can't have the same results here." She estimated the cost of subsidizing the vandal watchers at "no more than $2,500 a year at each school." The biggest obstacle to overcome: the school board will have to obtain variances from the Zoning Board to allow the use of trailers on school grounds, some of which are in neighborhoods zoned for single-family and other restricted usages.

4. What can you do to maximize the span of your life? Raymond W. Herron, author of a book titled "Centenarians," autographed copies of his book at area bookstores today and, during a press conference at 9:30 a.m. today, answered the questions of local reporters from newspapers and radio and television stations in the area. In response to their questions, he said a major factor is work. "Old age is not a time to be sedentary, but to be active. Work is an invaluable remedy against premature old age—hard work. If you study the background of people who live to be 100, you'll find

few of them are lazy. Most worked hard all their lives, and many are still working." Herron noted that the Soviet Union claims to have almost 20,000 centenarians, many more than any other country in the world, and that the highest age claimed by the Soviet Union is 167, attained by Shirali Mislimov, who passed away in the year 1972. Herron noted that the Soviet Union reports that healthy old people seem to have several characteristics in common. Most live in rural areas. More than 99 percent are married. Most have large families. All are moderate eaters and drinkers and stick to a regular diet of plain foods. Much of their work is physical. Other studies, Herron continued, have found that people seem to live longer if they live in high places, drink well water and talk a lot. In the United States, he continued, researchers often note the effects of "pension illness"—the fact that people who retire deteriorate quickly in health and mind and often die within a few years after reaching their 65th birthdays, whereas people who continue to work maintain a better health and enjoy considerably longer lives. What are the average American's chances of living to be 100? Less than 1 out of 50,000, responded Herron.

5. Roger and Carolyn Nunez say it is outrageous. Their son, Bobby, 14, says it is not fair. Fifteen other neighborhood children who helped Bobby build a treehouse in his front yard at 2280 Norwell Ave. are also upset. It was an elaborate split level 8 x 15-foot treehouse, painted green with a white frame. Bobby's father helped the children build the treehouse three years ago, but it was not until last month that a neighbor complained. He called a county building inspector and said the treehouse is an eyesore in the neighborhood and that all the kids make too much noise, especially late at night. A building inspector who visited the site and inspected the treehouse called it a "nonconforming structure." He said it does not meet the city's building code, which requires the same standard of construction in playhouses as in wood frame residences. He ordered it torn down by noon Saturday. If it is not torn down, Mr. and Mrs. Nunez, the property owners, can be hauled into court and fined up to $500. Mr. Nunez, an engineer, told reporters that the treehouse "is as sturdy as any house on the block." His son, Bobby, says, "I don't think it's fair. The city should have better things to do than mess with our clubhouse." The county building inspector, Walt Straiton, responds that the structure was built without a building permit and that the building code is clear and designed to protect the public from any structure that would be damaged by a heavy wind and collapse into "deadly flying missiles." Straiton also noted that, if the playhouse did collapse, anyone inside it at the time might be seriously injured. The playhouse is about 12 feet off the ground. Straiton adds, "I've explained the problem to the Nunez family at least a half dozen times during the past month, and we've suggested they take the playhouse down and rebuild it elsewhere. We've even offered to help with the plans. But as it stands now, the building is in violation. It's nonconforming, and it has to come down. So I've given them a Saturday deadline." Bobby and other children in the neighborhood begged scrap lumber from neighbors and built the playhouse with about $40 worth of paint, nails and glass. It has three windows. Bobby Nunez added: "At first, we were going to build it in a vacant lot, but we thought somebody might come in and take it down. We never thought they'd come in our own front yard and tear it down. It's a playhouse for kids around here. When you get bored at home, there's always something to do in it."

6. Employment figures announced by the Labor Department for last month showed that a record 47.2 million adult women held full-time jobs. The figure indicated that nearly half of all adult women in the United States now hold jobs or are looking for them. The figure is up from earlier years, when the figures were: 1950, 16.7 million; 1960, 21.2 million; 1970, 28.3 million; and 1980, 41 million. But a comprehensive four-year study issued today by the Labor Department suggests that women's new status and tendency to hold full-time jobs outside their homes is not altogether without risks. The Labor Department's new report said more women seem to be working

because many families need two incomes to maintain an acceptable standard of living. Also, fewer women are content to remain home, and homemaking requires less time than before. The report went on to say that women who work are more likely to have their marriages break up, particularly if they earn about the same as their husbands. On the average, however, the report pointed out that women earn 60 percent less than the average man. "If a marriage is troubled, a woman with an independent income may be more likely to separate—or her husband may be less reluctant to leave," the study said. In some cases, a smaller number, a working wife can help hold a marriage together because of the additional income she provides and the increase in her self-esteem and satisfaction, the report concluded.

7. The Department of Health and Human Services issued a 121-page report today. Congress recently passed a law which requires the department to issue a report on alcoholism each year, and this was the first such report. The report was prepared by a committee of 11 within HHS.

The report said losses caused by alcoholism are high. It said alcohol causes 23,000 traffic deaths a year, and the deaths cost the nation a total $15,000,000,000. Nearly 9 million people suffer from alcoholism or lesser drinking problems, and they constitute 10% of the work force within the United States.

The report also contained some statistics about the use of alcohol. It said that in the last year, the average American drinker drank the equivalent of 44 fifths of whiskey. The report concluded that alcohol is "the major drug problem in this country." It said HHS will spend $500,000 next year to pay for advertisements to warn the public about the dangers of excessive drinking. The liquor industry has endorsed the campaign. The advertisements will be used on radio and television and in newspapers and magazines. But an official added: "We will not tell people not to drink. That is a personal decision. What we are saying is that citizens have a responsibility not to destroy themselves or society."

The 121-page report suggests that the problem of alcoholism is not adequately understood by most Americans, who seem more concerned about other drugs, such as cocaine and heroin, even though those drugs do not cause as many problems as alcohol. To prove that point the report pointed out that New York City has an estimated 600,000 alcoholics but only 125,000 heroin abusers. Yet the city spends 40 times more to fight narcotics addiction than it does to fight alcoholism. The report explained that most people do not know much about alcoholism and do not consider alcohol a serious problem. People are also reluctant to admit they have a drinking problem or are alcoholics.

Alcoholism is a particularly serious problem among certain groups. For example, the report said that on some Indian reservations alcoholism has reached epidemic proportions. On some reservations 10 percent of the residents are alcoholics, twice the national average, and the rate of alcoholism rises to as much as 25 percent on some reservations.

Classics of Illiterature

Writers often violate the ideas discussed in this chapter, and their errors are often humorous—for readers, though editors are not amused when the errors appear in their publications. For example, a recent news story reported that, "Tucker's father died in 1952, and he left school several months later."

Similarly, an essay written by a high-school student insisted that, "Floods can be prevented by putting dames in the river." Another high-school student wrote that, "The difference between a king and a president is that a king is the

---

son of his father, but a president isn't." Other students have written about "navel" battles and about a play "in which the characters are ghosts, goblins, virgins and other mythical creatures."

Other Americans make similar mistakes. Insurance forms ask motorists who have been involved in accidents to briefly explain what happened. Their explanations have included:

"I thought my window was down, but I found out it was up when I put my head through it."

"I pulled away from the side of the road, glanced at my mother-in-law and headed over the embankment."

"I had been driving for 40 years when I fell asleep at the wheel and had an accident."

"The telephone pole was approaching. I was attempting to swerve out of its way when it struck the front end."

"To avoid hitting the bumper of the car in front, I struck the pedestrian."

"My car was legally parked as it backed into the other vehicle."

"An invisible car came out of nowhere, struck my car and vanished."

"I saw a slow-moving, sad-faced gentleman as he bounced off the roof of my car."

"I was thrown from my car as it left the road. I was later found in a ditch by some stray cows."

13 Specialized Types of Stories

In addition to the news stories discussed in previous chapters, reporters also write more specialized types of stories, including brights, followups, roundups and sidebars.

Brights

Brights are short, humorous stories that often have a surprise ending. Some brights are written in the inverted pyramid style; they begin with a summary lead, then report the remaining details in the order of their importance, with the most important details appearing first. Other brights have unexpected or bizarre twists, and reporters may try to surprise their readers by withholding those twists until the stories' final paragraphs. Brights that have a surprise ending are called "suspended interest stories" and, to keep their endings a surprise, usually begin with an interesting or suspenseful fact—some detail likely to interest readers. Because it would reveal their surprise endings, suspended interest stories cannot begin with summary leads.

Editors are always searching for humorous stories and publish the best on Page 1. Brights entertain readers, arouse their emotions and provide some relief from the seriousness of the world's problems. The following brights begin with summary leads:

MIAMI (UPI)—The lovely, naked blonde guzzling champagne and darting through the "no frills" section of National Airlines Flight 51 wasn't part of the planned entertainment, but the cheering, gaping, clapping passengers didn't complain a bit.

DAVENPORT, Iowa (AP)—Two Davenport men were arrested Wednesday on charges of riding a horse on a sidewalk, riding a horse without lights and failure to pick up manure.

Just after midnight, a crew for the National Park Services in Washington, D.C. begins to clean a year's grime from a 19-foot statue of Abraham Lincoln.

The suspended interest story that follows begins so routinely that at first it may mislead readers; its bizarre twist is not revealed until the final paragraphs:

> Police killed an intruder after he set off a burglar alarm in a clothing store on Main Street shortly after 1 a.m. today.
> Police entered the store after customers in a nearby tavern heard the alarm and surrounded the building until the officers arrived.
> Police found the intruder perched on a counter and killed it with a fly swatter.
> "It was my third bat this year," declared a police officer triumphantly.

Followups

"Followups," which are also called "second-day" and "developing" stories, report the latest developments in stories that have been reported earlier. Major stories rarely begin and end in a single day, and newspapers will publish fresh articles about the topics each time a new development arises. So stories about a trial, legislative session, political campaign or flight to the moon may appear in the media every day for weeks. Other stories remain in the news for years: stories about wars, inflation, terrorism and federal deficits, for example. However, each followup and its lead emphasize the latest developments. Followup stories may also summarize some previous developments, but that information is presented as concisely as possible and placed in a later paragraph.

Followup stories about disasters are especially common. On Monday, newspapers may report that an explosion trapped 47 miners in a West Virginia coal field. The papers will report later developments on Tuesday, perhaps that rescuers have found 21 bodies. On Wednesday, the papers may report that seven miners have been found alive. Followup stories published on Friday may describe funeral services held for the known dead. Rescue workers may find all the remaining bodies on Saturday, and work in the mine may resume the following Tuesday. Weeks later, another followup story may report that state and federal investigators have determined the cause of the explosion. Months later, the final followup may report that lawsuits filed against the mine's owners have been dropped in return for payments of $260,000 to each victim's family.

As is typical of followups, the following leads would appear on successive days, and each lead emphasizes a new development in a continuing story:

1. The principal of Roosevelt Elementary School was arrested Monday and charged with shoplifting $12.72 worth of food from a supermarket.

2. The School Board on Wednesday suspended with pay an elementary school principal charged with shoplifting $12.72 worth of food from a local supermarket.

3. Margaret Soole, the suspended principal of Roosevelt Elementary School, pleaded not guilty Friday to a charge of shoplifting.
Later Friday, the School Board approved her request for an unpaid leave of absence for the remainder of this school year.

4. Shoplifting charges filed against an elementary school principal were dropped Friday after she agreed to seek counseling and to pay a supermarket for the food she was accused of stealing.
Assistant District Attorney Helen Wehr explained: "We didn't feel a need to take this case to trial. The amount involved is rather small. We've also considered the fact that all the adverse publicity this case has attracted and the possible loss of her job seem to be a harsh enough penalty for the defendant to pay."

5. Margaret Soole, who was charged with shoplifting and was suspended from her job as principal of Roosevelt Elementary School, will return to work next fall but has been re-assigned to an administrative job in the School Board office.

Again, each of the following leads emphasizes a new development in a continuing story:

1. A 17-year-old junior at Kennedy High School collapsed and died while playing basketball during a physical education class Tuesday.

2. An autopsy Wednesday revealed that a junior who collapsed during a physical education class at Kennedy High School died of a heart attack.
The student, Brandon R. Cogeos, had passed his physical examination for the school's football team the day before his death.

3. The School Board has appointed five doctors to a committee that will study sports injuries and the sudden death of an athlete at Kennedy High School.

4. The physical examinations given athletes enrolled in the city's public schools are "generally inadequate and ineffective in detecting many pre-existing medical problems," five doctors told the School Board Monday night.

5. To prevent injuries and deaths, the School Board on Wednesday voted to require athletes in the city's junior and senior high schools to take more thorough physical examinations.

Followup stories are becoming more common, and some publications have established regular columns for them. Typically, Newsweek magazine has established a special section called "Update," which appears every week near its front cover. In the past, critics complained that journalists, like firefighters, raced from one major story to the next, devoting most of their attention to momentary crises. Critics added that when one crisis began to subside, reporters moved on to the next, so older stories disappeared from the news before they were fully resolved. To solve the problem, both newspaper and magazine reporters now return to important topics and tell readers what has happened since the topics dropped from the news. Followups may show that an area devastated by a hurricane has been rebuilt, or that the victims of an accident are still suffering from its consequences.

Roundups

To save space, newspapers publish roundup stories that summarize several different but related events. Traffic roundups are most common; instead of publishing separate stories about each traffic death that occurs during a single weekend, newspapers will summarize a dozen or more fatal traffic accidents in a single story. Newspapers may also report all the weekend crimes, fires, drownings, graduation ceremonies or football games in a single roundup.

Another type of roundup story deals with a single event but incorporates facts from several sources. Reporters may interview half a dozen people to obtain more information about a single topic, to verify the accuracy of facts they have obtained elsewhere or to obtain new perspectives. For example, if your mayor resigned unexpectedly, you might interview the mayor and ask him why he resigned, what he plans to do after leaving office, what he considers his major accomplishments and what problems will confront his successor. You might then: (1) ask other city officials to comment on the mayor's performance and resignation, (2) ask the city clerk how the next mayor will be selected and (3) interview leading contenders for the job. All this information would be included in a single roundup story.

The lead in a roundup story emphasizes the most important or unique developments and ties all the facts together by stressing their common denominator, as in the following examples:

> Eleven people, including three teen-agers who were driving to the state fair, were killed in traffic accidents reported in the region last weekend.

> Gunmen who robbed four service stations during the weekend escaped with a total of $3,600. All four stations are located along Highway 141 on the west side of the city.

Subsequent facts should be organized by topic, not source. After the lead, roundup stories usually discuss the most important topic—the most newsworthy accident, crime, fire or drowning—then move on to the second, third and fourth most important topics. As they discuss each topic, roundup stories usually report what every source said about it. If roundup stories report first every fact provided by one source, then every fact provided by the second, third and fourth sources, the stories will become too disorganized and repetitious, since each source is likely to mention the same topics, and their comments about similar topics will be scattered throughout the stories.

Sidebars

Sidebars are related to major news stories but are separate from them and are usually of secondary importance. The sidebars are set apart for clarity—so that the main stories do not become too long or complicated. Sidebars give readers some additional information about the main topic, usually from a different source or perspective. They may provide background information, explain a topic's importance or describe the scene, emphasizing its color and mood. If fire destroys a nightclub, newspapers may publish a sidebar that quotes several survivors and describes their escape. If a prominent person is given an award (or arrested or injured), a news story will describe that award, arrest or injury, and a sidebar may describe the person's character or accomplishments. Similarly, when a new pope is selected, sidebars may describe his personality, past assignments, philosophy and previous trips to the United States. Other sidebars may

Photographers seeking protection from strong winds and blowing sand huddle under wraps at the White Sands Missile Range. They were waiting for the space shuttle Columbia to land on a runway in the background.

describe his new home in the Vatican and problems confronting Catholic churches throughout the world.

Sidebars are usually briefer than the main news stories and are placed next to those stories. If, for some reason, the sidebars must be placed on a different page, editors will add tielines (a brief note) telling readers where they can find the related stories. Because some people read only the sidebars, most briefly summarize the main stories even when they are placed alongside them.

EXERCISE 1
Specialized Types of Stories

BRIGHTS

INSTRUCTIONS: Use the following information to write "brights," a series of short, humorous stories. Write some brights that have a summary lead and others that have a surprise ending.

1. Practical Joke

Two 16-year-old girls, both juniors at Kennedy High School, were arrested by police and charged with attempted robbery yesterday. Later in the day, the charges against both the girls were dropped. Police did not release either of their names. The girls were shopping at Colonial Mall and thought they recognized a friend, another student at their school, walking in front of them. They said they thought they recognized the classmate's coat, figure, hairstyle and purse, and then they decided to play a practical joke on her. They decided to sneak up closer behind the friend and to pretend to snatch her purse. So they ran up behind her and grabbed the purse but could not get it free because she was holding the handle in her hand and did not let go. When the girls tried to grab the purse, the woman screamed and turned around toward them. The girls said that they immediately realized that they had made a bad mistake. It was not their friend. It was a 32-year-old woman they had never seen before. The girls said they were too embarrassed to explain their mistake, so they released the purse and turned and ran. Several other customers shopping in the shopping center's stores, including an off-duty police officer, heard the woman's screams and saw the two girls trying to grab her purse. The off-duty officer then proceeded to stop and to detain the two girls until other police officers arrived on the scene, handcuffed the two girls and took them to jail, where they were interrogated for an hour before being released to their parents.

2. Infant's Arrest

Charles Todd Snyder was charged with drunken driving following a traffic accident in your city one week ago. He was also charged with driving without a driver's license in his possession. He was scheduled to appear in court at 9 a.m. this morning. He failed to appear in court. As a consequence, Judge Edward Kocembra ordered police to go to Snyder's home and to haul Snyder into court. Police went to the address Snyder had given officers at the time of the accident: 711 Broadway Avenue. The police returned to the court at approximately 10:15 a.m. and appeared before Judge Kocembra with Snyder. Snyder was in his mother's arms. He is a 13-month-old child, and his mother insisted that he drinks only milk and that the only vehicle that he ever drives is a stroller. So the judge apologized for the inconvenience and told the officers to give Snyder and his mother a ride back to their home. Snyder, apparently frightened by the unfamiliar surroundings and people, cried. Police said that whoever was stopped had falsely given the arresting officers Snyder's name and address when he signed the drunken driving ticket and the ticket for driving without a driver's license in his possession. They told the judge that they have no idea who that person might be.

3. Lie Detector

Some people just don't trust lie detectors. To prove a point, a psychology professor on your campus, Ahmad Aneesa, Ph.D., conducted an unusual experiment. Using funds provided by a small grant, he sought 10 volunteers to serve as subjects. He asked each of the subjects some questions about their backgrounds and interests and college majors and grades. He instructed each subject to tell a lie about one of those facts in their background and offered each subject a sum of money as a reward or incentive if the subject could stay with the lie and register "normal" on a highly sophisticated lie detector. Local police agreed to cooperate with the experiment. The city's police department has its own lie detector, and a sergeant is trained to use that detector. The police chief allowed Aneesa to bring 10 students, all psychology majors from your school, to the police department last Saturday. The lie detector normally is not used for regular police business on Saturday. The sergeant, who normally does not work on Saturdays, volunteered to come in on his normal day off to administer the tests without pay. Dr. Aneesa then offered to pay each student $50 for a successful lie. He announced the results today. He found that the sergeant, who asked that his name not be used, was unable to detect the lies of 7 of the 10 students even though he was given a list of questions to ask each student and was told, in advance, that each student was going to give a lie in response to one of those questions.

4. Tax Refund

Allen L. Stein is 43 years old. Stein did not work and did not earn any money last year: none, not a penny. To obtain some money, he obtained an income tax form from the Internal Revenue Service. Then he filled out the form and reported an income of $63,810.91. He also listed expenses and deductions and withholding credits that he did not legitimately and honestly have. According to his creative calculations, the IRS owed him a refund of $4,292.57. IRS records indicate that the refund for that amount was mailed to him on the 17th of June of last year. A recent audit revealed that the tax return and application for a refund were suspicious, but when Stein was asked to appear in the local IRS office to discuss his income taxes with an examiner there, he indicated that he would be unable to do so for 10 years. Stein is an inmate in one of your state prisons. In 1986 he was sentenced to serve a term of 20 years for forgery. It was the third time he has been convicted of that offense. He said he expects to be released from prison in about 10 years due to good behavior. Last week, he was formally charged with defrauding the federal government. Stein pleaded guilty in a federal court today and will be sentenced by the judge next month. He could be sentenced to an additional term of up to 20 years in a federal prison. In court today, Stein said: "Why did I do it? I read the newspapers. They always have stories about how citizens are cheating Uncle Sam out of money, so I thought I'd try it, and it was easy. So now I'll have to spend some time in a federal prison. So what? I'm already in prison, and I hear federal prisons are a lot nicer than state prisons."

5. Lost Evidence

A Pennsylvania man may deserve an award for being the smartest crook of the week. He appeared in a Pittsburgh court today. He was charged with changing a $1 bill into a $20 bill by doctoring it a bit. A government attorney prosecuting the defendant placed the evidence—the $1 bill—on a table in front of the defendant for a moment and then turned away from him and toward the judge. When the attorney turned back, the defendant was chewing on something, and the evidence was gone. The judge promptly dismissed the case for a lack of evidence. Prosecutors said the defendant will not be charged with tampering with the evidence because they cannot prove that he ate the bill. There was no jury, and only 5 or 6 people were in the courtroom, and no one saw the defendant actually take the bill or place it in his mouth. People did see him chewing something, but he swallowed whatever he was chewing on before anyone fully comprehended and checked to see what was occurring at the time.

6. Shoplifting Case

The woman, an attractive blonde, is 31 years old, divorced and the mother of four young children. She resides in San Jose, California. She was arrested at approximately 8 p.m. last evening and was charged with shoplifting. Her arrest and the alleged offense occurred at Pete's Market, a supermarket located at 1238 Sacramento Road. Today, she told reporters she picked up one or two seedless grapes to test them before deciding whether to buy some for her family. She explained: "Sometimes you find that the fruits and vegetables they're trying to sell you are old and spoiled, or that they don't taste good, so I decided to sample one. That's all. That's not a crime. Everyone does it. There's nothing wrong with that; it's just good common sense." However, the store manager said: "I was standing there watching, and she must have eaten a dozen grapes, at least, maybe lots more, and then she didn't buy any. If she'd eaten just one or two, or if she'd bought some, then I wouldn't be so mad, but it was like she was eating dinner or something. I've got thousands of customers coming into this store every week, and if they all sampled everything before they bought it, I'd go broke. It's stealing, and I decided to stop it. I stopped her as she was leaving the store and asked her to pay for the grapes. She refused. All I asked for was a dime, but she laughed at me, so I called the cops."

7. Bank Regulations

Abraham Burmeister is president of the First National Bank, the largest bank in your community. Each year, in accordance with new federal laws, the bank is required to send all its customers copies of some complex new federal rules concerning the regulation of banks and the procedures followed for money transfers by means of electronic banking. Consequently, the First National Bank prepared a 4,500-word pamphlet describing and summarizing those new federal rules and then sent copies of the rules to all its 40,000 regular depositors and customers. Like many other bankers, Burmeister objected to the federal law, saying it imposed a needless burden and needless expense on bankers since the federal laws that banks are being forced to explain are too complicated for the average person to understand and too dull and uninteresting for people to spend time trying to read. To prove his point, on the last page of 100 of the 40,000 copies of the rules he took a gamble and inserted a special extra sentence. That sentence said, "If you return this pamphlet to any of the bank's tellers within the next 30 days, they will give you $25." The 30 days passed yesterday, and not one person turned in a single copy of the 100 special pamphlets and requested the $25 due on demand, apparently because no one read the pamphlets. Bank officials calculated that it cost somewhere in the neighborhood of $15,000 to prepare, print, address and mail the pamphlets to the 40,000 bank customers, and they said that is a waste of money, yet they must do it every year, even though obviously no one reads the things, as they have just proven with their interesting little experiment.

8. Dogcatcher

Robert C. Gratne is the municipal dogcatcher in Reno, Nevada. At 4 p.m. yesterday he caught a dog running loose on a school playground. According to a recent law adopted by the Reno City Council, all dogs must be on a leash at all times they are not on their owners' property. Gratne's enforcement of the law has always been strict. The name of the dog he caught yesterday is "Sorrowful," and he was able to catch the dog by calling its name, which he knew. The dog is owned by Gratne's wife, Rebecca. Mrs. Gratne appeared in court at 9 a.m. today and pleaded innocent to a charge of letting her dog run loose. Because of her husband's testimony, she was convicted by the judge. The judge fined Mrs. Gratne $17.50 and ordered her to pay court costs of $38.50. Her dog was freed from the city pound after she paid the money.

EXERCISE 2
Specialized Types of Stories

BRIGHTS

INSTRUCTIONS: Use the following information to write "brights," a series of short, humorous stories. Write some brights that have a summary lead and others that have a surprise ending.

1. Nude Man

A vacationing couple was driving a pickup camper through Phoenix, Arizona, yesterday. When a traffic light suddenly turned red, the woman slammed on the camper's brakes, coming to a very fast stop. Her husband was sleeping in the camper at the time, nude, as he says he always sleeps, and the sudden stop threw him off a cot. Half asleep and thinking they had been involved in an accident and forgetting his lack of attire, the husband threw open the back door of the camper and jumped to the ground. At that moment, the light turned green and his wife, not knowing he had jumped from the camper, drove on. So as a consequence, her husband was left standing naked in the middle of the intersection, in broad daylight, without any identification, without anything. Police at first charged him with indecent exposure but dropped the charges when he was able to convince them of the truth of his story. Highway patrolmen stopped his wife 78 miles away. She returned to Phoenix to pick him up at a police station. The police did not release the couple's names.

2. Political Dinner

Reid R. Wentila is a candidate for governor. Last night he had an unusual fund-raising dinner in the city. It was a great success and raised a total of $17,800 for his statewide political campaign. Wentila and his aides got the idea after they noticed how reluctant people are to buy tickets for fund-raising dinners and to take an evening off to attend them. Worse, many people who buy tickets give them to someone else, and those people come and eat everything available, thus increasing a candidate's expenses. "The overhead is something terrible," one of Wentila's aides said. So they implemented a new idea. They sold tickets for a dinner scheduled for last night. They charged guests $25 if they promised not to attend and $50 if they planned to attend. No one bought any of the $50 tickets, and no one appeared at the dinner last night. "That's just the way we wanted it," Wentila said. "We raised more money this way, and we didn't impose on anyone's time."

3. Power Plant

The Municipal Power Plant is owned by the city and provides electrical power to all city residents at a cost about 23% lower than the cost of power which private companies provide to other residents of the state. William C. Davis is Utilities Director. Last night, he asked the city for an allocation of $82,000 to construct an air-conditioned, soundproof room for power plant operators. He said the room is needed to comply with insurance requirements concerning noise levels. However, the city gave him considerably less than he asked for. The city has a surplus of more than enough money to comply with the request of Mr. Davis but decided to use the money for other, more urgent needs. Mayor Paul Novarro explained, "We have to watch our spending very carefully." The Mayor suggested that instead of providing a soundproof room, Davis buy earplugs for each power plant operator at a cost of $25 a set. Total cost for 11 persons: $275. A quick check found that earplugs, properly fitted by a medical doctor, will satisfy the insurance requirements.

4. Truck Theft

There was a motor vehicle theft which occurred in the city at some time in the middle of last night. The vehicle was taken from a building located at 7720 Avonwood Dr. The building was unlocked at the time, and 12 occupants sleeping in an upstairs room said they heard nothing unusual. They were all in bed by midnight and the first got up at 6 a.m., discovering the theft at that time. Police describe the missing vehicle as a bright canary-yellow fire truck, marked with the name of the city fire department. The custom-made truck cost a total of $92,000 and was delivered to the city just three months ago. Firemen said it had a full tank of gas, about 50 gallons. However, it gets only 1½ miles to the gallon. It contained enough clothing and equipment for six firefighters, a dozen oxygen tanks, 1,000 feet of hose, four ladders (each up to 60 feet tall), plus miscellaneous other equipment. The people sleeping upstairs were all firefighters and the building was a fire station. The firefighters suspect that someone opened the station's main door, then either pushed or towed the truck silently outside and started its engine some distance away from the building. It is the first time in its history that the city fire department has reported that one of its trucks has been stolen. It was not insured. The keys are always left in the truck to reduce the response time when firefighters receive a call for help.

5. Inheritance

The will of a local man, Benjamin Satterwaite, 74, of 307 E. King Boulevard was filed in Probate Court today. Satterwaite died on the twentieth of last month of cancer. He had lived alone in his home, neighbors said, for at least the past 20 years. He was a retired postal clerk. According to the will, Satterwaite left a total estate of $1,071,400.38. Much of the money was earned in the stock market. Neighbors said they were surprised by the amount. Satterwaite was not a miser but lived frugally, and neighbors said they did not suspect that the deceased was a millionaire. Satterwaite left the entire estate to the U.S. government, explaining that, "Everybody seems to be living off the government, so maybe someone ought to help it out." He had no known relatives.

6. Child's Lawsuit

Thomas J. Haggerty has reached the age of 27 and lives in Chapel Hill, North Carolina. Yesterday he filed a $350,000 lawsuit complaining that he is poorly adjusted. The suit blames his parents and names them as defendants in the case. Haggerty explains in the lawsuit that his parents, Mr. and Mrs. Byron R. Haggerty, also of Chapel Hill, failed to raise him properly, neglecting his needs for food, clothing, shelter, love and psychological support at crucial periods in his life. Haggerty, who dropped out of college, lives on a trust fund established by his parents which provides him with the sum of $2,500.00 a month. He filed the suit in Chapel Hill. In the suit, he claims that he is unable to get along well with other people, is unable to experience the emotion of love, has been divorced three times and will require continuing psychiatric care for the rest of his natural life because of the cruel manner in which he was raised. His lawyer adds, "Basically, what we are doing is bringing a suit for malpractice of parenting." His parents are both veterinarians. Both refused to comment on the lawsuit.

EXERCISE 3
Specialized Types of Stories

FOLLOWUP LEADS

INSTRUCTIONS: Write a story summarizing the initial set of facts and then just the lead for each of the later developments. Or your instructor may ask you to write a complete news story about each day's developments.

Day 1

Twelve people have been selected to hear the murder trial of Sara Kindstrom, 27, of 4828 North Vine Street. She is charged with murdering her live-in boyfriend, Frederick C. Taylor, 25. Kindstrom is charged with first-degree murder. If convicted of the charge, she could be sentenced to life imprisonment and would have to serve at least 25 years before becoming eligible for parole. Taylor's death occurred last summer, on the 4th day of August, at about 7 p.m. in the evening. Taylor was shot and killed by shots fired from a .22-caliber pistol. This morning, assistant state attorney Donald Hedricks and Kindstrom's attorney, assistant public defender Marilyn Cheeseboro, spent several hours questioning 42 potential jurors before selecting an 8-man, 4-woman panel to hear the case. The trial is scheduled to begin at 9:00 a.m. tomorrow before Circuit Court Judge Randall Pfaff.

Day 2

Jurors seemed to be spellbound as they listened to the fascinating testimony of Sara Kindstrom today. She told a tearful story of bloody beatings and verbal, physical and sexual abuse at the hands of her live-in boyfriend, whom she is accused of killing. During her 5½ hours of testimony today, Kindstrom said: "He was going to kill me. It wasn't a matter of whether he'd kill me, but when he was going to do it. I met him a year ago, and he moved right in with me, and at first it was really nice. Then he lost his job and got sicker and sicker. We could sleep together for a month and not have sex. Then we'd fight and he'd force himself on me. I work as a waitress, and when I got home Aug. 4 he was waiting for me. He started calling me names and hitting me and accused me of running around with other men, and that's not true. I'd never do that, but he was jealous. He was always jealous. I tried to keep quiet and make supper, but he started drinking. Later, we started arguing again. He was telling me how dumb I was, that if I left, he'd move someone nice in. I said it was my house, and he said I'd be dead and then it would be his house. He was hitting me really hard, hitting my face, and I was bleeding. Then we were in the bedroom, and I just couldn't take it anymore. He kept a pistol in a bedroom closet, and I had it in my hand. I don't remember getting it out, but I must have, and it started going off. I don't remember pulling the trigger. He looked surprised and then he just fell to the floor without saying anything. I knew I'd hurt him, but I didn't think he was dead. I didn't mean to kill him."

Day 3

A neighbor, Martha Rudnick, testified: "My husband and I heard her screaming, but that wasn't unusual. They were always fighting over there, and everyone in the neighborhood heard it. The police had been there a dozen times, but it never seemed to do any good. This time I heard the gun. Right away I knew they were shots, but I thought he was shooting her. He was always threatening to kill her. My husband picked up the telephone and called the police, and I ran next door to see if I could help Sara. But when I got outside, Freddy was crawling out their front door, and she was coming after him with the gun, still shooting him. She was shooting him in the back, and he was just lying there, bleeding out on the sidewalk, and she was shouting and crying all at once. She kept pulling the trigger, but the gun must have been out of bullets and was clicking every time she pulled the trigger. Then the police came and arrested her. I could see her face was all red and swollen and bleeding where he'd hit her, and it wasn't the first time I'd seen her like that."

Day 4

Police Sergeant Michael Barsch said: "I interrogated her as soon as we got her to the police station. She told me she'd shot him and that she hoped she'd killed him. It was his gun, but we checked and found that she'd used it before. He'd taught her how to shoot it. He'd taken her target shooting and hunting with him. We also found a box of shells in her purse, with 9 shells missing, and found that she'd bought the box herself at a sporting goods store near her home about a week earlier, so she'd apparently been planning to use the gun."

Day 5

In his closing arguments, the prosecuting attorney said: "The defendant did not have to murder Fredrick Taylor. She could have called the police for protection. She could have charged Taylor with assault, and she could have forced him to leave her house. But she never sought help and consistently returned to the man who beat her. She may regret it now, but she killed him. She shot him, and she did it deliberately. If she only wanted to protect herself, she could have shot him once, possibly twice, and escaped. But she fired 9 bullets, and all 9 hit him—mostly in the back. She continued firing those bullets even after Taylor was obviously helpless and down on the ground, trying to crawl to safety. That's murder in the first degree."

In her closing arguments, the public defender said: "This woman is a victim who acted in self-defense. She was repeatedly and brutally beaten by Frederick Taylor during their 12-month relationship. We also know that Taylor was an extremely dangerous man, a brutal woman-hater who eventually would have killed Sara Kindstrom. She killed him to protect herself from rape and murder. Imagine yourself in that situation. You're being beaten, badly beaten. Dazed, confused, in need of protecting yourself, you pick up a gun and begin to shoot. You're acting in self-defense, to protect your own life, and you may not be entirely rational at a moment like that."

Day 7

After two days of deliberation, the jury returned with a verdict. The jury announced that it found the defendant guilty. However, the jury found the defendant guilty of murder in the second degree rather than of murder in the first degree. The maximum penalty for a conviction of that type is from 5 to 18 years in prison.

Day 10

The judge today sentenced the defendant, Sara Kindstrom. He sentenced her to a term in a state prison of the minimum sentence of 5 years. In sentencing Kindstrom to the minimum prison term the judge noted the extenuating circumstances in the case, including her brutal treatment at the hands of her victim and her apparent effort to defend herself. However, the judge complained that she used excessive force in that defense. She will be eligible for parole in as short a time as a period of 18 months, with time off for good behavior.

EXERCISE 4
Specialized Types of Stories

FOLLOWUP LEADS

INSTRUCTIONS: Write a story summarizing the initial set of facts and then just the lead for each of the later developments. Or your instructor may ask you to write a complete news story about each day's developments.

Day 1

There was a tragic plane crash late yesterday afternoon. Three state highway patrolmen assigned to work in your county were on a routine air traffic patrol. Your county sheriff's department asked them for assistance in the tracking down of some burglary suspects. Neighbors in the Oakwood subdivision had become suspicious about a strange car parked in the driveway of a home whose owners were on vacation. Sheriff's deputies chased the car, and several shots were fired during the high-speed chase. Several shots were fired at the deputies, and they then returned the fire with their service revolvers as the suspects fled east on State Route 141 at speeds up to 80 and 90 mph in a late-model brown Ford. The Ford skidded off the road, and the two suspects fled on foot from the vehicle and into a nearby field and woods. The highway patrolmen, who were in a twin-engine Cessna Skyhawk, were called for help and circled the area in an effort to help the deputies spot the suspects. Other law enforcement officials speculate that the plane had one of the suspects in sight and was banking. Exactly what happened next is unknown, but the plane came down nose first. There were reports from other law enforcement agents that shots were fired and that they may have disabled the plane. The victims were identified as the pilot, Sgt. Travis Orzuk, and Cpl. Bryan Flynne. The name of the third trooper was withheld pending notification of his next of kin. One suspect, Daniel Mims, 24, 872 Huron Avenue, was subsequently arrested by police searching the woods and is being held in the county jail on charges of burglary. Other charges are pending. A deputy sheriff, Julie Wilhelm, said: "I heard someone start yelling that the plane was down. When I got to the scene there were a couple of people there, and the front part of the plane was burning. We crawled over the tail of the plane and lifted up one wing to try to reach the men. The plane was torn open, and we could see them all inside. But when we lifted the wing, gasoline poured out, and the flames shot up. We had to wait a few minutes for firemen to come and douse the flames before we could get to them, but they were all dead. They'd apparently died in the crash."

Day 2

A second burglary suspect has been arrested in connection with the burglary of several homes in the Oakwood subdivision and a chase that caused the death of three highway patrolmen. The suspect was arrested at his home and has been identified as Marc Ibold, 27, 877 Huron Avenue. Three homicide charges were filed against Mims and Ibold. Under state law, if a death occurs in the commission of a felony, murder charges may be filed against the suspects involved, They were also charged with three counts of burglary and were held under $20,000 bond for those charges. No bond was set on the homicide counts, so they are being held in the county jail. The suspects were questioned in connection with a dozen home burglaries committed during the past year, including three that occurred in the subdivision yesterday. The third highway patrolman killed in the crash has been identified as Eli Aimini. A spokesman for the highway patrol said that Orzuk is survived by his wife and four children. Flynn is survived by his wife and one child. Aimini was not married and is survived by both his parents and several brothers and sisters. Funeral services for all three will be held jointly at 1 p.m. Saturday.

Day 3

Investigators from the Federal Aviation Administration and the National Transportation Safety Board have arrived in town and are inspecting the wreckage. They are trying to determine the cause of the crash. Such probes may take up to six months before a final determination is made. A spokesman for the sheriff's department said reports the plane was shot down appear to be false, since only 3 shots were known to be fired after the suspects left their car, and all three shots were fired by a sheriff's deputy in close pursuit of one of the suspects.

Two Months Later

Both suspects pleaded guilty today to three counts of forcible burglary of a residence during the daytime. Both were sentenced to three concurrent terms of 20 to 28 years in a state prison. As part of a plea-bargaining agreement, six other burglary charges and three homicide charges filed against them were dropped.

Five Months Later

The Federal Aviation Administration today issued a report on the cause of the crash. It said the plane may have been overloaded and was flying too low and too slowly. A spokesman for the highway patrol, which conducted its own independent investigation of the accident, Capt. Joseph Washington, added: "We've stopped short of calling it pilot error. We're not going to put any label on it. As to why the plane went down, the bottom line is that the aircraft was excessively low, too slow, and the troopers were trying to observe some suspects on the ground. Another factor may have been too much weight aboard the light plane. Three big men in a plane is very unusual in search operations."

EXERCISE 5
Specialized Types of Stories

FOLLOWUPS

INSTRUCTIONS: Write a story summarizing the initial set of facts and then just the lead for each of the later developments. Or your instructor may ask you to write a complete news story about each day's developments.

Original Story

To supplement their incomes, Herman Ansel and Cecil LaCette scavenge for aluminum cans, which they sell to recycling plants. Ansel is 20 and LaCette 23. Both live at 2814 Ambassador Drive in apartment number 61. They were looking for aluminum cans in a dumpster behind the Colonial Shopping Center at 8 p.m. last night. When LaCette looked inside a bag that had been dumped into the dumpster, he found a dead baby. Later, he talked to the police who responded to his call and he said to them: "Sometimes we find cans and other valuable stuff in all sorts of containers, so we open everything. So I started to tear open this bag, and at first I thought it was a doll inside, a baby doll. Then I got scared, real scared, and called you." Police said it was the body of a white male infant. It apparently was only a few hours old. An umbilical cord was still attached. The bag was a plain grocery bag. The baby was taken to Memorial Hospital, where it was pronounced dead. The county coroner will conduct an autopsy to determine the cause of death. However, detectives said it might be as long as a week before the cause of death can be determined unless there are some visible signs of abuse or maltreatment. A detective added that: "We're trying to determine if there was life before death. The baby could have died after birth, or it could have been born dead. So we may have a murder case here, but at this point we just don't know. The dumpster was emptied at 2 p.m. yesterday afternoon, and we do know the body had to be put in there sometime after that."

One Day Later

Detective Larry Chevez has been placed in charge of the case. During a press conference in his office today he revealed the following developments: "We've got nine men working on this case full time, and a lot of citizens who've heard about the baby are calling us with information, and we're tracking down all the leads they're giving us, but we don't have anything really substantial yet. It's a slow, tedious process. We've got some possibilities, some things to check on, but nothing that I could consider real good information. But we are working on the assumption the baby was murdered; there was some evidence it was beaten, but the autopsy hasn't been completed yet. Next Sunday, we've got 18 officers who've volunteered to come in on their own time to help check the neighborhood. We think the mother lives in the vicinity. There are about 2,500 homes in the area and, if we have to, we're going to knock on the door of every one of them." Chevez urges anyone with information about the baby or its mother to call the police department. His number is 841–4111.

The Following Monday

An autopsy was conducted, and the results were announced today by the coroner, Dr. Marlene Stoudnour, who held a press conference in her office at 8 a.m. today. Detective Chevez was present. At the press conference, she released copies of her autopsy report, then answered the questions asked by reporters. The autopsy report reveals that the baby was "murdered by repeated blows to the back of the head with a blunt instrument." Also, the autopsy adds that the white male infant was newborn and "lived for less than 24 hours before he was beaten to death." The baby was definitely alive before he was killed and thrown into the dumpster. He was slightly premature— probably the product of a seven- or eight-month pregnancy. Also, Detective Chevez said the house-to-house check of the neighborhood by police Sunday and the pursuit of leads phoned in by private citizens has thus far been fruitless. His office still requests any assistance possible from the public which might lead to the identification of the baby's mother. "People have called in, but we haven't gotten nowhere near the response we hoped we'd get," Chevez said. "We have a few leads, but none are promising." At the present time, Chevez said police officers are contacting all hospitals, clinics and other medical facilities in the area to learn the identities of women who have been treated in recent months for pregnancies. He said all the women will be contacted by the police in an effort to find a woman who was pregnant but doesn't have a baby to show for it. The dead baby's remains are being held in the county morgue.

Two Weeks Later

Police officers report they are continuing to investigate the case. Three officers are working on it full time. They have no solid clues. The officers are continuing to knock on doors and question pregnant women for leads. Literally hundreds of pregnant women have been eliminated from consideration. The officers have begun to consider the possibility that the mother may have been a transient, in which case there will be no local records of her pregnancy and it will be much more difficult to successfully identify and prosecute her. Detective Chevez said, "We're a long way from quitting, I can tell you that." He said the investigation is focusing on the mother because, "Whoever and wherever she is, we believe that either she killed the kid herself, or she knows who did it and can lead us to the guilty party."

One Year Later

Police officers say the case is still "open." It has not been shelved, and officers occasionally look into it when they have free time. No one is regularly assigned to the case. Officers have not been able to obtain any firm clues regarding the identity of the mother. They are now certain that she is not from the local area, since "it would have been impossible for a woman to hide a seven- or eight-month pregnancy from everyone she knew—her family and friends and neighbors and doctor and everyone else she ran into."

EXERCISE 6
Specialized Types of Stories

FOLLOWUPS

INSTRUCTIONS: Write a story summarizing the initial set of facts and then just the lead for each of the later developments. Or your instructor may ask you to write a complete news story about each day's developments.

Original Story

Bus drivers employed by the city—there are a total of 86 of them—are paid a total of $10.45 an hour. They receive the equivalent of an additional $3.82 an hour in fringe benefits, such as for pensions, health, life and disability insurance, paid vacations, and so forth. Each driver works 40 hours a week. Their contract will expire in 30 days. Negotiations for a new contract begin today. 73 of the 86 drivers are represented by the Teamsters Union. The union is demanding a 20% across-the-board raise in salaries, effectively immediately. It wants an additional 12% increase in pay in the second year of the contract and a reduction in the number of hours worked each week to 35. City negotiators, employed by the municipal bus company, citing the fact that the bus system is losing a total of $3 million a year, which the city's taxpayers must provide, have offered a 3% raise for the current 40-hour week. Both the city and union negotiators appear optimistic that a new contract can be signed before the old one expires.

15 Days Later

Negotiators report they are deadlocked. The city has offered the drivers a 4.5% raise and says it is its "absolute, final offer." The union is demanding a 14% raise in the first year and an 8% raise the second year with a reduction in hours worked from 40 to 35 in the second year. Last night union members voted to strike, if necessary. The vote was 63–4 with a few drivers absent from the meeting. Drivers who are not union members could attend the meeting but were not allowed to vote. Transit company executives say that, even if there is a strike, they will make every attempt to maintain their regular service, using office personnel and by hiring replacements for the strikers, if necessary.

30 Days Later

City bus drivers went out on strike at 12:01 a.m. today. No buses in the city are operating. Not even nonunion drivers reported for work. Company officials say the nonunion employees were intimidated and threatened with physical violence. The union denies the charges. Company officials say at least a dozen buses parked in the city garage have been "sabotaged"—that they are not in running condition because of deliberate damage to their engines. The officials estimate the damage to run to a total of $8,000 to $10,000. Union officials say the damage was not caused by union members and that the extent of the damage has been grossly exaggerated. Picket lines are up at the garage. Downtown stores report a decline in business of about 20% since some shoppers are unable to get there. The use of car pools is widely reported by workers in the city. The bus company has been deluged with irate phone calls from patrons who were unaware of the strike and who waited this morning for buses that never arrived. One woman who called the bus company said she waited nearly three hours. Then she had to call a cab. It cost her $6.80 to get to work, whereas the normal bus fare is 80 cents. Police say traffic appears to be only slightly heavier than usual, with little more than the normal difficulty of obtaining parking places. The police report no violence on the picket lines.

45 Days Later

Jeffery Rey, director of the municipal bus company, held a press conference in his office. He announced: "Negotiations continue deadlocked. We have made a final offer of a 6% raise for the next year and an additional 4% raise for the following year, all for the normal 40-hour week. The union has dropped its demands for a 35-hour week but is demanding a 10% minimum raise each year. With bus operations running in the red by more than $3 million a year, we can't afford to meet its demands. Effective immediately, we plan to begin hiring replacements for the striking drivers. This strike isn't fair to our regular patrons, and they're the ones being hurt most. They can't get to work, can't go shopping, can't move about town. We've received applications from more than 40 persons and started to process them. It'll take about a week to train new drivers. Eleven nonunion drivers have agreed to return to work, effective tomorrow, and we'll start by assigning them to the busiest runs, so bus service will resume, at least partially, first thing tomorrow morning. The police will be on hand to ensure that there's no violence."

60 Days Later

Jeffery Rey, director of municipal bus operations, held a press conference in his office this morning. He announced: "By tomorrow morning, we'll have 30 buses back on the road. We've got 12 of the 13 nonunion drivers back at work. Besides that, five union drivers have returned, and we've hired and trained 13 new drivers. In addition, we've gotten more than 100 applications for the remaining jobs, and we expect to train them and resume normal service within the next 10 days. By then, we'll have hired replacements for every striker and had time to train them. All the drivers are getting our best offer—an immediate 6% raise for this year, with an additional 4% raise promised for next year. As you know, we've resumed negotiations with the union, but their demands are so unreasonable that we haven't made any progress. Now they say they'll accept the raises we've offered; they recognize we've given them a fair offer, but they expect us to rehire every striker, and we're just not going to do it. We warned them that we'd hire replacements if they called a strike. If they ended the strike today, we'd take back as many drivers as we could, going strictly on a seniority basis. But we've made promises to the new drivers, and we're going to keep them."

An hour later, union representative Victor Butcavage held a press conference. He said: "They're anti-union. They're damn strikebreakers; that's the city's only real purpose—they wanted to destroy us, and I guess they have. They never negotiated; they just dictated. Now we've told 'em we'll take their stinking 6%, and they won't let us; they won't take us back. I mean, we've got men who've driven buses for the city for 20 and 30 years of their lives. They've got to get their jobs back; they've got too much invested in their jobs to start anything new at this stage of their lives. That Rey's a real shit. He doesn't have any right to dump these men out onto the street."

80 Days Later

Bus service is back to normal. All the city's buses are operating on their regular schedules. They are manned by the 12 nonunion drivers, a total of 14 union members who returned to work, and the rest of the drivers are new people hired since the strike began. All are receiving the initial 6% raise. The strike technically continues, but the strikers have clearly lost, all agree. Pickets continue to appear, but fewer, and some strikers say they have begun to look for positions elsewhere. Use of the city's buses is down 18% below its prestrike levels. Cause of the decline is uncertain. Bus company officials say people who began to use other means of transportation during the strike have not returned. Union leaders say their members and supporters are boycotting the bus system.

EXERCISE 7
Specialized Types of Stories

ROUNDUPS—MULTIPLE SOURCES

INSTRUCTIONS: Write a single roundup story that quotes the following sources:

Background

Ronald James Smitkinns, a 16-year-old youth, appeared in Circuit Court in your community today. He is charged with rape. His address is 417 Huron Avenue. He is the son of Marlene and Myron Smitkinns, also of 417 Huron Avenue. His victim is a junior high-school teacher. Police have not identified her or the junior high school at which she teaches. Last Sept. 3, Smitkinns asked the woman for help in her classroom after the end of the day's classes, police said. Then he turned out the lights, locked the classroom door and, brandishing scissors, raped her several times. Last Friday, he pleaded guilty to a charge of sexual battery, and today the judge had to decide whether to sentence Smitkinns as a juvenile or as an adult. As a juvenile, he could be sentenced to a maximum of three years at a youth facility, to be followed by two years of probation. The range of sentences for an adult convicted of the same offense, sexual battery, is 30 years to life imprisonment. The following remarks were made at a hearing which preceded the sentencing this morning. Under new state laws, the victim was allowed to testify about the crime and about the assailant at the pre-sentence hearing.

Ronald Smitkinns

"I'm sorry for what I did. I can't explain why I did it, but I know it's wrong, and it'll never happen again, I promise. I made a bad mistake, and I've learned from it. I want to repay society and the victim. All I need is another chance. I'm doing good in school, and I've never been in bad trouble like this before, you know. So you wouldn't ever have to worry about me again. It's just one dumb crazy thing I did and, you know, hey, it wouldn't ever happen again."

The Victim

"It was the most horrible, absolutely horrible, degrading experience of my life. I've needed psychiatric treatment and surgery, and I'm still not done with the counseling. I don't know if I can ever be done with it. My marriage has suffered, and I don't enjoy teaching any longer. All my life I wanted to be a teacher, and I was a good one. Now I'm nervous and afraid of the students, and I don't want to leave my home in the morning. But I'm not here today because I want vengeance. I just want protection. I want protection for me and for all the other women who work in the city's schools. You can't let this happen, especially in a school, and you can't let this rapist go free with a slap on the wrist. Rapists do it again because they get off on the violence, and he did."

Marlene Smitkinns, the Defendant's Mother

"I beg you, he's sorry. He's only 16, just a boy, and he didn't know what he was doing. If you send him to prison now, you'll destroy him. You'll ruin his whole life. You send a nice young boy like him, a good son, to prison for 30 years, and he'll never have a chance for a real, normal life. He'll be thrown in there with a lot of criminals, and they'll be a terrible influence on him."

Joel Greene, Defense Attorney

"This boy has no criminal record, had good grades in school and went to church. I agree there's a need to protect this victim and other potential victims, but the way to do it is not to send such a young boy to a state prison. In 10 years he'll come out 10 years older and stronger and full of hatred for society. That's not justice, that's not going to help society, and that's not going to help the victim. This young boy needs help, and he's not going to get it in prison. He's not a criminal now, but you put him in prison for 10 or 20 years, and you'll have a criminal on your hands when he gets out, and maybe a bad one. That just doesn't make sense."

Marlene Ostreicher, Judge

"I think those who are involved in the education and upbringing of young people should have some assurance that these matters will not be taken lightly by the court. Teachers are entitled to protection and some guarantee of their personal safety, and that thought is uppermost in my mind. This defendant is 16 years old, almost 17, and he's old enough to know better, to know right from wrong. Therefore I've decided to sentence him, as an adult, to a term of 30 years in the state prison. I recognize that he may suffer, but it's also obvious that he inflicted a great deal of undeserved suffering upon his victim, and that she may continue to suffer for years to come, perhaps for the rest of her life. Our society has to put a stop to this kind of behavior and maybe, just maybe, sentences of this nature will make some other youths pause and think about the consequences of their actions and know we're not going to let them engage in this kind of behavior and then come into our courtrooms and say they were too young to know what they were doing and that they are too young to be punished for their crimes."

Followup

Smitkinns and his attorney said they will appeal the sentence. If the appeal fails, Smitkinns must serve three years and nine months before he can be considered for parole. However, in cases of this kind parole is usually granted after the offender has served between 8 and 15 years; but Smitkinns may serve longer because he used the scissors as a deadly weapon in the commission of the felony. After the judge pronounced sentence, the victim said she felt like justice had been done. "I feel as if someone lifted a ton or two off me," she said. "Now I can stop worrying that he's coming back and that it'll happen again."

EXERCISE 8
Specialized Types of Stories

ROUNDUPS—MULTIPLE SOURCES

INSTRUCTIONS: A severe thunderstorm struck your city yesterday afternoon. Write a roundup story about the storm that summarizes all the information provided by the following sources. You may quote the sources.

U.S. Weather Bureau Employee

"We had a cold front moving in from the north, and it tangled with warm air masses that have been in the area for the last several days to create a severe thunderstorm, with hailstones that measured up to 1½ inches in diameter. Actually, two storms hit—one at about 4 p.m. and another 90 minutes later—and we expect another thunderstorm tonight, but it won't be nearly so bad. We recorded 3.1 inches of rain in four hours yesterday, starting at 4:10 p.m. Wind blasts reached 61 miles an hour. Those were the strongest blasts recorded in the city since 1954. The temperature fell 19 degrees in 15 minutes. We also received some reports of funnel clouds, although no touchdowns were reported."

Martin Guidema, Police Chief

"We're urging people to stay home today if at all possible. It'd really help alleviate the cleanup and traffic problems. We still have some traffic lights out, and the streets are a mess. We received about 250 calls related to the storm. We've had about 80 minor traffic accidents, a lot caused by slippery roads. A tree limb fell on a car at the intersection of Cedar Ave. and 35th St., killing the driver, Mrs. Kathy Murphy. Otherwise, there've been only minor injuries that I know of. About 100 calls we've received have concerned trees down and blocking roads. We referred those calls to the Department of Public Works, and it kept its crew out all night cleaning up the mess. They started on the main streets and still haven't been able to clear all the side streets. Some downtown store windows were blown out, and we've had officers stand guard until the windows could be boarded up. We've had only one report of looting, and that involved a liquor store that lost all its display windows due to the wind."

Reynold Hunt, Fire Chief

"We received 31 calls yesterday, and all but two related to the storm. Electric wires were reported down in eight locations. We watched the wires until the electric company was able to shut off power to repair them. Six homes were struck by lightning. The ligntning caused two small fires, but it didn't hurt anyone or cause much damage. We also helped some people whose homes were damaged by the winds and falling trees, and our rescue squads assisted the police at several traffic accidents."

Telephone Company Employee

"We had a widespread loss of telephone service from falling trees and heavy winds and rains. Probably, at one time or another, we had about 35,000 customers without service. We may not be able to get every phone back in order, especially in rural areas, for another day or two. Plus, with an unusually high calling rate, we had plenty of problems. We lost our regular power and some of our emergency system. During the 10 minutes just after 4:30, about half of all telephone calls didn't get through. We had a 92 percent dial tone delay, meaning that people had to wait up to 30 seconds just to get a dial tone. The worst thing about this is people call and can't get through, so they panic and keep on trying, tying up the lines even more. The lines were going crazy with calls late yesterday, and it still hasn't settled back to normal."

Power Company Employee

"Power has been off in several areas of the city. The power failures began at about 4 o'clock and, after that, we received hundreds of calls about the problem, so we had to call in linemen from neighboring counties to help restore the service. By midnight, we had the power restored to maybe 75 percent of the homes, and we kept the crews out working all night, and we still had 2,000 to 3,000 homes without power at 8 o'clock this morning. We'd hoped that we'd have everything restored by noon today, but it's going to take longer, until 6 p.m., or even until midnight. Some of our poles were struck by lightning, but most of the trouble was caused by the wind and by trees that fell on our lines. The wind was so strong that some poles toppled right over. Altogether, I'd estimate that, at one time or another, we had about 25,000 to 30,000 customers without service, but that's just a guess."

Marcia Pagozalski, Superintendent of Schools

"The information I've received so far is still preliminary, but it seems evident that the storm really hurt us. We just finished getting the steel beams and walls up for the new Eisenhower Junior High School on Eisenhower Drive, and everything came down last night. We're going to have to start all over again. I'd estimate damage at somewhere between $1 million and $1.2 million. The shell of the building had just about been finished. The walls measured 240 by 500 feet. They were concrete block but didn't have much support. The wind blew them all down; it just leveled everything. Also, children were sent home from five schools that didn't have any electrical power when their classes were scheduled to start this morning. A few of those schools still don't have any power, and their staffs have also been sent home, but they'll all have to make up the time next Saturday, the students and staff."

Patricia Bache, Manager of Bache Insurance Co.

"We've been deluged with calls. Our phones went out yesterday, but we must have gotten 200 calls this morning, and there's no way of knowing how many more people tried to call and couldn't get through because our lines were busy, and you have to keep in mind that we're just one small company. I'm sure that the other companies in town are getting just as many calls. We're calling in help from other districts to help with the damage estimates, but it's going to take a day or two for more adjusters to get here. And it'll probably take a week or longer before we can inspect all the damage suffered by our policyholders and start settling their claims. Some policyholders report that their cars and homes were hit by trees, and some people have trees in their swimming pools. But mostly people seem to be reporting broken windows and other wind and hail damage, plus a lot of water damage."

EXERCISE 9
Specialized Types of Stories

ROUNDUPS—MULTIPLE SOURCES

INSTRUCTIONS: A fire destroyed your city's old vocational-technical school last night. Write a roundup story about the fire that summarizes all the information provided by the following sources. You may quote the sources.

Marcia Pagozalski, Superintendent of Schools

"We haven't used the building for several years now. I've been told it was built in 1914 and was originally designed and used as a grammar school. Since the late 1920s, I don't have the exact date, it's been used as a vocational-technical school. In fact, it was the city's first vocational school. By the 1970s, it was just too small and old for our needs. We'd used the building for 60 years, and it was worn out. We went to the school board and asked for a new building, but at first they thought it would be cheaper to remodel VT. But it had already been remodeled a half dozen times, and the school board finally recognized that we needed a new building, and a much larger building, designed especially for our modern classroom programs and equipment. We moved out in 1986, and a few months later the School Board sold the building to a group of investors. They paid $820,000 for the building. I don't think the building was worth anywhere near that amount, but they wanted the land for a condominium. I've heard they had trouble getting the financing for it, so the school's been boarded up and sitting empty all this time."

Reynold Hunt, Fire Chief

"We got the first call shortly after 10 p.m. It's only a few blocks from our main downtown station, so we were there in a minute or two, but the flames had already broken out some first- and second-floor windows. The fire must have been smoldering for hours before that, before anyone noticed it, to break out so quickly. Our first men on the scene found the flames in the center of the building. At first, I thought we had a chance to save it. Sometimes we would gain control of one section, but then another blaze would spring up elsewhere. The flames spread to the upper floors, breaking through the roof and then engulfing the top of the building in about 90 minutes. Finally, I had to have my commanders tell our men to get out and to switch into a defensive mode—to fight the fire only from the outside. It was too dangerous inside because of the intensity of the blaze and the age of the structure. The whole thing could have collapsed at any time. Most of the interior structure was wood, and it'd been remodeled so often that once the fire got inside the walls, it could spread everywhere and we couldn't get at it, we couldn't reach it. Then the roof collapsed, and I knew we were going to lose the building. I had about 50 firefighters at the scene, but there wasn't anything we could do after that. Altogether, we had six fire engines, three tower trucks and two rescue vehicles at the scene. The fire was so intense you could feel the heat a half block away, and you could see it miles away. It's the worst fire I remember in the downtown area in the last 20 years, and we had our firefighters there all night. We had the fire out by 4 a.m., but there's always the danger that a big fire like that will start up again. It's still too hot and unstable to get inside, so it may be a few days before we can determine what started it."

Allen Smythe, Police Lieutenant

"The officers in one of our cruisers smelled smoke and then tracked it down to the school and sounded the alarm. Right away, we knew it was a bad one, so we cordoned off the whole block and assigned more than a dozen men, 16 I think, to directing traffic and holding back the crowd. It attracted a huge crowd, maybe 2,000 or 3,000 people, and the traffic problem was terrible, really terrible."

James Custodio, Attorney

"I'm one of the owners. So far as we know, the building was empty, so we didn't lose anything of value. We didn't have any insurance because we planned to tear the building down. It wasn't worth anything. This will just make it that much easier for us. But we're certainly grateful no one was hurt. I didn't even know anything about the fire until a reporter called me at home last night, and I still don't know what started it, although we've had reports that some transients have been living in the building. We've just recently got the financing, and we're putting together plans for a condominium high-rise with 110 units that we're planning to put on the site, probably starting sometime next summer."

EXERCISE 10
Specialized Types of Stories

ROUNDUPS—MULTIPLE EVENTS

INSTRUCTIONS: Write a single roundup story that summarizes all three of the following accidents.

Accident 1

One car was driven by T. J. Ortsen, 51, of 810 N. 14th St. The other car was driven by Sara Anne Talbertson, 34, of 3214 Riverview Drive. The two vehicles collided at the intersection of U.S. 141 and Carlton Avenue. The accident was reported to police at 12:35 a.m. today. The accident was investigated by Patrolmen Julius Tiller and Manuel Cortez. They reported that Ortson and his wife, Martha, 53, suffered head and chest injuries. An ambulance rushed the couple to Memorial Hospital, where both are reported in serious condition. Miss Talbertson was not injured, apparently, the officers said, because she was wearing a shoulder-type seat belt at the time of the accident. However, the officers charged Miss Talbertson with running a red light. Both cars were demolished. Ortson was driving a 3-year-old Toyota valued at approximately $5,000, and Miss Talbertson was driving a 10-year-old Plymouth valued at approximately $600.

Accident 2

Officers were called to the 4200 block of Wymore Road at 6:30 a.m. today to investigate a reported accident. Patrolman Cecil Roehl filed a report concerning the accident. The report said: "I arrived at the scene at 6:34 a.m. and, upon arrival, found the victim's motorcycle in the eastbound lane of traffic. The victim has been positively identified as Leon Merritt, 17, of 301 Wymore Road. Skid marks indicate that his motorcycle was traveling at excessive speeds and went out of control just past a dip in the road. Road signs warn of the dip. The posted speed limit is 45 miles an hour. The subject's motorcycle is estimated to have been traveling in excess of 60 miles an hour. The motorcycle went off the road and struck a telephone pole and then seems to have bounced back onto the road. The victim's body was thrown into a field and was lying 47 feet from the roadway. A truck driver went off the road to avoid striking the wrecked motorcycle. The driver, who was not injured, telephoned police from a nearby house. The truck had to be towed from a ditch, but no damage was apparent. The coroner pronounced Merritt dead at the scene. His motorcycle was totally destroyed."

Accident 3

The accident occurred at 8:20 a.m. today. Two vehicles were involved. A delivery van driven by Jay Gable of 1701 Woodcrest Drive and a car driven by Jean Janvier, 27, of 1883 Hope Ter. Gable was alone in his vehicle. A passenger in the Janvier vehicle has been identified as Reba Carvel. She was 23 years old. She also lived at 1883 Hope Ter. Miss Janvier and Miss Carvel taught at Colonial Elementary School, and they apparently were on their way to school when the accident occurred. Patrolman Nego, who investigated the accident, reported that: "We were unable to find any witnesses to the accident. Gable suffered a broken leg and possible head injuries and has been taken to Memorial Hospital for treatment. He seemed in shock so I couldn't talk to him much before an ambulance took him away. Gable had stopped to pick up another man who works with him. He identified himself as Melvin McCaully, 47, of 540 Osceloa Blvd. The accident occurred directly in front of his house. McCaulley said he heard Gable stop and honk. McCaully said he went to get his lunch bucket and then heard the crash. From skid marks at the scene, it appears that Gable hadn't pulled off the road and the Janvier vehicle rammed square into the back of his van. The van was pushed off the road and into a ditch, where it overturned. The car remained upright on the highway. Skid marks and the extent of the damage indicate that the car was traveling about fifty miles an hour at the time of impact. The speed limit on Osceola Blvd. at that point is fifty-five miles an hour. Both women were dead when I got to them and it took more than a half hour for the rescue squad to pry their bodies out of the wreckage. Both bodies were badly mangled, and Miss Janvier's legs were amputated just below the knees. Charges of manslaughter will probably be filed against Gable later today. The district attorney is looking at the evidence now."

EXERCISE 11
Specialized Types of Stories

ROUNDUPS—MULTIPLE EVENTS

INSTRUCTIONS: Write a single roundup story that summarizes all three of the following fires.

Fire 1

Two police officers patrolling Main St. reported a fire at Frishe's Bowling Alley, 4113 Main St., at 3:32 a.m. today. They smelled smoke, got out of their squad car and traced the smoke to the bowling alley. Firefighters said the fire was confined to an office, where it caused an estimated $10,000 damage. Firefighters found evidence of arson and notified police that the office apparently had been set on fire after it was burglarized. Two cigarette machines, a soft-drink machine and a door leading to the office had been pried open. Police said the thieves probably set the fire to hide the robbery. Art Mahew, manager of the bowling alley, estimated that $20 was missing from the three machines and $50 was taken from a cash box in the office. He added: "That's all the money we keep in the building at night. Except for some change for the next day's business, we just don't keep any money in the building at night. It's too risky. This is the third robbery we've had since I started working here four years ago."

Fire 2

Firefighters were called to 1314 Griese Drive at 8:23 a.m. today. They found a fire in progress on the second floor of the two-story home. The home is owned by Mr. and Mrs. Timothy Keele. Mr. and Mrs. Keel and their four children escaped from the home before firemen arrived. Firefighters extinguished the blaze within 20 minutes. The fire was confined to two upstairs bedrooms and the attic. Smoke and water damage were reported throughout the house. No one was injured. Damage was estimated at $20,000. Mrs. Keel told firemen she had punished one of her children for playing with matches in an upstairs closet earlier in the morning. Fire marshals said the blaze started in that closet and attributed the fire to the child playing with matches. Mrs. Keel added that she was not aware of the fire until a telephone repairman working across the street noticed smoke, came over and rang her doorbell. When she answered the door, he asked, "Do you know your house is on fire?"

Fire 3

Firefighters responded to a call at the Quality Trailer Court at 10:31 a.m. today after neighbors were alerted by screams from a trailer occupied by Mrs. Susan Kopp, age 71. Flames had spread throughout the trailer by the time firefighters arrived at the scene. The firefighters had to extinguish the blaze, then wait for the embers to cool before they were able to enter the trailer. They found Mrs. Kopp's body in her bedroom in the trailer. A spokesman for the Fire Department said she had apparently been smoking in bed, then awoke when her bedding caught fire. She died of suffocation before she could get out. Neighbors who heard her screams were unable to enter the trailer because of the flames, smoke and heat.

EXERCISE 12
Specialized Types of Stories

SIDEBARS

INSTRUCTIONS: Use the following information to write two separate stories: first a news story reporting the fire, then a sidebar based on the interview with Mrs. Noffsinger.

Main Story

The Grande Hotel is located downtown at the corner of Wisconsin and Barber Avenues. It is a seven-story structure with a total of 114 rooms. It was constructed and opened for business in the year 1924. In recent years the hotel has been in an obvious state of decline, unable to compete with newer facilities in the city and with the convenience of motels located along highways which now bypass the city. Many of the hotel rooms have been rented on long-term leases, often to elderly persons who like its downtown location, which is more convenient for them, since many facilities they use are in walking distance and buses are easily available for other trips they want to make. Three persons died in a fire at the hotel last night. The cause of the fire is undetermined. It started in a third-floor room. It spread and also destroyed the fourth, fifth, sixth and seventh floors before it was brought under control at 4:30 a.m. today. At about 11 p.m. a guest called the lobby to report the odor of smoke. A hotel employee used a passkey to enter the third-floor room where the fire originated and found it totally engulfed in flames. The room is believed to have been vacant at the time. The employee sounded a fire alarm in the hotel and called firefighters. It was the first five-alarm blaze in the city in more than 10 years. Every piece of fire equipment in the city was rushed to the scene, and off-duty firefighters were called in to assist. Fortunately, said Fire Chief Reynold Hunt, no other fires were reported in the city at the same time or he would have had to send a truck and men from the scene of the hotel blaze. Hotel records indicate that 62 persons were registered in the hotel at the time the blaze initiated; 49 had long-term leases and 13 were transients. All the transients were located on the second floor and escaped safely. The dead, all of whom had long-term leases, have been identified as Mildred Haserot, age 58; Willie Hattaway, age 67; and Pearl Petchsky, age 47. The bodies of all three victims were found on the fourth floor, where they lived. Fire Chief Reynold Hunt said this morning the hotel is a total loss and that some walls are in danger of collapse. He said: "The fire was already out of hand when our first units reached the scene. I was called from home, and by then the flames were breaking out through the third- and fourth-floor windows. We were really lucky there weren't more people killed, but the hotel people knocked on the door of every room that was occupied to get everybody out. Most guests used a back stairway, and we were lucky the elevators kept working for awhile even after my men got into the building, otherwise the loss would have been worse. I'm also told that the top two floors were empty, and that helped keep down the loss of lives."

The Red Cross is caring for survivors, finding them new rooms and providing clothes and emergency allocations of cash, a total of $250 per person. Five people were injured, including one fireman who suffered from smoke inhalation. The others suffered from burns, some serious, and also from smoke inhalation. Three are being treated at Mercy Hospital. Two have been released, including the fireman. Their names and conditions are unknown at this time.

Sidebar

Nora Noffsinger, 74, has been a resident of the hotel for the past nine years. She paid $480 a month rent for one room on the fifth floor. A retired bookkeeper, she said afterward: "It was dreadfully expensive, but it was a charming old building and I had lots of good friends living there. I was asleep last night when I heard someone pounding on my door. I don't know who it was, but he told me to get out fast, and I did. All I had on were my pajamas and a robe, but I could see the smoke, even up there on the fifth floor, and I was scared; I knew right away that it was bad. Everyone else was scared too, but we all knew what to do. We'd talked lots about what we'd do if there was ever a fire because you hear so often about fires in old hotels, and we wanted to be prepared. We all kept flashlights in our rooms and planned to go back down the back stairway unless the fire was there, and it wasn't. The lights were still on, so we didn't even need our flashlights. Now the Red Cross put me in a motel room a few blocks away, and I guess I should be happy I'm safe, but I lost everything—my clothes, a little money I'd kept hidden in a secret place, all my photographs. My husband's dead, you know, and I lost all my pictures of him. I don't know what I'll do now; I don't have any children. I'm all by myself, except for my friends, and they all lived at the hotel with me."

EXERCISE 13
Specialized Types of Stories

SIDEBARS

INSTRUCTIONS: Use the following information to write two separate stories: first a news story reporting the Senate's action, then a sidebar based on the interview with the sheriff.

Main Story

The state Senate today approved a bill overwhelmingly. The bill has already been approved by the House and now goes to the governor, who has indicated that he will sign it. The bill was passed almost unanimously by angry lawmakers who want inmates housed in jails throughout the state to help pay the costs of their room and board. There were only 2 votes against the measure in the Senate and none against in the House. The bill will go into effect next January 1st. It will require persons housed in a jail within the state to reveal their incomes and, if they can afford it, to pay the entire cost of their room and board behind bars, or whatever share of the cost they can reasonably afford. The bill requires the State Department of Offender Rehabilitation to draw up guidelines on how prisoners will disclose their finances and how much they will be required to pay. The department will consider a number of relevant variables, such as whether a prisoner must support a family and devote all his or her income to that family. The idea of the bill arose a number of months ago when lawmakers touring a state prison were told that some inmates received government benefits (mostly Social Security and veterans' benefits). The lawmakers were told that some prisoners opened bank accounts in the prisons and that the money they received piled up so they had thousands of dollars accumulated in the accounts when they were released. A subsequent survey requested by legislative leaders found 19,000 inmates in the state and that, of that total, 356 received government payments of some type. The same survey found that the inmates had a total of $3.1 million in inmate accounts at state prisons. Prison officials cautioned that the prisoners may have more money deposited in banks outside the prison system and that it would be difficult to locate those accounts. To enforce the new bill, lawmakers stipulated that prisoners who refuse to disclose their finances cannot be released early on parole. Officials have not yet determined how much each prisoner will be charged. Lawmakers also noted that some inmates may have other assets, such as farms, homes, automobiles, and stocks and bonds, and that those prisoners can also be expected to help defray their prison expenses.

Sidebar

Gus DiCesare is the county sheriff. He has held that position for 11 years. To retain the position, he must run for re-election every four years. As sheriff, DiCesare is in charge of the county jail, which has a capacity of 120 inmates, mostly men but also a few women. Criminals sentenced to terms of less than one year in prison are usually sentenced to the county facility rather than to a state prison. Despite its capacity of 120 persons, the county jail usually holds 140 to 150 persons—20 or 30 more than its rated capacity. When interviewed today about the legislature's approval of the bill in question, DiCesare said: "Hell, I think it's a great idea. Some of these prisoners got more money than I'll ever have. When we pick them up, they're driving big, fancy cars, living in big homes and carrying a thick wad of money. Not most of them, but there're always a few in here, mostly drug dealers. We sentence them to jail as punishment, but it punishes honest taxpayers who pay to keep them in here—pay for this building, their food, clothes, jailers and all the rest. A couple of years ago, we calculated that it cost about $35 to keep one prisoner here one day. Hell, if they can afford it, prisoners should help pay for it all; that could be part of their punishment. I'll bet our costs are up to nearly $80 a day apiece now, and they're still rising. It'd help me too. I've got a damned hard problem trying to run this place on the budget the county gives me. With a little more money, I could improve the food, come up with some more recreational facilities and maybe even try to rehabilitate a few prisoners—bring in some teachers and counselors and that type of thing. Now, all I really do is keep them locked behind bars all day, and that's not going to rehabilitate anyone."

14 Writing Obituaries

Obituaries are reports that people have died. Typically, obituaries describe the funeral arrangements and present brief information about the deceased.

Unfortunately, most obituaries are cold and impersonal. Few convey the impression that any of the people they describe possessed unique personalities and sets of experiences. But obituaries cannot easily be improved. One reason is that few newspapers can devote enough time, space or reporters to obituaries. Newspapers often assign a single reporter to write all their obituaries, and in a few hours each day that reporter may have to write the obituaries for a dozen or more people. Another reason is that newspapers traditionally have assigned obituaries to their newest and least experienced reporters. Some newspapers even hire people without any journalistic training to write obituaries, thus freeing experienced reporters for assignments thought to be more important. Obituaries are considered an ideal assignment for beginners because they seldom require any specialized knowledge; most are brief, simple and easy to write. Moreover, reporters can write obituaries without leaving their desks—or the close supervision of their editors.

Some newspapers expect experienced reporters to help write obituaries, but few reporters like the assignment. Reporters rarely know the people who died and complain that the assignment is unexciting and unimportant. Many also consider it unpleasant. Like most other Americans, reporters are uncomfortable with death and are reluctant to call the friends or relatives of people who just died. Reporters also realize that they are unlikely to receive many rewards for writing good obituaries.

Newspapers in small towns try to publish an obituary for everyone who dies in their geographical area. However, all the obituaries may have to fit into a limited amount of space, perhaps two or three columns (about 40 to 60 inches). Because some of that space is filled by headlines, only 3 to 4 inches are left for each obituary. Newspapers in larger cities do not have enough space to print an obituary for everyone; instead, they report only the deaths of the most prominent members of their communities.

Some people confuse the obituaries with news stories. If a newsworthy individual dies, or if someone's death is unusual, newspapers will publish a news story about the death. Newspapers may also publish an obituary, but the obituary may appear a day or two later. Also, the obituary will emphasize the individual's life, not death.

Other people confuse obituaries with paid funeral notices. Obituaries are separate stories written by newspaper reporters and published free. Because newspapers in large cities do not have enough space to publish everyone's obituary, funeral directors often place paid funeral notices in those newspapers. Most funeral notices are only one paragraph long and are published in alphabetical order among the newspapers' classified advertisements. The notices are written by funeral directors, and the fee for having them published is added to the cost of funerals. Funeral directors often place the paid notices in newspapers that also publish free obituaries.

Funeral homes give newspapers all the information they need to write most obituaries. The funeral homes, eager to have their names appear in the newspapers as often as possible, obtain the information when families come in to arrange funeral services. Some funeral homes fill out special forms provided by their local newspapers and immediately deliver completed forms to the papers. Just before their daily deadlines, reporters may call the funeral homes to be certain that they have not missed any obituaries.

If the person who died was prominent, reporters may learn more about the person by going to their newspaper's library and reading previous stories published about him or her. Reporters may also call the person's family and business associates to obtain some additional information and a recent photograph. Most people willingly cooperate with reporters; they seem to accept requests made by the reporters as part of the routine that occurs at the time of death. Many people also cooperate with the reporters because they want their friends and relatives' obituaries to be thorough and well-written.

The Content of Obituaries

An obituary usually begins by identifying the person who died. A typical lead reveals the person's name and identification and at least one unique or outstanding fact about that person's life, usually the person's major accomplishments. The inclusion of some unique or outstanding fact is essential; it makes obituaries more interesting and keeps them all from looking alike. For example:

Dr. Catherine Mekdeci of 4112 N. Lakeview Drive died of a heart attack at St. Nicholas Hospital Monday. She was 72.
REVISED: Catherine Mekdeci, who delivered more than 10,000 babies during the 40 years she worked as an obstetrician at St. Nicholas Hospital, died Monday at the hospital.

Russell C. Johnson, 73, of 4578 Davisson Ave., a retired businessman, died Monday at his home after a lingering illness.
REVISED: Russell C. Johnson, who began work as a mailroom clerk for the nation's largest insurance company and 30 years later became the company's president, died Monday at the age of 73.

The original leads stressed dull, routine facts: the people's ages, addresses and causes of death. The revisions contain more interesting facts about their lives and accomplishments. Other good leads might describe an individual's interests, goals, hobbies or personality. Here are two examples, written for more famous individuals:

TUCSON, Ariz.—Sports legend Jesse Owens, once known as "the world's fastest human" and winner of four gold medals at the 1936 Berlin Olympics, died Monday of cancer.

(United Press International)

COLUMBUS, Ohio—Woody Hayes, who for 28 seasons ruled his Ohio State University football teams like one of the generals he so admired, died in his sleep Thursday at home. He was 74.

(The Associated Press)

After the lead, an obituary should provide a chronology of an individual's life. Thus, information commonly presented in obituaries, and its approximate order of inclusion, is as follows:

1. Identification (full name, age, address)
2. Time and place of death
3. Occupation and employment history
4. Other major interests and accomplishments
5. Honors, awards and offices held
6. Educational history: schools attended and schools graduated from
7. Membership in churches, clubs and other civic organizations
8. Military service
9. Year and place of birth and marriage
10. List of surviving relatives
11. Religious services
12. Other burial and funeral arrangements, possibly including the names of the clergyman and pallbearers

If time and space are available, and if an individual merits a lengthy obituary, reporters may also include some anecdotes about the person's life and the recollections of friends and relatives, as well as other biographical highlights.

Normally, information about the religious services, burial and surviving relatives is placed at the end of an obituary. The information should be as specific as possible so that mourners will know when they can call on the person's family and when and where they can attend the funeral and burial. The list of survivors normally includes only an individual's immediate family. It begins with the name of the person's husband or wife, followed by the names of parents, brothers and sisters, and children. Newspapers may list the number (but not the names) of grandchildren and great-grandchildren. Few newspapers list more distant relatives, such as nieces, nephews and cousins, unless they are the only survivors or are themselves people of note. During the past 5 or 10 years, however, a few newspapers have also begun to list the names of other survivors: non-relatives, including live-in friends who played an important role in the person's life.

Newspapers usually report the specific street address of survivors who live in their local communities, but only the hometowns (not the street addresses) of people living elsewhere. The following typical obituaries illustrate this format:

David C. Curnutte, who owned and managed a downtown bookstore after serving as a fighter pilot in two wars, died at his home Monday. He was 73.

Curnutte opened the Classics Bookstore at 410 N. Main St. in 1966 and operated it until his retirement in 1983.

He was born in Seattle, Wash., and was an All-American basketball and football player in high school there. He attended Duke University on a football scholarship and majored in philosophy.

Curnutte joined the Army Air Corps before Pearl Harbor was attacked in 1941 and flew

132 combat missions in the South Pacific. He was recalled to active duty during the Korean War and flew 81 missions during that conflict. He retired from the Air Force in 1965.

He was a member of the Quiet Birdmen, the Retired Officers Association, the University Club and the American Association of Retired Persons.

Survivors include his wife, Helen; sons Leroy of 4810 N. Highland Road and James of Fresno, Calif.; daughter Mrs. Paul (Mary) White of Des Moines, Iowa; and seven grandchildren.

Memorial services will be conducted at 2 p.m. Thursday at the First Congregational Church, with the Rev. Randolph Schulz officiating. Burial will be in Evergreen Cemetery.

Margaret Joan Holleanna, 69, a teacher at Hawthorne Elementary School for 32 years, died at the Elder Kare Nursing Home early today.

She had been offered several jobs as an elementary school principal but never accepted them. She once explained: "I always love the children in my classroom, and they're the only children I have. I never want to leave my children."

She was born in Holland, Mich., and received her bachelor's and master's degrees from the University of Michigan before moving here in 1947.

She was a member and a past president of the City Women's Club and a past president of the State Federation of Women's Clubs.

She was also a member of St. Andrew's Catholic Church, the Sunshine Society, Chaminade Club and DAR.

Miss Holleanna never married. Survivors include a niece, Marlene Sanders of 4827 N. Garland Ave.

Funeral services will be held at 1:30 p.m. Saturday at the Pine Garden Chapel with Father Robert Kurber of St. Andrew's Catholic Church officiating. Interment will follow in Greenwood Cemetery.

Friends may call from 2 to 4 and from 7 to 9 p.m. Friday at the Pine Garden Chapel, 430 N. Kirkman Road.

In lieu of flowers, memorial contributions may be made to the American Cancer Society.

Some newspapers also try to report the cause of every death. However, others do not, often because that information is difficult to obtain. Many people are reluctant to reveal the cause of their relatives' deaths, particularly if they died of a dreaded disease, such as AIDS or cirrhosis of the liver (which may be caused by alcoholism). For years, people were also reluctant to mention cancer, so obituaries used the euphemism that people "died after a long illness." A similar euphemism—"died after a lingering illness"—is still used for victims of cirrhosis and AIDS.

Newspapers are most likely to report the cause of a celebrity's death. They also try to report the cause of violent, unusual and unexpected deaths.

Some newspapers report suicides in separate news stories, particularly when the suicides are bizarre, occur in public or involve a prominent individual. Other newspapers mention the cause of death, even when it is suicide, in routine obituaries rather than in separate news stories. Still other newspapers consider suicide a private matter, never to be reported in any manner. When newspapers do report suicides, they carefully attribute the determination of the cause of death to some authority, usually the coroner. Few newspapers describe in detail the methods used to commit suicide or any bloody details about the deaths. If you work for a newspaper, you will be expected to follow the policies set by its executives; in other cases, use your own judgment.

It often takes authorities several days to announce the official cause of death. When that problem arises, an initial story or obituary may report that the cause of death has not yet been determined, or that, "An autopsy will be conducted Thursday." A later story may report the results of the autopsy or inquest.

Additional Guidelines for Writing Obituaries

Obituaries become more interesting when reporters go beyond the routine and do more than list the events in a person's life—when they take the time to include additional details and to explain their significance. For example, instead of reporting that a man served in the Army and graduated from college, an obituary might tell what he did in the Army, where he attended college and what he studied. Similarly, instead of simply reporting that a man retired 10 years earlier, an obituary might reveal what he has done since his retirement.

Reporters are trained to avoid eulogies, euphemisms and sentimentality. They report that people have died, not that they passed away, departed, expired or succumbed. Obituary writers must also avoid the flowery language used by funeral directors and by grieving friends and relatives—terms such as "the deceased," "the remains" and "the loved one." Yet, as a sign of respect, newspapers often use a person's full name the first time he or she is mentioned and later refer to him or her as "Mr. Jones" or "Mrs. Smith."

Other problems encountered by obituary writers are unique. Many people are reluctant to reveal their relatives' ages, particularly if they had falsified them or kept them a secret during their lifetimes. Obituary writers will report that someone died in a hospital, but many hesitate to identify the hospital. Editors explain that deaths are rarely a hospital's fault, and that obituaries that repeatedly mention a specific hospital may unfairly harm its reputation. Because the statement might offend florists who advertise in their newspapers, many editors and publishers also hesitate to report that "The family requests no flowers." However, some permit the publication of more positive statements, such as, "The family requests that gifts be sent to the Heart Fund."

Readers often call newspapers and ask reporters to write obituaries for other people, and the callers usually provide all the necessary information. The callers may explain that they have not yet made any arrangements with a funeral home, and some have no intention of ever going to a funeral home, particularly if a body is to be cremated, disposed of by a private burial society or used for scientific or medical purposes. Other callers explain that the person they are describing died in another city but formerly lived in the local area, had many friends there or is related to a prominent resident of the area.

People described in the obituaries occasionally call newspapers the next day, demanding the publication of a correction. Because it is not uncommon for pranksters to call newspapers and give them obituaries for living people, editors often require their reporters to call a second source and confirm every obituary before it is published. Author Mark Twain experienced this problem while traveling in Europe. After learning that newspapers in the United States had reported that he died, Twain sent a cable insisting that, "Reports of my death have been greatly exaggerated."

Despite the problems that arise while writing them, obituaries are one of the most widely read features in newspapers; many people regularly scan them to learn who has died. Newspapers are the only medium to report them. Radio and television stations mention the deaths of a few celebrities, but only newspapers have the time, space and staff necessary to publish detailed obituaries—usually for everyone in their communities, not just the rich and famous.

Surveys have found that 40 to 50 percent of a newspaper's readers will look at the obituaries. The percentage increases with age. About 45 percent of the readers 18 to 24 express "at least some interest" in obituaries, compared to more than 60 percent of the readers over 60.

Few stories are so likely to be clipped, pasted in scrapbooks and mailed to friends. As a consequence, obituary writers must be especially accurate. Obituaries are usually the last stories written about a person and, if a reporter makes an error, it is likely to infuriate the person's friends and relatives.

Even the information provided by funeral directors should be checked for errors. Friends and relatives are likely to be upset when they make the arrangements for a funeral and consequently may be mistaken about some of the information they give to funeral directors. The friends and relatives may not know or remember some facts and may guess at others. The funeral directors may make some mistakes while recording the information and may misspell some names, especially the names of unfamiliar individuals and cities.

Other guidelines that reporters should consider while writing obituaries include the following:

- Detailed obituaries should begin with the highlights and most interesting facts in a person's life. Reporters should guard against writing lengthy obituaries that begin in chronological order with a description of the person's education and military service, then—10 or 20 paragraphs later—finally report that the person was elected mayor, governor or president.
- A man is said to be survived by his wife, not his widow. Similarly, a woman is survived by her husband, not by her widower.
- A Catholic funeral Mass is celebrated, said or sung, and the word *Mass* is capitalized.
- Many editors object to reporting that a death was "sudden," explaining that most deaths are sudden.
- Because burglars sometimes break into surviving relatives' homes while they are attending a funeral, some newspapers no longer print survivors' addresses in obituaries.

Obituaries for Celebrities

Newspapers publish more colorful obituaries for celebrities, such as politicians, athletes and entertainers. The Associated Press and United Press International provide obituaries for national celebrities. Some newspapers localize these obituaries, and they prepare the complete obituaries for local celebrities.

Obituaries written for celebrities are longer than obituaries written for other people and emphasize different types of information. Because few readers are likely to know a national celebrity and to attend that celebrity's funeral and burial, the obituary may not mention those services. Instead, it will emphasize the celebrity's personality and accomplishments.

Here are some typical leads for obituaries of famous people:

WASHINGTON—Werner von Braun, a dreamer whose love was the heavens and whose wizardry sent men to explore them, is dead.
He died of cancer at 3 a.m. Thursday in Alexandria Hospital in suburban Virginia. . . .

WASHINGTON—William O. Douglas, a mighty force for individual freedom during almost four decades as a Supreme Court justice, died Saturday at the Walter Reed Army Medical Center.

(The Associated Press)

NEW YORK—Andy Warhol, the pale prince of pop art who turned images of soup cans and superstars into museum pieces, died Sunday of a heart attack.

(The Orlando Sentinel)

Other obituaries for artist Andy Warhol quoted from a book he wrote. "In the future," Warhol predicted, "everyone will be world-famous for 15 minutes." The obituaries described Warhol's unhappy life as a youth, including three nervous breakdowns. Then—in 1968—an actress shot Warhol at his office. Bullets punctured his lungs, spleen, liver and stomach. After that, "Warhol was believed to have sent lookalikes to some public events." The obituaries also described his idiosyncracies—including the fact that he "was retiring to the point that he was said to shrink from human touch."

GENEVA, Switzerland—Richard Burton, the Welsh actor who juggled a spellbinding stage and screen career with alcoholism and a volcanic love life that included two marriages to Elizabeth Taylor, died Sunday. He was 58.

(The Associated Press)

Similarly, obituaries for actor Richard Burton noted his humble beginnings. He was a coal miner's son, born in South Wales, but educated at Oxford. Burton became "one of Britain's greatest Shakespearean stage performers and acted in more than 40 movies. . . ." Obituaries also described Burton's personal life, often quoting Burton's observations about himself. One of the obituaries revealed that Burton had said, "I rather like my reputation, actually, that of a drunk, a womanizer; it's rather an attractive image." Burton also said, "If I had a chance for another life, I would certainly choose a better complexion."

To help reveal a celebrity's character or philosophy, a good obituary may reprint the person's most interesting or controversial statements. Obituaries for actor John Wayne noted that he had been a patriotic figure and once said, "I am proud of every day in my life I wake up in the United States of America." Wayne rarely received good reviews for his film performances, and obituaries also reported that he had said, "Nobody likes my acting but the public." Other quotations reprinted at the time of his death include:

> I'm 53 years old and 6 feet 4. I've had three wives, five children and three grandchildren. I love good whiskey. I still don't understand women, and I don't think there is any man who does.

> Hell, I'm no saint. Never said I was. I thought of three things when I had the cancer operations. My wife, my kids and death. I was butchered. One lung gone, some of the other cut away. When the doctor came in to give me the news I was in the bed trying to be John Wayne and I gruffly said, "Doctor, you trying to tell me I've got cancer?" What a shock. I couldn't believe I was dying.

An obituary also may quote other people who knew the celebrity. The following quotation appeared in an obituary for Louis Armstrong, jazz trumpet player, singer, composer and orchestra leader:

> Armstrong's fourth wife, Lucille, once said of him:
> "Life with Louis is a laugh a day. Why, that man even wakes up happy. I tell him sometimes, 'Louis, it's against the law of averages for you to be so happy all the time.' But he always finds something to laugh about just the same."

> *(The Associated Press)*

Even on the day a celebrity dies, reporters may recall anecdotes likely to make readers laugh. However, the anecdotes serve a purpose—they help describe the famous person. When Newsweek published an obituary for Eddie Rickenbacker, a World War I ace who later became head of Eastern Airlines, the magazine reported that Rickenbacker had been badly injured years earlier when a DC-3 crashed as it approached Atlanta:

> In the hospital, he heard the radio voice of Walter Winchell announce that he was dying. "I began to fight," Rickenbacker recalled later. "They had me under an oxygen tent. I tore it apart and picked up a pitcher. I heaved it at the radio and scored a direct hit. The radio fell apart and Winchell's voice stopped. Then I got well."

Obituaries should not simply praise individuals, but should report their lives: both the good and the bad. An obituary for Liberace reminded readers that a 27-year-old chauffeur had filed a $113 million palimony suit, charging that Liberace promised to support him in exchange for sexual favors. The suit was settled out of court for $95,000, with Liberace insisting that the chauffeur was just a vengeful ex-employee.

Obituaries also described Liberace's early career at supper clubs, speak-easies and hotels. By the 1950s, Liberace had his own television show and—explaining his success—once said: "I came along right after Hopalong Cassidy. I was different. The timing was just great." On television and in person, Liberace "swathed himself in fur, feathers,

Should newspapers have reported the cause of Liberace's death?

sequins and rhinestones"—and told corny jokes about his outfits. An obituary added that Liberace's fans, many of them older women, adored him, giggling at his jokes and ignoring his offstage problems.

Similarly, the obituaries for boxer Joe Louis noted that he won the heavyweight crown and held it 12 years, defending his title a record 25 times. However, the obituaries also reported that he married three times, used cocaine, spent some time in a Denver mental hospital and spent the last year of his life working in a Las Vegas hotel, shaking hands and posing for pictures with gamblers, "a sad figure in a crumpled suit and golf cap."

Obituaries usually explain how the celebrities died. Jessie Owens, "a pack-a-day cigarette smoker for 35 years," died of lung cancer at the age of 66. Supreme Court Justice William O. Douglas entered a hospital on Christmas Eve, "suffering from pneumonia, and was treated for progressive respiratory and kidney failure." A publicist attributed Liberace's death "to cardiac arrest due to congestive heart failure." But obituaries also reported the rumors that he died of AIDS.

The best obituaries reveal the celebrities' character as well as their accomplishments, their successes and failures. Typically, a lead in the Los Angeles Times began by reporting:

> HOLLYWOOD—Sir Alfred Hitchcock, the master director who probably frightened more moviegoers than anyone in history with his 54 suspense-packed movies, died peacefully Tuesday at his home.

The obituaries written about Hitchcock also quoted him, quoted his friends and revealed interesting details about his personality and life. Hitchcock, who frightened millions of moviegoers, was himself a fearful man; he was afraid of burglars, crowds, darkness, Sundays, heights, closed spaces, open spaces and, above all, false accusation and arrest. The obituaries explained that Hitchcock feared the police because, as a youth, he had been taken to a police station and locked in a cell as an example of "what we do to naughty boys."

Newsweek magazine quoted another person who said, "Hitch is a gentleman farmer who raises gooseflesh." Newsweek also described Hitchcock's attitude toward sex and quoted one of his statements about it:

> Sex has never interested me much. I don't understand how people can waste so much time over sex: sex is for kids, for movies—a great bore.

Newspapers that publish negative information in obituaries do not have to fear lawsuits. A person who has died cannot sue the newspapers for libel; nor, in most cases, can the person's relatives. Thus, the decision to publish or to suppress critical information should be influenced by the information's newsworthiness, good taste or impact on the community, not by any legal considerations.

Newspapers are more likely to publish negative information about public figures than about private citizens. Also, large dailies are more likely than smaller daily and weekly newspapers to mention a person's indiscretions. Smaller newspapers tend to be more protective of their communities and of the people living in them. Journalists in smaller cities may know the people who died and fear that the critical information would anger the people's friends and relatives and be disturbing for the entire community.

Major news organizations prepare obituaries for some celebrities in advance, then bring them up to date periodically so that, for example, if a president dies, his obituary is immediately ready for dissemination to the public. Similarly, if a prominent individual becomes seriously ill, newspapers may prepare that person's obituary and even have it set in type. When the person dies, only the obituary's lead has to be written.

Thus, many obituaries are poorly written—but they do not have to be. Given enough time and space, reporters can produce well-written and interesting obituaries, and they regularly do so for celebrities. As you begin to write, critically examine the existing policies of your newspaper and work to improve the quality of every type of story you write, including every obituary.

EXERCISE 1
Obituaries

INSTRUCTIONS: Write obituaries based on the information given below and in the obituary forms printed on the following pages. After reading this chapter, use your own judgment while deciding whether to use the most controversial details.

Obituary 1: Lynn Marie Shepard

Identification: Lynn Marie Shepard. Age 20. Address: 854 Maury Road, Apt. 107B.

Circumstances of death: Taken to the emergency room at Mercy Hospital at 1 a.m. yesterday, where she died shortly thereafter. An autopsy conducted later in the day revealed that she died "of symptoms brought about by the ingestion of a large quantity of cocaine."

Funeral services: 5 p.m. tomorrow at Hines Brothers Funeral Home. Burial immediately following at Memorial Park Cemetery.

Survivors: Her parents, Frank and Helen Shepard of 107 Eastbrook Avenue. Three sisters, Patricia, Virginia and Carol, all at home. A brother, William, a soldier stationed in Germany. Also, her college roommate of the last two years: Timothy Bolankner, also of 854 Maury Road, Apt. 107B.

Accomplishments: Salutatorian of her senior class at Central High School, where she was a member of the girls' volleyball team, a member of the homecoming court during her senior year and also school treasurer during her senior year. Now, a sophomore studying business administration at your school. She compiled a 3.8 gpa during her first full year of college and was on the Dean's List. A member of Delta Delta Delta Sorority and the Business Honor Council. Worked part-time as a waitress at the Steak & Ale Restaurant. Hoped to someday own her own business.

Obituary 2: Miguel Acevedo

Identification: Miguel Acevedo. Age 27. Address: 812 Bell Avenue.

Circumstances of death: Died early today at Mercy Hospital of a bone marrow disorder.

Funeral services: The body will be cremated and the ashes scattered. A memorial service for friends and relatives will be held at sunrise Saturday under the pavilion overlooking Lake Charm at Ayers Park.

Survivors: Mothers and stepfather, Mercedes and Orlando Hernandez of Brooklyn, N.Y. Father and stepmother, Louis and Esther Acevedo of 8487 Highland Drive. Brothers, Juan and Francisco, both of Brooklyn. Sister Ramona of Buffalo, N.Y. Stepbrother Charles of Columbia, S.C. Stepsisters Felipa Cintron of Hollywood, Calif., and Carmen Santiesban of Los Angeles. Also, his roommate for the last two years, Sara Howard.

Accomplishments: Born in New York. Princeton University graduate and then a law graduate at the University of Texas. Moved here four years ago. A Democrat and a member of St. John Vianney Catholic Church. Employed by the city as a public defender until about four months ago when he became medically unable to continue working.

Obituary 3: Louis Perez

Identification: Louis Daniel Perez. Born in 1923. Address: 2027 Harrison Street.

Circumstances of death: Died at 2:30 a.m. today in General Hospital. Perez was admitted to the hospital almost five weeks ago and was being treated for cancer.

Funeral services: A memorial service at Redeemer Lutheran Church will be held at 8 p.m. Friday. Graveside services scheduled for 1 p.m. Saturday at Wildwood Cemetery. There will be no viewing of the body. The family requests no flowers and that expressions of sympathy be in the form of contributions to Redeemer Lutheran Church.

Survivors: Wife, Elfreda. Three sons: Robert of New York City; Peter of Miami, Florida; and Patrick of 2025 Harrison Street. One daughter: Pamela Perez of Sacramento, Calif. Three grandchildren.

Accomplishments: Born and attended elementary and high schools in Chicago. Graduated from the University of Illinois in 1944 and served as a lieutenant in the Marine Corps, fighting in the Pacific during World War II. Received a Purple Heart after being struck in the abdomen by a grenade fragment. Graduated from Marquette University law school in Milwaukee in 1949 and opened an office in this city in August of that year. Elected city councilman in 1958 and retained that post until 1964. Defeated in 1964 in a race for mayor. At the time of his death, was senior partner in the law firm of Perez, Sherman and Kinsel. He was a member of the County Bar Association, the American Bar Association, American Legion Post No. 14, the Defense Law Institute, and Phi Alpha Delta fraternity. He was also a member of the board of directors of the hospital in which he was a patient when he died.

Obituary 4: Theresa Goodwyn

Identification: Theresa Goodwyn. Born in 1894. Address: Doctor's Convalescent Home, 814 Cyers Lane.

Circumstances of death: Cause of death undetermined. Found dead in her bed at the nursing home at 8 p.m. yesterday.

Funeral services: At 4 p.m. Friday at Trinity Lutheran Church, with burial immediately following at Memorial Park Cemetery. Visitation from 7 until 9 p.m. Thursday at Pirkle Mortuary.

Survivors: One son, Donald, of Conemaugh, Pa. Four grandchildren. Eleven great-grandchildren.

Accomplishments: Born Theresa Rudnick in her parents' home at 2539 W. Oakridge Road in this city, and lived in this city all her life. Graduated from Washington Elementary School and Wilson High School. Married Kenneth R. Hutchinson in 1916. Hutchinson died during a flu epidemic following World War I. Married for a second time to Harold G. Goodwyn, a plumber, who also preceded her in death, dying in 1948. Until three years ago, she continued to live by herself in her family's original home, one of the oldest in the city. She was a member of Trinity Lutheran Church.

Obituary 5: Helen Marie Nemnich

Identification: Helen Marie Nemnich. Born in 1921. Address: 1231 Mt. Vernon Avenue.

Circumstances of death: Died of a stroke at her home yesterday. Her husband found her body lying on her bedroom floor when he returned home at 5:30 p.m.

Funeral services: Services will be held at 2 p.m. Sunday in Alton's Mortuary. Visitation will be from 3 to 5 and from 7 to 9 p.m. Saturday at the mortuary. Burial will be at 3 p.m. Sunday at Memorial Park Cemetery. The family requests no flowers and that memorials be given to the American Diabetes Association.

Survivors: Husband, Harlon. Two sons: Bernard, who lives at home, and John of Colorado Springs, Colo. Three daughters: Eileen Kubisak of 418 N. Wilkes Road; Hannah Kruckemeyer of 1601 Perkins Road; and Marilyn Bruce of 8241 Bellmont Avenue. Twelve grandchildren. One great-grandchild.

Accomplishments: Born Helen Marie Oliver in England. Married her husband, Harold, while he was serving in the Army during World War II and returned here with him after the war. A member of St. Paul's United Church of Christ. For 15 years, she worked as a clerk in the credit department of Sears Roebuck and Company. In 1952, she served as president of the PTA at Glenridge Junior High School. A long-time member of the choir at her church and of Alcoholics Anonymous.

Obituary 6: William David Raye

Identification: William David Raye. Born in 1922. Address: 112 Riverview Dr.

Circumstances of death: Suffered a stroke and died at his home Sunday evening while watching television.

Funeral services: 7 p.m. tomorrow at Hines Brothers Funeral Home. No burial, since his body will be cremated. No viewing or visitation.

Survivors: Wife, Beth. Two daughters, Mrs. Donna Moronese of 623 N. 5th Street and Mrs. Ruth Howland of 1808 Gadsden Blvd. Five grandchildren. Two brothers, Michael and Frank, both of Miami, Fla.

Accomplishments: Born in Normandy, Tenn. Graduated from the University of Tennessee in 1943. Served in the Army during World War II, rising to the rank of sergeant in an infantry company. Established the Raye Truck and Tractor Company here immediately after the war. Served as president of the State Trucking Association from 1950 to 1952. Company went bankrupt in 1957 and he was charged with embezzlement but acquitted by a jury. Joined Adler's Real Estate Co. in 1958 and rose from salesman to president. He retired from the presidency in 1987 after transforming it into the largest and most profitable real estate firm in the city.

OBITUARY NOTICE

Please supply the information asked for below and send to the newspaper office as quickly as possible after the death. Relatives, friends and neighbors of the deceased will appreciate prompt reporting of this news so that they may attend funeral services or send messages of condolences.

Full Name of Deceased Robynn Anne Richter

Address 42 Tusca Trail

Age Exact age unknown—estimated by friends to be about 60

Date of Death Late yesterday afternoon

Place of Death St. Nicholas Hospital

Cause of Death Injuries suffered during a fall at her home last week, including a broken hip.

Time and Date of Funeral The authorities are still trying to contact all her relatives.

Place of Funeral Unknown—to be determined by her relatives.

Place of Burial Unknown

Officiating Clergyman Unknown

Place of Birth Reidsville, N.C.

Places and Lengths of Residences After graduating from the University of South Carolina in 1948, where she majored in political science, she worked briefly in Charleston and in Boston. She moved here in 1951.

Occupation Retired stockbroker. After moving here in 1951, she taught civics and history at Roosevelt High School, working summers as a clerk at the local office of Merrill Lynch Pierce Fenner & Smith, Inc. In 1957, she became the first woman stockbroker employed at the office, rising to the position of office manager 7 years ago.

Did Deceased Ever Hold Public Office (When and What)? Long active in the Democratic party, she was appointed to the city's Library Board in 1954 and served 2 4-year terms. She was elected to the city council in '62 and re-elected to a second 3-year term in '65. At the time of her death, she was a member of the Mayor's Advisory Committee.

Name, Address of Surviving Husband (or Wife) Friends think she was separated or divorced when she moved here in 1951, but it was a topic she never discussed. Since 1953, she shared her home here with a friend, Patricia Richards.

Maiden Name (if Married Woman)

Marriage, When and to Whom Unknown

Names, Addresses of Surviving Children None

Names, Addresses of Surviving Brothers and Sisters A sister, Alvia Dey of Phoenix, Ariz. Three brothers, George of Reno, Nev., Robert of Stanhope, N.J. and Thomas of Modesto, Calif.

Number of Grandchildren (Great, Great-Great, etc.) None

Names, Addresses of Parents (if Living) Her father, Melvin, preceded her in death in 1958. Her mother, Sara, preceded her in death in 1973, both of Reidsville, N.C.

Additional Information A member of the Board of Directors of the Kenmore Home for Unwed Mothers. A member of the University Club, the ACLU and Amnesty International. The first woman to join this city's Rotary Club. Also a member of the County Democratic Executive Committee, and chairwoman of the committee, serving 3 2-year terms, from 1964–65 and from 1968–71. Actively involved in the campaigns for John F. Kennedy in 1960, Robert Kennedy, George McGovern and Eugene McCarthy, serving as Robert Kennedy's county campaign coordinator and as McGovern's state campaign coordinator. She once told a reporter: "I've never had any children, but then I've never had to change any diapers or wipe any noses. It's politics and travel that I love—that make me feel alive, and I've enjoyed the time I needed for both."

OBITUARY NOTICE

Please supply the information asked for below and send to the newspaper office as quickly as possible after the death. Relatives, friends and neighbors of the deceased will appreciate prompt reporting of this news so that they may attend funeral services or send messages of condolences.

Full Name of Deceased Beryl Anne Goetz

Address 1010 McLeod Road

Age 57

Date of Death Yesterday

Place of Death At home. She was transported from Mercy Hospital to her home 5 days ago at her insistence after being told she would soon die.

Cause of Death Breast cancer

Time and Date of Funeral 4 p.m. tomorrow

Place of Funeral Faith Baptist Church

Place of Burial Evergreen Cemetery

Officiating Clergyman The Rev. Harley O. Marchese

Place of Birth Boulder, Colo.

Places and Lengths of Residences Moved here with her husband in 1960.

Occupation Dentist/Authoress/Mother

Did Deceased Ever Hold Public Office (When and What)? No

Name, Address of Surviving Husband (or Wife) Separated after 22 years of marriage from her husband, Gerald Roy Goetz, now of Portland, Ore.

Maiden Name (if Married Woman) Beryl Anne Shenuski

Marriage, When and to Whom Married in 1957 at West Point to Lt. Gerald Roy Goetz, then a new graduate of the military academy.

Names, Addresses of Surviving Children___Daughters Patricia Anne
Cooper of Buffalo, N.Y., Elaine Marie McElhenny of Lexington, Ky.,
Betty Anne Dawsun of Kansas City, Mo. and Grace Stoops of Chicago,
Ill. Sons Patrick M. of Dallas, Texas, Frederick W. of Midlothian, Va.,
Anthony Roy of San Antonio, Texas, Christopher of Seattle, Wash. and
Charles of Minneapolis.

Names, Addresses of Surviving Brothers and Sisters___Stepbrothers
Steven and Richard both of Boulder, Colo. Stepsister Linda of Denver.

Number of Grandchildren (Great, Great-Great, etc.)___Seventeen
grandchildren and seven great-grandchildren.

Names, Addresses of Parents (if Living)___Mother, Gertrude, and
stepfather, Ernie, of Boulder.

Additional Information___Graduated from the University of Colorado,
receiving both her B.S. and dental degrees there. All 9 children born
here. Worked at dentistry part-time, mornings only, until her
youngest, Christopher, was in high school, then opened her own office
at 702 East Broadway Avenue. Started writing as a hobby, as she
created stories to entertain her own children and later began to write
them down for others. Began to write children's books and published a
total of 37. In 1974, she received the Newberry Medal, the highest
honor awarded to the author of books for children. A Baptist and
member of Faith Baptist Church. Told an interviewer several years
ago: "I get up at 5 and write until 7 every morning. It's a habit I
started when all 9 children were still at home. With 9 children, it was
the only time the house was quiet. Now they're gone, but that's still
when I write. It's a bad habit."

OBITUARY NOTICE

Please supply the information asked for below and send to the newspaper office as quickly as possible after the death. Relatives, friends and neighbors of the deceased will appreciate prompt reporting of this news so that they may attend funeral services or send messages of condolences.

Full Name of Deceased Jeffrey R. Ahson

Address 49 Groveland Ave.

Age Born August 4, 1923

Date of Death Sometime last evening

Place of Death Home

Cause of Death A lifelong smoker, he died of emphysema.

Time and Date of Funeral Funeral service to be at 10 a.m. Saturday

Place of Funeral At the Littleton Mortuary, to be immediately followed by burial. Viewing at the mortuary from 4-5:30 and 7:30-9 Friday.

Place of Burial Memorial Park Cemetery

Officiating Clergyman The Rev. Billy Lee West

Place of Birth Chico, Calif.

Places and Lengths of Residences Moved here after leaving the Navy in 1946

Occupation City firefighter, 1946–1966. After retiring from the fire department, he became a new car salesman for Romero Buick. At the age of 62, he retired from sales.

Did Deceased Ever Hold Public Office (When and What)? No

Name, Address of Surviving Husband (or Wife) Wife, Theresa Ahson

Maiden Name (if Married Woman)

Marriage, When and to Whom 1947, Therese Alpert

Names, Addresses of Surviving Children Three adopted children: son, Richard D. of Phillipsburg, Kan.; daughters Angela Molino of Omaha, Neb. and Lela Stalling of Pipe Creek, Texas.

Names, Addresses of Surviving Brothers and Sisters Brother Henry of San Francisco. Sisters Judith Eaker of Reidsville, N.C. and Shirley Solomon of Newark, N.J.

Number of Grandchildren (Great, Great-Great, etc.) Five grandchildren and five great-grandchildren

Names, Addresses of Parents (if Living) All deceased.

Additional Information Member VFW Post 4206. Served aboard a destroyer in the Pacific during World War II. Also a member of the Elks Lodge, the National Checkers Association and Gideons. Member and usher at John Calvin Presbyterian Church. Past commander of American Legion Post 702. During the 1950s, after becoming a fireman, he became interested in the history of firefighting in the city. He began to research the topic and to gather memorabilia, including a 1924 fire truck he restored with friends and used to carry his exhibits to the city's elementary schools. He was well known by young school children in the city, speaking to thousands of them about the history of firefighting, until overtaken by the illness that subsequently claimed his life. Two years ago, he donated firefighting collection to the city's public library, and all are now on permanent display there—including the fire truck. (The family wants no flowers.)

OBITUARY NOTICE

Please supply the information asked for below and send to the newspaper office as quickly as possible after the death. Relatives, friends and neighbors of the deceased will appreciate prompt reporting of this news so that they may attend funeral services or send messages of condolences.

Full Name of Deceased Ellen Jean Koch

Address 4214 Azalea Court

Age Approximately 60

Date of Death Last night

Place of Death Memorial Hospital

Cause of Death A recurrence of cancer for which she had been receiving medical treatment for the past 3 years.

Time and Date of Funeral 10 a.m. Friday. A mass will be said at 8 p.m.

Place of Funeral St. John Vianney Catholic Church

Place of Burial St. Andrews Cemetery

Officiating Clergyman The Reverend John Carey

Place of Birth Philadelphia

Places and Lengths of Residences Miss Koch resided at her family home in Philadelphia until graduating from the Philadelphia Musical Academy, then spent 3 years living in Europe. She returned to Philadelphia for 3 years, attending law school there, then moved here.

Occupation Attorney

Did Deceased Ever Hold Public Office (When and What)? Appointed to the city's Human Relations Commission, nonpaid, voluntary position. Served from 1966 until her death.

Name, Address of Surviving Husband (or Wife) Never married

Maiden Name (if Married Woman)

Marriage, When and to Whom Never married

Names, Addresses of Surviving Children None

Names, Addresses of Surviving Brothers and Sisters Two brothers: Warren and Richard, both of Philadelphia.

Number of Grandchildren (Great, Great-Great, etc.) None

Names, Addresses of Parents (if Living) Both are dead.

Additional Information Moving here in 1958, Miss Koch worked for the law firm of Ellis, Ballard, Searl and Associates. In 1960, she opened the Neighborhood Law Office at 818 Pershing Avenue, dispensing free legal aid to the poor from a donated office furnished with borrowed furniture. Clients were asked to donate what they could but she supported herself mainly from an inheritance from her parents and donations from foundations, a few law firms and other sources in the city. Served an estimated 250 needy clients and fielded more than 1,000 telephone calls for assistance monthly. She was also involved in the Democratic party. In 1962–63 she spent 14 months as a Peace Corps attorney in Addis Adaba, Ethiopia, where she said she found parallels between America's poor and the poor and their problems in Africa. During her absence, about two dozen colleagues in the city each volunteered their presence one day a month to continue her office's operations. In recent years, some also provided donations to it. Since 1971, the office has received some government grants and grown to a full-time staff of seven. In recent years, she urged the elderly to political activism and was a key organizer for the Gray Panthers and other older-citizen advocacy groups. Received dozens of awards for her work, and named to the boards of a dozen neighborhood and community organizations. (In lieu of flowers, friends are asked to make donations to the Neighborhood Law office.)

OBITUARY NOTICE

Please supply the information asked for below and send to the newspaper office as quickly as possible after the death. Relatives, friends and neighbors of the deceased will appreciate prompt reporting of this news so that they may attend funeral services or send messages of condolences.

Full Name of Deceased Frederick Daggett

Address 777 West Lancaster Rd.

Age 69

Date of Death 7:30 p.m. yesterday

Place of Death Home of daughter, Carolyn

Cause of Death Unknown. Autopsy scheduled for this afternoon.

Time and Date of Funeral 4 p.m. Friday

Place of Funeral Church of Christ

Place of Burial Evergreen Cemetery

Officiating Clergyman The Rev. Stuart Adler

Place of Birth West Berlin

Places and Lengths of Residences Parents moved to Milwaukee, Wisconsin, when he was four years of age. Graduated from the University of Wisconsin at Madison in 1941. Worked in Denver from 1946 to 1950, in Pocatello, Idaho from 1950–54 and in Columbia, Mo., 1954–61. Transferred here in 1962.

Occupation Manager, Sears Roebuck & Co.

Did Deceased Ever Hold Public Office (When and What)? Member, school board, 1968–74. Board chairman, 1970–74. Appointed to the county draft board in 1966. Resigned in 1970 because of his personal and growing opposition to the Vietnam War.

Name, Address of Surviving Husband (or Wife) Edith, 777 W. Lancaster Road

Maiden Name (if Married Woman)

Marriage, When and to Whom 1942 in Madison to Edith Prange, then a student with him at the University of Wisconsin.

Names, Addresses of Surviving Children Frederick Junior, a colonel in the Air Force, stationed in Spain

John of Sacramento, Calif.

Debbie, at home

Carolyn, a teacher in the suburb of Roseville

Names, Addresses of Surviving Brothers and Sisters 1 brother, Ernest, in Milwaukee, Wis.

Number of Grandchildren (Great, Great-Great, etc.) 17 grandchildren and 4 great-grandchildren

Names, Addresses of Parents (if Living) Gerhardt and Anna Daggett, both of Milwaukee, both deceased.

Additional Information Served as assistant manager of local Sears outlet from 1962 until 1966. Became manager in 1966 and held that position at the time of his retirement. Declined to transfer to another city even though new job meant promotion to a larger store. Also refused job as district manager for same reason—he liked living here. Active in civic affairs. Served as president of the city's Chamber of Commerce in 1978. Member of Church of Christ and American Legion Post #12. Also a member of the Rotary Club. Led United Fund Drive which surpassed goal of $4.1 million in 1976 by nearly 12%. Led $3,820,000 drive for new YMCA building. Drafted during World War II and awarded Purple Heart after losing left arm while commanding a tank during Italian campaign.

EXERCISE 2
Obituaries

MISCELLANEOUS ASSIGNMENTS

1. For one week, clip and analyze all the obituaries published by your local newspaper, then compare them to the obituaries that Time and Newsweek magazines publish for celebrities. Why are obituaries published by the news magazines so much more interesting? What types of information do the magazines emphasize?

2. Write an obituary for some person on your campus, possibly another student in your class. Assume that the person died of unknown causes early today and that the funeral arrangements have not yet been made. Do not write a news story about the person's death, but an obituary about the person's life. Include the following: the person's philosophy and goals, some interesting experiences or major accomplishments, and a quotation or anecdote provided by the person or by one of that person's friends. Avoid generalities and clichés.

3. Write an in-depth obituary for one of the following people. Briefly report that the person died of unknown causes at home last night and that the person's funeral service has not yet been scheduled. Do not make up any other facts, nor report only what you remember about the person. Instead, use your campus library to *thoroughly* research the person's career. Begin with an interesting lead that describes the person's character or major accomplishments. In the succeeding paragraphs, report additional highlights—interesting and important details. Your obituary should reveal the person's character. Avoid dull lists, and avoid reporting the information in chronological order. More routine facts and figures, such as the person's place of birth, education and survivors, should be placed near the end of the obituary, not near the lead.

   People about whom you might write an obituary include:

Athletes and Entertainers

Henry Aaron
Muhammad Ali
Johnny Carson
Jane Fonda
Billie Jean King
Paul McCartney
Eddie Murphy
Jack Nicholson
Leonard Nimoy
Brooke Shields
Barbra Streisand
Lee Trevino
Johnny Unitas
Vanna White

Authors and Journalists

Jack Anderson
Saul Bellow
Art Buchwald
William Buckley
Walter Cronkite
Katharine Graham
Charles Kuralt
Norman Mailer
Bill Moyers
Andrew Rooney
Pierre Salinger
A. Solzhenitsyn
Kurt Vonnegut Jr.
Barbara Walters

Political Figures

Spiro Agnew
Howard Baker
Menachem Begin
Joseph R. Biden
Jerry Brown
Rosalyn Carter
Fidel Castro
John Connally
Robert Dole
Betty Ford

John Glenn
Barry Goldwater
Mikhail Gorbachev
Gary Hart
Jesse Jackson
Thomas Jefferson
Lady Bird Johnson
Barbara Jordan
Edward Kennedy
Henry Kissinger
Edward Koch
Bert Lance
Eugene McCarthy
George McGovern
Walter Mondale
Sam Nunn
Daniel Ortega
Dean Rusk
Margaret Thatcher
Kurt Waldheim
George Wallace
George Washington
Andrew Young

Your mayor, governor or senator

Others

F. Lee Bailey
Jim Bakker
Tammy Bakker
Cesar Chavez
Princess Diana
Jerry Falwell
A. J. Foyt
Billy Graham
Patty Hearst
Lee Iacocca
Coretta King
Robert McNamara
Ralph Nader
Oliver North
Pat Robertson
Sally Ride
Gloria Steinem
Paul Volcker

15 Publicity Releases

Newspapers are besieged by individuals and organizations seeking publicity for themselves. Even daily newspapers located in small towns often receive hundreds of publicity releases a day in their mail. In addition, each of these papers may be telephoned by 20 people, and another 10 people may stop at their offices. Some larger dailies receive thousands of requests for publicity.

Business firms use publicity releases to describe their growth, to report their latest dividends and to solicit more customers. Charities use publicity releases to plead for money, politicians to win votes, colleges to attract more students and parents to obtain recognition for their children's achievements—and often for themselves as well.

Because most publicity releases are self-serving—written for the benefit of their sources rather than the public—journalists respond to them with skepticism. Journalists want to report the news: important stories that interest the public. They do not want to write publicity to advertise commercial products, or to praise even the most outstanding individuals and organizations in their communities. That is not their job.

It is not unusual for editors to discard 100 publicity releases for every three or four they accept. Some editors do not even open all the publicity releases; they glance at the return addresses on their envelopes and immediately throw away those coming from sources that regularly submit trivia. For example, the major auto makers often send out publicity releases announcing the promotions of executives in Detroit, yet few newspapers print stories about the promotions because they are of little interest in other cities and states. Newspaper editors reject other publicity releases because they are unimportant, poorly written and obvious advertisements.

The best publicity releases are submitted by major charities and corporations that employ professionals—often former reporters—to prepare their materials. Many government officials and government agencies also submit excellent publicity releases. The best are so good that it is difficult to distinguish between them and the stories written by a newspaper's own staff.

The worst publicity releases, usually those submitted by local groups unfamiliar with the media, are likely to be handwritten, inaccurate, incomplete and submitted days after the events they describe have ended. They fail to provide all the information that reporters need to write complete stories—and fail to provide the names and telephone numbers of people whom the reporters might call to obtain more information or explanations of facts that are unclear.

Regardless of their quality, most publicity releases are rewritten before their publication in newspapers. Some editors are reluctant to use any material provided by publicists and have publicity releases rewritten as a matter of principle. Other editors want the stories published by their newspapers to be distinctive. Also, most editors simply believe that publicity releases can and should be improved. Publicity releases are least likely to be rewritten at smaller papers that lack the necessary staff and sometimes the more critical standards of metropolitan dailies.

Reporters handle publicity releases much as they would any other type of story: they critically examine the information, then summarize it as clearly, concisely and objectively as possible. Their task is difficult because many publicity releases contain clichés, technical jargon, puffery, platitudes and loaded adjectives. Most also fail to use the proper style for capitalization, punctuation and abbreviations.

Reporters obviously prefer publicity releases about topics that are unusual, timely, relevant and important. Reporters also look for topics likely to affect thousands of readers. Action is more newsworthy than opinions, and a genuine or spontaneous event tends to be more newsworthy than a contrived one. Nowadays, for example, few newspapers publish publicity releases about ribbon-cutting and ground-breaking ceremonies.

Newspapers might use the three publicity releases below because they describe topics that would interest many readers. However, all three publicity releases would require some rewriting.

> This season's first musical-comedy by the Bay Street Players is "How to Succeed in Business Without Really Trying." The hit musical spoof of big business will play the State Theatre on the 9th thru 12th and 16th thru 19th of next month. Information and reservations are available through the Bay Street Players' 24-hour phone, 357-7777.

> All eyes will be skyward this Saturday and Sunday when the U.S. Navy Blue Angels, World Aerobatic Champion Leo Loudenslager and others take to the air. More than 20,000 people are expected to attend the 22nd Annual State Air Fair, sponsored by the Rotary Club. The weekend show features three acres of aviation displays and eight aerobatic acts.

> Programs making war violence exciting and fun entertainment are said to lead the new Fall programs, according to the National Coalition on Television Violence (NCTV). NCTV has just released its most recent monitoring results of prime-time network programs. Violence remains about seven violent acts per hour, with new programs taking three of the top four violent spots. ABC continued to be the most violent network for the fourth quarter in a row.
> The most violent programs were . . .

Newspapers would be less likely to use the following publicity releases because for most readers their topics are uninteresting and unimportant:

> Southern Fruit Distributors announced that Russell L. Odom has joined the company as its new Purchasing Director, according to Jim Caruso, Director of Marketing and Sales.

> The list of bus companies registered for the fifth annual American Bus Marketplace in Cincinnati, Nov. 30–Dec. 4, literally spans the alphabet (from Adirondack Trailways of Kingston, N.Y. to Zanetti Bus and Fast Express, Inc., of Rock Springs, Wyo.).

Similarly, reporters are likely to discard these publicity releases because they announce contrived events:

WASHINGTON—The President has joined with the blood bank community proclaiming January as National Volunteer Blood Donor Month and is urging everyone who is healthy to donate blood to help others.

The governor has proclaimed Nov. 14–20 American Education Week in the state. The theme of this year's event, observed since 1921, is "A Strong Nation Needs Strong Schools."

Every week and every month of the year is dedicated to some cause, and often to dozens of different causes. For example, May is Arthritis Month, National High Blood Pressure Month, National Foot Health Month, Better Speech and Hearing Month, National Tavern Month and American Bike Month. Thus, stories about how such occasions are observed are trite, dull, repetitive and of little news value.

Journalists are even more likely to reject the following publicity releases because both are blatant advertisements for commercial products:

A briefcase that can't be lost, can't be stolen and prevents others from secretly recording your conversations is one of several new security devices now available from Hammacher Schlemmer, the internationally famous New York emporium of luxurious, unusual and useful gadgetry.

SportaRub, a new Aloe Vera product, will be test marketed this fall by Warren Bridges, Inc. SportaRub is the amateur athlete's answer to weekend aches and pains.
Joggers, golfers and tennis players alike appreciate SportaRub's soothing qualities. . . .

When they are accepted, many publicity releases require extensive rewriting. Yet journalists might use the following leads because they begin with facts likely to interest a newspaper's readers:

Earth's climate may warm as much as 8 degrees Fahrenheit as a result of increasing carbon dioxide levels from burning coal, oil and gas.

The number of severe and fatal injuries dropped 39 percent during the first six months that drivers in the State of Michigan have been required to use their seat belts.

The stories' later paragraphs explained that an expert was going to speak about the earth's climate, and that safety experts wanted other states to adopt similar laws requiring the use of seat belts.

Other publicity releases are rewritten because their leads emphasize something other than the news they purport to announce. The following publicity releases issued by an ambitious state official all tend to sound alike because they all begin in the same manner—with the official's name:

State Insurance Commissioner Bill Gunter has fined seven insurance companies a total of $48,750 for alleged violations of the state statutes and rules of the Department of Insurance.

State Insurance Commissioner Bill Gunter today announced he will file an administrative complaint against the state's largest private passenger auto insurer—State Farm Mutual Auto Insurance Co.—charging that a recent rate increase filed by the company would circumvent the state's law against excess profits.

State Insurance Commissioner Bill Gunter this morning announced the issuance of warrants for five people, including an attorney, an insurance adjuster and an administrator of a medical treatment clinic, each charged with insurance fraud, first-degree grand theft and conspiracy.

Press releases issued by Sen. William Proxmire usually begin in the same manner—with his name. Proxmire often attracts publicity because of his Golden Fleece of the Month Awards, which he gives for "the biggest, most ironic or most ridiculous examples of wasteful spending." A student, asked to write a story about one of those awards, began her story with this lead:

> Sen. William Proxmire, D-Wis., has given his Golden Fleece of the Month Award for wasteful government spending to the National Aeronautics and Space Administration.

The lead is dull because it emphasizes the routine—the fact that Proxmire has given another of his awards for wasteful government spending, something he does 12 times a year. Moreover, the lead contains three names: Proxmire's, NASA's and the award's. Instead, the lead should emphasize the news—a specific description of the latest recipient:

> The Golden Fleece Award for February has been given for a $14 million to $15 million project designed to find intelligent life in outer space.
> Sen. William Proxmire, D-Wis., has complained that the project "is a low priority program that at this time constitutes a luxury that the country can ill afford."
> Proxmire presents the Golden Fleece Award each month to what he considers "the biggest, most ironic or most ridiculous example of wasteful spending." The project to find intelligent life in outer space was proposed by the National Aeronautics and Space Administration.

Notice that the revision mentions Proxmire in the second paragraph rather than in the lead, and that NASA is not mentioned until the third paragraph. Also, the introductory paragraphs carefully attribute Proxmire's claims; they do not present his claims as fact. However, the most important point is that the lead does not have to begin with Proxmire's name, since it is not the most interesting, the newest or the most newsworthy aspect of the story.

Other publicity releases may have to be rewritten because they state the obvious:

> For years, elderly Americans have worried about the rising cost of medical care.

> The state fire marshal today urged people to observe simple fire safety precautions.

Or, the news may be buried in a publicity release's second—or 22nd—paragraph:

> Choosing a college or a career can be a pretty traumatic experience. It's a major decision which will impact on an individual for the rest of their life.
> Recognizing this, the Jewish Community Center, located at 851 North Maitland Ave., has organized a professionally led two-day seminar beginning on Jan. 4, titled "Exploring Your Future." Open to the community, the program is geared to assisting high-school juniors and seniors plus college students.
> REVISED: The Jewish Community Center at 851 N. Maitland Ave. will conduct a two-day seminar to help students select a college or a career.

> "It's not easy to raise kids in today's fast-paced society, but that's all right," according to the Program Director of the Regional Medical Center's Child Protection Team. Doreen Mayer asserts that levels of stress inherent in child-rearing are normal.
> Mayer is among several child abuse professionals who will address a community service program titled "Help! My Kids Are Driving Me Crazy," which will be conducted next Wednesday from 7 to 9 p.m. in the RMC Auditorium.
> REVISED: The Regional Medical Center will offer a program to help parents who are having a difficult time raising their children. The program, titled, "Help! My Kids Are Driving Me Crazy," will begin at 7 p.m. Wednesday.

Reporters also eliminate puffery, especially laudatory adjectives. Every speaker does not have to be called a "guest speaker," and none should be labeled "famous," "prominent," "well-known" or "distinguished." Moreover, their appearances and topics should not be called "interesting" or "important." Similarly, no story—or publicity release—should call a program "wonderful," "successful," "timely" or "informative." Also avoid phrases such as "bigger and better," "the best ever" and "back by popular demand."

The puffery often appears in leads:

PUBLICITY RELEASE: Michael R. Zaslow, a nationally recognized and respected forecaster in the field of economics and financial investments, will speak in the city November 15.
REVISED: Economist Michael R. Zaslow will speak about financial investments—gold, stocks and real estate—at 8 p.m. Nov. 15 in Carr Auditorium.

PUBLICITY RELEASE: The Creative Art Gallery, devoted exclusively to fine art photography, proudly announces an event of international significance in the photographic community . . . an exhibition of the works of Jerry N. Uelsmann and Diane Farris.
REVISED: The Creative Art Gallery, 324 N. Park Ave., will exhibit the photographs of Jerry N. Uelsmann and Diane Farris from Jan. 4 to 29.

Reporters also delete the adjectives appearing in later paragraphs:

PUBLICITY RELEASE: A gala reception will be held at 8 p.m.
REVISED: A reception will be held at 8 p.m.

PUBLICITY RELEASE: The public is cordially invited to attend this enjoyable concert.
REVISED: The public is invited to the concert.

PUBLICITY RELEASE: A special treat will be in store for all. The carnival will have 24 exciting and fun-filled rides. We hope that you will be able to come and enjoy the festivities.
REVISED: The carnival will have 24 rides.

Platitudes and vague generalities are equally common in publicity releases. One political candidate pledged that he "will work for a community development plan that will maintain the community's natural assets and promote its growth." And when the U.S. Postal Service announced the purchase of some new computers, a publicity release it sent to newspapers called the computers "part of an ongoing program to improve service to customers while keeping rates at the lowest possible level."

The platitudes and generalities sound familiar because they are used so often. For example, the following platitudes are similar but appeared in publicity releases that different companies used to describe different employees:

We are fortunate to have a man with Russell's reputation and background as a member of the team. His knowledge and experience will be invaluable as we broaden our sales and marketing base.

We are extremely fortunate to have someone of his background and expertise join our program. He's joining our program at a most opportune time, when we are preparing to move forward with new vigor and emphasis.

Other sentences contain no facts, only generalities and self-praise. Reporters would delete all the following sentences:

It will be an exciting musical celebration.

An impressive lineup of speakers will share their expertise.

The library has a reputation as a friendly, pleasant place to visit.

The colorful costumes will make a memorable impression at this once-in-a-lifetime experience.

With a dazzling lineup of new entertainment, the fair is the best it has ever been.

Such gush often appears in quotations, but that rarely justifies its use. If a quotation lacks substance, reporters discard it, too:

> Blosser said, "It's an exciting time of quality entertainment and should not be missed."

> "We're very excited about the opening of the new store," said Mark Hughey, president. "The store represents a new direction for us and extends our commitment to provide customers with the highest-quality products at the lowest possible prices."

Other publicity releases show even less understanding of the media and their definitions of news. Some publicity releases are editorials that praise rather than report. Typically, a publicity release submitted by a state's beef producers declared that, "Red meat makes a contribution to America's health and vitality and should be saluted." The publicity release continued:

> We often overlook the fact that American meat products are known throughout the world for their quality, wholesomeness and delicious flavor. This week is National Meat Week, and it is an excellent opportunity to recognize the important contribution red meat makes to the diets of more than 200 million Americans who have made meat one of this country's favorite foods. Meat is more than a satisfying meal—it's part of a healthy, well-balanced diet.

Other publicity releases urge the public to act: to donate their time and money, to buy new products, to attend events, to join organizations:

> Come and enjoy the fair.
> Get into the "Spirit of the Season" by joining in the celebration.
> Please be generous. Send your contributions of $25, $50, $100 and more to help the needy.

Reporters must delete such editorial comments or rewrite them in a more factual manner. They may report a story and then—in the final paragraph—tell readers that they can respond. Reporters do not tell readers that they *should* respond, but only how people who want to respond can do so:

> PUBLICITY RELEASE: Everyone should bring their families to the picnic.
> REVISED: The picnic is open to the public and will be held from 10 a.m. until 8 p.m. at Central Park. Admission is $2 for adults and $1 for children.

> PUBLICITY RELEASE: Tickets for the Father Martin appearance are available to the public at the Bob Carr Performing Arts Center, and by calling 422-4896, for $5 each. Seating will not be reserved, so the public is urged to arrive early to hear this most important message on the subject of alcoholism.
> REVISED: Tickets cost $5 and can be obtained at the Bob Carr Performing Arts Center or by calling 422-4896.

Because of all the changes and deletions, and because of the need to save space for other material, reporters regularly condense four- and five-page handouts into three- and four-paragraph news stories. For example:

Publicity Release	News Story
Joyce Jones, organ virtuoso and concert artist, returns to perform her second concert on the Trexler Memorial Organ of St. Paul Lutheran Church at 8:00 P.M., Friday, November 19.	Organist Joyce Jones will perform at St. Paul Lutheran Church at 8 p.m. Nov. 19 as part of the Trexler Memorial Concert Series.
Her dazzling technique left the audience calling for more at her first performance in the Trexler Memorial Concert Series in 1980. Long before that appearance and certainly	Tickets cost $10 and are available at the Concert Series Office, 300 E. Church St. or by calling 425-6060, extension 7117, from 1 to 5 p.m. on weekdays.
	Her program will include: Toccata on "Loge den Herren," Fantasia and Fugue in G

many times since, she has thrilled audiences all over the United States and Europe.

"Utterly charming . . . dazzling bravura mingled with intelligence," said the Los Angeles Times. The Stuttgarter Nachrichten hailed her performances in Germany as displays of "phenomenal technique . . . played magnificently."

Studying piano at age 4 and composing by age six, her seemingly boundless energy and talent have earned her a wall full of accolades of international recognition. When she is not touring, she is organist in residence at Baylor University, Texas.

Her program will include: Toccata on "Loge den Herren," Fantasia and Fugue in G minor, Twilight at Fiesole, Sonata: The Ninety-fourth Psalm, In Paradisium and Pageant.

Like all Trexler Memorial Concerts, her performance will begin promptly at 8:00 P.M. Tickets are $10.00 each and are available at the Concert Series Office, 300 E. Church St. Telephone number is 425-6060, Ext. 7117, between the hours of 1:00 and 5:00 P.M. weekdays.

minor, Twilight at Fiesole, Sonata: The Ninety-fourth Psalm, In Paradisium and Pageant.

Ms. Jones is the organist in residence at Baylor University in Waco, Texas. She also performed here during the 1980 concert series.

Other problems are more difficult to resolve. People and organizations submit publicity releases to the media because they hope to benefit from the stories' publication. Virtually all their publicity releases are one-sided. They present only their sources' opinions, and they often present those opinions as fact. Publicity releases that do mention opposing viewpoints usually try to show that those viewpoints are wrong.

Because it is fast and easy, reporters are tempted merely to accept and publish information provided by the publicity releases. But if they do—if they fail to check the "facts"—they are likely to make some serious errors. For example, a college newspaper missed a major story because it received and immediately published a publicity release announcing the promotion of eight faculty members. The publicity release provided by the college failed to reveal that more than a dozen other faculty members had also sought promotions but were rejected by the college president. A single telephone call to a faculty representative would have uncovered the story.

Other publicity releases encourage controversy. Here, too, newspapers that publish those publicity releases allow themselves to be used. For example, Paul N. Strassels, a former tax law specialist for the Internal Revenue Service, has charged that the IRS uses the media to scare taxpayers. Each year, stories about tax evaders who have been sentenced to prison begin to appear in the media shortly before the April 15 deadline for filing income tax returns. Strassels explains: "It's the policy of the IRS public affairs office to issue such stories at the time you are figuring your taxes. The service knows that prison stories make good copy. It's simple manipulation." Similarly, a congressman recently accused the IRS of waging "a campaign of terror among the American people." He explained that the IRS uses tactics "carefully designed to threaten the American taxpayer, to keep him in a constant state of fear" so that fewer Americans will cheat on their taxes.

Despite the problems, publicity releases remain an important source of information. The publicity releases are easily available and provide some facts that journalists might be unaware of—or unable to obtain—in any other manner. So when properly used, publicity releases give newspapers the information necessary for legitimate news stories. They also help individuals and organizations obtain needed publicity. However, the process is never automatic, since most publicity releases are discarded by journalists, and others are extensively rewritten.

Some newspapers rarely publish any publicity releases—but use them to learn about important topics. The newspapers then assign their own reporters to obtain more information about the topics. The reporters confirm the information's accuracy and seek the viewpoints of a variety of sources. Thus, the newspapers try to provide a more objective, balanced and complete account of the news.

Good PR: A Journalist's View

What do journalists look for in public relations people?

Journalists look for people with good writing skills, people able to translate complicated information into clear, readable stories. Journalists also look for people who understand the media's definitions of news. The journalists want to be informed about major stories. They do not want to be bothered with stories that, rather obviously, are not newsworthy.

Good public relations people are available and cooperative. To help journalists meet their deadlines, they respond quickly, no matter what the question, and do their best to provide true and complete information at all times.

The best PR people are also well informed about their own companies and industries. They can find information quickly and will arrange interviews with experts and top executives. When an important issue arises, some anticipate journalists' questions and make sure that the right corporate officials will be available to answer them.

People at companies with reputations for bad public relations seem to be unfamiliar with newsroom procedures and uninformed about their own companies and industries. Some are unable—or unwilling—to arrange interviews with their top executives. They refuse to return phone calls, refuse to answer questions or respond with "no comment" to questions. They are also more defensive. They try to hide bad news, perhaps hoping that it will go away. Some deliberately mislead journalists—a tactic that often backfires.

EXERCISE 1
Publicity Releases

EVALUATING THE NEWSWORTHINESS OF PUBLICITY RELEASES

INSTRUCTIONS: Critically evaluate the newsworthiness of the following leads. Each lead appeared in a publicity release mailed to a daily or weekly newspaper. Rate each publicity release's newsworthiness on a scale of "1" (Not Newsworthy) to "10" (Extremely Newsworthy), then discuss the ratings with your class.

1. Nail polish remover is still being dropped into the eyes of conscious rabbits to meet insurance regulations, infant primates are punished by electric shocks in pain endurance tests and dogs are reduced to a condition called "learned helplessness" to earn someone's Ph.D.

   With the theme "Alternatives Now," People for the Ethical Treatment of Animals (PETA), is sponsoring a community rally on Friday—World Day for Laboratory Animals—at 1 p.m.

   RATING:_____ EXPLANATION:_____

2. A new device that alleviates pain by allowing each patient to administer his own medication is now available at Memorial Hospital.

   The hospital has purchased Harvard's Patient-Controlled Analgesia (PCA) Pumps that allow patients to safely and effectively control pain by pressing a button at their bedside.

   RATING:_____ EXPLANATION:_____

3. Dr. Paul Becton, who recently retired after 35 years with the U.S. Department of Agriculture, has assumed his new duties as Chief of the Bureau of Brucellosis and Tuberculosis with the State Department of Agriculture and Consumer Services, Commissioner Doyle Conner announced today.

   RATING:_____ EXPLANATION:_____

4. Demand for gas energy in the United States could, under the right conditions, increase as much as 50 percent to approximately 30 trillion cubic feet (Tcf) by the year 2000, according to a study by the American Gas Association (AGA).

   RATING:_____ EXPLANATION:_____

5. An eye disease that affects only diabetics nonetheless has such vision-destroying potential that it now ranks among the country's leading causes of blindness. The National Society to Prevent Blindness warns that all diabetics are at risk from the disease, diabetic retinopathy, that blinds some 4,700 of them each year. Right now, a million diabetics have eye changes that can lead to blindness if not treated—10 percent of the country's estimated 10 million diabetics.

   RATING:_____ EXPLANATION:_____

6. The Crime Prevention Commission has produced a brochure of crime prevention and safety tips that every child should know. This free brochure contains a handy list of home and bicycle safety guidelines as well as rules regarding "dangerous strangers" that should be taught to all youngsters. The cheerful yellow leaflet also includes a panel of emergency numbers for posting near the telephone.

   RATING:_____ EXPLANATION:_____

7. The State Supreme Court has suspended an attorney from the practice of law for three months and one day, effective immediately. The discipline resulted from action brought by the State Bar.

RATING:_____ EXPLANATION:_____

8. High interest rates, coupled with low prices for most agricultural commodities, are causing serious "cash flow" problems for farmers, pushing some toward bankruptcy, according to a study by the Institute of Food and Agricultural Sciences (IFAS) at your state university.

RATING:_____ EXPLANATION:_____

9. General Electric Company will establish the worldwide headquarters for its new Automation Systems Department near your city, James A. Meehan, General Manager of the Automation Systems Department, announced today.

   Automation Systems markets industrial robots designed for parts assembly, arc and spot welding, spraying, material handling, and process applications such as grinding, polishing, and deburring.

RATING:_____ EXPLANATION:_____

10. "The Changing Face of Men's Fashion" will be illustrated in a fashion presentation in Robinson's Men's Shops at 5:30 on Thursday. A special feature of the event will be commentary of the distinctive directions in men's designs by Pieter O'Brien, a fashion editor of Gentlemen's Quarterly magazine.

RATING:_____ EXPLANATION:_____

11. Fire safety education in the state's public schools should be stepped up, according to the State Fire Marshal.

RATING:_____ EXPLANATION:_____

12. The festive holiday season is upon us. Help defray Christmas expenses and ring in the new year by recycling aluminum.

   Save the many aluminum items found around the home during the holiday season and receive cash for them every Tuesday through Saturday (except December 24 through January 4, due to the holidays) from 9:30 a.m. to 4:30 p.m. at the Reynolds Aluminum Recycling Service Center, 3801 N. Young Parkway.

RATING:_____ EXPLANATION:_____

EXERCISE 2
Publicity Releases

EVALUATING THE NEWSWORTHINESS OF PUBLICITY RELEASES

INSTRUCTIONS: Critically evaluate the newsworthiness of the following leads. Each lead appeared in a publicity release mailed to a daily or weekly newspaper. Rate each publicity release's newsworthiness on a scale of "1" (Not Newsworthy) to "10" (Extremely Newsworthy), then discuss the ratings with your class.

1. Four minutes is all that stands between life and death in a person whose heart or breathing suddenly stops. Getting prompt medical help, such as cardiopulmonary resuscitation (CPR), can help save the victim's life.

     To help you learn the lifesaving technique of CPR, Memorial Hospital and the American Heart Association are teaming up to offer "CPR for Citizens" classes.

     RATING:_____ EXPLANATION:_____

2. OKLAHOMA CITY—The Federal Aviation Administration has announced a nationwide Air Traffic Controller recruiting program.

     The agency plans to hire 2,000 to 3,000 controllers in the next year and is actively seeking candidates through its "We Need More of the World's Best" recruiting campaign.

     RATING:_____ EXPLANATION:_____

3. We would like to inform you that our Fine Arts Theatre's third season offering, "The Rainmaker," has been replaced by Frank D. Gilroy's "The Subject Was Roses" which will be presented Wednesday, March 2, through Saturday, March 5 at 8 p.m., and Sunday, March 6 at 2 p.m. Performances will take place in the Fine Arts Theatre on the Seminole Community College campus.

     RATING:_____ EXPLANATION:_____

4. The Evans Group, architects and planners specializing in multifamily shelter design, walked off with the coveted Attached Home of the Year Award and six other prestigious Aurora Awards at the recently concluded Southeast Builders Conference.

     RATING:_____ EXPLANATION:_____

5. Women have made much progress against discrimination through social and legal reforms, but they are still the victims of a very disabling form of discrimination that largely goes unnoticed: arthritis.

     Of the more than 31 million Americans who suffer from arthritis, two-thirds are women, according to the Arthritis Foundation.

     RATING:_____ EXPLANATION:_____

6. Parents who refuse to let children believe in Santa Claus may be doing them harm, today asserted a Mt. Sinai School of Medicine psychologist.

     Dr. David M. Kelley stated in the current issue of Parents' magazine, "Being the only one in the classroom who knows for sure that there's no such guy could make a child feel very different, very strange." He said it "would be unusual" if the denial led to a sense of strength.

     RATING:_____ EXPLANATION:_____

7. Called "in a class by itself" and "a welcome addition to any fairy tale library," by the Christian Science Monitor, "Russian Folk Tales" is a collection of seven classic folk tales from Russia in a large format edition, featuring the brilliant, dynamic full-color graphics of Ivan Bilibin.

   RATING:_____ EXPLANATION:_____

8. "Recently declining interest rates make this a good time to buy," according to Pete Gaidis, senior vice president, residential loans, at Pioneer Federal Savings and Loan Association. Gaidis added that Pioneer has "plenty of funds to invest in the local community."

   RATING:_____ EXPLANATION:_____

9. People shopping for children's toys this holiday season should select gifts with a wary eye in order to spare a child's eyes, warns the National Society to Prevent Blindness. According to the society, an estimated 4,327 individuals were treated in hospital emergency rooms last year for toy-related eye injuries. More than 68 percent of them were less than 15 years old.

   RATING:_____ EXPLANATION:_____

10. Bring the entire family out for a day of zany fun at the 7-Up Bed Race for the Muscular Dystrophy Association.

    The festivities begin at 10:30 a.m. at the corner of Church Street and Garland Avenue on Saturday, with a parade of the decorated beds followed by the Bed Race at 11 a.m. There will be elimination heats, climaxing in a final runoff for the fastest bed.

    RATING:_____ EXPLANATION:_____

11. Pregnant women throughout the state are finding it more difficult to locate an obstetrician willing to deliver their baby because of the number of obstetricians—80 last year alone—who are discontinuing this practice because of the high cost of malpractice insurance, according to a survey by the State Obstetric and Gynecologic Society.

    RATING:_____ EXPLANATION:_____

12. The County Chapter of the American Red Cross has a new service for homebound senior citizens called Dial-A-Friend. Each day, at a previously arranged time, a Red Cross volunteer telephones the homebound senior to check and see that he or she is all right. If the telephone is not answered after the volunteer has tried three times within an hour, a call will be made to a neighbor or other backup person who will visit to see why the phone was not answered.

    RATING:_____ EXPLANATION:_____

EXERCISE 3
Publicity Releases: Leads

INSTRUCTIONS: The following are leads from publicity releases mailed to a daily or weekly newspaper. Rewrite the leads, using the proper style and only the facts—not the puffery.

1. "Fiesta On The Park," one of the largest outdoor arts and crafts shows in the state, will be held this Saturday and Sunday on Park Avenue. "Fiesta On The Park" is the perfect event for browsing, sampling different food, enjoying live entertainment, and finding that unique gift for yourself or for a loved one. Artists and craftsmen will display their work in more than 500 booths set up along the mile-long Park Avenue.

2. The Bay Street Players promise "haunts and howling good humor" in their season-opener at the State Theatre. A wild and woolly production of "Dracula" is scheduled Oct. 17–19 and 23–25, at 8:30 PM Thursday–Saturday and 2:30 Sunday.

3. The National Spa and Pool Institute will sponsor their Annual Pool and Spa Show at the Colonial Mall on Thursday through Sunday. Those interested in buying their own personal pool or spa can use this opportunity as an excellent shopping guide for searching for the item that best fits their needs. Customers can also register to win a free spa, valued at $12,500, and gather information from 62 dealers by visiting at this one central location.

4. If good Italian cooking tickles your tastebuds, the 1st annual ITALIAN FESTIVAL should be a must on your calendar this spring. The ITALIAN FESTIVAL will be held April 1 and 2 at Rollins Park, with food, fun, games and dancing for everyone.

5. Come and visit with Santa at Lake Lily on Sunday, Dec. 14. Santa and his helpers will arrive at the park's gazebo in a Fire Truck at 3:00 PM. Children can share their Holiday wishes with Santa from 3:00 PM until 6 PM. Enjoy a beautiful afternoon on Lake Lily listening to Christmas music, observing the wonderful holiday decorations and visiting with Santa himself.

6. David Hurcades, one of the many outstanding fishery biologists in our state, has been employed with the State Division of Fishery for 22 years. He is a fine speaker and provides an excellent program. He will present a slide program on the History and Future of Great Lakes Sports Fishing at 8 p.m. on Sept. 11. This is a program that a fishing family would certainly enjoy.

7. Holiday Fun Time for children six (6) through twelve (12) years of age will begin Dec. 22 at the Hill Recreation Center. This exciting program, running from 9:00 AM to 4:00 PM will include tennis, archery, gameroom activities, a cookout, a talent show, and much, much more!!! And one low price of $5 covers it all!

8. Some 4,000 Girl Scouts from your county's Council of Girl Scouts, Inc. will be collecting more than discards when they bring their Salvation Army bags to your door this Saturday. They will also be collecting HOPE for the men in the rehabilitation program at the Adult Rehabilitation Center on Colonial Drive. The discards you donate will be repaired, priced and put on sale in the Red Shield Thrift Stores. The proceeds support the whole program at the Center. When men see that the work they do on items you donate pays their way to a new life, they find HOPE. Help the Girl Scouts help The Salvation Army on this "Helping Hands Day".

EXERCISE 4
Publicity Releases

INSTRUCTIONS: These are actual publicity releases mailed to a daily or weekly newspaper. Only the locations and the names of some individuals have been changed. Your instructor may ask you to write only the lead for each publicity release—or to write the entire story.

1. Recovered Anorexic To Speak

"Understanding the Anorexic/Bulimic Family Member" will be the subject of a meeting sponsored by Memorial Hospital's Eating Disorders Unit Monday, Nov. 3, at 6:00 p.m. in the hospital auditorium.

Karen Balliet, a recovered anorexic and the president and director of the state chapter of the American Anorexia/Bulimia Assn., Inc., will be the speaker.

Anorexia nervosa, which is characterized by an intense fear of becoming obese, affects over 100,000 people in the U.S. alone. Bulimia, characterized by recurrent episodes of binge eating often followed by attempts to purge food by vomiting or laxative abuse, is especially prevalent in female high school and college students.

The Memorial Hospital Eating Disorders Unit has been open for two years. It is unique to this area in that it offers both in-patient and out-patient programs. Its staff is available to answer questions concerning these life threatening disorders and to assist patients and family members in coping.

For information about Balliet's talk or the Eating Disorders Unit, call the hospital at 767-2267.

2. Beauty Contest Entries

Mr. Carlos Zumbado, General Manager of the County Fair, announced that this year's County Fair Queen Beauty Contest will be held on October 22 at the Fashion Square Mall at 6:30 pm. The contestant must be a student and a resident of the county between the ages of 16–20.

The prizes will be as follows:

FIRST: $150.00 cash, free modeling course from MDM Studios, beautiful crown, banner and trophy, and two VIP tickets good for every fair concert, general admission and midway rides and many nice gifts from the Fashion Square Mall Merchants.

SECOND: $50.00 cash, two VIP tickets for any two concerts and free general admission every day and a gift from the Fashion Square Mall.

THIRD: $25.00 cash, two VIP tickets for any two concerts and free general admission every day and a gift from the Fashion Square Mall.

Entry forms can be picked up at any high school, Fashion Square Mall business office and the County Fair office at 500 Friday road.

Contestants must have their entry forms returned to the Fashion Square Mall office by October 10. The preliminary judging and interviewing will be held on October 15 at the Fashion Square Mall. The finals will be open to the public. For further information, contact Bonnie Whidden at 452-3270.

3. Halloween Creativefest

Colonial Mall is hosting a Halloween Creativefest Costume Contest and "safe" Trick-or-Treating on October 31st from 5:30–9:00 p.m. The contest will be for all ghosts and goblins 12 years of age and under. The costume categories include: Scariest, prettiest, funniest, and most original. In order to maintain crowd control the contest for children ages 6 and under will be at 5:30 p.m. while children ages 7–12 are encouraged to trick-or-treat during this time then return at 7:00 p.m. for their costume contest. Those wishing to participate must first register at the Colonial Mall information desk, located lower level center of the mall from 3–5:30 p.m. Other Halloween Creativefest events include thrilling entertainment such as face painting, clowns, mimes, and more!

4. Annual "Stop, Drop & Shop" Program

The city Parks & Recreation Dept. and the Public Library invite you to spend an afternoon of Christmas Fun, Sunday, December 14, 1 p.m.–5 p.m.

Parents can begin by *Stopping* off at the Public Library, *Dropping* off their school age children and *Shopping* for the holidays with their free time, knowing that their children are being well cared for and having fun.

The Public Library's annual *Stop, Drop & Shop* program will be held at the library from 1 to 5 p.m. Sunday, December 14. Games, films, stories and other activities for school age children will be featured to add to their holiday fun. It's all completely free of charge.

5. Senior Citizen's Club Festivities

The Senior Citizen's Club will host a weekend Pot Luck this Saturday, beginning at 12:00 noon. Anyone 55 years of age or older that is interested in enjoying good company and good food is invited to attend. Everyone is asked to bring a dish; the ham will be provided by the Club. The Pot Luck will be held at 210 Packwood Drive.

A trip is planned for February 5 to the State Fair. Cost will be $2.50 per person, and everyone is encouraged to attend.

New officers sworn in at the previous meeting, held last Saturday, are President Samuel Gibbson, Vice President Billy Joe Day and Treasurer Patricia Bulmahn.

The Club invites new members to join all its fun-filled activities. Interested parties should call President Samuel Gibson at 645-4071.

EXERCISE 5
Publicity Releases

INSTRUCTIONS: These are actual publicity releases mailed to a daily or weekly newspaper. Only the locations and the names of some individuals have been changed. Your instructor may ask you to write only the lead for each publicity release—or to write the entire story.

1. The Psychic Zone

Beyond the edge of understanding, yet just within the fringe of awareness. . . . Beyond the distant future though before the forgotten past, lies a little-understood territory of the human mind that is known as . . . The Psychic Zone!

Saturday April 23 and Sunday April 24th, THE HILTON INN will become part of The Psychic Zone, as a roving contingent of multi-talented psychics proudly present a Psychic Fair for your entertainment.

Many of the psychics will be available for private consultations. Come in and join us, whether you're serious about psychic phenomena, want to enjoy a FREE MINI SEMINAR, or have a private reading.

FREE MINI SEMINARS will be given at 10 AM, 12 Noon, 3 PM and 5 PM. On Saturday night, at 7:30 PM, there will be a PSYCHIC AWARENESS SEMINAR, teaching you how to Meditate, See Auras, Feel Auras, and learn how to reduce stress. Find out how to use your Psychic Abilities. This is a paid seminar, with the cost of admission set at $9.50 for one and all.

THE PSYCHIC ZONE is in your future, April 23rd and 24th, at THE HILTON INN.

2. First Community Respite Care Weekend

Alzheimer's, the fourth leading cause of death among adults in the U.S., has a profound impact on the entire family, thus leaving the primary care giver in a "high risk" category for stress related illnesses. Any time off, regardless of how little, is essential in helping reduce that stress.

Next week, on Saturday and Sunday, Sand Lake Hospital will offer the area's first "Community Respite Care Weekend," a new concept. Volunteers will offer time and loving care the entire weekend.

The Community Respite Care Project offers rest or relief to those families who are continually caring for an Alzheimer's loved one. This weekend will give those family members the opportunity to have a weekend off to do just as they please while their loved one is safe and in the caring hands of trained volunteers and nursing professionals.

After this weekend's respite, similar respite care will be offered on the first weekend of each month at the Sand Lake Hospital facility. The new program also offers in-home volunteer help and subsidized adult day care.

"Anyone who has an interest in volunteering their time is greatly needed," says Charlotte McFarland. Our program relies solely on volunteer power to staff both the in-home and hospital respite. We realize many people may find this type of volunteerism difficult, however, the devoted people we do have find much personal satisfaction and reward once they see how much they help and the difference they make to these families."

For more information, call Charlotte McFarland, Respite Project Director, at 425-2489.

3. Blood Donors Needed During Summer Months

Come roll up your sleeve and give a livesaving gift to a patient who needs you.

The summer is a time for enjoyment and relaxation, but for many local hospital patients who are ill or injured, the summer won't be so much fun. The Blood Bank asks that you help these patients return to good health by donating blood.

"The community blood supply traditionally decreases during this time of the year because many regular donors are on vacation or busy with other activities," said Linda Wallenhorst-Zito, director of communications and marketing at the Blood Bank. "However, accidents and emergencies increase during the summer, and many patients wanting elective surgery are forced to postpone it until more blood becomes available."

Any healthy person at least 17 years old may donate and there is no upper age limit. Donors complete a brief medical questionnaire and health screening that many find a good way to regularly monitor such factors as their heart rate and blood pressure.

For additional information, call your local Blood Bank branch. Come help save a live. Someday, someone may save yours.

4. 31st Annual Community Art Festival Begins Fall Season

Fall is the time to enjoy art festivals everywhere, and our community's 31st annual Fall Art Festival starts the season off right with a weekend show.

Sponsored by the Jaycees, the festival will be held this Saturday and Sunday. Hours are 10:00 A.M. to 5 P.M. each of the two days.

Enjoy first class original artwork in categories including ceramics, watercolors, oils, sculpture, photography and more. Last year's show exhibited 240 artists and drew about 22,000 visitors during the two-day festival.

Food will be available throughout the weekend, along with entertainment, all set along New York Avenue, between 9th and 12th Streets—a perfect setting to enjoy the fall weather and perhaps find that special painting you've been looking for.

For more art festival information, or for information on accommodations in the city, contact the Convention and Visitors Bureau, Box 2007. Call 847-5000.

EXERCISE 6
Publicity Releases

INSTRUCTIONS: The following are actual publicity releases that have been mailed to newspapers. Only the locations and the names of some individuals have been changed. Write a complete story for each publicity release. Or, your instructor may ask you to write only the leads.

The exercises contain numerous style, spelling and punctuation errors. Some are even inconsistent from one paragraph to the next.

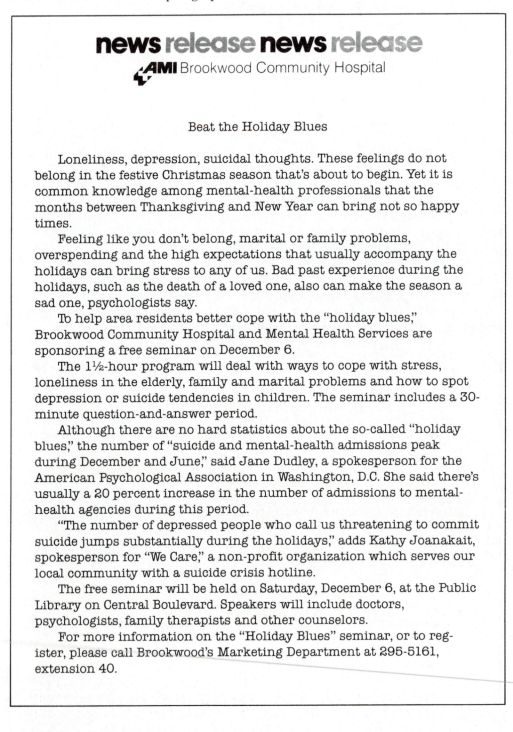

news release news release

AMI Brookwood Community Hospital

Beat the Holiday Blues

Loneliness, depression, suicidal thoughts. These feelings do not belong in the festive Christmas season that's about to begin. Yet it is common knowledge among mental-health professionals that the months between Thanksgiving and New Year can bring not so happy times.

Feeling like you don't belong, marital or family problems, overspending and the high expectations that usually accompany the holidays can bring stress to any of us. Bad past experience during the holidays, such as the death of a loved one, also can make the season a sad one, psychologists say.

To help area residents better cope with the "holiday blues," Brookwood Community Hospital and Mental Health Services are sponsoring a free seminar on December 6.

The 1½-hour program will deal with ways to cope with stress, loneliness in the elderly, family and marital problems and how to spot depression or suicide tendencies in children. The seminar includes a 30-minute question-and-answer period.

Although there are no hard statistics about the so-called "holiday blues," the number of "suicide and mental-health admissions peak during December and June," said Jane Dudley, a spokesperson for the American Psychological Association in Washington, D.C. She said there's usually a 20 percent increase in the number of admissions to mental-health agencies during this period.

"The number of depressed people who call us threatening to commit suicide jumps substantially during the holidays," adds Kathy Joanakait, spokesperson for "We Care," a non-profit organization which serves our local community with a suicide crisis hotline.

The free seminar will be held on Saturday, December 6, at the Public Library on Central Boulevard. Speakers will include doctors, psychologists, family therapists and other counselors.

For more information on the "Holiday Blues" seminar, or to register, please call Brookwood's Marketing Department at 295-5161, extension 40.

Crimeline Program Inc.

FOR IMMEDIATE RELEASE

This week's CRIMELINE case comes from the files of the County Sheriff's Office.

It was a relatively quiet night last October 18, while Sgt. David Aneja was riding in patrol. He normally worked in the Internal Affairs Section of the County Sheriff's Office, but he liked riding on the street periodically; so when he had the chance to fill in for a friend and fellow sergeant who was on medical leave, he readily volunteered.

Just a few minutes after midnight, Sgt. Aneji spotted a black Chevrolet Nova parked on a dead-end street north of Beville Road directly across from the Forest Lake subdivision.

The vehicle was jacked up in the rear, had wide tires and a Duval County tag. Both the lights and the engine were turned off.

Sgt. Aneji pulled his unmarked police car behind the Nova and got out. At the same time, a male in his mid 20's, 6' tall, 180 pds. got out of the other car. Even though Sgt. Aneja was in uniform, he wanted to make sure that there was no doubt that the man knew he was a police officer, so he reached back in his car to turn on the blue lights. When he stood back up, he heard a shot and felt a sharp pain in his left chest. The bullet struck the deputy's badge and, thankfully, his bulletproof vest. Sgt. Aneja fell to the ground behind his car door. The suspect fired five more rounds through the door, narrowly missing the deputy.

The gunman then jumped into his car and sped off, heading west on Beville Road, with Sgt. Aneja returning fire. Through the whole gun battle, not one word was spoken!

Who was this man, and why was he so bent on killing Sgt. Aneji? If you know, you could earn a reward of up to $1,000 by calling CRIMELINE at 423-TIPS. And, of course, you don't have to give your name. When only <u>you</u> know, we keep it that way.

Crimeline Program Inc.

FOR IMMEDIATE RELEASE

Last Thursday, at approximately 12:30 p.m., a 77-year-old white female was shopping at Colonial Plaza Mall. Mrs. Dorothy Kauffman was approached by a white female who told her that she had just found a bag containing $21,000 in cash and a note indicating the money was illegal as it was unreported tax money. The subject then told Mrs. Kauffman that she had a friend who was a lawyer and asked Mrs. Kauffman to wait while she called him. Upon returning, the white female subject was accompanied by a black female subject who identified herself as Angie Williams, secretary to Attorney Goldberg. The white female subject indicated that Miss Williams was instructed to advertise the found sum for 30 days and to pay taxes on said amount. Taxes would amount to $3,000, leaving a total of $18,0000, to be divided among them in equal shares of $6,000 for equal participation. But before doing that, Attorney Goldberg wanted to see if he could make a transaction of shares of stock in a computer. He would need more money, but just for a few hours. He requested that each participant withdraw $8,000 from their personal accounts and return to a parking space at a lot on Hillcrest Street. Mrs. Kauffman, accompanied by the white female, went to the Federal Credit Union and withdrew $8,000, saying she was using it for a down payment on a house. They then went to a bank at Colonial Plaza and cashed the check and went to the parking lot on Hillcrest Street where the black female was waiting. The white female asked Mrs. Kauffman for her part of the money so that the serial numbers could be entered into the computer. Mrs. Kauffman gave the white female the money and she went into the building. Upon returning, the two women responsible told Mrs. Kauffman that Mr. Goldberg wanted to meet her personally to return her money during which time they would wait for her in the car. Mrs. Kauffman then entered the building seeking a Mr. Goldberg, and upon finding no lawyers' offices, she returned to her car finding it empty.

The white female was described to be about 35 years old, 5'5" tall, and weighing approximately 130 pounds.

The black female was about 35 years old, dark hair, 5'4" tall, and weighing approximately 130 pounds.

How could anyone fall for something like that? It could never happen to me! That's exactly what Mrs. Kauffman had said before she was conned out of $8,000.

CRIMELINE is offering a reward of up to $1,000 for information leading to the arrest and conviction of this or any other unsolved felony crime in the area. If you have any information, call CRIMELINE at 423-TIPS. No one needs to know who you are, because with CRIMELINE, there are no names, no faces and no hassles! Your information will be held in absolute confidence and you will remain anonymous.

FRIENDS OF FATHER MARTIN

431 E. Central Boulevard, Suite 250

Your City

TO: ALL MEDIA

FROM: Friends of Father Martin/Jackie Lewis, President

RELEASE: Immediate

RE: FATHER MARTIN TO SPEAK AT CARR ON "ALCOHOLISM AND THE FAMILY"

Author and internationally acclaimed educator on alcoholism, Father Joseph Martin, will speak for one night only at the Carr Performing Arts Center next Monday and will address the problem of "Alcoholism and the Family" in a practical manner, offering guidelines for recovery from alcoholism.

Father Martin, who has lectured on alcoholism in all fifty states and several foreign countries, received national acclaim for his film, "Chalk Talk." The film, initially used by the armed services, has become a standard for use in government and private alcoholic rehabilitation centers throughout the United States. He received the first annual Marty Mann Award for Outstanding Achievement in Alcoholism Communications, presented by the "Alcoholism/The National Magazine" and his book, "No Laughing Matter" has just been released by Harper & Row, Publishers.

It has long been recognized that the alcoholic is not the only person affected by his disease. Drinking affects the family deeply, and reaches out to affect the alcoholic's relationships with his employer and fellow workers, friends and social habits. Alcoholism is quickly approaching being the number one concern in the nation, not only for the individual, but for the death and destruction caused as a result of the disease.

Friends of Father Martin in the area, realizing the need for information to combat the spread of alcoholism, organized this special appearance as a benefit for his rehabilitation center, Ashley, a non-profit, tax-exempt effort in Maryland, that will be utilized by alcoholics and their families from throughout the United States.

Tickets for the Father Martin appearance are available to the public at the Carr Performing Arts Center, and by calling 422-4896, for $5.00 each. Groups wishing to attend should call Friends of Father Martin in advance to arrange for blocks of tickets. Seating will not be reserved, so the public is urged to arrive early to hear this most important message on the subject of alcoholism.

-30-

NEWS RELEASE

BETTER BUSINESS BUREAU

For Immediate Release

As the film and modeling industries continue to make inroads in the area, more businesses preying on young hopefuls and their lack of industry knowledge are making their presence known. One look at the employment section of local newspapers confirms this.

Ads are glamorous and exciting; however, all too often many of the dreams are shattered by "promoters" and "con men" who hustle the naive with promises of fame and fortune.

The Better Business Bureau takes the position that no modeling or talent agency should advertise under "Help Wanted" unless they are hiring people to work for them. We urge consumers to be wary of any modeling or talent agency requiring a purchase or investment when responding to an advertisement for employment.

If you are considering employment in this area, you might contact employment managers who hire people in this field and possibly obtain their opinions on your chances of success as well as the requirements for employment.

A number of hopeful models have reported to the Better Business Bureau after responding to the "Help Wanted" ads in local newspapers, they learned that the firms were offering training on how to become a model or an actor and that there were no positions open. Other consumers have reported that in response to such ads some firms required them to pay for photographs to be put in a portfolio, which in turn would be sent to companies who may or may not be in the market to offer the consumer some kind of employment.

Therefore, we offer these guidelines to potential models and actors in dealing with such agencies:

1. Determine if the company actually has jobs available or if it's just a ploy to enroll you in a training course or to sell you photographs.

2. If the agency offers training, are they licensed by the State Board of Education? Ask to see a current license.

3. Determine whether the agency has an established reputation with reputable retailers, advertising agencies, and other persons and organizations who would be knowledgeable in this area.

4. Is the agency offering to serve as an agent? Real agents make their money on the amount of work they secure for their talent . . . not on the sheer number of models they represent.

5. Will the agent use the photographs from another agency or photographer? Be wary if they will only accept their own photographs or portfolio.

Twenty-Six Dead from Watching "Deer Hunter"; FCC Action Demanded

Twenty-nine Americans have shot themselves after watching **The Deer Hunter**, 28 from viewing the Hollywood film on television, according to the National Coalition on Television Violence (NCTV). Twenty-six of these young men, whose ages ranged from 8 to 31, have died. Police and press investigations have reported that the victims were influenced by the Russian roulette scenes graphically displayed in the movie. The danger of this violence was pointed out as early as 1978 after the first death. CBS and other networks agreed that the Russian roulette scenes were unfit for television. In spite of this, pay-cable and local television stations have been continuing to show the film across the nation.

The epidemic of deaths caused by **The Deer Hunter** was first noted by Linda Talbott of Handgun Control, Inc. NCTV was notified and has since been attempting unsuccessfully to get local broadcasters to delete the Russian roulette scenes in the interest of preserving human life. NCTV is now asking the Federal Communications Commission and the House Communications Subcommittee to require that the Russian roulette scenes be deleted from television and cable presentations of the movie.

Dr. Thomas Radecki, M.D., a psychiatrist with the Southern Illinois University School of Medicine and chairman of NCTV has also asked the FCC not to renew the broadcast license of WFLD-TV in Chicago (Channel 32), the station connected with the most recent deaths. He stated that he had warned WFLD before the broadcast of the serious threat to human life. Dr. Radecki had predicted a 50% chance of death in the Chicago area due to the broadcast. Two young men killed themselves playing Russian roulette on November 21st shortly after viewing the movie.

WFLD has since announced that it will show the film again this May in spite of the deaths. Dr. Radecki stated, "The sole reason that WFLD is showing this film is to maximize advertising profits. In spite of considerable protest in local print and radio media and in spite of the two deaths, WFLD still refuses to take the problem of human death seriously. It is clearly abusing the public airwaves. It should have its license to use the public airwaves revoked."

Dr. Radecki said, "Industrial self-regulation and the Federal Communications Commission have failed in their obligations to protect the public. Only citizen action against the advertisers is left. NCTV will be monitoring the next time if we can, at all, afford it." He stated that the repeated **The Deer Hunter** deaths raise the issue of legal liability where programs have been found to cause repeated deaths and when the station and producer have been forewarned. NCTV is cooperating with two separate law firms preparing to sue stations on behalf of families of two of the deceased young men.

Radecki noted that the natural human learning process is responsible for the numerous real-life replays of **The Deer Hunter** scenes. He said, "For every one to two million viewers, approximately one death is occurring. Other high violence movies are undoubtedly causing frequent deaths but the connections are harder to trace. Russian roulette is such an unusual way to die, and since witnesses are often available, the connection is much easier to trace. **The Deer Hunter** is typical of the distorted violence in Hollywood and TV entertainment. Not a single episode of such Russian roulette torture is reported to have occurred in Vietnam. But now, it has occurred 29 times in America."

Dr. Radecki stated that in no case of **The Deer Hunter** victims was there any report of mental illness or clear depression. However, he voiced considerable concern that America is becoming calloused to human death. "Many callers to NCTV act as if, had the people been depressed, those deaths were not to be taken seriously," he reported. Radecki noted that over 50% of Americans will have suicidal thoughts at some time. He attributed the growing calloused attitude toward death to the massive amounts of entertainment violence being presented in American movie and television programming.

News Release

ROTARY CLUB
P.O. Box 2185
Proud Sponsors of "The Official State Air Fair"

STATE AIR FAIR FACTS

WHAT: The 22nd Annual State Air Fair.

WHEN: This Saturday and Sunday. Gates will open at 9:00 a.m. and
           the show begins at 1:00 p.m., lasting 3–4 hours.

WHO: The U.S. Air Force Thunderbirds—Performing Sunday only,
           the U.S. Air Force's official air demonstration squadron will
           display precision flying maneuvers in their stunning F-16
           Fighting Falcons.

           The Eagles Aerobatic Flight Team—A trio of colorful
           biplanes specializing in loops, rolls and flips; the world's
           foremost civilian flight team.

           Bob Hoover—One of America's most prestigious pilots flying
           his Shrike Commander, sponsored by Evergreen
           International.

           The French Connection—Aerial Ballet Team, performing
           synchronized maneuvers in some of the closest formation
           aerobatics to be seen anywhere.

           Jim Franklin—Performs in his Waco Mystery ship, with
           Johnny Kazian, wingwalker.

           Leo Loudenslager—The seven-time U.S. National Aerobatic
           Champion displays his mastery in his Bud Light 200.

           The Golden Knights—The U.S. Army parachute team will
           plummet from 12,000 feet in the air with a variety of mid-air
           maneuvers.

           Plus—The Navy's F-18 Hornet demonstration team and the
           U.S. Air Force A-10 demonstration team.

WHERE: The Municipal Airport, located 15 minutes west of
           downtown off Hwy. 19.

ALSO: See acres of static displays, including many vintage
           airplanes and a special NASA exhibit. Plenty of food
           concessions, souvenir stands and chair rentals will be
           available. Free parking. Fly-ins are welcome and plane
           parking is available.

TICKETS: Gate prices are $7 for adults, $5 for juniors (ages 12–17)
           Saturday, $9 for adults, $7 for juniors Sunday. Children
           under 12 will be admitted free with an adult both days.

WHY: The State Air Fair is sponsored by the Rotary Club to benefit
           the United Way.

OFFICE OF
SENATOR WILLIAM PROXMIRE

WISCONSIN

Senator William Proxmire (D-Wis.) today awarded his Golden Fleece of the Month Award to the Department of Education for "permitting educational officials in Louisiana to misuse $912,678 earmarked to serve the educational needs of handicapped children."

Senator Proxmire is the ranking Democrat on the Senate Appropriations Subcommittee which approves the budget for the Department of Education. He approves a Fleece monthly to the most wasteful, ridiculous, or ironic use of the taxpayers' money for that period.

"No group deserves a 'fair deal' more than handicapped children. Instead these special needs young people were given the worst type of 'raw deal' by the people assigned to protect their interest. According to the Audit Report prepared by the Inspector General of the Department of Education:

'Our review of 13 projects disclosed that, overall, the handicapped children received little, if any, benefit from the projects, some expenditures were for unallowable activities, and some purchased services were not provided.'

"In spite of the fact federal law requires that the funds under this program be spent exclusively to serve the unique needs of handicapped children, the auditors found that $385,200 was spent on two highly suspicious computer projects for the <u>general</u> student population. After examining the project files, the federal auditors could not find any information to support either the choice of the contractor or his estimated cost. After reviewing the major subcontract the report of the Inspector General stated:

'In our opinion, the amounts paid for two of the major items were unreasonable. The first item was software development for which the subcontractor received $43,715. We requested a copy of the software to determine how it was designed to meet the unique needs of handicapped children. Our request was denied for the stated reason that the software had been marketed for general use in the classroom for some time and was proprietary. If no new software was developed to meet the special needs of handicapped children, the subcontractor should not be paid for research and design. The second item for which the subcontractor was paid $89,700, was consultant services. According to the teachers interviewed, the subcontractor provided only minimal guidance on the basic use of the computers and software. It is the general practice in the computer sales field to provide such services free of charge when a number of computers are purchased. Moreover, costs of $89,700 for such minimal guidance appears to us to be unreasonable.'

"The audit report goes on to describe many other instances of misuse of federal fundings including the hiring of inexperienced and non-certified personnel for unapproved projects and the paying of an individual for nine months when in fact he performed only minimal work for six weeks before falling ill.

"It is my understanding that officials from the Department of Education are now attempting to reach an agreement with Louisiana State education officials on refunding at least a portion of the misspent federal money. However, for permitting a gigantic, three year long, rip-off of funds for the education of handicapped children to take place, the U.S. Department of Education richly deserves to receive this month's Golden Fleece Award."

SENATOR WILLIAM PROXMIRE

Senator William Proxmire (D-Wis.) today in a statement released from his Washington office gave his Golden Fleece of the Month Award to the Federal Aviation Administration (FAA) for "landing a $47 million default on the taxpayer, with another $75 million on final approach, and still another $192 million in a holding pattern. This money is going to pay the debts incurred by bankrupt airlines which used federally-guaranteed loans to buy airplanes and spare parts.

"This sounds like 'plane' nonsense to me. The taxpayers should be making a flap over this loss."

Senator Proxmire is the ranking Democrat on the Banking, Housing, and Urban Affairs Committee and serves on the Appropriations Committee. He awards a Fleece monthly to the most wasteful, ridiculous, or ironic use of the taxpayers' money for that period.

"Congress established this federally-guaranteed loan program nearly 30 years ago, but it was not until the coming of deregulation that it ran into turbulence. Then, market demand instead of bureaucratic decisions, started determining which airlines would prosper. What had been a comfortably settled industry was thrown into turmoil.

"The taxpayers are paying for part of that turmoil. Since 1983, when the FAA stopped making these guaranteed loans, the agency has paid out about $47 million to cover the resulting defaults. This money comes straight from the Treasury and is not paid for by some sort of user fee or tax. Here is the record so far:

Air Carrier	Amount ($000)
Air Florida	$ 907
Altair	24
Cascade	13,436
Continental	11,824
Dorado Wings	11
Excellair	10,287
Golden West	298
Pocono	2,166
Wheeler	107
Subtotal	39,060
Interest paid	8,720
Grand Total	47,780

"The story continues. For this fiscal year, the FAA has set aside $75 million to pay for possible defaults. Which air carriers might need this money? The FAA says 'it would be inappropriate to speculate on the possibility of default for specific carriers in the absence of definitive information on that prospect.' Talk about flying blind. Why should the taxpayers have to take this trip to the wild blue yonder?

"How much could the taxpayers end up shelling out? They are potentially liable for '$267 million in active FAA guaranteed loans' again according to that agency. Tighten your seatbelts, taxpayers, the worst is yet to come.

"These loans have put the government in a 'heads, they win; tails, we lose' situation. Some air carriers are going to make a bundle from deregulation. Their owners will win. What about the losers? Let the taxpayers pick up part of those costs. For rigging this situation, the FAA deserves a 'Fleece.'"

FOR IMMEDIATE RELEASE   1507 Longworth House Office Building
Washington, D.C. 20515
202/225/2176

MARRIAGE FRAUD BILL PASSES THROUGH CONGRESS

The Senate today passed U.S. Rep. Bill McCollum's "Marriage Fraud Act", H.R. 3737, sending it to the President to be signed into law. The House of Representatives passed the bill three weeks ago. McCollum first proposed H.R. 3737 to close the marriage fraud loophole in our immigration laws. Senator Paul Simon introduced companion legislation in the Senate and helped shepherd H.R. 3737 to Senate passage.

McCollum said, "No legislation can completely stop immigration marriage fraud, but this bill will be a big help to law enforcement and slow marriage fraud down tremendously. I am very pleased the Senate has passed my bill without amendment and sent it to the President."

McCollum said, "Marriage has become the single largest qualifying mechanism for immigration because it is the easiest to pursue." By virtue of a simple ceremony taking only a few minutes, aliens can cut through the red tape and years of waiting to enter this country legally. Marriage to a United States citizen currently confers a "most favored alien" status on the beneficiary and in most cases instantly results in immigrant status as no visa number or certification from the Department of Labor is necessary.

McCollum's legislation puts a big dent in the "Buy a bride—get a green card" theory. Upon marriage, the alien spouse would be granted a conditional two year permanent resident alien status which would enable the alien to work and reside in the U.S.

However, 90 days prior to the expiration of the two year date, both spouses are required to file a petition with the Attorney General to remove the conditionality of the permanent resident status by listing all residences and employers of both spouses since the status was granted and stating under penalty of perjury that his/her marriage is still legally intact (except in the case of death) and the marriage was not entered into for purposes of immigration or for a fee. The couple must also appear for a personal interview with the INS to substantiate the petition. The Attorney General then has 90 days to review the matter and either remove the conditions or terminate the permanent resident status if fraud is found.

H.R. 3737 also creates criminal penalties to deter immigrant marriage fraud. An individual who knowingly enters into a marriage contract for the purpose of evading immigration laws could be imprisoned for not more than five years, fined not more than $250,000, or both. Also, no petition shall be approved if the petitioner has previously applied for permanent resident status by reason of marriage and it was determined that the marriage was entered into for the purpose of evading our immigration laws.

Furthermore, no one will be able to get a "K" fiance visa unless the alien and U.S. citizen have actually met in person. The "K" visa allows aliens who are engaged to Americans to enter our country to get married and is often the front line of marriage fraud.

McCollum's bill would effectively put a halt to the two types of marriage fraud flourishing in our country. One in which an alien marries a native US citizen for the purpose of obtaining a green card and immediately disappears, or a US citizen accepts payment for helping an alien obtain permanent residency by marriage.

McCollum said, "Marriage fraud is a thriving cottage industry in the underground economy. United States citizens who marry an alien view it as a great way to earn thousands of dollars quickly, and without penalty. Currently, the alien spouse who is caught could possibly be deported (although few are ever caught); the U.S. citizen spouse and the arranger who brings the two together are rarely penalized."

The increasing abuse of our immigration laws is clearly seen in the statistics: While total immigration to the US dropped 9.6% during the past six years, the percentage of immigrants acquiring status as the spouse of US citizens during that same time period increased 43%. Last year alone, 45% of 11,721 alien fiances have "disappeared" or were unaccounted for.

Sen. Simon said, "These sham marriages victimize our laws, they victimize others who are waiting their turns to come here, and they victimize U.S. citizens who are duped into such marriages. The fraud has to stop and now some of it will."

McCollum and Simon are confident the President will sign the bill into law in the next few weeks.

Facts for Consumers
from the Federal Trade Commission
BUREAU OF CONSUMER PROTECTION • OFFICE OF CONSUMER EDUCATION • WASHINGTON, D.C. 20580

Vacation Certificates

Immediate
Release

"Gift vacation for two. Have an exciting fun-filled holiday. Deluxe room accommodations for two days and three nights." Sometimes it's in Las Vegas. Or Reno. Or Miami. Or it might be in some other vacation spot.

It sounds too good to be true. And it sometimes is. Las Vegas law enforcement officials are warning consumers about vacation certificate promoters who make these claims.

Phone and
Mail Sales

According to these officials, about 100 firms make these offers either directly to consumers—through telephone or mail solicitations—or to businesses who use these vacation certificates as part of their own sales promotions. Consumers don't always get what they expected.

However, the files of Nevada Consumer Affairs Commissioner David Cook are filled with complaints from unhappy people who took the certificate promoter up on the "free vacation" offer. Cook tells of people who traveled to Las Vegas only to find out that—even though they had "confirmed" reservations—the hotel staff had never heard of them.

Deposits
Made in
Advance

Vacation certificates usually cost from $15 to $25. If you buy one—or a local merchant gives you one it bought— you would typically be entitled to a three-day, two-night vacation to Las Vegas or Reno or Miami. According to the conditions on the certificate, you would have to contact the promoter—not the hotel—to make your reservation and would probably have to make a deposit to "hold" it. You might even have to make another deposit when you confirm the reservation.

In some cases, the promoter has a good relationship with the hotel, and the hotel agrees to set aside a block of rooms so the certificates can be redeemed.

However, in some cases vacation certificate promoters get rooms from the hotel **only if the hotel is not already booked up**. If it is already booked up, consumers who want to redeem their certificates may not get their first choice of hotel. They may find promised "first class accommodations" aren't all that classy or that their "vacation site" may be some distance from the main attractions of the resort community.

In fact, as Commissioner Cook indicates, some promoters sell vacation certificates without reserving **any** rooms. They issue counterfeit certificates that are not honored by the hotel, restaurant, or casino indicated. These promoters rake in the money, go out of business overnight, and leave you holding the casino chips.

Some companies, more sophisticated in their sales techniques, simply make it virtually impossible for you to **use** your certificates. They do this by repeatedly refusing your requests for a specific vacation date. You may never get a confirmed reservation. They figure that after a while you'll just give up.

If you do get a date and take the vacation (one promoter said they figure fewer than 2% of the recipients actually do), you might have some unpleasant surprises. You will usually have to pay travel costs and the cost of your meals. Also, your "bonus coupons" for free meals, drinks, discount gambling, show tickets, or golf may not be a bargain at all. For example, an offer of free meals may be limited to the hours of 2 a.m.-5 a.m., and the free tickets for gambling might be available only from certain casinos at odd hours. Very often you'll have to spend your own money first; then the promoter will match it with an equal sum.

The Better Business Bureau of Southern Nevada released a typical standard vacation certificate coupon package showing that you would have to spend as much as $50 of your own money to get a $13.50 value in coupons.

Some vacation certificate offers are completely above board and plainly disclose any limitations they may have. But before you fly off to your free vacation, invest some time checking the reputation of the company. If you can't get straight answers to the questions you ask, don't go.

16 Speeches and Meetings

Many of the stories published by newspapers summarize the content of speeches and the actions taken at meetings. Even in small towns there are dozens of speeches and meetings every week; in large cities, there may be thousands. Some of these speeches and meetings involve government agencies; others are sponsored by clubs, schools, unions, churches, and business and professional organizations. Journalists attend only the most important—the speeches and meetings that affect or involve large numbers of people and that are therefore most likely to interest the public.

Newspapers normally publish at least two stories about each of the major speeches and meetings in their communities: an "advance" story before the speeches and meetings take place and a "follow" story afterward. The advance stories notify readers about future events, often helping them to prepare for events that they may want to attend, support or oppose. Most advance stories are published on the day speeches and meetings are announced, but (as a reminder to their readers) newspapers may publish a second advance story a day or two before the speeches and meetings are scheduled to take place.

Newspapers may publish a dozen or more advance stories about events of unusual importance. For example: if the president announced plans to campaign in your community, local newspapers would immediately report those plans and, as more information became available, the newspapers would publish additional advance stories about the president's itinerary, goals, security measures and companions.

Most advance stories emphasize the same basic facts: the stories tell readers what will happen, when and where it will happen, and who will be involved. Typically, advance stories for speeches identify the speakers, report the times and places they will appear, and describe their topics. Similarly, advance stories for meetings identify the groups scheduled to meet, report the times and places of their meetings, and describe the topics on their agendas. In addition, advance stories may explain why the speeches and meetings are important and may comment about their purposes or sponsors. Advance stories may also tell readers whether the public is invited, whether those who attend will be given an opportunity to participate and whether there will be a charge for admission.

The leads in advance stories should be interesting and as specific as possible. The leads emphasize the important and the unusual, not just the fact that someone has scheduled a speech or meeting. Often, they mention celebrities who will be involved in the events or the topics that will be discussed. For example:

> Singer and actress Barbra Streisand has agreed to perform in Washington, D.C. at a dinner expected to raise more than $5 million for the Cancer Society.

> Members of the American Civil Liberties Union will meet at 8 p.m. Friday in the YWCA to discuss charges that the Police Department has refused to promote a patrolman because he is a homosexual.

Advance stories are generally short; many contain no more than two or three paragraphs. Typically, a complete advance story might report that:

> Sen. Charles Kulifay, who has introduced a constitutional amendment that would force the federal government to balance its budget and repay the national debt, will discuss the amendment during a speech at 8 p.m. Sunday in the Municipal Auditorium.
> His appearance is being sponsored by the Republican Council of 1,000. The public is invited, and there will be no admission charge.
> Kulifay, a Texan elected to the Senate four years ago, introduced the amendment earlier this month and has said that it will curb wasteful federal spending and solve the problem of inflation.

To save space, some editors summarize advance stories in a single paragraph and place them in roundups or digests (often called "Community Calendars") that list all the newsworthy events scheduled during a forthcoming week.

Because each follow story may involve many participants or issues, the follow stories are generally longer than the advance stories and more difficult to write. For example: 14 council members may attend a council meeting, hear a dozen witnesses and then vote on several issues. Although many of those issues may be complex, reporters are expected to summarize all of them in a single story.

Reporters assigned to cover a speech or meeting usually try beforehand to learn as much as possible about its participants and issues. As a first step, the reporters may go to their newspaper's library and read previous stories written about the topic. Reporters can obtain agendas prior to most meetings and—if they are lucky—may obtain advance copies of some speeches. Then, instead of having to take notes, they can follow the printed texts, simply checking to be certain that the speakers are not departing from their prepared remarks.

To attract more publicity, groups often schedule press conferences immediately before or after speeches they are sponsoring so that reporters will have an opportunity to obtain additional information. If that is not done, reporters may arrange to see speakers for a few minutes immediately after their appearances. Similarly, reporters who cover a meeting should learn all the participants' names beforehand so that they will always know who is speaking and—so that they understand the issues being discussed—should also learn as much as possible about them. In case any unexpected or confusing issues arise during a meeting, reporters may arrange to see the leading participants after the meeting adjourns.

Follow story leads should summarize the latest developments—the speaker's comments about a topic or the action taken at a meeting. The leads must do more than report

After becoming president, Harry Truman held his first press conference on April 17, 1945. The reporters simply gathered around Truman's desk. Since then, press conferences have become much larger and more formal. They also attract more women—and seem to be dominated by television.

that a topic was "discussed" or "considered," since the topic may have been announced weeks earlier and reported in several advance stories. For example:

ADVANCE STORY LEAD: The Student Senate will meet at 4 p.m. Thursday and is expected to consider the University's decision to dismiss history professor Albert Calley.

FOLLOW STORY LEAD: After learning the reasons for his dismissal, the Student Senate voted 27 to 1 Thursday not to support Albert Calley, a history professor whose contract for next year has not been renewed by the University.

Reporters use the inverted pyramid style to write most follow stories. Consequently, the stories present information in the order of its importance, not the order in which it arises during a speech or meeting. Reporters can move statements around and may begin their stories with a statement made at the end of a two-hour speech, then shift to a topic discussed midway through the speech. If the topics mentioned during the first hour of a speech are unimportant, reporters may never mention them.

Particularly when writing about speeches, reporters should use some direct quotations for emphasis and a change of pace, and to help reveal more about the source's personality and manner of speaking.

Follow stories will inevitably repeat some of the facts reported in advance stories because some basic facts, such as the identity of a speaker, must be reported in follow as well as advance stories.

EXERCISE 1
Speeches and Meetings

SPEECHES

INSTRUCTIONS: Write separate advance and follow stories about each of the following speeches. Because these are verbatim accounts, you can use direct quotations.

1. FIREFIGHTER CONCERNS

Information for Advance Story

Reynold Hunt is scheduled to speak to the Downtown Rotary Club Monday of next week. The club meets every Monday noon at the Blackhawk Hotel. Lunch is served and costs $6.50 per person. The public is invited to the lunch, which begins promptly at noon, or the public may come for just the speech, which will begin promptly at 1 p.m. Reynold Hunt is your city's fire chief, and he will speak to the club members about the major concerns of today's firefighters.

Speech for Follow Story

Some of you don't know me. My name is Reynold Hunt. When I was 22 years old and had just been discharged from the Army, I didn't know what I wanted to do with the rest of my life. Two of my best friends wanted to join the Fire Department, and they talked me into taking all the physical and written tests along with them. I passed, but they didn't, and I've been associated with the Fire Department for the past 28 years. For the past 6 years, I've been chief.

The Fire Department is much different today than it was when I joined 28 years ago, and we've got much different problems today. I've been asked to talk to you about those problems. Our biggest problems, as you might expect, are low pay and long hours. But we're also concerned about the problems of arson and outdated gear. Now I'd like to talk to you about each of those problems, and in much more detail. As local business people, all of you are affected by the problems, and I hope that you'll be able to help us solve them.

First, the problem of arson. It's gotten completely out of hand. Property owners in this state alone lost at least $500 million in damaged and destroyed property due to arson last year. We'd estimate, conservatively, that right here in this city 10 to 20 percent of our fires are arson. It's hard to control because the conviction rate for arson is low. And that's because fires oftentimes destroy the evidence. You, as business people, lose money because arson causes higher insurance premiums for everyone. It also causes lower profits, lost wages to workers and lost tax revenue to the city.

Another big problem we face involves the gear we use in fighting fires. A good truck these days costs $100,000. If we want a good ladder truck, one that can reach some of the taller downtown buildings, it may cost twice that much. The city can't afford many, but if we don't have the trucks, then we can't rescue people trapped on the upper floors of those buildings.

Even the protective gear worn by our firefighters is getting terribly expensive. Until recently, all our protective clothing has been made of a highly flammable cotton coated with neoprene, usually black. Black is bad because it absorbs heat and because firefighters can't be seen if they fall and get into trouble inside a dark building or a building filled with smoke. Then take a look at our helmets; they're far from being the state of the art. They melt in temperatures above 700. In your average fire, the floor temperature is 200 and the ceiling is 1,800. The state-of-the-art helmets can resist heat up to 2,000 degrees, but they cost three times what we're paying now.

One reason why the injury and death rate among firefighters is so high—more firefighters die annually than police—is because our gear is so expensive, and cities won't buy it. They seem to think it's easier to replace firefighters than to outlay the money for better gear.

The heavy physical labor and working conditions also contribute to the high injury rate. When you send people into a fire, and you've got intense heat, broken glass, the danger of whole walls and floors collapsing, and the danger of explosions from unknown chemicals stored in these buildings, it's almost inevitable that you're going to have some injuries and possibly even some deaths. With the proper equipment, we could reduce the number and severity of injuries, but there's no way to completely eliminate them. Danger's a part of our job. We accept that.

Despite the fact we have a higher death rate than the police, firefighters start out earning $1,000 to $2,000 a year less than they do, and we object to that. It's not fair. When we ask the City Council why, they say because it's always been that way and it would cost too much to pay firefighters as much as the police. We don't think that's right, especially when you consider that the police work only 40 hours a week. Firefighters work 24-hour shifts and an average of 56 hours a week. So they work longer hours for less money.

The next time you hear anyone talking about these problems, and the next time you see us going to the City Council, requesting a larger budget, we'd appreciate your support. With your support, we'll be able to offer you, and everyone else in the city, better fire protection. It's already good, but with your help we can make it even better, and that benefits everyone.

2. ABORTION CRITIC

Information for Advance Story

John F. Palladino is an outspoken critic of abortion. He is scheduled to speak at a prayer breakfast next Sunday at the First Baptist Church, 412 North Eastland Ave. in your city. His topic will be, "Abortion: Our Greatest Sin." The public is invited free of charge for both the breakfast and speech. The prayer breakfast will be held in the church's social hall, starting at 7:30 a.m. Palladino is a Republican and unsuccessful candidate for governor in the last election in your state. He was defeated in the Republican primary. Previously, he served three terms in your State Senate. Currently, he lives in the state capital and operates his own real estate firm there. He is chairman of your state's Right to Life Committee, which opposes abortion.

Speech for Follow Story

I appreciate your invitation to speak to you today. I also appreciate the help that many of you have given our Right to Life Committee. I recognize that some of you have given us very generous financial donations, and that others of you have helped man our telephone lines and distribute our literature.

I'd like to begin this morning by telling you something of my personal views. Personally, I cannot understand how a woman can achieve sexual liberation by taking the life of her unborn child. I believe that abortion basically is a very selfish, self-centered remedy to those that think the birth of a child is an inconvenience. I think it is an inconvenience for only nine months. After that, there are 3- or 4-year waits to adopt children. I know of many families who go down to El Salvador to adopt children. I have other friends who adopted little babies from Korea and from many other countries of the world. So no child is unwanted; there's a loving home in this country for every child.

Now some people ask, "What about cases where the mother's life is threatened, or where the mother is impregnated through rape or incest?" My main concern is with the 99 percent of the abortions that do not deal with that, but merely with inconvenience.

When the mother's life is in question, and it's a true case of the life of a mother vs. the life of an unborn child, certainly the life of the mother should take precedence—the reason being that there is a good possibility that the mother is already a mother of other children. To say that we're going to deprive these already-born children of their mother to protect the life of an unborn child is improper.

But I find it difficult from a personal standpoint to say that I would agree to abortion in the case of rape or incest because, again, it's an innocent child no matter whether it's the product of a legitimate or illegitimate sexual union. So if I had the authority to stop all abortions, except those that involve the endangerment of the mother's life, then certainly I would agree to that.

Now, in talking about this issue, you have to remember one critical point. Life begins upon fertilization of the egg. If you don't agree with that, certainly at least you have the potential for life at that point, and therefore it should be jealously guarded as life itself.

The federal and state laws that permit abortion are wrong, absolutely and totally wrong. Abortions are a crime and a sin. When governments adopt these laws, they're saying that life doesn't exist, or that some forms of life aren't as important as others and don't deserve the same protection as others. So even from a political view, abortion is wrong because it allows governments to judge the value of life—to say that there's a point or condition under which some lives can be ended. I think that's a very dangerous position for government to be in. And you have to ask where it'll stop. What other lives will governments decide we can end? Next it could be the sick, the elderly, the insane, or the criminals from all our jails. That's not the kind of decision governments should be making. All life is precious. All life should be protected by the government—and by us, as individuals.

Thank you.

3. CITY PARKS

Information for Advance Story

The city's University Club meets at 8 p.m. every Monday night at its own building located at 428 Michigan Ave. During its regular meeting next Monday, the guest speaker will be Emil Plambeck. Plambeck is superintendent of the City Parks Commission. He has said that he will talk about the city's park system. All members of the club are urged to attend the meeting, which is sure to be interesting and informative. The public is also welcome. Admission is free to all club members and their families and is $1 for all other people.

Speech for Follow Story

I'm pleased to be here this evening and intend to discuss a topic of concern to all of us—the city's park system. All of you, as business people, know the value of an attractive community. It promotes growth and helps attract both new residents and new industry. An attractive community with a good park system also improves the quality of life for those of us already living here.

Members of this community long have boasted of one of the finest park systems in the United States. But now, because of financial problems, we are beginning to fall behind. We simply are not getting enough money to expand our park system to meet the needs of a growing community or even enough money to maintain our old system properly. As a result, the parks are becoming overcrowded and all the people utilizing them every weekend are endangering the vegetation and wildlife we've worked so hard to preserve.

We used to feel that we were among the top-ranking communities in the United States, but now there definitely are several other cities that have gone ahead of us, even within this very state. We still look pretty good on paper, but some of the statistics are misleading. Neighborhood parks in the new suburbs are lagging badly behind our needs. We do have several excellent parks, with a lot of acreage, but they're concentrated in the older sections of the city.

City planners recommend that we provide one acre of playground for each 100 people living in the city. We now have 1.3 acres—30 percent more than the minimum requirement. But that lead is slipping. Just five years ago we had 1.45 acres per 100 residents. And you have to keep in mind the fact that 1 acre for every 100 people is a minimum—not an ideal. An ideal ratio would be 1.5 acres for every 100 people, and we're falling farther and farther away from that goal.

We need some laws to force developers to provide property in new subdivisions for schools and playgrounds. My office is working on a new code to help the city obtain land for parks in each new suburb constructed around the city. I haven't revealed that fact before, but we expect to submit the proposal to the City Council within a few days. If the council accepts it, the developers will be required to set aside 3.5 percent of their land for miniparks. That way we'll be able to have wooded areas in every neighborhood, maybe with baseball diamonds or a few tennis courts.

The city hasn't been totally inactive in this area since I took office five years ago. We have acquired three parks. One of them—near Ridgeview School—has two ball fields and a large picnic area. The other new areas include Petersen Park, on West Dover Court and Hillandale Road, and Riverview Park. In the case of the Ridgeview and Petersen Parks, the land was purchased by the park board with funds provided by the City Council. The city inherited the land for Riverview Park. Altogether, the city now has 27 parks and playgrounds, which include 1,168 acres valued at more than $25 million. But I'd like to see the city develop at least a half-dozen more parks, all in the newer subdivisions.

EXERCISE 2
Speeches and Meetings

FIRE MARSHAL'S SPEECH: CPR

INSTRUCTIONS: Assume that Steven Chen, the training officer for your city's fire department, gave this speech to the Rotary Club at a breakfast meeting in your city today. Write a story that summarizes his comments. Because this is a verbatim copy of his comments, you can use direct quotes.

I've been asked to talk to you this morning about CPR: cardiopulmonary resuscitation. What we'd like to happen is for everyone to learn CPR themselves instead of counting on paramedics to revive someone in an emergency. A few weeks ago, we had a man drown in a hotel pool just a few blocks from here. He was pulled from the water by a woman sitting by the pool, but he died because no one knew CPR. When paramedics arrived, it was too late. The situation is a typical one, repeated somewhere almost every day. You can't fault the paramedics. They respond as quickly as possible.

Rarely can we save a victim that has not had CPR done to them before we arrive. Depending on the location, it takes our rescue squad from 1 to 10 minutes to respond to a call. The American Heart Association recommends that CPR be done in no more than 4 to 6 minutes to keep the person alive. After 10 minutes, we don't even try to start CPR. After 10 minutes, the brain damage is too severe for the person to lead a normal life if he were resuscitated.

There are exceptions to the 10-minute rule. Last winter, you may have read, a small boy was successfully resuscitated after 45 minutes. But he had been submerged in icy water. That rescue was possible because the cold temperature slowed down the boy's body responses enough so that no brain damage was done. If it's summer and hot and humid, the heat and humidity quicken the body's responses and make it impossible to survive without brain damage.

Most of our calls where we have to use CPR are near drownings. The more swimming pools people build in their backyards, the more calls we get. Statistics show that people have a better chance of drowning in their own backyard pool than in public swimming areas. The statistics show the safest place to swim is a patrolled beach, since all the lifeguards there are required to know CPR. Also, help gets to them quicker, and the lifeguards prevent trouble—horseplay and roughhousing—that could lead to serious accidents.

I would like to see us follow the footsteps of Seattle, where 1 out of every 3 people knows CPR, the highest rate in the country. Here, classes are offered by various schools and medical organizations, and at least once a year at each of the city's fire stations. Classes usually take about 8 hours to complete.

That's all I have to say, but I'll be happy to answer your questions.

Q: Do the classes cost anything?
A: No, just $4.99 for a workbook.

Q: What can you do to help if you don't know CPR?
A: The most important thing is to call for help and then to stay calm until help arrives.

Q: If you use CPR and there's a problem, if something goes wrong, can you be sued?
A: The state has a Good Samaritan law, and it covers possible lawsuits for injuring someone while trying to revive them. So if you've had the proper training and try it, you're fully protected. It's nothing to worry about.

EXERCISE 3
Speeches and Meetings

SPEECH TO SPJ, SDX

INTRODUCTION: Following a dispute between your city's reporters and police department, Police Chief Martin Guidema agreed to speak at 7:30 last night at a meeting of your local chapter of the Society of Professional Journalists, Sigma Delta Chi. This is a verbatim transcript of his comments and can be quoted directly.

You all know who I am and why I'm here. We've had a problem, and I'm trying to handle it as best I can. I have a responsibility to the residents of this city to maintain law and order. I've also got to run my department as efficiently as possible.

Some unfortunate things have happened during the last year, and they caused us to take a good look at the information we make available to the public. On the 1st of this month we instituted a new policy. Before then, we let any member of the public look at our daily events list: the blotter. It not only listed the events—the names and addresses of where they took place—but also included the officers' narrative. Since the 1st, people can still look at it, but the blotter now lists only the time, case number, patrol car number, event and a code for the disposition of the case. Narratives describing what happened are available to legitimate news people, but a clerk has to get them from the files for you. We don't want other people abusing them. That's the problem.

About a year ago, we started getting complaints from burglary victims. Private security agencies were checking our blotter every day to determine which homes were burglarized and picking up the victims' phone numbers—in some cases, unlisted numbers. Then they would call and try to sell burglar alarms to the victims. Other law enforcement agencies in the state report the same thing happening there.

That's not all of it. Insurance people were using our blotters for all sorts of things, and other people too. A few months ago, we had two burglars who confessed to a whole string of crimes. They told us they felt safe because one of their friends had come in and looked at a burglary report for them and learned we hadn't gotten their description. We also suspect that we had some ambulance chasers—lawyers looking for clients. So now we limit the blotter to the information required by state law. I've tried to explain that to our regular police reporters, but we're getting all sorts of complaints, and one editor called and threatened a lawsuit.

I've always thought I had a friendly relationship with reporters. It's been my philosophy that reporters have, as their primary vocation, to write a story. It's been my policy to do everything I can to help you. That hasn't changed. This was something we had to do.

Now, let me answer your questions.

Q: A lot of us didn't know what was happening. Why didn't you tell everyone before you started?
A: I thought if I told the regulars, they'd tell their editors and the others. I admit, if I had it to do over again, I'd do it different.

Q: If your clerk doesn't know us, what sort of identification will she want?
A: A press card or anything showing that you work for the media.

Q: How will you decide who's a legitimate reporter? What if someone comes in from a high-school paper, or says he's a freelance writer?
A: That hasn't happened yet. If there's a problem, the clerk is supposed to refer it to me. We may have to think more about that.

Q: Last week some of us had to wait 10 minutes until a clerk was there to help us.

A: That shouldn't happen, and I'll see that it's corrected. Thank you for listening to me. My department is anxious to work this out with you. There's nothing to get upset about.

EXERCISE 4
Speeches and Meetings

SPEECH: CAPITAL PUNISHMENT

INSTRUCTIONS: Write a news story about the following speech, which Russell Troutman gave last night to the Kiwanis Club in your city. Troutman is an attorney, former president of the Orange County Bar Association and former president of the Florida Bar. The following statements are his exact words and may be quoted directly.

I feel about capital punishment like I do about World War II. I oppose war and its needless slaughter of useful lives. But when Japan bombs Pearl Harbor, what is the state to do? At what point is reverence for life pre-empted by the necessity for retaliation? Pearl Harbor convinced us that killing the innocent as well as the guilty was necessary homicide. Murder is premeditated killing, and the massive bombings that followed were acts clearly within that definition. Yet, no one was conscious-smitten by annihilation at our hands; everyone accepted its necessity. Personally, I would save capital punishment for the lowest form of depraved killings similar to those committed by Manson, who mesmerized a cult into slicing and stabbing away at Sharon Tate and her friends, leaving bloody epitaphs on the mirrors and walls.

World War II and capital punishment have a common denominator: self defense. Self defense allows one to inflict death to repel serious bodily harm. No one advocates a change in that principle. The same principle is why the state carried out multiple executions, or capital punishment, if you will, during World War II. Self defense is based not only on the right of survival, but a sense of fair play. Justice means doing what is fair. It is not fair to permit a nation to drop bombs on innocent people and prohibit a similar response. It is not fair to allow sadists to rape and stab, and prohibit the victim from lethal retaliation.

There were no righteous outbursts imploring the state not to kill the invaders in World War II. Yet, the Pearl Harbor dead could not be restored by killing others. A lethal response was analogous to capital punishment. We wanted to prevent recidivism by the perpetrators, restore peace, and deter others from similar conduct. It is absurd to hold that when multiple murderers combine to kill multiple victims, the state can retaliate with deadly force, even if retaliation kills innocent victims, but should not do it when one murderer is involved, even though the retaliation is directed to the guilty party only.

In exercising the right to self defense, it is almost always a question of debatable fact as to when one is placed under threat of bodily harm. In my judgment, once an individual has cruelly and needlessly killed someone, the state, like it did in World War II, may take the life of that killer. The proven capability of a person to butcher lives is enough to place the state in fear it will happen again, so that self defense is justified. The state need not wait until a knife is thrust into the breast of another victim to defend itself any more than the state should have waited for another Pearl Harbor to defend itself.

When Hitler wrote "Mein Kampf," he told the world he intended to subjugate it. His book was comparable to a killer writing a note to his victim that eventually the killer would murder him. The book, coupled with the act of arming, impelled the world to do the same. However, the world waited and postponed self defense until the dagger was closer to the heart. Hitler began taking countries. Certainly by then, self defense was impelled but the world watched and waited. It was not until many murders by this Manson on the world stage that the rest of us responded with force consonant with the occasion. We were like the anguished crowds before an execution outside the prison walls wishing the world was not violent and killers could be appeased. Sadly, it was not true with Hitler, and it is not true with the maniac killers today. The sensible retort is to remove them from our midst, not for malice or for revenge, or for that matter, not just to deter or punish, but to assure society it won't happen again.

However, there is another reason to support capital punishment. The depraved act of chopping people to pieces or raping them first, and then dismembering them, calls for more than putting them in prison for life without hope of parole. To meet the infamy of perverted murder by relegating the sadists to a community of other lawbreakers is offensive to natural law. Besides, others in prison, including guards, are exposed to the murderers' killing disposition for a lifetime. A life sentence simply denies the brand of justice the offense compels, just as sentencing a bank robber to thirty days in a county jail. Revenge is not the goal here, but rather an appropriate remedy for the wrong.

It has been my experience that capital punishment deters brutal murders. There are statistics on both sides of this issue, and it has been said that based on statistics, the economy of this country can be equated to production of wheat in China. An argument can be made that imprisonment should be eliminated altogether since in those states that still imprison criminals, crime continues to rage with increased regularity.

Once I represented two tough guys charged with robbing a store. An accomplice turned state's evidence and testified against them. My two clients convinced me that only the death penalty prevented them from killing their friend. The deeply rooted instinct of survival makes the prospect of losing one's life a deterrent to crime.

EXERCISE 5
Speeches and Meetings

SPEECH: RAPE

INSTRUCTIONS: Write separate advance and follow stories about the following speech.

Information for Advance Story

Albert Innis is a lieutenant in the Detective Bureau of the city's police department. He will speak at the YWCA Friday about the topic of rape. The speech will be open to the public free of charge. Women, particularly, are urged to attend the meeting by the sponsor, the YWCA Young Adults Section. The speech will begin at 8 p.m. in Room 12. Innis has agreed to answer questions from the audience at the conclusion of his speech. Members of the Young Adults Section will hold their monthly business meeting after the conclusion of the speech, and the public is also welcome to attend the meeting. To be eligible for membership in the section, women must be between the ages of 18 and 35. The Young Adults Section is sponsoring the presentation because of public interest in the topic of rape and its importance to women, a club representative said. According to some estimates, there are 10 rapes for every one reported to the police.

Speech for Follow Story

I've been asked to come here tonight to talk to you about rape. I'd like to begin by discussing three myths about rape. Two concern the victim, another the rapist. According to one myth, the victim is always young and attractive; movies and television programs perpetuate this myth. The truth is that every woman is a potential victim. Last year, the victims in this city ranged in age from 2 to 91 years. A second myth is that the woman provokes the attack. But sexual assault isn't provoked by a woman's behavior or by the way she dresses. The truth is that the rapist selects his victim on the basis of opportunity. Most rapists select as their victims women who appear vulnerable and alone. Third, it's also a myth to think that rape is committed for sexual gratification. Sex is not the motivating factor. Rapists have feelings of hostility, aggression and inferiority, and they enjoy overpowering and degrading their victims; it raises their self-esteem.

Rape can occur virtually anywhere, but it is most likely to occur in the victim's home or in the home of the assailant. Often, the assailant is someone the victim knows either closely or by sight.

Most rapists are emotionally unstable, and all rapists have the potential to be violent. Outwardly, they appear to be normal, but most have difficulty relating to other people and establishing lasting relationships.

No one can predict how a woman will react when actually confronted with the threat of sexual assault. Panic and fear are perfectly normal responses. The first few moments you may be too terrified to utter a sound. That's perfectly normal. But if you have thought in advance about the possibility of sexual assault, the shock won't be as great. And if you mentally prepare yourself in advance and think about what you might do, you may be able to react more quickly and effectively.

One tactic available to women is making noise. Sometimes screaming "Fire!" or "Call the police!" or blowing a whistle if you have one with you may frighten away your assailant or bring help. But it may antagonize him. All the alternatives involve some dangers, and screaming can make an assailant angrier, and he may beat you or try to strangle you to keep you quiet. You have to weigh the odds, depending on the situation, of this tactic being successful.

A second tactic is trying to run to safety. But unless you are reasonably certain you can get a good lead and reach safety before he overtakes you, this may be too risky. Make sure you have a place to run where someone will help. If you try running away and your assailant overtakes you, it may make him even more violent.

A third tactic is trying to gain a psychological advantage. Try to defuse your assailant's anger and give yourself time to think. If you do something the rapist doesn't expect, it may stop or delay him because rapists want to be in control, and many can't cope with actions they don't expect. This tactic can take many forms—going limp, sinking to the ground and eating grass, hiding your face to stick your fingers down your throat and cause yourself to vomit, making yourself belch, even urinating on your attacker. Crying might be effective in some instances.

You should understand that rapists don't understand or recognize the rights of women as individuals. So it's important to teach them in a way that breaks their fantasies and allows them to see you as an individual with honest feelings and concerns—not as an object. Many of these men put women on a pedestal and, through sexual assault, feel they're cutting women down to size.

You might try to speak calmly and sincerely as one human being trying to reach out to another. Don't beg, plead, cower or make small talk. That's what these assailants expect to hear, and it may antagonize them even more. Talk about something that interests you—anything you can talk about comfortably—a pet, a recent movie you've seen, a book you're reading, a recent death in the family. The important thing is to convince your assailant you're concerned about him as a person.

The last tactic available to you is fighting, but you should keep in mind the fact that all rapists have the potential for inflicting serious harm; they are all potentially violent, so fighting is the last tactic to try if all the others have failed. And if you use this tactic, you have to be willing and able to inflict serious injury. If you try fighting and fail to completely incapacitate your assailant, your risk of receiving serious injury is greatly increased. Most studies show that about half of all rapists carry some weapon, and you have to always assume they're willing to use the weapons. If you are going to fight, use surprise and speed to your advantage. For instance, gently put your hands on the assailant's face and get your thumbs near his eyes, then press his eyeballs suddenly with your thumbs as hard as you can. This will put the assailant into shock and could blind him. Or grab his testicles, squeeze as hard as you can and jerk or pull to inflict immobilizing pain.

There is no universal prescription for foiling sexual assaults. No one can tell you what specific tactics to use. What worked for one woman may not work for you. It all depends upon the circumstances, your basic personality and your perceptions of the rapist. The way you react may depend upon your physical condition. The very thought of sexual assault makes some women so angry that they would rather face the risk of serious injury. Other women may want to escape with the least possible injury or may be more concerned about the safety of other members of their families than with rape or other injury to themselves.

Thank you.

EXERCISE 6
Speeches and Meetings

SPEECH: SHOPLIFTING

INSTRUCTIONS: Write separate advance and follow stories about the following speech.

Information for Advance Story

There will be a breakfast meeting of the Chamber of Commerce at 7 a.m. next Monday. The speaker will be Loretta Hemphill, director of security for the State Alliance of Businesspeople. Anyone is welcome to attend. Cost of the breakfast will be $3.50. However, persons who come only for the speech, which will begin at approximately 8:15, will be admitted free of charge. The affair is being held at the Downtowner Motel. Ms. Hemphill has been asked to talk about shoplifting, a continuing problem for merchants in the city and especially appropriate for this meeting, since most members of the Chamber of Commerce are merchants in the city.

Speech for Follow Story

U.S. retailers lose nearly $5 billion a year to thieves, and the losses at some stores now exceed their net profits. The problem is growing worse, and arrests of shoplifters in the state are rising an average of 15 percent a year. There are no easy solutions. The only sure way to eliminate shoplifting is to lock your stores and to fire all your employees.

The worst shoplifters are white, middle-class suburban girls. Housewives are next most likely to be shoplifters. We've found that a lot of the younger people, people under 18, are shoplifting because of peer pressure or are attempting to buy friendships by stealing gifts for their friends. Teenage girls often steal in groups, sometimes just for the thrill of it, and they usually take merchandise they can use: records, clothing, cosmetics, recreational items and furnishings for their rooms. Many of these young people consider shoplifting a minor thing that doesn't hurt anyone. Most are under the impression that, if they're caught, they'll be lectured and released.

Professionals take smaller, more expensive items they can quickly resell. True kleptomaniacs—people who steal because of psychological disorders—are rare.

Few people shoplift because they are poor. We've found that 95 percent of the persons arrested for shoplifting in the state either have the money or the means, such as a credit card, to pay for the things they've stolen.

As merchants, there are a number of things you can do to cut down on the problem. We think the best answer is to prosecute more offenders—and to let your customers and employees know about it. Shoplifters avoid stores with a reputation for tough prosecution and good security.

Another important step is to pay attention to your customers; never turn your backs on them. True customers will be flattered by the attention, and shoplifters will leave if they know they're being watched and never come back. Train your sales staffs to look for people with unusual clothing—people who wear baggy clothes, long dresses, heavy outer garments out of season, and raincoats when the sun's been out all day. Some thieves wear special hooks or straps to conceal merchandise. Others wear a dummy cast or sling. Also watch for shoppers carrying bags, boxes, briefcases, topcoats, umbrellas, oversized purses, and other possible hiding places for stolen items.

Some mothers hide things in their children's clothing, and other thieves work in pairs—they move merchandise to other areas so their accomplices can pick it up later without suspicion. Items such as jewelry are often stashed in dressing rooms. So keep your dressing rooms free of merchandise, and watch for people who frequent the dressing rooms and your stores' restrooms. Also watch for people who continually refuse service and seem on the alert or defensive.

It's a good policy to have shoppers check all their packages when they enter your stores, or at least to seal their packages. If they buy something in your stores, seal the packages you sell them so they can't put anything else in them.

There are lots of other safeguards, some more expensive than others. It's a good idea to buy price tags that can't be switched, even though they're somewhat more expensive. Magnetized or electronically sensitive tags that can be attached to merchandise are especially effective. Clerks can remove the tags when the merchandise is sold. If someone tries to carry an article out of your store with the tag still on, it'll sound an alarm. Of course, your clerks have to be conscientious about it; if they forget to clip off a tag or to demagnetize an item, one lawsuit for false arrest will wipe out all your profits.

You can also hire more security people, install two-way mirrors and try closed-circuit TV systems. Tie down display items and eliminate narrow, cluttered aisles where it's hard to observe customers. Keep everything as open and neat as possible, and set up cash registers so your clerks can see your display areas. If the merchandise you're selling comes in pairs, only show one of a pair. Keep valuable merchandise away from doors, and limit the number of entrances and exits to your store. Where possible, use separate doors for entering and exiting.

Another problem is proving that the shoplifters you've caught intended to steal the items found in their possession. When they appear in court, defendants often say they forgot to pay for the items. There's an average wait of two months between an arrest and a trial, so you should write or dictate as much as you remember about shoplifting incidents immediately after they occur. A lot will happen between the time of the incident and the trial, and you need to remember all the details.

But not all the thefts in your stores are caused by shoplifters. It's estimated that 75 percent of all the losses in some industries, especially restaurants and hotels, are due to stealing by employees, and many companies are resorting to lie detector tests. Most companies give the tests to new job applicants, but some companies require all their employees to take a test once a year.

EXERCISE 7
Speeches and Meetings

SURGEON GENERAL'S SPEECH: SMOKING

INSTRUCTIONS: Write a news story about the following speech given by the U.S. surgeon general. Assume that the surgeon general spoke last night to a convention of health experts in your city. Because this is a verbatim transcript of his comments, you can use direct quotations.

I'm here tonight to talk to you about our country's number one health problem. Every year, more than 340,000 Americans die from diseases related to cigarette smoking. Five thousand of these people are non-smokers.

We feel that we've succeeded in educating the smoker. He listens to us, but he doesn't do much about it. Why doesn't he? Because he's addicted to the most addictive drug in our society: nicotine. It's more addictive than cocaine or heroin.

There are 53 million Americans who smoke, and 87 percent want to quit. Many have tried over and over. Some have succeeded, but it's difficult, and we can't force them to. We are not a proscriptive people. We will not ban smoking at a federal level. But I do believe that, before the end of this century, smokers will no longer smoke in the presence of non-smokers without their permission.

Because of a confluence of an interest in smoking at the worksite, the effect of the militant non-smoker in bringing new smoke-restricting ordinances to bear on the smoking public at state, county and city levels, and the AMA's more active role in pressing for such a ban, the general public will see some striking changes that will be very important for the health of this country. Such changes could spell disaster for the tobacco companies.

You're all aware of the product liability suits being brought against tobacco companies. Smokers dying because of their habit—and also their survivors—are suing the tobacco companies. I'm not a prophet, but I would suspect that sometime, shortly, a plaintiff is going to win one of these cases. When that happens, I think the rest of them will be like falling dominoes, and we will see tremendous changes in this country in reference to smoking.

Now, the tobacco companies say the jury is still out on the effects of smoking. That is absolutely untrue. The jury is in, and the verdict is in, and the fact is that they are guiltier than charged because cigarette smoking is the single most preventable cause of death in this country. To have major industries, such as the tobacco industry, say that there is no evidence about this is ridiculous. There are in excess of 50,000 scientific articles, in every language which publishes science, written since 1964 that have linked cigarette smoking with the problems of health I'll be talking about.

One out of every 10 smokers dies of lung cancer, but the problem doesn't end there. That's a horrible figure. Three out of 10 of all cancer deaths in this country are due in some way to smoking. Lung cancer is what everybody thinks about, but we have very good evidence, direct evidence, about mouth, larynx, esophagus and stomach cancer, and indirect evidence about bladder, pancreas, cervical and other such types of cancer.

Coronary heart disease and stroke actually surpass lung cancer as a public health problem. About 170,000 a year in this country die of coronary heart disease due to smoking. About 120 to 130,000 die of lung cancer, and about 50,000 die of the problems of bronchitis and other forms of chronic obstructive lung disease, the most crippling and debilitating of which is emphysema.

I don't think people understand how deleterious smoking is to others—especially to the fetus. A recent longitudinal study in the United Kingdom indicates that the effects of smoking during pregnancy are discernible in the child through the 10th year of life, both in physical growth and in cognitive growth. There are very real reasons why people who are carrying a child should look not just to that particular nine-month period but to the long-term effects upon the youngster who will be their child.

Smoking is also becoming an issue at the worksite. Many are concerned about the effect of the smoker's smoke upon the non-smoker. This is called various things: ambiant smoke, sidestream smoke, or passive smoking. But the fact is, we now know that there is a deleterious effect upon the health of those who have to live with the smoke of the smoker, whether at the worksite or at home. If a smoker and a non-smoker work in the same office, one smoking two packs a day and the other none at all, the non-smoker smokes three cigarettes a day whether he wants to or not.

The sidestream smoke is much worse for the person who inhales it than the smoke is for the smoker himself. I know this sounds peculiar, but if you think about it this way, you hold a cigarette in your hand that's lit, the smoke comes off at a fairly low temperature. When the smoker inhales, the end of the cigarette lights up, the temperature rises to a tremendous height, around 1,200 degrees, and burns a lot of things away. Then the smoke goes through the cigarette, which filters a lot out. Seventy percent more tar comes out in the sidestream smoke than goes into the smoker's lungs, and 2.7 times the nicotine comes out the sidestream smoke as goes in the smoker's lungs. And there are many other things. There are 4,000 compounds in tobacco smoke. One of them is ammonia, and it is 73 times more concentrated in sidestream smoke than it is in direct smoke. We're not just talking about possibility. We're talking about serious things that are medically provable. So there are 5,000 people in this country who are non-smokers who die each year due to sidestream smoking from those with whom they live or work.

In addition, the cost of the smoking employee to his employer is, on the average, $4,500 a year. This takes into account the employee's life and health insurance, fire insurance on the building, workman's compensation, absenteeism, damage and depreciation of equipment. For example, people in the workforce between 24 and 64 have twice the death rate if they smoke. The smoker uses 50 percent more of the days of health care on insurance plans. Absenteeism is 100 percent more for the smoker than the non-smoker, and he is responsible for almost all damage to equipment that is burnable because of putting down a lighted cigarette on tables, coffee cups, floors, and so forth. Also, routine maintenance and cleaning is cheaper if you don't have a smoking group of employees, and the energy costs associated with the maintenance of air circulation drop remarkably when the building site goes smoke free.

The fascinating thing about it to me is that, when companies have installed a no-smoking policy, morale for both smokers and non-smokers goes up remarkably. I think that is something employers should be very much aware of. In fact, we're beginning to see some employers, especially police and fire departments, requiring new employees to sign affidavits stating that if they smoke—on or off the job—they will be dismissed. There is no grievance procedure for reinstatement.

Right now, there are ordinances in 11 states and more than 30 municipalities that have to do with smoking at the worksite, and I think this is just the beginning. But it's a good beginning, and accelerating. I hope, as you return to your jobs, especially those of you in supervisory positions, that you'll encourage it at your worksite. The smokers will complain, but you'll be saving their lives—and the lives of your non-smokers.

EXERCISE 8
Speeches and Meetings

INSTRUCTIONS: Write a separate news story about this speech and about each of the other speeches on the following pages. As you write the speeches, assume that a local newspaper would publish them the day after each speech. If time permits, research each speech and include some background information about it or about the speaker.

THE GETTYSBURG ADDRESS
By Abraham Lincoln

Four score and seven years ago our fathers brought forth on this continent, a new nation, conceived in Liberty, and dedicated to the proposition that all men are created equal.

Now we are engaged in a great civil war, testing whether that nation, or any nation so conceived and so dedicated, can long endure. We are met on a great battlefield of that war. We have come to dedicate a portion of that field, as a final resting place for those who here gave their lives that this nation might live. It is altogether fitting and proper that we should do this.

But, in a larger sense, we can not dedicate—we can not consecrate—we can not hallow—this ground. The brave men, living and dead, who struggled here, have consecrated it, far above our poor power to add or detract. The world will little note, nor long remember what we say here, but it can never forget what they did here. It is for us the living, rather, to be dedicated here to the unfinished work which they who fought here have thus far so nobly advanced. It is rather for us to be here dedicated to the great task remaining before us—that from these honored dead we take increased devotion to that cause for which they gave the last full measure of devotion—that we here highly resolve that these dead shall not have died in vain—that this nation, under God, shall have a new birth of freedom—and that government of the people, by the people, for the people, shall not perish from the earth.

(Delivered Nov. 19, 1863, at the dedication of the cemetery for Civil War dead at Gettysburg, Pa.)

EXERCISE 9
Speeches and Meetings

BLOOD, TOIL, TEARS AND SWEAT
By Winston Churchill

On Friday evening last I received His Majesty's commission to form a new administration. It was the evident wish and will of Parliament and the nation that this should include all parties, both those who supported the late Government and also the parties of the Opposition. I have completed the most important part of this task. A War Cabinet has been formed of five Members, representing, with the Opposition Liberals, the unity of the nation. The three party leaders have agreed to serve, either in the War Cabinet or in high executive office. The three fighting services have been filled. It was necessary that this should be done in one single day, on account of the extreme urgency and rigor of events. A number of other key positions were filled yesterday, and I am submitting a further list to His Majesty tonight. I hope to complete the appointment of the principal Ministers during tomorrow. The appointment of the other Ministers usually takes a little longer, but I trust that, when Parliament meets again, this part of my task will be completed, and that the administration will be complete in all respects.

I considered it in the public interest to suggest that the House should be summoned to meet today. Mr. Speaker agreed and took the necessary steps, in accordance with the power conferred upon him by the Resolution of the House. At the end of the proceedings today, the adjournment of the House will be proposed until Tuesday, May 21, with, of course, provision for earlier meeting if need be. The business to be considered during that week will be notified to Members at the earliest opportunity. I now invite the House, by the Resolution which stands in my name, to record its approval of the steps taken and to declare its confidence in the new Government.

To form an administration of this scale and complexity is a serious undertaking in itself, but it must be remembered that we are in the preliminary stage of one of the greatest battles in history, that we are in action at many points in Norway and in Holland, that we have to be prepared in the Mediterranean, that the air battle is continuous and that many preparations have to be made here at home. In this crisis I hope I may be pardoned if I do not address the House at any length today. I hope that any of my friends and colleagues, or former colleagues, who are affected by the political reconstruction, will make all allowance for any lack of ceremony with which it has been necessary to act. I would say to the House, as I said to those who have joined this Government: "I have nothing to offer but blood, toil, tears and sweat."

We have before us an ordeal of the most grievous kind. We have before us many, many long months of struggle and of suffering. You ask what is our policy? I will say: It is to wage war, by sea, land and air, with all our might and with all the strength that God can give us: to wage war against a monstrous tyranny [the Nazi regime of Adolf Hitler in Germany], never surpassed in the dark, lamentable catalogue of human crime. That is our policy. You ask, What is our aim? I can answer in one word: Victory—victory at all costs, victory in spite of all terror, victory, however long and hard the road may be; for without victory, there is no survival. Let that be realized; no survival for the British Empire; no survival for all that the British Empire has stood for; no survival for the urge and impulse of the ages, that mankind will move forward towards its goal. But I take up my task with buoyancy and hope. I feel sure that our cause will not be suffered to fail among men. At this time I feel entitled to claim the aid of all, and I say, "Come, then, let us go forward together with our united strength."

(Delivered May 13, 1940, to the House of Commons, three days after he became Prime Minister of England)

EXERCISE 10
Speeches and Meetings

REQUEST FOR A DECLARATION OF WAR
By Franklin D. Roosevelt

Yesterday, December 7, 1941—a date which will live in infamy—the United States of America was suddenly and deliberately attacked by naval and air forces of the Empire of Japan.

The United States was at peace with that nation and, at the solicitation of Japan, was still in conversation with its Government and its Emperor looking toward the maintenance of peace in the Pacific. Indeed, one hour after Japanese air squadrons had commenced bombing on Oahu, the Japanese Ambassador to the United States and his colleague delivered to the Secretary of State a formal reply to a recent American message. While this reply stated that it seemed useless to continue the existing diplomatic negotiations, it contained no threat or hint of war or armed attack.

It will be recorded that the distance of Hawaii from Japan makes it obvious that the attack was deliberately planned many days or even weeks ago. During the intervening time the Japanese Government has deliberately sought to deceive the United States by false statements and expressions of hope for continued peace.

The attack yesterday on the Hawaiian Islands has caused severe damage to American naval and military forces. Very many American lives have been lost. In addition American ships have been reported torpedoed on the high seas between San Francisco and Honolulu.

Yesterday the Japanese Government also launched an attack against Malaya. Last night Japanese forces attacked Hong Kong. Last night Japanese forces attacked Guam. Last night Japanese forces attacked the Philippine Islands. Last night the Japanese attacked Wake Island. This morning the Japanese attacked Midway Island.

Japan has, therefore, undertaken a surprise offensive extending throughout the Pacific area. The facts of yesterday speak for themselves. The people of the United States have already formed their opinions and well understand the implications to the very life and safety of our nation.

As Commander-in-Chief of the Army and Navy, I have directed that all measures be taken for our defense.

Always will we remember the character of the onslaught against us.

No matter how long it may take us to overcome this premeditated invasion, the American people in their righteous might will win through to absolute victory.

I believe I interpret the will of the Congress and of the people when I assert that we will not only defend ourselves to the uttermost but will make very certain that this form of treachery shall never endanger us again.

Hostilities exist. There is no blinking at the fact that our people, our territory and our interests are in grave danger.

With confidence in our armed forces—with the unbounded determination of our people—-we will gain the inevitable triumph—so help us God.

I ask that the Congress declare that since the unprovoked and dastardly attack by Japan on Sunday, December seventh, a state of war has existed between the United States and the Japanese Empire.

(Delivered Dec. 8 before Congress, which responded that same afternoon, declaring war on Japan without a dissenting vote)

EXERCISE 11
Speeches and Meetings

INAUGURAL ADDRESS
By John F. Kennedy

Mr. Chief Justice, President Eisenhower, Vice President Nixon, President Truman, reverend clergy, fellow citizens, we observe today not a victory of party, but a celebration of freedom—symbolizing an end, as well as a beginning—signifying renewal, as well as change. For I have sworn before you and Almighty God the same solemn oath our forebears prescribed nearly a century and three quarters ago.

The world is very different now. For man holds in his mortal hands the power to abolish all forms of human poverty and all forms of human life. And yet the same revolutionary beliefs for which our forebears fought are still at issue around the globe— the belief that the rights of man come not from the generosity of the state, but from the hand of God.

We dare not forget today that we are the heirs of that first revolution. Let the word go forth from this time and place, to friend and foe alike, that the torch has been passed to a new generation of Americans—born in this century, tempered by war, disciplined by a hard and bitter peace, proud of our ancient heritage—and unwilling to witness or permit the slow undoing of those human rights to which this Nation has always been committed, and to which we are committed today at home and around the world.

Let every nation know, whether it wishes us well or ill, that we shall pay any price, bear any burden, meet any hardship, support any friend, oppose any foe, in order to assure the survival and the success of liberty.

This much we pledge—and more.

To those old allies whose cultural and spiritual origins we share, we pledge the loyalty of faithful friends. United, there is little we cannot do in a host of cooperative ventures. Divided, there is little we can do—for we dare not meet a powerful challenge at odds and split asunder.

To those new States whom we welcome to the ranks of the free, we pledge our word that one form of colonial control shall not have passed away merely to be replaced by a far greater iron tyranny. We shall not always expect to find them supporting our view. But we shall always hope to find them strongly supporting their own freedom—and to remember that, in the past, those who foolishly sought power by riding the back of the tiger ended up inside.

To those peoples in the huts and villages across the globe struggling to break the bonds of mass misery, we pledge our best efforts to help them help themselves, for whatever period is required—not because the Communists may be doing it, not because we seek their votes, but because it is right. If a free society cannot help the many who are poor, it cannot save the few who are rich.

To our sister republics south of our border, we offer a special pledge—to convert our good words into good deeds, in a new alliance for progress, to assist free men and free governments in casting off the chains of poverty. But this peaceful revolution of hope cannot become the prey of hostile powers. Let all our neighbors know that we shall join with them to oppose aggression or subversion anywhere in the Americas. And let every other power know that this hemisphere intends to remain the master of its own house.

To that world assembly of sovereign states, the United Nations, our last best hope in an age where the instruments of war have far outpaced the instruments of peace, we renew our pledge of support—to prevent it from becoming merely a forum for invective—to strengthen its shield of the new and the weak—and to enlarge the area in which its writ may run.

Finally, to those nations who would make themselves our adversary, we offer not a pledge but a request: that both sides begin anew the quest for peace, before the dark powers of destruction unleashed by science engulf all humanity in planned or accidental self-destruction.

We dare not tempt them with weakness. For only when our arms are sufficient beyond doubt can we be certain beyond doubt that they will never be employed.

But neither can two great and powerful groups of nations take comfort from our present course—both sides overburdened by the cost of modern weapons, both rightly alarmed by the steady spread of the deadly atom, yet both racing to alter that uncertain balance of terror that stays the hand of mankind's final war.

So let us begin anew—remembering on both sides that civility is not a sign of weakness, and sincerity is always subject to proof. Let us never negotiate out of fear. But let us never fear to negotiate.

Let both sides explore what problems unite us instead of laboring those problems which divide us.

Let both sides, for the first time, formulate serious and precise proposals for the inspection and control of arms—and bring the absolute power to destroy other nations under the absolute control of all nations.

Let both sides seek to invoke the wonders of science instead of its terror. Together let us explore the stars, conquer the deserts, eradicate disease, tap the ocean depths, and encourage the arts and commerce.

Let both sides unite to heed in all corners of the earth and the command of Isaiah—to "undo the heavy burdens and to let the oppressed go free."

And if a beachhead of cooperation may push back the jungle of suspicion, let both sides join in creating a new endeavor, not a new balance of power, but a new world of law, where the strong are just and the weak secure and the peace preserved.

All this will not be finished in the first 100 days. Nor will it be finished in the first 1,000 days, nor in the life of this administration, nor even perhaps in our lifetime on this planet. But let us begin.

In your hands, my fellow citizens, more than in mine, will rest the final success or failure of our course. Since this country was founded, each generation of Americans has been summoned to give testimony to its national loyalty. The graves of young Americans who answered the call to service surround the globe.

Now the trumpet summons us again—not as a call to bear arms, though arms we need; not as a call to battle, though embattled we are; but a call to bear the burden of a long twilight struggle, year in, and year out, "rejoicing in hope, patient in tribulation"—a struggle against the common enemies of man: tyranny, poverty, disease, and war itself.

Can we forge against these enemies a grand and global alliance, North and South, East and West, that can assure a more fruitful life for all mankind? Will you join in that historic effort?

In the long history of the world, only a few generations have been granted the role of defending freedom in its hour of maximum danger. I do not shrink from this responsibility—I welcome it. I do not believe that any of us would exchange places with any other people or any other generation. The energy, the faith, the devotion which we bring to this endeavor will light our country and all who serve it—and the glow from that fire can truly light the world.

And so, my fellow Americans, ask not what your country can do for you: Ask what you can do for your country.

Finally, whether you are citizens of America or citizens of the world, ask of us the same high standards of strength and sacrifice which we ask of you. With a good conscience our only sure reward, with history the final judge of our deeds, let us go forth to lead the land we love, asking His blessing and His help, but knowing that here on earth God's work must truly be our own.

(Delivered Jan. 20, 1961)

EXERCISE 12
Speeches and Meetings

I HAVE A DREAM

By the Rev. Dr. Martin Luther King, Jr.

I am happy to join with you today in what will go down in history as the greatest demonstration for freedom in the history of our nation.

Five score years ago, a great American, in whose symbolic shadow we stand today, signed the Emancipation Proclamation. This momentous decree came as a great beacon light of hope to millions of Negro slaves who had been seared in the flames of withering injustice. It came as a joyous daybreak to end the long night of their captivity.

But one hundred years later, the Negro still is not free; one hundred years later, the life of the Negro is still sadly crippled by the manacles of segregation and the chains of discrimination; one hundred years later, the Negro lives on a lonely island of poverty in the midst of a vast ocean of material prosperity; one hundred years later, the Negro is still languished in the corners of American society and finds himself an exile in his own land.

So we've come here today to dramatize a shameful condition. In a sense we've come to our nation's capital to cash a check. When the architects of our republic wrote the magnificent words of the Constitution and the Declaration of Independence, they were signing a promissory note to which every American was to fall heir. This note was a promise that all men, yes, black men as well as white men, would be guaranteed the unalienable rights of life, liberty, and the pursuit of happiness.

It is obvious today that America has defaulted on this promissory note insofar as her citizens of color are concerned. Instead of honoring this sacred obligation, America has given the Negro people a bad check; a check which has come back marked "insufficient funds." But we refuse to believe that the bank of justice is bankrupt. We refuse to believe that there are insufficient funds in the great vaults of opportunity of this nation. And so we've come to cash this check, a check that will give us upon demand the riches of freedom and the security of justice.

We have also come to this hallowed spot to remind America of the fierce urgency of now. This is no time to engage in the luxury of cooling off or to take the tranquilizing drug of gradualism. Now is the time to make real the promises of democracy; now is the time to rise from the dark and desolate valley of segregation to the sunlit path of racial justice; now is time to lift our nation from the quicksands of racial injustice to the solid rock of brotherhood; now is the time to make justice a reality for all of God's children. It would be fatal for the nation to overlook the urgency of the moment. This sweltering summer of the Negro's legitimate discontent will not pass until there is an invigorating autumn of freedom and equality.

Nineteen sixty-three is not an end, but a beginning. And those who hope that the Negro needed to blow off steam and will now be content, will have a rude awakening if the nation returns to business as usual. There will be neither rest nor tranquility in America until the Negro is granted his citizenship rights. The whirlwinds of revolt will continue to shake the foundations of our nation until the bright day of justice emerges.

But there is something that I must say to my people, who stand on the worn threshold which leads into the palace of justice. In the process of gaining our rightful place, we must not be guilty of wrongful deeds. Let us not seek to satisfy our thirst for freedom by drinking from the cup of bitterness and hatred. We must forever conduct our struggle on the high plane of dignity and discipline. We must not allow our creative protests to degenerate into physical violence. Again and again we must rise to the majestic heights of meeting physical force with soul force. The marvelous new militancy, which has engulfed the Negro community, must not lead us to a distrust of all white people. For many of our white brothers, as evidenced by their presence here today, have come to realize that their destiny is tied up with our destiny. And they have come to realize that their freedom is inextricably bound to our freedom. We cannot walk alone. And as we walk, we must make the pledge that we shall always march ahead. We cannot turn back.

There are those who are asking the devotees of Civil Rights, "When will you be satisfied?" We can never be satisfied as long as the Negro is the victim of the unspeakable horrors of police brutality; we can never be satisfied as long as our bodies, heavy with fatigue of travel, cannot gain lodging in the motels of the highways and the hotels of the cities; we cannot be satisfied as long as the Negro's basic mobility is from a smaller ghetto to a larger one; we can never be satisfied as long as our children are stripped of their selfhood and robbed of their dignity by signs stating "For White Only"; we cannot be satisfied as long as the Negro in Mississippi cannot vote and a Negro in New York believes he has nothing for which to vote. No! No, we are not satisfied, and we will not be satisfied until "justice rolls down like waters, and righteousness like a mighty stream."

I am not unmindful that some of you have come here out of excessive trials and tribulations. Some of you have come fresh from narrow jail cells. Some of you have come from areas where your quest for freedom left you battered by the storms of persecution and staggered by the winds of police brutality. You have been the veterans of creative suffering. Continue to work with the faith that unearned suffering is redemptive. Go back to Mississippi. Go back to Alabama. Go back to South Carolina. Go back to Georgia. Go back to Louisiana. Go back to the slums and ghettos of our Northern cities, knowing that somehow this situation can and will be changed. Let us not wallow in the valley of despair.

I say to you today, my friends, that even though we face the difficulties of today and tomorrow, I still have a dream. It is a dream deeply rooted in the American dream. I have a dream that one day this nation will rise up and live out the true meaning of its creed, "We hold these truths to be self-evident, that all men are created equal." I have a dream that one day on the red hills of Georgia, sons of former slaves and sons of former slave owners will be able to sit down together at the table of brotherhood. I have a dream that one day even the state of Mississippi, a state sweltering with the heat of injustice, sweltering with the heat of oppression, will be transformed into an oasis of freedom and justice. I have a dream that my four little children will one day live in a nation where they will not be judged by the color of their skin, but by the content of their character.

I HAVE A DREAM TODAY!

I have a dream that one day down in Alabama—with its vicious racists, with its Governor having his lips dripping with the words of interposition and nullification—one day right there in Alabama, little black boys and black girls will be able to join hands with little white boys and white girls as sisters and brothers.

I HAVE A DREAM TODAY!

I have a dream that one day every valley shall be exalted, every hill and mountain shall be made low. The rough places will be made plain and the crooked places will be made straight, "and the glory of the Lord shall be revealed, and all flesh shall see it together."

This is our hope. This is the faith that I go back to the South with. With this faith we will be able to hew out of the mountain of despair, a stone of hope. With this faith we will be able to transform the jangling discords of our nation into a beautiful symphony of brotherhood. With this faith we will be able to work together, to pray together, to struggle together, to go to jail together, to stand up for freedom together, knowing that we will be free one day. And this will be the day. This will be the day when all of God's children will be able to sing with new meaning, "My country 'tis of thee, sweet land of liberty, of thee I sing. Land where my father died, land of the pilgrim's pride, from every mountain side, let freedom ring." And if America is to be a great nation, this must become true.

So let freedom ring from the prodigious hilltops of New Hampshire; let freedom ring from the mighty mountains of New York; let freedom ring from the heightening Alleghenies of Pennsylvania; let freedom ring from the snow-capped Rockies of Colorado; let freedom ring from the curvaceous slopes of California. But not only that. Let freedom ring from Stone Mountain of Georgia; let freedom ring from Lookout Mountain of Tennessee; let freedom ring from every hill and mole hill of Mississippi. "From every mountainside, let freedom ring."

And when this happens, and when we allow freedom to ring, when we let it ring from every village and every hamlet, from every state and every city, we will be able to speed up that day when all of God's children, black men and white men, Jews and Gentiles, Protestants and Catholics, will be able to join hands and sing in the words of the old Negro spiritual: "Free at last. Free at last. Thank God Almighty, we are free at last."

(Delivered at the Lincoln Memorial on Aug. 28, 1963, during the March on Washington for Civil Rights)

EXERCISE 13
Speeches and Meetings

CITY COUNCIL MEETING

INSTRUCTIONS: Write a news story that summarizes the comments and decisions made at this meeting. Assume that your city council held the meeting at 8 p.m. yesterday.

The first item on the agenda was the city's sign code. Mayor Paul Novarro informed the council members that several business owners have complained that the city's sign code is too restrictive. The present code states that a sign displayed on the front of a business may not exceed 32 square feet. Navarro said store owners want the size of signs to be determined according to the size of each store. This would give larger businesses bigger signs. Business owners also complain about a limitation on roadside signs—that the 200-foot required distance between roadside signs is unfair. "Since the city is growing, new stores are moving here, and they all have signs to put up," the mayor said. "Under the existing code, they can't put up a roadside sign if they're within 200 feet of an existing sign." The mayor concluded that some changes may be necessary and appointed a committee to meet with business owners to look into the problem. To the committee the mayor appointed council members Victor Wang, Madge Seechuk and Howard Piquet, warning them that, "Remember, we want to be cooperative, but we also want to keep clutter down and maintain a quality appearance throughout the community."

The second item on the agenda was a discussion of four possible sites submitted by the Parks and Recreation Advisory Board to be used for a community park. Council Member Keith So made a motion that the council make an offer to the owners of the board's number 1 choice, a 43-acre tract of land. The property has been appraised at $2.1 million, and that is what the city will offer the owners. The advisory board had four criteria for the sites. It said the land must be available, affordable, suitable and accessible. Council member Nina Pazzelli said, "This plot is flat, so it would need little improvement. And parts are wooded. That's an advantage for a park." Councilman Thomas Ciaravino opposed the motion and cast the only dissenting vote, so the vote was 6–1 in favor. He wanted a larger property. The city attorney advised the council that, if negotiations fail, the next step would be for the city to condemn the property. There is a problem, however. The land would also have to be annexed, since it now lies just outside the city's northern city limits. The city attorney said he would check to see if the council had authority to condemn property outside the city limits. However, if not, the city and county might work together and jointly condemn the property, since the county has that power. Plans for the park include several baseball fields, tennis, racquetball and volley-ball courts, jogging paths, playgrounds and picnic areas.

After considering it for nearly 30 minutes, the Council decided to put another matter on a back burner for awhile. Recently, the city council passed a resolution authorizing spending $500,000 in order to improve and repair the city's existing police station. Now, preliminary studies by architects have found that the building's deterioration is far more serious than previously known. So the city may have to build a new police station. Action on the issue was postponed until the architects make a formal report next month.

The final item concerned a parking ban. It was approved by a narrow margin: just 4–3, after having been considered and debated at 2 previous meetings. The ban prohibits commercial vehicles weighing more than 5,000 pounds to be parked on city streets overnight.

EXERCISE 14
Speeches and Meetings

COUNTY COMMISSION MEETING

INSTRUCTIONS: Write a news story that summarizes the comments and decisions made at this meeting. Assume that your county commission held the meeting at 2 p.m. yesterday.

The 11 members of your county commission began their meeting by listening to a presentation of plans for a luxury condominium development on Elkhart Lake. The new development will be called "SunCrest." It will be completed in 2 to 3 years. The property is owned by The Roswell Development Corporation, headquartered in Pittsburgh. Carlos Rey, a spokesman for the company, said: "We are planning a series of 10-story buildings overlooking the lake. None will exceed 100 feet in height. They will contain a total of 715 units, with 5 units per floor. Each unit will have two or three bedrooms. Estimated selling price of a unit will be $100,000 and upwards, perhaps to a top of $500,000 for the larger penthouse units. The development is about 5 miles from the nearest town, and we intend to promote it as a vacation and recreation center, possibly also for active retirees. We'll have our own well for water, and our own sewer system, with an extensive recreation system centered around the lake. We know that fire protection is a concern. The township fire department serving the area doesn't have a ladder truck capable of reaching the top of a 10-story building. We'll donate $320,000 for the purchase of one. It's the least we can do." The commission voted 9–2 to approve the plans and to rezone the land from agricultural to PUD: Planned Unit Development.

Next, at 3 p.m., the commission honored and presented plaques to two 15-year-old girls. The girls, Doreen Nicholls and Pamela Dezinno, were walking along a river in a county park last week and saw a young child fall from a boat. Both girls dove into the river and pulled her out. While Doreen then proceeded to administer CPR, Pamela called for help, thus saving a life.

Appearing next before the commission, Sheriff Gus DiCesar asked it to adopt a proposal imposing a three-day wait before a pistol could be bought from any gun dealer in the county. The proposed ordinance was drafted by sheriff's department officials. "I do not think that 72 hours is too long for someone to wait to buy a handgun," Sheriff DiCesar said. "There are a lot of cases where we can show that people went out and bought a gun with criminal intent and used it right away to shoot or rob someone. We want a cooling off period." There is no county law now regarding the sale of pistols. Under the proposed ordinance, a customer would also have to provide the dealer with his name, address, date of birth and other information, then wait 72 hours before picking up the pistol. The dealer would mail the information to the sheriff's department, where it would be kept on a computerized file. Sheriff DiCesar said it would speed the identification of the owner of a pistol found at a crime scene. A majority of the commissioners said they favor such a proposal but want to study it and get more information and possibly hold a public hearing to give every citizen an opportunity to speak his mind about it. They promised to seriously consider it at their next meeting.

The commissioners then decided not to give themselves a raise, rejecting a proposed pay raise on a 7–4 vote. It has been five years since the last pay raise for them. Then their salary went from $32,500 to $36,000 a year. Yesterday, the majority, led by

Commissioners Roland Graumann and Anita Shenuski, argued that a raise was "inappropriate." Ron Ryan argued a proposed increase to $42,500 was not out of line because commissioners in other counties earn more. "This is not asking too much," he said. "The county is getting a good deal for the time we put in." Derric Hadsee responded, "Our work should be done for community service, not just for how much we make." Haedsee warned that, if the commissioners gave themselves a big raise, other county employees would want one too.

EXERCISE 15
Speeches and Meetings

SCHOOL BOARD MEETING

INSTRUCTIONS: Write a news story that summarizes the comments and decisions made at this meeting. Assume that your school board held its monthly meeting at 7:30 p.m. yesterday.

The board opened its meeting by honoring seven retiring teachers: Shirley Dawsun, Carmen Foucault, Nina Paynich, Kenneth Satava, Nancy Lee Scott, Lonnie McEwen, and Harley Sawyer. Paynich worked as a teacher 44 years, longer than any of the others. Each teacher was given a framed "Certificate of Appreciation" and good round of applause.

The school board then turned to the major item on its agenda: the budget for next year. The budget totals $43.9 million, up 5% from this year. It includes $3.2 million for a new elementary school to be built on West Madison Ave. It will be completed and opened in two years. The budget also includes a 4.5% raise for teachers and a 6% raise for administrators. Also, the salary of the superintendent of schools was raised $10,000, to $88,000 a year. The vote was unanimous: 9–0.

The school board then discussed the topic of remedial summer classes. Board member Umberto Vacante proposed eliminating them to save an estimated $820,000. "They're just too expensive, especially when you consider we serve only about 900 students each summer. A lot of them are students who flunked their regular classes. Often, if they attend the summer classes, they don't have to repeat a grade. If we're going to spend that kind of money, I think we should use it to help and reward our most talented students. They're the ones we ignore. We could offer special programs for them." Supt. Marcia Pagozalski responded, "Some of these summer students have learning disabilities and emotional problems, and they really need the help. This would hurt them terribly. Without it, they might never graduate." The board then voted 7–2 to keep the classes one more year, but to ask its staff for a study of the matter.

During a one-hour hearing that followed, about 100 people, many loud and angry, debated the issue of creationism vs. evolution. "We've seen your biology books," said parent Claire Sawyer. "I don't want my children using them. They never mention the theory of creationism." Another parent, Harley Euon of 410 East Third Street, responded: "Evolution isn't a theory. It's proven fact. Creationism is a religious idea, not even a scientific theory. People here are trying to force schools to teach our children their religion." A third parent, Roy E. Cross of 101 Charow Lane, agreed, adding: "People can teach creationism in their homes and churches. It's not the schools' job." After listening to the debate, the board voted 6–3 to continue using the present textbooks, but to encourage parents to discuss the matter with their children and to provide in their individual homes the religious training they deem most appropriate for their families.

Finally, last on its agenda, the board unanimously adopted a resolution praising the school system's ADDITIONS: adult volunteers who contribute their spare time to help and assist their neighborhood schools. Last year, Supt. Marcia Pagozalski reported, there was a total of 897 ADDITIONS, and they put in a total of 38,288 hours of volunteer time helping the schools.

EXERCISE 16
Speeches and Meetings

ADVANCE AND FOLLOW STORIES: CITY COUNCIL MEETING

INSTRUCTIONS: Write separate advance and follow stories about the following city council meeting. Assume that the meeting was held in Roseville, a suburb of your community.

Information for Advance Story

City Clerk Wilma Durbin said: "There are three issues on the agenda for next Monday's meeting, but you never know. If the council wants to, it can consider other issues that come up. And then they always give everyone in the audience a chance to speak. The issues we've got listed now include a proposal to give city employees an 8 percent raise. That comes from the city manager's office. Then they will open bids and award a contract for the operation of concession stands at the Civic Center. Number 3 on the agenda, the council will vote on a proposal to limit the number of dogs that anyone can have in a home in a residential area without a permit. The proposal would limit the number of adult dogs in a household to four. That's a controversial topic. Everyone gets excited about dogs."

Information for Follow Story

TOPIC 1: The first issue on the city council's agenda last night was the city budget for next year. City council members debated the size of the raise that city employees will receive. City Manager W. E. Knowles started the discussion, saying: "I recommend an 8 percent across-the-board raise for city employees. Every employee deserves at least that much. We've got a total of 275 employees, and an 8 percent raise would cost the city a total of $320,000. The annual payroll is about $4 million, and this would increase it to $4,320,000. It's really a catch-up raise. If you look at the salaries the city pays today, and you compare those salaries with the salaries we paid 10 years ago, and then you compare them with the rise in the cost of living over those 10 years, then you'll find that city employees have fallen behind; they've lost 11.5 percent of their salaries to inflation. In constant dollars, they're earning 88.5 percent of what they did 10 years ago. We've also got to give them a good raise to maintain a competitive position in the local labor market. They haven't gotten a decent raise for years, and if we don't give them one this year, we'll begin to lose some key employees. Last year, they got a 3 percent raise, and the year before that they got 4 percent. That's not enough."

Mayor Brad Freeman said: "Eight percent is too much. Everyone agrees they're underpaid and deserve a raise. I don't question that. The real issue is whether we can afford to give them 8 percent. Where would the money come from? We'd have to raise property taxes, but they're already too high. We just don't have the money."

Council member Stacy Ruskiewicz said: "I don't know enough about the budget to say what we can and can't afford. Tax revenues might go up next year, or we might cut back somewhere else. I think this is important, but let's get some more information before deciding anything. I move that we ask the city treasurer to look into this and report back to us at our meeting next week." Her motion passed by a vote of 9–0.

TOPIC 2: The council then opened 14 bids for the right to operate concession stands at the city's Civic Center. The high bidder, Dehuer Catering, agreed to give the city 21.3 percent of its gross receipts if it was awarded the exclusive contract to operate all the concession stands at the Civic Center, and it was granted the contract. The next highest bidder offered the county 18.61 percent of its gross receipts. The low bid was 12 percent. It is estimated by Civic Center authorities that the total receipts at the concession stands may exceed $1.5 million on an annual basis. The contract is for a five-year period of time.

TOPIC 3: City Zoning Director Mack Felino offered a new ordinance that specifies that no homeowner in an area zoned for single- or multiple-family residences could keep more than four dogs that are older than 6 months without a license from the city. To obtain a license, dog owners would have to demonstrate that they have ample room and facilities for the dogs and that the dogs would not be a nuisance to neighbors. A license would cost $100.

Felino then added: "We have found that many city residents receive additional income from breeding and selling these animals, dogs especially, and it's often a nuisance for neighbors. We need to place some restrictions on the breeding of dogs. People shouldn't be allowed to have commercial kennels in residential neighborhoods. We don't permit any other kinds of businesses in residential neighborhoods, and we shouldn't permit these kennels."

City Commissioner Willie Ralph said: "I agree with all that's being said. We're going to have a lot of people angry with us if we adopt this law, but we need some guidelines for the number of animals kept in homes. I'd say this is my number 1 problem as a city commissioner. Every week, I've got people calling and complaining about barking dogs and strange dogs running loose in their yards, and I know the police get hundreds of these calls."

City Commissioner Duwayne Tutone said: "This isn't something we should rush into. I'm not convinced it's necessary, or even a good thing. There are lots of people living in this city that hunt and that raise dogs for show, and they have a right to as many dogs as they want. How many dogs someone has isn't any of our business. We've already got enough other laws, so if there's a real problem with noise or anything, it can be taken care of."

The City Commission approved the proposal, thus limiting people living in residential areas to a maximum of four dogs aged 6 months and older. The vote was 7–2 with Commissioners Duwayne Tutone and Larry Raftis voting against the proposal.

TOPIC 4: James Gracie is the city attorney. He has been the city attorney for the past nine years. He submitted his resignation at the end of the meeting. His resignation was a surprise. No one expected it. He said he wants to go into private law practice and has been offered a good job as a partner with a major law firm in the city. City commissioners asked him to continue working until his replacement can be found. He agreed. The job will be advertised, with a deadline for applications on the last day of next month. The job currently pays $45,600 per year and is a full-time position.

17 Interviews and Polls

Reporters interview people to learn their opinions and to obtain factual information about events in the news. Reporters like interviews because they provide a fast, easy way to obtain the news. Often there is no alternative to an interview. Reporters cannot personally observe every news event that occurs in their communities because there are too many events, and because many important events occur unexpectedly. So reporters interview other people who witnessed the events, who became involved in them or who are concerned about the consequences.

Unfortunately, interviews are notoriously unreliable. Sources may fail to notice important details or may misunderstand or forget the details. Because they want to promote a cause or gain recognition for themselves, other sources may reveal only their side of an issue and present that side as favorably as possible. Like their sources, the reporters conducting an interview may fail to recognize the importance of some details and may misunderstand or forget others. Reporters may also fail to consult a second source to verify the details and may make some factual errors while writing their stories.

Regardless of their training, it is difficult for reporters to be totally neutral observers during the interviewing process. Some personal prejudices may be unconscious but still affect what the reporters see, remember and consider important. Even the reporters' ages and physical characteristics may affect their sources. For example, older sources may not respect young reporters, regarding them as inexperienced and unreliable. Conversely, younger sources may be more responsive to young reporters. Researchers have also found that if a black and a white interviewer ask the same questions, they are likely to receive different answers.

The way reporters word questions also affects their sources' responses. Children are particularly susceptible to suggestion and often give the answers that interviewers seem to expect. Adults are more cautious and, to avoid embarrassment, are likely to give answers that are socially acceptable. If adults are unaware of a fact, they may pretend they know it so they will not seem uninformed.

Through months and years of practice, perceptive reporters improve their interviewing skills. By studying the advice provided by more experienced reporters, beginners can avoid many of the problems likely to arise during interviews. This chapter will discuss those problems and recommend solutions to them.

Arranging an Interview

Normally, reporters call in advance to make appointments for formal interviews. The reporters identify themselves and the newspapers they work for and explain why they want to conduct an interview. Then their source can prepare for the interview, perhaps by gathering information the reporters specifically requested.

Reporters try to arrange most interviews with top officials—with the presidents of businesses and with the mayors of cities—rather than with subordinates, such as secretaries, assistants or public information officers. Reporters want to interview people with first-hand knowledge of their topics, with experts who can immediately answer all their questions—and whose answers will be respected by the reading public.

In-depth interviews require a minimum of one hour and often take two or three hours. Reporters usually offer to go to the sources' homes or offices because, if the sources are in familiar surroundings, they are more likely to be comfortable and thus to speak more freely. Perhaps even more importantly, the site of an interview should be private, free of interruptions and distractions. If any other people—even friends or relatives—are present, they may interrupt or inhibit a source.

Reporters rarely schedule major interviews in their newsrooms. Most newsrooms lack privacy and seem too noisy and chaotic, especially for strangers. Reporters also avoid luncheon appointments. When they schedule interviews, reporters want to talk, not eat. Luncheon meetings require too much time, create too many distractions and create too much unnecessary expense.

Telephone Interviews

Reporters conduct most of their interviews by telephone, often without having had time to prepare their questions. People who have stories they want published in a newspaper often call the reporters unexpectedly, and the reporters may want to interview them immediately. Reporters may also be instructed to call immediately and interview people involved in spot news stories, such as crimes, accidents and fires.

Telephone calls save enormous amounts of time, since reporters do not have to leave their newsrooms, drive to the source's home or office, wait until the source is free, conduct the interview, then walk back to their cars, drive to their offices, find new parking places and return to their desks. Experienced reporters will cradle a telephone on one shoulder and type their notes directly onto a typewriter or video display terminal. When they hear the noise and realize that reporters are typing everything they say, some sources become upset; they begin to speak more cautiously and try to end the interview as quickly as possible. Reporters can try to soothe their fears and, if the noise continues to upset the source, can begin to take their notes more quietly in longhand. Sources used to dealing with reporters become accustomed to the noise.

Reporters for the nation's largest news media obtain many of their stories by calling sources throughout the United States. If your telephone rang and a reporter said, "This is CBS Television News," "The Washington Post," or "Time magazine," you would probably be likely to cooperate and give the reporter your full attention.

Telephone calls, however, are not a very satisfactory means of obtaining in-depth interviews about controversial or complex issues and personalities. It is difficult to cultivate sources known only by telephone and never seen face to face, and therefore difficult to persuade those sources to talk for a long time and to answer questions about embarrassing or personal matters. Thus, telephone interviews tend to be brief—only 4 or 5 minutes long—and relatively superficial. If reporters want to conduct longer, in-depth interviews, they try to visit the source in person.

Preparing for an Interview

To prepare for an in-depth interview, reporters may spend several hours learning all they can about their source and about the topics they want to discuss with that source. Reporters must be prepared to ask the right questions—meaningful, intelligent questions—and to understand their source's answers.

If reporters are well prepared, they will not waste any time by asking unnecessary questions about issues that have already been widely publicized, questions that might bore their sources and reveal their own ignorance. They are also more likely to recognize significant statements and are better able to ask intelligent followup questions about them. Reporters who prepare for an interview also are more likely to notice if their sources are avoiding certain topics or are presenting only one side of a controversial issue. Moreover, if reporters obviously understand an issue, their sources are likely to be more trusting and to speak more freely.

Reporters who fail to prepare for an interview are less likely to uncover interesting and important new information. Because of their ignorance, the reporters may be forced to rely on their sources for guidance and may be unable to detect their sources' biases. Reporters will not know what to ask, nor what is new, important or controversial. Inevitably, some sources will detect the reporters' ignorance and try to take advantage of it. The sources may avoid complex topics that they fear the reporters would not understand, or they may try to promote a cause or to hide their errors. If reporters are obviously unprepared, a source also may cancel the interview or lose interest in the interview and provide only a few perfunctory responses to the reporters' questions.

Thus, the preparation of good questions may be the single most important step in the interviewing process. Sources rarely reveal startling new information without some prompting. They may not want to discuss some issues or may be hesitant to speak freely with reporters whom they do not know. So reporters must pry the information (and more colorful quotations) from them.

Good interviewers write their questions in advance, then check off each question as they ask it so that they do not run out of questions or forget to ask an important question. All the questions should be arranged in a logical order, so that a source's answer to one question leads into the following question.

Some reporters like to list their most important questions first so that if they run out of time, only their least important questions will remain unanswered. Reporters also like to save their most embarrassing and difficult questions for the end of interviews. By then, their sources should be more trusting and in the habit of answering their questions. If a source refuses to answer the embarrassing questions and abruptly ends an interview, reporters will have already obtained most of the information needed for their stories.

At some time during their lives, most Americans will probably be interviewed for a consumer or public opinion poll. When the pollsters call you, notice that they usually begin with a few easy questions. Their last question will be the most personal—perhaps, "What is your annual income?" If such a question came first, people might immediately hang up their telephones or walk away. But if that is their last question, people are more likely to answer it, as well as all the preceding questions.

As you begin to prepare for an interview, ask yourself, "What questions would my readers want to ask?" Also ask yourself, "Which facts are new, important and most likely to interest or affect the public?" After deciding exactly what you want to know, ask your source about those specific points. If a fact is particularly important, begin with a general question about it, then prepare several followup questions designed to elicit more information about it.

The best questions tend to be short, simple and clearly relevant. They also should be specific. Vague questions elicit vague answers: abstract generalities. Specific questions elicit more specific, factual details. Sources may not answer long, complex questions because they do not understand them. Moreover, if reporters ask long questions, the questions will consume much of the time sources would need to answer them.

Reporters try to avoid asking questions that can be answered with a simple "yes" or "no." They want lively responses—colorful quotations and interesting details—and consequently ask questions that require sources to give more detailed answers. They may ask the sources to "describe" or to "explain" or to tell "how" or "why" some event occurred.

Conducting an Interview

After scheduling an interview, reporters should arrive promptly and should be appropriately dressed. Too many college students dress informally, regardless of the circumstances, then wonder why their sources failed to give them much time, information, trust or respect.

Reporters often begin important interviews by chatting quietly with the sources. They may mention a subject of mutual interest or ask about something interesting or unusual they noticed in the source's home or office. The reporters want to put the source at ease and to establish a friendly relationship so that the source will be more willing to answer their questions. That is especially important when a source is not used to answering reporters' questions.

Reporters should immediately take control of every interview and then remain in control. They should decide which matters are most important, then encourage the source to discuss those matters. If the source lapses into generalities, reporters should ask more specific questions. If the source strays from a topic, reporters should ask additional questions to return the conversation to it immediately. Reporters cannot let a source waste time or evade important questions.

Thus, good interviewers must also be careful listeners. They must listen carefully to ensure that a source has answered their questions—and to ensure that they understand the answers. Reporters must ask the source to repeat or to explain any comment that is unclear. If the source fails to provide some important information, reporters must ask followup questions. Or, if the source raises an interesting point that the reporters had not expected or known about, they must ask for more details, temporarily setting aside their remaining questions. Reporters must also ask the source to spell names and to repeat important numbers. Later, the reporters should verify the accuracy of these spellings and numbers.

Reporters occasionally ask a source to repeat important facts two or three times. Each time a source retells a fact, he or she may add a few additional, and sometimes important, details. However, reporters should not argue or debate with a source. Instead, they should encourage the source to express his or her opinions as fully and freely as possible. Few sources will continue to speak freely after reporters disagree with them.

After asking all their prepared questions, reporters should ask the source whether there is any other information that should be included in the story. Although some sources will have nothing to add, others will provide their interviews' most valuable information. A source may mention related issues, new developments of great importance or facts of personal interest, about which the source may begin to speak more candidly and enthusiastically.

Before ending an interview, reporters also should be certain that they understand everything that has been said. And as a precautionary measure, they should ask how and where they can contact the source if a question arises while they are writing the story.

Sometimes reporters decide to interview a second and third, and possibly even a fourth and fifth, person. When they interview someone, reporters often learn only what that person wants them to know or perceives to be the truth. By interviewing several other people, reporters can verify the source's remarks and obtain a more well-rounded account of the topic. The additional interviews are essential when reporters are writing about controversial issues.

Reporters also observe their sources so they can describe as well as quote them. Reporters may, when appropriate, describe a source's height, weight, posture, hair, voice, gestures, facial expressions, clothing, jewelry, home, car, office or family.

Some experts say reporters should also analyze and respond to their sources' non-verbal behavior. A cough, grin, shaking fist or nod of the head may reveal that a source is nervous or relaxed, sympathetic or angry, deceitful or truthful. Researchers have found that people speak more rapidly when they are anxious about a topic, and that they begin to stutter, repeat words, leave sentences unfinished and look away from their interviewers. Few beginning reporters possess the knowledge necessary to interpret accurately and take advantage of all these non-verbal cues. However, experienced reporters may begin to watch their sources' physical reactions to difficult questions and to consider those responses as they continue the interviews.

Dealing with Hostile Sources

Most people cooperate with reporters because interviews are mutually beneficial, enabling sources to achieve their goals at the same time they enable reporters to obtain information for news stories. Sources may enjoy seeing their names in print, welcome the opportunity to tell their side of a story, hope to promote some cause or want to inform the public about an issue they consider significant. Sources may also cooperate because they are flattered that reporters consider their opinions important or are curious about how the media operate.

However, some people are hostile and refuse to talk to reporters. They may distrust reporters and fear that a topic is too complex for reporters to understand or that reporters will be inaccurate or sensational. Hostile sources frequently complain— sometimes justifiably—that reporters have misquoted them and made other embarrassing errors in previous stories. Some people are too nervous to talk to reporters. Others may consider a topic unimportant, may dislike a particular newspaper or may fear that any story, regardless of its accuracy, may harm them.

When reporters encounter a hostile source, they may try to learn why the source is hesitant to speak to them. After learning the reason, they may be able to overcome that specific objection. Reporters may also try to convince sources that they will benefit from a story's publication—that favorable publicity will help them or help the organizations they represent. Reporters may argue that it would look bad if they had to say the source refused to comment about an issue. Similarly, reporters may argue that a story would be less damaging if the source explained his or her side of an issue.

As a last resort, experienced reporters may try to threaten or bluff a hostile source. Reporters usually begin by obtaining as much information as possible from other people, including the source's opponents. Then they confront the source and ask for a comment on the information. Alternatively, reporters may pretend that they want to talk about an unrelated issue, or that they have already obtained all the information they need for a story. Then the reporters may ask the hostile source to explain a few details or to respond to some minor allegations. By responding, the source may unintentionally provide more information and confirm the information's accuracy.

The Problem of Note-Taking

Another major problem, especially for beginners, is note-taking. A few experienced reporters do not take any notes during interviews, instead trying to remember everything their sources say and then writing their notes later. These reporters fear that, if they take notes during an interview, their sources will become nervous and speak less freely. They may find it too difficult to think of questions, listen to a source's answers and take thorough and accurate notes—all at the same time.

While writing the book "In Cold Blood," author Truman Capote was afraid that a tape recorder would inhibit the people he wanted to interview. So Capote trained himself to remember everything they said. Capote did this by talking to a friend or reading for a while, then writing down everything he heard or read. Later, he would compare his record with a recording of the conversation or with the actual reading material. Capote said, "Finally, when I got to be about 97 percent accurate, I felt ready to take on this book."

Unless they have photographic memories, however, most newspaper reporters need to take notes. Traditionally, reporters have used paper and pencil to record their notes in longhand, and most continue to do so. A recent survey found that 68 percent never use tape recorders and that only 12 percent use them frequently.

Good interviewers take copious notes, writing down much more information than they can possibly use. At the time they take the notes, reporters often do not know which facts they will need or which facts they will want to emphasize in their stories. If they record as much as possible, they are less likely to forget an important point or to make a factual error. Later, they can discard the unimportant and irrelevant items.

Few reporters know shorthand. Few, if any, schools of journalism in the United States teach or require it. However, many reporters develop a shorthand of their own. Because they cannot record everything a source says, they leave out some words and abbreviate others. They may take notes only on the most crucial points—key words, phrases and ideas—then fill in the details later. Reporters also write down every name, number and good quotation. Reporters can learn to recognize good quotations and key statements as they are spoken and train themselves to remember those quotations long enough to write them down, word for word.

If a source speaks too rapidly, reporters can ask the source to slow down or to repeat an important statement. Or reporters might say: "Could you wait a minute? That's an important point, and I'd like to write it down." Then, to be certain that they have recorded it accurately, reporters can read the statement back to their source. As another alternative, some reporters ask dummy questions. If a source is talking too rapidly for reporters to record an important statement, they ask the source an unimportant question, then catch up on their notes while the source answers it.

If their note-taking makes a source nervous, reporters can stop and explain that the notes will help them write more accurate and thorough stories. Reporters can also show or read their notes to the sources.

After completing an interview, reporters should review their notes as soon as possible, while everything is fresh in their minds. They may want to fill in some gaps or be certain that they understand everything a source said. Finally, reporters also should write their stories as soon as possible. The longer they wait, the more likely they are to forget some facts and to distort others.

Reporters interview basketball star Julius Erving. Newspapers are employing more women in their sports departments and, although none appear in this photo, women reporters are demanding the right to enter teams' locker rooms along with their male counterparts.

The use of tape recorders enables reporters to concentrate on the questions they want to ask and on their sources' responses to those questions. Recorders also provide verbatim and permanent records, so reporters make fewer factual errors and their sources are less likely to claim that they were misquoted. Moreover, when reporters replay the tapes, they are likely to find some important statements that they failed to notice during the original interviews.

Despite these advantages, few reporters use tape recorders, especially for routine stories, primarily because their use requires too much time. After taping a one-hour interview, for example, reporters would have to replay the entire one-hour tape at least once, and perhaps two or three times, before writing their stories. It would also be difficult to find a particular fact or quotation in the tape. By comparison, reporters can read their handwritten notes in a few minutes and find a particular fact or quotation in a few seconds.

In the past, reporters also feared that their sources might freeze at the sight of a tape recorder and that the recorders might break or run out of tape. Modern tape recorders, however, are reliable, unobtrusive and able to play for longer periods of time. Tape recorders have also become small enough to hide in a pocket—but they should be used openly. If reporters intend to record an interview, they have an obligation to inform their source of that fact.

As a final alternative, reporters may record major interviews but augment the tapes with written notes. The reporters can consult their notes to write the stories, then use the tape recordings to verify the accuracy of important facts and quotations.

Pat Washburn, a reporter and columnist for 10½ years in Georgia, New York, Texas, Virginia and Indiana, prepared these 11 tips for improved note-taking.

1. If possible, prepare in advance. It's ridiculous to sit at a speech or interview and write down background information that you already could have jotted down. If you're well prepared, you'll do better.

2. Work out a system of initials in advance that you can use in your notes. For example, if you're writing a story about a Zebediah Schwartenzeger, plan to write ZS in your notes when his name comes up. It'll save you a lot of time.

3. Skip small words (such as "the," "a" and "to") in your notes.

4. ALWAYS put quote marks around direct quotes. Then, there's no doubt later what is quoted and what is paraphrased.

5. If something in your notes appears important, mark it (perhaps with an asterisk) so you can find it quickly later on. Also mark any gaps in your notes where there's an unanswered question. Then you won't forget that you need more information.

6. As you're taking notes, try to make a preliminary judgment on what your lead should be. This will tell you what additional information you'll need.

7. Learn to listen and write at the same time. If you hear something that you want to write down and tune out the speaker while you note it, you might miss something even more important.

8. Don't depend solely on your ears in note-taking. Use your eyes, too. How someone looks while they're speaking (smiling vs. frowning) can put their words in a different context.

9. Practice writing while you're looking somewhere else (for example, at the speaker). If you want to take notes while someone is pointing out something on a chart, this skill is invaluable.

10. Immediately after a speech or interview, glance over your notes and make sure you understand what you've written down. Something that is clear originally may not be so clear 15 minutes later. If you have any questions, try to clear them up immediately after a speech or interview. It may be difficult to reach the person later over the telephone.

11. Finally, if you're covering any outdoor event, ALWAYS carry a pencil. Rain can be a disaster as anyone knows who has ever tried to write on wet paper with a ball-point pen.

Other Interviewing Problems

As they begin to write, reporters must examine critically all the information they have gathered, decide which facts are most newsworthy and then concentrate on those facts—discarding clichés, platitudes, and self-praise, as well as the repetitious, the irrelevant and the obvious. This task is more difficult than it may seem. A student interested in the U.S. space shuttle interviewed a representative of the National Aeronautics and Space Administration but lost control of the interview and was overwhelmed by facts promoting NASA. Because the student included much of that information in her story, it sounded more like a publicity release than a news story:

NASA has two major purposes, to develop transportation through the use of the space shuttle and to transfer technology from previous space programs into common use.
A spokesman for NASA gave several examples of technological innovations that resulted

from projects such as the Apollo and Skylab programs. These innovations include the development of Teflon, artificial limbs, global weather forecasting, communication satellites and computer technology.

The spokesman added that many of the computer systems that Americans take for granted today are a direct result of the Apollo project. He said the computers were developed for use in the Apollo program and that the technology learned as a result affects almost everyone in every day of their lives.

All the information included in the story is accurate, but much of that information is several years old and irrelevant to the student's topic, the U.S. space shuttle. (NASA depends on annual appropriations from Congress and, to win support for the space program, attempts to emphasize its benefits for the American public.)

Newspaper reporters rarely use a question-and-answer format for their stories; this format requires too much space and makes it more difficult for readers to grasp a story's highlights. Instead, reporters begin most interviews with a summary lead, then present their story's highlights in the following paragraphs. All the information is presented in the order of its importance, not in the order in which it was provided by a source. Background information is kept to a minimum and presented in later paragraphs. Also, reporters vary their style of writing so that every sentence and every paragraph does not begin with the source's name.

Reporters try to make their sources come alive through the use of quotations and description. After a newspaper editor spoke to a class of journalism students, one student effectively described the manner in which the editor answered questions as well as his exact words:

> Lewis answered questions quickly and sharply, speaking in short, clipped sentences, never wasting a word. Sometimes, anticipating questions, he interrupted the students with his answers.
>
> At one point, he told the students: "I don't know why you would want to get in to the newspaper profession. There are long hours, low pay, hard work and lots of pressure and strain."
>
> Why is he in the profession?
>
> "I like it all," he said.

Reporters should specify the rules they intend to follow at the beginning of an interview. If a source says that an interview is "off the record," reporters should ask what is meant by that term, since the source may be confused and really mean something else. Normally, information provided off the record cannot be published. Reporters may try to change the source's mind. If that fails, they may cancel the interview, then seek the same facts elsewhere.

If a source grants an interview and—at the end of the interview—says it was off the record, reporters are not obliged to cooperate. Most reporters probably would feel free to report all the information they had received under those circumstances.

As mentioned in Chapter 11, the use of unidentified sources, particularly outside Washington, D.C., is greatly exaggerated. However, if reporters believe that there is a legitimate need to withhold a source's name—to protect that source from undeserved embarrassment or retaliation—they can identify the source by an initial, a first name, a fictitious name or a descriptive phrase.

Again, some sources will want to review stories before they are published. Most newspapers prohibit this practice. Editors fear that it would take too much time, that some stories might be lost and that some people shown the stories would want to change them. Then the reporters, the editors and the sources would have to spend hours haggling over the changes. To avoid that problem, reporters can tell the source that deadline pressures make the practice impossible, or that it violates their newspapers' policies. If a source persists, reporters should tell that source to call an editor.

Feature-Story Interviews and Press Conferences

Reporters also interview people for personality or feature stories that describe people in the news. Personality and feature stories go into more depth than most news stories, and they are more colorful and descriptive. Reporters writing such stories usually want to reveal someone's personality, mannerisms, accomplishments or opinions. Reporters may talk to that person for several hours; talk to that person's family, friends and business associates; and then return and interview the source a second or third time. Reporters may also observe the source in action for several days, both at home and at work.

Press conferences are less personal and rewarding for journalists than one-to-one interviews. Most press conferences, including presidential press conferences, are more convenient for sources than for reporters. They enable sources to speak to dozens of reporters at once. It is usually impossible for a single reporter to ask several questions or to obtain any exclusive information at a press conference. Also, people used to dealing with the media may find it easier to manipulate reporters at press conferences. They may begin with long statements that consume much of the time and that present their side of an issue, then avoid recognizing reporters likely to ask hostile questions. If each reporter does not have an opportunity to ask followup questions, it may be easier for the source to evade their original questions.

Discussion Questions

1. How would you respond to a source who, several days before a scheduled interview, asked to see the questions you intended to ask?

2. Do you agree that reporters have an obligation to inform their sources when they plan to record an interview?

3. If a story's publication is likely to embarrass a source, do reporters have a responsibility to warn the source of that possibility? Does it matter whether the source is used to dealing with reporters?

4. Would you be willing to interview a mother whose son just died? Would it make a difference whether he drowned in a swimming pool, was murdered or was a convicted killer executed in a state prison?

5. Would you be willing to call a source at home at 2 a.m. to verify a fact or to ask that person's opinion of an issue in the news? Would it make a difference whether the source was a public figure or a private citizen?

6. If you promised to protect a source's identity, would you be willing to spend a year in jail rather than obey a judge's order to identify the source?

7. If several students in your class plan to become reporters, ask why all of them have not learned to type and to take shorthand. Do you think their answers are reasonable?

Class Projects

1. List 10 interviewing tips provided by other sources in your school's library.

2. Interview an expert on body language or non-verbal communication, perhaps someone in your school's psychology or speech department, then report on the usefulness of this knowledge to journalists. You might also invite the expert to speak to your class.

3. Find an expert on interviewing, perhaps a faculty member in your school's psychology department, then interview that expert. You might also invite the expert to speak to your class.

4. Interview government officials who frequently deal with reporters. Ask those officials what they like and dislike about interviews and how they try to handle the interviews and the reporters conducting those interviews.

5. Ask several government officials which local reporters are the best interviewers, then interview those reporters about their interviewing techniques. You might invite one of those reporters to speak to your class.

6. Ask every student in your class to write one paragraph about the three most newsworthy experiences in their lives. Then select the students with the most interesting experiences and have your entire class interview them and write news stories about their experiences.

Suggested Readings

Arlen, Michael J. "The Interview." *The New Yorker*, Nov. 10, 1975, p. 141.

Babb, Laura Longley. *Writing in Style*. Boston: Houghton Mifflin, 1975.

Best Newspaper Writing. St. Petersburg, Fla.: Modern Media Institute. (This book, published every year since 1979, contains prize-winning articles, followed by the editors' comments and question-and-answer sessions with the writers. Several of the writers have published exceptional interviews, and some discuss their interviewing techniques.)

Biagi, Shirley. *Interviews That Work: A Practical Guide for Journalists*. Belmont, Calif.: Wadsworth, 1985.

Brady, John. *The Craft of Interviewing*. Cincinnati: Writer's Digest, 1977.

Donaghy, William C. *The Interview: Skills and Applications*. Glenview, Ill.: Scott Foresman and Company, 1984.

Harrall, Stewart. *Keys to Successful Interviewing*. Norman: University of Oklahoma Press, 1954.

Hentoff, Nat, et al. "The Art of the Interview." *(More)*, July 1975, p. 11.

McCombs, Maxwell, Donald Lewis Shaw and David Grey. *Handbook of Reporting Methods*. Boston: Houghton Mifflin, 1976.

Metzler, Ken. *Creative Interviewing*. Englewood Cliffs, N.J.: Prentice-Hall, 1977.

Rivers, William L. *Finding Facts: Interviewing, Observing, Using Reference Sources*. Englewood Cliffs, N.J.: Prentice-Hall, 1975.

Sherwood, Hugh C. *The Journalistic Interview*. 2nd ed. New York: Harper & Row, 1972.

Sincoff, Michael Z., and Robert S. Goyer. *Interviewing*. New York: Macmillan Publishing Company, 1984.

Stewart, Charles J., and William B. Cash, Jr. *Interviewing Principles and Practices*. 3rd ed. Dubuque, Iowa: Wm. C. Brown, 1985.

Turkel, Studs. *Working: People Talk About What They Do All Day and How They Feel About What They Do*. New York: Pantheon, 1974.

Webb, Eugene J., and Jerry Salancik. *The Interview, or The Only Wheel in Town. Journalism Monographs*, no. 2. Austin, Texas: Association for Education in Journalism and Mass Communication, 1966.

Yates, Edward D. *The Writing Craft*. 2nd ed. Raleigh, N.C.: Contemporary Publishing, 1985.

EXERCISE 1
Interviews and Polls

INTERVIEW: ROBBERY VICTIM

INSTRUCTIONS: Write a news story based on the following interview with Michele Schipper, a sophomore majoring in journalism at your college. The interview provides a verbatim account of a robbery that occurred yesterday. "Q" stands for the questions Ms. Schipper was asked during an interview this morning, and "A" stands for her answers, which may be quoted directly. (This is a true story, told by a college student.)

Q: Could you describe the robbery?

A: I pulled up into the parking lot of a convenience store on Bonneville Drive, but I pulled up on the side and not in front where I should have, and I was getting out of my car, and I was reaching into my car to pull out my purse when this guy, 6 foot tall or whatever, approached me and said, "Give me your purse." I said, "OK." I barely saw him out of the corner of my eye. And then, I, um, so I reached in to get my purse. And I could see him approaching a little closer. Before then, he was 4 or 5 feet away. So I turned around and kicked him in the groin area, and he started going down, but I was afraid he wouldn't stay down, that he would seek some kind of retribution. So when he was down, I gave him a roundhouse to the nose. I just hit him as hard as I could, an undercut as hard as I could. And I could hear some crunching, and some blood spurted, and he went on the ground, and I got in my car, and I went away. I called the cops from a motel down the street. They asked where he was last I seen him, and I said, "On the ground."

Q: Did the police find him?

A: No, he was gone.

Q: Had you taken judo or some type of self-defense course?

A: No, but I used to be a tomboy, and I used to wrestle with the guys, my good friends, when I was young. It was a good punch. I don't know, I was just very mad. My dad, he works out with boxing and weightlifting and everything, and I've played with that, so I've got the power.

Q: Could you describe the man?

A: I didn't see him well enough to identify him, really, but I hope he thinks twice next time.

Q: What time did the robbery occur?

A: This was about 4 in the afternoon, broad daylight, but there were no other cars parked around, though.

Q: Did you see the man when you drove up, or was he hiding?

A: There was a dumpster, and I guess he came from behind the dumpster, like he was waiting there, just like he was waiting there. And I guess he was waiting around the dumpster, because no one was standing around when I pulled up, I remember that.

Q: Were there any witnesses who could describe the man?

A: There was no one around, there were no cars parked. The clerks were inside the store. I didn't see any pedestrians around and, after I did it, I didn't wait to find if there were any witnesses because I wanted to leave right away.

Q: Was the man armed?

A: Out of the corner of my eye I realized I didn't see any weapon. And I guess I thought he was alone. You register some things; you just don't consciously realize it.

Q: What was your first reaction, what did you think when he first approached and demanded your purse?

A: I didn't think of anything, really, you know. I just reacted. I was very, really indignant. Why, you know, just because he wanted my purse, why should he have it? There was really only $10 in there, and I probably wouldn't really do it again in the same situation. And my parents don't know about it because they would be very angry that I fought back.

Q: Had you ever thought about being robbed and about what you would do, about how you would respond?

A: It just came instinctively, and after the incident, you know, I was shaking for about an hour afterwards.

Q: About how long did the robbery last?

A: It really only lasted a second, just as long as it would take for you to kick someone and then to hit them and then drive away in the car. It really only lasted a second.

EXERCISE 2
Interviews and Polls

INTERVIEW: MURDER TRIAL

INSTRUCTIONS: Write a news story based on the following transcript from a murder trial. "Q" stands for the questions of District Attorney Jeffery Milan, and "A" stands for the answers of Frank Biegel, one of the defendants. The questions and answers are the men's exact words and may be quoted directly.

BACKGROUND INFORMATION: Biegel, 43, of 782 12th Ave. and Eric A. Knapp, 27, of 2314 N. 11th St. are accused of robbing a service station of $83 last July and of abducting and murdering the attendant, Larry Totmann, age 17. Biegel testified this morning, the second day of the trial.

Q: Well, let me ask you this. Did you commit a robbery at a service station on Baytree Road last July 14?
A: Yes sir, I did.

Q: And did you help take the attendant, Larry Totmann, out to a campground somewhere away from that station?
A: Yes sir.

Q: And did you personally see Eric Knapp, your co-defendant, shoot and kill that attendant?
A: Yes sir.

Q: Describe for us how you and Knapp went about robbing and murdering Totmann.
A: It wasn't me. It was Knapp that shot the kid, not me. We had gone up to the gas station, got my car filled with gas. While I was . . . I went in the bathroom. While I was in the bathroom some other people drove up in a car, young kids it sounded like, and they had an argument with the attendant about using the telephone. When it was all over, I came out, and I got back in the car while Knapp put a gun on him.

Q: All right. Did the young people who had driven up, did they leave before you got back into the car?
A: Yes sir.

Q: Then what happened?
A: I started the car, and Knapp made the kid take all the money out of the register, and he found a gun hidden under the counter and put it in a box with the money.

Q: Tell us what happened after that.
A: Well, sir, Knapp told the kid to get into the car with us, and, uh, I drove out of town about five miles.

Q: Where was Knapp all that time?
A: He was in the back seat with the kid. He had his gun on him, and the box with the money.

Q: And then what happened?
A: I was driving out toward a campground I use sometimes, and Knapp told me to stop. He told the kid to get out of the car and lay down in some bushes along the road.

I didn't know he was going to shoot the kid, I swear. The kid hadn't caused us any trouble, and I thought we'd just dump him there so he couldn't call the cops right away.

Q: But Knapp shot him, didn't he?
A: Yes sir.

Q: How many times?
A: Four. He fired four shots. I don't know how many times he hit him.

Q: Did Knapp shoot him in the head?
A: Well, sir, I couldn't see that. It was dark, and they were off the side of the road. I just heard the shots and saw like blue flames coming out of his gun.

Q: Uh, how far away from Totmann was Knapp when the shots were fired?
A: Not over three or five feet. He was standing right over him.

Q: Did Totmann say anything or try to run away?
A: No, he just kept lying there. He'd done everything we said, and I don't think he expected it. He just lay there; he never moved.

Q: What . . . well, what did you do after that?
A: I drove Eric home. We had a couple beers at his apartment and divided the money. There wasn't much, not even a hundred dollars.

Q: What did you do with the gun?
A: The next night we went out and threw both guns down a sewer. It was over on the other side of town, near a ballpark.

Q: Do you know why Knapp decided to kill Totmann?
A: He told me the kid recognized him, that the kid had seen him before. And he . . . he was afraid the kid might've seen my license number, the license number on my car.

Q: Why didn't you try to prevent the murder?
A: How could I? I didn't know he was going to shoot anyone, I really didn't. We'd never talked about that. I thought we'd just drop the kid there and leave.

Q: Can you tell us why you've decided to confess?
A: The murder wasn't my idea; I didn't pull the trigger. I didn't know Eric was going to shoot the kid. I don't think I should die, and I thought maybe if I cooperated, I wouldn't get the death penalty.

Q: Have the police or anyone else promised you anything in return for testifying against Knapp?
A: No sir. No one's promised me anything, nothing at all. I wish they would.

EXERCISE 3
Interviews and Polls

INTERVIEW: RAPE TRIAL

INSTRUCTIONS: Write a news story based on the following interview with District Attorney Jeffery Milan. "Q" stands for the questions he was asked during an interview in his office this morning, and "A" stands for his answers, which may be quoted directly.

BACKGROUND INFORMATION: On the 23rd of last month, Wilma Cele Dolezar, a 63-year-old widow, was raped in her home at 1947 S. Georgia Ave. Mrs. Dolezar, who lived alone, told police the assailant forced his way into her home shortly after 10 p.m. In addition to raping her, the assailant beat Mrs. Dolezar and took about $50 from her purse. Two days later, a former neighbor, Randall Sylvester Burrell, 23, no permanent address, was arrested and charged with the crime. Burrell is being held in county jail, and his trial on charges of rape, robbery and aggravated assault is scheduled to begin at 10 a.m. next Monday.

Q: We've just learned that Mrs. Dolezar has died. Have you been informed of that?
A: Yes, one of her daughters called my office about an hour ago.

Q: That's unusual, isn't it, for the victim's relatives to notify you?
A: Yes, but she's really upset. She thinks Burrell is responsible for her mother's death, and now she's afraid that he'll go free.

Q: That's why I'm here. There weren't any other witnesses, and you needed Mrs. Dolezar's testimony. What's going to happen now, with her dead?
A: I think that . . . we're going to find that we can't proceed without her.

Q: But wouldn't she be alive if it wasn't for the attack? Can't you charge Burrell with murder?
A: We've talked about that, but I don't think we could prove it. Mrs. Dolezar had a weak heart. You . . . she's had a couple heart attacks in the past, and she's been on medication for years. She survived the rape and beating—that was a month ago, so it'd be hard to tie the heart attack to Burrell at this date.

Q: Have you talked to her doctors?
A: Did that yesterday. We wanted to talk to her before the trial, and I sent someone to her home last week, and we found out she was in the hospital again, so we were getting ready to postpone the trial. When we learned she was seriously ill, that she might die, I called her doctor, and he said there's no way he could testify that the attack had anything to do with this, that she might have died anyway. Or, it may be murder. There's just no way of telling for certain in something like this.

Q: Was her testimony really that crucial?
A: There are some facts that she alone possessed knowledge of.

Q: Is there anything else you can do?
A: We'd been trying for the past two weeks to negotiate a plea with Burrell. Under the terms discussed, he'd have pleaded guilty to the charge of rape in exchange for a maximum sentence of 10 years, and we'd have dropped the other charges, but he's not going to do that now. He's not that stupid.

Q: Then there's nothing you can do?

A: We're going to try to salvage the case. We hope to persuade the judge to allow the state to use as evidence the deposition Mrs. Dolezar made shortly after the attack. But that's an iffy proposition, and Burrell's attorney will oppose it, will vigorously oppose it.

Q: When will you see the judge?

A: He's agreed to hear the matter at nine Monday morning. If he approves our motion, the trial will begin at 10 on all three charges. If not, Burrell goes free.

EXERCISE 4
Interviews and Polls

INTERVIEW: RESTAURANT MURDER

INSTRUCTIONS: Write a news story about the following interview with a bookkeeper at the North Point Inn. "Q" stands for the questions she was asked during an interview at her home this morning, and "A" stands for her answers, which may be quoted directly. (The interview is based upon an actual case: a robbery and murder at an elegant restaurant.)

Q: Could you start by spelling your name for me?
A: N-i-n-a C-o-r-t-e-z.

Q: You work as a bookkeeper at the North Point Inn?
A: Yes, I've been there seven years.

Q: Would you describe the robbery there yesterday?
A: It was about 9 in the morning, around 7 or 8 minutes before 9.

Q: Is that the time you usually get there?
A: At 9 o'clock, yes.

Q: How did you get in?
A: I've got a key to the employee entrance in the back.

Q: Was anyone else there?
A: Kevin Blohm, one of the cooks. He usually starts at 8. We open for lunch at 11:30, and he's in charge.

Q: Did you talk to him?
A: He came into my office, and we chatted about what happened in the restaurant the night before, and I asked him to make me some coffee. After he brought me a cup, I walked out to the corridor with him. That was the last I saw him.

Q: What did you do next?
A: I was just beginning to go through the receipts and cash from the previous night. I always start by counting the previous day's revenue. I took everything out of a safe, the cash and receipts, and began to count them on my desk.

Q: About how much did you have?
A: $6,000 counting everything, the cash and receipts from credit cards.

Q: Is that when you were robbed?
A: A minute or two or less, a man came around the corner, carrying a knife.

Q: What did you do?
A: I started screaming and kicking. My chair was on rollers, and when I started kicking, it fell. I fell on the floor, and he reached across my desk and grabbed $130 in $5 bills.

Q: Did he say anything?
A: No, he just took the money and walked out.

Q: Was he alone?
A: I don't think so. I heard someone—a man—say, "Get that money out of there." Then someone tried to open the door to my office, but I'd locked it. Three or four minutes later, the police were there.

Q: Is that when you found Mr. Blohm?
A: I went into the hallway with the police and saw blood on a door in the reception area. It was awful. There was blood on the walls and floor. Kevin was lying on the floor, dead. He had a large knife wound in his chest and another on one hand.

Q: Can you describe the man who robbed you?
A: He was about 5 feet 10, maybe 6 feet tall, in his early 20s, medium build.

Q: What was he wearing?
A: Blue jeans, a blue plaid button-up shirt and blue tennis shoes.

Q: Did you see his face?
A: He had a scarf, a floral scarf, tied around the lower part of his face, cowboy style. It covered the bottom half of his face.

Q: Did the man look at all familiar, like anyone you may have known or seen in the restaurant?
A: No.

Q: Did you notice anything unusual that day?
A: I saw a car in the parking lot when I came in, one I didn't recognize. It didn't belong to anyone who worked there, but that's all I remember.

Q: Do you have any idea why someone stabbed Blohm?
A: No. Kevin might have gotten in his way or tried to stop him or recognized him or something. I don't know. I didn't see it. I don't know anything else.

EXERCISE 5
Interviews and Polls

INTERVIEW: "OUT OF BODY"

INSTRUCTIONS: Write a news story about the following interview with Marty Murray. Assume that she returned to work today after recovering from surgery. "Q" stands for the questions you asked during an interview at her office this morning, and "A" stands for her answers, which may be quoted directly. (Again, this is a true story: a verbatim transcript of an interview taped with Mrs. Murray. Moreover, she consented to the use of her real name. While writing the story, assume that she works in your community.)

Q: Could you begin by describing what happened during your surgery?
A: I went into the hospital for surgery—tonsil and adenoid removal. I came out of my body and could look down on the operating table. I never exactly saw my body lying on the operating table, but I saw the people all around me, and I knew it was me on the operating table. I saw the attendants and the nurses and the person who was handling the anesthesia and the attending physician standing right there. Then I went like a corkscrew, right through the top of the hospital. I heard a very loud noise, like a rush of wind, and it was almost like a train going through a long tunnel. The noise was very loud. I don't recall being frightened, but was perplexed and puzzled by it. It didn't scare me in the least, mainly because the place where I wound up was so peaceful and quiet, and I remember it was kind of cold too. I remember the sensation of coldness. I don't know whether to call them people or beings, but the people communicated with each other, not through words, but with telepathy, and I could tell they were communicating with one another. I couldn't understand it, but they understood each other.

Q: Other people have had similar experiences at times they were near death. Did you feel that happened to you—that you nearly died during the operation?
A: I don't know. I was never told, but I was under a general anesthesia and could have been.

Q: The people you saw, what did they look like?
A: They were beings. I don't remember seeing them. I only remember being aware of their presence.

Q: What else do you remember?
A: I remember a light. It seemed like the light came after the loud noise, the whoosh and the very fast trip. I mean it was just—the speed the trip took—it was just incredible. It was just an incredibly quick journey that defied everything I had ever known about and, what was so convincing about it was that, in my wildest imagination, I never could have dreamed this up. That is why I am so convinced that it actually happened, because I am a practical person. I am a very practical, down-to-earth person, always wanting to find the scientific proof for this or that, and I have no explanation for what did happen except that it really did happen.

Q: Was it a frightening experience?
A: No, it was not frightening. It was not frightening at any time. Even though it was a strange and bizarre experience, it was never frightening. And it really was out of this world.

Q: It was off in space somewhere?
A: Somewhere away from here. Far away.

Q: Can you describe where it was?
A: It was up in the atmosphere. It wasn't on earth. It wasn't on clouds. It was in space.

Q: Have you ever met anyone who had a similar experience?
A: No, but when I've told people, I've had them tell me, "Well, my grandmother had that happen to her," or "I know of someone that happened to." I've never actually spoken to anyone else who had the experience.

Q: Were you always able to look down—even when you were off in space—look down into the operating room and see all those people around the table?
A: It seemed like the table itself went up. The whole insides of the operating room: the table, myself, the persons attending me and myself, out of the body, looking on the whole scene, were transported to a different place.

Q: The doctors and all went off in space with you?
A: Yes.

Q: Suddenly . . . and then you went back to sleep?
A: I woke up. I didn't see that scene anymore. I was in the recovery room trying to tell about the experience.

Q: Did you have any sense of time?
A: No, I really didn't. I had no concept of the time or of the distance traveled. It could have been one second, or it could have been an eternity.

Q: Has the experience changed your feelings about death?
A: Absolutely! I would not fear death. It was not a frightening thing. It was kind of a comforting thing and, I guess if I had to think about what death might be like, it was not anything to be frightened of. I would not want to leave two children—I have two children now—I would like to see the children raised to be adults themselves, but I would not be afraid to die. I'll never think that a person just dies with his body. There's much more to it than that. Basically, it made me not be afraid to die.

Q: And you seem to remember everything?
A: Yes, I sure do. It's something that a person could never forget. Never! Once something like that has happened to you, you could never forget the emotions. I'm kind of at a loss to express myself because so many of the things that happened to me—because we don't have those concepts on earth, we don't even have the words to describe what happened, and so the words themselves fail to describe the entire experience because it was so different from anything I have ever encountered.

EXERCISE 6
Interviews and Polls

INTERVIEW: ACCIDENT VICTIM

INSTRUCTIONS: Write a news story based on the following interview with Steven Michalano, a history major at your college. The interview provides a verbatim account of an actual auto accident and lawsuit. Only the names of the bar and the people involved in the story have been changed. "Q" stands for the questions Michalano was asked during an interview at his home this morning, and "A" stands for his answers, which may be quoted directly. In writing the story, emphasize not the accident, but the latest development—the settlement of Michalano's lawsuit.

Q: Could you tell me your name, age and address?
A: Steven Michalano. I'm 27. 132 East Muriel Street.

Q: Please describe the accident.
A: I was a passenger in a car and, and, a, uh, uh, a man in a pickup truck crossed the median, hit us head-on, and it was on, uh, the date was last year, May 26, about 6:30 at night, and, uh, it was a head-on collision.

Q: Were you driving?
A: I was in the, uh, front seat in a Ford Fiesta. My girlfriend was driving, and this guy, William Soistman, hit us.

Q: What is your girlfriend's name?
A: Beverly Leeson.

Q: How old is she, and what's her address?
A: Well, she was 19 at the time. She's 20 now. Her address is 471 Eastbrook Ave.

Q: Was she hurt?
A: She sustained, uh, scars, um, on her ear, on her right knuckle, middle knuckle, and some scars on her leg where she was cut, and she had a concussion. She was in the hospital for 4 days.

Q: Could you describe your injuries?
A: I was trapped in the wreck for about 40 minutes, and it was in the rain and all, and they had to cut me out. I did sustain injuries. My pelvis was broken, snapped in half, uh, front and back. My foot was broken. I had traumatic phlebitis in my left leg, and then complications developed because, uh, my blood clotted, and, uh, nerve damage.

Q: Could you describe your injuries again? I'm not certain that I understand all of them.
A: Pelvis, broken front and back. Left foot, broken. Nerve damage in my left leg, and traumatic phlebitis. And then, you know, just cuts and stuff.

Q: What's phlebitis?
A: It's just where the blood coagulates, and there was no blood flowing through my leg, and if it's not corrected, the leg has to be amputated.

Q: Were you in a hospital very long?
A: I was in the hospital for the summer. I was in there for a long time. But I was in intensive care, uh, for about 5 days, and they twice had that code 90 thing or

whatever it's called where, uh, they thought I was going to die. The bad thing was that, for the first week, I was on morphine, and, and I could talk to people and everything, but then after that, because of the blood clotting, I had to have blood thinner, and so I couldn't even take aspirin. And then the pain was unbelievable. It was till late July. It was May 26 to late July, about 2 months, about 2 solid months. I couldn't move. I mean I couldn't move. I mean I wasn't paralyzed, but I mean I just lay flat on my back, and they put me in a bed that rocked back and forth 24 hours a day. But I didn't, like, move until, I went actually seven and a half weeks without moving. And, and, and, yeah. My hospital bills were $26,000.

Q: Was the other driver injured?

A: The guy who hit me, he was, uh, he was, uh, in the hospital about a month. William Soistman. I don't know how old he was, about 50-something. He was driving a Ford pickup truck.

Q: Where did the accident occur?

A: We were coming back to my place, and this guy left a bar on State Route 50. I was going east on 50 in the right-hand lane, and this guy was heading west from the bar in the right-hand lane. It's a four-lane road, four lanes altogether. I was about 200 yards from the bar when we collided.

Q: Can you describe the accident?

A: I don't recall. I mean, I didn't even see it. I was just totally, the next thing I know I just remember, uh, being in the paramedics' van. Beverly didn't see it coming either.

Q: Later, were you able to learn what happened?

A: This guy left the parking lot of a bar, Johnny's Lounge, and he went, he only made it about maybe 200 yards, then he went across the road and plowed head-on into us.

Q: Were you going very fast?

A: We were going, I guess, 50, and then he was going, I guess, 45 or 50, and came across the median.

Q: Did the police give him any blood or breath tests to determine whether he was drunk?

A: He was so injured and everything that, uh, they just took him to a hospital.

Q: Why did you file a lawsuit against the bar, against Johnny's Lounge?

A: Well, because, uh, because, uh, I knew it wasn't my fault. I wasn't even driving. The reason I sued the bar was because of, because of, uh, what, uh, we consider gross negligence because the guy was passed out at the bar, just totally asleep. And they, uh, two assistant managers, grabbed, they took him, threw him into his, uh, truck, with the keys. And you know, just like he didn't even make it 200 yards down the road, so I sued.

Q: When did you file the lawsuit?

A: That, that is, uh, a little blurred, but I remember, um, but, um, so, so, my dad says that I said, when he came into the, uh, uh, emergency room, and I was in really bad shape, and he says that I said, "Get the attorneys." And I don't even remember saying that, but, uh, they immediately got an investigator out there. And they could tell, evidently there were witnesses that saw him come from the bar. And my, uh, investigator went into the bar that night and got interviews and depositions from, uh, from people that work there and from the customers. So we were very fortunate to have somebody see the guy come from the bar. But it took a long time. Uh, they finally settled out of court yesterday.

Q: Why did you accept an out-of-court settlement?
A: We didn't even go to court. When we finally let them know that they were being sued, my firm had done a year's amount of research and everything, so they hit them pretty hard. Like, you know: "This is what we have. We're taking you to court unless you want to settle out." And you know, they just didn't. My God, the money that bar has, and they didn't want to have a risk of every Friday night or Saturday night, you know, a potential precedent being set, and they could be sued on every given weekend if stuff like this went to court. But then I could have lost too, so I didn't want to press it.

Q: How much did they give you?
A: They said $40,000 and I said $60,000, and then, uh, we got up to finally $50,000, plus all my hospital bills were covered by my own car insurance.

Q: Did you also sue the other driver?
A: This William Soistman, he didn't have anything, but I sued his insurance company.

Q: Why did you file that suit?
A: Why not? I mean, the guy, the guy came across the median in a truck, drunk. The guy that hit me, he never called or anything, so I didn't really give a damn. To tell you the truth, he never even said he was sorry. He's dead now. He died about a month ago.

Q: Did you win that case?
A: Um, well, you know, I got $50,000 from them, but then you have to pay your attorney fees.

NOTE: Assume that, after this interview, you called the owner of Johnny's Lounge, John Tillotsen. He confirmed the fact that he settled out of court for $50,000 and said that he had fired the two assistant managers who helped Soistman to his truck. However, Tillotsen refused to answer any other questions or to provide any other information about the case.

EXERCISE 7
Interviews and Polls

POLLS

INSTRUCTIONS: Interview a minimum of 10 people, about half of them men and half of them women. Ask them a single question concerning a controversial issue; then write a news story about their opinions. The respondents may be students, professors, non-academic employees, visitors or anyone else you encounter on your campus. Conduct your interviews separately, not simultaneously with other members of your class—if only because it is disconcerting to be approached by two or three people, all asking the same controversial question. Identify yourself, explain why you are conducting the poll, then ask the single question selected by your instructor or class. You may want to use one of the following:

1. Do you believe that newspapers and radio and television stations in the United States report the news fairly and accurately?

2. Should faculty members be allowed to date their students, or should your institution adopt some rules prohibiting the practice?

3. Would you want your state legislature to adopt a law making it legal—or illegal—for women to serve as surrogate mothers: to have and sell babies to childless couples?

4. If you saw another student cheating on a test, would you try to stop the student or report the student to your teacher? Why?

5. If the administrators at your school learned that several students had AIDS, would you want them to allow the students to attend classes with you? Why?

6. Do you favor the execution of criminals convicted of murder and other serious crimes?

7. Should the government prohibit the sale of pornographic magazines or the showing of pornographic movies?

8. Should churches and other religious organizations be required to pay property taxes for the municipal services, such as police and fire protection, they receive?

9. Should women under the age of 18 be allowed to obtain abortions without their parents' knowledge or consent?

10. Should married women be allowed to obtain abortions without their husbands' knowledge or consent?

11. Do you think that movies and television programs place too much emphasis on crime, sex and violence?

12. Should the government do more to limit the sale and possession of handguns?

Your instructor may ask you to conduct the interviews and to write your story within a single class period, or you may be allowed to complete the assignment outside class. However, if you do the work outside class, you may be asked to interview more than 10 people.

Go beyond the superficial and encourage people to respond with more than a simple yes or no. Ask people why they favor or oppose the issues and—if they respond with vague generalities—ask them to be more specific. The responses you obtain are vital; if the responses are dull, vague or unclear, your story will be just as uninteresting.

Your lead should summarize your findings—the opinion expressed by a majority of the people you interviewed. The lead must do more than report that you conducted a poll or that the people you interviewed were "divided" about an issue. People are divided about every controversial issue, and the fact that you conducted a poll is not news-worthy; only the results are likely to interest your readers. Leads should also be as specific as possible. Instead of reporting that a "majority" of the people you interviewed favored or opposed an issue, report that majority's exact size. Was it 51 percent, 84 percent or 99.7 percent? For these reasons, three of the following leads need to be revised. Only the fourth is well-written:

> One hundred college students were polled Tuesday about the nation's pornography laws. (This lead fails to report the news—the results of that poll.)

> One hundred college students responded with varied answers Tuesday when they were asked, "Should Congress legalize the sale of pornography?" (This lead states the obvious—the fact that people disagree about a controversial issue.)

> One hundred college students were interviewed Tuesday, and a majority said the sale of pornography should be legalized for adults, but not for children. (This lead is too vague—it fails to reveal the size of that majority.)

> BETTER: Sixty-eight out of 100 college students interviewed Tuesday said the federal government should legalize the sale of pornography to adults, but not to children.

After the lead, present two or three paragraphs of introductory material before you begin to quote specific individuals. The second and third paragraphs in your story might summarize other highlights or trends, and the fourth paragraph might quote the exact question that you asked each respondent. Shifting directly from the lead to a quotation will be too abrupt a transition and will make your story seem disorganized. Also, if the quotation placed in the second paragraph reflects the opinion of a single individual, it is probably not important enough to merit that position in the story.

Fully identify every person you quote. In addition to their names, identify students by their major and year in school, faculty members by their rank and department, and non-academic employees by their jobs. If some people refuse to identify themselves or to answer your questions, ask them why they are reluctant to respond and try to identify them by some other means, such as their age.

You do not have to quote everyone you interview, only the people who say some-thing colorful, important or unusual. Paraphrase or discard responses that are awk-ward, wordy, unclear or repetitious. If two people make similar replies, combine their responses in a single sentence or paragraph. However, because two people are unlikely to use exactly the same words, you cannot attribute a direct quotation to both of them. Instead, paraphrase their responses or indicate that several people expressed the same opinion, then quote one of those people to illustrate that point of view. For example:

> Lionel Jackson and Eugene Bushnell, both seniors majoring in political science, said the state's sales tax discriminates against the poor.

> Three students said they had dropped out of college for a year or more. Marsha Dilte, a senior, explained: "I was running out of money, and I really wasn't certain what I wanted to do. After two years of working as a secretary, I had enough money to finish college and knew I wanted to be a nurse."

Organize all the quotations in a logical order, grouping similar responses together and placing transitions between those groups. Look for trends—perhaps consistent differences between the responses of men and women, young and old, students and nonstudents. First quote people who expressed the majority viewpoint, then people who expressed opposing viewpoints. Some quotations may be divided into even smaller groups. For example: if the respondents who favor an issue give four reasons for their beliefs, you might begin by quoting respondents who mentioned the most popular reason, then quote respondents who cited the second, third and fourth most popular reasons.

Transitions should be interesting. Many summarize the viewpoint of the group of quotations that reporters are about to present. The following transitions appeared in a poll about high-school students' opinions of the Army. The paragraphs following each of these transitions quoted students who expressed the viewpoint that the paragraph summarized:

> Fourteen students said they consider service in the Army a patriotic duty.

> Seven students said they plan to join the Army because they want to travel but cannot afford to go overseas by themselves.

> Four women said the Army offers higher salaries than civilian employers and is more willing to promote women.

Vary your sentence structure and avoid beginning every sentence and every paragraph with the name of the respondent you are quoting. Also decide which of the people you interviewed made the most interesting statements, then devote several paragraphs to their remarks. If you quote 10 or 20 people but devote only one paragraph to each of their remarks, your story will seem too choppy and superficial.

Avoid repeating the words "yes" and "no" when reporting the opinions expressed by your respondents. If the fourth paragraph in your story repeats the question that each respondent was asked, and the tenth paragraph reports that, "Mary Alton responded 'Yes,'" readers may not understand that she was responding to the question presented six paragraphs earlier:

> Mary Alton responded, "Yes."
> REVISED: Mary Alton agreed that the president's relationship with Congress is deteriorating.

> None of them said yes when asked if the women's movement has affected their lives.
> REVISED: None of them said the women's movement has affected their lives.

Be specific and clear, even if it means that you must briefly restate an idea:

> Gayle Prince echoed the opinions expressed by Drucker.
> REVISED: Gayle Prince agreed that apartment complexes have a right to reject couples that have children.

> Sandy Roach more or less agreed with Miss Hass.
> REVISED: Sandy Roach agreed that government workers are overpaid but said it is the fault of politicians, not of the unions representing government workers.

Never criticize or attach any labels to your respondents' answers. Do not refer to any answers as "interesting," "thoughtful" or "uninformed." Simply report whatever your respondents said, and let your readers judge their remarks for themselves (your readers' conclusions may be quite different from your own). Also avoid making comments about the manner in which people responded to your questions, and be especially careful to avoid trite generalities. For example, do not report that one person seemed "sincere," or that another seemed "apathetic." However, you can report specific details, such as the fact that one person paused for nearly a minute before answering your question and that person talked about the question for more than 30 minutes.

Some of the people you attempt to interview may be undecided on or unfamiliar with your topic. People who are undecided or uninformed usually constitute a small minority and can be mentioned in your story's final paragraphs. In the final paragraphs you might also describe the methods you used to conduct your poll: the exact number of people you interviewed and the way you selected those people. Never summarize or comment on your findings in the final paragraphs; a news story contains only one summary, and it belongs in the lead.

Newspapers often conduct informal polls of this type, because they are fast and cheap, but they are often inaccurate. The polls are so notoriously inaccurate that newspapers have begun to conduct more systematic studies, using techniques developed by social scientists. In the past, when reporters interviewed 50 or 100 people on a street corner, they could not generalize about the results of their poll because those 50 or 100 people were unlikely to be typical of everyone in their communities. For that reason, you can report only the opinions of the 10 or 20 people you interview; you cannot suggest that other people on your campus share their opinions. Using more scientific techniques, reporters at many newspapers now conduct their polls by selecting a random sample of the people living in their communities—usually a sample of several hundred people. Because of their more scientific procedures and carefully worded questions, the reporters can accurately determine the public's opinions about important issues and the way people will vote in elections.

18 Public Affairs Reporting

Previous chapters described the system of beats that reporters use to gather local news. Normally, the most important beats are government offices: police stations, city halls, courthouses and federal buildings, for example. Reporters assigned to those offices visit them daily, gathering information and cultivating sources among the people who work there.

New reporters are often assigned to their cities' police and fire departments. The stories that arise there tend to be simple, requiring little expertise. After a year or two, a small daily may transfer the reporters to more important beats, perhaps their city hall or county courthouse. At larger dailies, the reporters covering those beats are seasoned professionals. City hall and county courthouse reporters must be familiar with their communities and with the people who live there. They must also know their local officials and understand how cities work. In addition, the reporters must be able to write good, clear stories about complicated issues.

The best public affairs reporters do more than describe events. They explain why the events occurred and how they are related to other issues in the news. The best reporters also produce stories that are interesting—and that clarify the jargon used by government officials.

The Leads of Public Affairs Stories

Every lead should emphasize the news—the latest, most interesting and most important developments. Unfortunately, many of the stories written about public affairs are flat and lifeless. A typical lead might report that:

A development firm is being sued for breach of contract by its partner in a joint venture.

Reporters interview New York
Mayor Ed Koch.

The opening arguments were heard in Circuit Court in the trial of Willie Keaton of 4909 Leonard Drive on charges of burglary and petty theft.

A special task force appointed by the mayor has recommended the establishment of a central management group to coordinate housing programs, establish support services— such as job placement—and develop and support legislation that addresses the problems of the homeless.

These leads are dull and unintelligible because they contain unfamiliar terms and abstract generalities.

Some topics are less interesting than others, but that is rarely a valid excuse for writing a dull lead or weak story. Some reporters write dull leads because they do not understand a topic or fail to notice (and emphasize) its most interesting details:

The residue in an empty barrel exploded Monday, severely burning a 37-year-old man who was sawing it in half to make a barbecue pit.

A 73-year-old widow lay bound and gagged on a bed for nearly two days after burglars ransacked her home.

City commissioners voted Monday to rename a ball field in memory of a 13-year-old Little League shortstop killed by lightning.

Thus, public affairs reporters do not write good leads simply because they are given good topics. Good leads are a matter of thought and emphasis. Reporters from competing dailies often cover the same stories, and some of their leads are dull and unimaginative. Yet other leads—the leads written by their competitors—sparkle. Here are three more examples:

FIRST REPORTER: Burglars robbed the home of a 36-year-old man while he was sleeping.
SECOND REPORTER: Burglars entered a home occupied by a man, a dog and a talking parrot, and—without causing an alarm—managed to steal almost $3,000 worth of cash and household goods.

FIRST REPORTER: Donna Sokoler, 17, 5810 Cascade Way, was sentenced to three consecutive life terms after being convicted of three counts of murder, despite the defense of insanity.
SECOND REPORTER: A 17-year-old high-school senior who pleaded that television violence drove her insane has been convicted of poisoning her mother and two brothers.
She was sentenced to three life terms.

FIRST REPORTER: A local couple has filed suit against Sears, Roebuck & Co., charging that a single-mantle propane lantern malfunctioned and caused the death of their son.
SECOND REPORTER: A local couple is suing Sears, Roebuck & Co., charging that their son died of carbon monoxide poisoning because a propane lantern malfunctioned in an old school bus he used as a camper.

The following story illustrates the same principle. The first account emphasizes a squabble between government agencies. The second account emphasizes the story's impact upon teen-age girls:

FIRST REPORTER: The "squeal rule," the newest proposed amendment to the Public Health Service Act, comes into direct conflict with the philosophy of the County Health Department, according to its director, Kurt Scorse.
The squeal rule, introduced in Congress Monday, would require federally funded public health clinics to notify parents within 10 days if their children have been given prescriptive contraceptives.
SECOND REPORTER: County health officials fear that a new federal rule "will cause an epidemic of teen-age pregnancies."

To make your stories more interesting, demonstrate their relevance to your readers. During the 1930s, one of New York's most famous editors, Stanley Walker, explained that, "A good story is one in which the average reader, whoever he is, can imagine himself, and say, subconsciously, 'Why, that could happen to me!'" Frank Caperton, managing editor of The Indianapolis News, recently added that: "Reporters cover a lot of meetings and tell what happens, and that's very important—they need to do that. But they also should be able to transcend that, to tell why the actions are important for their readers."

Again, you can often demonstrate a story's relevance by changing the angle or emphasis in your lead:

A statewide study of 8,400 students aged 13 to 19 found that 34 percent had shoplifted.
REVISED: About one out of every three teen-agers you know may have shoplifted.

The County Commissioners last night voted 7–2 in favor of constructing a sewage plant that will cost $228 million and handle 140 million gallons of sewage each day.
REVISED: The County Commissioners last night voted 7–2 in favor of constructing a $228 million sewage plant. To pay for it, the average homeowner's sewer fees will triple to $90 a month.

Public affairs reporters with an eye for detail can also add some description to their stories. Good description makes even routine stories come alive:

. . . The jury deliberated nearly seven hours before deciding that Zaslow acted in self-defense when he kicked a police officer.

Zaslow waited nervously outside the courtroom. Dressed in a T-shirt and jeans, he paced the hallway, a cigarette in his hand all the while.

Zaslow showed no emotion when the jury announced its verdict. However, when Judge Joseph Miklosi said he was free to go, Zaslow turned to the back of the nearly empty courtroom and smiled at his father. He then walked out a side door.

Avoiding the Obvious and the Routine

Public affairs reporters must be careful to avoid emphasizing routine or unimportant details, especially in their leads. Every weekday, Americans file thousands of wills, lawsuits, bankruptcy petitions and other legal documents, and they file all those documents in a few government offices. Good leads should emphasize the documents' content, not the fact that they were filed:

Attorneys for Thomas J. Totten, a real estate agent who died last week, filed his will in Probate Court on Wednesday.
REVISED: Real estate agent Thomas J. Totten has left his entire estate, valued at more than $2 million, to the Salvation Army.

A lawsuit seeking $7.5 million for a 7-year-old girl today was filed in Circuit Court.
REVISED: A lawsuit filed today for a 7-year-old girl who was struck by three bullets seeks $7.5 million from a hunter who says he was aiming at a deer.

A local couple Tuesday filed a bankruptcy petition in the U.S. District Court here.
REVISED: A dentist and his wife, who listed $240,000 in debts and $47 in assets, filed for bankruptcy Tuesday.

Unless reporters are careful, the leads for other types of public affairs stories also may state the obvious or emphasize the routine:

Due to differences that cannot be worked out, a woman married 17 years has filed for a divorce from her husband.

A police officer who became suspicious during a routine patrol last night found a man's body in a parked car.

Paramedics treated a woman after she was struck by a car while crossing Elm Avenue today.

Most divorces are caused by "differences that cannot be worked out," and every woman wanting a divorce seeks it "from her husband." Similarly, the police routinely patrol the nation's cities, and paramedics routinely treat the accident victims in their cities. Thus, all three leads need to be rewritten. The first lead might specify the irreconcilable differences that caused the divorce. The second lead might emphasize the victim's death rather than the discovery of the victim's body during a routine patrol, and the third lead might provide a more specific description of the accident or the severity of the woman's injuries.

Reporters should also avoid leads that contain several names. Especially in large cities, few readers are likely to know the people involved in most news stories. But even if those people are well-known, leads containing three or four names are likely to be dull. Normally, reporters emphasize what was said or done, not who was involved:

E. D. Farnsworth has filed a suit in county court charging Majik Rides, Inc., with negligence.
REVISED: A college teacher whose right leg had to be amputated after a Ferris wheel he was riding with his children collapsed is seeking $850,000 in damages.

Christine Ann Mosher is suing Superintendent of Schools Marcia Pagozalski, Kennedy High School Principal Thomas R. Gurney and Standard Guaranty Insurance Co. in the drowning of her daughter, Margaret.

REVISED: A mother who charges that her 15-year-old daughter drowned in a high-school pool that was left unsupervised has filed a $2.5 million lawsuit against school officials and the company that insures them.

Mistakenly, other reporters begin too many public affairs stories in chronological order. As a consequence, they fail to emphasize the stories' most interesting and important details. Normally, the way a story ended—its consequences—is more newsworthy than the way it began:

An unidentified man called police late Friday night to report a disturbance in a parking lot at 541 Barton Ave.
REVISED: Three high-school students were hospitalized Friday night, and police say at least a dozen others suffered minor injuries, in a fight that started in a parking lot after a basketball game.

A murder trial began Monday with opening statements by the prosecution and defense.
REVISED: Prosecutors in the murder trial of Loretta Lorenzo Perry charged Monday that she fired three shots into her husband's back while he was sleeping, then set fire to his bed.

Before they were revised, both leads emphasized the obvious or unimportant. People normally call the police to quell disturbances, and many refuse to reveal their identities. Leads should emphasize the news—the fight and the injuries it caused—not the fact that an anonymous caller reported the disturbance to police. Similarly, most trials begin with opening statements by attorneys for the prosecution and defense. A good lead should summarize the attorneys' most newsworthy statements.

Emphasizing the Specific, Not the Technical, in Legal Stories

New police reporters often place too much emphasis on the technical charges filed against the defendants in criminal cases. News stories should describe the specific crimes involved, not just the legal charges. Because they are less specific, the legal charges often fail to state clearly what happened. Moreover, the same legal charges could be repeated in thousands of stories:

A businessman pleaded guilty Monday to a charge of attempted aggravated battery against his wife and son.
REVISED: A businessman pleaded guilty Monday to attacking his wife and son with a tire iron.

Three people arrested in a church parking lot Sunday morning were charged with petty larceny.
REVISED: Three people arrested in a church parking lot Sunday morning were charged with siphoning gasoline from a car.

When defendants appear in court, reporters should provide a specific summary of each day's proceedings. Mistakenly, beginners often emphasize a witness's identity or a general topic instead of specifically summarizing what the witness said about that topic. But if reporters fail to summarize the proceedings, their leads will be much less interesting and, once again, will sound too much like other leads. Leads usually do not have to reveal whether a witness testified for the state or for the defense; that can be reported later. The witness's testimony—a summary of the witness's most important remarks—is more important:

A 13-year-old girl testified for the state Wednesday in the murder trial of her mother.
REVISED: A 13-year-old girl testifying at her mother's murder trial Wednesday said she heard her parents arguing, then saw her mother chase her father into a bedroom and stab him with a steak knife.

The trial of William Allen Lee, who is accused of shooting his girlfriend, began Tuesday with the testimony of a prosecution witness who described what he saw on the day of the murder.

REVISED: A neighbor testified Tuesday that he saw William Allen Lee shoot his girlfriend, then carry her body into the house the couple shared at 914 W. 22nd St.

Similarly, stories about wills, lawsuits, bankruptcy petitions and other legal documents should summarize their specific content. The stories about most lawsuits explain why they were filed—why one person decided to sue another. And the stories about most wills describe an estate's value and disposition. However, the estate's recipients do not have to be identified by name in the lead:

The will of Marguerite Vernay, a long-time local resident, was filed in Probate Court on Wednesday.

REVISED: A 73-year-old woman who died last month left more than $160,000 to three neighbors who took her shopping once a week and invited her to their homes on holidays.

A woman who died last year has named her husband as the trustee and personal representative of her estate.

REVISED: A 37-year-old woman who established a chain of 82 restaurants left more than $800,000 to her husband but stipulated that he cannot remarry for at least five years.

In addition to emphasizing the unique content and specific details of a legal document, a lead should go on to emphasize unusual aspects of the document. The final paragraph in one news story revealed that a young man who robbed a restaurant apologized to the cashier, saying, "I'm sorry but my wife is going to have a baby, and I need your money." That quotation should have been moved to the story's lead. The following leads also emphasize the unusual, as opposed to routine, events:

Two police officers who charged a woman with shoplifting a $6.98 bottle of perfume Monday afternoon found more than $10,000 when they searched her purse.

The city is threatening to sue more than 700 people, including a member of the City Council and three police officers, because the checks used to pay their property taxes failed to clear their banks.

As all these examples indicate, the best leads tend to be the most specific ones. They provide a clear summary of each story's unique details. They clearly tell readers what happened or what was said or done:

GENERALITY: Beginning Jan. 1, county residents summoned for jury duty will be introduced to a new system.

REVISED: Beginning Jan. 1, county residents summoned for jury duty will be required to serve only two instead of five days.

GENERALITY: A local couple has filed a $500,000 lawsuit against Southern Airways, Inc., charging the airline with negligence.

REVISED: A 52-year-old man and his wife have filed a $500,000 lawsuit against Southern Airways, Inc., charging that the man was seriously injured when he fell 18 feet from a jetliner to a concrete runway.

GENERALITY: A suit filed in U.S. District Court charges the Moore Manufacturing Corp. with a violation of the Age Discrimination Employment Act of 1967.

REVISED: A 58-year-old salesman who says he was fired because of his age has filed a $600,000 lawsuit against Moore Manufacturing Corp.

Each of the following leads contains a number of errors, including generalities, routine details, technical charges and unfamiliar names. Notice how much more interesting the leads become after those errors are corrected:

Marilyn Curtin of 178 Crestview Circle was charged with one misdemeanor and two felonies following an altercation Friday night.

REVISED: A woman participating in an amateur topless contest at a local bar was charged with disorderly conduct, kicking a police officer and resisting arrest after she lost the contest Friday night.

Danny Doss Parker, 28, 122 Lake Sumpter Drive, was acquitted Monday of charges of sexual battery.

REVISED: After deliberating 16 hours, a jury found a 28-year-old attorney innocent of charges that he abducted and raped a neighbor.

Three college students, Frederick R. Little, Thomas Pohl and Mildred Cress, have been charged with grand theft in the second degree.

REVISED: Police have charged three college students with stealing $7 in coins and a cassette tape recorder from a parked car.

The Bodies of Public Affairs Stories

Avoiding Jargon

Public affairs reporters must be especially careful to avoid bureaucratic and technical jargon in the bodies of their news stories. The reporters covering government agencies gradually learn the jargon's meaning, become accustomed to its use and—if they are not careful—begin to use it in their stories. Much jargon is wordy and unnecessary. Moreover, many readers may not understand it:

By order of her last will and testament, the architect left her entire estate to her daughter.
REVISED: The architect left her entire estate to her daughter.

The men were released on their own recognizance.
REVISED: The men were released without having to post bail.

He asked the county to rezone the land from R-1AA to P-O and RMF-2.
REVISED: He asked the county to rezone the land from single-family residential (R-1AA) to professional office (P-O) and multiple-family residential (RMF-2).
OR: He asked the county to rezone the land to permit the construction of professional offices and multiple-family residences instead of single-family homes.

Jargon is also common in lawsuits. Plaintiffs frequently charge that they suffered "great mental and physical pain," and that defendants "acted in a careless and reckless manner." Other examples of the jargon found in lawsuits include:

She charges that she suffered permanent injury to her head, neck, torso, body and nervous system.
REVISED: She charges that she was permanently injured.

Mrs. Harris says the sidewalk was slippery, worn, cracked and unsafe to walk on.
REVISED: Mrs. Harris says the sidewalk was unsafe.

While writing about a lawsuit, there's rarely any need to go into the technical detail: to report that a couple is suing "individually and jointly," for example. If you add that the couple has charged a company "with strict liability, breach of implied warranty and negligence," few readers are likely to understand your story. Look for the specifics: the fact that the couple is upset because they found a bug in their beer.

There are thousands of other legal and technical terms—"ad valorem taxes," "capital outlays," "declaratory judgments," "perculation ponds," "promissory notes," "rapid infiltration basins," "secured and unsecured debts" and "tangible personal property," for example—that can be replaced by something simpler and more familiar. While writing about plans to fix a sewer system, one reporter explained that the repairs were necessary because of "groundwater infiltration." Another reporter explained, more clearly, that the sewer pipes were so old and cracked that water was leaking into them.

If a legal or technical term is essential to a story, define it:

> The store filed for protection under Chapter 11 of the federal bankruptcy laws. Chapter 11 will protect the store from creditors' lawsuits while it tries to reorganize.

> Police officers handcuffed the student and committed her to a hospital under the Baker Act. The Baker Act allows authorities to commit people for observation if they seem to be a threat to themselves or others.

Attributing Charges and Including Responses

Reporters assigned to cover government offices should critically examine all the information they are given and clearly attribute statements of opinion. This is especially critical in stories about lawsuits. Lawsuits present only the plaintiffs' charges; defendants are likely to deny those charges, and judges may rule (months or even years later) that the charges are unfounded. Consequently, reporters should carefully attribute those charges, clearly indicating that they are the plaintiffs' allegations, not accepted facts. For example:

> Because of the accident, Samuelson will require medical care for the rest of his life.
> REVISED: In the lawsuit, Samuelson says that because of the accident he will require medical care for the rest of his life.

> The passengers' personal baggage, which had been placed in racks above the seats, was not properly stored and, as a result of the careless driving of the bus driver, a heavy piece of baggage fell from one of the racks and struck Heinrich with great force and violence.
> REVISED: Heinrich's lawsuit charges that a suitcase fell from an overhead rack and struck his head.

Because of the danger of libel, few newspapers would report at an early stage of the proceedings that the bus driver acted carelessly. Consequently, that allegation was deleted when the sentence was revised.

Whenever possible, reporters should include the defendants' responses to the charges filed against them. If the legal documents do not include the defendants' responses, reporters can obtain them from the defendants or their attorneys. The following example and revision illustrate the inclusion of a defendant's response. However, they also illustrate the need to condense, to simplify and to attribute the claims made by a plaintiff:

> He was caused to slip, trip and fall as a direct result of the negligence and carelessness of the store because of a liquid on the ground. This fall injured his neck, head, body, limbs and nervous system and caused him to be unable to lead a normal life and to lose his normal wages for a prolonged period of time.
> REVISED: The suit charges that he slipped and fell on a wet sidewalk outside the store, dislocating his left arm and shoulder and tearing several ligaments.
> The store's manager has responded that, "He was running to get out of the rain, and he slipped on the wet pavement."

The Problem of Libel

Because many of the stories they write will harm someone's reputation, reporters covering the police and courts must be especially careful to avoid the problem of libel. As explained in Chapter 9, reporters can say that a person has been *charged* with a crime. However, reporters cannot say the person is *guilty* (regardless of any claims made by the police or other law enforcement officials) until *after* that person has been convicted by a judge or jury. Also, reporters must carefully identify everyone mentioned in their stories.

No one knows how many crimes occur each year; most are never reported to the police. Statistics compiled in one of the nation's largest states revealed that 803,509 crimes were reported in one year, and that the reports led to 438,222 arrests. But few of the arrests led to a trial or conviction. Only 20,020 of the cases—4.5 percent—resulted in a trial. And only 13,213 of the defendants—3.0 percent—pleaded or were found guilty.

Remember those statistics the next time you write about a crime. If you libel someone—if you report that a suspect arrested by the police is guilty—you may have a 97 percent chance of being wrong, of being unable to prove your allegation to a judge or jury.

Remaining Objective

Public affairs reporters also must be careful to avoid expressing their own opinions. They cannot editorialize or comment on the stories they cover. Their comments are rarely necessary and often confuse rather than clarify:

> Police are resting easier this morning after two bomb threats during the night proved to be hoaxes.

> A shopper learned Wednesday that taking too long to get through a grocery checkout line may lead to violence from those waiting impatiently behind her.

The first example seems to reflect a rather contrived attempt to update the story. But the statement is trite and simplistic. The same statement could be used in most crime and accident stories, since the police are usually happy when a case is resolved. Moreover, the statement is likely to be erroneous. Instead of resting after a hoax, the police normally respond to a number of other calls. The second lead fails to tell readers exactly what happened and is subjective (how does the reporter know whether or what the shopper learned?).

Other Guidelines

There are four additional guidelines that public affairs reporters should consider. First, reporters should be skeptical of the amounts of money demanded in lawsuits. Plaintiffs can demand any amount they want, even obviously exorbitant amounts. To attract more publicity, some lawyers encourage their clients to demand large amounts, often hundreds of thousands of dollars as compensation for minor injuries. The plaintiffs normally settle for much less, often a small fraction of the amounts they originally demanded. Consequently, leads generally should not emphasize any of those amounts.

Second, reporters often use too much attribution. You do not have to attribute uncontested facts provided by government officials, not even in leads:

> Two women entered the hotel at noon and robbed it of $640, according to a police report.
> REVISED: Two women entered the hotel at noon and robbed it of $640.

> Sheriff's deputies reported that one person was killed and three injured when two cars collided on State Route 17-92 at noon Friday.
> REVISED: One person was killed and three injured when two cars collided on State Route 17-92 at noon Friday.

You can often avoid excessive attribution by writing a summary lead, then adding a transition such as, "Witnesses gave this account. . . ." After the transition, you may be able to report the story without any further attribution.

Third, while describing a crime, do not mention the fact that it was committed by an "unidentified" man or woman. Criminals rarely announce their identities, and most crimes are never solved. Thus, most criminals are never "identified." Similarly, if the police do not know a criminal's identity, you cannot report that the police are looking for "a suspect." If the police do not know who committed a crime, they have no suspect.

Fourth, people normally "suffer" or "sustain" injuries. They "receive" gifts. While covering the police beat, also remember the differences between a robbery, burglary, theft and swindle.

Court documents, like police reports, provide all the information needed for routine news stories. Examples of such documents as well as sample police reports are reprinted in the following exercises, beginning with Exercise 3. Write a news story about each document, assuming that the police reports have been prepared by officers who investigated incidents in your community and that the legal documents have been filed in your city hall, county courthouse or federal building.

Most of the exercises use genuine copies of actual government documents. Even the most unusual police reports are based upon actual cases.

Write & Wrong ST. LOUIS POST-DISPATCH

By Harry Levins
Post-Dispatch Writing Coach

Reporters who write about government budgets find themselves working with numbers that stretch way past the experience of most people. In the coming year, for example, Missouri's state government will spend $4.5 billion. Putting that sort of total in perspective is tough; after all, it comes to $1 for every human being on Earth.

Terry Ganey faced the problem recently when he wrote that the state's budget left precious little in reserve. First, he spelled out the situation in the state's terms:

The budget . . . includes a $67.6 million operating reserve to maintain cash flow and handle emergencies.

But raw numbers mean little to the average reader. So Ganey decided to refine the numbers further:

While that sounds like a lot, it is less than 1.5 percent of the state's total spending and 2.8 percent of general tax revenue expenditures.

That helps considerably. Most readers grasp percentages more easily than whole numbers. Even so, Ganey decided to take one more step and put the numbers in terms that almost anybody could see clearly:

A comparison to the state's situation would be that of a family with a combined annual income of $30,000 setting a budget for a year that leaves $450 in the bank after all its anticipated bills are paid.

What a nice touch. Ganey had said in his lede that the state would have "a very thin bank account." And in his comparison with a middle-class family, Ganey drove home just how thin that bank account would be.

Some years back, Eliot Porter turned the same smooth trick in a story on the water supply in the St. Louis area. He mentioned how much water rolled by each day in the Mississippi River and then noted how much water St. Louis needed each day. The numbers were so big that they were, in effect, meaningless. But the next paragraph put the whole thing in focus. Porter wrote words to this effect:

In other words, a sightseer standing by the Arch to watch the river roll past need stand there only four minutes and 42 seconds to see all the water St. Louis needs that day.

The Coach is dredging the passage from memory, and the numbers are guesswork. But what the paragraph accomplished is clear:

1. It reduced big numbers to a total anybody could fit into perspective. Few people can picture millions of gallons of water, but most of us have a close idea of what four minutes and 42 seconds equals.

2. It gave the reader a specific frame for the numbers. Almost all of us have stood at the Arch and watched the river roll by. Porter's use of that image gave us something specific, something concrete to use as an aid to grasping the abstract concepts that we choose to call "numbers."

So good is Porter at this sort of thing that The New York Times lifted his explanation of how to visualize five parts of dioxin for each billion parts of soil:

That's the equivalent of five jiggers of vermouth in a thousand railroad tank cars of gin.

To help people grasp numbers, the people at Dow Chemical have put out a small pamphlet titled "How Big is 'Small'?" It says:

We often find reference to "parts per billion" or "parts per trillion" in our reading or conversations about trace impurities in chemicals.

What is a part per billion? How big is a part per trillion? And what about a part per quadrillion? Can we get a fix on these infinitesimally small quantities?

Well, if you're a 26-year-old male, for example, your heart beats about 72 times a minute . . . a part per billion is equal to one heartbeat out of all your heartbeats since birth (plus half of your prenatal experience)!

Let's start with a part per million, our largest scale . . . that's the equivalent of one automobile in bumper to bumper traffic stretching from Cleveland to San Francisco . . . or one drop of gasoline in a tankful of gas for a full-sized car . . . or one facial tissue in a stack of facial tissues higher than the Empire State Building. It's also one pancake in a stack of pancakes 4 miles high!

Still hungry? How about one 4-inch hamburger in a chain of hamburgers circling the Earth 2½ times at the Equator? That's equal to one part per billion . . . pass the mustard!

Some other comparisons . . . Part per billion
—One silver dollar in a roll of silver dollars stretching from Detroit to Salt Lake City . . .
—One kernel of corn in enough corn to fill a 45-foot silo, 16 feet in diameter . . .
—One sheet in a roll of toilet paper stretching from New York to London . . .
—One second of time in 32 years.

More comparisons . . . Part per trillion:
—One square foot of floor tile on a kitchen floor the size of Indiana . . .
—One drop of detergent in enough dish water to fill a string of railroad tank cars over 10 miles long . . .
—One second of time in the past 32,000 years.
—One mile on a 2-month journey at the speed of light (light travels at 186,000 miles per second).

How about something really small? Part per quadrillion:
—One postage stamp on a "letter" the size of California and Oregon combined . . .
—The palm of one's hand compared to the total land area of the United States . . .
—One human hair out of all the hair on the heads of all the people in the world . . .
—One mile on a journey of 170 light years . . .

To be sure, Dow has a vested interest in making big numbers look small. But we have our own vested interest: clarity. And in making things clear, we can go beyond Dow's comparisons and come up with our own.

We can use the volume of local landmarks like Busch Stadium; one billion equals a stadium sellout of every home game for almost 247 baseball seasons. For area, we can use the figures for St. Louis (61 square miles, or 39,040 acres), St. Louis County (500 square miles, or 320,000 acres) and Missouri (68,945 square miles, or 44,124,800 acres). Time—when expressed in local terms—is another handy device. For example, more than half a billion seconds have elapsed since the Arch was topped off.

Coming up with your own comparisons involves nothing more than a base figure and a calculator—or, as in Ganey's case, a pencil, a piece of paper and a touch of imagination.

(continued on next page)

☆ ☆ ☆

Two Roads Diverged Department

Here's the lede of a recent story; the emphasis is The Coach's:

BOSTON (UPI)—*Lead*, blamed for various mental and behavioral disorders in children, *has declined in the blood of Americans since unleaded gasoline became widely used, a federal study said today.*

No sentence can serve two ideas: for either it will distract from the one, and overemphasize the other; or else it will weaken the one, and lead the reader astray toward the other . . .

The lede above is a wearying example of the two-idea sentence. Reading a two-idea sentence can be like listening to a two-headed person when both heads are yakking at once. You get a lot of information, but sorting it out is difficult.

The main point of the UPI story was that Americans had less lead in their blood now that unleaded gasoline was widely used. That's a straightforward notion, simply grasped. So why clutter it up with the secondary information on what lead has been blamed for?

Fixing the lede would have been simple:

BOSTON (UPI)—*The level of lead in the blood of Americans has declined since unleaded gasoline became widely used, a federal study said today.*

Lead poisoning has been blamed for various mental and behavioral disorders in children.

The headline writer had no problem in slicing away the needless clause. The headline said: **Lead In Blood Down Since Fuel Shift**. That says it all—and says it without mentioning mental and behavioral problems in children.

Here's another example; pay special attention to the quotation in the second paragraph:

BEVERLY HILLS, Calif. (UPI)—Some of Richard M. Nixon's friends, con-ceding he made mistakes as president, *are forming a group to improve his image.*

"We all recognize that some mistakes were made," Pat Hillings, a former congressman and longtime Nixon friend said Wednesday . . .

The main point of the story is the formation of the group. Why clutter it up with the clause about mistakes? The point is secondary—and is made nicely in the following paragraph anyway. So leaving the clause in the lede amounts to redundancy. And redundancies are twice cursed: we can't afford the space, and our readers can't spare the time.

Wire services tend to overload stories with multi-idea sentences. The wire writers are rushed; the editors think that brevity takes priority over clarity. Besides, the wire service people can comfort themselves in the knowledge that editors at the receiving end can unscramble everything if they so choose.

After all, that's how it was done before the Teletype machine. The cable and telegraph editors would get cryptic messages—"Wilson arrive today crowd cheers Southampton"—and translate them into a news story: "President Woodrow Wilson stepped onto British soil at Southampton today to the cheers of a waiting crowd."

Today's wire and copy editors have the same privilege. We're under no obligation to publish two-idea sentences, just because the wire services send them. And reporters here are under no obligation to write two-sentence ideas, even though any edition of the Post-Dispatch carries a dismaying number of precedents.

☆ ☆ ☆

Typecast

A military atrocity has been making its way into our columns recently—the use of "-type" as a suffix. In the Army, a rifle becomes a "shoulder-type weapon." In newspaper writing, we see such examples as "suspension-type bridge," "modern-type architecture" and "office-type furniture." If some sort of extra word is needed—and in all three examples cited, none is—use "-style" or "type of."

Suggested Readings

Anderson, David, and Peter Benjaminson. *Investigative Reporting*. Bloomington, Ind.: Indiana University Press, 1976.

Bolch, Judith, and Kay Miller. *Investigative and In-Depth Reporting*. New York: Hastings House, 1978.

Hage, George S., Everette E. Dennis, Arnold H. Ismach and Stephen Hartgen. *New Strategies for Public Affairs Reporting.* 2nd ed. Englewood Cliffs, N.J.: Prentice-Hall, 1983.

Izard, Ralph S. *Reporting the Citizens' News: Public Affairs in Modern Society.* New York: Holt, Rinehart & Winston, 1982.

Kohlmeier, Louis Jr., John G. Udell and Laird B. Anderson. *Reporting on Business and the Economy.* Englewood Cliffs, N.J.: Prentice-Hall, 1981.

Lovell, Ronald P. *Reporting Public Affairs: Problems and Solutions.* Belmont, Calif.: Wadsworth, 1983.

Meyer, Philip. *Precision Journalism: A Reporter's Introduction to Social Science Methods.* 2nd ed. Bloomington, Ind.: Indiana University Press, 1979.

Mollenhoff, Clark R. *Investigative Reporting: From Courthouse to White House.* New York: Macmillan, 1981.

Schulte, Henry H. *Reporting Public Affairs.* New York: Macmillan, 1981.

Ullman, John H., and Steven Honeyman, eds. *The Reporter's Handbook: An Investigator's Guide to Documents and Techniques.* New York: St. Martin's Press, 1983.

EXERCISE 1
Public Affairs Reporting

EVALUATING LEADS

INSTRUCTIONS: Critically evaluate the following leads from public affairs stories. Discuss the leads in class and decide which are most effective, and why. As you evaluate the leads, look for general principles that will help you write better leads. For example: What common problems should you strive to avoid?

1. A man posing as a crime prevention officer tied and robbed an elderly woman Friday after she let him in to inspect her home.

2. The School Board has voted to grant teachers a 5.8 percent raise but complained that their union protects incompetent teachers and opposes merit pay for outstanding teachers.

3. The city's Crime Prevention Commission has completed its study and announced more than 60 recommendations Monday.

4. A local couple is suing a doctor and a hospital for brain damage suffered by their daughter as a result of improper monitoring during a routine operation.

5. A robbery victim opened testimony Wednesday in the first-degree murder and armed robbery trial of a 19-year-old woman.

6. An ad hoc committee Thursday made recommendations on zoning criteria for foster homes and foster group homes at a workshop session of the county commission.

7. Police say two men have been arrested and charged with burglary to a residence.

8. Two 16-year-old boys who heard burglars break into a neighbor's house Sunday night called the police, then deflated all four tires on the burglars' van.

9. A jury of four men and two women took only 15 minutes Thursday to convict a Montana man of selling 1,000 morphine tablets to undercover agents.

10. The First Federal Bank was evacuated Monday morning as police searched the premises for a bomb.

11. The county's Department of Community Affairs is presently undertaking several ambitious programs designed to benefit residents of the county.

12. A case involving a man who admitted committing three armed robberies may be dismissed because of a technical error.

13. A gunman jumped behind the customer service counter of a local department store Monday afternoon, grabbed a handful of money and ran down a fire escape.

14. A 27-year-old woman who admitted she lied to welfare officials has been ordered to repay $850.

15. A New Jersey manufacturing company is suing a local business and nine of its employees for breach of employment contract.

16. A man on trial in a federal court here sat expressionless as his brother testified against him.

17. An Indiana couple has filed a $1 million lawsuit against two chiropractors they claim are responsible for their son's birth defects.

18. A 24-year-old man convicted of the shooting deaths of his wife and two children was sentenced Thursday to 199 years in prison with no chance of parole.

EXERCISE 2
Public Affairs Reporting

AVOIDING AND DEFINING JARGON

SECTION I: Rewrite the following sentences, providing clear explanations or definitions of the terms that appear in italics.

1. The police *read Lewis his rights*.

2. The jury awarded her $60,000 in *compensatory damages*.

3. The jury awarded her $2 million in *punitive damages*.

4. The company's stockholders filed *a class action suit*.

5. The judge sentenced him to two 20-year terms to be served *concurrently*.

6. The judge sentenced him to two 20-year terms to be served *consecutively*.

7. The judge refused to grant *a change of venue* or to *sequester* the jury.

8. Government officials said 21 *civil suits*, but no *criminal charges*, were filed as a result of the bus accident.

SECTION II: Rewrite the following sentences, simplifying or eliminating the jargon.

1. She said the car was negligently, carelessly and improperly designed.

2. Police said thieves gained access to the premises by prying open a back door to the restaurant.

3. He says he suffered contusions in and about the head, neck, back, leg, body, spine and nervous system.

4. He says the libelous statements received widespread publicity and caused him extreme humiliation, mental anguish and physical deterioration.

5. Stevenson says he suffered and will continue to suffer great mental and physical pain, anguish, embarrassment and humiliation due to the verbal attack.

6. Brown charges that he suffered from bodily injury, disability, disfigurement and mental anguish; that he lost his ability to earn a decent living; that he lost the cost of his hospital bills; and, further, that the auto accident aggravated a previous medical condition.

SECTION III: Define the following terms, which frequently appear in public affairs stories. Use Black's Law Dictionary and other reference books in your campus and city libraries.

1. ad hoc committee _____

_____

2. ad valorem tax _____

_____

3. affidavit _____

_____

4. arraignment _____

_____

5. common law _____

_____

6. defendant _____

_____

7. deposition _____

_____

8. felony _____

_____

9. grand jury _____

_____

10. habeas corpus _____

_____

11. indictment _____

_____

12. injunction _____

_____

13. nolo contendere _____

_____

14. preliminary hearing _____

_____

15. probate _____

_____

EXERCISE 3
Public Affairs Reporting

Submitting Agency __Sheriff's Dept.__	Victim's Name (last - first - middle) Burmester, Herman Andrew	Comp. No. 867041

Descrip-tion of Victim	Sex M	Descent Cau.	Age 43	Height 6
Weight 180	Hair Brown	Eyes Blue	Build Med.	Complexion Tanned

Identifying Marks and Characteristics
Missing tips of two fingers on left hand.

Clothing & Jewelry Worn
Jeans, T-shirt, denim jacket

Location of Occurrence Holden Rd. one mile north of the city	Dist. 23	Type Suburban

Date & Time Occurred 9:30 a.m. today	Date & Time Reported To. P.D. 9:32 a.m.

Type of Premises (loc. of victim) Construction site	Cause of Injury (instr. or means) Fall of about 30 feet

Reason (Acc.-Ill health, etc.) See narrative below	Extent of Injury (Minor or Serious) Very serious

Remove To (address) Memorial Hospital	Removed By Alco Ambulance

Investigative Division or Unit Notified & Person(s) Contacted
Rittmann Engineering Co.

Wife, Sally Burmester

INJURY REPORT	UCR

CODE	R- Person Reporting	D- Person Discovering	W- Witness

	Residence Address	City	Res. Phone	X	Bus. Phone	X
Victim's Occupation Iron worker	1214 S. 23rd St.	(Yours)	671-2108		644-2842	X
Name R&W Bill McGowin	4842 S. Conway Rd.	(Yours)	671-7022		644-2842	X
W James Randolph	654 Harrison St.	(Yours)	644-0814		644-2842	X
W Floyd Leidigh	1218 Dickens Ave.	(Yours)	644-6817		644-2842	X

(1) Reconstruct the circumstances surrounding the injury. (2) Describe physical evidence, location found, & give disposition.

All those persons involved are construction workers and employed by Rittmann

Engineering Co. They were putting up I-beams on the third floor and some steel supports

for the roof of a new warehouse being built on Holden Road, and were working about 30

feet off the ground at the time the accident occurred. Leidigh was operating a crane,

and McGowin and Randolph were up on the third level working with Burmester when there

was a sudden gust of wind while Burmester was standing on a beam, and they report that

he seemed to lose his balance, stumble for a minute and then fall backward, landing on

the structure's concrete base. It rained in the area last night, and everything was

obviously still wet and slippery this morning. There were no rails or safety lines on

the site yet. Only the steel frame for the building has been put up, and the beam

Burmester was standing on measures only 14 inches in width. He was about 8 feet from

the nearest crossbeam. Burmester never lost consciousness, and paramedics in the

ambulance say both his legs are broken. He also seemed to be experiencing some
paralysis of his other extremities. He's being treated in intensive care. Because

of his condition, we were unable to interview him.

Supervisor Approving E.G.	Emp. No. 941	Interviewing Officer(s) Wilcox	Emp. No. 1618	Person Reporting Injury (signature) Bill McGowin

602-07-23A   INJURY REPORT

EXERCISE 4
Public Affairs Reporting

Submitting Agency	Police Department				Victim's Name (last - first - middle) Levy, Mark T.	Comp. No. 428-91A

Descrip- tion Of Victim	Sex M	Descent C	Age 34	Height 6' 2"
Weight 180	Hair Brown	Eyes Blue	Build Med.	Complexion Tanned

Location of Occurrence 429 Holden Avenue Dist. 3 Type 6

Date & Time Occurred 7 p.m. yesterday **Date & Time Reported To P.D.** 7 p.m. yesterday

Type of Premises (loc. of victim) Home **Cause of Injury (instr. or means)** .38 caliber bullet

Reason (Acc.-ill health, etc.) Discharge of firearm **Extent of Injury (Minor or Serious)** Very serious

Remove To (address) St. Nicholas Hospital **Removed By** Paramedics

Identifying Marks and Characteristics

Beard, mustache

Clothing & Jewelry Worn
Blue plaid dress shirt, dark

blue pants, tie, black shoes.

Investigative Division or Unit Notified & Person(s) Contacted

Detective Bureau

INJURY REPORT UCR

CODE R- Person Reporting D- Person Discovering W- Witness

	Victim's Occupation	Residence Address	City	Res. Phone	X	Bus. Phone	X
	Managed lumber company	429 Holden Avevenue	Yours	420-6182		365-2681	
W	**Name** Karl Medina	542 Holden Avenue		420-7683		644-0229	
R	Sarah Medina	Same as above					

---

(1) Reconstruct the circumstances surrounding the injury. (2) Describe physical evidence, location found, & give disposition.

Karl Medina, a brother-in-law of the victim, said he and his wife, Sarah, had been

invited for dinner and had been visiting the victim and his family.   After the meal, the

victim showed Medina a new pistol he had recently purchased for the protection of his

family and home, a .38 caliber Colt revolver.   Medina got the pistol from a bedroom

closet, and both men handled the weapon while seated in a family room in Levy's home.

The victim had cautioned Medina that the weapon was loaded since he always kept it that

way in a locked cabinet in the bedroom, but the safety was on.   All this was supported

by Medina's wife and by the victim's wife, although the latter was somewhat incoherent

at times and will have to be questioned again at a later date.   The two men then set

the loaded gun down on a coffee table.   The two men were drinking coffee and began

discussing other topics.   Medina recalls that a short time later the victim's 6-year-old

son, Jason Levy, said something like "Daddy, look at me, daddy.   Watch me, I'm going to

shoot you."   The boy pointed the gun at his father, apparently in play and not realizing

that it was a real and loaded weapon.   Whereupon the weapon fired one round, striking

the victim in the chest.   Medina said it all happened so fast that they were unable to

say anything to the boy or take the gun away from him.   Paramedics treated the victim

at the scene, then transported him to St. Nicholas Hospital, where he was reported to

be in very serious condition.

If additional space is required use reverse side.

Supervisor Approving E.L.	Emp. No.	Interviewing Officer(s) Meeske	Emp. No.	Person Reporting Injury (signature)
			X	

602-07-23A **INJURY REPORT**

EXERCISE 5
Public Affairs Reporting

						Victim's Name (last - first - middle)			Comp. No.	
Submitting Agency	Police					Cortez, Roberto			78-14788	

Submitting Agency ___ Police

Descrip-tion Of Victim	Sex	Descent	Age	Height
Weight	Hair	Eyes	Build	Complexion

Identifying Marks and Characteristics

Clothing & Jewelry Worn

Victim's Name (last - first - middle)	Comp. No.
Cortez, Roberto	78-14788

Location of Occurrence	Dist.	Type
Dunkin Donuts, 1218 Sherwood Drive	2	

Date & Time Occurred	Date & Time Reported To. P.D.
00:30 today	00:30 today

Type of Premises (loc. of victim)	Cause of Injury (instr. or means)
Donut shop parking lot	Gunfire

Reason (Acc.-ill health, etc.)	Extent of Injury (Minor or Serious)
Shooting	Minor

Remove To (address)	Removed By
Park Memorial Hospital	Squad Car #12

Investigative Division or Unit Notified & Person(s) Contacted

Detective Bureau

Internal Affairs

INJURY REPORT   UCR

CODE   R- Person Reporting   D- Person Discovering   W- Witness

	Victim's Occupation	Residence Address City	Res. Phone	X	Bus. Phone	X
	Patrolman	1118 Tiffany Lane	671-9996		671-1234	
	Name					
	Roberto Cortez					

---

(1) Reconstruct the circumstances surrounding the injury. (2) Describe physical evidence, location found, & give disposition.

At approx. 00:30 hrs. an armed robbery was committed at a donut shop on Sherwood Drive. Backup officers Hill and Renko filed a separate robbery report, #87327. While on routine patrol, slowly cruising by the shop, I observed a male suspect inside the premises and apparently holding a gun on the two waitresses. After radioing for backup, I circled a vehicle parked outside to get the tag number. Just after I exited my vehicle and approached the door, the arrestee came out. I ordered him to put his hands on the trunk of his vehicle. As he started to do so, he pulled out a nickel plated short barrel revolver. He pointed the revolver at me and said, "Now what are you going to do." I retreated in a zig-zag fashion to put more distance between us. The arrestee began shooting at me. I ducked behind my car and began returning fire. I felt bullet or glass fragments strike me in the face. The arrestee got into his vehicle and fled south on Sherwood. A search was made with negative results. Two hours after the incident, the arrestee, Jerrod Robert Gianangeli, 34, 1104 Bumby Avenue, called the dept. to report his vehicle stolen. When he came to the station, he was arrested and charged with armed robbery, attempted murder and possession of a firearm by a convicted felon. He is now on probation for armed robbery. The arrestee signed a sworn statement in which he admitted to shooting 6 times at me. I was treated at the hospital for minor wounds and released.

If additional space is required use reverse side.

Supervisor Approving	Emp. No.	Interviewing Officer(s)	Emp. No.	Person Reporting Injury (signature)
J.L.	403		X	

602-07-23A   **INJURY REPORT**

EXERCISE 6
Public Affairs Reporting

Submitting Agency Fire Department	Name of Deceased (last, first, & middle) Lora Anne and Karen Lynn Dolmovich			Comp. No. 82471

Description Of Deceased	Sex	Descent	Hair	Eyes
Height	Weight	Age	Build	Complexion

Identifying Marks & Characteristics	Date/Time Original Ill./Inj. 8 p.m. yesterday	Occupation of Deceased None	Date & time Rptd to P.D. 8:05 p.m.

See below

Location of Occurrence
714 N. 23rd Street — Dist. 7 — Type (Trf, Nat) Accident

Location of Original Illness or Injury
714 N. 23rd Street — Dist. 7 — Type Orig. Rpt.

Date/Time Deceased Discovered 8:05 p.m. yesterday | Date/Time Death Occurred 8 p.m. yesterday | Relatives Notified By Were on scene

Clothing and Jewelry Worn
None

Removed To (Address)
Mercy Hospital — Removed By Paramedics

Probable Cause of Death
Electrocution — Reason (quarrel - illness - revenge - etc.) Accidental

Deceased's Residence Address
714 N. 23rd Street

Investigation Division or Unit Notified & Persons Contacted
Coroner's Office

Deceased's Business Address
None

DEATH REPORT — UCR 48-B-8216

CODE: R- Person Reporting Death   D- Person Discovering Death   I- Person Identifying Deceased   W- Witness   Day Phone —— X

CODE	Nearest Relative	Relationship	Address	City	Phone	X
RDI	Sandra M. Dolmovich	Notified ☐YES ☐NO	Res. 714 N. 23rd St. / Bus. 2318 N. Main Street	Yours / Yours	824-2791 / 365-7884	
	Name		Res. / Bus.			
			Res. / Bus.			

Doctor in Attendance
None — Business Address — Phone

Source of Call (How notified & By Whom)
Call came from girls' mother. Rescue Squad paramedics dispatched at 8:06 p.m.

Medical Examiner's Name
Marlene Stoudnour — Medical Examiner Case No. SD-24-8928

DISPOSITION OF PROPERTY	[X] RELEASED TO M.E. ☐ RELEASED TO RELATIVES	RECEIPT [X]YES ☐NO ADDRESS_____ NAME_____

(1) Reconstruct the circumstances surrounding the death. (2) Describe physical evidence, location found & give disposition.

Sandra M. Dolmovich, natural mother of Lora Anne Dolmovich, age 3, and Karen Lynn Dolmovich, age 5, reports that shortly after dinner last night she left her two girls playing in a bathtub as she straightened up the kitchen. After a few minutes, when the mother could not hear the girls splashing around, she went into the bathroom to check. She found both the girls lying face down in the water. A hair dryer, which was plugged in, was also in the water. The victims' mother says she normally kept the hair dryer on a radiator next to the bathtub. She says she immediately pulled the cord and then pulled both girls from the water and called the Fire Department Rescue Squad. The dispatcher received the call at 8:05 p.m. and paramedics Svendsen and Povacz reached the scene at 8:11 p.m. They report finding no heartbeat and immediately administered CPR and oxygen at the scene. Not getting any response, they took the victims to Mercy Hospital, where they were both pronounced dead on arrival at the emergency room. The victims' mother says she used the hair dryer in the bathroom each morning and that her girls sometimes played with it. It has a warning against immersion imprinted in the plastic body of the dryer. Autopsies are scheduled for tomorrow.

If additional space required, use reverse side.

Supervisor Approving Haskell	Emp. No. 1481	Interviewing Officer(s) Svendsen and Povacz	Emp. No.	Person Reporting Death (signature) X
				Indexed Yes	Checked Yes

602-07-21A — DEATH REPORT

EXERCISE 7
Public Affairs Reporting

						Name of Deceased (last, first, & middle)		Comp. No.
Submitting Agency		Police				Hillier, Carolyn E.		82723

Description Of Deceased

Description Of Deceased	Sex	Descent	Hair	Eyes
	F	W	Brown	Blue
Height	Weight	Age	Build	Complexion
5'6"	350	30	Fat	Clear

Identifying Marks & Characteristics
Overweight, pregnant

Clothing and Jewelry Worn
Simple blue dress, white sweater,

watch & 3 rings

Deceased's Residence Address
841 Richland Avenue

Deceased's Business Address
Unknown

Location of Occurrence	Dist.	Type (Trf, Nat)
Colonial Mall	7	Nat.
Location of Original Illness or Injury	Dist.	Type Orig. Rpt.
Colonial Mall		

Date/Time Original Ill./Inj.	Occupation of Deceased	Date & time Rptd to P.D.
7:30 p.m. yesterday	Unknown	7:45 p.m.
Date/Time Deceased Discovered	Date/Time Death Occurred	Relatives Notified By
7:30 p.m. yesterday	8:10 p.m.	Hospital

Removed To (Address)	Removed By
Park Memorial Hospital	Ambulance

Probable Cause of Death	Reason (quarrel - illness - revenge - etc.)
Weak heart	

Investigation Division or Unit Notified & Persons Contacted
N/A

DEATH REPORT

UCR
D2-784-L

CODE: R- Person Reporting Death   D- Person Discovering Death   I- Person Identifying Deceased   W-Witness   Day Phone-------- X

CODE	Nearest Relative	Relationship		Address	City	Phone
	Sandra Hillier, sister	Notified XX YES ☐ NO	Res.	3282 East Broadway		671-7838 XX
			Bus.	None		
	Name		Res.	2202 Eighth Avenue		671-0983
W	Theo Bronsen		Bus.	Colonial Mall		671-8303
			Res.			
			Bus.			

Doctor in Attendance	Business Address	Phone

Source of Call (How notified & By Whom)
Bronsen, a clerk at Mayer's Jewelers in the Mall

Medical Examiner's Name	Medical Examiner Case No.
Hildebrand	6014-832

DISPOSITION OF PROPERTY
XX RELEASED TO M.E.   RECEIPT ☐ YES ☐ NO   ADDRESS_____
☐ RELEASED TO RELATIVES   NAME_____

---

(1) Reconstruct the circumstances surrounding the death. (2) Describe physical evidence, location found & give disposition.

Theo Bronsen is a clerk at Mayer's Jewelers and states she was showing the victim
some bracelets when the victim complained of feeling ill and was assisted to a chair
in the rear of the premises.   Bronsen states that the victim seemed to be feeling
better a few minutes later and declined offers of help.   Bronsen and a second clerk
say they offered to get the victim a glass of water or to call a relative to pick her
up, not realizing at the time that she was pregnant or the serious nature of the
problem.   They returned to their business and when they checked back approximately
5 minutes later they found the victim losing consciousness.   At that time they
summoned an ambulance.   Victim was taken to Park Memorial Hospital in apparent
cardiopulmonary arrest.   CPR was performed enroute and a cesarean section was
performed at the hospital to save an 8 month fetus.   The baby was alive and is doing
well at this time.   Victim was pronounced dead at 20:10 by Dr. Jane Yanorini.   A
sister says the victim had a long history of diabetes and seizures and weighed 350
pounds.   The sister adds that she was seeing a doctor and taking medication for

the problems.
If additional space required, use reverse side.

Supervisor Approving	Emp. No.	Interviewing Officer(s)	Emp. No.	Person Reporting Death (signature)
JL	403	Wilcox	627	X
				Indexed: Yes	Checked: Yes

602-07-21A

DEATH REPORT

POLICE DEPARTMENT

STOLEN PROPERTY

	CASE NO. 83-4751		
SHIFT NO. 1			
CR NO. 14			

U.C.R. CLASSIFICATION FR-721-83-4498	OCCURRED (DATE & TIME) 11 a.m. yesterday	DAY OF OFF. Yesterday	DISP. 9:07a	ARR. 9:15	IN SER. 9:40	DATE OF REP. Today

OFFENSE (GRAND OR PETIT) Grand

NAME AND ADDRESS OF OCCURRENCE Bert's Shell Station, 4800 Conway Road   **AREA** 7

OWNER OF PROPERTY Rene J. Firment   **AGE - SEX - RACE** 19 M W   **RESIDENT ADDRESS** 2474 Colyer Road   **RES. PHONE** 350-6974   **BUSINESS ADDRESS** 4800 Conway Road   **BUSINESS PHONE** 644-0292

REPORTED BY Same as above

DISCOVERED BY Same as above

WITNESSED BY None

OWNERS OCCUPATION Service station attend.   **TYPE OF PREMISES (RES. OR BUS.)** Service Station

METHOD USED TO COMMIT CRIME Swindle   **MODUS OPERENDI**   **MAKE AND MANUFACTURER**   **LOCATION OF PROPERTY STOLEN**

MODEL NO. - SERIAL NO. - CALIBER   **GENERAL TYPE OF PROPERTY TAKEN** Cash   **INSURANCE COMPANY**

COST OF PROPERTY (NEW AND AT TIME OF THEFT) $100

VEHICLE USED BY OFFENDERS None seen	MAKE	MODEL	YEAR	BODY STYLE	COLOR	LICENSE STATE YEAR	NO. PRIOR THEFTS REPORTED

	AGE - SEX - RACE	RESIDENCE ADDRESS Unknown		INCARCERATED YES NO No	WHERE	OCCUPATION
☐ SUBJECT ☐ SUSPECT ☐ JUVENILE				DETECTIVE NOTIFIED -- DATE AND TIME		

KIND OF PROPERTY RECOVERED None   **VALUE**   **PROPERTY RECEIPT**

REMARKS (INCLUDED DETAILED DESCRIPTION OF PROPERTY TAKEN) Firment said a very well dressed young couple, both about 30, walked into the service station at about 11 a.m. yesterday, and the woman asked to use the restroom. While she was in the restroom, the phone rang, and Firment said he answered it in the station office from a man who told him his wife had left her wedding ring on a bathroom sink at the station. The caller said the ring was a genuine diamond worth $2,000 and offered a $200 reward if the ring was found. As Firment was still on the telephone, the woman then walked out of the restroom with a ring, and Firment told her of the offer. The couple said they were on their way to a friend's wedding and couldn't wait for the reward. The caller, who was still on the phone at that point, told Firment to give the couple $100 and said Firment would receive the $200 when he came down to pick up the ring later in the afternoon, so the couple and Firment would split the reward 50-50. Firment said he then proceeded to give the couple the suggested amount, and they left, walking south on Conway Road. The caller never came to the station yesterday, and Firment said he went to a jeweler early today and determined that the ring was a fake and worth only about $6. He called the department at about 9 a.m. today. He was unable to provide clear descriptions of either perpetrator and said he didn't see them get into a vehicle of any kind. Detectives will interview him later today and try to get some kind of description.

REPORTING OFFICER'S SIGNATURE (A) Cullinan	NO. 4281 3	AREA	APPROVED BY Forsythe	AREA	PERSON REPORTING CRIME Rene Firment
(B)					STATE TWX MSG. NO.
					LOCAL TWX MSG. NO

REFERRED TO: Detective Bureau

SUPERVISOR: E. G.

DISPOSITION ☐ CLEARED BY ARREST ☐ EXCEPTIONALLY CLEARED ☐ UNFOUNDED ☐ PENDING

CT 284

EXERCISE 9
Public Affairs Reporting

POLICE DEPARTMENT

STOLEN PROPERTY

			CR NO. 11	SHIFT NO. 2		CASE NO. 89306411

OFFENSE (GRAND OR PETIT): Grand

U.C.R. CLASSIFICATION: 84762.41

AREA: 7

OCCURRED (DATE & TIME): Sometime in the past week

DAY OF OCC: Unknown

DISP. 8:20a | ARR. 8:32 | IN SER. 10:12a | DATE OF REP. Today

NAME AND ADDRESS OF OCCURRENCE: 3405 Virginia Ave.

OWNER OF PROPERTY: Dr. William J. Gulas — AGE · SEX · RACE: 46 M B — RESIDENT ADDRESS: 3405 Virginia Ave. — RES. PHONE: 273-1364 — BUSINESS ADDRESS: 851 Morse Boulevard — BUSINESS PHONE: 442-8090

REPORTED BY: Mrs. Gulas — AGE · SEX · RACE: 29 F B — " — "

DISCOVERED BY: Mrs. Gulas and family

WITNESSED BY: No known witnesses

OWNER'S OCCUPATION: Medical doctor

TYPE OF PREMISES (RES. OR BUS.): Residence

LOCATION OF PROPERTY STOLEN:

MODEL NO.- SERIAL NO. CALIBER: Checking serial numbers presently

METHOD USED TO COMMIT CRIME: Front door pried open, pry marks found

MAKE AND MANUFACTURER:

GENERAL TYPE OF PROPERTY TAKEN: Household furnishings

MODUS OPERANDI: Used truck to move everything out of home

INSURANCE COMPANY: Prudential

COST OF PROPERTY (NEW AND AT TIME OF THEFT): $20,000

VEHICLE USED BY OFFENDERS: Exact vehicle unknown, but probably a large truck — MAKE — MODEL — YEAR — BODY STYLE — COLOR — LICENSE STATE YEAR

NO. PRIOR THEFTS REPORTED: Two

☐ SUBJECT ☐ SUSPECT ☐ JUVENILE — AGE · SEX · RACE — RESIDENCE ADDRESS — INCARCERATED YES NO — WHERE — OCCUPATION

KIND OF PROPERTY RECOVERED: None — VALUE: None

PROPERTY RECEIPT

DETECTIVE NOTIFIED — DATE AND TIME

REMARKS (INCLUDED DETAILED DESCRIPTION OF PROPERTY TAKEN) The family, including four children, had been vacationing in New Orleans for a week and got home at about 8:20 this morning and found the house totally looted. Almost everything is gone. All their furniture, clothes, appliances, yard tools, dishes, etc. Even the rugs were pulled up. About the only thing left were the drapes, so everything looks normal from the outside. Whoever was responsible must have had plenty of time, since they even took food from the kitchen shelves, plus the kitchen stove, refrigerator, a washer and a dryer, and a freezer the family says was half full of meat. Neighbors don't report hearing anything unusual, but the house is isolated on a 1½ acre lot. The house has been robbed twice before, and the family installed a burglar alarm system they say they paid $840 for just before leaving on vacation. It's been tampered with and silenced. Even some interior doors are missing from the home. Because of the previous robberies, much of the property was new, bought as replacements for property stolen earlier. Tire marks are apparent on the front lawn but are too old to make a good impression. We're continuing to interview people in the neighborhood. Because of the previous break-ins, the family hadn't told anyone that they wouldn't be home, and no one was checking the house while they were out of town. The break-in is similar to one of the previous entries, and the same thieves may have returned with a truck. Little was taken in that previous entry.

REPORTING OFFICER'S SIGNATURE (A): George Oldaker — BADGE NO.: 310 — AREA: 2 — APPROVED BY: D.N.

PERSON REPORTING CRIME: Mrs. Gulas

STATE TWX MSG. NO.

LOCAL TWX MSG. NO.

REFERRED TO: Detective Bureau

SUPERVISOR: Griffin

(B)

DISPOSITION: ☐ CLEARED BY ARREST ☐ EXCEPTIONALLY CLEARED ☐ UNFOUNDED ☒ PENDING

CT 284

EXERCISE 10
Public Affairs Reporting

POLICE DEPARTMENT

ROBBERY

4A. Offense	Armed robbery
4. U.C.R. Classification	84-19721
11. CR No.	18
1. Command No.	4
2. Case No.	13817674

10. Address of Occurrence	1634 Holden Ave.
12. Zone	8
9. Occurred	8:40 p.m.
5. Day	Yesterday
6. Disp.	On stakeout
7. Arr.	On stakeout
8. In Ser.	10:40 p.m.
3. Date	

14. Victim's Name	Thomas A. Golay
Age-Sex-Race	M 57 W
Res. Address	1203 Texas Avenue
Res. Phone	671-8437
Bus. Address	1634 Holden Ave.
Bus. Phone	671-4744

15. Reported by	Officers Skinner & Boysie
17. Witnessed By	Officers Skinner & Boysie
49. Owner	Thomas A. Golay

63. Victim's Occupation (14)	Liquor store owner
42. Type of Premises	Liquor store
129. Protect. Dev.	Silent alarm
135. Sobriety of Victim	Sober ☒ H.B.D. ☐ Intox. ☐

35. Weapon or Means Used — Serial No.	2 handguns L4387162 SB8231442
34. Method Used to Commit Crime	Strongarm robbery
37. General Type of Property Taken	Cash
130. Value	$312

45. Trade Mark or Unusual Event (Modus Operendi) One suspect entered the store when it appeared to be empty, 64. Weather Clear except for the owner, showed a gun and demanded the money.

50. Vehicle Used	Make	Model	Year	Body Style	53. Color	52. license	State	Year	55. Ident. Marks	47. Storage Receipt
By Offenders:	Ford	Mustang		Sedan	White	D812-175	Cur.	Yes	Badly rusted	84-3822

68. What Did Offenders Say "Give me all the money you've got in the register, all of it, and 136. No. of Offenders Two do it fast. This gun is loaded, and I'll shoot."

31. ☐ Suspect ☒ Subject Juv. ☐	Calvin Louis Winkler
Sex-Race-Age	M W 27
Res. Address	Louisville, Kentucky
Incarcerated ☐ Yes ☒ No	Where
Occupation	Unknown

138. Disguises	Bandana over face
72. How Offender Approached — Flight	Car driven by accomplice
41. Person or Unit Notified — Time	Shift commander 8:45
67. Hospital (14)	Memorial
95. Condition	Very grave

131. Kind of Property Recovered	Cash
132. Value	$312
48. Property Receipt	☒ Yes ☐ No

33. Remarks: We were on a routine stakeout, hiding in a back room in the liquor store when the suspect entered. When he displayed his weapon and grabbed the money we entered the area, identified ourselves and ordered the suspect to drop his weapon. The suspect turned toward us, seemingly pointing his gun at us, and we both opened fire. Skinner fired one shot from a shotgun and Boysie three shots from his service revolver. The shotgun blast struck the suspect in his groin area and one shot from the revolver struck him in the stomach and another in his right arm. The second suspect, who made no attempt to flee, was apprehended outside in their car. He has been identified as Norman F. Piezul, also of Louisville. Winkler is in the hospital's intensive care unit. Piezul is being held in the county jail.

20. Reporting Officer's Signature	Badge No.	87. District	19. Approved By	21. Person Reporting Crime
(a) Roger Skinner	482	3	R.N.	Skinner and Boysie
(b) Lee Boysie	789	3		22. State TWX Msg. No.
				23. Local TWX Msg. No.

Referred To	Detective Bureau and District Attorney
Signature	
27. Recorded	Yes
25. Indexed	
29. Statistics	
Assigned To	Detective Bureau
Supervisor	Griffin

30. Disposition: ☒ Cleared by Arrest ☐ Unfounded ☐ Exceptionally Cleared ☐ Pending

Date _____ Date _____

C T-78

EXERCISE 11
Public Affairs Reporting

SHERIFF'S DEPT.

☒ ROBBERY ☐ CRIME GENERAL
☒ CRIME AGAINST PERSON

2. CASE NO. 8476l003

14. VICTIM'S NAME Scott Pinchal
DOB 9-4-40   A __ S __ R __   RES. PHONE 644-9284

ADDRESS 737 Dean Road
CITY (Yours)   STATE __   ZIP __   BUS. PHONE 834-7868

15. REPORTED BY Deputy Cullinan
DOB __   A __ S __ R __   RES./BUS. PHONE

ADDRESS Sheriff's Dept.
CITY __   STATE __   ZIP __

16. DISCOVERED BY Deputy Cullinan

49. OWNER Scott Pinchal
DOB __   A __ S __ R __   RES./BUS. PHONE

ADDRESS 737 Dean Road
CITY (Yours)   STATE __   ZIP __

9. DATE AND TIME OF OCCURRENCE 8 p.m. yesterday

4. UCR CLASSIFICATION 841,72,A3

34. WHAT TOOL, WEAPON OR MEANS USED TO COMMIT CRIME Knife

45. TRADEMARK OR UNUSUAL EVENT (MODUS OPERANDI)
Hitchhiker pulled knife, demanded victim's money

OCCUPATION __   INCARCERATED ☐ YES ☐ NO   STATE __   VR EXPIRES __   WHERE __

55. IDENTIFYING MARKS

67. HOSPITAL (14) Memorial   Current   Damage to rear bumper

95. CONDITION Fair

132. VALUE

133. RECOVERY-FULL/PARTIAL

38. EXACT LOCATION OF VICTIM OR PROPERTY Victim found in car stopped alongside SR 17, badly wounded

134. CHANGE OF VALUE

90. PARENT (IF 14-15 JUVENILE)

10A. ADDRESS DISPATCHED TO

13B. WAS SCENE PROCESSED ☒ YES ☐ NO

OFFICER'S ASSIGNED __   I.D. NO.

21. PERSON REPORTING CRIME Cullinan   SIG. __

29. REPORT PREPARED BY Cullinan   SIG. __

25. INDEXED BY __   I.D. NO.

24. STATISTICS

DATE __
DATE __

4A. OFFENSE Aggravated Assault

11. RADIO NO. 432   12. ZONE 18   5. DAY Today   6. DISP.   7. ARR 3:40a.   8. IN SERV 5:05a.   74. DATE   1A. VICE VIOLATION ☐ YES ☒ NO

10. ADDRESS OF OCCURRENCE State Route 17

64. WEATHER Raining

3. HOW ASSIGNMENT RECEIVED ☐ RADIO ☐ SUPERVISOR ☐ CITIZEN   ☒ REQUESTED BY OFFICER

17. WITNESSED BY No known witnesses
DOB __   A __ S __ R __   RES./BUS. PHONE

PERMANENT ADDRESS
CITY __   STATE __   ZIP __

TEMPORARY ADDRESS
CITY __   STATE __   ZIP __

EMPLOYERS NAME
ADDRESS   CITY __   STATE __   ZIP __   EMPLOYERS PHONE

NEXT OF KIN
DOB __   A __ S __ R __   RES./BUS. PHONE

ADDRESS
CITY __   STATE __   ZIP __

63. VICTIM'S OCCUPATION Auto mechanic

42. TYPE OF PREMISES ☐ R ☐ B ☐ C ☐ D ☐ O   129. PROTECTIVE DEVICE ☐ OCCP ☐ ALARM ☐ S ☐ A   135. VICTIM'S SOBRIETY ☐ SOBER ☒ H.B.D. ☐ INTOX.

35. HOW USED TO COMMIT CRIME Stabbing

37. GENERAL TYPE OF PROPERTY TAKEN Money   130. VALUE $2

31. ☐ SUSPECT ☐ JUV. ☐ UNK.   NAME Unknown
DOB __   A __ S __ R __

54. VEHICLE USED ☒ BY VICTIM   MAKE Buick   MODEL Skylark   YEAR '78   BODY STYLE Sedan   53. COLOR Blue   LICENSE TAG NO. R372-814   131. KIND OF PROPERTY RECOVERED   VEHICLE ☐ FOOT ☒ OTHER ☐ UNKNOWN

136. WHAT DID OFFENDERS SAY Hitchhiker unknown to victim pulled a knife on the edge of town, demanded money. Victim had only $2, and assailant stabbed him in anger.

72. HOW OFFENDERS APPROACHED & FLED ☒ N ☐ E ☐ S ☐ W   FLIGHT DIRECTION,STREET,MEANS   68. APPROACH DIRECTION,STREET,MEANS ☒ N ☐ E ☐ S ☐ W

41. PERSON OR UNIT NOTIFIED __   ON __   BY __   TIME __   71. VICTIM REFERRED TO

69. ATTENDING PHYSICIAN Hitchell

65. NATURE OF INJURIES & LOCATION ON BODY Ambulance (Victim not married, lives alone) Stabbed in right arm, side, abdomen, at least five times

70. WILL VICTIM PREFER CHARGES ☒ YES ☐ NO

84. NEXT OF KIN NOTIFIED __   BY WHOM Cullinan   DATE Today   TIME 4:45a.   73. FURTHER POLICE ACTION REQUIRED ☒ YES ☐ NO   136. HAS VICTIM VIEWED MUG FILES ☐ YES ☒ NO   137. DISGUISES None: assailant was a female, thin, blonde, about 20

48. PROPERTY RECEIPT ☐ YES ☐ NO

13. DISTRICT 7

ID NO. 42813

150. MIRANDA WARNING READ ☐ YES ☐ NO

60. CONTACT INFORMATION

ID NO. __

36. GRID

20. REPORTING OFFICER'S SIGNATURE (A) Charles Cullinan
(B) __

19. APPROVED BY Forsythe

22. FOREIGN AGCY

23. LOCAL MSG NO

27. RECORDED BY __

SIGNATURE

28. REFERRED TO Detectives

30. DISPOSITION ☐ CLEARED BY ARREST ☒ EXCEPTIONALLY CLEARED ☐ UNFOUNDED ☒ PENDING

18. MULTIPLE CLEAR UP RET. CASE NO.

ASSIGNED TO __
SUPERVISOR __

PRESS DOWN — YOU ARE MAKING 5 COPIES

STATE ATTORNEY

564   Public Affairs Reporting

SHERIFF'S DEPT. — MISCELLANEOUS INCIDENT

2. CASE NO. 84761004

1. RADIO NO 42 12. ZONE 15
5. DATE Yesterday
6. DISP. 4:25 p.
7. ARR. 4:31 p.
8. IN SERV. 5:15 p.
6A. WEATHER Clear, sunny
14. VICTIM'S NAME Gregory L. Herwarth
RES. 641-7838 BUS. 644-2360
DATE 7/11/34

7A. FURTHER POLICE ACTION REQUIRED ☒ YES ☐ NO

ADDRESS 4401 Baltimore Avenue CITY (Yours)

48. PROPERTY RECEIPT ☐ YES ☐ NO
19A. MIRANDA WARNING READ ☐ YES ☒ NO

15. REPORTED BY Unknown caller ADDRESS CITY (Yours)

41. PERSON OR UNIT NOTIFIED

4A. NATURE OF INCIDENT Victim struck by motorboat

80. VEHICLE USED 18 foot motor boat, 45 horsepower motor
MODEL MAKE YEAR BODY STYLE YEAR EXPIRES

9. ADDRESS OF OCCURRENCE South end of Crystal Lake
9. OCCURRED Yesterday

32. LICENSE TAG NO. SB45-721-63 STATE (Yours)
47. STORAGE RECEIPT ☐ YES ☐ NO

53. COLOR White

55. IDENT. MARKS (ACCESSORIES, DAMAGE, ETC.)

CITY AND STATE (Yours)

4. U C R CLASSIFICATION (WHERE APPLICABLE)

31. ☐ SUBJECT ☐ JUV. ☐ UNK. NAME Vernon Sindelar
ADDRESS 4164 Mandar Drive
RES. 293-5495 BUS. 644-6648
OCCUPATION Salesman
3/28/60
INCARCERATED ☒ YES ☐ NO

WHERE County jail, freed on $1,000 bail at 10 p.m. yesterday

DISTURBANCES NO ASSAULT
☐ NEIGHBOR DISPUTE ☐ LOUD PARTY ☐ LOUD NOISE (VEH.)
☐ TENANT-LANDLORD ☐ LOITERING ☐ DOMESTIC
☐ JUVENILE ☐ PROWLER ☐ LOUD RADIO, STEREO, ETC.
☐ SHOOTING IN AREA ☐ BARKING DOG ☐ OTHER
☐ HEALTH LAW VIOLATION ☐ STRAY ANIMAL ☐ DISORDERLY CONDUCT ☐ FIREWORKS

POLICE SERVICE
☐ OBSCENE OR THREATENING CALLS ☐ MENTAL ILLNESS ☐ INDECENT EXPOSURE
☐ FOUND PROPERTY (DRUGS, ETC.) ☐ VANDALISM ☐ LOSS PROPERTY
☐ DAMAGE TO PROPERTY ☐ ACCIDENTAL NON-TRAFFIC
☐ DANGEROUS OR HAZARDOUS SITUATION ☐ LOST ☐ TAG ☐ HUMANE SOCIETY

POLICE SERVICE
☐ SUSPICIOUS PERSON ☐ SOLICITORS ☐ SUSPICIOUS VEHICLE
☐ SUSPICIOUS INCIDENT ☐ DOG BITE ☐ OTHER
☐ DRUNK DRIVER ☐ DRUNK PEDSTN ☐ BOATING TROUBLE
☐ INFORMATION ☒ MAKE INVESTIGATION ☐ ASSIST OTHER AGENCY
WHAT AGENCY? ☒ ACCIDENT ☐ CAPIAS ☐ OTHER

PUBLIC SERVICE
☐ OPEN DOOR/WINDOW (NO ILLEGAL ENTRY) ☐ BUILDING CHECK ☐ SCENE SECURED ☐ NO ADDRESS / COMPLAINANT
☐ CONTACT MSG ☐ VERBAL ☐ NOTE
☐ UNABLE ☐ ESCORT ☐ SP. DETAIL
☐ ROBBERY ☐ BURGLAR
☐ SILENT ☐ FIRE ☐ AUDIBLE
FAULTY, ACCIDENTAL/UNINTENDED ALARMS

ACTION TAKEN
☐ ALL PARTIES G O A ☐ CIVIL MATTER-ADVISED ☐ UNFOUNDED
GENERAL INFO. ☒ SEE NARRATIVE

7A. WILL VICTIM PREFER CHARGES ☒ YES ☐ NO

1. ODCN

60. CONTACT INFORMATION Other witnesses: Darla and Savilla Gould, 4178 N. 11th Ave.

33. NARRATIVE Herwarth was riding on an innertube being towed by a boat operated by his wife, Ruth. Another couple, Mr. and Mrs. Wayne Morrill of 382 Arlington Circle was in the boat with her. They say the boat operated by Sindelar approached from the west at high speed, suddenly veered straight at Herwarth, its propeller striking him and amputating his right arm at the shoulder. Herwarth was unconscious when we arrived at the scene, and an ambulance took him to St. Nicholas Hospital. His wife and the two Morrills pulled him from the water. They and witnesses allege that Sindelar stopped after the accident but did nothing to help. He appeared to be drunk, and we administered a Breath Analyzer test. He flunked, the alcohol in his blood being .14%, and we charged him with operating a power boat while under the influence of alcohol. Doctors at the hospital say Herwarth also suffered a broken collar bone and several broken ribs but is expected to survive.

26. REPORTING OFFICER'S SIGNATURE Charles Cullinan ID NO. 42813
28. REFERRED TO County attorney ID NO.
21. PERSON REPORTING CRIME Unknown caller

30. DISPOSITION (WRITE IN)
(A) SIGNATURE
(B)

19. APPROVED BY Forsythe
24. STATISTICS
22. FOREIGN AGCY.
23. LOCAL MSG NO.
27. RECORDED BY C.R.
25. INDEXED BY M.A.
29. RELEASE REPORT ☒ YES ☐ NO

RECORDS

PRESS DOWN — YOU ARE MAKING 5 COPIES

EXERCISE 13
Public Affairs Reporting

SHERIFF'S OFFICE

ZONE ___1___ UNIT ___#17___ **COMPLAINT REPORT** CASE NO. ___131-8864___

GRID ___14___ PAGE ___One___ OF ___One___ OTHER AGCY CASE NO. _____

MESSAGE NUMBER ___131-148___ DATE ___Today___ MONTH DAY YR

TIME RECEIVED ___11:35 p.m.___ TIME DISPATCHED ___11:37 p.m.___ TIME ARRIVED ___11:42 p.m.___ TIME IN-SERVICE ___1:20 a.m.___ WEATHER ___OK___

NATURE OF CASE ___Armed Robbery___ CHANGED TO _____ F.S.S.___ FEL. ___XX___ MISD.___

LOCATION OF OCCURRENCE (INCL. NAME OF BUSINESS/SCHOOL) ___McDonald's Restaurant 3220 McCoy Road___

VICTIM: ___Taylor___ (LAST) ___Marsha___ (FIRST) ___Lynn___ (MIDDLE) AGE ___29___ R/S___ DOB MO. DAY YR.

HOME ADDRESS ___2012 Lincoln Avenue___ PHONE ___420-9780___

CITY ___(Yours)___ STATE _____ ZIP _____

BUSINESS ADDRESS ___3220 McCoy Road___ PHONE ___420-6064___

CITY ___About 1 mile south of the city on McCoy Road___ STATE _____ ZIP _____

REPORTER ☐
WITNESS ☐ ___Six other employees, all available at the restaurant___ PHONE ___420-6064___

CITY ___(Yours)___ STATE _____ ZIP _____

		PROPERTY MISSING/STOLEN	EST. VALUE $	
QUAN.	ITEM	DESCRIPTION - SERIAL NO. - MFG NO. - ETC	STOLEN	RECOVERED
		Approximately $3,700 in cash	$3,700	None

■ MISSING ■ SUSPECT ■ ARRESTED ■ WITNESS ■ OTHER

NAME ___Unknown___ (LAST) _____ (FIRST) _____ (MIDDLE) AGE ___ R/S___ DOB MO. DAY YR.

ADDRESS _____ PHONE _____

CITY _____ STATE _____ ZIP _____

BUSINESS OR SCHOOL ADDRESS _____

HEIGHT ___ WEIGHT ___ HAIR ___ EYES ___ COMPLEXION ___ OCCUPATION _____

CLOTHING, ETC., _____

VEHICLE INVOLVED

☐ USED ☐ STOLEN ☐ TOWED ☐ DAMAGED ☐ BURGLARIZED ☐ WRECKER ☐ OTHER _____

YEAR ___ MAKE ___ MODEL ___ BODY STYLE ___ COLOR ___ DECAL _____

LICENSE TAG NO. _____ STATE ___ YEAR EXPIRES ___ I.D. OR VIN NO. _____

REMARKS: _____

ENTERED FCIC/NCIC ☐ YES ☐ NO BOLO ☐ YES ☐ NO MESSAGE NO. _____

NARRATIVE: Taylor, manager of the restaurant, was taking inventory with two assistant managers in a back room. Four other employees were cleaning the restaurant which had closed at 11 p.m. The front doors were locked, but when an employee opened a back door to take out some trash, three robbers wearing Halloween masks forced their way in. One gunman put a revolver to Taylor's head. Another of the managers was told to round up the other employees in the building. Taylor was forced to open a safe at gunpoint while the other six employees were taken to a small lounge used by employees. The two assistant managers were made to lie face down on the floor, and the other employees were seated at a table and told to put their heads down. Taylor was brought into the room after five cash register drawers in the safe had been emptied of about $3,700. The gunmen then ordered the employees to place their pocketbooks and jewelry on the table and took them as well. The employees then were warned they would be shot if they moved as the men left. The victims waited about five minutes before leaving the room and calling for help.

DISPOSITION: ___Referred to Detective Bureau___

FURTHER POLICE ACTION TAKEN YES ☐ NO ☐ REFERRED TO ___Detective Bureau___

___Deputy Cullinan___ ___Forsythe___
REPORTING OFFICER'S NAME (PRINT) I.D. NO. (INITIAL) APPROVED BY

RECORDS

EXERCISE 14
Public Affairs Reporting

SHERIFF'S OFFICE

COMPLAINT REPORT

ZONE __4__ UNIT __#23__

CASE NO. __AR-83-46241__

GRID __2__

PAGE __One__ OF __One__

OTHER AGCY CASE NO.

MESSAGE NUMBER __1-17-486__

DATE __Yesterday__ MONTH DAY YR

TIME RECEIVED __11:15 p.m.__ TIME DISPATCHED __11:17 p.m.__ TIME ARRIVED __11:30 p.m.__ TIME IN-SERVICE __2:15 a.m.__ WEATHER __Good__

NATURE OF CASE __Armed Robbery__ CHANGED TO _____ F.S.S. ___ FEL. __XX__ MISD. ___

LOCATION OF OCCURRENCE (INCL. NAME OF BUSINESS/SCHOOL) __Quik Shoppe   (Convenience Store)__

VICTIM: __Jimenez__ (LAST) __Edward__ (FIRST) __Carl__ (MIDDLE) AGE __48__ R/S ___ DOB MO. DAY YR.

HOME ADDRESS __3611 N. 31st. Street__ PHONE __365-0038__

CITY __(Yours)__ STATE _____ ZIP _____

BUSINESS ADDRESS __4760 Forest Road__ PHONE __420-5083__

CITY __About 1½ miles south of city__ STATE _____ ZIP _____

REPORTER ☒ WITNESS ☐ __Linda M. Smith, 1814 N. Third Street__ PHONE __422-4562__

CITY __Yes (Yours)__ STATE _____ ZIP _____

| PROPERTY MISSING/STOLEN | | | EST. VALUE $ | |
QUAN.	ITEM	DESCRIPTION - SERIAL NO. - MFG NO. - ETC	STOLEN	RECOVERED
		About $250 in cash	$250	None
		The victim is conducting an inventory. He says he's probably missing several cases of wine, beer and cigarettes. The inventory is due later today.	$400	None

☐ MISSING ☒ SUSPECT ☐ ARRESTED ☐ WITNESS ☐ OTHER

NAME __Unknown__ (LAST) ____ (FIRST) ____ (MIDDLE) AGE __30__ R/S ___ DOB MO. DAY YR.

ADDRESS _____ PHONE _____

CITY _____ STATE _____ ZIP _____

BUSINESS OR SCHOOL ADDRESS _____

HEIGHT __5' 6"__ WEIGHT __220__ HAIR __Black__ EYES __Brown__ COMPLEXION __Bad__ OCCUPATION _____

CLOTHING, ETC. __Green jacket, tan pants, wire-rimmed glasses. No rings or jewelry visible.__

VEHICLE INVOLVED

☐ USED ☐ STOLEN ☐ TOWED ☐ DAMAGED ☐ BURGLARIZED ☐ WRECKER ☐ OTHER _____

YEAR ____ MAKE ____ MODEL ____ BODY STYLE ____ COLOR ____ DECAL ____

LICENSE TAG NO. ____ STATE ____ YEAR EXPIRES ____ I.D. OR VIN NO. ____

REMARKS: __Use and make of vehicle unknown at this time__

ENTERED FCIC/NCIC ☐ YES ☐ NO   BOLO ☐ YES ☐ NO   MESSAGE NO. _____

NARRATIVE: __Last night at approximately 22:50 hours, a white male entered the convenience store at 4760 Forest Road. The suspect moved right to the register and was met by the store manager Jimenez who thought he was a customer. As Jimenez moved to the counter, the suspect pulled up the right side of his coat and produced from the area of his waist band a black hand gun. Holding the gun in his right hand the suspect told Jimenez the manager "let's go into the back room." As Jimenez approached the register, the suspect said "hold it, open the register," which was complied with by Jimenez. The suspect then forced Jimenez into a back storage room of the business where Jimenez was cuffed to the pipes of a sink. The suspect then warned Jimenez to keep quiet and shut the storage room door and went back into the store where Jimenez heard him moving about. A few minutes later, a white female entered the store and upon finding it empty called this department at which time we responded. The suspect's way of exiting the scene and direction of travel are unknown at this time. The fire dept. cut Jimenez free.__

DISPOSITION: __NOTE: This case resembles a robbery 3 weeks ago, Case #AR-83-46018.__

FURTHER POLICE ACTION TAKEN   YES ☐   NO ☐   REFERRED TO __Detective Bureau__

__Horan__ _____ __879__

REPORTING OFFICER'S NAME (PRINT)   I.D. NO. (INITIAL)

__K. W.__

APPROVED BY

RECORDS

EXERCISE 15
Public Affairs Reporting

SHERIFF'S OFFICE

COMPLAINT REPORT

ZONE __3__ UNIT __10__

CASE NO. __813-47-C28__

GRID __7__

PAGE __One__ OF __one__

OTHER AGCY CASE NO. __None__

MESSAGE NUMBER __842 - DN__

DATE __Yesterday__
MONTH   DAY   YR

TIME RECEIVED __9:10 p.__ TIME DISPATCHED __9:12 p.__ TIME ARRIVED __9:17 p.__ TIME IN-SERVICE __10:23 p.__ WEATHER _____

NATURE OF CASE __Strongarm robbery__ CHANGED TO _____ F.S.S.____ FEL.____ MISD.____

LOCATION OF OCCURRENCE (INCL. NAME OF BUSINESS/SCHOOL) __Mr. Grocer   4740 Hobson Street__

VICTIM: __Hessling__ (LAST) __Dorothy__ (FIRST) __L.__ (MIDDLE) AGE __27__ R/S __B__ DOB MO. DAY YR.

HOME ADDRESS __8197 Locke Avenue__ PHONE __671-3071__

CITY __Local__ STATE _____ ZIP _____

BUSINESS ADDRESS __4740 Hobson Street__ PHONE __671-1047__

CITY __Local__ STATE _____ ZIP _____

REPORTER ☐
WITNESS ☐ _____ PHONE _____

CITY _____ STATE _____ ZIP _____

PROPERTY MISSING/STOLEN

QUAN.	ITEM	DESCRIPTION - SERIAL NO. - MFG NO. - ETC	EST. VALUE $ STOLEN	RECOVERED
		$1,690 in cash, mostly small bills, nothing larger than a $20. Includes about $100 in loose change.	$1,690	None

■ MISSING ■ SUSPECT ■ ARRESTED ■ WITNESS ■ OTHER

NAME _____ (LAST) _____ (FIRST) _____ (MIDDLE) AGE ____ R/S ____ DOB MO. DAY YR.

ADDRESS _____ PHONE _____

CITY _____ STATE _____ ZIP _____

BUSINESS OR SCHOOL ADDRESS _____

HEIGHT ____ WEIGHT ____ HAIR ____ EYES ____ COMPLEXION ____ OCCUPATION _____

CLOTHING, ETC., _____

VEHICLE INVOLVED

☒ USED ☐ STOLEN ☐ TOWED ☐ DAMAGED ☐ BURGLARIZED ☐ WRECKER ☐ OTHER _____

YEAR __New__ MAKE __Unknown__ MODEL _____ BODY STYLE __Station wagon__ COLOR __White__ DECAL _____

LICENSE TAG NO. _____ STATE _____ YEAR EXPIRES _____ I.D. OR VIN NO. _____

REMARKS: _____

ENTERED FCIC/NCIC ☐ YES ☐ NO   BOLO ☐ YES ☐ NO   MESSAGE NO. _____

NARRATIVE: __Hessling said she was carrying the day's bank deposit for the store to her car when she was robbed. Victim reports seeing a man in a white station wagon parked near her car in the parking lot alongside the store. He was described by the victim as in his mid 30s, had a dark beard and something over his head, possibly the hood of a sweatshirt. As the victim opened her car door, the man got out of the station wagon and asked her for directions. When she turned to look at him, he sprayed her in the face with a chemical substance, probably mace. Victim was temporarily blinded and said he grabbed the money from her, and she heard his vehicle exit the parking lot in an apparent easterly direction. Victim states that the perpetrator seemed to know who she was and to be familiar with her routine as he went right for her and the bank receipts whereas he could have robbed any number of customers or other employees leaving the store that night.__

DISPOSITION: _____

FURTHER POLICE ACTION TAKEN   YES ☐   NO ☐   REFERRED TO __Detective Squad__

__Henderson, Leon__   __782__   __C.K.__
REPORTING OFFICER'S NAME (PRINT)   I.D. NO. (INITIAL)   APPROVED BY

RECORDS

EXERCISE 16
Public Affairs Reporting

SHERIFF'S OFFICE

COMPLAINT REPORT

ZONE __3__ UNIT __10__

GRID __7__   PAGE __1__ OF __1__

MESSAGE NUMBER __891- DN__

CASE NO. __A874-389224__

OTHER AGCY CASE NO. __Collier Cty #82411__

DATE __Today__   MONTH   DAY   YR

TIME RECEIVED __8:50 a.__   TIME DISPATCHED __8:52 a.__   TIME ARRIVED __9 a.__   TIME IN-SERVICE __11:20 a.__   WEATHER _____

NATURE OF CASE __Apparent hit and run__ CHANGED TO __Unavoidable accident__ FSS ____ FEL ____ MISD ____

LOCATION OF OCCURRENCE (INCL. NAME OF BUSINESS/SCHOOL) __Called to Allison Ford (service dept.)__

VICTIM: __Welke__ (LAST) __Milan__ (FIRST) __J__ (MIDDLE) AGE __52__ R/S ____ DOB MO. DAY YR.

HOME ADDRESS __Unknown. Original case handled by Collier County__ PHONE _____

CITY _____ STATE _____ ZIP _____

BUSINESS ADDRESS _____ PHONE _____

CITY _____ STATE _____ ZIP _____

REPORTER [X] WITNESS [ ] __Robert Allen Barlow, mechanic, Allison Ford__ PHONE __671-0202__

CITY _____ STATE _____ ZIP _____

PROPERTY MISSING/STOLEN

QUAN.	ITEM	DESCRIPTION - SERIAL NO. - MFG NO. - ETC	EST. VALUE $ STOLEN	RECOVERED

■ MISSING ■ SUSPECT ■ ARRESTED ■ WITNESS ■ OTHER

NAME __Mentzer-Meyer__ (LAST) __Sonya__ (FIRST) __M.__ (MIDDLE) AGE __47__ R/S ____ DOB MO. DAY YR.

ADDRESS __811 Moore Street__ PHONE __782-8137__

CITY __Local__ STATE _____ ZIP _____

BUSINESS OR SCHOOL ADDRESS __None__

HEIGHT __5'8"__ WEIGHT __130__ HAIR __Brown__ EYES __Brown__ COMPLEXION __Clear__ OCCUPATION __Housewife__

CLOTHING, ETC., _____

VEHICLE INVOLVED

[ ] USED [ ] STOLEN [ ] TOWED [X] DAMAGED [ ] BURGLARIZED [ ] WRECKER [ ] OTHER _____

YEAR __88__ MAKE __Buick__ MODEL __LeSabre__ BODY STYLE __4-door__ COLOR __Tan__ DECAL __Yes__

LICENSE TAG NO. _____ STATE _____ YEAR EXPIRES _____ I.D. OR VIN NO. _____

REMARKS: _____

ENTERED FCIC/NCIC [ ] YES [ ] NO   BOLO [ ] YES [ ] NO   MESSAGE NO. _____

NARRATIVE: At approx. 8:30 hrs. Robert Barlow, a mechanic for Allison Ford, began work on the Mentzer-Meyer vehicle. Barlow noticed on the undercarriage what appeared to be human hair, blood, flesh, and clothing. At that time he called another mechanic. After they both observed the undercarriage of the vehicle, it was determined that the police should be called. Further investigation and questioning of the owner revealed that she had driven to another part of the state last weekend to visit a daughter at night. Along the way on a dark strip of highway a man tried to flag her down. Afraid she drove around him and continued. After having arrived at her daughter, the woman contacted the local sheriff who said nothing had been reported but he would look into it. The Collier Cty. sheriff confirms the woman's story and says he had trouble getting back to her but intends to do so. After her call he learned the man waving his arms on the highway had hit a pedestrian and was trying to stop the woman for help. She apparently then unknowingly ran over the already-hit pedestrian accidentally. No charges have been filed against anyone. The sheriff says several vehicles hit the deceased, who appears to have been drunk, and it is impossible to determine what vehicle killed him. No further action is contemplated.

DISPOSITION:

FURTHER POLICE ACTION TAKEN YES [ ] NO [X] REFERRED TO _____

__Henderson, Leon__   __782__   __C.K.__

REPORTING OFFICER'S NAME (PRINT)   I.D. NO. (INITIAL)   APPROVED BY

RECORDS

EXERCISE 17
Public Affairs Reporting

TRAFFIC ACCIDENT REPORT
MAIL TO: ACCIDENT RECORDS BUREAU, DEPT. OF HIGHWAY SAFETY & MOTOR VEHICLES

TIME & LOCATION

| DATE OF ACCIDENT: | Month | Day | Year | DAY OF WEEK Yesterday | | TIME OF DAY 11:40 p. | M |

COUNTY (Yours)

CITY, TOWN OR COMMUNITY

LOCAL ACCIDENT REPORT NUMBER 34178004

IF ACCIDENT WAS OUTSIDE CITY LIMITS, INDICATE DISTANCE FROM NEAREST TOWN ... 1½ — [ ] Feet [X] Miles [ ][X][ ][ ] N S E W Of (Your City) City, Village or Township

ROAD ON WHICH ACCIDENT OCCURRED S. R. 17 — Use State or County Road Number or Name — [ ] Exit Ramp — At its intersection with [ ] Entrance R. — Influenced by intersection — Highway Number or Name of Intersecting Street and Node

IF NOT AT INTER- SECTION 400 — [X] Feet [ ] Miles [ ][X][ ][ ] N S E W Of County Road 41 — Show nearest intersecting street or highway, bridge, RR crossing, underpass or curve

[ ] Feet [ ] Miles N S E W of Node

IS ENGINEERING STUDY NEEDED (if so explain) No

DO NOT WRITE IN SPACE ABOVE

| TYPE MOTOR VEHICLE ACCIDENT | OVERTURNING | OTHER NONCOLLISION | PEDESTRIAN | MV IN TRANSPORT | MV ON OTHER ROADWAY | HIT AND RUN |
| | PARKED MV | RAILWAY TRAIN | PEDALCYCLIST | ANIMAL | FIXED OBJECT XXX | OTHER OBJECT | NON-CONTACT |

VEHICLE 1

| TOTAL NO. MOTOR Vehicles Involved | YEAR 1978 | MAKE Ford | TYPE (Sedan, Truck, Bus, etc.) Sedan | VEHICLE LICENSE PLATE NO. B678-510 | STATE Yes | YEAR Cur. | VEHICLE IDENTIFICATION NO. 811-423084 |

| Area of Vehicle Damage | 1 | 2 | 4 | | Damage Scale 1 | Damage Severity 1 | AMOUNT (Approximate) | Safety Equip- ment | VEHICLE REMOVED BY Bob's Shell |

NAME OF INSURANCE (Liability or PIP) Allstate — POLICY NO. 963-818-59 — Owner [ ] Driver [XX] — [ ] Owner's Request [ ] Other (Explain) — [XX] Rotation List

OWNER (Print or type FULL name) Alton J. Reimer — ADDRESS (Number and street) 2529 Barbados Avenue — CITY and STATE /Zip Code (Yours)

DRIVER (Exactly as on driver's license) Same as above — ADDRESS (Number and street) — CITY and STATE /Zip Code

| OCCUPATION Student | Driver's License Type A | DRIVER'S LICENSE NUMBER 471380059 | STATE Yes | DATE (Month, Day, Year) OF BIRTH Age 17 | RACE W | SEX M | Safety E. | Eject. X | Injury X |

OCCUPANTS	Name	ADDRESS – Number and Street	City and State /Zip Code	AGE	RACE	SEX	Safety E.	Eject.	Injury
Front center	Marlene Anne Guyer	4043 S. 28th Street		17	W	F			X
Front right									
Rear left									
Rear center									
Rear right									

VEHICLE 2 or PEDESTRIAN

| YEAR | MAKE | TYPE (Sedan, Truck, Bus, etc.) | VEHICLE LICENSE PLATE NO. | STATE | YEAR | VEHICLE IDENTIFICATION NO. |

| Area of Vehicle Damage | | | | | Damage Scale | Damage Severity | AMOUNT (Approximate) | Safety Equip- ment | VEHICLE REMOVED BY |

NAME OF INSURANCE (Liability or PIP) — POLICY NO. — Owner [ ] Driver [ ] — [ ] Owner's Request [ ] Other (Explain) — [ ] Rotation List

OWNER (Print or type FULL name) — ADDRESS (Number and street) — CITY and STATE /Zip Code

DRIVER (Exactly as on driver's license) — ADDRESS (Number and street) — CITY and STATE /Zip Code

| OCCUPATION | Driver's License Type | DRIVER'S LICENSE NUMBER | STATE | DATE (Month, Day, Year) OF BIRTH | RACE | SEX | Safety E. | Eject. | Injury |

OCCUPANTS	Name	ADDRESS – (Number and Street)	City and State Zip Code	AGE	RACE	SEX	Safety E.	Eject.	Injury
Front center									
Front right									
Rear left									
Rear center									
Rear right									

| PROPERTY DAMAGED–Other than vehicles Utility pole | AMOUNT $500 | OWNER – Name | ADDRESS – Number and Street State Power & Light, 2480 S. Main Street | CITY and STATE /Zip Code |

| INVESTIGATOR – Name and rank (Signature) Cpl. Alvarez | BADGE NO. 3814 | I.D. NO. 684172 | DEPARTMENT Highway Patrol | [ ] F.H.P. [X] C.P.D. [ ] S.O. [ ] Other | DATE OF REPORT |

SHEET One OF Two SHEETS

INDICATE NORTH
WITH ARROW

POINT OF IMPACT

Vehicle	1	2	
	☒	☐	Front
	☐	☐	Right front
	☐	☐	Left front
	☐	☐	Right side
	☐	☐	Left side
	☐	☐	Rear
	☐	☐	Right rear
	☐	☐	Left rear

DESCRIBE WHAT HAPPENED – (Refer to vehicles by number)

Reimer was trying to pass a truck driven by J. Vernon Flavell, 827 N. Pigeon Road. Flavell estimates he was traveling about 50 mph and the car was going 60 to 70 mph at the time. Skid marks confirm the car was going 59 mph. Reimer apparently lost control of the car as he pulled alongside Flavell's vehicle and his car ran off the left side of the road, struck a utility pole and stopped, rightside up, in a field 87 feet from the edge of the pavement. Neither occupant was wearing a seat belt, and Reimer was ejected through the windshield, apparently on impact with the utility pole. Guyer remained in the vehicle. Hospital officials say Reimer died of massive head injuries. The girl has been admitted to the hospital's intensive care unit with multiple internal injuries and is listed in serious condition. We were unable to interview either victim at the scene of the accident, Reimer being dead when we arrived at the scene.

*WHAT VEHICLES WERE DOING BEFORE ACCIDENT

VEHICLE No. 1 was traveling ☒☒☐☐☐ On S.R. 17 at 59 Approximately M.P.H.

VEHICLE No. 2 was traveling ☐☐☐☐ On at M.P.H.

Vehicle 1 2		Vehicle 1 2		Vehicle 1 2		Vehicle 1 2	
☐ ☐	Going straight ahead	☐ ☐	Making right turn	☐ ☐	Slowing or Stopping	☐ ☐	Starting from parked position
☒☒ ☐	Overtaking	☐ ☐	Making left turn	☐ ☐	Changing lanes	☐ ☐	Stopped or parked
						☐ ☐	Other (explain above)

*WHAT PEDESTRIAN WAS DOING

PEDESTRIAN was going ☐☐☐☐ (check one)

☐ Along

☐ Across or into from to (Street name, highway no.) (N.E. corner to S.E. corner, etc.)

Color of Clothing ☐ ☐ Dark Light

☐ Crossing at Intersection	☐ Stepped into path of Vehicle	☐ Getting on or off Vehicle	☐ Playing in roadway
☐ Crossing not at Intersection	☐ Standing in roadway	☐ Hitching on Vehicle	☐ Other roadway
☐ Walking in roadway – with traffic	☐ Standing in safety zone	☐ Pushing or working on Vehicle	☐ Not in roadway
☐ Walking in roadway – against traffic	☐ Lying or Sitting on roadway	☐ Other working in roadway	☐ Other (explain above)

DRIVERS AND VEHICLES

		VEHICLE 1	VEHICLE 2
PHYSICAL DEFECTS (Driver)	}		
VEHICLE DEFECTS	}		
CONTRI- BUTING	}		
CIRCUM- STANCES	}		

ACCIDENT Characteristics	LIGHTING CONDITION	Dark	ROAD DEFECTS	None	TRAFFICWAY CHARACTER	Light	CLASS OF TRAFFICWAYS	7
	WEATHER	Overc	TRAFFIC CONTROL	None	TRAFFICWAY LANES	Two	TYPE TRAFFICWAY	3
	ROAD SURFACE	Dry	TYPE LOCATION	Str.	VISION OBSCURED	No		

WITNESSES other than occupants

NAME	ADDRESS – Number and street	City and State /Zip Code
J. Vernon Flavell, 827 N. Pigeon Rd.		(Yours)

FIRST AID GIVEN BY

J. Vernon Flavell

☐ Doctor or Nurse ☐ Cert. First Aider
☐ Cert. First Aider (Police) ☐ Other (Explain)

CHEMICAL TEST: YES NO
Driver No. 1 ☒ ☐ Not yet in
Driver No. 2 ☐ ☐

TEST RESULTS:

INJURED TAKEN TO
Memorial Hospital

BY:
Cleary Ambulance

☒ Priv. Ambulance ☐ Other (Explain)
☐ Gov't. Ambulance

ARREST

NAME	CHARGE	Citation No.
NAME	CHARGE	Citation No.

PHOTOGRAPHS TAKEN
☒ Yes ☐ No
☐ Invest. Agency
☐ Other (Explain)

TIME NOTIFIED OF ACCIDENT	TIME ARRIVED AT SCENE	WAS INVESTIGATION MADE AT SCENE (If not where)	IS INVESTIGATION COMPLETE (If not why)
11:44 19 P. M	12:03 A. M	Yes	Need to interview surviving passenger

EXERCISE 18
Public Affairs Reporting

TRAFFIC ACCIDENT REPORT
MAIL TO: ACCIDENT RECORDS BUREAU, DEPT. OF HIGHWAY SAFETY & MOTOR VEHICLES,

TIME & LOCATION	DATE OF ACCIDENT — Month / Day / Year	DAY OF WEEK — Yesterday	TIME OF DAY — 11:35 p. M
	COUNTY (Yours)	CITY, TOWN OR COMMUNITY	LOCAL ACCIDENT REPORT NUMBER 34178005
	IF ACCIDENT WAS OUTSIDE CITY LIMITS, INDICATE DISTANCE FROM NEAREST TOWN 4	☐ Feet ☒ Miles — ☐☐☒☐ N S E W	of (Your city) City, Village or Township
	ROAD ON WHICH ACCIDENT OCCURRED U.S. 141 — Use State or County Road Number or Name	☐ Exit Ramp ☐ Entrance R. At its intersection with / Influenced by intersection	Highway Number or Name of Intersecting Street and Node
	IF NOT AT INTERSECTION 2	☐ Feet ☒ Miles — ☐☐☒☒ N S E W	of State Route 19 — Show nearest intersecting street or highway, bridge, RR crossing, underpass or curve
		☐ Feet ☐ Miles — ☐☐☐☐ N S E W of Node	IS ENGINEERING STUDY NEEDED (if so explain) None — DO NOT WRITE IN SPACE ABOVE

TYPE MOTOR VEHICLE ACCIDENT	OVERTURNING	OTHER NONCOLLISION	PEDESTRIAN	MV IN TRANSPORT	MV ON OTHER ROADWAY	HIT AND RUN
	PARKED MV xxx	RAILWAY TRAIN	PEDALCYCLIST	ANIMAL	FIXED OBJECT	OTHER OBJECT	NON-CONTACT

VEHICLE 1

TOTAL NO. MOTOR Vehicles Involved	YEAR 1977	MAKE Buick	TYPE (Sedan, Truck, Bus, etc.) Sedan	VEHICLE LICENSE PLATE NO. 7D-8434	STATE Yes	YEAR Cur.	VEHICLE IDENTIFICATION NO. 817-93200745

Area of Vehicle Damage	4	5	6	Damage Scale 1	Damage Severity 1	AMOUNT (Approximate)	Safety Equipment	VEHICLE REMOVED BY Halston Towing

NAME OF INSURANCE (Liability or PIP) Liberty Mutual — POLICY NO. 84-992-8341 — Owner ☒☒ Driver ☐ — ☐ Owner's Request ☐ Other (Explain) — ☒☒ Rotation List

OWNER (Print or type FULL name) Mr. and Mrs. Harry Ralph Novogroski — ADDRESS (Number and street) 2891 Norris Avenue — CITY and STATE / Zip Code (Yours)

DRIVER (Exactly as on driver's license) Harry R. Novogroski — ADDRESS (Number and street) 2891 Norris Avenue — CITY and STATE / Zip Code (Yours)

OCCUPATION Machinist	Driver's License Type A	DRIVER'S LICENSE NUMBER 74-892-4837	STATE Yes	DATE (Month, Day, Year) OF BIRTH 3/23/27	RACE B	SEX M	Safety E.	Eject.	Injury X

OCCUPANTS	Name	ADDRESS – Number and Street	City and State/Zip Code	AGE	RACE	SEX	Safety E.	Eject.	Injury
Front center									
Front right									
Rear left	Mary Ruth Novogroski	2891 Norris Ave.		15	B	F			X
Rear center	Margaret Sue Novogroski	2891 Norris Ave.		11	B	F			X
Rear right	Matthew Harold Novogroski	2891 Norris Ave.		9	B	M			X

VEHICLE 2 or PEDESTRIAN

YEAR 1978	MAKE Chevy	TYPE (Sedan, Truck, Bus, etc.) Pickup truck	VEHICLE LICENSE PLATE NO. 7d-3680	STATE Yes	YEAR Cur.	VEHICLE IDENTIFICATION NO. 935-8780341

Area of Vehicle Damage	1	2	3	Damage Scale 1	Damage Severity 1	AMOUNT (Approximate)	Safety Equipment	VEHICLE REMOVED BY Halston Towing

NAME OF INSURANCE (Liability or PIP) Not yet determined — POLICY NO. — Owner ☐ Driver ☐ — ☐ Owner's Request ☐ Other (Explain) — ☒☒ Rotation List

OWNER (Print or type FULL name) Donald Edward Guerin — ADDRESS (Number and street) 1045 Eastview Road — CITY and STATE / Zip Code (Yours)

DRIVER (Exactly as on driver's license) Same as above — ADDRESS (Number and street) — CITY and STATE / Zip Code

OCCUPATION City fireman	Driver's License Type A	DRIVER'S LICENSE NUMBER 62-311-3828	STATE Yes	DATE (Month, Day, Year) OF BIRTH 11/3/56	RACE W	SEX M	Safety E.	Eject.	Injury

OCCUPANTS	Name	ADDRESS – (Number and Street)	City and State/Zip Code	AGE	RACE	SEX	Safety E.	Eject.	Injury
Front center									
Front right									
Rear left	None								
Rear center									
Rear right									

PROPERTY DAMAGED–Other than vehicles None — AMOUNT — OWNER – Name — ADDRESS – Number and Street — CITY and STATE / Zip Code

INVESTIGATOR – Name and rank (Signature) Cpl. Alvarez	BADGE NO. 3814	I.D. NO. 684172	DEPARTMENT Highway Patrol	☐ F.H.P. ☒ C.P.D. ☐ S.O. ☐ Other	DATE OF REPORT

SHEET One OF Two SHEETS

DIAGRAM WHAT HAPPENED – (Number each vehicle and show direction of travel by arrow)

↑ INDICATE NORTH WITH ARROW

POINT OF IMPACT		
Vehicle		
1	2	
☐	☒	Front
☐	☐	Right front
☐	☐	Left front
☐	☐	Right side
☐	☐	Left side
☒	☐	Rear
☐	☐	Right rear
☐	☐	Left rear

#2   #1

DESCRIBE WHAT HAPPENED – (Refer to vehicles by number)

Novogroski had experienced a flat tire and drove onto the shoulder, completely leaving the roadway with his vehicle, to change it. His wife was outside with him, apparently holding a light of some type, when vehicle #2 struck the rear of their car, crushing the couple between the two vehicles, apparently killing them outright. Guerin was not injured and was wearing a seatbelt at the time. Three children in vehicle #1 were injured and taken to Eastbrook Hospital, although the extent of their injuries was not immediately determined. Gasoline ignited, setting both vehicles totally ablaze, burning one of the children who had not yet gotten out of the car. Bystanders helped pull the child out, as did Guerin.

---

*WHAT VEHICLES WERE DOING BEFORE ACCIDENT

VEHICLE No. 1 was traveling ☐☒☐☐ N S E W   On U.S. 141 at 0 M.P.H.   Approximate's

VEHICLE No. 2 was traveling ☐☐☒☐ N S E W   On U.S. 141 at 50 M.P.H.

Vehicle 1 2		Vehicle 1 2		Vehicle 1 2		Vehicle 1 2	
☐ ☒	Going straight ahead	☐ ☐	Making right turn	☐ ☐	Slowing or Stopping	☐ ☐	Starting from parked position
☐ ☐	Overtaking	☐ ☐	Making left turn	☐ ☐	Changing lanes	☒ ☐	Stopped or parked
						☐ ☐	Other (explain above)

*WHAT PEDESTRIAN WAS DOING   ☐ Along

PEDESTRIAN was going ☐☐☐☐ (check one) N S E W   ☐ Across or into _____ (Street name, highway no.) from _____ to _____ (N.E. corner to S.E. corner, etc.)   Color of Clothing Dark ___ Light

☐ Crossing at intersection	☐ Stepped into path of Vehicle	☐ Getting on or off Vehicle	☐ Playing in roadway
☐ Crossing not at intersection	☐ Standing in roadway	☐ Hitching on Vehicle	☐ Other roadway
☐ Walking in roadway – with traffic	☐ Standing in safety zone	☐ Pushing or working on Vehicle	☐ Not in roadway
☐ Walking in roadway – against traffic	☐ Lying or Sitting on roadway	☐ Other working in roadway	☐ Other (explain above)

	DRIVERS AND VEHICLES	
	VEHICLE 1	VEHICLE 2
PHYSICAL DEFECTS (Driver)		
VEHICLE DEFECTS		
CONTRI-BUTING CIRCUM-STANCES		

ACCIDENT **Characteristics**	LIGHTING CONDITION	Dark	ROAD DEFECTS	None	TRAFFICWAY CHARACTER	Quiet	CLASS OF TRAFFICWAYS	4
	WEATHER	Normal	TRAFFIC CONTROL	None	TRAFFICWAY LANES	2 lane	TYPE TRAFFICWAY	2
	ROAD SURFACE	Dry	TYPE LOCATION	Hwy.	VISION OBSCURED	No		

WITNESSES other than occupants	NAME	ADDRESS – Number and street	City and State / Zip Code
	None		

FIRST AID GIVEN BY			
Donald Guerin	☐ Doctor or Nurse ☒ Cert. First Aider ☐ Cert. First Aider (Police) ☐ Other (Explain)		

CHEMICAL TEST:		TEST RESULTS:
	YES NO	
Driver No. 1	☐ ☐	
Driver No. 2	☒ ☐	Negative

INJURED TAKEN TO	BY
Eastbrook Hospital	Cleary Ambulance ☒ Priv. Ambulance ☐ Other (Explain) ☐ Gov't. Ambulance

ARREST	NAME	CHARGE	Citation No.	PHOTOGRAPHS TAKEN
	Donald Edward Guerin	Manslaughter	8320816	☒ Yes ☐ No
	NAME	CHARGE	Citation No.	☐ Invest. Agency ☐ Other (Explain)

TIME NOTIFIED OF ACCIDENT	TIME ARRIVED AT SCENE	WAS INVESTIGATION MADE AT SCENE (If not where)	IS INVESTIGATION COMPLETE (If not why)
11:47 19 ___ P.M	11:54 M	Yes	Yes

EXERCISE 19
Public Affairs Reporting

In the Circuit Court of
The 9th Judicial Circuit
in and for (your) County

Division: Civil

Case No.: C971-7782

FRENCHIE'S RESTAURANT, INC.,

by Maria and Roy Menut, *Plaintiffs*,

vs.

WOWL CHANNEL FOUR, *Defendant.*

COMPLAINT

COME NOW the Plaintiffs by and through the undersigned attorney, and sue the Defendant and say:

1. This is an action for damages of $1 million.

2. Plaintiff, FRENCHIE'S RESTAURANT, INC., was a corporation duly organized under the Laws of the State which was dissolved by operation of law by virtue of a discharge in Bankruptcy on or about the 12th of this year.

3. The Plaintiffs, MARIA AND ROY MENUT, are the successors and assigns of the Plaintiff, FRENCHIE'S RESTAURANT, INC.

4. The Defendant, WOWL CHANNEL FOUR, is a television broadcasting station which conducts business in the State.

5. On or about September 2 of last year, the Defendant, WOWL CHANNEL FOUR, a television broadcasting station, by an agent known to the general public and the Plaintiffs as the "Mystery Diner," did utter and publish and broadcast to the general public in this and other surrounding Counties in the area defamatory statements about the Plaintiffs, alleged to be a review of the meals served at said restaurant, to wit:

(a) The Defendant stated that "A Coca Cola cost $3".

(b) The Defendant stated that a meal for two cost $94.10. "Wow, that's almost $100.00".

(c) The Defendant stated that "The house wine tasted like a cheap domestic brand" thereby falsely implying that Plaintiff attempted to mislead and cheat its customers.

(d) The Defendant stated that "The fish was advertised as fresh but tasted as though it had been frozen" thereby falsely implying that Plaintiff attempted to cheat its customers, and further, that Plaintiff was guilty of false advertising.

(e) The Defendant stated that "The seafood medley I ordered was supposed to contain shrimp, scallops, fish and lobster, but I couldn't find the lobster" thereby falsely implying that Plaintiff attempted to cheat its customers.

6. The statements made by the Defendant were false at the time they were made,

were broadcast with a malicious intent to injure the business of the Plaintiffs, and did so injure the Plaintiffs in its business and reputation in the community, to wit:

(a) During the week immediately following the broadcast of said review, the Plaintiffs received a total of forty-three (43) cancellations.

(b) During the month immediately following the broadcast of said review, the number of meals served by the restaurant dropped by fifty (50) percent and never recovered.

(c) That the restaurant, which had been earning sizable profits until the date of broadcast, was forced into bankruptcy due to the sudden and immediate loss of business caused solely and directly by said broadcast.

7. A written request for a retraction or correction and apology was made to the Defendant more than five (5) days prior to the filing of this suit. No such retraction was made.

WHEREFORE, THE PLAINTIFFS demand trial by jury on all issues so triable, Judgment against the Defendant for damages, compensatory and punitive, attorneys fees, costs of Court, and such other and further relief as this Court deems just.

_____

Roy Menuet

_____

Dennis F. Dealfonso
710 Sunbranch Road
Attorney for Plaintiffs

EXERCISE 20
Public Affairs Reporting

**In the Circuit Court of
The 9th Judicial Circuit
in and for (your) County**

Division: Civil

Case No. C971-7783

TONY DEWITTE,   *Plaintiff,*

vs.

BUDDY RICHBOURG
d/b/a BUDDY'S LOUNGE, *Defendant.*

COMPLAINT

COMES NOW the Plaintiff and sues the Defendant and says:

1. This is an action for damages in the amount of SIX HUNDRED THOUSAND ($600,000) DOLLARS, plus all costs and reasonable attorneys' fees.

2. That at all times material to this cause, Defendant, BUDDY'S LOUNGE, was a business operating in this county.

3. That at all times mentioned herein, the Defendant operated and controlled a bar known as BUDDY'S LOUNGE located in this county, to which the general public was invited for the purpose of obtaining recreation and alcoholic beverages for compensation to be paid to Defendant.

4. On or about December 10 of last year, TONY DEWITTE was a patron in Defendant's bar.

5. At that time and place, and without provocation, a man unknown to the Plaintiff, and others, all in a highly intoxicated condition, willfully and maliciously assaulted and beat TONY DEWITTE and struck him repeatedly, breaking his nose, jaw and arm, and causing him the traumatic loss of several teeth.

6. The assault on TONY DEWITTE was caused by the negligence of Defendant in failing to exercise proper supervision and control over the persons in the bar, when the Defendant knew or should have known that such persons were intoxicated and belligerent and posed a threat to Plaintiff and others.

7. The negligence of Defendant, in addition to that hereinabove alleged, consisted of failing to provide an employee or employees to maintain proper order and exercise reasonable care for the safety of patrons, or the failure of such an employee to perform his duties and prevent injuries sustained by the Plaintiff.

8. The negligence of Defendant, in addition to that hereinabove alleged, consisted of continuing to sell known intoxicants to the assailants long after they had become loud, abusive and argumentative.

9. The negligence of Defendant, in addition to that hereinabove alleged, consisted of failing, once the altercation had commenced, to promptly come to the aid of the Defendant and to seek the assistance of the police and other appropriate law enforcement officials.

10. That as a direct and proximate result of the negligence of the Defendant, TONY DEWITTE sustained a broken nose, jaw and arm, and the traumatic loss of several teeth.

11. At the time of his injuries, the said TONY DEWITTE was of good health, industrious and thrifty, and enjoyed a substantial earning capacity and was acquiring property and resources.

12. As a result of Defendant's negligence, TONY DEWITTE incurred medical expenses, a loss of earnings and a permanent disability as well as pain and suffering, mental anguish, and humiliation and future medical expenses.

WHEREFORE, THE PLAINTIFF sues the Defendant and demands judgment for damages, costs, trial by jury and such other relief as the Court deems just.

Enrique Diaz
208 Baxter Avenue
Attorney for Plaintiff

EXERCISE 21
Public Affairs Reporting

In the Circuit Court of
The 9th Judicial Circuit
in and for (your) County

Division: Civil

Case No.: CI-74-8614

RONALD R. DEMPSEY,
PEGGY ALBERT DEMPSEY
d/b/a DEMPSEY'S
RESTAURANT,   *Plaintiffs,*

vs.

(YOUR) CITY,   *Defendant.*

COMPLAINT

COME NOW the Plaintiffs, RONALD R. DEMPSEY and PEGGY ALBERT DEMPSEY, by and through their undersigned counsel, and sue the Defendant, (YOUR) CITY, and as grounds therefor would show and allege as follows:

1. This is an action for damages of $820,000 and is within the jurisdiction of this Honorable Court.
2. All conditions precedent pursuant to State Statute #768.28 have been complied with.
3. The Fire Department serving the city is a department of the Defendant.
4. RONALD R. DEMPSEY and PEGGY ALBERT DEMPSEY, at all times relevant to this Complaint, owned and operated a business known as, DEMPSEY'S RESTAURANT, located at 4840 Colonial Drive in this city.

COUNT I

1. On or about the evening of September 23 of last year, the City Fire Department responded to an alarm at 4840 Colonial Drive.
2. The City Fire Department found an obviously minor fire in the kitchen of DEMPSEY'S RESTAURANT shortly after their arrival at 4840 Colonial Drive.
3. The City Fire Department then attempted to extinguish the fire.
4. After the City Fire Department supposedly extinguished the fire, they made a brief examination of the premises.
5. The City Fire Department then left the scene of the fire.
6. The fire was not extinguished or the same fire was reignited or the effects of the fire, heat and smoke, created a new fire in the early morning hours of September 24 which caused extensive damage to the premises located at 4840 Colonial Drive and all the objects located within those premises.
7. The City Fire Department owed a duty to the public and Plaintiffs, to prevent control and inspect for fire, and to take reasonable precautions to prevent reignition of a fire.

8. The City Fire Department owed a duty to the Plaintiffs not to mislead the Plaintiffs into believing there was no danger of reignition and the original fire was completely extinguished. The Plaintiffs were misled by the Fire Department that there was no further potential for fire damage.

9. The Defendant was negligent in the following respects:
   (a) By not fully extinguishing the first fire prior to their departure;
   (b) By improperly inspecting for fire after the occurrence of the first fire;
   (c) By taking inadequate safeguards to prevent reignition of another fire after the first fire;
   (d) By failing to maintain a fire watch for a sufficient time after the first fire;
   (e) By failing to periodically recheck to determine if the first fire had been extinguished fully or the effects of the first fire caused another fire;
   (f) By misleading the Plaintiffs into believing the fire had been extinguished, that it was safe to leave the premises, and that there was no further danger of another fire occurring; and
   (g) By failing to take reasonable precautions to prevent the reignition of the first fire or its effects.

10. As a direct and proximate cause of the Defendant's negligence, the Plaintiffs' business located at 4840 Colonial Drive, and the contents within that business, were absolutely and totally destroyed, so that the building became unsafe for human use and, by order of building inspectors, had to be razed. In addition, the Plaintiffs lost the value and use of their business during the time required to construct a totally new building and to secure additional equipment and supplies.

WHEREFORE, THE PLAINTIFFS sue the Defendant and demand judgment for damages, costs, trial by jury and such other relief as the Court deems just.

Respectfully submitted

DAVID CASIO & ASSOCIATES
831 Forester Road
Attorneys for Plaintiffs

BY: *Bruce R. Washington*

BRUCE R. WASHINGTON

EXERCISE 22
Public Affairs Reporting

In the Circuit Court of
The 9th Judicial Circuit
in and for (your) County

Division: Probate

Case No.: PR 67-1381

IN RE: GUARDIANSHIP
OF PATRICIA JEAN
WILLIAMS, an Incompetent

JOHN RUSSELL
WILLIAMS, as Guardian
of the Person of
PATRICIA JEAN
WILLIAMS,   *Plaintiff,*

vs.

MERCY HOSPITAL;
ROSS R. GRAHAM,
M.D.; RICHARD M.
CESSARINI, M.D.;
SHERRY ANGERMEIR,
DISTRICT ATTORNEY,   *Defendants.*

FINAL DECLARATORY JUDGMENT

THIS CAUSE came for hearing upon the Complaint for Declaratory Relief because of the uncertainty of the law by JOHN RUSSELL WILLIAMS as Guardian of the Person of PATRICIA JEAN WILLIAMS, an Incompetent, against MERCY HOSPITAL; ROSS R. GRAHAM, M.D.; RICHARD M. CESSARINI, M.D.; and SHERRY ANGERMEIR, DISTRICT ATTORNEY for the city, the Defendants, wherein Plaintiff seeks a Declaratory Judgment as to the following:

Authorization for JOHN RUSSELL WILLIAMS, as Guardian of the Person of PATRICIA JEAN WILLIAMS, an Incompetent, to direct MERCY HOSPITAL; ROSS R. GRAHAM, M.D.; RICHARD M. CESSARINI, M.D.; and all other attending physicians and health care providers to discontinue and to withhold all extraordinary measures such as mechanical ventilators, respirators, antibiotics, cardiovascular or similar type drugs; that these extraordinary measures should not be utilized, but be discontinued or withheld, in that the doctors agree there is no reasonable possibility of the Ward ever recovering from her present, persistent, "vegetative" (coma-like) state, which is irreversible;

That your Petitioner, JOHN RUSSELL WILLIAMS, surviving son; MERCY HOSPITAL; ROSS R. GRAHAM, M.D.; RICHARD M. CESSARINI, M.D.; and all other treating and consulting physicians and health care providers shall not be held civilly or criminally liable for taking the above action; and

That an appropriate restraining order be issued restraining the Defendant, SHERRY ANGERMEIR, DISTRICT ATTORNEY, from prosecuting any of the above named individuals and organizations for withdrawing or withholding all extraordinary measures such as mechanical ventilators, respirators, antibiotics, cardiovascular or similar type drugs.

The Court makes the following findings of fact:

1. That this action is properly brought as a suit for declaratory judgment and relief, and that Plaintiff is the proper party to bring this action.

2. That at all times material hereto, the Plaintiff is a resident of the county in which this action is brought, and PATRICIA JEAN WILLIAMS, the Ward, has been maintained at MERCY HOSPITAL since she was involved in a serious motor vehicle accident 73 days prior to the issuance of this order.

3. That the following findings are based upon reasonable medical certainty and derived from the testimony of ROSS R. GRAHAM, M.D.; RICHARD M. CESSARINI, M.D.; and the records of MERCY HOSPITAL:

    (a) That four electroencephalograms, commonly referred to as EEGs, were performed on PATRICIA JEAN WILLIAMS, the Ward. None of the electroencephalograms indicated any cortical response. The only indication was a flat line.

    (b) That the Ward has suffered severe brain damage, which brain damage is totally irreversible and untreatable with no hope of recovery; and that the Ward is in a chronic and persistent "vegetative" (coma-like) state.

    (c) That the testimony of the doctors revealed that it was their respective medical opinion that all measures which are considered extraordinary lifesaving measures should not be utilized with respect to the Ward, but be discontinued or withheld; however, the decision to withdraw or withhold extraordinary lifesaving measures should be made by the Plaintiff and the family of the Ward.

    (d) That PATRICIA JEAN WILLIAMS, the Ward, requires constant care, and will so require IN THE FUTURE.

4. That PATRICIA JEAN WILLIAMS, the Ward, requires constant care, which care invades the Ward's body and violates the Ward's right to privacy as guaranteed by the Constitution of the United States of America and of this State; and that the State does not have an overriding interest it needs to protect, nor is there overriding medical interests that need to be protected.

5. That the son, JOHN RUSSELL WILLIAMS, has determined, subject to the approval of this Court, that all extraordinary lifesaving measures should not be utilized with respect to the Ward, but be discontinued or withheld from the Ward, PATRICIA JEAN WILLIAMS, and that MERCY HOSPITAL has no objection.

It is, therefore, ORDERED AND ADJUDGED:

1. That JOHN RUSSELL WILLIAMS, as the Guardian of the Person of PATRICIA JEAN WILLIAMS, an Incompetent, has full power to make decisions with regard to the identity of the Ward's treating physicians.

2. That MERCY HOSPITAL; ROSS R. GRAHAM, M.D.; and RICHARD M. CESSARINI, M.D., are authorized to discontinue or to withdraw all extraordinary measures and life-support systems upon written direction of JOHN RUSSELL WILLIAMS, as Guardian of the Person of PATRICIA JEAN WILLIAMS, an Incompetent.

3. That no one shall be held civilly or criminally liable for taking action authorized by this Order.

4. That the Defendant, SHERRY ANGERMEIR, as District Attorney for the city, shall be bound by this decision.

DONE AND ORDERED in Chambers.

BY: _Randall Pfaff_____

RANDALL PFAFF, Circuit Judge

EXERCISE 23
Public Affairs Reporting

In the Circuit Court of
The 9th Judicial Circuit
in and for (your) County

Division: Civil

Case No.: I-78-1439

JOHN H. WARD and
FRANCIS B. WARD,
individually and as next friends
and parents of KAREN
WARD, a minor,   *Plaintiffs,*

vs.

EILEEN BARTON and
BARTON SCHOOL
OF DANCE,   *Defendants.*

C O M P L A I N T

COME NOW the Plaintiffs and sue the Defendants and say:

1. This is an action for damages in the amount of $1,000,000 (One Million Dollars).
2. That at all times material to this cause, the Plaintiffs, JOHN H. WARD and FRANCIS B. WARD, were and are husband and wife residing together in this county, and that KAREN WARD is their natural born daughter.
3. That at all times material to this cause, the Defendants do business in this county and advertise the BARTON SCHOOL OF DANCE as a reputable institution, suitable for the enrollment of young children, and these advertisements further assert that lessons provided by said school will favorably promote the development of children's poise, health, happiness, personality and character.
4. That, to enrich the life of Plaintiff KAREN WARD, a minor and only daughter, Plaintiffs JOHN H. WARD and FRANCIS B. WARD enrolled the child in the BARTON SCHOOL OF DANCE and, at the personal urging of Defendant EILEEN BARTON, kept her in the school for a second year, regularly and at great personal sacrifice to themselves, paying a monthly fee of $48.50 for ballet lessons for Plaintiff KAREN WARD, during the course of both years.
5. That Willis A. Boyette was employed as a janitor by the Defendant, BARTON SCHOOL OF DANCE, and, due to the nature of his work, often came in close proximity to students.
6. That, on at least three separate occasions, Willis A. Boyette took Plaintiff KAREN WARD into a school restroom and violently and without her consent raped her.
7. That Plaintiff KAREN WARD was, at the time in question, only 9 years of age and a fourth-grade student at Croft Elementary School.
8. That the Plaintiff KAREN WARD did not immediately tell anyone of the attacks because of her confusion and shame and because she feared Boyette, who threatened her with further harm.

9. That Plaintiff KAREN WARD contracted a venereal disease and, when she was taken to a doctor for treatment of such disease, confided in that doctor and then in her parents about the attacks.

10. That, as a result of these attacks, the Plaintiff KAREN WARD has and continues to be very traumatized, fearful and unhappy, requiring psychiatric care of a continuing nature.

11. That the Defendants, EILEEN BARTON and BARTON SCHOOL OF DANCE, are solely responsible for the actions of Willis A. Boyette; that Boyette was personally hired by Defendant EILEEN BARTON, who thereupon failed to investigate adequately his background and to provide the proper supervision of his work.

12. That Willis A. Boyette has since been tried, convicted and sentenced to serve three to nine years in prison following his conviction in a criminal trial of carnal knowledge.

WHEREFORE, THE PLAINTIFFS, JOHN H. WARD and FRANCIS B. WARD, individually and as next friends and parents of KAREN WARD, a minor, sue the Defendants, EILEEN BARTON and BARTON SCHOOL OF DANCE, both jointly and severally, for compensatory damages in an amount within the jurisdictional limits of this Court, and demand trial by jury of all issues triable as of right by a jury.

DAVID CASIO & ASSOCIATES
831 Forester Road
Attorneys for Plaintiffs

BY: *Bruce R. Washington*
BRUCE R. WASHINGTON

EXERCISE 24
Public Affairs Reporting

**In the Circuit Court of
The 9th Judicial Circuit
in and for (your) County**

Division: Civil

Case No.: I-78-1440

THADDEUS DOWDELL
and LAURA DOWDELL,
individually and as next friends
and parents of JAMES
DOWDELL, a minor,   *Plaintiffs,*

vs.

MARVIN FERRELL,
GEORGE DISTELHORST
and (YOUR CITY'S)
SCHOOL DISTRICT,   *Defendants.*

COMPLAINT

COME NOW the Plaintiffs, THADDEUS DOWDELL and LAURA DOWDELL, individually and as next friends and parents of JAMES DOWDELL, a minor, by and through their undersigned counsel, and sue the Defendants, MARVIN FERRELL, GEORGE DISTELHORST and (YOUR CITY'S) SCHOOL DISTRICT, jointly and severally, for damages and allege:

1. That this is an action for damages of $500,000, exclusive of interest, costs and further demands.
2. That at all times material to this cause, JAMES DOWDELL was and is the minor son of THADDEUS DOWDELL and LAURA DOWDELL, residing together with them in a family relationship as residents of this county.
3. That at all times material to this cause, the Defendant MARVIN FERRELL held and now holds the position of Principal of Kennedy High School, and that the Defendant GEORGE DISTELHORST held and now holds the position of School Superintendent.
4. That the minor JAMES DOWDELL is and has been a student in Kennedy High School for the past three years and has been told that he will graduate from that school on or about the First Day of next June.
5. That the minor, JAMES DOWDELL, of this date, can barely read or do simple arithmetic and obviously has not learned enough to be graduated from high school or to function successfully in a society as complex as ours.
6. That the problem is not the fault of the minor JAMES DOWDELL, who, according to tests administered by guidance counselors at the high school, enjoys a normal IQ of 94.

7. That the failure of the minor JAMES DOWDELL to master the skills expected of high school students is the fault of the Defendants, MARVIN FERRELL, GEORGE DISTELHORST and (YOUR CITY'S) SCHOOL DISTRICT, that said Defendants failed to employ competent teachers, to maintain discipline, to provide remedial help, and to provide an atmosphere in which learning might take place.

WHEREFORE, the Plaintiffs, THADDEUS DOWDELL and LAURA DOW-DELL, individually and as next friends and parents of JAMES DOWDELL, a minor, sue the Defendants MARVIN FERRELL, GEORGE DISTELHORST and (YOUR CITY'S) SCHOOL DISTRICT, jointly and severally, for compensatory damages in the amount of $500,000, exclusive of interest and costs.

FURTHER, the Plaintiffs demand that the minor JAMES DOWDELL be retained in Kennedy High School until he masters the skills expected of a high school graduate.

FURTHER, the Plaintiffs demand trial by jury of all issues triable as of right by a jury.

PILOTO and HERNDON, Attorneys
1048 Westmore Drive
Attorneys for Plaintiffs

BY: *Kenneth T. Piloto*
KENNETH T. PILOTO

EXERCISE 25
Public Affairs Reporting

In the Circuit Court,
(your) County

Division: Criminal

Case No.: CR75-3564

(YOUR STATE),	*Plaintiff,*
vs.	
WALTER E. HAUGHEE, JR.,	*Defendant.*

ORDER ON CHANGE OF VENUE

THE COURT has considered the affidavits, exhibits and testimony presented by the Defendant, who is accused of murdering his wife by gunfire on the Fourth Day of December of last year, as well as arguments advanced by both the Defendant and the State.

The State has advanced a very practical position in opposition to the Motion, namely, the great cost and expense to the County in moving the trial to another County. While this observation is an accurate one, it nevertheless is not, and cannot be the criterion by which this Motion must be gauged. The only criterion by which this Court can be guided in considering this particular Motion is whether or not a change in venue is necessary to assure to the Defendant a fair and impartial trial before "indifferent" jurors, thus affording him the due process mandated by both the Federal and the State Constitutions.

The thrust of Defendant's argument is that the newspaper, radio and television coverage or publicity attending this case has been so pervasive as to have inflamed the minds of the public against the accused.

Both the State and Defense have cited, and heavily rely on, the case of *Singer* vs. *State*, 100 So2d 7, decided by the State Supreme Court on February 13, 1959, the principles enunciated therein, however, being as cogent today as when written.

While not necessary to a decision on the Motion here under consideration, a word on "fair trial" versus "free press" is in order. I do not believe that these two constitutionally guaranteed rights are in hopeless conflict, but rather that each may and, indeed, must exist without infringement on the other. In appropriate situations, to ensure or guarantee a "fair trial" to an accused, a trial Judge should focus upon the personnel and agencies over which he has immediate, summary and plenary power, namely, the prosecutor and defense lawyers (plus their agents and employees) and the law enforcement agencies. An attempt to impose "gag" rules on the news media should be imposed only as a last resort, and then only after due notice and opportunity to the news media to voice their position. I have, in this proceeding, made requests of the State Attorney and defense counsel to desist in making statements or news releases on any evidentiary facet of this case to the end that the guilt or innocence of the accused may be determined in the proper forum, namely, in the courtroom, and not in the press; since being requested to do so, both have complied in an appropriate manner. However, this controls future conduct. The question still remains if the publicity attendant this case, in the past, is so pervasive as to require granting the Defendant's Motion to Change the Venue of the Trial.

In *Singer* vs. *State*, 100 So2d 7, the Court said:

"In this case, as in most of those cited above, one of the grounds of the Motion for Change of Venue was that newspaper publicity had inflamed the minds of the public against the accused. As pointed out in those and other cases such publicity has been held to not necessarily require a change of venue, since, in this day of extended distribution of news, a sensational crime incurs great publicity not only in the County in which it occurred, but throughout most, if not all, the State. In such cases it would be difficult to find a County in which the residents thereof had not heard or read of the crime and formed opinions thereon . . ."

In *Irvin* vs. *Dowd*, 366 U.S. 717 (1961), the United States Supreme Court stated, at page 722:

"In essence, the right to jury trial guarantees to the criminally accused a fair trial by a panel of impartial 'indifferent' jurors. . . . A fair trial in a fair tribunal is a basic requirement of due process. . . . In the ultimate analysis, only the jury can strip a man of his liberty or his life. In the language of Lord Coke, a juror must be as indifferent as he stands unsworne.

"It is not required, however, that jurors be totally ignorant of the facts and issues involved. In these days of swift, widespread and diverse methods of communication, an important case can be expected to arouse the interest of the public in the vicinity, and scarcely any of those best qualified to serve as jurors will not have formed some impression or opinion as to the merits of the case. This is particularly true in criminal cases. To hold that the existence of any preconceived notion as to the guilt or innocence of an accused, without more, is sufficient to rebut the presumption of a prospective juror's impartiality would be to establish an impossible standard. It is sufficient if the juror can lay aside his impression or opinion and render a verdict based on the evidence presented in Court."

In examining the newspaper articles attached to the Motion in this case, as well as transcripts of certain of the radio and TV reports, it is apparent that a large percentage thereof is statements made by counsel for the Defendant, and one is an interview with the Defendant himself wherein he in fact asserts his innocence as to the crimes charged. The fact that Defendant or his counsel may be responsible for a great deal of the "press" heretofore generated in this case is not dispositive of the question now under consideration. The main question remains: Has the pretrial publicity been so pervasive (regardless of who precipitated the story) as to require a change of venue?

In the opinion of the Court, the answer to the foregoing question, based upon the information presented, must be answered in the negative. If at the time of jury selection, it becomes apparent that a fair and impartial jury cannot be seated, the Defendant may renew his Motion.

One last matter in passing. Defendant has filed numerous affidavits of individuals who have attested to their belief that the accused cannot receive a fair trial in this County which, while not ignored by this Court, nevertheless, are not in conformity with the law in that the affidavits do not "fully state the facts upon which he founds such belief"—See: *Irvin* vs. *State*, 19 Fla. 872.

IT IS ORDERED that the Motion for Change of Venue is DENIED.

Samuel F. Gunter
_____
Circuit Judge

EXERCISE 26
Public Affairs Reporting

INSTRUCTIONS: Write a news story about the following bill. Assume that the state senator for the district in which you live introduced the bill in the State Senate today.

HOUSE BILL 319

An act relating to cable television; providing legislative intent; prohibiting persons from sending, transmitting, or retransmitting by a cable television system any material which is indecent; providing definitions; providing penalties; providing an effective date.

Be It Enacted by the Legislature of the State:

Section 1. Legislative intent.—

(1) It is the intention of the Legislature in adopting this act to apply to cable television the prohibition against indecent programming, which was upheld by the United States Supreme Court in FCC vs. Pacifica Foundation. Subsequent judicial decisions had construed the Communications Act of 1934 as placing in doubt the ability of the federal or state governments to regulate indecency on cable television, as distinguished from radio and over the air television broadcasting. The "Cable Communications Policy Act" has now clarified the right of states to regulate indecent programming on cable television within their state. It is thus the intention of this act to restore the prohibition against indecent programming to cable television.

(2) The violence against and degradation of women and children in our society are increasing. There are many causes of this, but the most powerful communications media cannot escape responsibility for its part in this phenomenon. Just as cable operators have rights, so have parents, children, women, victims of crime, and society itself. This act seeks to balance and protect all those rights.

Section 2. (1) No person shall send, transmit, or retransmit by a cable television system material which is indecent. For the purposes of this section, material is indecent when, under contemporary community standards for cable television, it is patently offensive and is a representation or verbal description of:
(a) Ultimate sexual acts, normal or perverted, actual or simulated;
(b) Masturbation;
(c) Human sexual or excretory organs or functions; or
(d) A display, description, or representation in lurid detail of the violent physical torture or dismemberment of a person.

(2) For the purpose of this section, the term "material" includes visual and audible material and "community standards" means standards of the community encompassed within the territorial area covered by the franchise.

(3) Any person who violates the provisions of this section is guilty of a misdemeanor of the first degree, punishable by fines of up to $10,000 and 6 months in jail. A person who, after having been convicted of a violation of this section, thereafter violates any of its provisions, is guilty of a felony of the third degree, punishable by fines of up to $25,000 and 15 years in prison.

EXERCISE 27
Public Affairs Reporting

INSTRUCTIONS: Write a news story about the following bill. Assume that the state senator for the district in which you live introduced the bill in the State Senate today.

CHAPTER 82-58

An act relating to highway safety; creating s. 316.268, State Statutes; providing child restraint requirements; amending s. 318.18 (2), State Statutes; providing for notice; providing a penalty; providing an effective date.

Be It Enacted by the Legislature of the State:

Section 1. Section 316.268, State Statutes, is created to read:

316.268 Child restraint requirements.—

(1) Each parent or legal guardian of a child while transporting his or her child in a passenger car, van, or pickup truck registered in the State and operated on the roadways, streets, or highways of this state, shall, if the child is 5 years of age or younger, provide for protection of the child by properly using a crash-tested, federally approved child restraint device. For children through 3 years, such restraint device must be a separate carrier. For children 4 through 5 years, a separate carrier or seat belt may be used. Failure to provide and use a child passenger restraint shall not be considered comparative negligence, nor shall such failure be admissible as evidence in the trial of any civil action with regard to negligence.

(2) It is the legislative intent that all state, county, and local law enforcement agencies, and safety councils, in recognition of the problems with child death and injury from unrestrained occupancy in motor vehicles, conduct a continuing safety and public awareness campaign as to the magnitude of the problem. No person charged with violating this section shall be convicted if, prior to or at the time of his court or hearing appearance, he produces in court, or submits to the clerk of the court in which the charge is pending, proof of acquisition of required child restraint. The clerk of the court is authorized to dismiss such cases at any time if proof of acquisition is produced prior to the defendant's scheduled court or hearing appearance.

(3) The Division of Motor Vehicles shall provide notice of the requirement for child restraint devices, which notice shall accompany the delivery of a motor vehicle license tag.

Section 2. Subsection (2) of section 318.18, State Statutes, is amended to read:

318.18 Amount of civil penalties.—The penalties required for a noncriminal disposition pursuant to s. 318.14 (1), (2) and (4) shall be as follows:

(2) Fifteen dollars for all nonmoving traffic violations and for all violations of s. 320.07 (3) and s. 316.268.

Section 3. This act shall take effect on the 90th day following its adoption.

EXERCISE 28
Public Affairs Reporting

ORDINANCE NO. 20505

An Ordinance of (Your) City, Amending Chapter 31 "Zoning Ordinance" by Repealing Section 31-21, "General Provisions," Paragraph 14, Entitled "Walls and Fences," and Substituting Therefor a New Paragraph Entitled "Walls and Fences."

Be It Enacted by the People of (Your City):

SECTION 1. Pursuant to Section 31-24 thereof, Chapter 31 of the Code of Ordinances of the City is hereby amended and modified by repealing Paragraph 14 of Section 31-21, entitled, "Walls and Fences" and substituting the following therefor:

"14. Walls and Fences.

(a) Permits. Requests for permits for walls and fences must be accompanied by a site plan and drawings clearly showing the locations and heights for which approval is asked.

(b) Height. In front yards, and in side yards with street frontage, walls and fences shall not exceed (3) feet in height above the street curb elevation. In the rear yard of a corner lot, fences in excess of three (3) feet in height above the street curb elevation shall be set back from the street right-of-way the same distance as is prescribed for accessory buildings in the rear yard of corner lots. In all other side and rear yard areas, walls and fences may be a maximum of six (6) feet in height above the ground. Where compliance with these height limits would cause a hardship due to the natural topography of a particular lot, the Administrative Official may permit portions of a fence or wall to be up to eight (8) feet in height in areas where the normal maximum height would be six (6) feet; and where fences are normally limited to three (3) feet in height above the street curb elevation, he may permit the fence height to be measured from the underlying natural ground level rather than the curb. However, no wall or fence shall be permitted which would in any way obstruct the visibility of automobiles at intersections and points of ingress and egress to the public right-of-way.

(c) Materials Permitted in Residential Districts. In any single-family residential district, fences in the front yard or in a side yard with street frontage shall be decorative. Chain link, chicken wire or similar type fences shall be prohibited. Barbed wire or electrically charged fences shall not be erected in any residential district. Neither shall any wall, fence, or similar structure erected in any residential district contain any material or substance such as broken glass, spikes, nails, barbs or similar materials designed to inflict pain or injury on any person or animal.

(d) Designs and Materials Permitted in Non-residential Districts. In any non-residential districts, barbed wire may be incorporated in or used as a fence above the level of six (6) feet from the ground. Any barbed wire shall be placed so that it does not project outward over any street, sidewalk, public way, or adjacent property.

SECTION 2. This Ordinance shall take effect immediately upon its final passage and adoption.

ADOPTED at a regular meeting of the City Council (last night).

Paula M. Novarro
Mayor

EXERCISE 29
Public Affairs Reporting

ORDINANCE NO. 20732

An Ordinance of the City Enacting Chapter 2A, "Alarm Devices," Relating to Privately Owned General Alarm Devices: Defining Terms; Imposing upon the Owner or Manager of the Premises the Responsibility of Deactivating Alarms upon Notification to Do So; Requiring Corrective Action and the Filing of Reports; Prescribing Fees; Providing for Disconnection of Faulty Alarm Devices; Prohibiting the Installation of Telephone Alarm Devices Connected to the Police Department; and Providing for an Effective Date.

WHEREAS, malfunctions of privately owned alarm devices are causing substantial misuse of the manpower and resources of the Police Department of the City by provoking responses to numerous false alarms; and

WHEREAS, telephone alarm devices regulated or programmed to make connection with the Police Department could seize and hold Police Department telephone lines to the exclusion of other calls; and

WHEREAS, false alarms and use of telephone alarm devices create a threat or potential threat to the health, safety and welfare of the people of the City,

NOW, THEREFORE, BE IT ENACTED BY THE CITY COUNCIL THAT:

SECTION 1. Chapter 2A, "Alarm Devices," of the Code of Ordinances of the City is hereby enacted to read as follows:

Sec. 2A-1. Definitions. For purposes of this ordinance, the following terms shall have the following meanings:

(a) False alarm—the activation of a telephone alarm device or general alarm device by other than a forced entry or attempted forced entry to the premises and at a time when no burglary or hold-up is being committed or attempted on the premises, except acts of God.

(b) First response—a response to a false alarm to premises at which no other false alarm has occurred within the preceding six (6) month period.

(c) Telephone alarm device—any device which, when activated, automatically transmits by telephone lines a recorded alarm message or electronic or mechanical alarm signal to any telephone instrument installed in any facility of the Police Department.

(d) General alarm device—any alarm bell, light or other signaling device which, when activated, is designed to indicate a burglary or hold-up.

Sec. 2A-2. Duty of owner or manager of premises. Prior to the installation or use of any type of telephone device or general alarm device, the owner or manager of the premises shall furnish to the Police Department information regarding the full names, addresses and telephone numbers of at least two (2) persons who can be reached at all times and who are authorized to enter the premises and deactivate the alarm device. Owners or managers of premises with telephone alarm devices or general alarm devices already installed shall have thirty (30) days from the effective date of this ordinance to comply with the above notice requirement. If any such person shall fail to appear and reset any such alarm within one (1) hour after being notified by the Police Department to do so, then the owner or manager of the premises shall be charged a fee of twenty dollars

($20.00) for the first such occurrence, and a fee of fifty dollars ($50.00) for each succeeding occurrence within six (6) months of the last failure to appear.

Sec. 2A-3. Responses to false alarms; corrective action and reports required; fees charged.

(a) Corrective action and report required. For each response by the Police Department to a false alarm, the owner or manager of the premises involved shall, within three (3) working days after notice to do so, make a written report to the Chief of Police, on forms provided by him, setting forth the cause of the false alarm, the corrective action taken, the name, address and telephone number of the service man, if any, by whom the device has been inspected or repaired, and such other information as the department may reasonably require to determine the cause of the false alarm and what corrective action has been taken or may be necessary.

(b) Fees charged. There shall be no fee charged for a first response to premises or for a second or third response within six (6) months after a first response. For a fourth response to premises within six (6) months after a third response, there shall be a fee of twenty dollars ($20.00), and for all succeeding responses within six (6) months of the last response, a fee of fifty dollars ($50.00) for each such response shall be charged. Upon a failure to pay any such fee within ten (10) days after the notification for which it is charged, the Chief of Police shall be authorized to disconnect or deactivate the alarm device involved.

(c) Authority to disconnect. Upon failure of an owner or manager of premises to pay any fee specified above within ten (10) days after the occurrence for which the fee is charged, or upon a determination by the Chief of Police that any false alarm, other than a false alarm caused by the act of God, to which a first response is made has resulted from a failure on the part of the owner or manager of the premises to take necessary corrective action, the Chief of Police shall be authorized to disconnect the telephone alarm device or general alarm device, and it shall be unlawful to reconnect such telephone alarm device or general alarm device unless and until appropriate corrective action has been taken and such reconnection is authorized by the Chief of Police; provided, however, that no disconnection or deactivation shall be ordered or made as to any premises required by law to have an alarm device in operation.

Sec. 2A-4. Telephone alarm devices prohibited. It shall be unlawful for any person, firm, corporation or association to install any telephone alarm device after the effective date of this ordinance.

SECTION 2. All ordinances or parts of ordinances in conflict herewith are hereby repealed.

EXERCISE 30
Public Affairs Reporting

SENATE BILL 143

(Legalizing heroin for terminally ill cancer patients)

BACKGROUND: Two U.S. senators, Dennis DeConcini and Daniel Inouye, have introduced Senate Bill 143, which would allow doctors to prescribe parenteral diacetylmorphine (heroin) "to relieve the excruciating pain of terminally ill cancer patients." Although most pain associated with cancer is controllable by drugs such as morphine and dilaudid, estimates are that in the United States 8,000 people a year die in intractable pain from cancer. "For many of these victims, the closing days of their lives are ones of prolonged agony," explains Sen. DeConcini. "They cannot function in a normal way and their families often endure great trauma. Medical studies that have been conducted abroad and in this country suggest that heroin can be used very effectively to control the extreme pain of cancer patients. If there is a beneficial use of the drug, we should not let our normal instincts of aversion to its use unreasonably affect our thinking." This bill proposes an experimental program operating "under the strictest controls of production and distribution." The authors add that, "In five years we will have a solid body of facts and experience upon which to decide whether the program should be extended, modified, or terminated."

S.143

Be it enacted by the Senate and House of Representatives of the United States of America in Congress Assembled, That this Act may be cited as the "Compassionate Pain Relief Act".

Sec. 2. The Congress finds the following:

(1) Cancer is a progressive, degenerative, and often painful disease which afflicts one out of every four Americans and is the second leading cause of death.

(2) In the progression of terminal cancer, a significant number of patients will experience levels of intense and intractable pain which cannot be effectively treated by presently available medication. The effect of the pain often leads to a severe deterioration in the quality of life of the patient and heartbreak for the patient's family.

(3) The therapeutic use of parenteral diacetylmorphine is not permitted in the United States but extensive clinical research has demonstrated that it is a potent, highly soluble painkilling drug when properly formulated and administered under a physician's supervision.

(4) Making parenteral diacetylmorphine available to patients through controlled channels as a drug for the relief of intractable pain due to terminal cancer is in the public interest. Diacetylmorphine is successfully used in Great Britain and other countries for relief of pain due to cancer.

(5) The availability of parenteral diacetylmorphine for the limited purposes of controlling intractable pain due to terminal cancer will not adversely affect the abuse of illicit drugs or increase the incidence of pharmacy thefts.

(6) The availability of parenteral diacetylmorphine will enhance the ability of physicians to effectively treat and control intractable pain due to terminal cancer.

(7) It is appropriate for the Federal Government to establish a temporary program to permit the use of pharmaceutical dosage forms of parenteral diacetylmorphine for the control of intractable pain due to terminal cancer.

Sec. 3 (a) Not later than three months after the date of the enactment of this Act, the Secretary of Health and Human Services (hereinafter in this Act referred to as the

"Secretary") shall issue regulations establishing a program under which parenteral diacetylmorphine may be made available to hospital pharmacies and other such pharmacies as may be prescribed by the Secretary for dispensing pursuant to written prescriptions of physicians to individuals for the relief of intractable pain due to terminal cancer (hereinafter in this section referred to as "the program"). For purposes of the program, an individual shall be considered to have terminal cancer if there is histologic evidence of a malignancy in the individual and the individual's cancer is generally recognized as a cancer with a high and predictable mortality. It is the intent of Congress that the Secretary primarily utilize hospital pharmacies for the dispensing of parenteral diacetylmorphine under the program, but the Congress recognizes that humanitarian concerns might necessitate the provision of parenteral diacetylmorphine through pharmacies other than hospital pharmacies in cases in which a significant need is shown for such provision and in which adequate protection is available against the diversion of parenteral diacetylmorphine.

(b) The Secretary shall provide for the manufacture of parenteral diacetylmorphine for dispensing under the program using adequate methods in, and adequate facilities and controls for, the manufacturing, processing, and packing of such drug to preserve its identity, strength, quality, and purity.

(c) Under the program parenteral diacetylmorphine may only be made available upon application to pharmacies registered under section 302 of the Controlled Substances Act that also meet such qualifications as the Secretary may by regulation prescribe. An application for parenteral diacetylmorphine shall—

(1) be in such form and submitted in such manner as the Secretary may prescribe, and

(2) contain assurances satisfactory to the Secretary that—

(A) the applicant meets such special requirements as the Secretary may prescribe respecting the storage and dispensing of parenteral diacetylmorphine, and

(B) parenteral diacetylmorphine provided under the application will be dispensed through the applicant upon the written prescription of a physician registered under section 302 of the Controlled Substances Act to dispense controlled substances in schedule II of such Act.

(d) Requirements prescribed by the Secretary under subsections (b) and (c)(2)(A) shall be designed to protect against the diversion into illicit channels of parenteral diacetylmorphine distributed under the program.

(e) A physician registered under section 302 of the Controlled Substances Act may prescribe parenteral diacetylmorphine for individuals for the relief of intractable pain due to terminal cancer. Any such prescription shall be in writing as prescribed by the Secretary by regulations.

(f) The Federal Food, Drug, and Cosmetic Act and titles II and III of the Comprehensive Drug Abuse Prevention and Control Act of 1970 shall not apply with respect to—

(1) the importing of opium,

(2) the manufacture of parenteral diacetylmorphine, and

(3) the distribution and dispensing of parenteral diacetylmorphine in accordance with the program.

Sec. 4. (a) Not later than the second month beginning after the date of the enactment of this section and every third month thereafter until the program is established under section 3, the Secretary shall report to the Committee on Energy and Commerce of the House of Representatives and the Committee on Labor and Human Resources of the Senate on the activities undertaken to implement the program. Each year after the program is established and while the program is in effect, the Secretary shall report to such committees on the activities under the program during the period for which the report is submitted.

(b) Upon the expiration of fifty-six months after the date the program is established, the Comptroller General of the United States shall report to the committees referred to in subsection (a) on the activities under the program during such fifty-six month period.

Sec. 5. The program established under section 3 shall terminate upon the expiration of sixty months after the date the program is established.

Sec. 6. The Secretary of Health and Human Services shall transmit a report to the Committee on Energy and Commerce of the House of Representatives and the Committee on Labor and Human Resources of the Senate not later than six months after the date of the enactment of this Act—

(1) describing the extent of research activities on the management of pain which have received funds through the National Institutes of Health,

(2) describing the ways in which the Federal Government supports the training of health personnel in pain management, and

(3) containing recommendations for expanding and improving the training of health personnel in pain management.

Sec. 7. The Secretary may at any time six months after implementation of the program modify or terminate the program if in the Secretary's judgment the program is no longer needed or if modifications or termination is needed to prevent substantial diversion of the diacetylmorphine.

EXERCISE 31
Public Affairs Reporting

CITY BUDGET

WHEREAS, on October 1, the City will start a new budget for the next fiscal year; and

WHEREAS, the City Council of the City wishes to adopt a final budget for that fiscal year and that on September 2 at a legally called public hearing the Council did adopt a tentative budget; and

WHEREAS, the City Council made a study of the needs for expenditures in each of the City Departments and determined that this amount for the coming year, including the Federal Revenue Sharing Budget, will be $2,850,777; and, in the same study, the Council has determined that the expected income will be a like amount, including the Federal Revenue Sharing budget; and

WHEREAS, the City Council has set the tax millage rate at 3.99, this being a decrease in the rolled back millage from a rate last year of 4.16,

NOW, THEREFORE, BE IT RESOLVED that the City Council of this City hereby adopts a final budget for next year as follows:

Revenues	Amount
Ad Valorem Taxes	$ 422,609
One-half Cent Sales Tax	262,046
Franchise and Utility Taxes	558,400
Licenses and Permits	42,500
Intergovernmental Revenue	936,031
Service Charges	272,615
Fines and Forfeitures	32,600
Miscellaneous	105,107
Redesignated Capital Improvement Funds	73,761
Federal Revenue Sharing	145,108
TOTAL	$ 2,850,777

EXPENDITURES	FEDERAL REVENUE SHARING	OTHER FUNDS	TOTAL
Bond Requirements	——	$ 55,500	$ 55,500
Administration	$ 55,000	243,135	298,135
City Clerk's Office	——	42,518	42,518
Building and Zoning	——	52,416	52,416
Finance & Utility Accounts	——	178,495	178,495
Police Department	——	784,068	784,068
Fire & Ambulance	——	820,464	820,464
General Maintenance	——	33,318	33,318
Street Maintenance	16,700	154,799	171,499
Recreation Department	——	100,961	100,961
Recreation/Special Projects	——	45,052	45,052
Parks and Cemetery	——	116,637	116,637
Garage	——	78,306	78,306
Capital Improvements	73,408	——	73,408
TOTALS	$145,108	$2,705,669	$2,850,777

PASSED AND ADOPTED by the City Council of this City.

19 Statistical Material

Much of the information given to newspaper reporters comes in the form of statistics, so reporters must learn how to present those statistics to the public in a form that is both interesting and intelligible. Statistics appear almost daily in news stories concerning budgets, taxes, census data, profits, dividends and annual reports. Other news stories concerning rates of crime, productivity, energy consumption, unemployment and inflation are based largely on statistics.

When you are given a collection of numbers and asked to write a news story about them, critically analyze the data and translate as many of the numbers as possible into words, since readers can understand words more easily than statistics. Thus, instead of simply reporting the statistics, you should explain their significance. Look for and emphasize major trends, record highs and record lows, the unusual and the unexpected. For example:

> The Fire Department's annual report states that last year it responded to the following numbers and types of calls: bomb threats, 60; electrical fires, 201; false alarms, 459; first aid, 1,783; mattress fires, 59; burned pots left on stoves, 78; rescues, 18; washdowns, usually of leaking gasoline at the scene of automobile accidents, 227; and water salvage, 46.
>
> REVISED: The Fire Department responded to a total of 5,024 calls last year. According to the department's annual report, calls for first aid were most common, followed by false alarms and washdowns.
>
> The five leading types of calls included, in the order of their frequency: first aid, 1,783; false alarms, 459; washdowns, usually of leaking gasoline at the scene of automobile accidents, 227; electrical fires, 201; and burned pots left on stoves, 78.
>
> Other common types of calls included: bomb threats, 60; mattress fires, 59; water salvage, 46; and rescues, 18.
>
> For the first time in seven years, no one died in any fires reported in the city.

Go beyond the superficial. If you are writing about a city election, do more than tell your readers who won and the number of votes that each candidate received. Search for

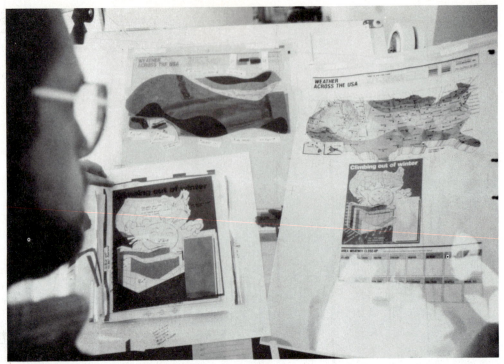

An employee prepares a weather map for USA Today. Since its establishment on Sept. 15, 1982, USA Today has become the second largest daily in the United States, with a circulation of 1.5 million. Signals from its headquarters in Washington, D.C. are transmitted to a satellite 22,300 miles above the Earth, then back to 30 printing plants in the United States and to two abroad (one in Switzerland and one in Singapore).

additional highlights: for example, did incumbents (or women, blacks, youths or conservatives) tend to win or lose? Did any candidates win by unusually large or small margins? Also, compare the votes cast in different wards and look for significant differences from the outcomes of previous elections.

When you must include some statistics in your news stories, present those statistics as simply as possible. Avoid a series of paragraphs that contains nothing but statistics. Use transitions, explanations and commentary to break up long strings of numbers and to make the information clearer and more interesting for your readers. For example:

> In the races for city councilmen, George McDuff defeated Carl Lasher 7,614 to 3,581 in the First Ward, Marian V. Fleck defeated David S. DiMassimo 5,432 to 5,401 in the Second Ward, Michael J. Stewart defeated Kenneth Dunihue 4,802 to 3,781 in the Third Ward, John M. Scroggins defeated Royce R. LaChapelle 7,814 to 1,801 in the Fourth Ward, and Mary M. Tilton defeated Jeffery Pratt 5,041 to 4,014 in the Fifth Ward.
>
> REVISED: All three male incumbents seeking re-election to the City Council were defeated, two of them by women.
>
> In the Second Ward, incumbent David S. DiMassimo was defeated by 31 votes by Marian V. Fleck, 5,432 to 5,401. Another woman, Mary M. Tilton, defeated incumbent Jeffery Pratt in the Fifth Ward by more than 1,000 votes.
>
> The third incumbent, Royce E. LaChapelle of the Fourth Ward, was defeated by John Scroggins, 7,814 to 1,801. Police charged LaChapelle with drunken driving and resisting arrest after he was involved in an automobile accident on Chapman Road last month. He has not yet been tried on the charges.
>
> George McDuff and Michael J. Stewart, who campaigned against higher property taxes, also won.
>
> McDuff defeated Carl Lasher in the First Ward by a vote of 7,614 to 3,581, and Stewart defeated Kenneth Dunihue in the Third Ward by a vote of 4,802 to 3,781.

EXERCISE 1
Statistical Material

INSTRUCTIONS: Write a news story about the results of the following national opinion poll about certain American presidents, based on a random sample of 2,400 people aged 18 and older. Assume that the interviews were conducted by telephone last week by members of the National Association of Political Scientists, and that the results were announced today. All the figures are percentages.

	Most Loved	Most Powerful	Highest Moral Standards	Did Most to Improve U.S.	Best in Domestic Affairs	Best in Foreign Affairs
Franklin D. Roosevelt	26	25	29	29	27	22
Harry S. Truman	9	12	13	8	7	14
Dwight D. Eisenhower	18	11	13	13	12	17
John F. Kennedy	24	10	16	16	14	14
Lyndon B. Johnson	4	16	5	11	16	6
Richard M. Nixon	3	9	3	6	4	11
Gerald R. Ford	2	3	3	4	6	4
James E. Carter	4	3	7	4	5	3
Ronald Reagan	6	8	8	6	7	5
Undecided or no answer	4	3	3	3	2	4

EXERCISE 2
Statistical Material

CRIME STUDY COMMISSION RESIDENT SURVEY

INTRODUCTION

According to a survey of 8,000 residents of your community conducted last month by a crime study commission appointed by the mayor, the incidence of crime in the city is taking its toll on their daily lives. Of the questionnaires returned, an overwhelming majority are extremely concerned about the rising lawlessness and some even claim they no longer leave their homes except when absolutely necessary.

Degree of Citizen Concern (in percentages)

CRIME	NOT AT ALL CONCERNED (1)	(2)	(3)	(4)	EXTREMELY CONCERNED (5)
Assault	16.0	3.9	9.9	10.4	59.8
Breaking/Entering (home)	6.7	1.2	4.5	9.2	78.4
Breaking/Entering (business)	33.8	4.2	10.7	9.4	41.9
Drug Abuse	20.4	4.4	11.2	10.0	54.0
Larceny	23.8	4.4	13.6	13.3	44.8
Vehicle Theft	20.6	5.7	15.0	13.5	45.2
Murder	17.5	2.6	5.9	6.7	67.3
Prostitution	33.9	8.4	12.0	7.3	38.3
Rape	14.9	1.8	5.1	7.3	70.8
Robbery/Mugging	12.7	2.1	6.6	11.5	67.1
Vandalism	13.3	2.4	9.2	14.0	61.0
Other	73.9	0.3	0.9	1.3	23.6

Sex of respondents: Male: 41.9 Percent Female: 55.7 Percent Not Stated: 2.4 Percent
Average age of respondents: 53

NOTE: Based on 6400 responses.

Survey Methodology

In the survey, respondents were asked to rate all concerns on a scale ranging from "Not at all concerned" to "Extremely concerned."

Write-in Responses

In a write-in portion of the survey, the fear of crimes against children and the elderly are widely reflected while drug abuse gets the blame for contributing to many infractions of the law.

Many citizens wrote in that they think the courts and criminal justice system are too lenient and, in some cases, neglectful in handling the five percent of those arrested who ever do appear before a judge. Plea bargaining and bail bonding also come under attack as court actions that favor the criminal over the victim and free offenders who are charged with serious crimes.

Less than three percent of those responding say they have been victims in the past year of crimes that they did not report to police. Most of the unreported offenses are of a minor nature such as garden vandalism or petty theft, but others tell of more serious offenses, such as spouse or child abuse. A few list rape, however, and will not report the attacks out of embarrassment or for fear of harassment. Those who fail to report child or spouse abuse claim to fear further abuse since the offender most likely will not be jailed even when reported.

EXERCISE 3
Statistical Material

UNITED STATES DEPARTMENT OF EDUCATION
WASHINGTON, D.C. 20202

UPDATE ON ADULT ILLITERACY

THE SOURCE

The English Language Proficiency Survey was commissioned by the U.S. Department of Education and conducted by the Bureau of the Census during the last summer. At that time, simple written tests of English comprehension were administered in the home to a national sample of 3,400 adults, ages 20 and over.

MAJOR FINDINGS

Between 17 and 21 million U.S. adults are illiterate, for an overall rate of nearly 13 percent. In contrast to traditional estimates of illiteracy based on completion of fewer than six years of school, this new study shows that illiterate adults are now much more likely to be located in our major cities, and most are under the age of 50. Immigration and reliance on a non-English language are also major factors; nearly half of all adults using a non-English language at home failed the test of English proficiency. More specifically,

- Of all adults classified as illiterate:

  —41 percent live in central cities of metropolitan areas, compared to just 8 percent in rural areas;
  —56 percent are under the age of 50; and
  —37 percent speak a non-English language at home.

- Among native English-speakers classified as illiterate:

  —70 percent did not finish high school;
  —42 percent had no earnings in the previous year; and
  —35 percent are in their twenties and thirties.

- Among illiterate adults who use a non-English language:

  —82 percent were born outside the United States;
  —42 percent live in neighborhoods where exclusive reliance on English is the exception rather than the rule;
  —21 percent had entered the U.S. within the previous six years; and
  —About 14 percent are probably literate in their non-English language (judging from their reported education).

THE TEST AND THE DEFINITION OF ILLITERACY

The test employed is called the Measure of Adult English Proficiency (MAEP). The written portion of MAEP consists of 26 questions which test the individual's ability to identify key words and phrases and match these with one of four fixed-choice alternatives. Based on an analysis of the number of questions answered correctly out of 26, a literacy cutoff of 20 was selected as providing the best discrimination between high and low risk groups. Specifically, among native English speakers, less than 1 percent of those completing some college scored below 20, in contrast to a failure rate of more than 50 percent for those with fewer than 6 years of school.

ACCURACY OF THESE ESTIMATES

The standard error of our point estimate (18.7 million) is about 1 million. Thus, we can be quite confident (95 chances out of a 100) that the true figure is in the range of 17 to 21 million.

IDENTIFICATION OF HIGH-RISK GROUPS

Six factors were found to be strongly correlated with performance on the written test: age, nativity, recency of immigration for non-natives, race, poverty status, amount of schooling, and reported English speaking ability (of persons who use a non-English language at home).

Illiteracy Rate Estimates*

	Rate	Inverse Rank		Rate	Inverse Rank
United States	13				
			MISSOURI	12	25
ALABAMA	13	31	MONTANA	8	4
ALASKA	7	2	NEBRASKA	9	9
ARIZONA	12	25	NEVADA	9	9
ARKANSAS	15	40	NEW HAMPSHIRE	9	9
CALIFORNIA	14	33	NEW JERSEY	14	33
COLORADO	8	4	NEW MEXICO	14	33
CONNECTICUT	12	25	NEW YORK	16	47
DELAWARE	11	17	NORTH CAROLINA	14	33
DIST. OF COLUMBIA	16	47	NORTH DAKOTA	12	25
FLORIDA	15	40	OHIO	11	17
GEORGIA	14	33	OKLAHOMA	11	17
HAWAII	15	40	OREGON	8	4
IDAHO	8	4	PENNSYLVANIA	12	25
ILLINOIS	14	33	RHODE ISLAND	15	40
INDIANA	11	17	SOUTH CAROLINA	15	40
IOWA	10	14	SOUTH DAKOTA	11	17
KANSAS	9	9	TENNESSEE	15	40
KENTUCKY	15	40	TEXAS	16	47
LOUISIANA	16	47	UTAH	6	1
MAINE	11	17	VERMONT	10	14
MARYLAND	12	25	VIRGINIA	13	31
MASSACHUSETTS	11	17	WASHINGTON	8	4
MICHIGAN	11	17	WEST VIRGINIA	14	33
MINNESOTA	9	9	WISCONSIN	10	14
MISSISSIPPI	16	47	WYOMING	7	2

*Rates apply to the adult population age 20 and over. All rates have been rounded to the nearest whole percent.

EXERCISE 4
Statistical Material

FROM THE OFFICE OF THE GOVERNOR

The annual survey of legislative appropriations for the arts, conducted by the National Assembly of State Arts Agencies, is being released nationwide today. The results show how our state compares to others in the nation.

The complete survey follows:

National Assembly of State Arts Agencies

	Per Capita (¢)		Appropriations ($)			% of State	
	This Year	Last Year	This Year	Last Year	% Change	General Fund	Rank
Alabama	24.1	26.2	969,020	1,045,000	−7.2	.0374	42
Alaska	420.3	800.2	2,189,800	4,000,000	−45.2	Not available	
Arizona	35.9	33.1	1,144,800	1,010,200	13.3	.0452	37
Arkansas	42.7	35.6	1,006,754	836,226	20.3	.0588	27
California	47.7	46.0	12,589,000	11,793,000	6.7	.0411	40
Colorado	50.8	30.6	1,640,647	971,459	68.8	.0820	17
Connecticut	52.5	46.0	1,666,166	1,479,000	12.6	.0388	41
Delaware	97.1	80.9	603,900	496,000	21.7	.0647	24
Dist. of Columbia	378.3	283.3	2,368,000	1,765,000	34.1	.1032	13
Florida	111.8	88.9	12,710,386	9,761,077	30.2	.1639	5
Georgia	45.0	37.7	2,687,779	2,200,588	22.1	.0506	32
Hawaii	216.5	208.9	2,282,092	2,170,485	5.1	.1230	8
Idaho	13.5	13.3	134,000	131,400	1.9	.0223	49
Illinois	75.9	57.0	8,758,300	6,559,400	33.5	.0857	15
Indiana	33.4	33.3	1,836,923	1,830,576	0.3	.0551	28
Iowa	34.0	18.0	981,590	522,593	87.8	.0452	38
Kansas	24.6	24.5	602,707	596,288	1.0	.0335	45
Kentucky	53.2	42.0	1,983,300	1,564,400	26.7	.0659	23
Louisiana	20.1	27.0	900,000	1,205,431	−25.3	.0212	50
Maine	40.7	36.4	473,503	420,292	12.6	.0456	36
Maryland	108.7	43.9	4,776,096	1,909,382	150.1	.1079	11
Massachusetts	313.7	282.5	18,265,924	16,379,066	11.5	.2738	1
Michigan	125.5	113.4	11,404,000	10,291,500	10.8	.1863	4
Minnesota	65.7	60.1	2,755,083	2,502,961	10.0	.0539	31
Mississippi	15.8	17.9	411,986	465,827	−11.5	.0277	47
Missouri	87.6	137.9	4,403,292	6,904,051	−36.2	.1316	9
Montana	109.2	78.8	901,745	649,068	38.9	.2457	2
Nebraska	36.5	36.3	585,891	582,749	0.5	.0676	22
Nevada	19.1	19.1	178,642	174,270	2.5	.0338	44
New Hampshire	32.6	33.1	325,500	323,000	0.7	.0712	21
New Jersey	177.9	138.3	13,453,000	10,391,000	29.4	.1488	6*
New Mexico	48.2	50.1	698,800	713,500	−2.0	.0481	33
New York	273.2	249.3	48,590,702	44,218,900	9.8	.2081	3
North Carolina	64.8	63.8	4,050,637	3,936,067	2.9	.0734	20
North Dakota	34.8	34.7	238,268	238,268	0.0	.0421	39
Ohio	84.2	69.7	9,050,963	7,493,265	20.7	.0855	16

Oklahoma	46.5	55.2	1,535,253	1,821,462	− 15.7	.0900	14
Oregon	18.4	18.2	494,421	487,048	1.5	.0286	46
Pennsylvania	65.6	56.3	7,780,000	6,724,000	15.7	.0805	18
Rhode Island	62.0	46.2	599,854	444,357	34.9	.0539	30
South Carolina	85.7	77.4	2,869,596	2,555,563	12.2	.1039	12
South Dakota	40.5	40.2	286,873	283,912	1.0	.0775	19
Tennessee	29.0	76.7	1,382,500	3,615,800	− 61.7	.0476	35
Texas	18.2	30.3	2,983,955	4,846,064	− 38.4	.0546	29
Utah	100.1	94.9	1,646,000	1,568,200	4.9	.1242	10
Vermont	49.5	45.8	264,900	242,902	9.0	.0622	26
Virginia	52.2	34.6	2,979,540	1,947,865	52.9	.0637	25
Washington	38.5	43.2	1,697,395	1,879,419	− 9.6	.0360	43
West Virginia	115.8	106.5	2,241,793	2,117,238	5.8	.1488	6*
Wisconsin	24.1	24.2	1,148,600	1,151,500	− 0.2	.0226	48
Wyoming	33.2	28.3	169,275	144,605	17.0	.0447	34

*New Jersey and West Virginia are tied for sixth.

EXERCISE 5
Statistical Material

Kasten
News

U.S. Senator Robert W. Kasten Jr.   Senate Office Bldg.   Washington, D.C.

WASHINGTON, D.C.—"THE 159 MEMBER STATES OF THE UNITED NATIONS VOTED AGAINST U.S. INTERESTS IN THE GENERAL ASSEMBLY LAST YEAR AN AVERAGE OF NEARLY 80 PERCENT OF THE TIME," U.S. SENATOR BOB KASTEN SAID TODAY IN ANNOUNCING THE FINDINGS OF THE THIRD ANNUAL "KASTEN REPORT."

Kasten released preliminary details of the report, an annual study of U.N. voting patterns done by the U.S. State Department, at a hearing of the Senate Appropriations Subcommittee on Foreign Operations. American Ambassador to the U.N. Vernon Walters testified before Kasten's panel, which focused on the U.S. contribution to the United Nations budget.

The Kasten Report is required by legislation authored by the Wisconsin Republican. It pays particular attention to the ten issues that the Administration determines to be most critical to U.S. interests.

**

U.N. VOTING RECORD
ALL UNGA PLENARY VOTES
Percent Coincidence
With U.S. Votes (Yes/No)

THE AMERICAS

Grenada	71.7	Haiti	23.8
Canada	69.8	Jamaica	22.7
St. Christopher & Nevis	50.0	Barbados	20.3
Belize	37.8	Panama	19.7
Paraguay	35.4	Venezuela	19.0
St. Vincent & Grenadines	32.7	Bahamas	18.6
Chile	31.4	Bolivia	18.5
El Salvador	30.2	Uruguay	18.1
Honduras	29.8	Trinidad & Tobago	17.9
Costa Rica	29.1	Peru	17.8
Columbia	27.9	Argentina	16.4
St. Lucia	26.2	Suriname	16.2
Guatemala	25.2	Brazil	16.0
Antigua & Barbuda	25.0	Mexico	14.5
Dominican Republic	25.0	Guyana	13.9
Ecuador	24.6	Nicaragua	8.4
Dominica	24.2	Cuba	6.2
		Group Average	23.7

WESTERN EUROPE

United Kingdom	86.6	Denmark	58.3
Federal Rep. Germany	84.8	Spain	55.6
France	82.7	Ireland	51.0
Belgium	82.3	Sweden	42.2
Italy	81.9	Austria	40.0
Luxembourg	80.2	Finland	39.8
Netherlands	76.3	Turkey	38.1

Portugal	65.0	Greece	33.3
Iceland	62.4	Malta	16.5
Norway	61.2		
		Group Average	59.2

NO AFFILIATION

Israel	91.5		

EASTERN EUROPE

Poland	14.8	Czechoslovakia	12.2
Romania	14.6	German Democratic Rep.	12.2
Hungary	12.3	USSR	12.2
Ukraine	12.3	Yugoslavia	11.9
Bulgaria	12.2	Albania	6.7
Byelorussian S.S.R.	12.2		
		Group Average	12.4

AFRICA

Ivory Coast	27.3	Gambia	14.9
Malawi	26.9	Zambia	14.9
Liberia	23.7	Nigeria	14.7
Zaire	23.1	Zimbabwe	14.6
Mauritius	22.1	Djibouti	14.3
Swaziland	22.0	Tunisia	13.9
Equatorial Guinea	21.2	Ghana	13.2
Central African Rep.	20.9	Uganda	13.2
Gabon	19.7	Burkina Faso	13.1
Senegal	19.3	Guinea-Bissau	12.2
Togo	19.0	Comores	12.1
Sierra Leone	18.3	Guinea	12.1
Cameroon	18.0	Cape Verde	11.9
Chad	18.0	Seychelles, The	11.9
Niger	17.6	Congo	11.3
Botswana	17.4	Tanzania	11.3
Rwanda	17.4	Mali	11.1
Kenya	16.7	Madagascar	10.6
Somalia	16.3	Sao Tomé & Príncipe	10.3
Mauretania	16.1	Ethiopia	9.3
Lesotho	16.0	Benin	8.8
Burundi	15.9	Libya	6.9
Morocco	15.9	Mozambique	5.9
Sudan	15.5	Algeria	5.1
Egypt	15.3	Angola	3.5
		Group Average	15.1

ASIA AND THE PACIFIC

Japan	66.3	Bhutan	13.9
Australia	60.2	Oman	13.6
New Zealand	55.3	Saudi Arabia	13.6
Solomons	48.1	Vanuatu	13.4
Samoa	27.4	Lebanon	13.1
Fiji	26.0	Bahrain	12.8
Singapore	23.6	Qatar	12.8
Papua New Guinea	23.1	Emirates	12.8
Thailand	22.4	Maldives	12.5
Philippines	22.3	Kuwait	12.2
Kampuchea	21.4	Cyprus	11.6

Nepal	18.0	Iran	11.3
Burma	17.1	Mongolia	9.9
Sri Lanka	16.8	Yemen (A.R.)	9.0
Malaysia	16.3	India	8.9
Bangladesh	16.1	Iraq	8.7
Pakistan	16.1	Syria	8.1
China	15.9	Viet Nam	6.5
Brunei	15.3	Afghanistan	6.2
Indonesia	14.3	Laos	5.9
Jordan	14.2	Yemen (P.D.R.)	5.7
		Group Average	17.0

EXERCISE 6
Statistical Material

INSTRUCTIONS: Write a story based on this comparison of prices in five local supermarkets.

Item	Size	Supermarket				
		Saver's Mart	Mayfair*	Jerry's	G&O	Samuelson's*†
FOOD PRODUCTS						
Idaho Potatoes	10 lb.	$ 2.19	$ 2.38	$ 2.29	$ 2.19	$ 2.25
Tomatoes	1 lb.	.68	.79	.75	.69	.69
Bananas	1 lb.	.39	.39	.37	.35	.37
Tetley Tea Bags	100 ct.	1.99	2.19	2.08	1.97	1.99
Wesson Oil	1 gal.	5.79	5.98	5.99	5.84	5.88
Eggs	1 doz.	.87	.89	.89	.87	.83
Heinz Dill Pickles	32 oz.	1.39	1.47	1.49	1.28	1.29
Mazola Margarine	1 lb.	.89	.99	.98	.86	.89
Coca-Cola	6-pack	1.59	1.59	1.69	1.58	1.49
Welch's Grape Jam	20 oz.	1.49	1.69	1.59	1.47	1.58
Old Milwaukee Beer	12-pack	3.79	3.98	3.78	3.59	3.68
Brim Decaffeinated Coffee	4 oz.	3.39	3.39	3.59	3.25	3.28
Jif Peanut Butter	28 oz.	2.99	3.29	3.19	2.87	2.89
Kraft Miracle Whip	32 oz.	1.39	1.48	1.49	1.35	1.39
Planter's Peanuts	14½ oz.	2.39	2.48	2.49	2.19	2.25
TOTAL:		$31.22	$32.98	$32.66	$30.35	$30.75
MEAT						
Chicken	1 lb.	.59	.59	.69	.57	.65
Ground beef	1 lb.	1.49	1.62	1.59	1.45	1.47
Pot roast	1 lb.	1.99	2.29	2.25	1.99	1.97
Spare ribs	1 lb.	1.87	1.95	2.19	1.79	1.79
Cube steaks	1 lb.	2.99	3.59	3.48	3.09	3.19
Oscar Mayer Wieners	1 lb.	1.99	2.29	2.17	1.99	2.09
Armour Canned Ham	3 lb.	6.99	7.39	7.19	6.84	7.09
Chuck roast	1 lb.	2.25	2.59	2.67	2.19	2.39
Pork chops	1 lb.	2.29	2.29	2.49	2.29	2.35
Armour Bacon	1 lb.	1.89	1.99	1.98	1.74	1.87
Turkey	1 lb.	.99	.98	1.09	.92	.97
TOTAL:		$25.33	$27.57	$27.79	$24.86	$25.83

*Gives trading stamps.   †Open 24 hours a day.

Item	Size	Supermarket				
		Saver's Mart	Mayfair*	Jerry's	G&O	Samuelson's*†
MISCELLANEOUS PRODUCTS						
Raid House & Garden Bug Killer	13.5 oz.	2.79	3.19	2.99	2.87	2.89
Listerine Antiseptic	24 oz.	2.19	2.29	2.19	1.98	2.17
Anacin Tablets	100 ct.	2.59	2.67	2.69	2.18	2.37
Ivory Liquid	22 oz.	1.29	1.49	1.47	1.29	1.39
Purina Dog Chow	5 pd.	2.79	2.98	2.99	2.84	2.89
Kleenex	280 ct.	1.39	1.39	1.35	1.27	1.29
Wisk Liquid Detergent	1 qt.	1.89	1.99	1.89	1.74	1.79
Sparky Charcoal	5 pd.	1.79	2.09	2.09	1.75	1.99
Colgate Toothpaste	6 oz.	2.19	2.19	2.09	1.98	2.09
Pampers Diapers	38 ct.	9.19	9.68	9.37	9.19	9.59
TOTAL:		$28.10	$29.96	$29.12	$27.09	$28.46
GRAND TOTAL:		$84.65	$90.51	$89.57	$82.30	$85.04

*Gives trading stamps.   †Open 24 hours a day.

EXERCISE 7
Statistical Material

INSTRUCTIONS: Write a news story based on the following statistics. Assume that the figures were released today by the Office of Institutional Research at your school, summarizing the distribution of grades given during last year's fall term at your school. The statistics are real ones released by a medium-sized university. For two reasons, the statistics do not always add up to 100 percent. First, they do not include grades of "Satisfactory" and "Unsatisfactory." Second, they are rounded off to the nearest tenth.

College and Department	Percentage of Grades							Total No. of Grades
	A	B	C	D	F	WP*	I	
Business Administration								
Accountancy	15.6	29.9	26.1	7.9	7.9	11.9	0.5	949
Economics	19.4	38.5	21.3	6.7	4.4	8.3	1.4	361
Finance	17.6	34.8	24.7	9.3	4.7	8.0	0.9	1,091
Management	15.4	33.4	32.0	7.7	4.9	4.3	2.3	1,489
Marketing	13.6	35.9	37.1	5.0	3.7	4.3	0.4	515
TOTAL	16.1	33.7	28.7	7.7	5.3	7.2	1.2	4,405
Education								
Elementary Education	39.8	35.4	14.2	3.2	2.2	2.6	2.6	1,285
Physical Education	53.2	24.4	8.6	3.0	2.9	3.4	4.5	837
Professional Lab	11.9	6.4	2.2	0.6	0.0	1.2	1.2	328
Secondary Education	39.1	36.4	9.2	1.1	1.5	2.7	10.0	261
Teaching Analysis	41.4	33.6	14.4	1.6	2.4	2.9	3.7	804
TOTAL	40.7	29.7	11.4	2.4	2.1	2.7	3.8	3,515
Engineering								
Civil	20.2	39.4	24.4	4.5	3.8	6.6	1.1	287
Electrical	27.6	32.5	22.7	9.2	3.1	4.3	0.6	163
Engineering Mathematics and Computer Science	21.5	36.6	19.3	11.8	4.3	6.5	—	93
Engineering Core	18.7	31.0	27.3	7.7	4.8	9.5	1.0	1,626
Engineering Technology	37.0	33.9	15.4	5.6	3.6	3.8	0.7	573
Mechanical	13.4	20.5	40.2	15.2	6.2	3.6	0.9	112
TOTAL	22.9	32.3	24.6	7.5	4.4	7.4	0.9	2,854
Health-Related Professions	38.8	34.1	9.9	1.9	2.4	2.4	3.0	1,338
Humanities & Fine Arts								
Art	31.4	34.8	13.7	2.1	4.6	8.5	4.9	328
English	32.0	35.8	14.1	1.7	5.2	8.2	3.0	696
Foreign Languages	34.0	38.2	13.9	3.5	2.1	4.8	3.5	144
History	10.7	31.3	27.5	10.5	8.4	6.2	5.4	726
Humanities	41.8	29.3	12.0	1.2	3.7	5.8	6.2	242
Music	57.1	22.3	10.9	2.7	2.7	2.3	2.0	615
Theatre	41.3	28.3	15.2	0.0	0.0	6.5	8.7	46
TOTAL	33.0	31.0	16.7	4.3	5.0	6.0	4.0	2,797

*Withdraw Passing

College and Department	Percentage of Grades							Total No. of Grades
	A	B	C	D	F	WP*	I	
Natural Sciences								
Biological Sciences	24.1	33.1	19.7	8.7	8.7	3.8	1.9	366
Chemistry	21.3	23.5	25.6	8.9	12.5	7.0	1.2	328
Computer Science	23.3	29.3	23.3	9.0	6.9	6.0	2.2	1,157
Geology	8.9	26.9	23.9	3.0	11.9	25.4	—	67
Math & Statistics	11.2	17.8	24.3	13.3	15.4	16.8	1.2	1,372
Physics	20.8	36.5	28.0	6.0	2.8	5.3	0.6	318
TOTAL	18.1	25.4	23.9	10.2	10.6	10.3	1.5	3,608
Social Sciences								
Air Force ROTC	26.9	45.5	16.7	2.6	5.1	1.9	1.3	156
Communications	21.4	43.5	21.0	4.6	3.9	4.2	1.2	1,115
Political Science	30.3	32.0	19.1	4.2	4.8	6.8	2.8	456
Psychology	35.6	34.4	16.6	4.0	3.2	4.5	1.1	1,185
Public Service Admin.	34.2	29.0	23.1	3.6	2.9	3.4	2.1	1,219
Sociology	27.0	36.0	21.5	4.1	5.1	3.3	2.8	967
TOTAL	29.8	35.5	20.3	4.1	3.8	4.1	1.8	5,098

*Withdraw Passing

EXERCISE 8
Statistical Material

INSTRUCTIONS: Write a news story based on the following summary released today by your state's Council of Better Business Bureaus, Inc. It lists the 70 types of complaints that the Better Business Bureaus in your state receive most frequently and the percentage of those complaints that are resolved. All the numbers are authentic; they were provided by an actual Council of Better Business Bureaus.

| Type of Business | Last Year | | | | Two Years Ago | | | |
	Rank	Total	Percent of Total	Percent Settled	Rank	Total	Percent of Total	Percent Settled
TOTAL		369,703	100.00%	71.3%		401,476	100.00%	71.9%
Mail Order Companies	1	76,076	20.57	77.8	1	82,264	20.49	79.5
Franchised Auto Dealers	2	16,461	4.45	82.4	2	18,974	4.72	79.9
Home Furnishings Stores	3	11,832	3.20	69.6	4	11,643	2.90	70.3
Magazines, Ordered by Mail	4	10,437	2.82	72.4	6	10,379	2.58	77.4
Misc. Home Maintenance Co.'s	5	10,230	2.76	58.3	5	10,672	2.65	55.5
Indep. Auto Repair—Except Transmissions	6	9,713	2.62	64.7	3	13,054	3.25	56.8
Department Stores	7	9,262	2.50	88.5	7	10,306	2.56	89.3
Misc. Automotive	8	8,276	2.23	65.5	8	8,082	2.01	65.9
Television Servicing Co.'s	9	7,028	1.90	70.1	10	7,352	1.83	70.3
Insurance Companies	10	6,797	1.83	82.4	11	7,156	1.78	83.8
Dry Cleaning/Laundry Co.'s	11	6,371	1.72	63.6	12	6,737	1.67	67.0
Home Remodeling Contractors	12	6,131	1.65	58.3	9	7,825	1.94	60.6
Apparel & Accessory Shops	13	5,647	1.52	70.7	14	5,505	1.37	73.3
Appliance Service Co.'s	14	5,537	1.49	63.7	13	6,064	1.51	66.2
Real Estate Sales/Rental Services	15	4,360	1.17	61.9	18	4,339	1.08	63.9
Misc. Health & Personal Services	16	4,345	1.17	67.9	19	4,175	1.03	75.0
Appliance Stores	17	4,215	1.14	70.9	15	5,061	1.26	74.2
Roofing Contractors	18	4,201	1.13	53.7	16	4,557	1.13	54.2
Floor Coverings Stores	19	4,147	1.12	66.1	20	4,142	1.03	66.7
T.V. & Radio/Phone Shops	20	3,989	1.07	71.5	24	3,825	.95	71.2
Heating & Central Air Cond'g Co.'s	21	3,727	1.00	66.6	21	4,111	1.02	70.4
Auto Tire, Battery, Accessory Shops	22	3,369	.91	73.9	22	3,965	.98	72.3
Direct Selling—Magazines	23	3,352	.90	77.5	28	3,452	.85	81.0
Jewelry Stores	24	3,200	.86	74.1	23	3,914	.97	76.2
Gasoline Service Stations	25	3,100	.83	65.3	26	3,587	.89	67.6
Auto Dealers—Used Only	26	2,994	.80	66.6	17	4,519	1.12	74.5
Direct Selling—Misc.	27	2,886	.78	70.7	27	3,498	.87	72.0
Auto Transmission Shops	28	2,758	.74	69.5	35	2,506	.62	69.7
Photographic Studios	29	2,741	.74	69.9	38	2,470	.61	65.1
Moving/Storage Companies	30	2,712	.73	66.7	29	3,321	.82	69.5
Plumbing Contractors	31	2,644	.71	61.7	30	3,121	.77	66.5
House/Apt. Rental—By Indiv.	32	2,486	.67	62.8	25	3,722	.92	54.1
Health Studios	33	2,423	.65	65.4	48	1,931	.48	69.8
Photographic Processing Co.'s	34	2,421	.65	75.7	39	2,437	.60	69.9
Gardening/Nursery Products	35	2,378	.64	68.9	40	2,388	.59	66.3
Vacation Certificate Co.'s	36	2,354	.63	40.3	51	1,853	.46	66.9
Mobile/Modular Home Dealers	37	2,352	.63	69.6	31	3,015	.75	68.3
Banks	38	2,278	.61	87.1	42	2,238	.55	86.3
Misc. Financial	39	2,263	.61	66.3	43	2,256	.56	71.8
Exterminating Service Co.'s	40	2,221	.60	75.1	36	2,504	.62	76.0

Type of Business	Last Year				Two Years Ago			
	Rank	Total	Percent of Total	Percent Settled	Rank	Total	Percent of Total	Percent Settled
TOTAL		369,703	100.00%	71.3%		401,476	100.00%	71.9%
Travel Agencies	41	2,187	.59	68.0	37	2,500	.62	68.9
Direct Selling—Photography	42	2,146	.58	67.7	45	1,987	.49	67.3
Credit Card Companies	43	2,116	.57	87.4	41	2,329	.58	88.3
Home Builders—New Construction	44	2,030	.54	65.8	32	2,919	.72	66.8
Utility Companies	45	2,021	.54	84.0	56	1,500	.37	88.3
Advertising Soliciting Orgs.	46	1,971	.53	56.6	47	1,962	.48	58.5
Swimming Pool Companies	47	1,922	.51	66.6	34	2,742	.68	59.0
Credit Collection Companies	48	1,884	.50	77.8	46	1,965	.48	80.1
Waterproofing Companies	49	1,682	.45	57.4	53	1,600	.39	56.0
Reupholstering Shops	50	1,548	.41	54.9	57	1,472	.36	56.1
Carpet & Upholstery Clng. Co.'s	51	1,530	.41	60.8	44	2,202	.54	67.2
Consumer Finance & Loan Co.'s	52	1,489	.40	78.2	52	1,831	.45	80.9
Paving Contractors	53	1,393	.37	50.5	50	1,856	.46	48.3
Homework Companies (Work-at-Home)	54	1,358	.36	51.5	33	2,757	.68	56.2
Buying Clubs/Group Purch.	55	1,321	.35	78.8	60	1,419	.35	66.7
Siding Contractors	56	1,305	.35	63.6	49	1,889	.47	62.7
Trade/Vocational Schools	57	1,283	.34	80.4	62	1,199	.29	77.5
Building Material/Supply Co.'s	58	1,277	.34	75.0	55	1,505	.37	76.9
Employment Services	59	1,270	.34	63.0	58	1,467	.36	69.2
Telephone Companies	60	1,226	.33	82.0	67	894	.22	80.4
Airlines	61	1,190	.32	75.3	59	1,454	.36	80.9
Recreational Vehicle Dealers	62	1,142	.30	65.8	54	1,514	.37	68.4
Hospitals/Clinics	63	1,079	.29	80.9	63	1,079	.26	83.8
Music/Record Stores	64	1,018	.27	72.5	61	1,268	.31	76.0
Alarm Systems Dealers	65	990	.26	67.7	66	919	.22	69.3
Misc. Food Companies	66	887	.23	69.1	65	1,012	.25	66.2
Electrical Contractors	67	790	.21	69.4	64	1,017	.25	68.0
Land Development Co.'s	68	699	.18	77.3	70	741	.18	71.5
Doctors	69	667	.18	81.5	72	712	.17	77.2
Hair Product Improvement Co.'s	70	647	.17	67.9	68	855	.21	64.9

EXERCISE 9
Statistical Material

INSTRUCTIONS: Write a news story based on the following returns from the municipal elections that were held yesterday in the suburb of Roseville. "I" stands for "incumbent," "U" means the candidate ran unopposed, and "W" indicates a write-in candidate.

Office	Ward 1	Ward 2	Ward 3	Ward 4	Ward 5	Totals
Mayor						
Alfred Bingston	7,891	3,911	11,824	7,787	9,123	40,536
Thomas Field (I)	6,041	5,886	9,348	4,016	9,007	34,298
Stephen Hamilton (W)	438	521	147	21	86	1,213
City Attorney						
George McCartney	11,121	6,780	9,987	9,987	12,067	49,942
Louis Swanson	3,041	4,844	10,711	1,641	5,291	25,528
City Treasurer						
Joseph Alvito (I, U)	12,942	9,041	21,431	10,039	16,441	69,894
City Clerk						
Henry Wong (I, U)	12,734	9,119	21,402	10,114	16,434	69,803
Superintendent of Schools						
Walter Pfaff	8,824	6,779	13,466	6,004	11,612	46,685
Peter Wilke (I)	5,129	3,412	7,854	4,387	8,941	29,723
Municipal Court Judge						
Frederick Cole	3,824	2,711	6,409	2,878	4,731	20,553
Richard Kernan (I)	9,743	7,443	14,385	8,562	13,862	53,995
Council Member, First Ward						
Mary Hyatt	5,014					
Ralph Issac (I)	8,279					
George Reynolds (W)	482					
Council Member, Second Ward						
Paul Putnam (I)		4,003				
Louis Ramirez		4,019				
Norman Shumate (W)		46				
Council Member, Third Ward						
Alan Kline			10,831			
Jerome Mack			10,176			
Council Member, Fourth Ward						
Howard Elton (I)				8,260		
Leonard Pollard				3,642		
Council Member, Fifth Ward						
Jerry Crum					7,469	
Michael Kelly (I)					8,944	

EXERCISE 10
Statistical Material

INSTRUCTIONS: The following budget is an actual copy of the budget for a small town. Assume that the town is Roseville, a suburb of your community, and that the figures for next year's budget were approved today by the Roseville City Council. Write a news story about the budget. The city's revenues are listed on this page, and its expenditures are listed on the following page.

CITY OF ROSEVILLE BUDGET REVENUES

Fiscal Year	Actual Budget Two Years Ago	Actual Budget Last Year	Actual Budget This Year	Adopted Budget for Next Year
Tax Levy Net	1,686,982	1,724,207	1,767,730	1,783,550
Occupational License	140,099	133,358	150,000	150,000
Building Permit Fees	38,137	53,570	60,000	60,000
Registration Fees	8,529	8,054	7,000	7,000
Fines and Forfeitures	169,748	146,333	80,000	120,000
Franchise Taxes	409,187	524,250	550,000	579,900
Interest on Deposits	76,517	68,299	60,000	60,000
Office of Civil Defense	729	475	—	—
Sewer Revenue Funds	732,661	1,024,844	1,080,480	1,083,500
Improvement Rev. Fund	416,107	430,516	391,310	413,500
Cigarette Tax Revenue	164,222	143,527	155,000	155,000
Motor Fuel Tax Revenue	182,454	217,831	201,540	202,000
Other Revenue	90,935	47,016	40,000	45,000
Golf Course	30,000	30,000	30,000	30,000
Total Revenue	4,146,307	4,552,280	4,573,060	4,689,450
Federal Revenue Sharing	389,000	—	379,352	260,700
Prior Year Surplus	—	119,090	164,633	84,300
GRAND TOTAL	4,535,307	4,671,370	5,117,045	5,034,450
Ad Valorem Tax Rate	5.32 mills	5.32 mills	5.5 mills	5.5 mills

CITY OF ROSEVILLE BUDGET EXPENDITURES

Fiscal Year	Actual Budget Two Years Ago	Actual Budget Last Year	Actual Budget This Year	Adopted Budget for Next Year
General Government	101,756	119,131	112,950	93,450
Office of City Manager	56,828	59,893	62,400	74,150
Finance	111,561	127,552	138,850	136,450
Planning	21,982	24,477	21,700	28,650
Building & Zoning	68,485	72,926	74,300	70,550
Administration	68,633	72,989	56,750	65,300
Engineering	102,618	106,474	100,300	107,900
Streets	385,531	396,117	493,652	425,200
Lakes Management	163,747	270,142	252,600	240,700
Public Building Maint.	325,176	366,531	367,500	351,200
Police	1,221,688	1,248,862	1,226,900	1,325,900
Fire	634,116	706,383	826,450	850,300
Civil Defense	5,535	8,520	9,200	—
Parks	384,712	408,085	468,200	444,400
Forestry	96,027	107,231	118,800	117,350
Cemetery	38,662	50,614	48,400	58,800
Recreation	169,034	171,343	115,400	158,600
Community Centers	45,408	41,218	44,600	50,050
Organizational Support	97,922	101,500	182,500	197,700
Transfer to Other Funds	254,411	211,019	311,283	237,800
TOTAL	4,353,832	4,671,007	5,032,735	5,034,450
Personnel	317	310	301	303

20 Feature Stories

Most news stories describe a recent *event*: a meeting, crime, fire or accident, for example. Earlier chapters have shown that news stories also inform the public about topics that are *important*, *local* or *unusual*. Many of the topics are *relevant* to people's lives, providing useful information that makes their lives easier and more enjoyable.

Feature stories place a greater emphasis upon facts that are interesting—facts likely to amuse and entertain their readers. Because of that emphasis, feature stories are also called "human interest" and "color" stories. They are published by magazines as well as by newspapers and often describe a person, place or idea rather than an event. So long as the stories are interesting, their topics may be older, less important and less relevant than the topics of news stories. Similarly, some feature stories concern distant rather than local topics, and many appeal to their readers' emotions rather than to their intellect.

There is no single formula or style of writing, such as the inverted pyramid form, which reporters must use while writing every feature story. However, features generally explore their topics in greater depth than news stories and place a greater emphasis upon colorful details, anecdotes, quotations and descriptions, for example.

In addition, feature stories share two characteristics with news stories: both must be factual and original. Feature stories are not a form of fiction; like news stories, they must be based on facts. They must also be objective—they are not essays or editorials. Moreover, reporters must personally gather the facts for their stories. They cannot copy or rewrite the stories already published elsewhere. Few editors want to republish facts that their readers may have seen months earlier.

Characteristically, the following features emphasize new, interesting and factual details:

DALLAS—Just after noon July 12, Bill and Anita Keeler finished counting the collection money at Schreiber Memorial United Methodist Church in north Dallas. Three blocks away, their son, David, waited for them at home.

The Keelers got into their car and drove north a mile to the Town North National Bank, just across the Lyndon B. Johnson Freeway, then turned back for the short drive to their ranch-style brick home on Ridgeside Drive. They arrived about 12:15 p.m.

The Keelers walked into the hallway leading to the bedrooms. David, 14, was in his room. He was holding his father's Remington 1100 semi-automatic shotgun.

Police say they believe the first shots hit Bill Keeler, president of Arco Oil and Gas Co., in the chest and neck. David quickly reloaded, investigators say. Anita Keeler was hit in the abdomen. David reloaded a second time and fired one more shot, police say. He fled out the back door, leaving behind the weapon and seven spent shells.

At 12:40 p.m., Lee Walden, a patrolman with the Addison Police Department was watching for speeders along a road about 4 miles north of the Keelers' home. A handsome teen-ager wearing blue shorts and a green sweatshirt rode up to the car on a green Schwinn Varsity 10-speed. Walden rolled down the window and asked if he could help.

"I just shot and killed my parents at home with a shotgun," Walden reported David Keeler as telling him. A week later, the mystery remains. More than a family has been shattered by the tragedy. A church, a school, a corpora-tion, a neighborhood, a community, society asks the same question: What went wrong?

(The Washington Post)

They come, three and four young men packed into a dusty car with ripped seat covers and taillights dangling.

Chances are, they have driven all night from Wyoming or Texas or New Mexico, with their only stops for gas and a burger greasier than the spot the old car left in the diner parking lot.

If they have the entry fees, they're guaranteed a few seconds of work for the night, but there's nothing that says they'll get paid for it—not even if they do their jobs well. Tomorrow night, it will be another town, another try.

They are the professional rodeo cowboys, and they come—at their own expense—to entertain you.

(Deseret News)

TRENTON, N.J.—The arrival of Gary Maik's Social Security disability payment is one of the big events of his month. He gets fidgety if the check is late. With careful management, he has saved over $6,000 in the last four years.

Maik receives his checks at Trenton Psychiatric Hospital, where he has been an inmate since a judge overturned his manslaughter conviction and found him not guilty by reason of insanity. According to court records, he stabbed his best friend 66 times with a hunting knife while under the influence of LSD.

The disability for which Maik is compensated at the rate of $214 a month is the insanity that put him in the state prison. He is eligible because, based on a psychiatric report, he was found "unemployable in American society."

Maik is one of a growing number of inmates of state and federal prisons who receive Social Security payments. . . .

(The New York Times)

None of the stories begins with a summary lead. Instead, all three begin with the details most likely to interest readers: the human element—people rather than abstract problems or ideas. If you reread the first story about the Texas teen-ager, you will note a number of specific details in the first three paragraphs. Those paragraphs tell you when the story occurred, the name of the church, the name of the bank, the distance to the couple's home, the type of home (a brick ranch-style) and even the brand of shotgun.

Types of Feature Stories

The most crucial step in beginning to write a good feature is the selection of a good topic. Ideally, every topic should be fresh, dramatic, colorful and interesting. You may, of course, write a feature story about a topic that has already been in the news, but you must then approach the topic from a new point of view, emphasizing a new development or angle.

Feature writers find appropriate topics simply by being curious and observant. A college student read several news stories about the homeless—the street people—in her community and noticed that none of the stories quoted the homeless. Instead, reporters relied upon the authorities in their community. Police blamed the homeless for a series of minor crimes. Welfare agencies wanted more money to care for the homeless. Church leaders wondered about their responsibilities.

The student drove to the area where the homeless congregated, sat on a curb and began to interview one of them. Others gathered around her, so that in an hour she was able to complete a dozen interviews. Her feature story revealed that the homeless were not primarily adult males—or bums and criminals. Rather, families with small children had become homeless. For years, many of the families had lived in their own homes. Then a husband or wife became ill or lost a job, often because a factory closed or moved. The couples came to the city looking for work, but were unable to find new jobs or low-cost housing.

Another news story may report that your city is hiring a private business to build or operate its prisons. You might write a feature about the trend. If a criminal's sentence seems too lenient (or too harsh), you might ask how long the average murderer, rapist or robber remains in your state's prisons. If, each week, a local group called "Crime Watch" or "Crime Stoppers" asks the public to help solve a crime, you might ask about the group's success.

Other feature stories are based upon reporters' personal experiences—and their friends'. If, after little or no training, one of your friends is given a gun and hired as a guard, you might ask about the training and qualifications of other "rent-a-cops." In many cities, they outnumber the police. Students have also written about unwed fathers, student suicides, unusual classes and unusual teachers.

After selecting a general topic, reporters must limit it to a manageable size, perhaps by emphasizing a single individual, theme or episode. For example: a profile might discuss just one aspect of a person's life or character—a single experience, trait or achievement. If reporters fail to limit their topics, their stories are likely to become too long, disorganized and superficial. They may ramble from one idea to another, without adequate transitions and without explaining any of the ideas in adequate detail.

While gathering the information for feature stories, reporters are likely to consult several sources—perhaps a half dozen or more—to obtain a detailed and well-rounded account of their topics. Good reporters gather two or three times more information than they can possibly use, then discard all but the most interesting details.

The following pages describe the most common types of feature stories. As you read about them, you may think of a topic that you could write about.

Profiles or Personality Features

Profiles describe interesting people. The people may have overcome a handicap, pursued an unusual career, achieved success or become famous because of their colorful personalities. To be effective, profiles must do more than list an individual's achievements or important dates in the individual's life. They must reveal the person's character. To gather the necessary information, feature writers often watch their subjects at work; visit them at home; and interview their friends, relatives and business associates. Completed profiles then quote and describe their subjects. The best profiles are so revealing that readers feel as though they actually know and have talked to the people.

Some sources may surprise you by revealing their most personal and embarrassing secrets. However, a few may ask you to keep their identities a secret. Their stories are compelling. But you need *their* stories. Instead of interviewing the police about a drug problem, or faculty members about students who cheat, interview the drug users and cheaters themselves—specific individuals who seem to be representative of a larger problem.

The following profile uses a single individual to reveal the problems of the elderly. Notice how the use of quotations enables the woman to tell much of the story in her own words:

> She is old—86—but doesn't like to admit it. "It's like admitting defeat," Rilla says. "Why does old age have to be such a hardship? It's supposed to give you time to enjoy things."
>
> Rilla was the oldest of 10 children but is the only one still alive. The youngest died three months ago at the age of 72.
>
> "One of the hardest things I've had to face is watching my family and friends die," she says. "Even my own children are middle-aged and in ill health."
>
> Rilla seems reluctant to discuss old age, but considers herself an authority on the subject. "I've been old for a long time now," she explains. "I just see myself get a little older every day. I guess I'm what's kindly referred to as 'fragile.'"
>
> She lives with a daughter and her husband. "I used to have a lot of friends in the neighborhood," she adds, "but they're all dead.
>
> "There's nothing for me to do anymore. I can't see to read. I have such bad arthritis that I can't hardly walk from the living room to the kitchen. My garden has all gone to weeds because I can't bend over far enough to work in it."
>
> Rilla says there are a few benefits to old age: "I don't worry about my figure anymore. I eat as much as I want as often as I want.
>
> "Of course, I've been able to watch my children and grandchildren grow and develop and become good people. And too, there have been times when I've wanted to die."

Historical Features

Historical features commemorate the dates of important events, such as the attack on Pearl Harbor, the bombing of Hiroshima or the assassination of Dr. Martin Luther King Jr. The following story, distributed by the North American Newspaper Alliance, typifies that type of historical feature:

> MATEWAN, W. Va.—The most infamous episode in the annals of Appalachia erupted on Blackberry Creek 100 years ago.
>
> The feud between the Hatfields and McCoys, two powerful mountain clans, lasted for about 15 years. When the fighting finally subsided, more than 100 men, women and children had been killed or wounded, and the region's residents generally were viewed by the rest of the country as a bunch of murderous moonshine-swilling hillbillies who liked nothing better than to loll about the front porch, picking their toes and taking potshots at each other.

Newspapers also publish historical features on 100th birthdays and on the anniversaries of the births and deaths of famous people. Other historical features are tied to current events that generate interest in their topics. If a tornado, flood or earthquake strikes your city, newspapers are likely to publish feature stories about earlier tornadoes, floods or earthquakes. When President Kennedy was assassinated, newspapers published historical features about the assassinations of Presidents Lincoln, Garfield and McKinley. When the space shuttle exploded, killing seven astronauts, newspapers published features about the astronauts killed in previous accidents. Other historical features describe famous landmarks, pioneers and philosophies; improvements in educational, entertainment, medical and transportation facilities; and changes in an area's racial composition, housing patterns, food, industries, growth, religions and wealth.

Every city (and every school) is likely to have experienced some interesting events at some time in its history. A good feature writer will learn more about those events, perhaps by consulting historical documents or by interviewing the people who witnessed or participated in them.

Adventure Features

Adventure features describe unusual and exciting experiences—perhaps the experiences of someone who survived an airplane crash, climbed a mountain, sailed around the world, served in the Peace Corps or fought in a war. In this type of feature story, too, quotations and descriptions are especially important. After a catastrophe, for example, feature writers often use the survivors' eyewitness accounts to recreate the scene. Many writers begin with the action—their stories' most interesting and dramatic moments. Here are two examples:

Visibility was unlimited as the single-engine Cessna sped westward, climbing to 10,500 feet as it approached the snow-capped Sierra, a rugged mountain range that separates Nevada and California.

Then the airplane's motor stopped: suddenly, completely, without warning.

"After all these years of flying, I'm going to crash," the pilot thought. "And it's going to happen at the worst spot in the United States and at the worst time of year—midwinter in the High Sierra."

"It was the 10th of July, 1969, approximately 5 p.m.," said Steve Jefferson, one of the Vietnam veterans attending classes here. "Myself and two sergeants were driving down the road in a Jeep. Theoretically, we shouldn't have been in this situation. We should have been accompanied by more men in another Jeep, but I always thought that when my time was up, it was up. It was going to happen no matter what.

"There was a white flash and a pop, and the next thing I knew I was lying in the middle of the road.

"I thought we had hit a hole, and that I had flipped out of the Jeep. I always rode kind of haphazardly in the Jeep, with one leg hanging out one side of it. I really thought I had fallen out, and they had kept going without me; you know, as a joke.

"Then I turned and saw the Jeep overturned and on fire by the side of the road. I touched my arm with my good hand, and it was all bloody. It finally dawned on me that it was an ambush. I heard some rifle fire but, at the time, didn't realize they were shooting at me.

"I crawled over to the side of the road, away from the Jeep, and hollered for the other guys. There was no answer. . . ."

Seasonal Features

Reporters are often assigned to write feature stories about seasons and holidays: about Christmas, Easter, St. Patrick's Day, Friday the 13th and the first day of spring. Such stories are difficult to write because, in order to make them interesting, reporters must find a new angle.

A reporter in Madison, Wis., was asked to write about June weddings, and her story was interesting because it went beyond the routine. The reporter learned that the county clerk did issue more wedding licenses in June than during any other month of the year. However, the reporter continued questioning the clerk and also learned that the couples applying for marriage licenses are getting older. Most are in their mid-to-late 20s. Applicants under the age of 18 need their parents' consent, but fewer are getting married. As the interview continued, the reporter also learned that, "Not every couple that applies for a marriage license gets as far as the wedding ceremony." The county clerk recalled one applicant, a man, who seemed unusually nervous. The next day, he called back and asked whether he could get a refund. He could—and did.

Explanatory Features

Explanatory features are also called "local situation" and "interpretive" features. They attempt to provide a more detailed description or explanation of topics in the news. Explanatory features may examine a specific organization, activity, trend or idea. For example, after news stories describe an act of terrorism, an explanatory feature may examine the terrorists' identity, tactics and goals.

News stories provide the ideas for thousands of other explanatory features. After a bank robbery, an explanatory feature might examine the training that banks give their employees to prepare them for robberies. Or, an explanatory feature might reveal more about a typical bank robber, including the robber's chances of getting caught and probable punishment. If you see several news stories about a new diet, you might ask why so many dieters lose weight—but seem unable to keep it off. Or, if you notice that more people are driving pickup trucks—and riding in the back of them—you might ask about the trucks' safety.

Another followup won a Pulitzer Prize. In 1947, an explosion killed 111 men in an Illinois mine, and Joseph Pulitzer—editor of the St. Louis Post-Dispatch—asked his staff to thoroughly review the tragedy. Pulitzer wanted to know what was likely to be done to improve mine safety. What would be done for the miners' families? Also, who was responsible for the tragedy, and were they likely to be punished for it? Notice that the story starts with the action. Also notice the reporter's use of specific detail:

> The clock in the office of the Centralia Coal Company's Mine No. 5 ticked toward quitting time on the afternoon of March 25. As the hands registered 3:27 and the 142 men working 540 feet under ground prepared to leave the pit at the end of their shift, an explosion occurred.
>
> The blast originated in one of the work rooms in the northwestern section of the workings. Fed by coal dust, it whooshed through the labyrinth of tunnels underlying the town of Wamac, Ill., on the southern outskirts of Centralia. Thirty-one men, most of whom happened to be near the shaft at the time, made their way to the cage and were brought out alive, but the remaining 111 were trapped. Fellow-workmen who tried to reach them shortly after the explosion were driven back by poisonous fumes.

Another explanatory feature, recently published by the Chicago Tribune, examined the problems of young lawyers. A Tribune reporter found that law students look forward to exciting, glamorous careers. But when they actually begin work—often 12 to 14 hours a day—many are disillusioned:

> SAN FRANCISCO—They are young, bright and well paid with big futures. They are also very unhappy.
>
> They are the many young lawyer associates who enter the profession out of law school with high hopes of an interesting career and expectations of all the good things life has to offer.
>
> Instead, they find long hours of boring work, often under the thumb of a senior partner who is more a taskmaster than teacher, unwilling to give needed feedback and support.
>
> Some of them drop out of the profession, move to another law firm or end up in a hospital or on a psychiatrist's couch.

How-To-Do-It Features

How-to-do-it features tell readers how to perform some task: how to buy a house, find a job, plant a garden, repair a car or strengthen a marriage. Such stories are often shorter than other types of features and more difficult to write. Inexperienced reporters tend to preach or dictate to readers—to present their own opinions—instead of consulting expert sources and providing detailed, factual advice.

Types of Feature Leads

The lead is the most important part of any feature story and must immediately capture its readers' interest. The lead must also reveal a story's theme and suggest how that theme will be treated. However, the lead should never exaggerate, mislead or sensationalize.

Mistakenly, some reporters save their best material. They present it later, often on the second or third page. Yet most readers will never see it there; they quit before getting that far. If a lead is dull or poorly written, readers will not go any further. So begin with your best material: your most interesting details.

Like news stories, many features begin with summary leads. However, features may also begin with quotations, anecdotes, questions, action, descriptions, shocking facts or a combination of these techniques. Again, the only requirement is that the leads interest readers, luring them into the stories.

As you read the following examples, also notice that a feature lead can be a unit of thought that contains two, three or even four paragraphs.

Summaries

It gets great gas mileage and is fun to ride—for those who survive. It is seven times more dangerous than a car.

Yet the motorcycle's popularity continues to soar.

(Chicago Tribune)

Nothing works. Judges and jailers, cops and robbers, reformers and reactionaries are increasingly coming to the same dismal conclusion about a century and a half of prison reform in the United States. No matter what we do to fight crime by trying to reform criminals, nothing works.

Quotations

"My husband died of a heart attack," said Mrs. H. "I don't know what was wrong with me after that. I lost a few years in my life somewhere. I can't remember. Maybe I don't want to."

(The Orlando Sentinel)

"When it hit me, I was unconscious for three days, and when I came to I couldn't remember a thing. I asked my boy what happened, and he told me, 'You were hit by lightning.'"

(The Orlando Sentinel)

Anecdotes and Examples

NEW YORK—A high school graduate on Long Island sues the local school system because he cannot read above the third-grade level.

The chief of personnel for the Navy reports $250,000 in damage to a diesel engine because a sailor who worked on it could not read the maintenance manual.

The National Assessment of Educational Progress shows a group of 17-year-olds a replica of a traffic ticket, and more than half cannot determine the last day the fine can be paid.

Such anecdotes are being heard with increasing frequency and point to a conclusion that is becoming painfully obvious to employers, educators, politicians and the general public alike: the United States has a serious problem with illiteracy.

(The New York Times)

Martha, a 28-year-old, began to suffer from ulcers, headaches and high blood pressure. A doctor advised her to change jobs and, three days later, she became a travel consultant.

Kim, 32, was divorced with four children to support. To increase her income, she began to sell real estate. She earned $29,000 last year—and expects to earn $50,000 this year.

Allison, 25, disliked taking orders from doctors. Moreover, she thought some doctors were lazy and uncaring. So she returned to college and is studying to become an English professor.

Until last year, all three women were nurses. Like thousands of others, they became frustrated by the job's stress, low pay, hard work and irregular hours.

Questions

How much longer will you live?
What are your chances of becoming a millionaire?

Action or Narratives

Dust rose from the track as the race car increased its speed to 100, 120 and then 130 miles an hour.

Then, disaster.

Bill McDill hasn't forgotten that moment at Sebring. It was his most frightening on a race track.

"I was heading for the hairpin turn at about 130 mph," McDill recalls. "To get around that corner you have to slow to 15 or 20 miles an hour, but when I stepped on my car's brakes, nothing happened."

An overnight train ride turned into a seven-day horror-filled trip when William Kraslawsky, now an American citizen, fled from the Russians during World War II.

"Early on Jan. 23, 1945, my father sent word for my mother and me to pack up and go to a railroad siding outside my town, Ratibor, which is located in Eastern Germany. There they had been evacuating wounded German soldiers from the Ratibor hospital onto a Red Cross train," Kraslawsky said.

His father learned of the evacuation while working at the hospital and realized it would be his family's last chance to escape. . . .

Shockers

Cancer will kill someone in your family.

Within the lifetime of today's people, humans may be in touch with beings on other worlds.

(Christian Science Monitor)

Description

Neighbors say the frail and gray-haired woman rarely goes out of the house and sometimes refuses to come to the door or answer the telephone.

Occasionally, struggling with a garden hose, she waters her yellow-green lawn on one of Southern California's hot summer days. Once in awhile she beats out a rug on the porch.

But mostly she sits alone inside the old white frame two-story house, her only fellowship the company of two of her five bachelor sons.

One of her sons is Sirhan B. Sirhan, under life sentence at San Quentin Prison for assassinating Sen. Robert F. Kennedy.

(The Associated Press)

HOUMA, La.—The eight men, shotguns in hand, crept close to the thousands of geese feeding in a rice field. On signal, they stood up and fired three shots each into the mass of birds, most of which took to the air as soon as the first shots were fired. A ninth man recalls the outcome:

"The flock was enormous—there must have been ten thousand geese. Some were dead, some were flopping around, and cripples were falling out of the sky as far as the eye could see."

The death toll: 168, more than four times Louisiana's legal limit of five geese per hunter per day.

This wasn't a scene from a distant, presumably crueler age. It took place only a few months ago and was openly photographed with a video camera by the ninth man—an agent of the U.S. Fish and Wildlife Service, David Hall. Mr. Hall had duped the eight into taking him along as "an outdoor writer," and he has filed a variety of poaching charges against them.

(The Wall Street Journal)

A Less Effective Lead

The following lead, written by a student, is less effective than the previous examples. Why?

"It's something that I imagine happens every day, somewhere or another, but for me it's got to be the most harrowing experience in my life."

Elizabeth Gerdt is a 21-year-old college student: a junior studying to become a nurse.

Her story is an unusual one, and probably no one can tell it as well as Beth (she feels uncomfortable being called "Elizabeth"—too formal, she says) herself.

"I decided to visit some friends last weekend," she explains. "I don't have a car, so I decided to hitchhike."

How many facts—specific details—can you find in the lead? Do the introductory paragraphs tell you what happened? Do they arouse your interest in the topic, or do they occasionally confuse you? Why?

The story's most interesting details appeared later. Two paragraphs on the third page explained:

"An older man picked me up, and he seemed like someone I could trust. Then, while passing a truck, we saw a car coming right at us and swerved back into the right lane to avoid a collision.

"The man lost control, and we drove straight down the shoulder at 50 miles an hour and right into a fence. We hit a fence post, and then drove directly, head on, into a tree."

The student was wearing a seat belt and escaped serious injury. The driver was badly hurt, and the student's medical training helped save his life. Those facts are interesting, unusual and dramatic. They belong in the lead.

The Body of a Feature Story

Like the lead, the body of a feature story can take a number of forms. The inverted pyramid style is most appropriate for some features, and chronological order for many others. Regardless of the form or style of writing you decide on, every feature must be coherent. All the facts must fit together smoothly and logically. Transitions must guide readers from one segment of the story to the next and clearly reveal the relationship between those segments. Transitions should be brief. They may ask a question; shift to a new time or place; or repeat a key word, phrase or idea.

Also remember to be concise: never waste your newspaper's space or your readers' time. Emphasize lively details—the action. And provide an occasional change of pace. A good writer rarely composes an entire story of all quotations or all summaries. Instead, you might use several paragraphs of summary, then some quotations to explain an idea, then some description, and then more quotations or summary.

Also be specific. Instead of saying that a person is generous or humorous, give specific examples of the subject's generosity and humor. Similarly, instead of simply stating that "President Calvin Coolidge was a taciturn man," it would be better to illustrate his reluctance to speak by quoting Coolidge himself:

A woman meeting President Coolidge for the first time said to him, "My friends bet that I couldn't get you to say three words."

The president replied, "You lose."

Dialogue can be used to reveal such important story elements as time, place, circumstance and theme:

"Hi Charley! How many days do you have left?" a woman asked as she entered the small grocery store at 2636 Brady St.

"Until Jan. 1. We're selling out, you know," replied Charles Kur, who started selling groceries 56 years ago.

One student used quotations to reveal the problems facing her city's first pregnant firefighter. The city had never granted its firefighters any maternity benefits, and the young woman had not been employed long enough to accumulate many vacation or sick days. Instead, she wanted to take some days from her station's "sick leave bank." The city allowed its firefighters to voluntarily give up, or "bank," some of their vacation and sick leave. Then, if anyone at the station was injured and used up all of his or her own vacation and sick leave, the injured firefighter could draw extra time from the bank. A committee of five firefighters decided who was eligible to use the time:

"My doctor says I'll need about six weeks to recover from the pregnancy," the woman continued. "He says I won't be medically able to work during that time.

"But everyone on the sick leave committee at my station is a man, and they don't want a woman around. They feel like firefighting is a man's job. So I've always had trouble, and yesterday they voted against me. They won't give me any days from our bank."

The men responded that they do not consider a maternity an accident or illness.

"If she was hurt, I would be more than willing to let her take off," a lieutenant said. "But our bank is reserved for people who have been badly injured. In her case, it was a deliberate thing. She wanted to get pregnant."

Another firefighter agreed, adding: "If she gets days from our bank for a pregnancy, then I should too, if my wife gets pregnant. A man should be entitled to at least a month off to be with his wife after their baby is delivered. A man ought to be at his wife's side at a time like that."

Description—what the reporter sees, feels, smells and tastes, as well as what he or she hears—adds even more color to the body of feature stories. However, description should be spread throughout a story rather than packed into a single paragraph or two. Description must also be used judiciously; too much bores readers and delays the presentation of more important facts. The description must be specific, composed of factual details as opposed to generalities and personal opinions.

Anecdotes are short and often humorous stories. Like quotations, they can illustrate a point, reveal character or supply interesting details. Anecdotes can also help sustain readers' interest in a story. To be effective, the anecdotes should be specific, mentioning names, times and places, as in these examples:

In addition to being a gifted diplomat and scientist, Benjamin Franklin was also a sly businessman. Franklin wanted to publish an almanac but worried about the competition from a talented rival. To ruin the rival, Franklin reported that he was dead.

When asked to describe the most romantic thing that ever happened to her, a woman said her boy friend unexpectedly stopped at her home last Christmas. He gave her a big box. Inside was a satin pillow topped by a little box which held an engagement ring. Then, with her relatives gathered around—some unknown to him—her boy friend got down on one knee and proposed.

Karen, a 25-year-old college student, said she received a single white rose twice a week for two months. "At first, there was no card," she said. "Then I found out it was the man upstairs, who I was dating."

A 42-year-old hairdresser, tired after standing on her feet all day, said her husband often draws her a bubble bath. Then he plays soft music, lights candles and rubs cream on her feet.

Reporters should not attempt to persuade or advocate in feature stories, but they occasionally draw some conclusions about their topics. After presenting a conclusion, reporters may use examples, anecdotes, quotations or dialogue to demonstrate the conclusion's validity. Or, reporters may present the details first, then draw the conclusion from them. In either case, the conclusion becomes more credible when it is accompanied by solid evidence. For example, the following leads do more than report facts; they draw certain conclusions about those facts. However, the conclusions are reasonable, supported by evidence presented later in the stories:

Julie is a 19-year-old college student. Two years ago she made a decision that could haunt her for the rest of her life: she had an abortion.

He packs a stainless steel .25-caliber pistol in the pocket of his judicial robes and stalks to the bench in pointed-toe cowboy boots.

Policemen generally adore him, defense attorneys generally hate him, and defendants both fear and admire him.

Judge Robert L. Hamilton, 31, has been Municipal Court judge for less than five months, but he has carved a reputation as a flamboyant and fearsome judge.

(The Orlando Sentinel)

News stories are usually written in the third person, with the reporter a neutral observer or outsider. Feature stories, however, can be written in the first person, with the reporter appearing in the story, or in the second person, with the reporter addressing readers directly. At times, these styles can be extremely effective. Note the following lead, taken from a feature story written by a young woman. During a storm, the woman and three companions tried to swim ashore after their boat sank two miles from the coast of California:

It felt like an endless battle. I paddled as hard as I could but thought we'd never reach shore. My arms ached and Jip's legs were numb. All I wanted was to be warm again. Every time a wave splashed over us the chill ran through our bodies.

It was horrible, not really knowing if we were going to make it to shore, or if we should stop trying because we were going to drown anyway.

It is tempting to write about your own experiences because it seems easy; you do not have to interview anyone, spend any time digging for information or do any other research. But you should use the first person cautiously, especially in your first feature stories. While describing your own experiences, you run a greater risk of selecting poor topics and dwelling upon insignificant details and dull generalities, as in the following leads, either of which merits a passing grade:

During the summer, 20 ardent cyclists (I among them) biked through 300 miles of the Canadian Rockies. In the course of our journey, we encountered many exciting experiences.

The clock read 6:30. I was already 30 minutes late for the fishing date. Waking up will never be easy for me, especially when I am to go fishing.

I have never been enthusiastic about fishing. The aversion probably began when I was a boy and every vacation was spent in the same fishing camp. I had decided to give the sport one more chance, however.

The following story is also written in the first person—but is more interesting because it describes a truly unusual experience. Also, the story emphasizes specific details, descriptions and anecdotes. It was written by M. Timothy O'Keefe, a successful free-lancer and one of the first Americans to visit modern China:

Any time any of us walked down a street alone, we drew tremendous interest. If we stopped to talk or eat an ice cream bar, we drew a crowd. If we did something interesting, like change the film in a camera, we drew a horde.

The Chinese paid especially close attention to our feet. Leather shoes are a sign of great wealth among the Chinese, and one of the things the crowds discussed about us was how wealthy we might be. The quality of our shoes was a clue.

If we wanted to talk seriously with the Chinese in a particular city, all we had to do was stand on a street corner near our hotel at dusk when the work day was done. In a short time some young man—never a woman—would stop to talk. Often his English was broken and halting simply because he hadn't had sufficient opportunity to practice. Other times the English was amazingly fluent.

Their questions were direct and blunt. They wanted to know how much money we made, what our sex practices were and, in general, what interested young people in the United States. They were especially interested in our music.

Sometimes the Chinese would make strange requests of us. Several wanted to rub our arms to see if our freckles were permanent or would come off. They also were intrigued about the amount of hair on our arms (the guys', of course). And they were always impressed at our larger size, which they ascribed to our different diet.

As for the conclusion to feature stories, some writers say that features should end like news stories, by reporting the last solid chunk of information. Other writers, particularly those who work for magazines, say that features should end with a satisfying conclusion, perhaps a quote, anecdote, or key word or phrase repeated in some surprising or meaningful way. In any case, you should avoid ending feature stories with a summary; summary endings are too likely to state the obvious, to be repetitious, flat and boring.

After finishing a feature, a professional is likely to edit and rewrite it, perhaps five, six or even 10 times. A professional will also slant the feature for a particular publication and audience, emphasizing its relevance and importance to them.

Newspapers probably publish more features than any other medium, and many editors expect every reporter to write one or two features a week, often for publication in their Sunday editions. Typically, the reporters employed by an afternoon daily will work on feature stories every afternoon, after their papers have been published for that day.

Most reporters enjoy writing features. They can select their own topics, examine the topics in depth and experiment with different styles of writing. The reporters who free-lance during their spare time usually write more features, submitting them to magazines.

Interesting Leads and Techniques from The Wall Street Journal

Many of the country's best feature stories appear daily in The Wall Street Journal. As you read the following examples, ask yourself why these stories are so interesting and readable.

Notice that the reporters used different techniques—and emphasized different elements—in the stories' leads. Also notice that a sentence summarizing each story often appears in its third or fourth (not its first) paragraph.

TOKYO—Campbell Soup Co. ships more soup to Albuquerque than to all Japan.

But thanks to the 89 percent rise of the Japanese yen against the U.S. dollar over the past two years, that could change. The Camden, N.J., company has been able to cut its soup prices below those of Japanese competitors—increasing its sales and market share. "We have a great opportunity to make Campbell's part of the Japanese consciousness," says James T. Conte, the managing director of Campbell Japan Inc.

Ronald, a 44-year-old resident of Newport, R.I., assumed for a decade that "it was all in my mind," before finding out it wasn't. Similarly afflicted, John, 22, of Birmingham, Ala., quit dating, became depressed and developed a drinking problem. And Bruce MacKenzie, 64, of Maryville, Tenn., found a simple surgical remedy for the same thing only after frustrating years of psychotherapy.

Their problem was impotence, one of America's most widespread but least talked-about disorders. It affects an estimated 10 million American men, for many of whom it is a painful secret. "You can tell your best friends you have cancer," says Mr. MacKenzie. "But who can you tell you're impotent? So you live a lie."

GLOUCESTER, Mass.—For several days, two federal agents have been prowling the piers here in unmarked cars. Now, they scan the horizon with binoculars, waiting to make their bust. In a nearby hotel room, another agent, acting as backup, sits next to a citizens' band radio.

Informants have tipped them about a boat allegedly carrying contraband. Finally, the agents spot the boat. But as they prepare to go aboard, they notice that it is riding high in the water. The cargo has already been unloaded.

"Even when we get the right information and we check every detail, something goes wrong," complains John McCarthy, the agent in charge, as he calls off the raid. "We're always outnumbered and we're always outplayed."

So goes the war—not on drug smuggling but on scallop smuggling. . . .

Every morning as soon as he gets to work, a Johnson & Johnson manager makes a beeline for the bathroom. He gargles with mouthwash and downs mints. Then, to mask any lingering odor, he douses his face and hands with skin cream.

But he still worries that he will be reprimanded or passed over for a promotion if his boss ever learns that his closet vice is cigarette smoking.

"I've become almost like a junkie, sneaking around as if I take illegal drugs," says the manager, who works at Johnson & Johnson headquarters in New Brunswick, N.J. "In a (corporate) culture like ours, where everyone is looking good and smelling good, the last thing you do is stick a cigarette in your mouth."

In corporate America, cigarette smoking is becoming hazardous to careers. Increasingly, smokers express anxiety that their prospects for getting hired and promoted are being stunted by their habit. Many of them fear they face both covert and overt discrimination in the workplace.

Linda Barbanel is still fuming. To get a silk blouse dry-cleaned, the New Yorker recently paid $6, up 33% from the $4.50 she paid less than a year ago. "You can buy the blouse in China for what they now want to clean it," she complains.

Although economists are just beginning to worry that inflation is reawakening after a five-year slumber, consumers such as Ms. Barbanel say they noticed its early stirrings months ago.

That's because prices of commonly used goods and services that shape consumers' perceptions about inflation—things such as toothpaste, coffee, haircuts and taxi rides—are soaring even though the overall rise in the cost of living continues moderate.

Suggested Readings

Alexander, Louis. *Beyond the Facts: A Guide to the Art of Feature Writing*, 2nd ed. Houston, Texas: Gulf Publishing Company, 1982.

Babb, Laura Longley, ed. *Writing in Style*. Washington, D.C.: The Washington Post Co., 1975.

Cappon, Rene J. *The Word: An Associated Press Guide To Good News Writing*. New York: The Associated Press, 1982.

Emerson, Connie. *Write on Target*. Cincinnati, Ohio: Writer's Digest Books, 1981.

Franklin, Jon. *Writing for Story: Craft Secrets of Dramatic Nonfiction by a Two-Time Pulitzer Prize Winner*. New York: Atheneum, 1986.

Gunther, Max. *Writing the Modern Magazine Article*. Boston: The Writer, 1968.

Harral, Stewart. *The Feature Writer's Handbook*. Norman, Okla.: University of Oklahoma Press, 1958.

Hughes, Helen McGill. *News and the Human Interest Story*. New Brunswick, N.J.: Transaction Books, 1981.

Jacobs, Hayes B. *Writing and Selling Non-Fiction*. Cincinnati, Ohio: Writer's Digest Books, 1967.

Martindale, David. *How to be a Freelance Writer: A Guide to Building a Full-time Career*. New York: Crown, 1982.

Nelson, Roy Paul. *Articles and Features*. Boston: Houghton Mifflin, 1978.

Patterson, Benton Rain. *Write to Be Read: A Practical Guide to Feature Writing*. Ames, Iowa: The Iowa State University Press, 1986.

Rivers, William L., and Alison R. Work. *Free-Lancer and Staff Writer: Newspaper Features and Magazine Articles*. 4th ed. Belmont, Calif.: Wadsworth Publishing, 1986.

Ruehlmann, William. *Stalking the Feature Story*. Cincinnati, Ohio: Writer's Digest Books, 1978.

Schoenfeld, A. Clay, and Karen S. Diegmueller. *Effective Feature Writing*. New York: Holt, Rinehart and Winston, 1982.

Williamson, Daniel R. *Feature Writing for Newspapers*. New York: Hastings House, 1975.

EXERCISE 1
Feature Stories

EVALUATING FEATURE LEADS

INSTRUCTIONS: Critically evaluate the following leads. Decide which topics are most interesting and which leads are most effective. As you evaluate the leads, try to formulate guidelines—"Do's and Don't's"—that you can apply to your own stories.

1. It may be one of the smallest pieces of real estate that you will ever buy, but chances are that your cemetery plot will also be the most expensive.

    The price of cemetery property goes up at least 10 percent a year, said Robert Neel, president of Woodlawn Memorial Park. The current starting price for a 5- by 10-foot plot is between $1,200 and $1,500 at most cemeteries.

2. There was no hesitation. The bowler picked up his ball and smoothly let it roll down the alley. Nine pins fell, leaving just one standing. Alfred Hershey took careful aim and knocked that one down too.

    Perfectly ordinary.

    Except that Hershey is blind.

3. "How about if I just sit on the floor with you?" asked Judge Clarence Dubreff after a child complained that he "always sits higher than anybody else."

    The juvenile court judge took off his coat, rolled up his sleeves and sat on the classroom floor.

4. Twenty teen-agers plan their own curriculum and live and work at Freedom House School. All 20 are from welfare families, and most have police records.

5. The student governments at most universities in the state are having problems.

6. Rudy Willging, Rick Kaeppler and Don Zitto aren't foresters and don't diagnose sick trees, and they aren't firefighters in the traditional sense, but are rather a combination, intensively trained to battle forest fires, perhaps the most dangerous fires of all.

7. Pancho is a short, dark-skinned, curly-haired 20-year-old with flashing black eyes, a bouncing step and a Spanish accent.

8. "It must be the most peculiar house in the city," said Katie Erhmann.

9. David, 44, was learning to write his name. Karen, 7, repeatedly practiced buttoning her sweater. Despite the difference in their ages, they have a common plight. Both are mentally retarded.

10. Sgt. David Blaren's first and favorite assignment was at Fort Meade, Md., where he was a member of the color guard at all Washington Redskins home football games. Between Fort Meade and his current assignment were 11 busy years in the U.S. Army.

11. A group of Californians, hoping to reduce the number of suicides, which some experts believe claim more lives than automobile accidents, is offering "love, concern and a sympathetic audience" for people intent on destroying themselves.

12. Almost 18,600 students are enrolled in the city's public schools, but 26 never leave home.

    The students are unable to attend school because of accidents and illnesses. All are tutored by three teachers from the school system's House Instruction Department.

EXERCISE 2
Feature Stories

EVALUATING FEATURE LEADS

INSTRUCTIONS: Critically evaluate the following leads. Decide which topics are most interesting and which leads are most effective. As you evaluate the leads, try to formulate guidelines—"Do's and Don't's"—that you can apply to your own stories.

1. Few college students today seem to be concerned with the old adage, "You are what you eat."

2. The concept of "night watchman" has been redefined.

3. An alcoholic doesn't want to drink but cannot help himself. What can he do? Who can he turn to?

4. "As I passed the Statue of Liberty, I got a cold chill. For the first time I felt I was really alone."

   Henry H. Sleczkowski, 70, came to the United States in 1940 to start a new life. He had no idea he would be so successful.

5. A 19-year-old coed has an interesting, if not unusual, job.

6. Garbage, garbage everywhere, and not an end in sight.

7. Tractors filled the yard as dozens of farmers, most dressed in light denim jackets and trousers, helped harvest 155 acres of corn on the Victor Stalling farm 18 miles northwest of here.

   "This is the custom around here," one of the farmers explained. "If somebody dies or has an accident, everyone pitches in to help."

   Stalling, 47, died of a heart attack 10 days ago.

8. As couples get older, they are more likely to join a church and to attend its Sunday services.

9. The powerful role that mayors once had is declining, according to three local political figures.

10. Mrs. McNeely keeps her kitchen knives hidden under her mattress. It is a safeguard she has taken since that day her son, Joseph, threatened her husband with a bread knife.

11. Ronald Oalmann is pessimistic about the future of the United States. Intermittently pounding on his desk with large, pale hands, the radio commentator explains: "No democratic republic in the history of the world has existed for 200 years. Why should we? There are too many things squeezing the middle class."

    Oalmann says: "The revolutionary is going to be the white, middle-class 45-year-old woman. She won't be able to get the rats out of her back yard. She won't be able to get groceries because they'll be too expensive. She won't be able to feed and clothe her children."

12. The practice of witchcraft is as old as man himself. It is called by some the "old religion." It deals with the powers of nature and the environment that can be controlled by the mind.

EXERCISE 3
Feature Stories

WRITING FEATURE LEADS

INSTRUCTIONS: First, write a straight news lead for each of the following stories. Your leads should concisely summarize each story. Second, write a feature lead for each story. Or, your instructor may ask you to write a complete feature based upon one of these sets of facts.

1. A study at the University of Michigan shatters some myths. The results were announced today. Women have a reputation for gossiping and talking, yet the study found the reputation is undeserved. The study, which required researchers to observe a number of people at work, found that women work both longer and harder than men—that men spend more time goofing off on the job. The study found that the average employed man spends 52 minutes, or 11 percent of each working day, not working: in scheduled coffee breaks, unscheduled rest breaks, at lunch beyond the normal hour and so forth. The average working woman spends only 35 minutes, or 8 percent of her working day, in such scheduled and unscheduled rest breaks. The same study found that the amount of effort expended by women at work is 112 percent that of men. The discrepancy is more dramatic than the statistics indicate because men earn more than women for the same type of work. The average man in the study earned $11 an hour, compared to $7.34 for the average woman. The women tended to hold mainly clerical jobs, but those in managerial positions also outperformed their male counterparts.

2. Many freebies no longer are free. Because of rising expenses and other problems, American business establishments are eliminating many services and other amenities once offered their customers free of charge. For example, the attendants at many gasoline stations no longer wash windshields, and one station owner has explained that his attendants were using too many cleaning towels, which cost a penny each. Service stations have also discontinued free giveaways: free car washes with a fillup, free glasses and steak knives, free trading stamps and road maps. Some restrict the use of their washroom facilities and charge for the air used to inflate tires. When you buy new clothes, you can no longer expect to receive a free wooden or plastic hanger. When men buy a pair of slacks, alterations—once universally free—may cost several dollars. Free gift-wrapping, once a blessing for last-minute shoppers, has largely disappeared. Coffee refills, once free at many restaurants, no longer are free. Other restaurants serve water only upon request. And matchbooks that once rested in each table ashtray are now hidden near the cashier.

3. Someone called 18 people in the city last night. The caller identified himself as the president of Rutherford Ford, Inc., 2780 Doss Boulevard. He told each of the people that they had just won a new car from his dealership. Interviewed by reporters today, most of the people who received the calls said that at first they just couldn't believe it. And they were right. They couldn't. The person who called was a prankster, and Allen Ruthorford, president of the dealership, says he has no idea who placed the calls, and that he's spending all his time today trying to explain the situation to those 18 people. "Someone apparently has a sick idea of humor," Ruthorford said. After convincing people they had won a new car, the caller asked them to drop by the dealership this morning to pick it up. All 18 were there when the dealership opened its doors at 9 a.m. "I told them we never offered to give away a

car," Rutherford said. "One woman told me she couldn't believe she'd won, and then she told me she couldn't believe it when I told her she hadn't. Two other women began to cry, and a man is threatening to sue me."

4. The police in this municipality received a call at 3:45 p.m. yesterday afternoon. A woman shouted at the sergeant who answered the telephone. She said: "My son's been beaten. His teacher whipped him this afternoon, and he's all red where she paddled him. Can teachers do that? That's assault and battery, and I want her arrested." Two police officers were sent to the home. They questioned the boy, who is 9 years old. At his mother's insistence, the police officers also inspected the boy's reported injuries. They reported: "We couldn't tell that the boy had been paddled. His fanny didn't look red to us, but we did notice that his pants legs were wet and muddy. As we talked, it became obvious that the boy was lying. He finally admitted that he had stopped to play on the way home from school, forgot the time and got home late. He told his mother that the teacher had spanked him and kept him after school. His mother was there with us and heard the whole story. She said she'd take care of the situation, and we're quite certain that she will, as she was very embarrassed. In fact, we could hear her giving the kid a real paddling as we left—and a hard one."

5. Thomas J. Serle works for Parker Bros. Circus, which is in town this week. Performances are scheduled at 2 p.m. and 7:30 p.m. every day through Sunday, beginning today. Serle, who maintains a home in Fort Lauderdale, is a laborer who helps care for the animals at the circus, including 10 elephants. During a conversation with a reporter, he said: "Some people look on work with a circus as a glamorous job. It ain't. But I been doing it all my life, and it's too late for me to change. I'll be 60 next year. I was born into it. Both my folks were circus people. I started out as an acrobat until I fell and busted a leg. It never healed quite right, so they offered me this job, and I took it. What else could I do? There's all kinds of myths about circuses, like about these elephants here. Some people say they're afraid of mice, but that's crazy. When we pen the elephants up for the winter there's always mice that get in their hay, and it don't bother them none. The elephants never try to run away or stomp them or anything. They share the same cages all winter. And then some people say elephants got a good memory. Hell, some of the ones we got are so dumb they can't remember a simple trick from one year to the next."

EXERCISE 4
Feature Stories

WRITING FEATURE LEADS

INSTRUCTIONS: First, write a straight news lead for each of the following stories. Your leads should concisely summarize each story. Then write a feature lead for each story. Or, your instructor may ask you to write a complete feature based upon one of these sets of facts.

1. An armored truck was traveling down Orange Avenue during this morning's rush hour. The truck hit a particularly bad pothole, and the back door of the vehicle flew open. The truck contained approximately $20,000 in change the city had collected from its parking meters. The money fell to the pavement. Several bags burst open. Police halted traffic. City workers summoned to the scene used brooms to sweep up the coins, then shoveled them back into the truck. But, before the police and other city employees arrived at the scene, dozens of other motorists and bystanders stopped at the scene. Some offered to help. When city officials later counted the money retrieved by the workers, they found they had exactly $18,482.17. The remainder seems to have been stolen.

2. Lt. James Robbins of your city's police department has made a study of everyone convicted of robbery in your city during the last year. He has written up a 19-page report. The police were looking for answers—anything that might help them detect or prevent crimes. Robbins surveyed a total of 250 people, including jail inmates. He also interviewed people from other police departments, the sheriff's department, the district attorney's office and the Probation and Parole Commission. He questioned people on how their agencies deal with burglaries and on their opinions of the characteristics of burglary suspects. The inmates he interviewed said they burglarized homes most often to get "quick and easy money," the report says. It adds that, "There was a significant amount of input which indicated that the money was to be used to support a drug or alcohol problem." Robbins also found that 95 percent of home burglars are men, most have less than a high-school education, and most are between 14 and 23 in age, have no job and live in the neighborhood they burglarize. The average residential burglar was caught after robbing 28 houses. The report adds that: "Almost half were caught because of dumb luck. They made a stupid mistake, like breaking into a house when the residents were there and had a gun. Or, they did something that made it easy to find them, like making a lot of noise, so the neighbors heard them, or using their real names while selling a piece of merchandise that was easy to identify. Others were caught for traffic violations, like speeding, and had everything they'd stolen piled up in plain sight in the back seat. No more than a third were caught because of good police work."

3. There is a trend in dogs. People no longer like full-sized dogs. Big dogs—those over 40 pounds, especially 5-year-old-and-up dogs—are about as much in demand these days as big cars. "About the only people who come in here and want to adopt a big dog are businesses or crime victims—after something has happened to them," says the Humane Society's director, Rika Brill. Even then, people tend to tire of the animal and return it to the shelter once their fear abates. Full-sized dogs, like Great Danes, Saint Bernards, Russian wolfhounds and German shepherds, are being unloaded for some of the same reasons: cost and space. The cost of owning a big dog averages about $500 a year—just for the bare essentials. Also, more and more apartment

complexes are banning or restricting pets. Most limit the size of pets to no more than 15 or 20 pounds, and charge a refundable damage deposit—in many cases, several hundred dollars. Some charge a $250 non-refundable pet fee. Other apartment complexes charge a monthly pet fee of $10 to $20. So fewer people are willing to adopt a big dog. Also, people are turning big dogs in to the shelter at an alarming rate. Each year, the county's Humane Society takes in more than 20,000 homeless animals. Only 27 percent are adopted. Of the 27 percent fortunate enough to find new homes, fewer and fewer are large dogs. Which means they constitute the majority of the nearly 200 dogs and cats put to sleep each week at the Humane Society.

4. Charlotte Lopez owns The Gift Shoppe at 1010 Main Street in your city. Yesterday she took a fraudulent check to the city attorney. "I got a big surprise," Lopez said. "They told me if I couldn't positively identify the person who wrote it, they couldn't prosecute. There was no way that I could identify anyone—not with a couple hundred customers a day coming through my store. A third of them write checks." Other shop owners said they have the same problem. They have tried to get the city to prosecute people who write a worthless check but learned that it would take at least a year before the district attorney's overworked staff could get to it. Most decided it was not worth the effort. So today, as a matter of policy, most will not take out-of-town or temporary checks. Others cash checks only for their regular customers. Most require identification, including a driver's license and a credit card—especially if the amount is more than $50. Businesses given a worthless check can either take a loss or hire a collection agency to find the customer. State law makes it difficult to prosecute if improper or no information is available about the person who wrote the check. The district attorney explains that his office gets about 300 worthless check complaints a month. If prosecutors cannot identify the specific individual who wrote it, judges and law enforcement officers will refuse to sign a warrant or make an arrest for fear they will be held liable for false arrest. Even when investigators gather all the necessary information, only one in 200 cases is prosecuted. That's why so many stores no longer accept checks or require so much identification from people cashing checks, recording even their hair color and approximate age, height and weight. If a check is bad and they want to prosecute, they must be able to identify the specific individual who wrote it.

5. Two students in a psychology class at your school conducted an interesting experiment yesterday afternoon. One was a male and one was a female, both juniors. They drove to your city's largest shopping center. The male approached 100 strangers, and the female later interviewed all 100 of them. The male, Scott Lupa, explained: "It was for a class project. We wanted to see what would happen. I went up to 100 strangers, one at a time, and asked them for directions to a testing clinic for AIDS. Then, no matter what the people said, I thanked them and tried to shake their hand. Most of the people really tried to help me; almost everyone gave me directions to a nearby hospital, but shaking hands concerned them. When I put my hand out, a lot automatically grabbed it. They didn't stop and think what they were doing until later. Then they realized they had touched me and began worrying about it—about getting AIDS."

The second journalism student, Maryann Lathan, added: "These are some of the things people said when I interviewed them. I took down their exact words." An elderly woman said: "What was I supposed to do when he asked for directions? Scream and run?" A 50-year-old man said: "He looked normal to me. If someone needs help, I don't mind doing what I can." A 25-year-old man said: "I don't know for sure that you can get AIDS by shaking hands, but I don't like to take chances." Another man said: "As I shook his hand, it dawned on me that he said 'AIDS.' Then I did feel uncomfortable. But I think everyone is wary when it comes to AIDS." An elderly woman said: "I didn't mind shaking his hand. I'm more worried about catching colds than I am about catching AIDS." A 30-year-old woman said: "I'm always kissing my gay friends. I guess if I should be concerned about anything, it would be getting AIDS that way. I've lived in San Francisco, and I had a lot of gay friends there. I try not to judge people. I think anyone could get AIDS, not just gays."

EXERCISE 5
Feature Stories

MISCELLANEOUS EXERCISES

1. Clip five feature stories from a newspaper or magazine and write a two- or three-page paper that critically analyzes the stories' topics, leads and style of writing, particularly their organization and development of color.

2. Rewrite the introductory paragraphs of five news stories as feature leads.

3. Rewrite the introductory paragraphs of five feature stories as news leads.

4. Read and report on a magazine article or a chapter in a book that discusses feature writing.

5. Outline three new feature stories that you might write.
   a. Explain why each topic is newsworthy, if it is new and of interest, or has relevance to most of the readers in your community.
   b. List at least five sources for each story.
   c. Describe your major theme and list the questions you intend to ask each source.
   d. Discuss the outlines with your instructor and perhaps also with the other members of your class, then write the feature story that seems most promising. As you write the feature, be sure to use some quotations, description, examples and revealing anecdotes.
   e. Write a second feature story, then submit it to a newspaper or magazine.

21 Advanced Reporting Exercises

This chapter consists of a variety of advanced reporting exercises. These exercises tend to be longer and more complex than the exercises in previous chapters. However, they are the types of assignments that reporters are likely to encounter during their first years of employment. To do well on the assignments, you will have to apply all the skills developed in the earlier chapters of this book.

Every exercise in this chapter is genuine. Only a few names and dates have been changed. Unless the exercises mention another time and location, assume that each story occurred today in your community.

Briefly, the exercises include:

1. A notice sent to every real estate agent in the state, warning them about two robbers.
2. A presidential order establishing a commission to investigate the explosion of the space shuttle Challenger.
3. A report the Centers for Disease Control issued about youth suicide.
4. A state attorney general's annual report to his governor and legislature.
5. A sociological report about the families of death row inmates.
6. A proposal to deter crime by preventing some criminals from consuming alcoholic beverages.
7. An extortion note left at a Nevada casino.
8. A San Francisco booklet warning about the danger of nuclear war.
9. Verbatim transcripts of interviews with three people involved in a major fire.
10. A report about juvenile shoplifters.

EXERCISE 1
Advanced Reporting

INSTRUCTIONS: Write a news story about the following warning. Assume that the robbery occurred in your community and that your state's Board of Realtors issued the warning today.

Realtor Alert: Realtor, Client Robbed at Gunpoint

The executive officer of the State Board of Realtors in (your) community reported that a Realtor was robbed at gunpoint while showing a house last Saturday in the Fairgreen Development.

A couple had called the Realtor's office about a month ago inquiring about a specific listing. The couple was shown the house one time before Saturday. On the day of the robbery, the couple insisted that the owner of the house be present at the time of the showing. When the Realtor, the owner, and the couple were inside the house, the man pulled a gun and robbed the owner of her jewelry (valued at $35,000 according to the report). The couple also stole money and credit cards from the Realtor. They also stole the Realtor's car. (Which was recovered the next day.)

On the previous visit to the house the couple had no car. They said the car was in a garage for repairs. The Realtor drove them to a nearby service station following the showing. The next day (day of the robbery) they again came without a car saying the "car broke down."

The couple seemed to know something about real estate sales as they asked questions regarding abstracts and title insurance.

The couple used the name Gonzales first, and the name Garcia the next time. The man was reported to be 35–45 years old with black hair and brown eyes. He was wearing black jeans and a plaid jacket. He weighs about 180 pounds and is more than 6′ tall. No description of the woman.

PLEASE BE ON THE LOOKOUT FOR THIS COUPLE. Contact the Police if you think you are involved with this couple.

State Board of Realtors
Office of the President

EXERCISE 2
Advanced Reporting

INSTRUCTIONS: On Jan. 28, 1986, seven U.S. astronauts were killed when the space shuttle Challenger exploded after its launch in Florida. An executive order issued by President Reagan established a presidential commission to investigate the explosion. Assume that President Reagan issued the order today, and write a news story summarizing its content.

EXECUTIVE ORDER

- - - - - -

PRESIDENTIAL COMMISSION ON THE
SPACE SHUTTLE CHALLENGER ACCIDENT

By the authority vested in me as President by the Constitution and statutes of the United States of America, including the Federal Advisory Committee Act, as amended (5 U.S.C. App. I), and in order to establish a commission of distinguished Americans to investigate the accident to the Space Shuttle Challenger, it is hereby ordered as follows:

Section 1. <u>Establishment</u>. (a) There is established the Presidential Commission on the Space Shuttle Challenger Accident. The Commission shall be composed of not more than 20 members appointed or designated by the President. The members shall be drawn from among distinguished leaders of the government, and the scientific, technical, and management communities.

(b) The President shall designate a Chairman and a Vice Chairman from among the members of the Commission.

Sec. 2. <u>Functions</u>. (a) The Commission shall investigate the accident to the Space Shuttle Challenger, which occurred on January 28, 1986.

(b) The Commission shall:

(1) Review the circumstances surrounding the accident to establish the probable cause or causes of the accident; and

(2) Develop recommendations for corrective or other action based upon the Commission's findings and determinations.

(c) The Commission shall submit its final report to the President and the Administrator of the National Aeronautics

---

2

and Space Administration within one hundred and twenty days of the date of this Order.

Sec. 3. Administration. (a) The heads of Executive departments and agencies shall, to the extent permitted by law, provide the Commission with such information as it may require for purposes of carrying out its functions.

(b) Members of the Commission shall serve without compensation for their work on the Commission. However, members appointed from among private citizens of the United States may be allowed travel expenses, including per diem in lieu of subsistence, to the extent permitted by law for persons serving intermittently in the government service (5 U.S.C. 5701-5707).

(c) To the extent permitted by law, and subject to the availability of appropriations, the Administrator of the National Aeronautics and Space Administration shall provide the Commission with such administrative services, funds, facilities, staff, and other support services as may be necessary for the performance of its functions.

Sec. 4. General Provisions. (a) Notwithstanding the provisions of any other Executive Order, the functions of the President under the Federal Advisory Committee Act which are applicable to the Commission, except that of reporting annually to the Congress, shall be performed by the Administrator of the National Aeronautics and Space Administration, in accordance with guidelines and procedures established by the Administrator of General Services.

(b) The Commission shall terminate 60 days after submitting its final report.

Ronald Reagan

THE WHITE HOUSE

EXERCISE 3
Advanced Reporting

INSTRUCTIONS: This report was issued by the Centers for Disease Control in Atlanta. Assume that the report was issued today, and write a news story summarizing its content.

Surveillance Summary

Youth Suicide—United States, 1970–1980

Between 1970 and 1980, 49,496 of the nation's youth (15–24 years of age) committed suicide. The suicide rate for this age group increased 40% (from 8.8 deaths per 100,000 population in 1970 to 12.3/100,000 in 1980), while the rate for the remainder of the population remained stable. Young adults (20–24 years of age) had approximately twice the number and rate of suicides as teen-agers (15–19 years old).

This increase in suicide for persons 15–24 years of age is due primarily to an increasing rate of suicide among young males: rates for males increased by 50% (from 13.5 to 20.2) compared with a 2% increase for females (4.2 to 4.3), so that by 1980, for this age group, the ratio of suicides committed by males to those committed by females was almost 5 to 1. Most (89.5%) young male suicide victims were white. Moreover, the white male group showed a marked upward trend in suicide rates from 1970 to 1980; in fact, suicide rates for young white men have increased in each of the past three decades. Although rates increased for young males of black and other races, their rates remained lower than rates for young white males. Rates for young white females and for females of black and other races were approximately equal and relatively stable over time.

The western United States had consistently higher youth suicide rates from 1970 to 1980 than the other three regions (North Central, Northeastern, and Southern). However, this difference in rates had narrowed substantially by 1980 because rates for each of the other regions increased over the period.

The method of suicide changed significantly from 1970 to 1980. The proportion of suicides committed with firearms increased for both young males and females (15–24 years old), and the proportion of both males and females committing suicide by poisoning declined. The changes were more marked among females, who, in the past, have most commonly committed suicide by poisoning.

Data show that among persons 15–24 years of age, young white male adults (20–24 years old) have the highest suicide risk. Further research is needed to explain the marked increase in suicide among young white males, to characterize their deaths more precisely, and to develop and evaluate effective ways to prevent these deaths.

EXERCISE 4
Advanced Reporting

INSTRUCTIONS: Each year, state Attorney General Jim Smith is required to submit an annual report to his governor and legislature. Write a news story that summarizes the report's highlights. As you write the story, assume that Smith is the attorney general for your state and that he released this year's report today.

Department of Legal Affairs
Office of the Attorney General
The Capitol

Prison overcrowding is potentially the most expensive criminal justice problem facing the state. Intake is at an unprecedented level, and the system already is under a federal population cap. The effectiveness of our entire criminal justice system is threatened by the urgency of the prison overcrowding situation.

After four years of close association with criminal justice issues, I have concluded that we need to review our thinking in light of the realities that confront us. Can we continue on the same course, or is fundamental change necessary?

For my part, I opt for change. We concede that our criminal justice system too often has been uncertain. Various components—the policing, convicting, sentencing, imprisoning and paroling of criminal offenders—clearly function independently of their impact on the rest of the system, making that system increasingly unworkable and complex.

We have allowed the system to grow without coherence, laying on methods, philosophies and criteria until it has lost its ability to mesh. It is neither understood nor feared by those who are breaking our laws. A criminal justice system that fails to inspire public confidence or deter illegal acts is not delivering what hundreds of millions of taxpayer dollars are spent to buy.

In my judgment, specific shortcomings in several areas need to be addressed without delay. My recommendations are more pragmatic than theoretical. Their purpose is to dispense direct and unequivocal justice, both for the offender who must go to prison and for the public that must pay to keep him there.

The comments I hear from those who are in the field, working within the system, indicate to me that the process of dealing with criminal defendants needs fundamental revision to attain predictability, swiftness, simplicity and, to the greatest degree possible, economy.

Given these goals for the state's criminal justice system, I make the following recommendations:

Sentencing: Offenders should know with certainty that, if convicted, their opportunities for probation will be limited. When granted, probation will be accompanied by supervision under provisions that contain "teeth." Probation should continue to encompass a range of options that serve the needs of justice, among them community service, restitution and restriction of freedom. Generally, initial terms of incarceration should be for short, fixed periods determined from within a narrow range of guidelines related to both the offender and the offense. A second conviction would result in a doubling of the first sentence, and the third would make the offender eligible for twice the term of the second offense. I believe that a sentencing policy articulated in this way—and carried out by our courts—brings accountability to the system. To an extent defined by the range, it would limit the discretion of judges and prosecutors. But it would be easily understood, and it would deal honestly with those who violate our criminal laws.

Parole: Under a policy of fixed sentences, there would be no need for supervised parole. Inmates would exit the system at the completion of their terms, less gain time accrued. Parole violations would no longer result in re-sentencing, a practice I think has contributed to the system's much criticized inequities and lack of public confidence. The resources now used in parole functions would be transferred to probation supervision, with strict regulation and clear consequences for those who stray.

Gain Time: A sentencing scheme that acts realistically and consistently in applying the consequences of criminal behavior must also deal fairly with inmates who accept those consequences, and who show a willingness to conform and benefit from the incentives offered for good behavior. The chief incentive is gain time. If it is to work as desired, the gain time plan must be easily understood and to a certain degree automatic, so that inmates can mark off days from a known release date. There should also be liberal provisions for discretionary gain time as an added incentive.

Judiciary: Judges should have discretion to aggravate or mitigate sentences for reasons related to the offender or the offense. Nevertheless, they should be limited to rendering "real" sentences—a term of years that the offender will remain in prison and that constitute his debt to society for the offense committed. Under circumstances that warrant it, judges could impose sentences of natural life.

State Prisons: Primarily, prisons must be places where the most serious offenders are incarcerated. They are where society will warehouse habitual offenders, major drug dealers, and those whose crimes were characterized by violence or who are inherently violent themselves. The initial impact of these proposals, inasmuch as they are premised on certainty of punishment, may be to exacerbate overcrowding. Surely this would be the case if we employed certainty with the current sentencing procedures. However, I am of the opinion that a change in sentencing philosophy, coupled with shorter first sentences, will over time reduce the inmate population and contribute to a drop in recidivism, inasmuch as the tempted offender will know in advance the penalty for repeat offenses. Incarceration will best serve the inmate and the state if we see to it that the time spent is productive. Maximum use of the prison industries program must be made if the idleness that characterizes so much of prison life is to be defeated and if the inmates who will return to the streets will be prepared to earn an honest living.

Emergency Release Mechanism: One of the characteristics of the state's criminal justice system with the Parole and Probation Commission as it now functions is an unwillingness or inability to act—or react—in response to overcrowding emergencies. The state needs new prison space to accommodate today's population, provide for normal expansion tied to growth in the general population, and maintain humane conditions within the institutions. However, we obviously cannot continually build to match the current pace of admissions. The system needs a more expeditious way to stay within the inmate population cap imposed by a federal district court and avoid the unpredictability of a judgment imposing substantial new costs on the state. A mechanism for emergency release is essential. I am recommending changes to ensure that when the inmate population reaches maximum capacity (a number directly related to the availability of facilities), early release can be granted to inmates from a list of those deemed eligible by the Department of Corrections. Such a list might, for instance, select inmates with less than 90 or 60 days remaining to serve who have records free of disciplinary reports. The Parole Commission as it exists today is limited by statute and resources to a slower and more methodical course.

Fundamental revisions, such as I have described, require careful planning and implementation and the support, acceptance and participation of everyone in the system. Judges, prosecutors, legislators, members of the executive branch—all must articulate realistic expectations of what the system can accomplish and must work toward appropriate long-term goals. The Task Force on Prison Overcrowding, the Advisory Committee on Corrections and the Sentencing Commission will be issuing reports soon that may bring us closer to those goals.

EXERCISE 5
Advanced Reporting

INSTRUCTIONS: Write a news story that summarizes the content of the following report about the families of death row inmates. The report was written by Michael L. Radelet and Felix M. Berardo of the Department of Sociology at the University of Florida and by Margaret Vandiver of the School of Criminology at Florida State University.

The Families of Death Row Inmates

Since 1930 nearly 4,000 people have been executed in the United States, and the 1,900 people now awaiting execution constitute the largest number of inmates living under a death sentence in the history of the United States. Florida leads the country with over 250 men sentenced to death. This report focuses on the families of death row inmates. Information was obtained from several hundred hours of visiting men sentenced to die in Florida, by weekly correspondence with a dozen of the men, and by discussions with several of the men's family members, friends, and attorneys.

A. The Psychological Impact of the Death Sentence. The men sentenced to death in Florida experience a variety of physical constraints beyond those encountered by other prisoners. The condemned men are each housed in a separate 6 × 9 cell, which they usually are permitted to leave only three times per week for brief showers and once per week for a two-hour exercise period. Men with death sentences are not permitted to visit the prison library or chapel, and no phone calls are allowed except in rare emergencies. More painful than these physical restraints, however, are the psychological consequences of being formally condemned as unfit to live. The men are often seen by outsiders, prison officials, and each other only as condemned murderers, and other aspects of their identity are not regularly recognized or nurtured. The death sentence carries with it an all-encompassing personality label, and there are few opportunities to escape this label. In short, while awaiting physical death the men may experience a slow social death, with various aspects of their self-identity quietly eroding through lack of social outlet and reinforcement.

B. The Importance of Family Contact. It is in relation to this identity struggle that families provide their most valuable functions for the men sentenced to die. Families can respond to the non-deviant aspects of the inmate's personality and encourage him to maintain dignity and self-respect. The family recognizes the man as a person with a unique history and individuality, and thereby draws out aspects of his identity that are dormant in everyday prison interactions. Because some inmates have little or no contact with their relatives, it is not uncommon for close friends and correspondents outside the prison to assume functional importance as quasi-family members.

Families offer not only social release from the identity crisis of a death sentence, but also physical release from the cell through a visit. While less than half of the men sentenced to death receive a visit in a given year, we estimate that this rate is double that of visits to other inmates in the maximum security prison where death row inmates are housed. This higher rate of visits for the condemned may indicate that their families perceive the death sentence as a threat which must be met by the family as well as the condemned man. Visits are held in a large room in which there are 30 four-person tables, and are permitted for up to six hours each holiday and Saturday or Sunday (longer visits are granted for out-of-state visitors). A visit is usually the highlight of the prison stay for the man, for it offers the opportunity to leave the cell, see women and children, and talk in confidence. It also offers the opportunity for the man to assume a different role than that of condemned inmate.

C. The Stresses of the Family. A major barrier to visits is the time and expense involved in getting to the prison, which is located in a rural area of north Florida some 350 miles from Miami. No public transportation to the prison is available. One inmate's 78-year-old illiterate mother, who suffers from arthritis and a variety of other physical problems, reported that she occasionally would hitchhike the final 15 miles to the prison when rides were unavailable. Nearly all the families of condemned prisoners are poor, and many live in other states. The expenses of travel make visits nearly impossible for many families.

To visit a condemned prisoner requires an initial formal application for placement on the inmate's visiting list, a thorough search when entering the prison, and a tolerance for the noise, heat, smoke and uncomfortable seats in the visiting room. Visits can be emotionally and physically draining, and it is not uncommon for a pattern of visits set early after confinement to gradually taper off. The prisoners are aware of the difficulties of visiting and frequently express concern at the strains their families endure to see them.

A second source of stress for the family members is the uncertainty of their family member's fate. Like the families of those suffering chronic or terminal disabilities, of workers facing unemployment or of those in areas of natural disaster, a great deal of anxiety is produced by the inability to predict and control the future and by the effort to fight despair. There is also outright fear, particularly as legal appeals are exhausted, other inmates are executed, and the family member's execution date is set. The families are caught between a strong desire to do something to help and the feeling that whatever they can do is not enough to redirect the legal process. Yet, unlike some families coping with chronic uncertainty, the families of men sentenced to death are not organized to support or communicate with each other. This is in part due to the geographic dispersion of families, but is augmented by prison restrictions against families talking with each other in the visiting room. Their agony is therefore experienced in solitude.

Several other stresses confront the families of death row inmates. Almost all are poor, and the others quickly exhaust their monetary resources on legal expenses. Many do not understand the complex legal issues involved in trying and appealing capital cases, further augmenting their uncertainty. Perhaps most demoralizing is the stigma attached to having a loved one sentenced to die and the knowledge that a majority of the public supports executions. Crank letters and phone calls to families (and those who write about them) are not uncommon, and cries for executions by public officials or in newspaper editorials can have marked impacts on the families. Rather than receiving public sympathy, as do for example the families of the terminally ill, the families of the condemned must face their loss knowing the public actively desires the death of their relatives.

Facing such hardships, some family members resolve their uncertainty by abandoning their condemned relative and terminating visits and correspondence. For the inmate, erosion of this contact can be the most stressful aspect of imprisonment. The diminution in family contact threatens that part of the social identity which the family reinforces. Similarly, part of the inmate is also destroyed when a family member dies or develops a serious illness.

Other family members, however, remain committed and devoted to their loved ones. Part of this devotion can be explained by their strong belief in the injustice of capital punishment. Convinced that capital punishment has no deterrent effect and built-in racial and class disparities, the families are often united to their condemned relatives in their outrage at this form of punishment. They also believe the death penalty is cruel and unusual, and justifiable only as a primitive form of vengeance. Anger at prison officials and regulations is sometimes evident, although most believe that the prison personnel are usually decent. Instead the families direct the brunt of their anger at state officials and a public that they perceive as uninformed about the realities of capital punishment. While most family members insist that their loved one is innocent of the crime, others believe that there are major mitigating circumstances that were not considered by the judge or that their relative was severely sentenced because of an inability to hire a highly skilled lawyer.

Conclusion. There is a wide range of patterns in family-inmate relationships, and differences are as abundant as similarities. The crisis which the death sentence presents to the condemned and their families can result in abandonment of the prisoner, or in a family drawn closer together. Common patterns include chronic uncertainty, an overwhelming sense of injustice, sensitivity to public hatred, and feelings of responsibility to each other. Whatever one's position on the death penalty, the families' experiences remind us all that the impact of capital punishment is not confined to the condemned men themselves.

EXERCISE 6
Advanced Reporting

INSTRUCTIONS: This proposal was prepared by probation officer Derek J. Gallagher and assistant state attorney Steven "Woody" Igou. Assume that Gallagher and Igou work in your community and today submitted the proposal to your state legislature. Write a story summarizing its content.

Alcohol and Crime

Alcohol and crime are cozy bedfellows. Statistics show that alcohol consumption is by far the most common contributing factor in the commission of violent crime. A recent study indicated that alcohol was involved in 71% of all criminal arrests nationwide. In regard to specific crimes, the breakdown of those which were alcohol related include:

70% of all murders
70% of all manslaughters
64% of all assaults on police officers
62% of all assaults
60% of all sex crimes against children
60% of all child abuse cases
50% of all residential burglaries

The toll of driving under the influence (DUI) alone is staggering. Last year the residents of this state were involved in 35,000 alcohol-related accidents, during which some 1,294 people lost their lives.

Alcohol also plays a large part in the current drug abuse epidemic. Data from rehabilitation centers indicate that a substantial percentage of those treated for cocaine and other drug abuse are also abusing alcohol. Drug abusers alone account for millions of dollars in property crimes (thefts) each year as well as a plethora of violent crimes.

There is presently no *effective* judicial method of keeping alcohol out of the hands of criminals who abuse it. A person convicted of DUI, once back on the street, can immediately walk into a bar and begin the cycle of criminal behavior all over again. Under current methods of probation an offender can be ordered not to drink or enter bars. These warnings are meaningless, however, for there is no method to *enforce* the orders of the Court other than relying upon the will of the offender *not* to drink. Thus, citizens are protected from alcohol-related crime only by a criminal's flimsy willpower—a protection that often ends in inevitable violence or death. Rehabilitation efforts ordered by the Courts, through AA or other agencies, are of some benefit, yet due to underfunding and lack of motivation on the part of criminals, they do not provide an adequate solution to the problem of alcohol-related crime.

The Solution: Criminal Alcohol Probation (CAP)

This proposed package of legislation would represent a strong commitment on the part of the legislature to place a cap on the fuel to crime. In a nutshell this proposal would allow judges to place on alcohol probation all persons found guilty of criminal acts in which it is determined that alcohol was a contributing factor. The alcohol probation would last the length of the probation imposed in criminal cases and the length of the driver's license suspension in DUI cases.

Basically the legislation would operate as follows:

1. All judges sentencing convicted offenders would be required to determine if alcohol played a part in the offense. This would be done by consulting the arrest report,

family members, the victim, etc. Law enforcement officers would be on notice to look out for the presence of alcohol on all persons arrested and to note it in arrest reports. *All* persons convicted of DUI would face CAP as part of their probation.

2. If it is determined that alcohol was a factor, the sentencing judge would be required to impose Criminal Alcohol Probation (hereafter CAP) as a part of the offender's probation. The courts would retain discretion over the length of CAP imposed *above* a minimum mandatory time of six months for misdemeanors and one year for felonies. The courts would then take possession of the offender's driver's license. The offender would then be required to report to the Department of Motor Vehicles to receive a CAP license.

3. The Department of Motor Vehicles would issue the probationer a special driver's license which clearly denotes that person as having CAP status. The license would, for example, have a conspicuous (i.e., red) background for easy identification.

4. State law would prohibit persons on CAP from purchasing, possessing, or consuming any alcoholic beverages within the State. In addition, it would be unlawful for any person to knowingly purchase or provide alcohol to someone on CAP status.

5. State law would require vendors of alcoholic beverages to check the identification of every person purchasing alcohol within the State. Thus no persons on CAP would be able to purchase alcohol or order a drink in a bar or restaurant. Failure to comply with this carding requirement would subject the vendors to the penalties now in force for non-compliance with checking the identification of minors.

6. An *optional* provision of CAP would be to require universal carding upon *entry* into any bar or tavern, excluding bona fide restaurants. In that way persons on CAP would be kept out of bars altogether. This is a common condition of current criminal probation, but only through CAP could it be enforced.

7. Because CAP is done through the Department of Motor Vehicles there would be an updated computer list of all persons under CAP, just as persons with suspended licenses are currently listed. This would give law enforcement officers an invaluable tool in both pre-empting crime and enforcing CAP. For example, if a driver is stopped on a traffic infraction the license check would indicate CAP status and if that person were on CAP and if they smelled of alcohol, whether or not DUI, they could be arrested, thus averting a possible DUI accident. Similarly, if an officer came upon a fight or disturbance a routine ID check could indicate CAP status and the person could be arrested before violence escalated.

8. Persons caught violating the terms of CAP status could be dealt with in two ways. At the time the person is found in possession of alcohol (including alcohol already consumed, as evidenced by drunkenness or smell of alcoholic beverages or breath-alyzer test results) or purchasing alcohol, they would be arrested for violating State law prohibiting those with CAP from possessing or purchasing alcohol. This would be a misdemeanor crime and law enforcement would have the option of arresting the individual or issuing a citation. The second tier of enforcement would be through a violation of probation hearing. Evidence of possession of alcohol on the part of the defendant would be brought before the judge and the probation officer. As part of CAP probation each individual would be required to submit to a breathalyzer test upon request of law enforcement if they have probable cause to believe a person on CAP has been drinking. A refusal to submit would be an automatic violation of probation. Results of such a test would be submitted as evidence in any violation of probation hearing. Upon a finding of a violation the Courts could impose sanctions ranging from prison to in-house alcohol treatment.

EXERCISE 7
Advanced Reporting

INSTRUCTIONS: A bomb caused extensive damage at Harvey's Resort Casino-Hotel in Stateline, Nev., a plush gambling casino. The casino was being remodeled, and the bomb was planted by two men posing as computer technicians. The bomb was about the size of a desk and supposedly contained 1,000 sticks of dynamite. However, there were no injuries.

The bombers were trying to extort $3 million from the casino and left a three-page letter. An attempt to make the payoff apparently failed when a helicopter pilot, aloft in darkness, failed to see the bombers' prearranged signs at the delivery point. The pilot returned with the money, and the bomb exploded as experts tried to disarm it by remote control.

Assume that the bomb exploded today. Write a news story summarizing the letter's content.

Stern Warning to the Management and Bomb Squad:

Do not move or tilt this bomb, because the mechanism controlling the detonators in it will set it off at a movement of less than .01 on the open-end Richter scale. Don't try to flood or gas the bomb. There is a float switch and an atmospheric switch set at 26.00–33.00. Both are attached to detonators. Do not try to take it apart. The flathead screws are also attached to triggers and as much as 1/4 to 3/4 of a turn will cause an explosion. In other words, this bomb is so sensitive that the slightest movement either inside or outside will cause it to explode.

The bomb can never be dismantled or disarmed without causing an explosion. Not even by the creator. Only by proper instruction can it be moved to a safe place where it can be deliberately exploded, or where the third automatic timer can be allowed to detonate it. There are three automatic timers each set for three different explosion times. Only if you comply with the instructions of this letter will you be given instructions on how to disconnect the first two automatic timers and how to move the bomb to a place where it can be exploded safely.

Warning:

I repeat, do not try to move, disarm or enter this bomb. It will explode.

If exploded this bomb contains enough TNT to severely damage Harrah's across the street. This should give you some idea of the amount of TNT contained within this box. It is full of TNT. It is our advice to cordon off a minimum twelve hundred foot radius and remove all people from that area.

Demands:

We demand three million dollars in used one hundred dollar bills. They must be unmarked, unbugged and chemically untreated. If we find anything wrong with the money we will stop all instructions for moving the bomb.

Instructions for Delivery:

The money is to be delivered by helicopter. The helicopter pilot is to park at 2300 hours as close as possible to the LTA building by the light at Lake Tahoe Airport. It is to face the east. The pilot has to be alone and unarmed. The pilot is to get out and stand by chain link fence gate. He is to wait for further instructions which will be delivered by a taxi that will be hired. The driver will know nothing. They may also be delivered by a private telephone or through the nearby public phone at exactly 0010 hours. At 0010 hours the pilot will receive instructions about where to go and what to do.

Before the pilot enters the helicopter, he has to take a strong flashlight and shine it around the inside of the helicopter so that it will light up the entire inside. We must be able to see it from a distance with binoculars. We want to be able to see everything that is inside the helicopter so that we can be sure there is no one hiding inside and that there is no contraband inside.

Conditions of the Business Transaction:

These conditions must be followed to the letter. Any deviation from these conditions will leave your casino in a shambles. Also remember that even a very small earthquake will detonate the bomb so do not try to delay the delivery of the money.

(1) All news media, local or nationwide will be kept ignorant of the transactions between us and the casino management until the bomb is removed from the building.

(2) The helicopter will be manned only by the pilot. He must be unarmed and unbugged. We do not want any misunderstanding which might cause us to have to take lives unnecessarily.

(3) Fill the helicopter up completely with gas.

(4) The helicopter pilot after he receives the first instructions cannot communicate with anyone except the necessary instructions given and taken by the tower. All channels from 11.80 to 17.00 will be monitored.

The designer of this bomb will not participate in the exchange. So it will be completely useless to apprehend any person making the exchange because they will not know how it works. They perform their duty for a reward. And again if you don't want to be stuck with a thousand pounds of TNT do not allow any investigation by local agencies, FBI or any other investigative action before the bomb is removed. If the instructions are violated in any way by any authority the secret of the handling of the bomb would definitely not be revealed. If the money is received without any problem, six sets of instructions regarding the removal of the bomb will be given to you at different times. The pilot will receive the first set of instructions. He can carry it back with him. If the money is sold to the buyer without complications you may receive the remaining five sets of instructions one by one via the Kingsbury Post Office by general delivery, or you may receive them all at once. The extent of your cooperation will make the difference. If you cooperate fully it will insure a very speedy exchange. We don't want to burden your business opportunities or cause more loss of money than is necessary.

Attention:

There will be no extension or renegotiation. Demands are firm regardless. The transaction has to take place within 24 hours. If you do not comply we will not contact you again and we will not answer any attempts to contact us. In the event of a double-cross there will be another time sometime in the future when another attempt will be made. We have the ways and means to get another bomb in.

To the Pilot:

The helicopter has to be filled up with gas. Do not come armed with any weapon. Do not bring a shotgun rider. All radio channels will be monitored. You are to have no communication with anyone after you reach the airport. Do not try to be a hero. Arlington is full of them and they can't even smell the flowers. Follow the orders strictly. You will make five stops, none of which will be at an airfield. You will have ample light for landing. All sites are fairly level. One has about 2 degrees pitch. There will be a clearance of more than two hundred feet radius. We don't want any trouble but we won't run away if you bring it.

HAPPY landings.

EXERCISE 8
Advanced Reporting

INSTRUCTIONS: As a community service, the mayor and Board of Supervisors of San Francisco issued this booklet about the danger of nuclear war. The mayor and board explained that they are responsible for public safety and have a duty "to inform the people of any imminent danger and to take steps to prevent harm from occurring." Their booklet adds that: "The danger is real. The risks are great. You should read this booklet to learn what is at stake. Then you can decide what you wish to do about it."

The mayor and board also issued a proclamation calling for a "temporary suspension of nuclear weapons production, while seeking a permanent international nuclear weapons ban." Assume that the mayor and Board of Supervisors released the booklet today. Write a news story summarizing its content.

THE NUCLEAR THREAT TO SAN FRANCISCO

1. Nuclear Weapons: How Many? How Powerful?

The United States and Soviet Union have the most weapons. France, Great Britain and China have them as well. India, Pakistan, Israel, South Africa and other nations are trying to get them or may already have them. The United States has about 30,000 nuclear warheads; the Soviet Union has approximately 20,000. Both the U.S. and the U.S.S.R. can hit each other with nuclear weapons carried by missiles launched from land or sea or air.

Each nuclear warhead is, of course, extremely powerful. The explosive power of a bomb or warhead is measured in "megatons." One megaton equals a *million* tons of TNT. The bombs which destroyed the Japanese cities of Hiroshima and Nagasaki had the explosive power of "only" 10 to 20 *thousand* tons of TNT. So, a one-megaton bomb—the size of the kind which could hit San Francisco—is 50 to 100 times more powerful.

The United States and Soviet Union have nuclear weapons ranging in size up to 20 megatons. If used, all these weapons would produce nearly a *million* times the explosive power used against Hiroshima. Thus, if a nuclear war were started—by accident or on purpose—the destruction would be beyond anything ever before experienced by the human race. The following sections describe what would happen.

2. Suppose a One-Megaton Bomb Were Exploded Near Ground Level at San Francisco City Hall

Almost every child, every woman and every man would be killed. The Civic Center, the Opera House and most of the elderly housing nearby would disappear as a crater 20 stories deep was formed. A deadly cloud of radioactive soil would be thrown thousands of feet into the air while the blast created winds up to 500 mph. Nothing recognizable would remain from the Old Mint on Mission to St. Mary's Cathedral and Japantown. Little of significance would remain standing from the Mission and Potrero Districts on the south, to Russian Hill on the north, from the Panhandle on the west to the Financial District and Chinatown on the east. This destruction would occur in seconds.

If you were farther away from City Hall (1.5 to 5.0 miles from the bomb blast)

Imagine instead you were fortunate enough to be farther from City Hall, driving across a bridge to Marin or the East Bay, shopping at Serramonte or Stonestown, at home in the Sunset or attending a game at Candlestick. The heat from the explosion and the instant burning of clothing would cause third-degree flash burns over much of the body for most people in this area, killing at least half. Brick and wood frame buildings would be destroyed. Vast firestorms could be caused by the intense heat, fanned by 160 mph winds. Such fires would suck up so much air that thousands could die from a lack of oxygen. Even underground shelters, if there were any, would become ovens from the heat. Pressure from the blast would shatter glass and turn it into missiles traveling at over 100 mph. Almost all transportation of any kind would be destroyed or made useless. Emergency medical equipment and supplies would be destroyed.

If you were anywhere in the extended Bay Area (5.0 miles and beyond)

The intense light from the explosion could cause retinal damage and even blindness to those who see the blast. Among the wounded survivors, many could be deaf because of ruptured eardrums. For up to hundreds of miles away, depending upon wind patterns, the nature of the bomb and other factors, radiation would kill many more. The radiation would be spread by tons and tons of contaminated soils and debris floating and drifting away from the blast area. The deaths may be rapid or slow. Radiation would also affect unborn generations because of its effects on genetic characteristics. For those of us who survive, the recovery would be long and painful, perhaps with permanent disability. The survivors may very well envy the dead.

3. What A Nuclear War Would Do

What we have just described are the effects of a single one-megaton attack on San Francisco. The probability, however, is that an attack would not be limited to one bomb or to San Francisco, but rather would be a part of a full-scale attack on the United States.

In such an all-out attack, over one-half of the population of the United States would be killed or injured. In the long run, millions more people would die from injuries, exposure to radiation, burns, and lack of food, water or adequate shelter. The Bay Area as a financial center and with a higher than average concentration of military and industrial facilities, unquestionably would be a prime target.

With many hospitals destroyed and many doctors and nurses killed and injured, we would have almost no medical care and few facilities for the hundreds of thousands of people suffering from burns, radiation sickness, blast effects, shock or other injuries. Epidemics of plague, typhus, cholera or other diseases could break out. There would be hundreds of thousands of human corpses to dispose of in San Francisco alone.

Our economic structure would be devastated. There would be drastic food shortages with foodstuffs largely destroyed and little hope of replacing them quickly. With roads clogged or damaged, there would be a breakdown of transportation. Most communications would be cut off. Basic services such as fire, police, sanitation and water would be disrupted. There would be severe energy shortages. Because of lingering radiation, people would not be able to return to their homes for weeks, months or even years—that is, if their homes were left standing.

The Worst May Be Unknown

It is almost impossible to calculate the effects of a nuclear war on the environment. The oceans, air and land may be too contaminated to sustain life. Entire species of plants and animals may die out. Certain insects and bacteria which are more immune to radiation will multiply.

The effects on the minds of the people who witness this holocaust can only be guessed.

4. What Can We Do?

Neither the continued arms race, nor civil defense programs can banish the threat of a nuclear disaster. Being involved in the prevention of a nuclear holocaust is more realistic than trying to deny the danger. After reviewing these facts about nuclear war and the nuclear weapons, the Mayor and the Board of Supervisors felt a responsibility to act. The first step was to endorse this booklet and have it distributed throughout San Francisco to inform you of the risks and dangers we all face.

Here are some steps you can take:

Learn More. There are lots of materials on nuclear weapons, nuclear war and related issues available in our public libraries.

Discuss the Problem. Engage in discussions with your family, friends, at your school, work, club or religious institution. Children too young to participate in activities to prevent nuclear disaster should have the support and reassurance which the involvement of their parents can provide.

Contact Groups in Your Neighborhood. Offer to arrange for a speaker and film presentation on the nuclear weapons issue.

Vote Appropriately. Make sure those persons for whom you vote will do all in their power to promote peace and avoid nuclear war, and actively oppose the nuclear arms race.

Call and Write the News Media. Ask for coverage of the issue. Praise as well as criticize where indicated. The press needs and wants to hear from their viewers/readers.

Write Your Elected Officials Frequently. Elected representatives in Washington, D.C. and Sacramento are YOUR voice. Make sure that *your* voice is heard. Jot two or three sentences on a postcard and urge them to support negotiations with the Soviet Union for an immediate bilateral and verifiable nuclear weapons freeze and the reduction and elimination of nuclear stockpiles as well as opposition to the development and deployment of any new nuclear weaponry.

EXERCISE 9
Advanced Reporting

INSTRUCTIONS: Write a news story based on the following interviews. The interviews provide verbatim descriptions of an actual fire. Only a few names have been changed. The story is more difficult than many of the previous assignments because information about the fire is provided by three sources, whose information is sometimes inconsistent. As you write the story, assume that the fire occurred yesterday at the Greenbrier Apartments just outside your community.

First Source

Q. Could you tell me your name and address, please?

A. Peg Hanson. 824 Greenbrier Drive. The Greenbrier Apartments.

Q. Could you describe the fire that occurred there yesterday?

A. Well, about 9 o'clock in the morning a friend of mine stood just opposite, uh, the carport visiting, and we were looking across at the carport and we noticed a car starting to smoke but we didn't pay too much attention. The, uh, manager of the apartment complex came by, uh, with a girl in a little golf cart, and the girl had a fire extinguisher in her hand, but I didn't see her using it. Uh, then a man came along and tried to open the car door, and I don't know what he was trying to do, but, uh, he got a little worried about the, uh, uh. There was so much smoke around the car that he backed off, so the apartment manager, the girl with the fire extinguisher in her hand and another man that works around the place, all three of them, just stood there looking at the car, and, uh, it was smoking more and more. Pretty soon flames, uh, came out the roof of the car. Next thing, I counted five more cars in the carport, and the next thing I knew they were on fire. There was smoke all around them and flames coming out of the roof of the car. And, uh, there wasn't any sign of a fire truck, no sign of any help of any kind. Big crowd of people coming around, sirens, ambulances, police cars, crowds of people.

   The roof of the carport is now on fire. It's smoking, smoking, lots of smoke. Uh, pretty soon flames. The sounds of it, uh, sounded like explosions, small explosions. And then flames rolling up out of the top of the carport. Flames reaching up into the sky the clear length of the carport. It was really very, it was terrifying to look at, and the heat was just terrific.

   Still no fire engines, no help. Uh, uh, people began to back away. They said, "Back away, get away, get away, they are all going to explode." So, and the heat was so bad that we walked back almost to Highway 436 because of the heat.

Q. About how many feet was that?

A. Fifty feet from the carport maybe.

Q. Then what happened?

A. Pretty soon a fire engine arrived. It looks like a very small fire engine. They attached the hose to a fire hydrant, and a little stream of water came out. Hardly went across the street. It, uh, so they, so they stood there and held it, and it, uh, uh, it didn't even reach the roof of the carport. There was no pressure apparently.

Q. About how long did it take the first fire trucks to get there?

A. When the fire first started in the car, it was around 9 o'clock. Around 9:30 there still wasn't any fire department there. And, uh, I wouldn't know when exactly, I shouldn't say exactly when the fire engine arrived. I couldn't say. It seemed as though it were about a quarter of 10, but I guess I shouldn't say, and, um, so, uh, at that point the heat was so bad, and it was such a terrible, terrible, awful, awful thing to look at, that I decided to come on home. And then I went upstairs and, uh, looked out the window, and here was the fire department. They had one of these great big cherry pickers they call them. Two men were up there, and they had some water with some pressure with it, and they were directing the stream on the houses, the apartments that were in back of the carport. But by then they had, most all of them were destroyed. And it did seem as though if the, uh, if it had been possible to, to put water between the carport and those houses early in the game to protect the apartments that it wouldn't have been necessary for them to have burned down. It doesn't seem as though it would have been necessary.

Second Source

Q. What's your name and position?
A. Harry Miller. Employee at Greenbrier Apartments.

Q. Could you describe the damage at the apartment complex?
A. There was 12 units in the building. Eight of 'em were completely destroyed. The two on each one of the ends probably totally, smoke damage would probably cause the destruction of those but, so far as the fire was concerned, it didn't destroy any of their walls or anything.

Q. How many cars were destroyed?
A. Twelve cars were burned.

Q. Could you describe the carport?
A. It's a carport that holds about 16 cars. Two of the people who have had cars in there for the last couple of months, that have just rented the carports, were gone, so two of the cars, uh, weren't in the carport at the time.

Q. Was anyone living in the apartments hurt?
A. No one was injured, and that's mostly thanks to a couple of the yard workers that broke some of the doors down with people that didn't know the fire was going on. And one couple was both at work, and they had a dog inside the apartment of which one of the yard workers broke the chain off the door and went in and got the dog.

Q. If their apartments were destroyed, where did the people stay last night?
A. Most are staying with, uh, friends or relatives, or they put them up at a hotel, uh, indefinitely, I guess, you know, until they get them situated in another apartment.

Q. The apartment complex is paying their bills?
A. Yeah.

Q. Do you know what started the fire?
A. Well, yesterday when I got to work, we had to start immediately in securing the place off and keeping everyone away from it because there were so many lookers. And after the firemen had got the fire out, I checked the lady's car out, and there was not a carburetor on it, so, so I figure someone must have taken the carburetor off the car, and that would cause the, uh, gasoline to come out of the engine and not go into the carburetor. It would just shoot out and, if the spark got hot enough, it would probably just start the fire.

Q. Why did the fire spread so quickly?

A. The wood, uh, on the carport is just like a wooden frame carport which would burn very quickly. Light wood, too. It's not really heavy wood. It just, uh, seemed to go.

Q. Could you estimate the damage?

A. They said $500,000 damage, but I probably think it's a little more than that.

Q. Have you learned why the fire department didn't respond more quickly?

A. The way I understand it, a lady from the apartment complex next door saw it. One of the first ones that saw it. And called the telephone operator to get ahold of the fire department. The fire department she called said that it wasn't in its jurisdiction, and they would have to call the county Fire Department. We're not in the city here. We're just east, just outside, maybe 6, 8 blocks outside the city limits. So she had to start all over again with the operator and then call the county. And they said something about, the firemen I talked to, said something about the dispatcher was a little late. And she reported it as a single-car fire in which they only send out one fire truck for that. She didn't say that it was in a carport or possibly a structure fire where it could spread into the apartment complex.

Third Source

Q. What's your name and title?

A. John Inscho. District 3 chief, county Fire Department.

Q. Could you tell me how many men and trucks you had at the fire?

A. On the initial response we had, uh, two, had two fire pumpers and one rescue and one district commander that responded. When the first, uh, engine arrived on the scene and noticed the involvement of the fire, he immediately called for a second-alarm response, which is a response that just doubles the first-alarm response. And then under a mutual aid pact we have, we called some other departments for help, and they sent some more engines.

Q. About how long did it take to extinguish the fire?

A. Actually, to bring the fire under control was about an hour and a half after we arrived on the scene. Total suppression of the fire was about 4 hours into the fire.

Q. Have you been able to determine how the fire started?

A. The fire originated, uh, from a car fire. A carburetor, uh, had apparently been stolen off one of the cars and when the, uh, owner of the vehicle went to start it, it backfired, and the engine caught on fire, and being in a covered type of garage, and that fire not being suppressed, that fire spread quickly to other cars on either side of it, plus the garage became involved very rapidly.

Q. Did the cars' gas tanks explode?

A. None of the gas tanks I don't think exploded, but they ruptured, and when they ruptured, they dumped the gasoline on the ground, and you just have a hot fire.

Q. There seems to be some question about how long it took the fire department to respond. Do you know why there was a delay?

A. The lady whose car originally caught on fire, she didn't know what to do, so she went to get the apartment manager and, by the time she found him, which was several minutes later, he came, and he saw that they had a fire, so he went to get some fire extinguishers. And he came back and he used two, uh, soda-acid extinguishers on the fire. They didn't put it out, so I guess he decided he better call the fire department. So he summoned somebody to call the department. And I understand, uh, uh, a lady called the city's fire department. And prior to her doing that, she also called the operator, and the operator said she would have to call her local department via 911. So then when she called 911 and there was a problem in the computer, it routed her back to the city, and the city told her, "Madam, we told you to call the county department." And by then she was kind of upset and hot, and rightly so. So then when she did make contact with the department, it was a considerable time had gone by. But from the time the fire department received the call, we were, were on the scene within 3 minutes, which is the normal response time.

Q. Were any of your officers injured during the fire?
A. One of 'em had, um, minor smoke inhalation, and another had second, uh, degree burns on his legs from steam coming up off the pavement getting on his legs.

Q. Was it an unusual fire for you, or did you have any unusual problems in extinguishing it?
A. It was a routine fire. Of course, the fire started from a car fire which involved other cars parked next to it which involved the garage structure, and then the building that was behind it, which was an apartment building. And because of the intensity of the fire, that building caught on fire very, very quickly. And the fire spread very fast throughout the building. In the building codes now, a building of this type has to have firewalls separating the attic area of the building, which this one did not have.

Q. Did that make the fire more difficult to extinguish?
A. In these buildings which have a big common attic, which this one has, once a fire gets up in that attic it's very hard to control because there's no way of stopping it. So usually when the fire gets into the attic area, you have total involvement of the roof area. That's a problem that people that are living in these buildings or buying these buildings may want to be aware of, checking to see that the building is up to fire codes, that it meets fire code requirements.

EXERCISE 10
Advanced Reporting

INSTRUCTIONS: Write a news story that summarizes this report about shoplifters. Newspapers received copies of the report exactly as it appears here.

The Juvenile Shoplifter

Shoplifting is the largest monetary crime in the nation. Annual retail losses have been recently estimated at $16 billion nationally and as high as 7.5% of dollar sales. Shoplifting-related costs have been cited as a prime cause in one-third of all bankruptcies in small businesses. Shoplifting losses are on the rise, with a 300 percent increase in the incidence of this crime during the 1970s alone.

Juveniles make up the largest percentage of shoplifters. Several studies have revealed that juvenile shoplifters account for approximately fifty percent of all shoplifting.

To gain further insight into the shoplifting problem, George P. Moschis, Professor of Marketing at Georgia State University, and Professor Judith Powell of the University of Richmond, surveyed 7,379 students ages 7 to 19 in urban, suburban and rural areas using methods that insured anonymity of responses.

Some key findings:

• Approximately one out of three juveniles said they had shoplifted.

• Among teen-agers ages 15 to 19, about 43% had shoplifted.

• Male youths shoplift more than females; approximately 41% of the males and 26% of the females reported having shoplifted at some time.

• A large amount of shoplifting is done by relatively few juveniles. Approximately 14 percent of those who admitted to shoplifting indicated repeat shoplifting behavior.

• In comparison with non-shoplifters, youths who shoplift are more likely to believe that shoplifting is not a crime.

• Motives for shoplifting are primarily social rather than economic, especially among girls.

• A great deal of shoplifting is done because of peer pressure, especially among girls.

• About half of the time shoplifting takes place in the presence of peers. Shoplifting with peers is more common among girls than among boys (61% vs 47%).

• Females show greater tendency to shoplift with others with age than males.

• Females tend to shoplift more frequently in the presence of others with age.

• Boys tend to shoplift more frequently alone (less frequently with others) with age.

• Shoplifting done by juveniles is primarily impulsive; four times out of five it is done on impulse.

• Female juveniles who shoplift are more likely to shoplift on impulse. Approximately 87% of females and 76% of males who admitted they had shoplifted decided to shoplift after they entered the store.

• Older teen-age girls are more likely to shoplift on impulse than older teen-age boys. Older boys tend to plan out shoplifting more than girls.

- There is a decline in impulse shoplifting with age and an increase in planned shoplifting among boys. No decline in impulsive shoplifting behavior is shown for girls.

- Impulsive (unplanned) shoplifting in the presence of others is not only more common among girls but it also becomes more frequent with age. Impulsive shoplifting among boys in the presence of others does not increase with age.

The findings regarding differences in shoplifting behaviors due to age and sex characteristics are expected to apply to other parts of the country, and they are consistent with the results of previous studies.

The authors recommend two broad strategies for reducing shoplifting losses: shoplifting prevention and shoplifting detection. Among shoplifting prevention methods the authors suggest promotional campaigns that would increase awareness of the seriousness of the crime, and methods that would increase the difficulty of shoplifting. Proposed shoplifting detection strategies focus on educating security-detection personnel to be alert to the shoplifter's early warning signals, including knowledge of characteristics of youths most likely to shoplift.

APPENDIX A
City Directory

Like other city directories, this directory lists only the *adults* living in the *local* community. It does not list children, and it does not list people living in other cities. Similarly, it may not list people who moved to the local community within the past few months. When the information presented in this directory conflicts with the information presented in a story, assume that the city directory is correct and that the story is incorrect. If a name is not listed in the directory, assume that it is used correctly in the story. As you check the names of people involved in news stories, check those peoples' addresses and occupations too, since sources are likely to make some errors while supplying that information.

Abbreviations

acct	accountant	det	detective
adm	administration	dir	director
adv	advertising	dispr	dispatcher
agt	agent	dist	district
apt	apartment	dr	drive/driver
archt	architect	ele	elementary
asmbl	assembler	emp	employee
assoc	associate	eng	engineer
asst	assistant	est	estate
attnd	attendant	exec	executive
atty	attorney	facty	factory
av	avenue	fed	federal
bkpr	bookkeeper	gdnr	gardener
blvd	boulevard	hairdrsr	hairdresser
brklyr	bricklayer	hospt	hospital
bros	brothers	hwy	highway
capt	captain	inc	incorporated
cc	community college	ins	insurance
ch	church	insptr	inspector
chiro	chiropractor	jr	junior
cir	circle/circuit	jtr	janitor
clk	clerk	jwlr	jeweler
clns	cleaners	la	lane
co	company	librn	librarian
colm	council member	lt	lieutenant
com	commissioner	mach	machinist
const	construction	mech	mechanic
cpl	corporal	med	medical
ct	court	mfg	manufacturing
ctr	center	mgr	manager
cty	county	min	minister
custdn	custodian	mkt	market
dent	dental/dentist	muncp	municipal
dept	department	nat	national

ofc	office		serv	service
ofer	officer		sgt	sergeant
opr	operator		slsm	salesman
pcpl	principal		soc	social
pers	personnel		sr	senior
pharm	pharmacist		st	street
phys	physician		stat	station
po	post office		studt	student
pres	president		supm	supermarket
prof	professor		supt	superintendent
ptlm	patrolman		supvr	supervisor
ptr	painter		tchr	teacher
pub	public		tech	technician
rd	road		tel	telephone
recpt	receptionist		ter	terrace
rel	relations		treas	treasurer
rep	representative		univ	university
repr	repairman		vet	veterinarian
restr	restaurant		vp	vice president
retd	retired		watr	waiter
schl	school		watrs	waitress
sec	secretary		wid	widow
secy	security		widr	widower
sen	senator		wkr	worker

Sample Entry

Hurley Carl J (Jeanne dispr Yellow Cab) printer Weisz Printing Co 140 Kings Point Dr

    1   2   3   4   5   6   7

1 = Name of man, last name first
2 = First name of wife
3 = Wife's occupation, if other than housewife
4 = Name of wife's employer
5 = Man's occupation
6 = Name of man's employer
7 = Home address

Abare Ann recpt 855 Tichnor Way

Acevedo Louis (Esther) retd 8487 Highland Dr

Acevedo Miguel pub defender 812 Bell Av

Adcock George (Lydia soc wkr) ofc mgr 141 N Cortez Av

Adler Debra assoc Watson Realty 1847 Oakland Blvd

Adler Stuart (Sandra) min Ch of Christ 1847 Oakland Blvd

Adles John (Dora) rep Bache & Co 1218 S 23rd St

Ahl Thomas C facty wkr 2634 6th St #382

Ahrens Tommy (Joan ofc mgr) managing editor The Daily Courier 1097 Leeway Dr

Ahsonn Jeffrey R (Theresa) retd 49 Groveland Av

Aimini Eli state hwy patlm 1784 Collins Av

Albertson Esther facty wkr 4100 Conway Rd #14

Alicea Carlos cty emp 1920 Leisure Dr

Allen James D (Martha atty) 28 Rio Grande Rd

Allen Michael city assessor 524 Adirondack Av #1074

Allerson Harold (Margaret tech) vet 524 Adirondack Av

Alten Jesse (Lynda asst mgr First Federal Bank) pharm 9102 Meadow Creek Dr

Alvarez Harold (Tina Marie tchr) po wkr 4338 Hargarve St

Alvarez Jose cpl state hwy patrol 1982 Elmwood Dr

Anders Ralph univ prof 5212 Eldridge St

Andrews Ira (Paula acct) auto mech 4030 New Orleans Av

Aneesa Ahmad (Bea tchr) univ prof 1184 3rd Av

Aneja David (Tracie studt) sgt sheriff's dept 488 Tulip Av

Angermeir Sherry R dist atty 241 Michigan Av

Ansell Herman clk Blackhawk Hotel 2814 Ambassador Dr #61

Aparico Bruce (Marilyn) phys 3415 Hennessy Ct

Arico James K ptr 9950 Turf Way #703C

Avassa Mario chef Mario's Italian Restr 714 Lancaster Rd

Bache Alex (Patricia mgr Bache Ins) rep Watson Realty 842 West Av

Bailee Maggy welder Halstini Mfg 810 N Ontario Av

Baliet Thomas (Karen adv exec) pres Republican Bldrs 1440 Walters Av

Ball James C studt 1012 Cortez Av #870

Banks Julian Army pvt 9950 Turf Way #302

Banks Myron (Beatrice) mayor 1050 Treasure Dr

Barlow Kevin (Janet hairdrsr) ptlm 2886 Moor St

Barlow Robert Albert (Suzanne ch sec) auto mech Allison Ford 112 Hope Circle

Barsch Michael (Margaret asst mgr Kraft's Supm) police sgt 1489 Hazel La

Barton Eileen owner/mgr Barton Schl of Dance 1012 Treasure Dr

Basis Leon tchr 2457 S Conway Rd

Batcheldar Randall (Diana) dent 1792 Nairn Dr

Baugh Roger (Marcia state consumer advocate) mgr Baugh Linen Serv 350 Meridan Av

Bazinett Cira phys 2032 Turf Way #1410

Beasly Ralph (Lindsay sheriff's deputy) serv stat attnd 810 Howard St

Becker Ricky (Maurine sheriff's deputy) publisher The Daily Courier 1521 Cole Rd

Becker Thomas (Norma city recreation dir) mayor 5135 Westwinds Dr

Beghor Glenn R retd 415 W Hazel Av

Belcuore Paul (Christine watrs Holiday House Restr) librn 497 Fern Creek Dr

Belini Ed const wkr 2047 Princeton St #811

Belini Marie med tech 1010 Bumby Av

Bellochi Sidney (Myrtle) fire chief 2508 S Conway Rd

Biaggi Allison ptlm 2634 6th St #906B

Biegel Frank custdn Filko Furniture 782 12th Av

Blaron David (Allison clk) Army recruiter 6714 West Dr

Blohm Kevin (Monica rep Watson Realty) cook North Point Inn 5604 Woodland St

Bogard Mark studt 4100 Conway Rd #105D

Bolanker Timothy studt 854 Maury Rd #107B

Boyette Willis A jtr Barton Schl of Dance 2121 Biarritz Dr

Boyssie Lee (Betty bkpr Allstate Ins) ptlm 1409 3rd Av

Brame Don city emp 3402 Virginia Av

Brennan Rosemary city librn 1775 Nair Dr

Brill Mark (Rikka dir Humane Society) assoc Watson Realty 5604 Dockside Dr

Bronson Theo clk Mayer's Jewelers 2202 8th Av #4

Brookes Oliver (Sunni technical writer) univ prof 5402 Andover Dr

Brown Howard (Betty city recreation dir) ins slsm Prudential Ins Co 1745 Collins Av

Bruce Paul (Marilyn nurse Mercy Hospt) cab dr 8241 Bellmont Av

Bulman Patricia (wid) retd 3220 Clay Av

Burmeister Abraham (Esther) pres First Nat Bank 4439 Harding Av

Burmester Herman A (Sally) const wkr Rittman Eng Co 1214 S 23rd St

Burrall Randall S dispr Harris Trucking Inc 814 Central Av

Butcavage Victor union rep 9111 Alton Rd

Carey John priest St. John Vianney Catholic Ch 2020 Oak Ridge Rd

Carey Myron (Ruth operations supvr Social Security Adm) univ prof 614 N Highland Dr

Carig Craig (Susan) dir Woodlands Camp 453 Twisting Pine Cir

Carig James Roger (Alice bkpr) gdnr 453 Twisting Pine Cir

Carlisle John (Marion atty) atty 48 N Meridian Av

Carvel Reba tchr Colonial Ele Schl 1883 Hope Ter

Casey William (widr) police chief 763 Tiffany Dr

Casio David (Getta) atty 7111 N 31st St

Cessarini Richard M (Maxine univ prof) phys 1484 Cypress Av

Cheesbro Marilyn asst public defender 1010 Eastview Rd

Chenn Stephen (Denise mgr Sizzling Steak House Restr) fire dept training ofer 703 E Pine Av

Chevez Larry police det 4747 Collins Rd

Chmielewski Albert nurse Mercy Hospt 2814 Ambassador Dr #82

Ciravano Thomas (Sandra asst mgr First Federal Bank) colm/pres Thomas Plastics 711 Harding Av

Cisneroes Andrew (Lillian) min Redeemer Lutheran Ch 818 Bell Av

Claunch Andrew (Betty rep Watson Realty) asst fire chief 1619 West Av

Cohen Abraham (Estelle pub rel rep) asst dir computer serv city schl system 1903 Conway Rd

Cortez Manual (Nina bkpr North Point Inn) ptlm 1242 Alton Rd

Cortez Roberto (Evelyn clk Tom's Liquors) ptlm 1118 Tiffany La

Courhesne Adolph (Gloria nurse) mech 1186 N Highland Av

Cremrad Dennis (Beth) univ football coach 2702 Patty Way

Crenisky Dale (Myrtle tchr) dir city libraries 8112 West Av

Crosby Charles (Susan min Clemson Presbyterian Ch) pres Crosby Enterprises 200 Hillcrest St

Cross Lee (Andrea dent asst) acct Rittman Industries 124 Ingram Cir

Cross Ron E (Martha) hospt administrator 101 Charrow La

Cullinan Charles A (Susan) sheriff's deputy 615 Pennsylvania Av

Cullinan Charles R (Theresa) ptlm 230 W Lancaster Rd

Custodia James (Shirley asst mgr Textile World) atty 1198 Meridian Av

Cyler Richard (Alice colm) atty 7842 Toucan Dr

Daggett Deborah technical writer Cargill Industries 777 W Lancaster Rd

Daggett Fredric (Edith) retd 777 W Lancaster Rd

Davis William C (Rosa clk Belks Dept Store) dir Municipal Power Plant 411 Jamestown Dr

Dawkins Ronald (Valerie cty com) brklyr 1005 Strathmore Dr

Dawson Shirley (wid) tchr Colonial Ele Schl 492 Melrose Av

Day Billy Joe (Agnes insptr Holten Mfg) retd 257 Beloit Av

Deacosta Michael (Peggy) pres Deacosta's Restr 3154 Virginia Av

Dealfonso Dennis F (Heather eng) atty 1502 Jemima Av

Deamud Fredrick watr Deacosta's Restr 2212 DeLaney Av

Deamud Theodore (widr) retd 2212 DeLaney Av

Deboar Jack R (Ann dir emp relations Rittman Industries) supm mgr 1415 Idaho Av

Dees Karen program coordinator Alcohol Information Center 1212 DeLaney Av

Delevaux Maggie (wid) pres Delevaux Jewelers 1712 Townhall La

Dempsey Ronald (Peggy) pres Dempsey's Restr 3154 Virginia Av

DeVittini Ronald (Brenda asst min Redeemer Lutheran Ch) muncp emp 313 Coble Dr

DeWitte Tony studt 1012 Cortez Av #828

Deyo Ralph (Ashley graphic designer) dent 2047 Princeton St #844

Dezinno Marc (Nancy) asmbl 105 Rockingham Ct

Diaz Enrique (Lisa po wkr) atty 3224 Mt Semonar Av

DiCesare Gus (Henrietta) cty sheriff 1804 Atlantic Av

Dillan Martha atty Westinghouse Corp 702 S Kirman Av

Distelhorst George (Cele dent asst) supt of schls 1620 W 27th St

Dolezaar Wilma (wid Gerhard) 9147 S Georgia Av

Dolmovich Sandra M clk K Mart 714 N 23rd St

Dowdell Thaddeus (Laura clk Dowdell Jewelry) jwlr Dowdell Jewelry 620 Lexon Av

Dubriff Clarence (Susan ofc mgr) judge 554 Village La

DuFaule Jeffery clk Weiss Bros Warehouse 1994 Hazel La

Duncan Edward (Jean) truck dr 533 Oak Park Way #372

Durrence Mark capt sheriff's dept 2308 S 14th Av

Durst Albert (Alice clk Belks Dept Store) facty insptr 2731 S Kirman Rd

Dwyer Margaret studt 2047 Prince St #405

Edwards Tracy R psychiatrist 529 Pinar Dr

Einhorn Adam (Arlene vp loans First Nat Bank) eng 4120 Rio Grande Av

Elam Roger A (Dorothy tchr) landscape contractor 2481 Santana Av

Ellerbe Robert (Lisa) pres Ellerbe's Boats 3213 Hidalgo Dr

Erhmann Katy dr Yellow Cab 811 N 11th St #542

Eulon Harley (Martha) acct St. Nicholas Hospt 410 E 3rd St

Evans Timothy (Nikki loan ofer First Federal Savings & Loan) ofc mgr Allstate Ins 806 Citrus St

Favata John (Karen financial planner) soc wkr 8724 Joyce Dr

Ferrell Marvin (Fannie atty) pcpl Kennedy High Schl 1284 West Av

Finkbeiner Clayton (Marie) archt 414 Ivanhoe Blvd

Firmet Rene J serv stat attnd 2474 Colyer Rd

Fishner Jo-Anne nurse Memorial Hospt 682 S 28th St

Flavell J Vernon (Lucille dispr Becker Trucking Co) truck dr 827 N Pigeon Rd

Flynn Bryan (Linda) state hwy patrol cpl 4182 Eastland Dr #582

Focault Carmen (wid) tchr Aloma Ele Schl 1452 Penham Av

Forsythe Scott (Carolyn) cpl sheriff's dept 2414 S 14th Av

Friendly Daniel exec dir Community Action Center 853 Bellmont Av

Fusner Charles (Tillie) lineman 1892 Meridian Av

Gable Jay (Frances exec sec Prudential Ins Co) truck dr 1701 Woodcrest Dr

Gaidis Peter (Donna rep Watson Realty) vp Pioneer Federal Savings & Loan Association 8724 Joyce Dr

Gallagher Derek J probation ofer 1420 Penham Av

Gardepe Elaine serv mgr Derek Chevrolet 210 Lake Dr

Gianangeli David gdnr 524 Adirondack Av #482C

Gianangelli Jerrod Robert 1104 Bumby Av

Giangeli Marlene P pres Pestfree Inc 214 Lake Dr

Gibson Samuel (Rebecca librn) retd 2207 17th Av

Goetz Beryl dent 1010 McLeod Rd

Golay Thomas A (Evelyn cashier Tom's Liquors) owner/mgr Tom's Liquors 1203 Texas Av

Goodwynn Theresa (wid Harold) retd 814 Cyers La

Goree Timothy (Leigh) nat rep Kohler Plumbingware 1402 Alabama Av

Gould Savilla (Darla) slsm Anchor Realty Co 2178 N 11th Av

Graham Ross R (Estella cty com) phys 710 Harding Av

Grauman Roland (Tina asst supt for pub education) cty com 3417 Charnow La

Green Joel atty 604 Michigan Av

Guempil Alvin J (Dolly) police capt 1010 Atlantic Av

Guerin Donald Edward (Anita) city fireman 1045 Eastvue Rd

Guerria David R (Suzette) min Redeemer Lutheran Ch 3418 N Oakland Blvd

Guikema Martin (Sandra) police chief 8340 North Av

Guiterman Daniel bartender Jim's Lounge 553 Oak Park Way #7

Gulas William J (Gail studt) phys 3405 Virginia Av

Gunter Samuel F circuit ct judge 820 3rd St

Guyer Joseph (Rita photographer) artist 4043 S 28th St

Habber Thomas R clk Family Hut Lumber 366 Clemson Dr

Hadsse Derric cty com 344 Huron Av

Haile Jeffrey ptlm 2634 6th St #847

Halso Geoffrey (Beverly pres Halso Public Rel) vet 879 Tichnor Way

Hamill Kimberly clk Albertson's supm 811 N Cortez Av

Hammar Margaret J secy ofer Belk's Dept Store 1181 6th St

Hammill Margaret studt 811 N Cortez Av

Hanson Edward (Peg) retd 824 Greenbrier Dr

Hanzel Myron sheriff's deputy 312 Adirondack Av

Harmon Rhonda watrs 816 Westwinds Dr #8

Harnish David (Cheryl supvr sales Cargell Corp) state sen 388 Hillcrest St

Harris Gerald R slsm Derek Chevrolet 2245 E Broadway Av

Harris Jewel C recpt 2245 E Broadway Av

Haselle Richard (Jennifer loan ofer First Nat Bank) pres Haselle Development Corp 554 Beloit Av

Haserott Mildred (wid John) ticket agt Greyhound Lines 411 Wisconsin Av

Haskell Thomas lt fire dept 1010 Oak Ridge Rd #711

Hattaway Willie (widr Claire) retd 411 Wisconsin Av

Haughe Walter E Jr barber 1040 7th St #B4

Hedricks Donald asst state atty 4232 Elsie Dr #884

Hemphill Loretta dir secy State Alliance Businesspeople 429 Conway Rd

Henderson Leon (Diane dir pub rel city schl system) sheriff's deputy 902 Patty Way

Henricks Florence tchr Risser Ele Schl 423 E Marble Rd

Herman Andrew J (Jennifer teller First Nat Bank) acct 1888 Hope Ter

Hernandez Ronald (Martha alderman) baker Kalini Bros 798 Tichnor Way

Herndon Joyce atty 310 Mills Av

Herrin Raymond W univ prof 410 Park Av

Hershey Alfred (Allison asst branch mgr Liquor World) 2047 Princeton St #78A

Herwarthe Gregory L (Ruth asst mgr Harrington & Co Investments) pres Knight Realty 4410 Baltimore Av

Hesselin Dorothy L asst mgr Mr. Grocer 8197 Locke Av

Hesslen Christopher (Allison dispr Webb Plumbing) studt 811 Rockinham Ct

Higginbotham Gladies A (wid Paul) mgr Security Federal Bank 811 E Newsome Rd

Hildebrand L C (Nancy) cty medical examiner 4749 Elm Dr

Hill Robert (Donna) ptlm 564 Tiffany Dr

Hillier Carolyn E 841 Richland Av

Hillier Sandra 3228 E Broadway Av #283

Hodgins John custdn Wymore Ele Schl 9214 Turf Way

Hodgson Ralph (Janet) dist supvr Getty Oil 882 Village La

Hoequist Thomas owner/mgr The Jewelry Shoppe 2418 Collins Av

Hoffman Melody Ann 481 E Brittany Rd

Hoffmyer Vivian clk Quik Shoppe 711 Meadow Creek Dr

Holmann Leonard (Evelyn) phys 4366 Normandy Dr

Holmann Saul (Frances nurse Park Memorial Hospt) univ prof 1440 Elmwood Dr

Holton Elizabeth owner Mom's Donuts 1743 N 3rd St

Holtzclaw Norma J (wid Elmer) Realtor 739 West Av

Horan Roger sheriff's deputy 118 Hillside Dr #C3

Horton Robert J (Maxine) dist atty 1130 11th St

Horvath Joseph L (Destiny sales rep Horvath Realty) min Ch of God 778 Hyuer Av

Hotelin Stephen (Miriam watrs) 4112 American St

Howard Sara tchr Risser Ele Schl 812 Bell Av

Howeland Terry (Ruth bkpr Blackhawk Hotel) secy guard Memorial Hospt 1808 Gladsden Blvd

Hunt Reynold (Edna) city fire chief 33 Venetian Way

Hurcads David (Nancy) state biologist 547 Collins Av

Hyde Roger (Marie asst schl supt) slsm Ross Chevrolet 2481 Lakeview Dr

Ibold Marc schl custdn 877 Huron Av

Igou Steven asst state atty 2841 Gadsden Blvd

Innis Alvin (Sarah) lt det city police 1305 Atlantic Blvd

Inscho John (Delores tchr) dist 3 chief Cty Fire Dept 4484 Rio Grande Av

Jacbos Todd (Martha) min Community United Methodist Ch 1889 32nd St

Jacobs Bill (Carol) sgt city police 2481 Lakeview Dr

Janviere Jean tchr Colonial Ele Schl 1883 Hope Ter

Jeffreys Michael (Katherine realtor) dir Humane Society 2781 Collins Av

Jimenez Edward C mgr Quik Shoppe 3611 31st St

Johnson Edgar (Marcie legal sec) cty judge 148 West Av

Jonakait Erin (Cathy asst dir We Care) phys 2442 Collins Av

Julastic James (widr Marlane) supt of schls 3117 Collins Av

Kaehler Karl (Cynthia city com) cc tchr 2242 2nd Av

Kaeppler Rick (JoAnn judge) state forester 11 N Cortez Av

Kalani Andrew (Lynne) mgr Kalani Bros Bakery 2481 Kaley Way

Kalani Charles (Mary cashier) pres Kalani Bros Bakery 2470 Kaley Way

Kasandra Kelli retd 9847 Eastbrook La

Kaufmann Dorothy retd 2814 Ambassador Dr #108

Kazyk N B fire marshal 228 2nd St

Keel Timothy (Sally) barber Plaza Barber Shop 1314 Girese Dr

Kehole Marvin 182 W Broadway Rd

Kernan Russell (Carolyn clk Quikke Clns) mach 168 Lake St

Kindstrom Sara watrs 4828 N Vine St

Kirby Buddy po wkr 2032 Turf Way #118

Knapp Erik cook Frisch's Restr 2314 N 11th St

Kocembra Edwin (Alyce) judge 714 Euclid Av

Kock Ellen Jane atty Neighborhood Law Ofc 4214 Azalea Ct

Kopez Frank (Lisa) mech 1067 Eastland Av

Kopp Susan (wid Arthur) retd Quality Trailer Ct 4200 S 11th St

Kruckmeir Hannah clk Schwalk's Bootery 1601 Perkins Rd

Krueger William (Elizabeth recpt) pres Aladdin Paints 48 Michigan Av

Kubik Ralph (Marilyn tchr North High Schl) tchr North High Schl 1452 N 3rd St

Kubisak Henry Sr (Eileen) mkt dir Schultz Inc 418 N Wilkes Rd

Kuhlman Audrey studt 2814 Ambassador Dr #84

LaCette Cecil serv stat attnd 2814 Ambassador Dr #61

Lasitor James (Harriet tchr) tchr 374 Walnut Dr

Lathan Mary Ann studt 1012 University Dr #88D

Layoux Michael E studt 212 N Wisconsin Av

LeClair George D (Heather chiro) judge 374 Walnut Dr

Leeson Beverly studt 471 Eastbrook Av #52

Leidigh Floyd (Rose) const wkr 1812 Dickins Av

Levine Thomas L cir ct judge 4100 Conway Rd #510

Levy Mark (Lynn pcpl Rosemont Ele Schl) mgr Clary's Lumber Co 429 Holden Av

Lewis Jonnie (Jackie watrs) facty insptr 1840 Maldren Av

Lewis Ralph const wkr 8182 Kings Point Dr

London Glenda sheriff's deputy 2202 8th Av #890

Lopez Stephen (Charlotte owner/mgr The Gift Shoppe) ins adjuster 4308 E Highland Dr

Lubinskas Mark (Rebecca) tailor Breslers Dept Store 2914 Byron Av

Lucas Frank (Laura hairdrsr) cpl hwy patrol 2417 Country Club Dr

Luppa Scott studt 1012 University Dr #404

Lydin Charles R (Dana cc vp) asst mgr LaCorte Printing Co 888 Melrose Av

MacDonald Herbert J (Rosalie) 1842 Hazel La

MacDowell William ptr 1429 Highland Dr

Mahew Arthur (Annette clk typist Kennedy High Schl) mgr Frishe's Bowling Alley 1918 Pacific Rd

Majorce Albert (Monica) archt 2882 Ambassador Dr

Marchese Harley O (Joyce organist) min Faith Baptist Ch 1481 Cole Rd

McAuliffe Claire clk Handy Shop 100 N Wilshire Av

McCartney James (Mildred watrs Mom's Donuts) welder 1019 6th St

McCaulley Melvin (Veronica) truck dr 540 Osceola Blvd

McEwen Lonnie (Victoria retd) tchr 1024 Nancy Cir

McFarland Charlotte nurse Sand Lake Hospt 1090 Timberline Trail

McFarlane Brunson (Joyce pers dir Belks Dept Store) exec dir State Dairy & Food Nutrition Council 901 East Blvd

McGowin Bill (Rosalind maid Grande Hotel) const wkr 4842 S Conway Rd

McGregor Samuel (Carol mgr trainee Food Fair) cir ct judge 1501 Southwest Ct

McIntry Eugene (Irene) pres McIntry Realty 2552 Post Av

McNeely Todd (Sandra sales rep Tupperware) vet 7203 Minnesota Av

Mears Andrew C food mgr Memorial Hospt 1190 Euclid Av

Medina Carl (Sara sec) jtr First Nat Bank 542 Holden Av

Meeske Peter det 905 S Conway Rd

Meir Sharon studt 810 Kalani St

Mejia Colette pcpl Risser Ele Schl 415 Ivanhoe Blvd

Menuet Roy (Maria) owner Frenchie's Restr 432 Hemlock Dr

Merritt Jacob (June) eng WTMC-TV 301 Wymore Rd

Meyer Gary (Sonya) plumber 811 Moor St

Michelano Steven studt 132 E Muriel St

Milan Jeffrey (Maggy) dist atty 1884 Byron Av

Millan Timothy cook Grande Hotel 1112 Huron Av

Miller Harry (Sandra sec) gdnr Greenbrier Apts 4428 Meridian Av

Mims Daniel secy guard Grande Hotel 872 Huron Av

Moronesi Donna slsm Adler's Real Estate 623 N 5th St

Morovchek Albert (Dorothy clk city police dept) fireman 4287 N 14th St

Morrell Wayne (Cathy) mgr Bon Voyage Travel Agency 382 Arlington Av

Murhana Thomas laborer 40 W Hillier Av

Murphy Joseph (Kathy) city colm 114 E Harvard St

Murray Blair (Patricia) mgr Beneficial Finance 1748 N 3rd St

Murray Marty curriculum resource tchr 1801 Hillcrest St

Neel Robert pres Woodlawn Memorial Park 782 Wilkes Rd

Neely Myron A det 1048 Jennings Rd

Nego David (Peggy studt) ptlm 655 Euclid Av #43

Nemnich Bernard mgr Kinney Shoe Store 1231 Mt Vernon Av

Nemnich Harlon (Helen) electrician 1231 Mt Vernon Av

Nicholls John (Tracie) ins adjuster 1801 Kalurna Ct

Nichols Cheryl fed emp 1287 Belgard Av

Noffsinger Nora (wid Nicholas) retd 411 Wisconsin Av

Norbratten Maria (wid Harry) pharm 6684 Jennings Rd

Norbratten Ronald L (Sandra mach) mech cty garage 3772 Euclid Av

Norbratten Rosemary K eng 2742 Douglas Rd

Novarro James E (Paula mayor) eng 234 E Markham Dr

Novogreski Harry R (Melba) mach 2891 Morris Av

Nunez Roger (Carolyn) eng Keele-Baldwin Corp 2820 Norwell Av

Oalmann Donald (Samantha) emp WGN Radio 1022 N Kentucky Av

O'Hara Allison sec Rittman Industries 1515 East Blvd

Oldaker George ptlm 2107 Wisconsin Av #488

Oldaker Thomas (Lori) ptlm 411 11th St #3

Oliver Franklin R (Jeannette mgr trainee Food Fair) exec Gill Assoc Inc Pub Rel 1121 Elm Blvd

Onn Tom C (Esther) dir City Housing Authority 3869 Jefferson Av

Ortson T James (Martha) vp Secy First Federal Bank 810 N 14th St

Orzigg James (Tracy univ prof) computer consultant 108 Hillcrest St

Orzuk Travis (Diane sec) sgt state hwy patrol 818 N Atlantic Av

Ostreicher Marlene (wid Mack) judge 449 Ferncreek Dr

Paddock Thomas C (Cynthia credit mgr Belks Dept Store) 1736 Hinkley Rd

Pagozalski Howard (Marcia supt of schls) rep Bache & Co 1484 2nd St

Palomino Ralph R (Molly) vp Genesco Inc 374 Douglas Rd

Paynick Stanley (Nina tchr) owner Paynick's Carpets 901 2nd St

Pazelli Robert (Nina colm) retd 5821 Brantmore Ct

Perakist Michael (Ethel mgr Pix Shoes) atty 876 Collins Av

Perez Louis D (Elfreda) atty 2027 Harrison St

Perez Patrick (Anne) bartender 2025 Harrison St

Petchski Pearl asst cashier Morrison's Cafeteria 411 Wisconsin Av

Peterson Sara (wid Conrad) 1671 Drexel Av

Pfaff Randall (Evelyn cashier Drays Supm) cir ct judge 2134 Oak Ridge Rd

Phillips Jay (Teresa) mgr Pix Shoes 1814 Arlington Cir

Picardo Marie 510 Concord St #48

Picciolli Alfred J fcty wkr 411 Robinson Rd

Pickaid Margaret (wid Ralph R) 819 Superior Av

Picott Marilyn cir ct judge 901 2nd St

Piloto Kenneth T (Claire interior decorator) atty Piloto and Herndon 1472 Bayview Rd

Pinchal Scott mech 737 Dean Rd

Pinder Ralph (Julie city assessor) electrician 211 Jefferson Av

Pinero J T (Elizabeth recpt Kemper Ins) pres Stanhope Development Corp 36 Cypress Way

Piquett Howard colm 258 Pennsylvania Av

Plambeck Emil (Dolly) supt City Park Com 6391 Norris Av

Povacz Julius city paramedic 210 E King Blvd

Propes Richard E asst mgr Safeway Supm 1012 2nd St

Raintree Donald supm clk 366 Clemson Dr

Ramirez Louis (Harriet dental asst) city colm 982 Euclid Av

Ramirez Michael A adm Memorial Hospt 4814 E Harvard St

Randolph James const wkr 654 Harrison St

Raye William David (Beth) retd 112 Riverview Dr

Reeves E Charlton (Polly) state health ofer 658 Lennox Av

Reimer Maurice acct 2529 Barbados Av

Renko Andrew (Dawn) ptlm 820 Starke Circle

Rey Jeffery (Rhonda) dir Municipal Bus Co 1607 Michigan Av

Richards Patricia 42 Tusca Trail

Richardson Thomas E (Inez) ptlm 5421 Jennings Rd

Richbourg Bud (Kathleen pharm) owner Buddy's Lounge 1014 Turkey Hollow

Richter Robynn Anne retd 42 Tusca Trail

Riggs Gladys Ann (wid George) retd 1080 Harvard Rd

Rittzmann Roger (Donna) mgr Municipal Airport 645 Euclid Av

Riveras Max (Ruth) lineman 2342 Harding Av

Robbitzsch John W psychiatrist 1014 Bear Creek Cir

Robins James (Para) police lt 443 Tucker Av

Rodriguez Mary Helen vp personnel Rasbach's Dept Store 2900 Lando La

Roehl Cecil (Esther) ptlm 1228 Euclid Av

Romain Nickolas H (Gerri) welder 2876 Post Av

Rossi Earl (Margaret chiro) day mgr Internatl Hse of Pancakes 817 Hennessy Ct

Rudnick Marvin (Carolyn) police chief 111 Longbranch Rd

Rudnike Harold (Martha sales mgr Vallrath Industries) 4830 N Vine St

Rue Wesley dent 4713 Bell Av #582

Ruiz George (Lila studt) ptlm 263 9th St

Ruiz Guillermo (Harriet asst dir public affairs Regional Medical Center) cty medical examiner 4718 Bell Av

Rutherford Allen (Susan) pres Rutherford Ford Inc 727 Dickens Av

Ryan Don (Dianna computer programmer) cty com 1713 Kaley St

Rybinski Kim owner Kim's Pets 2634 6th St #710

Sanchez Gumersinda mgr beauty salon 173 Burgasse Rd

Sasser Maurice (Doris) phys 1602 Meridian Av

Satava Kenneth (widr Kathy) tchr Kennedy High Schl 2204 Marcel Av

Satterwaite Benjamin (widr Edith) retd 307 E King Blvd

Sawyer Harley (Betty) tchr 2032 Turf Way #510

Sawyer Randy (Claire) butcher Safeway Markets 1320 Embrey Cir

Schauffler Anna studt 1014 Mission Rd

Schiffini Destiny vp Sun Bank 581 Lima Place

Schipper Michele studt 4100 Conway Rd #814

Schroeder Warren (Leigh housekeeper) 1012 Cortez Av #4

Scott Kerry (Nancy Lee tchr) slsm Kohler Lightingware 10 Magee Ct

Seechuk Madge colm 1210 Jasper Ct

Shadgott Frank D phys 8427 Chestnut Dr

Shatuck Dennis A (Christina mgr Perkins Restr) emp city garage 532 3rd St

Shearer Ethel cocktail watrs 408 Kasper Av #718

Shenuski Fredric (Anita cty com) dis mgr IRS 1230 Embre Cir

Shepard Frank (Helen) reporter The Daily Courier 107 Eastbrook Av

Shepard Lynn Marie studt 854 Maury Rd #107B

Shisenaunt Arthur (Lillian pharm) secy consultant 1243 Washington Av

Silverbach Daniel J (Jill) ptlm 3166 Wayne Av

Sindelair Vernon (Elaine) slsm Aetna Life Ins Co 4164 Mander Dr

Skinner Roger (Dorothy clk typist Lawton Bros) ptlm 1080 Washington Av

Skurow Melville carpenter 4138 Hennessy Ct

Slater David (Carolyn) chiro 8443 Turkey Hollow

Sleczkowski Henry H (Victoria) retd 642 Ridgewood St

Smith Ronald (Linda) cty treas 814 N 13th St

Smitkins Myron (Marlane sec) mach 417 Huron Av

Smythe Allen (Esther) police lt 1085 Washington Av

Smythe Grady wkr Greenbrier Apts 8213 Perch St

Smythe Terry mech McInerny Ford 2900 Lando La #410

Sneidermann Martin S mgr Beef & Ale Restr 5247 Riverview Dr

Snow Dale (Terri nurse Mercy Hospt) 4381 Hazel St

Snowden Benjamin (Beth clk state employment ofc) slsm 952 Kasper Av

Snyder Fredric (Valorie studt) studt 711 Broadway Av

Sobik Arthur (Mildred state sen) eng 1283 Byron Av

Sobolewski Robert (Kathy) brklyr 1031 Hidden La

Soistmann William (Janette recept) city librn 4824 E Pine Av

Soo Keith (Laura dir pub rel city library) colm 1010 Hillcrest St

Stevenson Harold med tech St. Nicholas Hospt

Stoudnour John (Marlene cty coroner) mgr Rexall Drugs 1350 41st St

Straiten Walter (Karen watrs Maison Des Crepes Restr) city building insptr 4450 Richmond Rd

Stricklan Julian (Cynthia) judge 1913 Oak La

Svendson Wayne (Lillian tel supvr) city paramedic 814 Washington Av

Swidell Roger atty 4183 Mandar Dr

Talbertsen Sara A artist 3214 Riverview Dr

Tartagilla Paul Jr (Angela univ pers dir) dist atty 2916 Oak La

Taylor Fredric C 4828 N Vine St

Taylor Marsha L mgr McDonald's Restr 2012 Lincoln Av

Temple Roger ptlm 2032 Turf Way #818

Thistell Dirk (Mildred R counselor Roosevelt High Schl) eng Rittman Industries 528 Kennedy Blvd

Thomas Joseph (Tina tchr Washington Ele Schl) tchr Kennedy High Schl 2848 Santana Av

Thompsen Yvonne studt 1012 University Dr #812

Tifton Albert (Marsha) eng Rittmann Industries 2814 Ambassador Dr #417

Tijoriwali Cathy 1320 S Embrey Cir

Tiller Julius (Ida) ptlm 539 Sheridan Blvd

Tillman Randall C (Marion) city health insptr 818 N 41st St

Tillotson John mgr Johnny's Lounge 4437 Richmond Rd

Tontenott Eldred L (Lisa hairdrsr) barber 2634 6th St #17

Toore Ralph Jr writer 4941 Pine Hills Rd

Totmann Marvin (Gloria dent asst) secy guard 1818 4th St

Troutman Russell atty 1792 Harding Av

Ungarient James R (Margaret atty) atty 7314 Byron Av

Vacante Carlos (Carol) ptlm 4910 Magee Ct

Vacante Umberto (Para) tech writer 3202 Joyann St

Van Den Shruck Margaret pub serv rep Allstate Ins 7663 Robinhood Dr

Wagnor Timothy Sr (Kristine) mgr coffee shop 418 N Wilkes Rd

Wang Victor (Laura treas Stambaugh Industries) colm 2704 Central Blvd

Ward Brenda 7214 Ollin Way

Ward John (Frances) Army recruiter 3113 DeLaney Av

Ward Lonnie D apt wkr 2814 Ambassador Dr #22

Warniky Wayne (Clara mgr beauty salon) ptlm 418 N Wilkes Rd

Washington Bruce R atty David Casio & Associates 1104 Esplada Av #19

Washington Howard 4008 Kasper Av #618

Washington Joseph capt hwy patrol 3281 11th St

Web George (Barbara Denise writer) pres Empire Room Restr 3210 Joyann St

Webber Nancy (wid) tchr 44 E Princeton St

Weinor Jason (Susan nurse) min Calvary Baptist Ch 811 N Holbrook Dr

Weinor Leonard (Margaret) univ dean 283 N Grove St

Weiskoph Herman asst min John Calvin Presbyterian Ch 4817 Twin Lakes Blvd

Welshans Charles (Bea ofc sec Smith Realty) owner/mgr Conway Lounge 814 Collins Av

Wentilla Reid R (Lorrie) pres Keele-Baldwin Corp 640 Clayton Av

West Billy Lee (Ruth) min John Calvin Presbyterian Ch 452 Central Blvd

Whiddon Kerry (Bonnie sec) mgr Blackhawk Hotel 2913 Oak La

Whisenant Jerrod Army recruiter 1012 Cortez Av #20

White Catherine asst mgr Blackhawk Hotel 4218 Bell Av

Wiese Robert Alvin wkr Belks Moving & Storage Co 2032 Turf Way #338

Wilcox Ronald sheriff's deputy 1230 Hillside Dr

Wildez Tiffany sheriff's deputy 1230 Hillside Dr

Wilhelm Judy sheriff's deputy 847 Elmwood Dr #481

Wilke James (Laura owner/pres Laura's Maids) 2420 Highland Av

Willging Marty (Tessie sec city schls) dir YMCA 1808 Gadsden Blvd

Willging Rudy state forester 1423 5th St

Williams Jon Russell welder 814 Harding Av

Williams Patricia J retd 1338 Biarritz Dr

Williamson William L phys 4794 Hazel St

Wilson Kurt (Catherine) po wkr 1882 Village Dr

Wong Steven I (Maxine tchr) asst mgr Belks Dept Store 441 S 28th St

Wymore Paul (Barbara) auto mech 2020 Lorry La

Yanorini Elias L (Rosa sec) city fireman 811 Washington Av

Zitto Ron state forester 2103 Stanley St

Zitto Thomas (Linda dir communications Blood Bank) serv rep Cargill Industries 452 Glenmoor Ct

Zlatkiss Ralph (Janet cty com) treas Baldwin Industries 1414 White Av

Zozulli Wesley (Carol) ptlm 5219 Ranch Rd

Zumbado Carlos general mgr cty fair 1902 White Av

APPENDIX B
The Associated Press Stylebook

The following pages summarize the most commonly used rules in The Associated Press Stylebook and Libel Manual. These selected rules have been reprinted with the permission of The Associated Press. United Press International, the nation's second major news agency, uses a similar stylebook, and most newspapers in the United States—both dailies and weeklies—follow the rules they recommend.

Complete copies of The Associated Press Stylebook and Libel Manual can be ordered from most bookstores or from: The Associated Press, 50 Rockefeller Plaza, New York, N.Y. 10020. The United Press International Stylebook can be ordered from most bookstores or from: United Press International, 220 E. 42nd St., New York, N.Y. 10017.

SECTION 1: ABBREVIATIONS

1.1 **COMPANY.** Abbreviate and capitalize *company, corporation, incorporated, limited* and *brothers* when used after the name of a corporate entity. Do not capitalize or abbreviate when used by themselves: *He works for the company*.

1.2 **DEGREES.** Generally avoid abbreviations for academic degrees. Use instead a phrase such as: *John Jones, who has a doctorate in psychology*. Use an apostrophe in *bachelor's degree, a master's*, etc. Use abbreviations as *B.A., M.A., LL.D.* and *Ph.D.* only when the need to identify many individuals by degree on first reference would make the preferred form cumbersome.

1.3 **DO NOT ABBREVIATE:** *Assistant, association, attorney, building, district, government, president, professor, superintendent* or the days of the week, or use the ampersand (&) in place of *and* in news stories.

1.4 **INITIALS.** Use the initials of organizations and government agencies that are widely recognized: *NATO, PTA, CIA, FBI* (no periods). The first time you mention other organizations, use their full names. On second reference, use their abbreviations or acronyms only if they would be clear or familiar to most readers.

1.5 **JUNIOR/SENIOR.** Abbreviate and capitalize *junior* and *senior* after an individual's name: *John Jones Jr.* (no comma).

1.6 **MPH/MPG.** The abbreviation *mph* (no periods) is acceptable in all references for miles per hour. The abbreviation *mpg* (miles per gallon) is acceptable only on second reference.

1.7 **STATES.** Do not use postal abbreviations for states. Eight states are never abbreviated: *Alaska, Hawaii, Idaho, Iowa, Maine, Ohio, Texas* and *Utah*. Abbreviations for other states include: *Ala., Ariz., Ark., Calif., Colo., Conn., Del., Fla., Ga., Ill., Ind., Kan., Ky., La., Md., Mass., Mich., Minn., Miss., Mo., Mont., Neb., Nev., N.H., N.J., N.M., N.Y., N.C., N.D., Okla., Ore., Pa., R.I., S.C., S.D., Tenn., Vt., Va., Wash., W. Va., Wis.* and *Wyo*.

1.8 **TITLES.** Abbreviate the following titles when used before a full name outside direct quotations: *Dr., Lt. Gov., Mr., Mrs., Ms., Sen., the Rev.*, and military titles such as: *Pfc., Cpl., Sgt., 1st Lt., Capt., Maj., Lt. Col., Col., Gen., Cmdr.* and *Adm.* Spell out all except *Dr., Mr., Mrs.* and *Ms.* when used before a name in direct quotations.

1.9 **U.N./U.S.** Spell out *United Nations* and *United States* when used as nouns. Use *U.N.* and *U.S.* (no space between initials) only as adjectives.

SECTION 2: ADDRESSES

2.1 **ADDRESSES.** Always use figures for an address number: *9 Morningside Circle*.

2.2 **DIRECTIONS.** Abbreviate compass points used to indicate directional ends of a street or quadrants of a city in a numbered address: *562 W. 43rd St., 600 K St. N.W.* Do not abbreviate if the number is omitted: *East 42nd Street*.

2.3 **STREETS.** Spell out and capitalize *First* through *Ninth* when used as street names; use figures with two letters for *10th* and above: *7 Fifth Ave., 100 21st St.*

Use the abbreviations *Ave., Blvd.* and *St.* only with a numbered address: *1600 Pennsylvania Ave.* Spell them out and capitalize when part of a formal street name without a number: *Pennsylvania Avenue.* All similar words (*alley, drive, road, terrace,* etc.) are always spelled out.

SECTION 3: CAPITALIZATION

In general, avoid unnecessary capitals. Use a capital letter only if you can justify it by one of the principles listed here.

3.1 **ACADEMIC DEPARTMENTS.** When mentioning an academic department, use lowercase except for words that are proper nouns or adjectives: *the department of history, the department of English, the English department.*

3.2 **AWARDS/EVENTS/HOLIDAYS/WARS.** Capitalize awards (*Medal of Honor, Nobel Prize*), historic events and periods (*the Great Depression, Prohibition*), holidays (*Christmas Eve, Mother's Day*) and wars (*the Civil War, World War II*).

3.3 **BIBLE/GOD.** Use *Bible* (no quotation marks) and *God* (but lowercase pronouns referring to the deity: *he, his, thee*).

3.4 **BRAND NAMES.** Capitalize brand names: *Buick, Ford, Mustang.* Lowercase generic terms: *a Volkswagen van.* But use brand names only if they are essential to a story.

3.5 **BUILDINGS/ROOMS.** Capitalize the proper names of buildings, including the word *building* if it is an integral part of the proper name: *the Empire State Building.* Also capitalize the names of specially designated rooms: *Blue Room, Oval Office.* Use figures and capitalize *room* when used with a figure: *Room 2, Room 211.*

3.6 **CAPITOL.** Capitalize *U.S. Capitol* and *the Capitol* when referring to the building in Washington, D.C. or to state capitols.

3.7 **CONGRESS.** Capitalize *U.S. Congress* and *Congress* when referring to the U.S. Senate and House of Representatives. Lowercase when used as a synonym for convention. Lowercase *congressional* unless it is part of a proper name.

3.8 **CONSTITUTION.** Capitalize references to the *U.S. Constitution*, with or without the *U.S.* modifier. Lowercase *constitutional* in all uses.

Also capitalize *Bill of Rights, First Amendment* (and all other amendments to the Constitution).

3.9 **DIRECTIONS/REGIONS.** In general, lowercase *north, south, northeast* when they indicate a compass direction; capitalize when they designate geographical regions: *the Atlantic Coast states, Deep South, Sun Belt, Midwest. He drove west. The cold front is moving east. The North was victorious. She has a Southern accent.*

3.10 **DO NOT CAPITALIZE:** *administration; first lady; first family; government; presidential; presidency; priest;* seasons of the year: *winter, spring, summer, fall;* and years in school: *freshman, sophomore, junior, senior.*

Also lowercase the common noun elements of all names in plural uses: *the Democratic and Republican parties, Main and State streets, lakes Erie and Ontario.*

3.11 **EARTH.** Generally lowercase *earth*; capitalize when used as the proper name of the planet.

3.12 **GOVERNMENT.** Capitalize *city, county, state* and *federal* when part of a formal name: *Dade County, the Federal Trade Commission.* Retain capitalization for the name of a specific body when the proper noun is not needed: *the County Commission.* Generally lowercase elsewhere.

Also capitalize *city council, city hall, courthouse, legislature, assembly,* etc., when part of a proper name: *the Boston City Council.* Retain capitalization if the reference is to a specific city council, city hall, etc., but the context does not require the specific name: *The City Council met last night.*

3.13 **HIGHWAYS.** Use these forms, as appropriate in the context, for highways identified by number: *U.S. Highway 1, U.S. Route 1, Route 1, Illinois 34, Illinois Route 34, State Route 34, Route 34, Interstate Highway 495, Interstate 495.* On second reference only for Interstate: *I-495.* When a letter is appended to a number, capitalize it but do not use a hyphen: *Route 1A.*

3.14 **MILITARY.** Capitalize names of the U.S. armed forces: *the U.S. Army, the Navy, Marine regulations.* Use lowercase for the forces of other nations.

3.15 **NATIONALITIES/RACE.** Capitalize the proper names of nationalities, races, tribes, etc.: *Arab, Caucasian, Eskimo.* However, lowercase *black, white, mulatto.* Do *not* use the word "colored." In the United States, the word is considered derogatory.

3.16 **PLURALS.** To form the plural of a number, add *s* (no apostrophe). To form the plural of a single letter, add *'s.* To form the plural of multiple letters, add only *s: 1920s, Mind your p's and q's. She knows her ABCs.*

3.17 **POLITICAL PARTIES.** Capitalize both the name of a political party and the word *party*: the *Democratic Party.* Also capitalize *Communist, Conservative, Republican, Socialist,* etc., when they refer to a specific party or to individuals who are members of it. Lowercase when they refer to a political philosophy. After a name, use this short form, set off by commas: *D-Minn, R-Ore.*

3.18 **PROPER NOUNS.** Capitalize proper nouns that constitute the unique identification for a specific person, place or thing. Lowercase (do not capitalize) common nouns when they stand alone in subsequent references: *the party, the river, the street.*

3.19 **SATAN.** Capitalize *Satan,* but lowercase *devil* and *satanic.*

3.20 **TITLES.** Capitalize formal titles, including academic titles, when used immediately before a name: *president, chairman, professor.* Lowercase formal titles used after a name, alone or in constructions that set them off from a name by commas. Use lowercase at all times for terms that are job descriptions rather than formal titles: *astronaut John Glenn, movie star John Wayne, peanut farmer Jimmy Carter.*

SECTION 4: NUMERALS

For general purposes, spell out whole numbers below 10, use figures for 10 and above. Exceptions: figures are used for all ages, betting odds, dates, dimensions, percentages, speeds and times. Also, spell out a number at the beginning of a sentence, except for a calendar year.

4.1 **AGES.** Use figures for all ages. Hyphenate ages expressed as adjectives before a noun or as substitutes for a noun: *a 5-year-old boy,* but *the boy is 5 years old. The boy, 7, has a sister, 10. The woman is in her 30s* (no apostrophe).

4.2 **CENTS.** Spell out the word *cents* and lowercase, using numerals for amounts less than a dollar: *5 cents, 12 cents.* Use the *$* sign and decimal system for larger amounts: *$1.01.*

4.3 **DECADES/CENTURY.** Use Arabic figures to indicate decades of history. Use an apostrophe to indicate numbers that are left out; show the plural by adding the letter *s: the 1890s, the '90s, the Gay '90s, the mid-1930s.* Lowercase *century* and spell out numbers less than 10: *the first century, the 20th century.*

4.4 **DOLLARS.** Lowercase *dollars.* Use figures and the *$* sign in all except casual references or amounts without a figure: *The book cost $4. Dollars are flowing overseas.* For amounts of more than $1 million, use the *$* and numerals up to two decimal places: *He is worth $4.35 million. He proposed a $300 million budget.*

4.5 **ELECTION RETURNS.** For election returns, use the word *to* (not a hyphen) in separating different totals listed together: *Jimmy Carter defeated Gerald Ford 40,287,292 to 39,145,157.*

4.6 **FRACTIONS.** Spell out amounts less than *1*, using hyphens between the words: *two-thirds, four-fifths, seven-sixteenths.* For precise amounts larger than 1, convert to decimals whenever practical.

4.7 **MEASUREMENTS.** Use figures and spell out *inches, feet, yards,* etc. Hyphenate adjectival forms before nouns: *He is 5 feet 6 inches tall, the 5-foot-six-inch man. The rug is 9 feet by 12 feet, the 9-by-12 rug.*

4.8 **MILLION/BILLION.** Do not go beyond two decimals: *7.51 million people, $2.56 billion.* Decimals are preferred where practical: *1.5 million.* Not: *1½ million.*

Do not drop the word *million* or *billion* in the first figure of a range: *He is worth from $2 million to $4 million:* Not *$2 to $4 million,* unless you really mean *$2.*

4.9 **NUMBER.** Use *No.* as the abbreviation for *number* in conjunction with a figure to indicate position or rank: *No. 1 man, No. 3 choice.*

4.10 **ODDS.** Use figures and a hyphen for betting odds: *The odds were 5-4, he won despite 3-2 odds against him.*

4.11 **PERCENTAGES.** Use figures: *1 percent, 2.56 percent.* For amounts less than 1 percent, precede the decimal point with a zero: *The cost of living rose 0.6 percent.* The word "percent" should be spelled out; never use the symbol "%."

4.12 **RATIOS.** Use figures and a hyphen for ratios: *The ratio was 2-to-1, a ratio of 2-to-1, 2-1 ratio.*

4.13 **SCORES.** Use figures exclusively for scores, placing a hyphen between the totals of the winning and losing teams: *The Reds defeated the Red Sox 4-1, the Giants scored a 12-6 victory over the Cardinals, the golfer had a 5 on the last hole but finished with a 2-under-par score.*

4.14 **TEMPERATURES.** Use figures for all temperatures except *zero.* Use a word, not a minus sign, to indicate temperatures below zero.

SECTION 5: PUNCTUATION

5.1 **COMMA/AGE.** An individual's age is set off by commas: *Phil Taylor, 11, is here.*

5.2 **COMMA/CITY-STATE.** Place a comma between the city and the state name, and another comma after the state name, unless the state name ends a sentence: *He was traveling from Nashville, Tenn., to Albuquerque, N.M.*

5.3 **COMMA/HOMETOWN.** Use a comma to set off an individual's hometown when it is placed in apposition to a name: *Mary Richards, Minneapolis, and Maude Findlay, Tuckahoe, N.Y., were there.* However, the use of the word *of* without a comma between the individual's name and the city name is generally preferable: *Mary Richards of Minneapolis and Maude Findlay of Tuckahoe, N.Y., were there.*

5.4 **COMMA/NUMBERS.** Use a comma in most figures higher than 999. The major exceptions are street addresses, telephone numbers and years.

5.5 **COMMA/QUOTATION.** Use a comma to introduce a complete, one-sentence quotation within a paragraph: *Wallace said, "She spent six months in Argentina."* Do not use a comma at the start of an indirect or partial quotation. Always place commas and periods inside quotation marks.

5.6 **COMMA/SERIES.** Use commas to separate elements in a series, but do not put a comma before the conjunction in a simple series: *The flag is red, white and blue. He would nominate Tom, Dick or Harry.*

5.7 **COLON.** The most frequent use of a colon is at the end of a sentence to introduce lists, tabulations, texts, etc: *There were three considerations: expense, time and feasibility.*

Use a colon to introduce direct quotations longer than one sentence within a paragraph and to end all paragraphs that introduce a paragraph of quoted material.

5.8 **POSSESSIVES.** Appendix C contains the rules for forming possessives.

5.9 **SEMICOLON.** Use a semicolon to separate elements of a series when individual segments contain material that also must be set off by commas: *He leaves a son, John Smith of Chicago; three daughters, Jane Smith of Wichita, Kan., Mary Smith of Denver, and Susan, wife of William Kingsbury of Boston; and a sister, Martha, wife of Robert Warren of Omaha, Neb.* Note that the semicolon is used before the final *and* in such a series.

SECTION 6: PREFERRED SPELLINGS

Adviser
Afterward (Not *afterwards*)
All right (Never *alright*)
Ax (Not *axe*)
Baby-sit, baby-sitting, baby sitter
Backward (Not *backwards*)
Damage (For destruction; *damages* for a court award)
Employee (Not *employe*)
Forward (Not *forwards*)
Goodbye
Gray (Not *grey*)
Kidnapping
Likable (Not *likeable*)
Percent (One word, spelled out)
Teen, teen-ager, teen-age. Do not use *teen-aged*.
Vice president (No hyphen)
Whiskey

SECTION 7: TIME

Use figures except for *noon* and *midnight*. Do not put a *12* in front of them. Use a colon to separate hours from minutes: *11:15 a.m., 1:45 p.m., 3:30 p.m.* Avoid such redundancies as *10 a.m. this morning* or *10 p.m. Monday night*. Use *10 a.m. today* or *10 p.m. Monday*. The hour is placed before the day: *a.m.* and *p.m.* are lowercase, with periods.

7.1 **DAYS.** Use the words *today, this morning, tonight,* etc. in direct quotes, in stories intended for publication in afternoon newspapers on the day in question, and in phrases that do not refer to a specific day: *Customs today are different from those of a century ago.* Use the day of the week in stories intended for publication in morning newspapers and in stories filed for use in either publishing cycle. Use *yesterday* and *tomorrow* only in direct quotations and in phrases that do not refer to a specific day.

7.2 **DAYS/DATES.** Use *Monday, Tuesday,* etc. for days of the week within seven days before or after the current date. Use the month and a figure for dates beyond this range. Avoid such redundancies as *last Tuesday* or *next Tuesday*.

7.3 **MONTHS.** Capitalize the names of the months in all uses. When a month is used with a specific date, abbreviate only: *Jan., Feb., Aug., Sept., Oct., Nov.* and *Dec.* Spell out when using alone, or with a year alone. When a phrase lists only a month and a year, do not separate the year with commas. When a phrase refers to a month, day and year, set off the year with commas: *January 1972 was a cold month. Jan. 2 was the coldest day of the month. His birthday is May 15. Feb. 14, 1976, was the target date.* Do not use *st., nd., rd.* or *th* after the date.

SECTION 8: TITLES

Formal titles that appear directly before a name are capitalized and abbreviated. After a name or alone, lowercase and spell out: *The president issued a statement. The pope gave his blessing.* Do not repeat a title the second time you use a person's name: *Sheriff Sam Smith, Smith* (not *Sheriff Smith*).

8.1 **BOY/GIRL.** The terms *boy* and *girl* are applicable until the age of 18. Use *man, woman, young man* or *young woman* afterward.

8.2 **COMPOSITIONS.** Capitalize the principal words in titles of books, movies, operas, plays, poems, songs, television programs, lectures, speeches and works of art. Put quotation marks around the names of all such works. Do not underline the titles of any of these works.

8.3 **CONGRESSMAN.** Use *congressman* and *congresswoman* only in references to members of the U.S. House of Representatives.

8.4 **COURTESY TITLES.** In general, do not use the courtesy titles *Miss, Mr., Mrs.* or *Ms.* on first reference. Instead, use the first and last names and middle initial of the person.

For a married woman, the preferred form on first reference is to identify her by her own first name and her husband's last name: *Susan Smith.* Use *Mrs.* on the first reference only if a woman requests that her husband's first name be used or if her own first name cannot be determined: *Mrs. John Smith.*

On the second reference, use *Miss, Mrs.* or *Ms.* before the last name of a woman, depending on her preference.

If a woman is divorced or widowed, use *Mrs.* or no title, if she prefers it. But, if a woman returns to the use of her maiden name, use *Miss, Ms.* or no title if she prefers it.

On the second reference, use only the last name of a man. Use *Mr.* only when it is combined with *Mrs.: Mr. and Mrs. John Smith.*

8.5 **INITIALS.** In general, use middle initials. Particular care should be taken to include middle initials in stories where they help identify a specific individual. Examples include casualty lists and stories naming the accused in a crime.

Use periods and no space when an individual uses initials instead of a first name: *H.L. Mencken.* Do not give a name with a single initial (*J. Jones*) unless it is the individual's preference or the first name cannot be learned.

8.6 **MAGAZINES.** Capitalize magazine titles but do not place in quotes. Lowercase *magazine* if it is not part of the publication's formal title: *Newsweek magazine.*

8.7 **NEWSPAPERS.** Capitalize *the* in a newspaper's name if that is the way the publication prefers to be known. If the location is needed but is not part of the official name, use parentheses: *The Huntsville (Ala.) Times.* Do not underline or add quote marks.

8.8 **REFERENCE MATERIALS.** Capitalize, but do not use quotation marks around, books that are primarily catalogs of reference materials. These rules also apply to almanacs, directories, dictionaries, handbooks and encyclopedias.

8.9 **REVEREND.** When using the title *Rev.* before a name, precede it with the word *the.*

SECTION 9: WORDS

9.1 **INJURIES.** Injuries are *suffered* or *sustained*, not *received.*

9.2 **INNOCENT/NOT GUILTY.** Use *innocent* rather than *not guilty* in describing a defendant's plea or a jury's verdict to guard against the word *not* being dropped inadvertently.

9.3 **MASS.** It is *celebrated, said* or *sung.* Always capitalize when referring to the ceremony, but lowercase any preceding adjectives: *high Mass, low Mass, requiem Mass.*

9.4 **NOUNS/VERBS.** Nouns that denote a unit take singular verbs and pronouns: *class, committee, family, group, herd, jury, team. The committee is meeting to set its agenda. The jury reached its verdict.* When used in the sense of two persons, the word *couple* takes plural verbs and pronouns: *The couple were married Saturday.*

9.5 **PERSON/PEOPLE.** Use *person* when speaking of an individual. The word *people* is preferred in all plural uses. For example: *Some rich people pay few taxes. There were 17 people in the room.*

9.6 **RAISED/REARED.** Only humans may be *reared.* Any living thing, including humans, may be *raised.*

9.7 **REALTOR.** The term *real estate agent* is preferred. Use *Realtor* only if the individual is a member of the National Association of Realtors.

9.8 **WORDS TO AVOID.** Do not use the following words in news stories: *kids, irregardless, ladies* (as a synonym for *women*), *cop* (except in quoted matter) or *entitled* (when you mean *titled*).

APPENDIX C
Rules for Forming Possessives

1. Always begin by writing the correct form of the word that you want to use. This rule applies to both the singular and to the plural form of the word.

2. If the word, regardless of whether it is singular or plural, does not already end in the letter "s," add an apostrophe and "s" to form the possessive. For example:

SINGULAR	man	child	person
SINGULAR POSSESSIVE	man's	child's	person's
PLURAL	men	children	people
PLURAL POSSESSIVE	men's	children's	people's

3. If the word already ends in the letter "s," add only an apostrophe to form the possessive. Note that this rule also applies to proper nouns, such as a person's name.

SINGULAR	fraternity	lady	Ralph	Smith
SINGULAR POSSESSIVE	fraternity's	lady's	Ralph's	Smith's
PLURAL	fraternities	ladies	Ralphs*	Smiths**
PLURAL POSSESSIVE	fraternities'	ladies'	Ralphs'	Smiths'

*Refers to two different people whose first name is Ralph.
**Refers to two different people whose last name is Smith.

4. If an object is hyphenated, add an apostrophe and the letter "s" to the last word only.

SINGULAR	father-in-law	He is my father-in-law.
SINGULAR POSSESSIVE	father-in-law's	It is my father-in-law's car.
PLURAL	fathers-in-law	They are your fathers-in-law.
PLURAL POSSESSIVE	fathers-in-law's	They are your fathers-in-law's cars.

5. If an object is owned by two or more people, add an apostrophe and the letter "s" to the latter name only.

   Mary and Fred's entry won a prize.

   My mother and father's home was destroyed by fire.

6. If the objects are not jointly owned—if you are describing separate objects owned or possessed by different people—add an apostrophe and the letter "s" to both nouns.

   Mary's and Fred's entries won a prize.

   My mother's and my father's luggage was lost.

7. Indefinite pronouns such as "everyone" follow the same rules. However, personal pronouns have special forms that never use an apostrophe. The personal pronouns include such words as: "his," "mine," "ours," "theirs," "whose" and "yours."

8. Generally avoid using an apostrophe and the letter "s" for inanimate objects. Instead, try to rewrite the passage, either dropping the apostrophe and the letter "s" or converting the passage to an "of" phrase.

   WRONG: the table's leg
   RIGHT: the table leg   Or: the leg of the table

   WRONG: the book's chapter
   RIGHT: the book chapter   Or: the chapter of the book

9. When mentioning the name of an organization, group or geographical location, always use the common or preferred and official spelling. Some of the names use the possessive case but others, such as Pikes Peak, do not.

10. The word "it's," spelled with an apostrophe, is a contraction of "it is." The possessive form, "its," does *not* contain an apostrophe.

APPENDIX D
Answer Keys for Exercises

Chapter 1: Format and Style
Exercise 6

1. The President of the U.S., a member of the republican party, announced yesterday that income taxes will be lowered eight per cent, effective at 12:01 a.m. on the morning of January 1st of next year. (Change "yesterday" to the specific day of the week.)

2. Atty. James M. Murphy, of Detroit, Michigan, estimated that 1/3 of the members of the United states congress are lawyers and members of the American Bar Assn.

3. time Magazine, which was established during the Twentieth [20th] Century, costs about three dollars a copy, has a circulation of 5,500,000 [5.5 million], and favors the Republican party.

4. Henry Kubisak, age eight, of 418 North Wilkes rd., sipped a coke at 11 A.M. yesterday morning while his father read a copy of the New York Times (Also: change "yesterday" to the specific day of the week. Because Kubisak is a child, his name does not appear in the city directory—only his parents'. Similarly, the city directory does not list the names of people who live in other cities.)

5. The Jiffey Loan company, formerly located at 841 South Jefferson Boulevard, has moved to the intersection of Colonial and Nye roads.

6. 12 police officers it helped capture the 19 year old boy [man]. One officer said the youth [man] was carrying three dollars, a bible, and a letter addressed to the overnor governor of the State. [women]

7. The girls [women], who were born in Austin, Texas, during the 1950s, agreed to hold their first reunion in Fla. on December 21st at 7:30 p.m. in the evening.

8. After serving four years in the Army, became he a united states citizen and then earned a B.A. from Harvard university.

9. Asst. Prof. Saul Holmann, a member of the Political Science dept., said the 1960s

were a decade of turmoil, caused by a revolutin among blacks and youths opposed to the Vietnam war.

10. Author Ralph toore, junior, who has an office in room 411 of the Lakeshore Heights Bldg., won a pulitzer prize for his first boook, which is entitled Ecology and You.

11. Despite the temperature, which Fell to twenty degrees below 0 in Minneapolis, Minnesota, 82% of the city's voters turnd out last tuesday and defeated Rev. Louis C. Salvaggio, an avowed homosexual candidate for mayor, by a vote of 142,619 to 81,710.

Chapter 1: Format and Style
Exercise 7

1. The president, speaking in Wis., Minn, and Neb. lsat saturday, said he opposes any further increased in social security taxes during the 20th cenTtury.

2. Roger Ritzmann, chairman of the Better Schools Assn., scheduled the group's next meeting for Tuesday, March 21, at 7:00 P.M. The Association's annfual dues are $25.00 ("The Associated Press Stylebook" uses the words "chairman" and "chair-woman," but rarely "chairperson." Also, Rittzmann's name is misspelled.)

3. After inheriting $2,300,600, the 20 year old girl established Fashions, Incorporated, a store at the intersection fo Conway and Anderson Sts.

4. Mr. Andrew c. Mears, a member of the republican party, said the Federal Government should give the army an additional $6 to $8 billion for the purchase of three thousand new Tanks.

5. The city council met at 12 noon last Tues. Afterwards, Councilwoman Maggy delevaux said it will meet at 7:30 p.m. tomorow night to reconsider the appointment of Mrs. Ralph Pinder as City Assessor. (Change "tomorrow" to the day of the week.)

6. Colonel Andrew Smith, who emnlisted in the army as a private on December 7th, 1941, retired in Sept. 1976 at the age of fifty three and now lives on the west coast.

7. The Hospital, located at 581 W. 89 Street, treatde one hundred person for food poisoning.

8. The woman is five feet, seven inches tall, weights 132 pounds AND has four sisters, Rosemary, Linda, Ruth, and Doris.

9. Mary Wilson, age eight, said, "the baseball game was rather dull?"

10. John Jones, Junior, of Rock Island, Illinois, arrived September 1 and helped raise almost $1,400,000 for the church new.
   $1.4 million

11. Mr. John Adams, A wir writer from Mont. will re ceive his B.A. next Monday and then fly to the midwest at 7:00 P.M. at night.

12. He is seven years old, four feet tall, weighs fifty-five pounds and has saved $74.00.

13. The pres ident of the u.s. his wife, and 2 daughters have announced plans to visit the city on August 7.

14. The gen. has retired from the army and is President of Globe Electronics company. The Company has an office e on Central Avenue.

Chapter 2: Newswriting Style
Exercise 6

Section I

1. facts
2. close
3. bodies
4. dropped
5. began
6. gifts
7. to
8. innovation
9. history
10. revert
11. strangled
12. tracked
13. unique
14. winter
15. child

Section II

1. stopped
2. ignored
3. because
4. believes
5. before
6. soon
7. near
8. possesses
9. investigated
10. studying
11. considered
12. married

Section III

1. The debt was smaller then.

2. The mayor said he favors the law's passage.

3. The agency recommended annexing the 40 acres.

4. Students using the library complained that two people talked too loudly.

5. The suspect said he had been drinking that Saturday night and could not remember what happened.

Section IV

1. The mental health clinic is trying to support itself.

2. Church officials estimate that the chapel will cost $320,000.

3. Three years ago, she decided to earn a bachelor's degree.

4. He said police are investigating the crime.

5. People at the clinic want to offer individual and group counseling to abused women.

6. Witnesses said the woman escaped in a new Ford.

Section V

1. Police said burglars pried open the home's back door.

2. Audrey Kuhlman and freshman Mark Bogard disagreed about abortion. (Note: the city directory spells Bogard's name with one "g," not two.)

3. He said the United States' conventional military forces in Europe are weaker than the Soviet Union's.

4. During a party the day she retired, co-workers gave the librarian a trip to Paris.

5. The conference revealed that Israelis dislike the agreement.

Chapter 2: Newswriting Style
Exercise 7

1. The club needs more members.

2. The new program will provide medical services for the poor.

3. A short circuit in electrical wiring at the church caused the fire.

4. The youths planned never to tell their parents about the near drowning.

5. Participants in the workshop agree that high school students need classes in sex education.

6. A teacher at the school said most students avoid algebra classes.

7. The report said people of all ages can enjoy water skiing.

8. The radio station also billed customers twice for the same advertisements.

9. The senator said the plan would help protect the elderly against inflation.

10. Police officers said a hook-shaped wire was jimmied through the vent window and used to pull up the door latch.

11. The city abandoned its plans to expand the school partly because of financial problems.

12. The report said alcohol causes 28,000 traffic deaths a year in the United States.

13. The sheriff said he will resign primarily because of overcrowded conditions in the county jail.

14. Patrons complain that city buses are often late.

15. People in the town do not get good television reception because the nearest television station is 60 miles away.

Chapter 2: Newswriting Style
Exercise 8

1. He lost his right eye.

2. They settled the debt.

3. Brown has a wife and four children.

4. The school is in Berkeley, Calif.

5. She received the money in late August.

6. The carpenters received an 8 percent pay raise.

7. Witnesses estimated that the boys drowned at 4:10 p.m.

8. This article examines students' problems.

9. The politician thanked his supporters.

10. The state Legislature will decide how to spend the money.

11. Applications must be submitted by March 1.

12. The fire started near the high school at about midnight.

13. The couple received a loan to buy a new home.

14. The woman testified that her husband often beat her.

15. Officials hope the medical program will be self-supporting, a representative said. (The Associated Press Stylebook recommends using the word "representative," not "spokesperson," if you do not know the sex of the individual.)

16. Four men and four women serve on the committee.

17. Property taxes will be raised 5 percent.

18. As cars become more expensive, sales decline.

19. Police found the child at 6 p.m.

20. Despite firefighters' efforts, the building burned to the ground. Or: Fire destroyed the building.

21. The company obtained an injunction to stop the strike.

22. Eight men assaulted the new sheriff.

Index

N

names
  accuracy of, 188
  in leads, 542
narrative lead, 626
National Aeronautics and Space
    Administration (NASA), 444,
    516–17
National Enquirer, 244, 270, 272, 273
NBC News, 269, 278
NBC Nightly News, 276–77
Nelson, Harold L., 249
Neshoba Democrat, 283
New York Daily News, 287
New York Journal, 182
New York Sun, 183
New York Times, 6, 29, 31, 77, 79, 84,
    118, 120, 122, 181, 189–90, 228,
    237–38, 256, 258, 319, 346, 348,
    349, 619–20, 625
New York Times Dispatch, 148
New York Times rule, 238
New York Times vs. *Sullivan* (1964),
    237–38, 251
New York World, 183
New Yorker, The, 251
news editor, 227
news peg, 176
news services, careers with, 217
news story format, 1, 2–3
Newsday, 140, 145
Newspaper Guild, The, 281
newspapers
  careers with, 211–19
  and libel suits, 244
newsrooms
  electronic revolution in, 227–29
  organization of, 225–27
Newsweek, 385, 423, 424
Nixon, Richard, 189, 306
North American Newspaper Alliance,
    622
note-taking, 514–16
numerals, 678–79

O

obituaries, 417–25
  of celebrities, 420, 422–25
  content of, 418–20
objectivity, 31–32, 39, 181–82, 365, 547
  in leads, 81–83
obscenity, 183
oddities, 179–80. *See also* unusual,
    stressed in leads
Ohio State University, 209
ombudsman, 246
Onassis, Jacqueline Kennedy, 250
opinions, 81–83, 236. *See also*
    quotations, attributing
Orlando Sentinel, 75, 117, 120, 121, 123,
    282, 422, 626, 629
orphan quotes, 307
outlines, 363
Owens, Jessie, 424

P

paragraphs, 27–28, 137–40
parallel form, 149, 364
partial quotations, 305, 306–7
personality features, 621–22
Peterson, Paul V., 209–10, 214–15
photography, 268, 274–76, 277, 278,
    279, 287, 387
plagiarism, 366
platitudes, 352–54, 445
Playboy, 230
police beat, 225–26
policies, 181
polls, 534–37
Port Reyes Light, 246
possessives, rules for forming, 683
Powell, Lewis F., 241
precision, 30–31
present tense, 361
press conferences, 476, 477, 518
pretrial settlements, 248
printers, 227
privacy, 248–52, 271–74
privilege, in libel suits, 236
Proctor & Gamble Company, 283
profanities, in quotations, 310
profiles, 621–22
prominence, as news characteristic,
    179
proofreading, 227, 228
proximity, as news characteristic, 179
Proxmire, William, 240, 444
public affairs reporting, 539–50
public relations, 448
  careers in, 217
publication, in libel suits, 235
publicity, 282
publicity releases, 441–48
Pulitzer, Joseph, 183, 624
punctuation, 316–18, 362, 679–82
punitive damages, in libel suits, 237
Pyle, Ernie, 28, 349

Q

question-and-answer format, 517
questions
  in leads, 119–20, 625
  as transitions, 144–45
quotations, 305–18, 478
  attributing, 305–16, 321–23
  capitalization and punctuation of,
    316–18
  explaining, 311–12
  in leads, 82, 118–19, 625
  in obituaries, 423

R

radio. *See* broadcasting, careers in
Rather, Dan, 177, 225
readership demographics, 173–74
Reagan, Ronald, 175, 177, 274, 347
reference materials, 191
repetition, 142